JOHN WILLIS'

THEATRE WORLD

1972-1973 SEASON

Volume 29

Crown Publishers, Inc.
419 Park Avenue South
New York, N.Y. 10016

TO

ALEXANDER H. COHEN

in recognition of his genius, perception, and impeccable taste in theatrical presentations; his dedication to the theatre in the face of diminishing productions, decreasing audiences, and shrinking profits; and his invaluable contribution to introducing Broadway to millions of viewers, and to cultivating new theatre audiences in The States, and throughout the world, with his superlative and exemplary television specials.

Paul Sorvino, Richard A. Dysart, Charles Durning, Walter McGinn in "That Championship Season"

Winner of 1972 Drama Critics Circle Award, 1973 "Tony" Award, and 1973 Pulitzer Prize for Best Play

CONTENTS

EDITOR: JOHN WILLIS
Assistant Editor: Raymond Frederick
Staff Photographers: Bert Andrews, Friedman-Abeles, Louis Mélançon,
Van Williams

THE SEASON IN REVIEW
June 1, 1972—May 31, 1973

As the curtain fell on the 1972–1973 theatre season, only 14 of Broadway's 49 openings during the year were still playing, and four had posted closing notices. The boxoffice gross was the lowest in a decade, and only 25% of Equity's members had been employed during the year. Nevertheless, it was a much more optimistic and distinguished season than the preceding one. There were five more Broadway productions than in 1971–72, and a majority of them was of higher quality. It was a strange observation, however, that except for an occasional week or two, none achieved a "Standing Room Only" status. At the end of the season, however, two musicals, "A Little Night Music" and "Irene," were registering capacity business. The former deservedly received both the New York Drama Critics Circle citation and a "Tony" for best musical. It also received "Tonys" for best libretto, score, and costumes, and Glynis Johns and Patricia Elliott for best actress and supporting actress in a musical. "Irene" had film star Debbie Reynolds making an impressive Broadway debut, and George S. Irving giving a "Tony" Award supporting performance. Among the other commendable musicals was "Seesaw" with excellent performances by Michele Lee, Ken Howard, and Tommy Tune. Mayor Lindsay made a guest appearance, giving impetus to its deserved gun. The extraordinarily imaginative "Pippin" was awarded "Tonys" for best actor (Ben Vereen in a virtuoso performance), best direction, choreography, scenery, and lighting.

Adding to last season's Drama Critics Circle Award as best play (before it moved to Broadway), "That Championship Season" received a "Tony" for best play, and the Pulitzer Prize for playwright Jason Miller. The entire cast deserved an award for its beautiful performance. The Drama Critics also cited the British import "The Changing Room" as best play for this season, and Off Broadway's "The Hot 1 Baltimore" as best American play. There was superb ensemble playing in "The Changing Room," and John Lithgow won a "Tony" for best supporting actor. Alan Bates received a "Tony" for his outstanding performance in the otherwise rather dull play "Butley." Best actress and supporting actress "Tonys" for non-musicals went to Julie Harris and Leora Dana for their roles in "The Last of Mrs. Lincoln." Two less memorable plays about Mary Todd Lincoln were presented during the season, "The Lincoln Mask" with Eva Marie Saint, and "Look Away" with Geraldine Page. Neil Simon had another comedy success with "The Sunshine Boys" in which Sam Levene, Jack Albertson, and Lewis J. Stadlen gave laudable performances. Tennessee Williams' "Out Cry," and Arthur Miller's "The Creation of the World and Other Business" were below their playwrights' usual standard, but had superior performances by Michael York, Cara Duff-MacCormick, George Grizzard, and Zoe Caldwell.

Another optimistic note for the season was the opening of three new theatres in the Times Square area, all in high-rise office buildings. "Irene" opened the Minskoff, the musical disaster "Via Galactica," but with critically applauded Keene Curtis and Raul Julia, opened the Uris, and Coleen Dewhurst in a revival of "Mourning Becomes Electra" initiated the Circle in the Square-Joseph E. Levine Theatre.

There were five holdovers from previous seasons, among them "Fiddler on the Roof." Before its closing, it had achieved an all-time record run for either a play or musical with 3242 performances.

Among the actors who received critical praise during the season, and not mentioned previously, were Maureen Stapleton, Rex Harrison, Len Cariou, Jane Alexander, Robert Morse, Alexis Smith, Christopher Plummer, Brock Peters, Marcia Rodd, Brian Farrell, Laurence Guittard, D. Jamin-Bartlett, Hermione Gingold, Monte Markham, John McMartin, Leland Palmer, Terry Kiser, Susan Browning, Jerry Orbach, Kelly Garrett, and John Rubinstein.

The Repertory Theater of Lincoln Center had its final, and, ironically, its most successful season financially and artistically. For its farewell production, and marking the twenty-fifth anniversary of the premiere of "A Streetcar Named Desire," the Repertory Theater gave it a noteworthy revival. Its success warranted an extended run. The always-brilliant Rosemary Harris was Blanche, and James Farentino an impressive Stanley. Next season, the two theatres used by the company will be under the direction of Joseph Papp as another of his ever-expanding New York Shakespeare Festival Public Theater projects.

Again this season, Mr. Papp transferred two of his off Broadway productions to "the Great White Way." They were the award-winning "That Championship Season" and the delightfully musicalized "Much Ado about Nothing." The latter was forced to close when audiences failed to appear after it was televised nationally. Two other successful off Broadway productions were moved uptown. "The River Niger" from the Negro Ensemble Company continued its success, but "The Play's the Thing" from the Roundabout Theatre failed to attract playgoers.

The season Off Broadway was not as encouraging as in previous years. Perhaps because of soaring costs, there were thirteen less productions than last year, and generally of inferior quality. The exceptions, in addition to those previously noted, were the musicals "Berlin to Broadway with Kurt Weill," "Oh Coward!," "National Lampoon's Lemmings," and such plays as "Wedding Band," "Green Julia," and the six productions presented in repertory by the new City Center Acting Company. Noteworthy performances off Broadway were given by Mari Gorman, Victor Garber, Trish Hawkins, Maya Angelou, Alice Playten, Ruby Dee, Jerry Lanning, Rue McClanahan, Jack MacGowran, James Earl Jones, Earle Hyman, Gloria Foster, Roderick Cook, Jamie Ross, and Barbara Cason.

Toward the close of the season, an innovation was sponsored in Duffy Square on Broadway. Unsold tickets were offered at discounts for the day of performance. Hopefully, it will help fill the theatres, prolong runs, and cultivate audiences. Curtain time for most productions remained at 7:30. However, some producers exercised their option to begin performances at 8 P.M.

According to *Variety*, touring companies continued to out gross Broadway, reaching the highest peak of revenue in ten years. Regional theatres continued to flourish, and there was an appreciable increase in the number of dinner theatres throughout the U. S. Perhaps this encouraging trend will help revitalize the hub of the theatre, and re-create the excitement that Broadway once epitomized.

Julie Harris

Alan Bates

BROADWAY CALENDAR

June 1, 1972 through May 31, 1973

Ben
Vereen

Debbie Reynolds

Robert Morse

Glynis Johns

BROADHURST THEATRE
Open Wednesday, June 7, 1972.*
Kenneth Waissman and Maxine Fox in association with Anthony D'Amato present:

GREASE

Book, Music and Lyrics by Jim Jacobs and Warren Casey; Director, Tom Moore; Musical Numbers and Dances Staged by Patricia Birch; Musical Supervision and Orchestrations by Michael Leonard; Musical Direction, Vocal and Dance Arrangements, Louis St. Louis; Scenery, Douglas W. Schmidt; Costumes, Carrie F. Robbins; Lighting, Karl Eigsti; Sound, Jack Shearing; Hairstyles, Jim Sullivan; Production Assistant, Carolyn Ciplet; Original Cast Album, MGM Records.

CAST

Miss Lynch	Dorothy Leon†1
Patty Simcox	Ilene Kristen
Eugene Florczyk	Tom Harris
Jan	Garn Stephens†2
Marty	Meg Bennett
Betty Rizzo	Adrienne Barbeau†3
Doody	James Canning
Roger	Walter Bobbie†4
Kenickie	Timothy Meyers†5
Sonny LaTierri	Jim Borrelli
Frenchy	Marya Small
Sandy Dumbrowski	Carole Demas†6
Danny Zuko	Barry Bostwick
Vince Fontaine	Gardner Hayes†7
Johnny Casino	Alan Paul
Cha-Cha Gregorio	Kathi Moss
Teen Angel	Alan Paul

UNDERSTUDIES: Female roles: Joy Rinaldi, Alaina Warren; Male Roles, Jeff Conaway, Richard Gere

MUSICAL NUMBERS: "Alma Mater," "Summer Nights," "Those Magic Changes," "Freddy, My Love," "Greased Lightnin'," "Mooning," "Look at Me," "I'm Sandra Dee," "We Go Together," "Shakin' at the High School Hop," "It's Rainin' on Prom Night," "Born to Hand-Jive," "Beauty School Dropout," "Alone at a Drive-In Movie," "Rock 'N' Roll Party Party Queen," "There Are Worse Things I Could Do," "All Choked Up," Finale

A musical in two acts and 12 scenes. The action takes place at the reunion of the Class of 1959 of Rydell High School.

General Manager: Edward H. Davis
Press: Betty Lee Hunt, Henry Luhrman, Harriett Trachtenberg, Maria C. Pucci
Company Manager: Leo K. Cohen
Stage Managers: T. Schuyler Smith, John Fennessey, Tom Harris

* Still playing May 31, 1973. For original Off-Broadway production, see THEATRE WORLD, Vol. 28.
† Succeeded by: 1. Sudie Bond during vacation, 2. Jamie Donnelly, 3. Elaine Petricoff, 4. Richard Quarry, John S. Driver, 5. John Fennessy, 6. Ilene Graff, 7. Jim Weston

Friedman-Abeles Photos

Left: Barry Bostwick, Carole Demas
Above: Ilene Kristen, Tom Harris, Dorothy Leon

Ilene Kristen, Katie Hanley, Tom Harris, Adrienne Barbeau, Barry Bostwick, Kathi Moss, Marya Small, James Canning

Katie Hanley, Jim Borrelli, Walter Bobbie, Timothy Meyers, Garn Stephens, Adrienne Barbeau, Barry Bostwick, James Canning, Marya Small

Walter Bobbie, Jim Borrelli, Timothy Meyers, James Canning, Barry Bostwick
Top: (L) Barry Bostwick, Walter Bobbie, Joy Garrett, James Canning
(R) Garn Stephens, Marya Small, Joy Garrett, Meg Bennett

9

BOOTH THEATRE
Open Thursday, September 14, 1972.*
The New York Shakespeare Festival (Joseph Papp, Producer) presents:

THAT CHAMPIONSHIP SEASON

By Jason Miller; Director, A. J. Antoon; Setting, Santo Loquasto; Costumes, Theoni V. Aldredge; Lighting, Ian Calderon; Associate Producer, Bernard Gersten; Production Assistant, Deloss Brown

CAST

Tom Daley	Walter McGinn
George Sikowski	Charles Durning†1
James Daley	Michael McGuire
Phil Romano	Paul Sorvino†2
Coach	Richard A. Dysart†3

UNDERSTUDIES: James, Tom, Bernie McInerney; Phil, Joe Mascolo; George, Ron McLarty

A Comedy-Drama in two acts. The action takes place in Coach Sikowski's house, somewhere in the Lackawanna Valley at the present time.

General Managers: Eugene Wolsk, Emanuel Azenberg
Company Manager: Edmonstone Thompson
Press: Merle Debuskey, Faith Geer
Stage Managers: Ron Abbott, Joseph Kavanagh

* Still playing May 31, 1973. Winner of 1972 Drama Critics Circle Award, 1973 "Tony" Award, and 1973 Pulitzer Prize. For original Off-Broadway production see THEATRE WORLD Vol. 28.
† Succeeded during vacations by: 1. Richard McKenzie, 2. Joseph Mascolo, 3. Harry Bellaver

Friedman-Abeles Photos

Michael McGuire, Richard A. Dysart, Paul Sorvino, Charles Durning, Walter McGinn
Top Left: Michael McGuire, Paul Sorvino, Charles Durning

Charles Durning, Michael McGuire
Top: Richard A. Dysart, Walter McGinn

Richard A. Dysart, Walter McGinn
Top: Paul Sorvino, Walter McGinn, Michael McGuire

JACQUES BREL IS ALIVE AND WELL AND LIVING IN PARIS

Production Conception, English Lyrics, Additional Material, Eric Blau, Mort Shuman; Based on Brel's Lyrics and Commentary; Music, Jacques Brel; Director, Moni Yakim; Musical Direction, Mort Shuman; Music Arranged and Conducted by Wolfgang Knittel; Scenery, Les Lawrence; Original Cast Album by Columbia Records.

CAST

Elly Stone	Joe Masiell
George Ball	Henrietta Valor
Janet McCall	Joseph Neal

MUSICAL NUMBERS: "Marathon," "Alone," "Madeleine," "I Loved," "Mathilde," "Bachelor's Dance," "Timid Frieda," "My Death," "Girls & Dogs," "Jackie," "The Statue," "Desperate Ones," "Sons of," "Amsterdam," "The Bulls," "Old Folks," "Marieka," "Brussels," "Fannette," "Funeral Tango," "Middle Class," "You're Not Alone," "Next," "Carousel," "If We Only Have Love"

A Musical Entertainment presented in two acts.

General Manager: Lily Turner
Press: Ivan Black
Stage Managers: Phillip Price, Joseph Neal

* Closed Oct. 28, 1972 after 51 performances. It had closed Off-Broadway July 2, 1972 after 1847 performances. See THEATRE WORLD Vols. 24–28.

Elly Stone (also top right), Joe Masiell, Henrietta Valor, George Ball

FROM ISRAEL WITH LOVE

Producer, Colonel Saul Biber; Director, Avi David; Musical Director, Rafi Ben-Moshe; Choreography, Yakov Kalusky; Executive Producers, Jerome M. Lapin, Regina A. Lapin; Executive Director, David A. Toben; Executive Assistant, William Dean; Director International Operations, Herman E. Schner

COMPANY

Micha Adir	Nathan Okev
Dani Amihud	Gadi Oron
Chaya Arad	Varda Sagy
Itzik Barak	Reuven Shenar
Shara Badishy	Yonnith Shoham
Eti Brechner	Nurit Zeevi
David Dardashi	David Rosenthal
Irith Esched	Izhack Litchtenfeld
Tami Gall	Juda Asher Shkolnik
Israel Klugman	Oded Pintus
Elis Menahemi	Shymel Aroukh
Malli Noy	Ilan Gilboa
Yacov Noy	

PROGRAM

"Israel Israel," "From the South Good Will Come," "Call for Freedom," "Three Legs," "We Take Whatever Comes," "Ballet," "Jerusalem of Gold," "Natasha," "A Beach Song," "Night, Night, A Lullaby," "From Across the River—Coffee Song," "The Parachutist," "My Dear Son," "Potpourri, Israel Style," "I Am Dying," " A Song of Peace"

A revue in two acts.

General Manager: Paul Vroom
Press: Gifford/Wallace, Michael Albert, Marlene Carter
Stage Managers: Alan Cossey, Garth Browne

* Closed Oct. 8, 1972 after a limited engagement of 10 performances.

WINTER GARDEN THEATRE
Opened Thursday, October 5, 1972.*
The Shubert Organization presents:

NEIL DIAMOND ONE MAN SHOW

Producer, Ken Fritz; Direction and Lighting, Joe Gannon; Sc
Design, Jim Newton; Sound, Stan Miller; Musical Conductor, Lee
dridge; Musical Coordinator, Tom Catalano; Wardrobe, Bill Whi
Associate Manager, David Wyler
A program of songs performed by Neil Diamond.

General Manager: Marvin A. Krauss
Press: Paul Wasserman, Lawrence Eisenberg, Jim Mahoney
Associates

* Closed Oct. 21, 1973 after limited engagement of 21 performanc

14

Opened Monday, October 9, 1972.*
Adela and Peter Holzer present:

DUDE

The Highway Life

Book and Lyrics, Gerome Ragni; Music, Galt MacDermot; Directed and Staged by Tom O'Horgan; Designed by Eugene Lee, Roger Morgan, Franne Lee; Costumes, Randy Barcelo; Musical Arrangements and Orchestrations by Horace Ott; Musical Direction, Thomas Pierson; Production Associate, Margaret E. Kennedy; Original Cast Album by Columbia Records

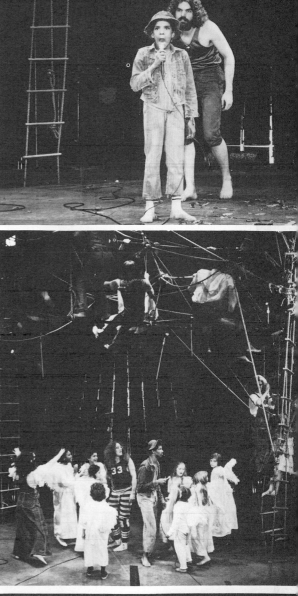

CAST

The Theatre Stars:

#33	Allan Nicholls
Dude	Ralph Carter
Mother Earth	Salome Bey
Bread	Delores Hall

The Shubert Angels:
Karen-Maria Faatz, Katie Field, Helen Jennings, David Kruger, Gary Mark, Mark Perman, Aida Random, Lynn Reynolds

The Theatre Wings:

Hero	Alan Braunstein
Halo	Sandra Loys Toder
Echo	Dawn Johnson
Solo	Michael Jason
Reba	Rae Allen
Harold	William Redfield
Suzie Moon	Nell Carter
Zero	James Patrick Farrell III
Nero	Leata Galloway
Sissy	David Lasley
Electric Bill	Jim Turner
Shadow	Dale Soules
Shade	Barbara Monte-Britton
Esso	Bobby Alessi
Extra	Billy Alessi
Meadow	Michael Meadows
World War Too	Georgianna Holmes
Noname	Carol Estey
Texaco	Dennis Simpson
Dude	Nat Morris

MUSICAL NUMBERS: Overture, "Theatre/Theatre," "A-Stage," "The Mountains," "Pears and Peaches," "Eat It," "Wah Wah," "Suzie Moon," "Y. O. U.," "I Love My Boo Boo," "Hum Drum Life," "Who's It?," "Talk to Me about Love," "Goodbyes," "I'm Small," "You Can Do Nothing about It," "The Handsomest Man," "Electric Prophet," "No-one," "Who Will Be the Children," "Go Holy Ghost," "A Song to Sing," "A Dawn," "The Days of This Life," "I Never Knew," "Air Male," "Undo," "The Earth," "My Darling I Love You March," "So Long Dude," "Peace Peace," "Jesus Hi," "Baby Breath," "Sweet Dreams"

A Musical in two acts.

General Managers: George W. Thorn, Leonard A. Mulhern
Press: Michael Alpert, Marianne Persson
Stage Managers: Michael Maurer, Robert Currie, Robert Vandergriff

Closed Oct. 21, 1972 after 16 performances and 16 previews.

Cosmos Photos

Bobby Alessi, Nat Morris, Billy Alessi
Top Right: Ralph Carter, James Patrick Varrell III

Rae Allen, William Redfield Above: (C) Allan Nicholls, Nat Morris

RITZ THEATRE
Opened Thursday, October 12, 1972.*
Peter Grad presents:

HURRY, HARRY

Book, Jeremiah Morris, Lee Kalcheim, Susan Perkis; Music, Bill Weeden; Lyrics, David Finkle; Director, Jeremiah Morris; Choreography, Gerald Teijelo; Scenery, Fred Voelpel; Lighting, Martin Aronstein; Costumes, Sara Brook; Orchestrations and Musical Supervision, Lee Norris; Musical Direction, Arthur Azenzer; Associate Producer, Ed Lewis

CAST

Harrison Fairchild IV	Samuel D. Ratcliffe
Harrison Fairchild III	Phil Leeds
Patience Fairchild	Liz Sheridan
Muffy Weathersford	Mary Bracken Phillips
Nick	Louis Criscuolo
Marco	Jack Landron
Stavos	Robert Darnell
Helena	Randee Heller
Mama	Liz Sheridan
Town Drunk	Phil Leeds
Melina	Donna Liggitt Forbes
Exodus	Robert Darnell
Genesis	Jack Landron
Deutronomy	Louis Criscuolo
Dr. Krauss	Phil Leeds
Writers	Louis Criscuolo, Robert Darnell, Randee Heller, Jack Landron, Liz Sherman
Starlet	Donna Liggitt Forbes
Natives	Robert Darnell, Donna Liggitt Forbes, Liz Sheridan, Randee Heller, Jack Landron
Witch Doctor	Louis Criscuolo
Chief	Phil Leeds
Grand Lama	Robert Darnell
Star	Liz Sheridan
Chorus Boys	Louis Criscuolo, Robert Darnell, Jack Landron, Phil Leeds
Winston	Robert Darnell
Gypsy	Randee Heller
Uncle Larry	Phil Leeds

MUSICAL NUMBERS: "I'm Gonna," "When a Man Cries," "A Trip through My Mind," "Life," "Love Can," "Africa Speaks," "Somewhere in the Past," "Hurry, Harry," "Goodby," "You Won't Be Happy," "He Is My Bag," Finale

A Musical in two acts and 19 scenes.

General Manager: Marvin A. Krauss
Press: Lee Solters, Harvey B. Sabinson, Marilynn LeVine
Company Manager: David Wyler
Stage Managers: Victor Straus, Harvey Landa, Don Fenwick

* Closed Oct. 13, 1972 after 2 performances and 9 previews.

Bert Andrews Photos

Phil Leeds (L), Samuel D. Ratcliffe (C)

Mary Bracken Phillips
Top: Donna Liggitt Forbes

Opened Monday, October 16, 1972.*
Irving Sudrow presents the New Zealand Maori Company Ltd.
production of:

PACIFIC PARADISE

Director, Jack Regas; Maori Cultural Director, Arapata Whaanga;
Choral Director, Kelly Harris; Opening Narration Compiled and Edited
Kit Regas; Technical Director, Herman Rudin; Executive Assistant,
William Dean

PROGRAM

Maori Welcome Ceremony, Legend of the Great Maori Migration,
Village Life in the New Land, Maori Festival

A Musical in two parts.

General Manager: Paul Vroom
Press: Karl Bernstein, Gifford/Wallace

Closed Oct. 21, 1972 after 5 performances.

Right: Maori Warrior

Maori Maidens Trio

HELEN HAYES THEATRE
Opened Tuesday, October 17, 1972.*
(Moved to Lunt-Fontanne Theatre Jan. 30, 1973)
Alexander H. Cohen and Bernard Delfont present:

6 RMS RIV VU

By Bob Randall; Director, Edwin Sherin; Scenery, William Ritman; Costumes, Ann Roth; Lighting, Marc B. Weiss; Production Associate, Hildy Parks; Associate Producer, Roy A. Somlyo; Production Supervisor, Jerry Adler; Associate Manager, Seymour Herscher; Production Assistant, Jane Tishman

CAST

Superintendent	Jose Ocasio
Pregnant Woman	Anna Shaler
Expectant Father	F. Murray Abraham
Anne Miller	Jane Alexander
Paul Friedman	Jerry Orbach
Woman in 4-A	Francine Beers
Janet Friedman	Jennifer Warren
Richard Miller	Ron Harper

STANDBYS: Paul, Richard, F. Murray Abraham; Anne, Anna Shaler; Janet, Woman in 4A, Lynda Myles

A Comedy in two acts and three scenes. The action takes place at the present time in an empty Riverside Drive Apartment in New York City.

General Manager: Roy A. Somlyo
Press: James D. Proctor, Louise Weiner Ment, David Powers
Stage Manager: Alan Coleridge

* Closed May 19, 1973 after 239 performances and 9 previews. Opened Monday, May 21 in Toronto, Canada for three weeks.

Friedman-Abeles, Secunda/Zarmati Photos

Jane Alexander, Jerry Orbach
Top: Jerry Orbach

Jerry Orbach, Jane Alexander

Francine Beers, Jerry Orbach Top: Jane Alexander,
Ron Harper, Jennifer Warren, Jerry Orbach

Jerry Orbach, Jane Alexander
(also top)

BELASCO THEATRE
Opened Thursday, October 19, 1972.*
Roger Ailes presents Ray Golden's production of:

MOTHER EARTH

Sketches and Lyrics, Ron Thronson; Music, Toni Shearer; Director, Ray Golden; Musical Staging, Lynne Morris; Consultant, Kermit Bloomgarden; Scenery, Alan Kimmel; Costumes, Mary McKinley; Lighting, Paul Sullivan; Musical Direction and Supervision, Sande Campbell; Associate Producers, Howard Butcher IV, Graeme Howard; Production Assistant, Madeleine Adams; Entire Production Supervised by Roger Ailes

CAST

Gail Boggs
Frank T. Coombs
Kimberly Farr
Kelly Garrett
Will Jacobs

Carol Kristy
Laura Michaels
John Bennett Perry
Rick Podell
Charlie J. Rodriguez

SKETCHES AND MUSICAL NUMBERS: "Out of Space," "Mother Earth," "The Client," "The Time of Our Life," "Corn on the Macabre," "The Mask Parade," "Too Many Old Ideas," "The Cheerleader," "Uneasy Rider," "Landscape with Figures," "Room to Be Free'.. "Model Wife," "Rent a Robot," "A Hike in the Woods," "Flash Gordon," "Plow It All Under," "Ewe Turn," "The Offal Truth," "The Killathon," "Taking the Easy Way Out," "Joggers," "Ozymandias," "Talons of Time," "The Nursery," "Save the World for Children," "Sail on Sweet Universe," "Mater Terra," "Xanadu," "Breath-Out," "Ecology Waltz," "Chic Diners," "Women Shoppers," "The Swan," "Good Morning World," "The Last Redwoods," "The Animals," "Tiger! Tiger!," "The Concrete Proposal," "Happy Mother's Day, Mother Earth," "Radioactive Terminate," "Pills," "The Billboards," Finale

A Musical in two acts and 18 scenes.

Company Manager: Robert P. Cohen
Press: Max Eisen, Milly Schoenbaum
Stage Managers: Donald W. Christy, Lanier Davis

* Closed Oct. 28, 1972 after 12 performances.

Gail Boggs, John Bennett Perry, Kelly Garrett, Kimberly Farr

Kelly Garrett, Charlie J. Rodriguez, Rick Podell

YMOUTH THEATRE
Opened Monday, October 30, 1972.*
Albert W. Selden and Jerome Minskoff present:

THE LINCOLN MASK

y V. J. Longhi; Director, Gene Frankel; By arrangement with John
sythe; Sets, Kert F. Lundell; Costumes, Patricia Quinn Stuart; Light-
Thomas Skelton; Music, Ezra Laderman; Audio, Jack Shearing;
rstyling, Ted Azar; Masks, Betsy Potter; Technical Director, John P.
gins; Assistant to Director, Nancy New

CAST

r American Cousin"

Edward	Joseph Warren
d Dundreary	Alek Primrose
rence	Ronnie Claire Edwards
rgina	Jean Bruno
ry Meredith	Patricia Cope
non	Eric Tavaris
Trenchard	Earl Hindman
coln at Ford's Theatre	Ray Stewart

Play:

ian Edwards	Thomas Barbour
elds	Albert Henderson
iam Herndon	Tom Rosqui
hen A. Douglas	W. B. Brydon
abeth Edwards	Tanny McDonald
ry Todd	Eva Marie Saint
aham Lincoln	Fred Gwynne
Henry	Alek Primrose
kins	Eric Tavaris
. Shields	Jean Bruno
in M. Stanton	Joseph Warren
vart	Eric Tavaris

DERSTUDIES: Lincoln, Ninian, Asa, Ray Stewart; Mary, Todd,
nie Claire Edwards; Herndon, Shields, Vernon, Jenkins, William
rles Reilly; Douglas, Stanton, Dundreary, Dr. Henry, Al Leberfeld;
ence, Georgina, Mary Meredith, Tanny McDonald

Drama in eight scenes performed without intermission. The action
s place between 1840 and 1865 in Springfield, Illinois, and Washing-
D.C.

General Manager: Walter Fried
Company Manager: Vincent McKnight
Press: Gifford/Wallace
age Managers: Frank Hamilton, William Charles Reilly, Al
Leberfeld

osed Nov. 4, 1972 after 8 performances and 19 previews.

Friedman-Abeles Photos

Eva Marie Saint, Fred Gwynne
(also top right)

IMPERIAL THEATRE
Opened Monday, October 23, 1972.*
Stuart Ostrow presents:

PIPPIN

Book, Roger O. Hirson; Music and Lyrics, Stephen Schwartz; Director-Choreographer, Bob Fosse; Scenery, Tony Walton; Costumes, Patricia Zipprodt; Lighting, Jules Fisher; Musical Direction, Stanley Lebowsky; Orchestrations, Ralph Burns; Dance Arrangements, John Berkman; Sound, Abe Jacob; Hair Stylist, Ernest Adler; Original Cast Album on Motown Records

CAST

Leading Player	Ben Vereen
Pippin	John Rubinstein
Charles	Eric Berry
Lewis	Christopher Chadman
Fastrada	Leland Palmer
Musician	John Mineo
The Head	Roger Hamilton
Berthe	Irene Ryan†
Beggar	Richard Korthaze
Peasant	Paul Solen
Noble	Gene Foote
Field Marshall	Roger Hamilton
Catherine	Jill Clayburgh
Theo	Shane Nickerson

STANDBYS AND UNDERSTUDIES: Pippin, Walter Willison; Leading Player, Northern A. Calloway; Berthe, Lucie Lancaster; Theo, Will McMillan; Charles, Robert Hamilton; Catherine, Ann Reinking; Fastrada, Candy Brown; Leading Player, Gene Foote; Dance Alternates, Cheryl Clark, Roger A. Bigelow

MUSICAL NUMBERS: "Magic to Do," "Corner of the Sky," "Welcome Home," "War Is a Science," "Glory," "Simple Joys," "No Time at All," "With You," "Spread a Little Sunshine," "Morning Glow," "On the Right Track," "Kind of Woman," "Extraordinary," "Love Song," Finale

A Musical Comedy in eight scenes, performed without intermission. The action takes place in 780 A.D. and thereabouts, in the Holy Roman Empire and thereabouts.

General Managers: Joseph Harris, Ira Bernstein
Press: Solters/Sabinson/Roskin, Cheryl Sue Dolby
Stage Managers: Phil Friedman, Lola Shumlin, Paul Phillips

* Still playing May 31, 1973.
† Succeeded by Lucie Lancaster, Dorothy Stickney.

Top Left and Below: Ben Vereen (C)

Irene Ryan

John Rubinstein

Ben Vereen (C) Above: (L & R) John Rubinstein (C)
Top: (L) Leland Palmer (R) Eric Beery

MOROSCO THEATRE
Opened Tuesday, October 31, 1972.*
Lester Osterman Productions (Lester Osterman-Rich
Horner) in association with Michael Codron presents:

BUTLEY

By Simon Gray; Director, James Hammerstein; Designed by Ei
Diss; Lighting and Costumes, Neil Peter Jampolis

CAST

Ben Butley	Alan Ba
Joseph Keyston	Hayward M
Miss Heasman	Geraldine Sherr
Edna Shaft	Barbara Le
Anne Butley	Holland Ta
Reg Nuttall	Roger Newr
Mr. Gardner	Christopher Hasti

STANDBYS AND UNDERSTUDIES: Ben, Ron Randell; Miss H
man, Andrea Stonorov; Joseph, Reg, Gardner, David Leary

A Comedy in two acts. The action takes place at the present tim
a college of London University.

General Manager: Leonard Soloway
Press: Abby Quinn Hirsch, Tobi Louis
Stage Managers: Harry Young, Andrea Stonorov

* Closed Feb. 24, 1973 after 128 performances and 7 previews.

Friedman-Abeles Photos

Left: Barbara Lester, Alan Bates, Hayward Morse
Top: Alan Bates

Alan Bates, Christopher Hastings

Holland Taylor, Alan Bates

Hayward Morse, Alan Bates, Roger Newman
Top: (L) Alan Bates (R) Alan Bates, Geraldine Sherman

WINTER GARDEN

Opened Saturday, November 11, 1972.*
The New York Shakespeare Festival (Joseph Papp, Producer) presents:

MUCH ADO ABOUT NOTHING

By William Shakespeare; Director, A. J. Antoon; Setting, Ming Cho Lee; Costumes, Theoni V. Aldredge; Lighting, Martin Aronstein; Music, Peter Link; Dances, Donald Saddler; Musical Supervision, John Morris; Associate Producer, Bernard Gersten; Production Assistant, Mary Colquhoun; Technical Director, Mervyn Haines, Jr.; Production Associate, Meir Zvi Ribalow; Sound, Peter Erskine; Music Conductor, Peter Phillips

CAST

Leonato	Mark Hammert†
Messenger	Charles Bartlett
Beatrice	Kathleen Widdoes
Hero	April Shawhan
Don Pedro	Douglass Watson
Benedick	Sam Waterston
Claudia	Glenn Walken
Don John	Jerry Mayer
Antonio	Arny Freeman
Conrade	Jack Gianino
Borachio	Frederick Coffin
Margaret	Jeanne Hepple
Balthasar	Marshall Efron
Ursula	Bette Henritze
Dogberry	Barnard Hughes
Verges	Will Mackenzie
First Watch	George Gugleotti
Second Watch	David Lenthall
Other Watches	Richard Casper, James McGill, Leland Schwantes
Friar Francis	Tom McDermott
Sexton	Charles Bartlett

TOWNSPEOPLE: Richard Casper, Lindsay Ann Crouse, Joan Jaffe, Rosamond Lynn, James McGill, William Robertson, Barbara Rubenstein, Richard Schneider, Leland Schwantes, Cathy Greene

STANDBYS AND UNDERSTUDIES: Dogberry, Albert Quinton; Benedick, Will Mackenzie; Pedro, Maury Cooper; Beatrice, Jeanne Hepple; Leonato, Maury Cooper; Borachio, Don John, Jack Gianino; Verges, George Gugleotti; Balthasar, David Lenthall; Claudio, Richard Casper; Ursula, Joan Jaffe; Conrade, Watch, Leland Schwantes; Sexton, Messenger, Watch, Richard Schneider; Margaret, Barbara Rubenstein; Hero, Linsay Ann Crouse; Antonio, William Robertson; Friar, Albert Quinton

A Comedy in two acts.

General Managers: Eugene Wolsk, Emanuel Azenberg
Company Manager: Robert Kamlot
Press: Merle Debuskey, Robert Larkin
Stage Managers: David Eidenberg, Tom Gardner, Dan Sedgwick

* Closed Feb. 11, 1973 after 116 performances. Opened Aug. 16, 1972 in Central Park's Delacorte Theater where it played 20 performances.
† Succeeded by Paul Sparer

Lawrence Fried, George E. Joseph Photos

Top Left: Kathleen Widdoes, Sam Waterston, also below with April Shawhan, Tom McDermott, Glenn Walken

Sam Waterston, Douglass Watson

Barnard Hughes, Will Mackenzie

Finale   Above: Mark Hammer, April Shawhan, Bette Henritze, Kathleen Widdoes,
Glenn Walken, Sam Waterston

BROOKS ATKINSON THEATRE
Opened Monday, November 13, 1972.*
David Black and David Seltzer present:

LYSISTRATA

By Aristophanes; Adapted and Directed by Michael Cacoyannis; Music, Peter Link; Sets, Robin Wagner; Costumes, Willa Kim; Lighting, Jules Fisher; Sound, Abe Jacob; Hairstyles, Ted Azar; Associate Producer, Ira Resnick; Musical Director, Henry "Bootsie" Normand

CAST

Lysistrata	Melina Mercouri
Kalonike	Evelyn Russell
Myrrhine	Priscilla Lopez
Lampito	Madeleine Le Roux
Corinthian Woman	Lynda Sue Marks
Theban Woman	Andrea Levine
Policewoman	Marylou Perhacs
Omicron	John Bentley
Phi-Chi	Gordon Connell
Omega	Joseph Palmieri
Upsilon	David Thomas
Gamma	Jane Connell
Alphabeta	Avril Gentles
Deltazeta	Mary Jo Catlett
Theta	Patti Karr
Iota	Gayla Osbourne
Commissioner	Philip Bruns
Woman A	Cynthia Bullens
Woman B	Joanne Nail
Woman C	Joy Franz
Kinesias	Richard Dmitri
Spartan Herald	Stephen Macht
Spartan Delegate	Charles E. Siegel

UNDERSTUDIES: Kalonike, Lampito, Patti Karr; Myrrhine, Joanne Nail; Kinesias, Stephen Macht; Men, Charles E. Siegel; Commissioner, John Bentley.

SONGS: "A Woman's Hands," "On, On, On," "Many the Beasts," "Are We Strong?," "And We Are In," "Lysistrata," "I Miss My Man," "To Touch the Sky," "Eels Are a Girl's Best Friend," "Let Me Tell You a Little Story," "Kalimera"

A Comedy performed without intermission. The action takes place in ancient Greece.

General Manager: Norman Maibaum
Company Manager: John J. Miller
Press: Betty Lee Hunt, Henry Luhrman, Harriett Trachtenberg, Maria C. Pucci
Stage Managers: Mortimer Halpern, Nicholas Russiyan

* Closed Nov. 18, 1972 after 8 performances and 35 previews.

Friedman-Abeles Photos

Melina Mercouri, Priscilla Lopez
(rehearsal shots only photos taken)

Phillip Bruns, Melina Mercouri
Top: Director Michael Cacoyannis, Melina Mercou

T-FONTANNE THEATRE
Opened Sunday, November 19, 1972.*
Gene Dingenary, Miranda d'Ancona, Nancy Levering present:

AMBASSADOR

ok, Don Ettlinger, Anna Marie Barlow; Based on novel "The Am-
dors" by Henry James; Music, Don Gohman; Lyrics, Hal Hackady;
tor, Stone Widney; Mucisal Staging and Choreography, Joyce
r; Sets and Costumes, Peter Rice; American Production Supervised
bert Guerra; Costumes Supervised by Sara Brook; Lighting, Martin
stein; Musical Direction and Vocal Arrangements, Herbert Gross-
Orchestrations, Philip J. Lang; Dance Arrangements, Trude Ritt-
; Associate Producer, Dan Rodden; Hairstylist, Ronald DeMann;
ant to the Producers, Shelly Maibaum; Production Assistant, Marie
ews; Assistant Choreographer, Elizabeth Hodes

CAST

er Girl	Patricia Arnell
s Lambert Strether	Howard Keel
marsh	David Sabin
e de Vionnet	Danielle Darrieux
ani	Carmen Mathews
er	Dwight Arno
m	Michael Goodwin
	Michael Shannon
ne de Vionnet	Andrea Marcovicci
ing Master	Larry Giroux
	Larry Giroux
e	Jack Trussel
er	Robert L. Hultman
eper's Wife	Marsha Tamaroff
oy	Nikolas Dante
in Park	Dixie Stewart
ia Newsome	M'El Dowd
aine	Patricia Arnell
ret Dancers	Alex Hoff, Phillip Filiato, Suzanne Sponsler, Larry Giroux
waiter	Robert L. Hultman
Manager	Jack Trussel

LE OF PARIS: Janis Ansley, Patricia Arnell, Dwight Arno,
a Brooks, Nikolas Dante, Richard Dodd, Vito Durante, Phillip
, Lynn Fitzpatrick, Larry Giroux, Charlie Goeddertz, Gerald Has-
Alexis Hoff, Robert L. Hultman, Douglas E. Hunnikin, Genette
Betsy Ann Leadbetter, Nancy Lunch, Linda-Lee MacArthur,
Petroski, Dean Russell, Salicia Saree, Elie Smith, Suzanne
er, Dixie Stewart, Marsha Tamaroff, Jack Trussell, Chester Walker

DBYS AND UNDERSTUDIES: Strether, Steve Arlen; Marie,
Moser; Gloriani, Linda-Lee MacArthur; Amelia, Marsha Tama-
Vaymarsh, Jack Trussell; Chad, Michael Goodwin; Jeanne, Patricia
; Bilham, Dean Russell; Flower Girl, Lynn Fitzpatrick

CAL NUMBERS: "Lilas," "Lambert's Quandary," "I Know the
"The Right Time, The Right Place," "She Passed My Way,"
," "Something More," "Love Finds the Lonely," "Kyrie Eleison,"
ise," "Happy Man," "Lilas, What Happened to Paris," "Young
im," "Too Much to Forgive," "Why Do Women Have to Call It
" "Mama," "What's What I Need Tonight," "Maxixe-Habanera,"
p," "Not Tomorrow," "All of My Life," "Thank You, No"

Musical in two acts and 19 scenes. The action takes place in Paris
6.

General Manager: Norman Maibaum
Company Manager: Malcolm Allen
Press: Reginald Denenholz, Timothy A. Burke
ge Managers: Alan Hall, Mary Porter Hall, Lynn Guerra,
Robert L. Hultman

ed Nov. 25, 1972 after 9 performances and 20 previews.

Martha Swope Photos

**'op Right: (R-L) Danielle Darrieux, Howard
el, Michael Goodwin, David Sabin, Carmen
hews, M'El Dowd, Andrea Marcovicci, Michael
non Right Center: Andrea Marcovicci, Michael
Goodwin**

Carmen Mathews, David Sabin

AMBASSADOR THEATRE
Opened Tuesday, November 14, 1972.*
James B. McKenzie and Spofford J. Beadle present:

THE SECRET AFFAIRS OF MILDRED WILD

By Paul Zindel; Director, Jeff Bleckner; Setting, Santo Loquasto; Costumes, Carrie F. Robbins; Lighting, Thomas Skelton; Sound, James Reichert; Hairstylist, Ernest Adler; Choreography, Edward Roll; Production Assistants, John Neville, Greg Nash; Assistant to the Producers, Linda Ford; Special Musical Arrangements, Rudolph Bennett

CAST

Mildred Wild	Maureen Stapleton
Roy Wild	Lee Wallace
Bertha Gale	Florence Stanley
Helen Wild	Elizabeth Wilson
Carroll Chatham	Neil Flanagan
Sister Cecelia	Joan Pape
Miss Manley	Doris Roberts
Rex Bulby	Bill McIntyre
Louis Garibaldi	Pat Corley
Warren, TV Host	Paul DeWitt
Evelyn, TV Hostess	Joan Pape

UNDERSTUDIES: Mildred, Doris Roberts; Carroll, Garibaldi, Warren, Bill McIntyre

A Comedy in three acts and five scenes. The action takes place at the present time in the living quarters in the rear of a dilapidated candy store in Greenwich Village in New York City operated by Roy and Mildred Wild.

General Manager: Ralph Roseman
Press: Solters/Sabinson/Roskin, Sandra Manley
Stage Managers: Frank Hartenstein, Bill McIntyre

* Closed Dec. 2, 1972 after 23 performances and 5 previews.

Bert Andrews Photos

Left: Elizabeth Wilson, Lee Wallace, Maureen Stapleton

Top: Maureen Stapleton

Doris Roberts, Elizabeth Wilson, Florence Stanley, Maureen Stapleton, Neil Flanagan, Joan Pape, Lee Wallace

Lee Wallace, Maureen Stapleton
Top: Maureen Stapleton

Lee Wallace, Doris Roberts, Maureen Stapleton
Top: Maureen Stapleton, Neil Flanagan

CIRCLE IN THE SQUARE
JOSEPH E. LEVINE THEATRE
Opened Wednesday, November 15, 1972.*
Circle in the Square (Theodore Mann, Artistic Director;
Libin, Managing Director) presents:

MOURNING BECOMES ELECTRA

By Eugene O'Neill; Director, Theodore Mann; Scenery, Marsh
Eck; Lighting, Jules Fisher; Costumes, Noel Taylor; Production
ciate, Linda Howes

CAST

Seth Beckwith	William H
Amos Ames	Hansford
Louisa Ames	Eileen
Minnie	Jocelyn Br
Christine Mannon	Colleen Dew
Lavinia Mannon	Pamela Payton-W
Hazel Niles	Lisa Ric'
Capt. Peter Niles	Jack Ry
Capt. Adam Brant	Alan M
Brigadier General Ezra Mannon	Donald
Josiah Borden	Hansford
Emma Borden	Jocelyn Br
Rev. Everett Hills	Eileen
Dr. Joseph Blake	Daniel K
Orin Mannon	Stephen McH
Chatyman	John
Abner Small	William
Ira Mackel	John

SERVANTS: Eileen Burns, Jocelyn Brando, William Bush, D
Keyes, Hansford Rowe, John Ridge

A Dramatic Trilogy in 3 acts and 13 scenes. The action takes pla
New England during 1865 and 1866.

Company Manager: William Conn
Press: Merle Debuskey, Leo Stern
Stage Managers: Randall Brooks, Charles Roden

* Closed Dec. 31, 1972 after 55 performances and 14 previews.

Friedman-Abeles Photos

Colleen Dewhurst, Stephen McHattie
Top Left: Pamela Payton-Wright, Colleen Dewhurst

Colleen Dewhurst, Donald Davis, Pamela Payton-Wright
Top: Alan Mixon, Colleen Dewhurst

Colleen Dewhurst, Pamela Payton-Wright

33

SHUBERT THEATRE
Opened Thursday, November 30, 1972.*
Robert Whitehead presents:

THE CREATION OF THE WORLD AND OTHER BUSINESS

By Arthur Miller; Director, Gerald Freedman; Settings and Pr-
tions, Boris Aronson; Lighting, Tharon Musser; Costumes, Hal Geo
Music, Stanley Silverman; Assistant to Producer, Doris Blum; Produc
Assistants, Bill Becker, Jean Bankier; Hairstylists, Steve Atha, Bob
bott; Vocal Director, Roland Gagnon; A Dowling-Whitehead-Ste
Production.

CAST

Adam	Bob D
God	Stephen El
Eve	Zoe Cald
Chemuel Angel of Mercy	Lou Gil
Raphael	Dennis Co
Azrael Angel of Death	Lou P
Lucifer	George Griz
Cain	Barry Pri
Abel	Mark La

STANDBYS: Lucifer, God, Timothy Jerome; Adam, Wayne Car
Abel, Dennis Cooley; Cain, Angels, Ira Lewis

A Comedy in three acts, answering three questions on the hu
dilemma: Since God made everything and God is good, why did He r
Lucifer? Is there something in the way we are born which makes us
the world to be good? When every man wants justice, why does he g
creating injustice?

General Manager: Oscar E. Olesen
Company Manager: Max Allentuck
Press: James D. Proctor
Stage Managers: Frederic de Wilde, Wayne Carson, Ira Lev

* Closed Dec. 16, 1972 after 20 performances and 21 previews.

Inge Morath Photos

George Grizzard, Zoe Caldwell
Top: Zoe Caldwell

Bob Dishy, Zoe Caldwell

Mark Lamos, George Grizzard, Bob Dishy, Zoe Caldwell, Barry Primus
Top: Stephen Elliott, Bob Dishy, Zoe Caldwell

Virginia Vestoff, Keene Curtis

URIS THEATRE
Opened Tuesday, November 28, 1972.*
George W. George and Barnard S. Strauss in association with
Nat Shapiro present:

VIA GALACTICA

Book, Christopher Gore and Judith Ross; Music, Galt MacDermo
Lyrics, Christopher Gore; Conceived and Directed by Peter Hall; De
signed by John Bury; Lighting, Lloyd Burlingame; Associate to Mr. Hall
Geoffrey Cauley; Musical Director and Vocal Arrangements, Joyc
Brown; Directorial Assistant, Patrick Libby; Orchestrations, Horace Ott
Bhen Lanzaroni, Danny Hurd; Hairstyles and Makeup, Ted Azar; Sound
Jack Shearing; Associate to Producers, Arthur Gorton

CAST

Clair	Irene Car
On Earth:	
Spokesman	James Dyba
Old Man	Chuck Cise
Blue People	Mark Baker, Jacqueline Britt, Melan
Chartoff, Richard DeRusso, Sylvia DiGiorgio, Edloe, Livi	
Genise, Marion Killinger, Toni Lund, Bob Spence	
Bonnie Walke	
Gabriel Finn	Raul Juli
Hels Mikelli	Damon Evan
April Whitney	Louise Heat
On Ithaca:	
Omacha	Virginia Vesto
Dr. Isaacs.	Keene Curti
Provo	Bill Sta
Diane	Livia Genis
Nicklas	Peter Nisse
Roustabout	Alex Ande
Cook	Mark Bake
Mute's Friend	Robert Blankshin
Gypsy	Jacqueline Bri
Boy	Ralph Carte
Geologist	Melanie Charto
Student	Chuck Ciss
Mute	Lili Cockeril
Lady	Lorrie Dav
Mechanic	Richard DeRuss
Teacher	Sylvia DiGiorg
Entertainer	James Dyba
Artist	Edl
Writer	Livia Geni
Politician	Marion Killing
Child	Toni Lur
Cripple	Veronica Red
Tailor	James River
Carpenter	Richard Ryd
Doctor	Stan Sha
Gambler	Leon Spelma
Janitor	Bob Spenc
Old Man	Bill Sta
Nurse	Bonnie Walk
Grandmother	J. H. Washingto

UNDERSTUDIES: Gabriel, Richard DeRusso; Omaha, Veronica Red
Isaacs, James Dybas; April, Edloe; Hels, Stan Shaw; Swing Dancer, Jor
Diaz

MUSICAL NUMBERS; "Via Galactica," "We Are One," "Helen
Troy," "Oysters," "The Other Side of the Sky," "Children of the Sur
"Different," "Take Your Hat off," "Ilmar's Tomb," "Shall We Friend?
"The Lady Isn't Looking," "Hush," "Cross on Over," "Gospel of Gabr
Finn," "Terre Haute High," "Life Wins," "The Great Forever Wagon
"The Worm Germ," "Isaacs' Equation," "Dance the Dark Away
"Four Hundred Girls Ago," "All My Good Mornings," "New Jerus
lem"

A Musical in two acts and seven parts. The action takes place in t
future.

General Manager: George Thorn, Leonard A. Mulhern
Press: Solters/Sabinson/Ruskin, Sandra Manley

Morty Lefkoe Photos

Top Left: Virginia Vestoff (L), Raul Julia (C)

LYCEUM THEATRE
Opened Monday, December 11, 1972.*
The New Phoenix Repertory Company (T. Edward Hambleton, Managing Director; Harold Prince, Stephen Porter, Michael Montel, Artistic Directors) presents:

DON JUAN

By Moliere; Director, Stephen Porter; Scenery, John J. Moore; Costumes, Nancy Potts; Lighting, Tharon Musser; Music, Conrad Susa; Fight staged by David Dukes; Hairstylist, Steve Altha

CAST

Sganarelle	John McMartin
Gusman	Clyde Burton
Don Juan	Paul Hecht
Dóna Elvira	Katherine Helmond
LeRamee	Robert Phelps
Ragotin	Thomas A. Stewart
Charlotte	Charlotte Moore
Pierrot	John Glover
Mathurine	Marilyn Sokol
Poor Man	James Greene
Robbers	Robert Ginty, Thomas A. Stewart, Robert Phelps
Don Carlos	David Dukes
Don Alonso	Curt Karibalis
Commander	Peter Friedman
La Violette	Clyde Burton
Monsieur Dimanche	James Greene
Don Luis	Bill Moor
Veiled Woman	Bonnie Gallup

UNDERSTUDIES: Don Juan, Curt Karibalis; Elvira, Veiled Woman, Ellen Tovatt; Charlotte, Mathurine, Bonnie Gallup; Carlos, Peter Friedman; Poor Man, Dimanche, Thomas A. Stewart; Luis, Gusman, Alonso, Robert Phelps; Pierrot, Clyde Burton; La Violette, Ragotin, LaRamee, Commander, Robert Ginty.

A comedy in five acts performed with one intermission. The action takes place in the house of Don Juan, on a seashore, and in a forest.

General Manager: Marilyn S. Miller
Company Manager: Gintare Sileika
Press: Daniel Langan
Stage Managers: Daniel Freudenberger, Kathleen A. Sullivan

* Closed Jan. 14, 1973 after 7 previews and 41 performances in repertory with "The Great God Brown."

Van Williams Photos

Top Left: David Dukes, Paul Hecht, John McMartin
Below: Marilyn Sokol, Paul Hecht, Charlotte Moore

Paul Hecht, Bill Moor

Paul Hecht, Katherine Helmond

LYCEUM THEATRE
Opened Sunday, December 10, 1972.*
The New Phoenix Repertory Company (T. Edward Hambl-
ton, Managing Director; Harold Prince, Stephen Porter, M-
chael Montel, Artistic Directors) presents:

THE GREAT GOD BROWN

By Eugene O'Neill; Director, Harold Prince; Scenery, Boris Aronsc
Costumes and Masks, Carolyn Parker; Lighting, Tharon Musser; Ass-
tant Director, Ruth Mitchell

CAST

William Brown	John Glov
Mrs. Brown	Bonnie Gall
Mr. Brown	Paul Hec
Dion Anthony	John McMart
Mrs. Anthony	Charlotte Moc
Margaret	Katherine Helmo
Cybel	Marilyn Sok
Older Son	Robert Phel
Younger Son	Thomas A. Stewa
Older Draftsman	Bill Mo
Younger Draftsman	Clyde Burt
Committee	David Dukes, Peter Friedman, Ellen Tov
Policeman	Curt Kariba

UNDERSTUDIES: William, David Dukes; Dion, Clyde Burton; Brow
Anthony, Bill Moor; Mrs. Brown, Mrs. Anthony, Ellen Tovatt; Margar
Charlotte Moore; Cybel, Bonnie Gallup; Sons, Draftsmen, Committ
Policeman, Robert Ginty

A Drama in three acts. The action takes place, variously, on the p
of a casino, in Dion Anthony's sitting room, in William Brown's office a
adjoining drafting room, and in Cybel's parlor. It spans the years fr
1916 to 1936.

General Manager: Marilyn S. Miller
Press: Daniel Langan
Stage Managers: Daniel Freudenberger, Kathleen A. Sullivan

* Closed Jan. 14, 1973 after 41 performances and 7 previews in report
with "Don Juan."

Van Williams Photos

John Glover Top Left: Katherine Helmond, John McMartin

John McMartin, John Glover Top: (L) David Dukes, Ellen Tovatt, Peter Friedman, Bonnie Gallup, John Glover (R) John McMartin, Marilyn Sokol

ANTA THEATRE
Opened Tuesday, December 12, 1972.*
Theater 1973 (Richard Barr/Charles Woodward) and the
American National Theatre and Academy present:

THE LAST OF MRS. LINCOLN

By James Prideaux; Director, George Schaefer; Settings and Lighting
William Ritman; Costumes, Noel Taylor; Hairstylist, Ray Iagnocco; Associate Producer, Michael Kasdan; Assistant to Producers, Jack Custer;
Production Assistant, Bolen High; Associate Producer, Harold Endicot

CAST

Senator Austin	Richard Wood
Robert Lincoln	David Round
Tad Lincoln	Tobias Halle
Mary Lincoln	Julie Harri
Ninian Edwards	Ralph Clanto
Lizzie Keckley	Dorothi Fo
Mary Harlan	Maureen Anderma
Mr. Keyes	Macon McCalma
Young Senator	Dennis Coone
Man	Joseph Attle
Boy	Marc Jefferso
Lewis Baker	Brian Farrel
Elizabeth Edwards	Leora Dan
Mrs. McCullough	Kate Wilkinso
Attendant	Louis Schaefe

STANDBYS AND UNDERSTUDIES: Mary Lincoln, Leora Dana;
Robert, Dennis Cooney; Elizabeth, Mrs. McCullough, Lois de Banzie;
Lizzie, Urylee Leonardos; Mary Harlan, Madelon Thomas; Tad, Lewi;
George Connolly; Ninian, Austin, Macon McCalman

A Drama in two acts.

General Manager: Michael Kasdan
Company Manager: Oscar Abraham
Press: Betty Lee Hunt, Henry Luhrman, Harriett Trachtenberg,
Maria Pucci
Stage Managers: Mark Wright, Charles Kindl, Allen Williams

* Closed Feb. 4, 1973 after 63 performances and 5 previews.

Martha Swope Photos

Julie Harris, Brian Farrell, Leora Dana, Kate Wilkinson

Julie Harris (also top left)

Maureen Anderman, Tobias Haller, Julie Harris, Dorothi Fox, David Rounds
Top: (L) Julie Harris, David Rounds (R) Julie Harris

BROADHURST THEATRE
Opened Wednesday, December 20, 1972.*
Emanuel Azenberg, Eugene V. Wolsk present:

THE SUNSHINE BOYS

By Neil Simon; Director, Alan Arkin; Scenery, Kert Lundell; C
tumes, Albert Wolsky; Lighting, Tharon Musser; Hairstylist, Jo
Quaglia

CAST

Willie Clark	Jack Albertso
Ben Silverman	Lewis J. Stad
Al Lewis	Sam Leven
Patient	Joe You
Eddie	John Bat
Sketch Nurse	Lee Mered
Nurse	Minnie Gen

UNDERSTUDIES: Al, Clem Fowler; Ben, John Batiste; Eddie, Patie
George Rando; Nurse, Cynthia Belgrave; Sketch Nurse, Darlene Pa

A Comedy in two acts. The action takes place at the present tim

Manager: Jose Vega
Press: Solters/Sabinson/Roskin, Cheryl Sue Dolby
Stage Managers: Tom Porter, George Rondo

* Still playing May 31, 1973.
† Played by Harold Gary during illness.

Martha Swope Photos

Lee Meredith, Sam Levene, Jack Albertson
Top Left: Lewis J. Stadlen, Sam Levene

Jack Albertson, Lewis J. Stadlen, Sam Levene

BILLY ROSE THEATRE
Opened Wednesday, December 27, 1972.*
Philip Rose presents:

PURLIE

Book, Ossie Davis, Philip Rose, Peter Udell; Music, Gary Geld; Lyr
Peter Udell; Based on play "Purlie Victorious" by Ossie Davis; Scene
Ben Edwards; Director, Philip Rose; Choreography, Louis Johns
Lighting, Thomas Skelton; Costumes, Ann Roth; Hairstylist, Ernest ▪
ler; Orchestrations and Choral Arrangements, Garry Sherman, Lut▪
Henderson; Musical Supervisor, Garry Sherman; Musical Conduc▪
Charles Austin; Dance Music Arranged by Luther Henderson; Prod▪
tion Supervisor, Mortimer Halpern; Technical Adviser, John P. Higg▪
Original Cast Album by Ampex Records.

CAST

Purlie	Robert Guillau▪
Church Soloist	Shirley Mon▪
Lutiebelle	Patti▪
Missy	Laura Coo▪
Gitlow	Sherman Hems▪
Field Hands	Every Hayes, Lonnie McNeil, Ted R▪
Charlie	Douglas Norw▪
Idella	Helen Mar▪
Ol'Cap'n	Art Wall▪

DANCERS: Darlene Blackburn, Deborah Bridges, Raphael Gilb▪
Linda Griffin, Every Hayes, Reggie Jackson, Alton Lathrop, Robert M▪
tin, Karen E. McDonald, Lonnie McNeil, Debbie Palmer, Andre P▪
Zelda Pulliam

SINGERS: Demarest Grey, Barbara Joy, Ursuline Kairson, Shi▪
Monroe, Alfred Rage, Beverly G. Robnett, Ted Ross, Frances Salisb▪
Vanessa Shaw, David Weatherspoon, Joe Williams, Jr.

STANDBYS AND UNDERSTUDIES: Purlie, Ra Joe Darby; L▪
belle, Demarest Grey, Ursline Kairson; Cap'n, Bill Nunnery; Cha▪
John Hammil; Gitlow, Ted Ross; Swing Dancer, Reggie Jackson; M▪
Beverly G. Robnett, Barbara Joy; Idella, Frances Salisbury

MUSICAL NUMBERS: "Walk Him Up the Stairs," "New Fan▪
Preacher Man," "Skinnin' Cat," "Purlie," "The Harder They F▪
"Charlie's Songs," "Big Fish, Little Fish," "I Got Love," "Great W▪
Father," "Down Home," "First Thing Monday Mornin'," "He Can▪
It," "The World Is Comin' to a Start," Finale.

A Musical Comedy in two acts and six scenes with prologue ▪
epilogue. The action takes place in South Georgia, not too long ag▪

General & Company Manager: Helen Richards
Press: Merle Debuskey, Maurice Turet
Stage Managers: Steven Zweigbaum, Lou Rodgers III, Ra J▪
Darby

* Closed Jan. 7, 1973 after 14 performances and 2 previews. Returne▪
national tour. For original production, see THEATRE WORLD, ▪
26.
† Succeeded by Louise Stubbs

Friedman-Abeles Photo

44
Patti Jo
Top: Robert Guillaume, Patti Jo

Laura Cooper, Sherman Hemsley

Robert Guillaume, Patti Jo Top: Carol Jean Lewis,
Patti Jo, Sherman Hemsley, Robert Guillaume

Art Wallace, Douglas Norwick

ALVIN THEATRE
Opened Monday, January 8, 1973.*
Herman Levin presents:

TRICKS

Book and Direction, Jon Jory; Based on play by Moliere; Music, Jerry Blatt; Lyrics, Lonnie Burstein; Choreography, Donald Saddler; Scenery, Oliver Smith; Costumes, Miles White; Lighting, Martin Aronstein; Orchestrations, Bert De Coteau; Dance and Incidental Music Arranged by Peter Howard; Conductor, David Frank; Sound, Jack Shearing; Associate Producer, Samuel Liff

CAST

Property Mistress	Adale O'Brien
Octave	Walter Bobbie
Sylvestre	Christopher Murney
Scapin	Rene Auberjonois
Hyacinthe	Carolyn Mignini
Argante	Mitchell Jason
Geronte	Tom Toner
Leandre	Randy Herron
Zerbinetta	June Helmers
Pantanella	Suzanne Walker
Isabella	Jo Ann Ogawa
Carmella	Lani Sundsten
Gondolier	John Handy

The Commedia:

Arlecchino/Lead Singer	Joe Morton
Charlotta	Charlotte Crossley
Ernestina	Ernestine Jackson
Shezwae	Shezwae Powell

UNDERSTUDIES: Scapin, Sylvestre, Eric Tavares; Argante, Geronte, Joe Hill; Zerbinetta, Adale O'Brien; Octave, Randy Herron; Leandre, John Handy; Hyacinthe, Property Mistress, Susan Dyas; Pantanella, Carmella, Isabella, Vicki Frederick

MUSICAL NUMBERS: "Love or Money," "Who Was I?," "Trouble's a Ruler," "Enter Hyacinthe," "Believe Me," "Tricks," "A Man of Spirit," "Where Is Respect," "Somebody's Doin' Somebody All the Time," "A Sporting Man," "Scapin," "Anything Is Possible," "How Sweetly Simple," "Gypsy Girl," "Life Can Be Funny"

A Musical Comedy in two acts. The action takes place in and around Venice.

General Manager: Philip Adler
Company Manager: Milton M. Pollack
Press: Frank Goodman, Arlene Wolf, Margaret Wade
Stage Managers: Mitchell Erickson, John Handy, Joe Hill

* Closed Jan. 13, 1973 after 8 performances and 5 previews.

Right: Randy Herron, Rene Auberjonois, Christopher Murney,

Top. Rene Auberjonois, Christopher Murney

Walter Bobbie

Walter Bobbie, Carolyn Mignini

LACE THEATRE
Opened Monday, January 15, 1973.*
Lee Orgel and William J. Griffiths present:

DON JUAN IN HELL

By George Bernard Shaw; Director, John Houseman; Production As-
ant, Jeffrey Richards; Miss Moorehead's gown by Nolan Miller

CAST

mmander	Paul Henreid
n Juan	Ricardo Montalban
vil	Edward Mulhare
na Ana	Agnes Moorehead

Understudy: Ricardo S. Ramos

A Comedy presented in two parts.
General Manager: Harry Zevin
Company Manager: James O'Neill
Press: Howard Newman, Jeffrey Richards
Stage Managers: Richard Wessler, Ricardo S. Ramos

Closed Feb. 4, 1973 after 24 performances.

Right: Paul Henreid, Agnes Moorehead

Edward Mulhare, Ricardo Montalban, Agnes Moorehead, Paul Henreid

BILTMORE THEATRE
Opened Tuesday, January 16, 1973.*
Michael and Barclay MacRae present:

LET ME HEAR YOU SMILE

By Leonora Thuna and Harry Cauley; Director, Harry Cauley; Scenery, Peter Larkin; Costumes, Carrie F. Robbins; Lighting, Neil Peter Jampolis; Hairstylist, Hector Garcia; Assistant to Producers, Christi Hatcher

CAST

Hannah Heywood .... Sandy Dennis
Neil Heywood .... James Broderick
Willy Farmer .... Paul B. Price

STANDBYS: Hannah, Nancy Chesney; Neil, Philip Cusack

A Comedy in three acts. The action takes place in the Heywood home in a small New Jersey town today, on Christmas Eve 1940, and in the summer of 1905.

General Manager: Richard Seader
Company Manager: Malcolm Allen
Press: Betty Lee Hunt, Henry Luhrman, Harriett Trachtenberg, Maria Pucci
Stage Managers: Ben Janney, Philip Cusack

* Closed Jan. 16, 1973 after one performance and 7 previews.

Friedman-Abeles Photos

Right: James Broderick, Sandy Dennis

Sandy Dennis, James Broderick

**CIRCLE IN THE SQUARE-
JOSEPH E. LEVINE THEATRE**
Opened Wednesday, January 17, 1973.*
Circle in the Square (Theodore Mann, Artistic Director; Paul
Libin, Managing Director) presents:

MEDEA

By Euripides; Adapted and Directed by Minos Volanakis; Scenery,
Robert Mitchell; Lighting, Marc B. Weiss; Costumes, Nancy Potts; Choral Music, Michael Small; Electronic Environment, Tempi; Production
Associate, E. J. Oshins; Production Assistant, Jill Farren

CAST

Nurse	Tally Brown
Old Man	Ron Faber
Two Children (Alternating)	Kirsten Aimee, Eric Faber, Eric John Roden
Medea	Irene Papas
Kreon	Ron Faber
Soldiers	Rob Evan Collins, Bill E. Noone
Jason	John P. Ryan
Aegeus	Albert Stratton
Messenger	Al Freeman, Jr.

CHORUS: Geraldine Court, Irene Frances Kling, Betty Lester, Julienne
Marshall, Marsha Meyers, Dina Paisner, Elaine Sulka, Florence Tarlow,
Nancy Zala.

UNDERSTUDIES: Medea, Elaine Sulka; Nurse, Florence Tarlow; Jason, Kreon, Rob Evan Collins; Old Man, Messenger, Bill E. Noone

A Drama performed without intermission.

Company Manager: William Conn
Press: Merle Debuskey, Leo Stern
Stage Managers: Randall Brooks, Charles Roden

* Closed March 18, 1973 after 79 performances and 8 previews.

Friedman-Abeles Photos

Al Freeman, Jr., Irene Papas
Top Right: John P. Ryan, Irene Papas

CORT THEATRE
Opened Wednesday, January 24, 1973.*
The John F. Kennedy Center for the Performing Arts by arrangement with Peter Saunders Ltd., London, presents:

THE JOCKEY CLUB STAKES

By William Douglas Home; Director, Cyril Ritchard; Seenery and Lighting, Paul Morrison; Costumes, Albert Wolsky; Produced by Roger L. Stevens and J. Charles Gilbert in association with Moe Septee

CAST

Marquis of Candover	Wilfrid Hyde-White
Lord Coverley de Beaumont	Geoffrey Sumner
Colonel Sir Robert Richardson	Robert Coote
Capt. Trevor Jones	Philip Kerr
Miss Hills	Joan Bassie
P. Brown	Norman Allen
Lady Ursula Itchin	Carolyn Lagerfelt
Lord Green	Lee Richardson
Tom Glass	Christopher Bernau
Charlie Wisden	Dillon Evans
Perch Graham	Albert Sanders
Sir Dymock Blackburn	Thayer David
Lady Green	Enid Rodgers

STANDBYS: Richardson, Beaumont, Blackburn, Alexander Reed; Green, Trevor, Glass, Jay Lanin; Miss Hills, Lady Green, Ethel Drew

A Comedy in two acts and four scenes. The action takes place at the present time in the Jockey Club rooms during the summer.

General Manager: J. Charles Gilbert
Press: Michael Sean O'Shea
Stage Managers: Nikos Kafkalis, Jay Lanin, Ethel Drew

* Closed March 24, 1973 after 69 performances and one preview.

Bert Andrews Photos

Left: Geoffrey Sumner, Robert Coote, Wilfrid Hyde-White

Wilfrid Hyde-White, Philip Kerr, Carolyn Lagerfelt

Dillon Evans, Enid Rodgers, Lee Richardson, Thayer David
Geoffrey Sumner, Wilfrid Hyde-White, Robert Coote

Robert Coote, Wilfrid Hyde-White, Geoffrey Sumner Top: (L) Geoffrey Sumner, Joan Bassie (R) Carolyn Lagerfelt, Lee Richardson, Thayer David

PLYMOUTH THEATRE

Opened Thursday, February 8, 1973.*

Robert Whitehead and Roger L. Stevens present:

FINISHING TOUCHES

By Jean Kerr: Director, Joseph Anthony; Scenery and Lighting, Ben Edwards; Costumes, Jane Greenwood; Production Assistant, Bill Becker A Whitehead-Stevens-Matthaei Production.

CAST

Katy Cooper	Barbara Bel Gedde
Jeff Cooper	Robert Lansing
Hughie Cooper	Scott Fireston
Kevin Cooper	Oliver Conan
Fred Whitten	Gene Ruper
Steve Cooper	James Wood
Felicia Andrayson	Pamela Bellwoo
Elsie Ketchum	Denise Gali

STANDBYS: Katy, Martha Randall; Jeff, Fred, Michael Fairman; Felicia, Elsie, Marsha Wishusen; Steve, Kevin, Brian Brownlee; Hughie, Kevin Smith

A Comedy in three acts. The action takes place in the Cooper home in an eastern university town at the present time.

General Manager: Oscar E. Olesen
Press: Seymour Krawitz
Stage Managers: Frederic de Wilde, Wayne Carson

* Closed July 1, 1973 after 164 performances and 2 previews.

Friedman-Abeles Photos

Left: Barbara Bel Geddes, Robert Lansing

Gene Rupert, Barbara Bel Geddes

Scott Firestone, Barbara Bel Geddes, Oliver Conant, Robert Lansing Above: Robert Lansing, Barbara Bel Geddes

Barbara Bel Geddes, Robert Lansing Above: Pamela
wood, Barbara Bel Geddes, James Woods, Denise Galik

Robert Lansing, Pamela Bellwood

53

JOHN GOLDEN THEATRE
Opened Tuesday, February 6, 1973.*
Richard Fields and Peter Flood present:

SHELTER

Book and Lyrics, Gretchen Cryer; Music, Nancy Ford; Director, Austin Pendleton; Settings, Costumes, Projections, Tony Walton; Lighting and Projections, Richard Pilbrow; Orchestrations and Electronic Arrangements, Thomas Pierson; Music Direction and Vocal Arrangements, Kirk Nurock; Associate Producer, Julie Hughes; Production Manager, John Actman; Musical Staging, Sammy Bayes; Original Cast Album by Columbia Records; Production Associate, Deborah Leschin; Technical Supervisor, David J. Nash; Hairstylist, John Quaglia; Sound Effects, Terry Ross

CAST

Maud	Marcia Rodd
Michael	Terry Kiser
Wednesday November	Susan Browning
Gloria	Joanna Merlin
Television Crew	Charles Collins, Britt Swanson
Arthur	Tony Wells
Voice of the Director	Philip Kraus

STANDBYS: Michael, David Snell; Maud, Gloria, Lucy Martin; Wednesday, Britt Swanson; Arthur, Charles Collins

MUSICAL NUMBERS: "Changing," "Welcome to a New World," "It's Hard to Care," "Woke Up Today," "Mary Margaret's House in the Country," "Woman on the Run," "Don't Tell Me It's Forever," "Sunrise," "I Bring Him Seashells," "She's My Girl," "He's a Fool," "Going' Home with My Children," "Sleep, My Baby, Sleep"

A Musical in two acts. The action takes place at the present time in a television studio set.

General Managers: NR Productions: Norman E. Rothstein, Patricia Carney, Bob MacDonald
Press: Solters, Sabinson, Roskin Inc., Marilynn LeVine
Stage Managers: John Andrews, Charles Collins

* Closed March 4, 1973 after 31 performances and 16 previews.

Martha Swope Photos

Joanna Merlin, Susan Browning, Marcia Rodd, Terry Kiser
Top: Terry Kiser, Marcia Rodd

AMBASSADOR THEATRE

Opened Wednesday, February 14, 1973.*
Anthony D'Amato in association with the Organic Theater Company of Chicago presents:

WARP

Episode I:
"My Battlefield, My Body"

By Bury St. Edmund, Stuart Gordon; Director, Stuart Gordon; Scenery, Robert Guerra; Lighting, Jane Reisman; Costumes, Laura Crow, Cookie Gluck; Supervised by Neil Peter Jampolis; Music, William J. Norris, Richard Fire; Visuals, Khamphalous Lightshow; Vocal Sound Effects, Flying Frog; Art Director, Neal Adams; Production Associates, Leo K. Cohen, Charlotte W. Wilcox, Robb Lady, Vicki Stein; Technical Supervisor, Mitch Miller

CAST

Desi Arnez	Andre De Shields
Penny Smart/Sargon	Cordis Fejer
Sheila Fantastik	Jane Fire
Mrs. O'Grady/Psychiatric Director/Bank Teller/Lugulbanda/Yggthion	Richard Fire
Mary Louise/Valaria	Carolyn Gordon
David Carson/Lord Cumulus	John Heard
Bank President/Dr. Victor Vivian/Symax	William J. Norris
Attendant/Young David Carson	Keith Szarabajka
Janitor/Prince Chaos	Tom Towles

Understudies: Kathleen Rostrom, Keith Szarabajka

A science fiction epic adventure play in two acts.

General Manager: Edward H. Davis
Press: Betty Lee Hunt, Henry Luhrman, Harriett Trachtenberg, Maria Pucci
Stage Managers: Frank Marino, Lynne Guerra, Flying Frog

* Closed Feb. 18, 1973 after 8 performances and 7 previews.

Andre De Shields

BROOKS ATKINSON THEATRE

Opened Sunday, February 18, 1973.*
George Keathley and Jack Lenny present:

STATUS QUO VADIS

Written and Directed by Donald Driver; Scenery, Edward Burbridge; Costumes, David Toser; Lighting, Thomas Skelton; Production Associate, Joy Welfeld; Co-Producers, Richard Jansen, Aaron Gold; Hairstylist, Randy Coronato

CAST

Mr. Grammerky	John C. Becher
Horace Elgin	Bruce Boxleitner
Mrs. Elgin	Geraldine Kay
Mr. Elgin	Roberts Blossom
Laporski	Charles Welch
Reinke	Ralph Strait
Paul Regents III	Ted Danson
Barbara	Lee Zara
Joyce Crishaw	Rebecca Taylor
Don Walgren	Don Marston
Irene Phillips	Gail Strickland
Professor Russel	Kenneth Kimmins
Choir Boys	Sue Renee, Diana Corto
Rev. John Purdy	William Francis
Father Mathais	Robert E. Thompson
Coffman	James S. Lucas, Jr.
Sarah	Katherine Korla
Detective	John C. Becher

STANDBYS: Irene, Carolyn Kirsch; Horace, Paul, Michael Sullivan; Mrs. Elgin, Sarah, Naomi Riseman; Joyce, Barbara, Karin Woodward

A Comedy in two acts. The action takes place at the present time in any familiar city in the United States.

General Manager: Ben Rosenberg
Press: Solters/Sabinson/Roskin, Marilyn LeVine
Stage Managers: Murray Gitlin, James S. Lucas, Jr.

* Closed Feb. 18, 1973 after one performance and six previews.

Gail Strickland, Bruce Boxleitner
(also above)

SAM S. SHUBERT THEATRE
Opened Sunday, February 25, 1973.*
Harold Prince in association with Ruth Mitchell presents:

A LITTLE NIGHT MUSIC

Book, Hugh Wheeler; Suggested by Ingmar Bergman's film "Smiles of a Summer Night"; Music and Lyrics, Stephen Sondheim; Director, Harold Prince; Choreography, Patricia Birch; Scenery, Boris Aronson; Costumes, Florence Klotz; Lighting, Tharon Musser; Musical Director, Harold Hastings; Orchestrations, Jonathan Tunick; Production Supervisor, Ruth Mitchell; Sound, Jack Mann; Hairstylist, Charles LaFrance; Production Assistant, Harold Apter

CAST

Mr. Lindquist	Benjamin Rayson
Mrs. Nordstrom	Teri Ralston
Mrs. Anderssen	Barbara Lang
Mr. Erlanson	Gene Varrone
Mrs. Segstrom	Beth Fowler
Fredrika Armfeldt	Judy Kahan
Madame Armfeldt	Hermione Gingold
Frid, her butler	George Lee Andrews
Henrik Egerman	Mark Lambert
Anne Egerman	Victoria Mallory
Fredrik Egerman	Len Cariou
Petra	D. Jamin-Bartlett
Desiree Armfeldt	Glynis Johns
Malla, her maid	Despo
Bertrand, a page	Will Sharpe Marshall
Count Carl-Magnus Malcolm	Laurence Guittard
Countess Charlotte Malcolm	Patricia Elliott
Osa	Sherry Mathis

STANDBYS AND UNDERSTUDIES: Fredrik, Count, Len Gochman; Desiree, Barbara Lang; Madame, Despo; Anne, Fredrika, Sherry Mathis; Countess, Petra, Beth Fowler; Henrick, Frid, Will Sharpe Marshall

MUSICAL NUMBERS: Overture, "Night Waltz," "Now," "Later," "Soon," "The Glamorous Life," "Remember?," "You Must Meet My Wife," "Liaisons," "In Praise of Women," "Every Day a Little Death," "A Weekend in the Country," "The Sun Won't Set," "It Would Have Been Wonderful," "Perpetual Anticipation," "Send in the Clowns," "The Miller's Son," Finale.

A Musical in two acts. The action takes place in Sweden at the turn of the century.

General Manager: Howard Haines
Company Manager; Ralph Roseman
Press: Mary Bryant, Bill Evans
Stage Managers: George Martin, John Grigas, David Wolf

* Still playing May 31, 1973. Winner of 1973 "Tony" Award, and Drama Critics Circle Award.

Van Williams, Martha Swope, Friedman-Abeles Photos

Left: Laurence Guittard, Patricia Elliott Top: Patricia Elliott, Judy Kahan, Sherry Mathis, Laurence Guittard, Glynis Johns, Len Cariou, Victoria Mallory

George Lee Andrews, Hermione Gingold, Judy Kahan

Len Cariou, Victoria Mallory, Mark Lambert, Patr Elliott, D. Jamin-Bartlett, Laurence Guittard

atricia Elliott, Victoria Mallory Above: D. Jamin-
Bartlett Top: Barbara Lang, Benjamin Rayson,
Teri Ralston, Beth Fowler, Gene Varrone

Judy Kahan, Glynis Johns, Despo Above: Glynis Johns

57

RITZ THEATRE

Opened Tuesday, Februrary 20, 1973.*
Tom Mallow by arrangement with John Gale presents:

NO SEX PLEASE, WE'RE BRITISH

By Anthony Mariott and Alistair Foot; Director, Christopher Hewett;
Scenery, Helen Pond, Herbert Senn; Lighting, John Harvey; Costumes,
Jeffrey B. Moss

CAST

Peter Hunter	Stephen Collins
Frances Hunter	J. J. Lewis
Brian Runicles	Tony Tanner
Eleanor Hunter	Maureen O'Sullivan
Leslie Bromhead	Ronald Drake
Superintendent Paul	John Clarkson
Delivery Man	Robert Jundelin
Mr. Needham	Leon Shaw
Susan	Jill Tanner
Barbara	Jennifer Richards

STANDBYS: Eleanor, Carol Raymont; Brian, Peter, Robert Jundelin;
Frances, Jill Tanner; Leslie, John Clarkson; Paul, Needham, Robert
Bruce Holley; Susan, Jennifer Richards

A Comedy in two acts and three scenes. The action takes place at the
present time in the Hunters' apartment above a sub branch of the National
United Bank in Royal Windsor, England.

General Manager: James Janek
Company Manager: Marshall Young
Press: Max Gendel
Stage Managers: Roger Franklin, Robert Bruce Holley, Carol
Raymont, Robert Jundelin

* Closed March 4, 1973 after 14 performances and 24 previews.

Bert Andrews Photos

Right: Leon Shaw, Stephen Collins, J. J. Lewis
Below: John Clarkson, J. J. Lewis, Stephen Collins

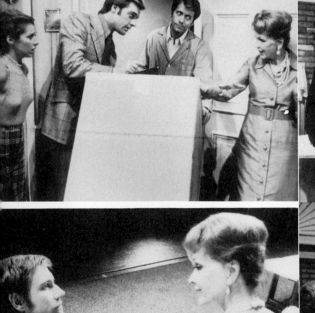

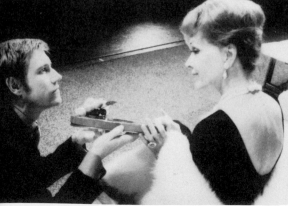

Tony Tanner, Maureen O'Sullivan Above: J. J. Lewis,
Stephen Collins, Robert Jundelin, Maureen O'Sullivan

J. J. Lewis, Stephen Collins, Tony Tanner, Maureen
O'Sullivan

LYCEUM THEATRE

Opened Thursday, March 1, 1973.*
David Merrick Arts Foundation and Kennedy Center Productions, Inc. Present:

OUT CRY

By Tennessee Williams; Director, Peter Glenville; Lighted and Designed by Jo Mielziner; Costumes, Sandy Cole; Production Associate, Lucia Victor; Staff Associates, Mark Bramble, Sandy Mandel, Shelly Faden; Sculpture, Nancy Grossman

CAST

Felice .... Michael York
Clare .... Cara Duff-MacCormick
Standbys: James Keach, Jane Hallaren

A Drama in two acts. The action takes place "in the State Theatre of a state unknown."

General Manager: Jack Schlissel
Company Manager: Fred Cuneo
Press: Harvey B. Sabinson, Sandra Manley
Stage Managers: Alan Hall, James Keach

* Closed March 10, 1973 after 13 performances and one preview.

Martha Swope Photos

Right: Michael York

Cara Duff-MacCormick, Michael York

MOROSCO THEATRE
Opened Tuesday, March 6, 1973.*
Charles Bowden, Lee Reynolds, Isobel Robins presents the
Long Wharf Theatre production of:

THE CHANGING ROOM

By David Storey; Director, Michael Rudman; Set, David Jenkins; Costumes, Whitney Blausen; Lighting, Ronald Wallace; Production Coordinator, Diana Shumlin

CAST

Harry Riley, the Cleaner	Louis Beachne
"Patsy" Turner #2	Doug Stende
Fielding #10	Rex Robbin
"Mic" Morley #13	Jack Schult
"Kenny" Kendal #12	John Lithgov
Luke, The Masseur	Jake Denge
"Fenny" Fenchurch #5	William Rhy
Colin Jagger #3	John Tillinge
Trevor #1	George Hear
Walsh #8	Tom Atkin
"Sandy," Assistant Trainer	John Brade
Barry Copley #7	James Sutoriu
Jack Stringer #4	Richard D. Masu
Bryan Atkinson #11	James Hummer
Billy Spencer #15	Mark Winkwort
John Clegg #9	Ron Sieber
Frank Moore #14	Alan Castne
Clifford Owens #6, Captain	Robert Murc
Danny Crosby, the Trainer	George Ed
Tallon, the Referee	Peter DeMai
Sir Frederick Thornton, Owner	William Swetlan
Mackendrick, Club Secretary	Ian Marti

STANDBYS AND UNDERSTUDIES: Thornton, Harry, Mackendric Crosby, Sandy, John Beal; Clegg, Atkinson, Fenchurch, Moore, Spence Tallon, Patsy, Steve Karp; Copley, Luke, Walsh, Fielding, Owens, Je David; Stringer, Morley, Kendal, Jagger, Trevor, Edwin J. McDonoug

A Play in three acts. The action takes place at the present time in th changing room of a Rugby League team in the North of England.

General Manager: Diana Shumlin
Company Manager: Robert I. Goldberg
Press: Seymour Krawitz, Patricia Krawitz
Stage Managers: Anne Keefe, Edwin J. McDonough

*Closed Aug. 18, 1973 after 191 performances and 3 previews. **Winner of 197** Drama Critics Circle Award.

William L. Smith Photos

Left: John Braden, John Lithgow, Rex Robbins, James Sutorius Top: John Braden, Tom Atkins, James Sutorius

Ian Martin, Louis Beachner, William Swetland

Robert Murch, William Swetland

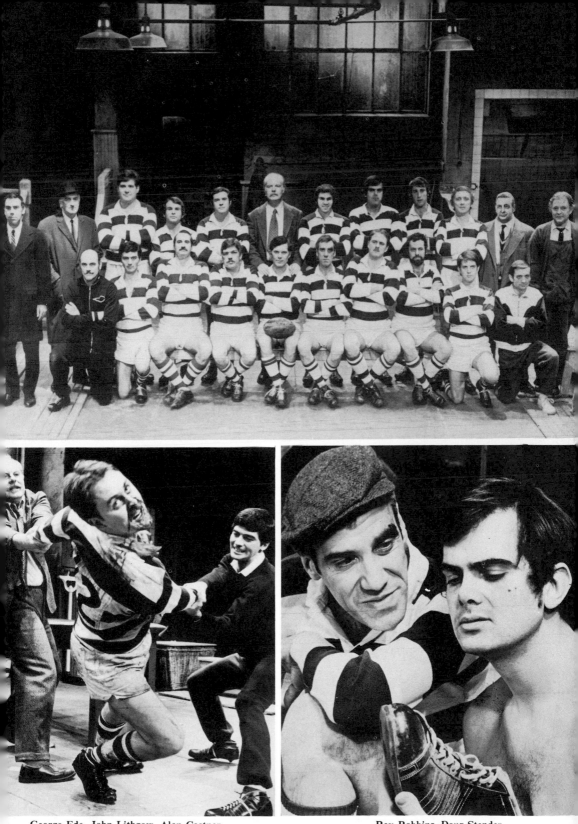

George Ede, John Lithgow, Alan Castner

Rex Robbins, Doug Stender

61

MINSKOFF THEATRE
Opened Tuesday, March 13, 1973.*
Harry Rigby, Albert W. Selden and Jerome Minskoff presen

IRENE

Book, Hugh Wheeler, Joseph Stein; From an Adaptation by Har
Rigby; Based on original play by James Montgomery; Music, Har
Tierney; Lyrics, Joseph McCarthy; Additional Lyrics and Music, Charl
Gaynor, Otis Cleme:ıts; Director, Gower Champion; Musical Numbe
Staged by Peter Gennaro; Production and Costumes Designer, Rao
Pene duBois; Miss Reynolds' Costumes, Irene Sharaff; Lighting, David
Segal; Music and Vocal Direction, Jack Lee; Orchestrations, Ralp
Burns; Dance Arrangements and Incidental Music, Wally Harper; Soun
Tony Alloy; Hair styles, Ted Azar, Pinky Babajian; Music Consultant an
Co-ordinator, Joseph A. McCarthy; Associate Producer, Steven Beckle
Production Associate, Constance Montgomery; Technical Director, Joh
Higgins; Assistant Choreographers, Mary Ann Niles, Tony Stevens; Pr
duction Assistant, Jeffrey Mont; Production Coordinator, Maggie Mi
skoff; Original Cast Album by Columbia Records.

CAST

Mrs. O'Dare	Patsy Kel
Jane Burke	Janie S(
Helen McFudd	Carmen Alvar
Jimmy O'Flaherty	Bruce L
Irene O'Dare	Debbie Reynol
Emmeline Marshall	Ruth Warri
Clarkson	Bob Fresc
Donald Marshall	Monte Markhan
Ozzie Babson	Ted Pu;
Madame Lucy	George S. Irvi
Arabella Thornsworthy	Kate O'Bra

DEBUTANTES: Arlene Columbo, Meg Bussert, Carrie Fisher, Dorot
Wyn Gehgan, Marybeth Kurdock, Frances Ruth Lea, Jeanne Lehma
Kate O'Brady, Julie Pars, Pamela Peadon, Pat Trott, Sandra Voris, Je
nette Williamson, Penny Worth

NINTH AVENUE FELLAS: Paul Charles, Dennis Edenfield, Dav
Evans, Bob Freschi, John Hamilton, Bruce Lea, Joe Lorden, Bryan Nic
olas, Robert Rayow, Dennis Roth, Kenn Scalice, Ron Schwinn, Dav
Steele, Albert Stephenson

STANDBYS AND UNDERSTUDIES: Mrs. O'Dare, Mrs. Marsha
Justine Johnston; Mme. Lucy, Emory Bass; Irene, Janie Sell; Dona
John Hamilton; Jane, Dorothy Wyn Gehgan; Helen, Penny Worth; Ozz
Bob Freschi; Swing Dancers, Frances Ruth Lea, Kenn Scalice

MUSICAL NUMBERS: "The World Must Be Bigger than an Avenu(
"The Family Tree," "Alice Blue Gown," "They Go Wild, Simply Wil
Over Me," "An Irish Girl," "Stepping on Butterflies," "Mother An¿
Darling," "The Riviera Rage," "The Last Part of Every Party," "We
Getting Away With It," "Irene," "The Great Lover Tango," "You Ma
Me Love You," Finale

A Musical in two acts and ten scenes.

General Manager: Walter Fried
Company Manager: G. Warren McClane
Press: John Springer, Ruth Cage, Suzanne Salter
Stage Managers: James Gelb, Robert Schear, Steven Beckler, J(
Lorden

* Still playing May 31, 1973. Original production opened Nov. 18, 19
and played 675 performances with Edith Day.
† Succeeded by Ron Husmann

Friedman-Abeles Photos

Top Left: Debbie Reynolds

Ruth Warrick, Monte Markham, Debbie Reynolds,
George S. Irving, Patsy Kelly

Ron Husmann, Debbie Reynolds

Debbie Reynolds, George S. Irving Above: (C)
Debbie Reynolds, and Top with Monte Markham

Monte Markham, Debbie Reynolds
Top: Ruth Warrick, Debbie Reynolds, Ron Husmann

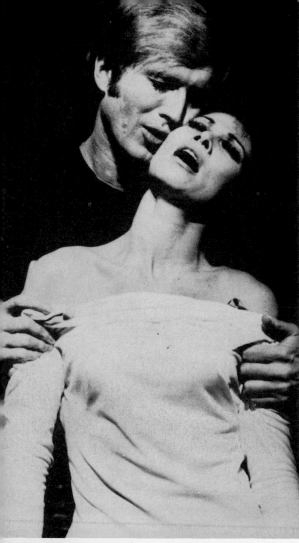

URIS THEATRE
Opened Sunday, March 18, 1973.*
Joseph Kipness and Lawrence Kasha, James Nederlander
George M. Steinbrenner III, Lorin E. Price present:

SEESAW

Music, Cy Coleman; Lyrics, Dorothy Fields; Written, Directed, and Choreographed by Michael Bennett; Co-Choreographer, Grover Dale Associate Choreographers, Bob Avian, Tommy Tune; Scenery, Robin Wagner; Costumes, Ann Roth; Lighting, Jules Fisher; Musical Director Vocal Arrangements, Don Pippin; Orchestrations, Larry Fallon; Dance Arrangements Supervised by Cy Coleman; Hairstylist, Ernest Adler; Media Art and Photography, Sheppard Kerman; Sound, Dick Maitland, Bob Ring, Lou Gonzales; Production Associate, Charlotte Dicker; Production Assistant, Gary Keeper; Assistant Conductor, Skip Redwine; Assistant to Director, Robert Peitscher

CAST

Jerry	Ken Howard†
Gittel Mosca	Michele Lee
David	Tommy Tune
Sophie	Cecelia Norflee
Julio Gonzales	Giancarlo Esposito
Sparkle	LaMonte Peterson
Nurse	Judy McCauley
Ethel	Cathy Brewer-Moore

CITIZENS OF NEW YORK CITY: John Almberg, Steve Anthony Cathy Brewer-Moore, Eileen Casey, Wayne Cilento, Patti D'Beck, Terry Deck, Judy Gibson, Felix Greco, Mitzi Hamilton, Loida Iglesias, Bobby Johnson, Baayork Lee, Amanda McBroom, Judy McCauley, Anita Morris, Gerry O'Hara, Michon Peacock, Frank Pietri, Yolanda Raven, Michael Reed, Orrin Reiley, Don Swanson, William Swiggard, Tom Urich, Dona D. Vaughn, Clyde Walker, Thomas J. Walsh, Chris Wilzak STANDBY: Gittel, Patti Karr; Swings, Jerry Yoder, Merel Poloway

MUSICAL NUMBERS: "Seesaw," "My City," "Nobody Does It Like Me," "In Tune," "Spanglish," "Welcome to Holiday Inn!," "You're a Lovable Lunatic," "He's Good for Me," "Ride Out the Storm," "We've Got It," "Poor Everybody Else," "Chapter 54, Number 1909," "The Concert," "It's Not Where You Start," "I'm Way Ahead"

A Musical in 2 acts and 18 scenes. The action takes place at the present time in New York City.

General Manager: Phil Adler
Company Managers: Max Allentuck, Paul Rackley
Press: Bill Doll & Co., Dick Williams, Virginia Holden
Stage Managers: Robert Borod, Tony Manzi, Nicholas Russiyan Gerry O'Hara

* Still playing May 31, 1973.

† Succeeded by John Gavin

Left: Ken Howard, Michele Lee

Giancarlo Esposito, Ken Howard, Michele Lee

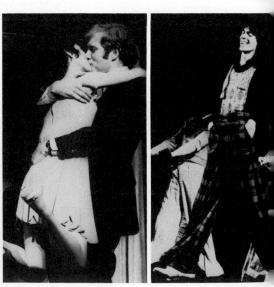

Michele Lee, Ken Howard   Tommy Tune

Michele Lee, Giancarlo Esposito, John Gavin, Cecelia Norfleet
Center: (L) Michele Lee, Tommy Tune, John Gavin (R) Giancarlo Esposito
Top: (L) Judy Gibson, Michon Peacock, Baayork Lee, Anita Morris (R) Michele Lee, John Gavin

BROOKS ATKINSON THEATRE
Opened Tuesday, March 27, 1973.*
The Negro Ensemble Company, Inc. presents:

THE RIVER NIGER

By Joseph A. Walker; Director, Douglas Turner Ward; Set, (
James Wheeler; Costumes, Edna Watson; Lighting, Shirley Prender
Incidental Music, Dorothy Dinroe; Scenery and Costumes supervise(
Edward Burbridge; Production Coordinator, Gerald S. Krone; Pro
tion Assistant, Sandra Ross; Technical Director, Michael Farrell

CAST

Grandma Wilhelmina Brown	Frances F(
Johnny Williams	Douglas Turner W
Dr. Dudley Stanton	Graham Br
Ann Vanderguild	Grenna Whit
Mattie Williams	Roxie R
Chips	Lennal Wainw
Mo	Neville Ri(
Gail	Saundra McC
Skeeter	Charles We
Al	Dean
Jeff Williams	Les Ro
Voice of Lt. Staples	Wyatt D

UNDERSTUDIES: Taurean Blacque, Barbara Clarke, Arthur Fr(
Louise Heath

A Drama in three acts and five scenes. The action takes place a
present time in the Williams' brownstone house on 133 Street in Ha

General Management: Dorothy Olim Associates
Press: Howard Atlee, Clarence Allsopp, Charles E. House
Chuck Artesona
Stage Managers: Garland Lee Thompson, Wyatt Davis

* Still playing May 31, 1973. Opened Off-Broadway at St. Marks
house Dec. 5, 1972 and played 118 performances before movii
Broadway.

Bert Andrews Photos

**Left: Grenna Whitaker, Frances Foster, Les Rober
Roxie Roker, Graham Brown**

Graham Brown, Douglas Turner Ward, Grenna Whitaker

Les Roberts, Grenna Whitaker, Saundra McClai

Grenna Whitaker, Les Roberts
Top: Dean Irby, Charles Weldon

Douglas Turner Ward, Roxie Roker Top: Roxie Roker,
Les Roberts, Frances Foster

67

ETHEL BARRYMORE THEATRE
Opened Wednesday, March 28, 1973.*
S. Hurok presents the Elliot Martin Production of:

EMPEROR HENRY IV

By Luigi Pirandello; Director, Clifford Williams; English transla▮
Stephen Rich; Scenery and Costumes, Abd'el Farrah; Lighting, and ▮
nery Supervision, Neil Peter Jampolis; Costumes supervised and exec▮
by Ray Diffen; Associate Producer, Herbert Wasserman; Production ▮
sistant, William Bond

CAST

First Guard	Michael Diam▮
Second Guard	Thom Christo▮
Secret Counselors:	
Landolph	Stephen D. New▮
Berthold	Reno R▮
Ordulph	Michael Du▮
Harold	George Ta▮
Giovanni, a butler	Douglas S▮
Countess Matilda Spina	Eileen H▮
Baron Tito Belcredi	Paul H▮
Dr. Dionysius Genoni	David H▮
Frida	Linda de ▮
Marquis Carlo Di Nolli	Rudolph Wil▮
"Henry IV"	Rex Harr▮

UNDERSTUDIES: Countess, Frida, Ruth Hunt; Baron, Stephe▮
Newman; Genoni, Douglas Seale, Michael Diamond; Marquis, T▮
Christopher; Landolph, Berthold, Thom Christopher, George Boyd; ▮
old, Ordulph, Michael Diamond, George Boyd; Giovanni, Gua▮
George Boyd

A Play in two acts and three scenes. The action takes place in a re▮
villa in Italy in 1922, in the throne room, and in the council cham▮

General Managers: George W. Thorn, Leonard A. Mulher▮
Company Manager: Maurice Schaded
Press: Ben Washer
Stage Managers: William Weaver, George Boyd

* Closed April 28, 1973 after limited engagement of 37 performance▮
3 previews.

Martha Swope Photos

Eileen Herlie
Top: Rex Harrison

David Hurst, Rex Harrison

Rex Harrison, Eileen Herlie
Top: Eileen Herlie, Rex Harrison, David Hurst

CIRCLE IN THE SQUARE
JOSEPH E. LEVINE THEATRE
Opened Thursday, March 29, 1973.*
Circle in the Square, Inc. (Theodore Mann, Artistic Director;
Paul Libin, Managing Director) presents:

HERE ARE LADIES

From the works of Irish Writers; Directed and Designed by Sean
Kenny; Music, Sean O'Riada; Production Associate, E. J. Oshins; Production Assistant, Jill Farren; Lighting Associate, Robert Kellogg.

with

SIOBHAN McKENNA

The women of Joyce, Shaw, O'Casey, Yeats, Synge, Stephens, and
Beckett presented in a two part solo performance.

Company Manager: William Conn
Press: Merle Debuskey, Leo Stern
Stage Manager: Robert Kellogg, Charles Roden

* Closed May 13, 1973 after 54 performances and 3 previews.
Originally presented Feb. 22, 1971 by The New York Shakespeare Festival at the Public Theatre for 67 performances.

Friedman-Abeles Photos

Right: Siobhan McKenna

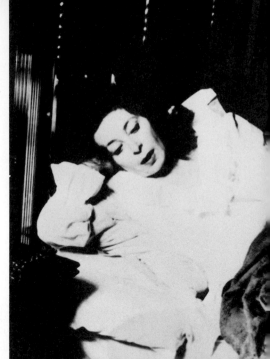

Siobhan McKenna

Siobhan McKenna

MARTIN BECK THEATRE
Opened Sunday, April 8, 1973.*
Orin Lehman, Joseph Kipness, Lawrence Kasha present:

NO HARD FEELINGS

By Sam Bobrick, Ron Clark; Director, Abe Burrows; Scenery and
Lighting, Robert Randolph; Costumes, Theoni V. Aldredge; Production
Associate, Charlotte Dicker; Production Assistant, Gary Keeper

CAST

George Bartlett	Eddie Albert
Roberta Bartlett	Nanette Fabray
Jimmy Skouras	Conrad Janis
Alex Springer	A. Larry Haines
Fred	David Marlow
Bunny Sutton	Beverly Dixon
Anna Wilkins	Stockard Channing
Policeman	Dino Narizzano
Voice of Judge	Alan Manson

STANDBYS AND UNDERSTUDIES: George, Alex, Alan Manson;
Anna, Bunny, Laura May Lewis; Roberta, Beverly Dixon; Jimmy, Dino
Narizzano; Policeman, Fred, Phillip Price

A Comedy in two acts. The action takes place at the present time in
and around Manhattan and one of its suburbs.

General Manager: Marvin A. Krauss
Company Manager: David Wyler
Press: Frank Goodman, Arlene Wolf, Susan L. Schulman
Stage Managers: Lanier Davis, David Marlow, Phillip Price

Closed April 8, 1973 after one performance and 21 previews.

Bert Andrews Photos

Right: Nanette Fabray, Eddie Albert

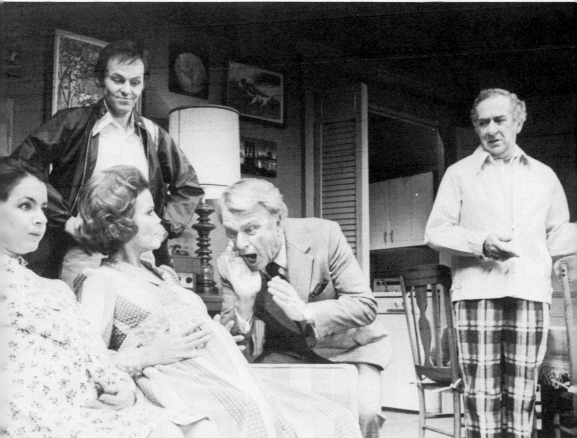

Stockard Channing, Nanette Fabray, Conrad Janis, Eddie Albert, A. Larry Haines

Jan Miner, Rhonda Fleming, Marian Hailey,
Kim Hunter, Alexis Smith

FORTY-SIXTH STREET THEATRE
Opened Wednesday, April 25, 1973.*
Jeremy Ritzer and Joel Key Rice in association with John W
Merriam and Milton Moss present:

THE WOMEN

By Clare Boothe Luce; Director, Morton Da Costa; Designed by Oliv
Smith; Clothes, Ann Roth; Lighting, John Gleason; Costume Supervisio
Ray Diffen; Hairstylist, Joe Tubens; Makeup, Joe Cranzano; Associa
Producers, Michael Frazier, William L. Livingston; Production Assistar
H. Julian Cohen; Presented by arrangement with Lester Osterman Pr
ductions

CAST

Peggy (Mrs. John Day)	Marian Haile
Nancy Blake	Mary Louise Wilso
Jane	Regina Re
Edith (Mrs. Phelps Potter)	Dorothy Loudo
Sylvia (Mrs. Howard Fowler)	Alexis Smi
Mary (Mrs. Stephen Haines)	Kim Hunt
Mrs. Wagstaff	Camila Ashla
Olga	Bobo Lew
First Hairdresser	Claudette Sutherla
Second Hairdresser	Louise Shaf
Pedicurist	Caryll Co
Customer	Elizabeth Per
Shirley	Jeanne De Ba
Mudmask	Lynne Stua
Little Mary	Cynthia Lis
Mrs. Morehead	Myrna L
First Girl	Caryll Co
Second Girl	Connie Forslu
Miss Shapiro	Patricia Whe
Miss Curtis	Polly Row
First Model	Lynne Stua
Crystal Allen	Marie Walla
A Fitter	Leora Da
Second Model	Louise Shaf
Third Model	Elizabeth Per
Princess Tamara	Jeanne De Ba
Exercise Instructress	Claudette Sutherla
Mat Girl	Connie Forslu
Miss Watts	Leora Da
Miss Trimmerback	Elizabeth Per
Nurse	Doris Dowl
Lucy	Polly Row
Countess De Lage	Jan Min
Miriam Aarons	Rhonda Flem
Helene	Caryll Co
Sadie	Camila Ashla
Cigarette Girl	Louise Shaf
First Girl	Jeanne De Ba
Second Girl	Elizabeth Pe
First Woman	Claudette Sutherla
Second Woman	Leora Da
Dowager	Bobo Lev
Debutante	Connie Forslu
Girl in distress	Caryll Co

UNDERSTUDIES: Camila Ashland, Caryll Coan, Leora Dana, T.
Darney, Jeanne De Baer, Doris Dowling, Connie Forslund, Susan Jay
Elizabeth Perry, Louise Shaffer, Lynne Stuart
    A Comedy in two acts and eleven scenes. The action takes place in
mid-'Thirties.

General Manager: Marvin A. Krauss
Company Manager: David Wyler
Press: Shirley E. Herz, Stuart Fink
Stage Managers: Victor Straus, Nick Malekos, Suzanne Egar

* Closed June 17, 1973 after 63 performances and 7 previews. Orig
  production opened Dec. 26, 1936 at the Ethel Barrymore Theatre w
  Ilka Chase, Margalo Gillmore, Betty Lawford, and Phyllis Povah

Friedman-Abeles Photos

Top Left: Myrna Loy, Kim Hunter
Left Center: Dorothy Loudon, Marian Hailey,
Myrna Loy, Jan Miner, Kim Hunter, Rhonda
Fleming, Mary Louise Wilson

nda Fleming, Jan Miner, Alexis Smith Above: Polly
les, Jan Miner Top: Alexis Smith, Rhonda Fleming

Dorothy Loudon, Marian Hailey Above: Myrna Loy, Leora
Dana, Elizabeth Perry Top: Alexis Smith, Polly Rowles **73**

Christopher Plummer, Leigh Beery

PALACE THEATRE
Opened Sunday, May 13, 1973.*
Richard Gregson and APJAC International present:

CYRANO

Book based on Anthony Burgess' adaptation of "Cyrano de Bergera
by Edmond Rostand; Music, Michael J. Lewis; Lyrics, Anthony Burge
Director, Michael Kidd; Costumes, Desmond Heeley; Settings, John J
sen; Lighting, Gilbert V. Hemsley, Jr.; Musical Direction, Thomas Pi
son; Orchestrations, Philip J. Lang; Sound, Abe Jacob; Incidental Mu
Arranged by Clay Fullum; Hairstylist, Ray Iagnocco; Duelling staged
Patrick Crean, Erik Fredricksen; Assistant to Producers, Diana Solom
Original Cast Album by A & M Records

CAST

Candle Lighters	Paul Berget, Anthony Inn
Doorman	Bob He
Foodseller	Tovah Feldsh
Marquis in yellow	Danny V
Musketeer	Michael No
Cavalryman	Donavan Sylv
Pickpocket	Geoff Garla
Citizen	James Richards
Citizen's Brother	Tim Nis
Marquis in red	Alexander Orf
Marquis in beige	Joel Cr
Ragueneau	Arnold Sobo
Christian de Neuvillette	Mark Lan
Madame Aubry	Betty Leigh
Madame de Guemene	Janet McC
Barthenoide	Patricia R
Felixerie	Mimi Wall
Urimedonte	Mary Stra
Le Bret	James Blend
Roxana	Leigh Be
Roxana's Duenna	Anita Dang
Count de Guiche	Louis Ture
Viscount de Valvert	J. Kenneth Camp
Actors	Anthony Inneo, Richard Schnei
Actresses	Vicki Frederick, Jill R
Jodelet	Michael Good
Montfleury	Patrick H
Cyrano de Bergerac	Christopher Plumr
Lise	Betty Leigh
Boys	Tim Nissen, Paul Be
Theophraste Renaudot	George Spe
Cyrano's Pages	Paul Berget, Tim Nis
Capucine Monk	Geoff Garl
Sister Marguerite	Betty Leigh
Sister Marthe	Anita Dang
Sister Claire	Patricia R

NUNS: Tovah Feldshuh, Vicki Frederick, Janet McCall, Jill Rose, M
Straten, Mimi Wallace

CADETS AND SOLDIERS: J. Kenneth Campbell, Joel Craig, Mic
Goodwin, Bob Heath, Anthony Inneo, Gale McNeeley, Michael No
James Richardson, Richard Schneider, Donovan Sylvest, Danny Vi

UNDERSTUDIES: Roxana, Janet McCall; Le Bret, de Guiche, Will
Metzo; Duenna, Betty Leighton; de Guiche, Alexander Orfaly; de
vert, Anthony Inneo

MUSICAL NUMBERS: "Cyrano's Nose," "La France, La Fran
"Tell Her," "From Now Till Forever," "Bergerac," "Pocapdedio
"No, Thank You," "Roxana," "It's She and It's Me," "You Have M
Me Love," "Thither, Thother, Thide of the," "Paris Cuisine," "Lov
Not Love," "Autumn Carol," "I Never Loved You"

A Musical in two acts and five scenes. The action takes place in P
in 1640, and 1654.

General Manager: Victor Samrock
Company Manager: James Awe
Press: Gifford/Wallace, Tom Trenkle
Stage Managers: Robert D. Currie, Christopher Kelly, Lani E

* Closed June 23, 1973 after 49 performances and 5 previews.

Top Left: Christopher Plummer
Below: Leigh Beery, Mark Lamos

Paul Berget, Tim Nissen, Christopher Plummer, Leigh
Beery, Anita Dangler

BIJOU THEATRE
Opened Monday, May 7, 1973.*
Robert J. Gibson and The Roundabout Theatre Company
(Gene Feist, Producing Director; Michael Fried, Executive Director) present:

THE PLAY'S THE THING

By Ferenc Molnar; Adapted by P. G. Wodehouse; Director, Gene Feist; Setting, Holmes Easley; Lighting, R. S. Winkler; Costumes, Mimi Maxmen; Original Score, Philip Campanella; Lighting and Costumes supervised by Holmes Easley; Production Assistant, Robert Ellowitz; Technical Supervisor, Arthur Siccardi

CAST

Sandor Turai	Hugh Franklin
Mansky	Humphrey Davis
Albert Adam	David Dukes
Ilona Szabo	Elizabeth Owens
Almady	Neil Flanagan
Johann Dwornitschek	Fred Stuthman
Mell	Philip Campanella

A Comedy in three acts. The action takes place in a room in a villa on the Italian Riviera, on a Saturday in the summer of 1926.

General Management: Gatchell & Neufeld
Company Manager: Maribeth Gilbert
Press: Cheryl Sue Dolby, Sandra Manley
Stage Manager: John Hagan

* Closed May 26, 1973 after 23 performances and 14 previews. Opened Jan. 9, 1973 at the Roundabout Theatre and played 64 performances before moving to Broadway. Original production opened Nov. 3, 1926 at the Henry Miller Theatre and played 260 performances with Holbrook Blinn and Catherine Dale Owen.

Martha Swope Photos

Right: Neil Flanagan, Humphrey Davis, Elizabeth Owens, David Dukes, Hugh Franklin

Elizabeth Owens, Hugh Franklin

ELEN HAYES THEATRE
Opened Thursday, May 17, 1973.*
Les Schecter and Barbara Schwei in association with SRO Enterprises and Arnold Levy present:

NASH AT NINE

Verses and Lyrics, Ogden Nash; Music, Milton Rosenstock; Conceived
d Directed by Martin Charnin; Orchestrations and Musical Supervi-
n, John Morris; Musical Direction, Karen Gustafson; Sets, David
apman; Costumes, Theoni V. Aldredge; Lighting, Martin Aronstein;
oduction Associate, Michael Hoover; Production Assistant, Terry Lilly

CAST
E. G. Marshall
Bill Berber
Richie Schechtman
Virginia Vestoff
Steve Elmore

ANDBYS: Mr. Marshall and Mr. Elmore, John Stratton; Miss Vestoff,
e Gable; Mr. Gerber and Mr. Schechtman, Jess Richards

A "Wordsical" presented without intermission.

General Manager: Sherman Gross
Press: Frank Goodman, Arlene Wolf, Susan L. Schulman
Stage Managers: Janet Beroza, Mary Porter Hall

Closed June 2, 1973 after 21 performances and 5 previews.

Friedman-Abeles Photos

Right: E. G. Marshall, Virginia Vestoff, Bill Gerber
Top: E. G. Marshall, Steve Elmore, Virginia Vestoff,
Richie Schechtman

E. G. Marshall, Virginia Vestoff

E. G. Marshall, Bill Gerber

BROADWAY PRODUCTIONS FROM OTHER SEASONS
THAT RAN THROUGH THIS SEASON

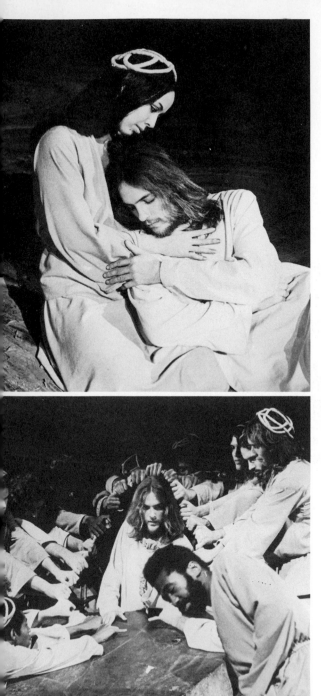

MARK HELLINGER THEATRE
Opened Tuesday, October 12, 1971.*
Robert Stigwood in association with MCA Inc., by arra
ment with David Land presents:

JESUS CHRIST SUPERSTAR

Lyrics, Tim Rice; Music and Orchestrations, Andrew Lloyd We
Conceived for the stage and directed by Tom O'Horgan; Associate
ducers, Gatchell and Neufeld; Scenery, Robin Wagner; Lighting, .
Fisher; Costumes, Randy Barcelo; Sound, Abe Jacob; Musical Superv
Mel Rodnon; Sound, Richard Mowdy; Assistant Conductor, Seyr
Miroff; Staff Assistant, David Relyea

CAST

Judas Iscariot	Ben Veree
Jesus of Nazareth	Jeff Fenho
Mary Magdalene	Yvonne Ellim
First Priest	Alan Braunste
Second Priest	Michael Meadov
Caiaphas	Bob Bingha
Annas	Phil Jeth
Third Priest	Steven B
Simon Zealotes/Merchant/Leper	Dennis Buckl
Pontius Pilate	Barry Denne
Peter/Merchant/Leper	Michael Jaso
Maid/Leper	Linda
Soldier/Judas' Tormentor	Tom Stoval
Old Man/Apostle/Leper	Peter Schl
Soldier/Judas' Tormentor	Paul Sylva
King Herod/Merchant/Leper	Paul Air
Cured Leper/Temple Lady	Robin Grea
Cured Leper/Apostle/Merchant	James S
Cured Leper/Temple Lady	Laura Michael
Cured Leper/Apostle/Merchant	Clifford Li
Cured Leper/Temple Lady/Reporter	Bonnie S
Cured Leper/Apostle/Reporter	Pi Dou
Cured Leper/Apostle Woman/Temple Lady	Celia
Cured Leper/Apostle/Tormentor	Dennis Co
Reporter/Apostle Woman/Temple Lady	Anita M
Reporter/Leper	Ted N
Reporter/Apostle Woman/Temple Lady	Kay
Reporter/Leper	Kurt Yag
Reporter/Leper	Margaret War
Reporter/Apostle/Leper	Willie Win
Reporter/Apostle Woman/Temple Lady	Ferne
Reporter/Apostle/Leper	Samuel E. W
Apostle Woman/Temple Lady/Leper	Denise Delap
Apostle/Merchant/Reporter	Robalee B
Apostle/Reporter/Tormentor	Doug L
Soul Girl/Leper	Charlotte Cro
Soul Girl/Leper	Janet P
Soul Girl/Leper	Cecelia No
Judas' Tormentor/Soldier	Edward Barto
Judas' Tormentor/Soldier	Tony Gardne

UNDERSTUDIES: James Sbano, Reggie Mack, William Daniel C
Shriely Sypert, Christopher Allen, William Parry, Randy Wilson,
Bailey, Doug Lucas, Lynn Gerb, Anthony White, Michael Lamont
ward Q. Bhartonn, Lorraine Feather, Laura Michaels

MUSICAL NUMBERS: Overture, "Heaven on Their Minds," "W
the Buzz," "Strange Thing Mystifying," "Everything's All Right," "
Jesus Must Die," "Hosanna," "Simon Zealotes," "Poor Jerusal
"Pilate's Dream," "The Temple," "I Don't Know How to Love H
"Damned for All Time," "The Last Supper," "Gethsemane," "The
rest," "Peter's Denial," "Pilate and Christ," "King Herod's S
"Could We Start Again, Please," "Judas' Death," "Trial before Pil
"Superstar," "The Crucifixion," "John 19:41"

A musical in two acts. The action depicts the last seven days in th
of Jesus of Nazareth.

General Managers: Gatchell & Neufeld
Company Manager: John Corkill
Press: Merle Debuskey, Leo Stern
Stage Managers: Galen McKinley, Frank Marino, William S
Robert W. Pitman

* Closed July 1, 1973 after 711 performances and 13 previews. For
nal production, see THEATRE WORLD, Vol. 28.
† Succeeded by: 1. Patrick Jude, 2. Dennis Cooley, 3. Marta H
Kathye Dezina, 4. Jeffrey Hillock, 5. Roger Lawson, 6. Stephen I
7. William Daniel Gray, 8. William Parry, 9. Reggie Mack, 10.
Allen, W. P. Dremak, George Mansour, 11. Robert Brandon, 12.
nis Simpson, 13. Edward Q. Bhartonn, 14. Christina Putnam, 1!
nelope Bodry, 16. Alan Blair, 17. Clifford Lipson, and Dan Gi
Mark Shannon, Christopher Allen, Randy Wilson, Lynn Gerb,
Bailey, Victor Vail, Bob Bingham, Martha Deering, Carol Estey
chael Lamont, Linda Ribbach, Realinda Farrell, DeMarest Grey,
liam Gestrich, Anthony White

Jeff Fenholt, Ben Vereen
Above: Yvonne Elliman, Jeff Fenholt

80

Friedman-Abeles Photos

Jeff Fenholt Top: Jeff Fenholt, Alan Braunstein,
Paul Ainsley, Michael Meadows

Patrick Jude Top: Kathye Dezina, Dennis
Cooley, Patrick Jude

EUGENE O'NEILL THEATRE
Opened Thursday, November 11, 1971.*
Saint-Subber presents:

THE PRISONER OF SECOND AVENU

By Neil Simon; Director, Mike Nichols; Set, Richard Sylbert; C
tumes, Anthea Sylbert; Lighting, Tharon Musser; Hairstylist, He
Chevrier; Produced by Nancy Enterprises; Sound, Dennis Maitland

CAST

Mel Edison	Peter Falk
Edna Edison	Lee Grant
Harry Edison	Vincent Gardeni:
Pearl	Florence Stanley
Jessie	Tresa Hughe:
Pauline	Dena Dietr

Standbys: Henry Sutton, Carol Morley

A Comedy in two acts. The actions takes place at the present time
a New York City apartment building.

General Manager: C. Edwin Knill
Company Manager: James Turner
Press: Solters/Sabinson/Roskin, Cheryl Sue Dolby, Milly
Schoenbaum
Stage Managers: George Rondo, Susan Lehman

* Still playing May 31, 1973. Vincent Gardenia received "Tony" for I
Supporting Actor, and Mike Nichols for Best Director.
† Succeeded by: 1. Art Carney, Hector Elizondo, 2. Barbara Bar
Phyllis Newman, Barbara Barrie, 3. Jack Somack, Harry Goz, 4. Jer
Ventriss, 5. Jean Barker, 6. Ruth Manning

Martha Swope Photos

Left: Peter Falk, Lee Grant

Dena Dietrich, Tresa Hughes (foreground), Florence
Stanley, Vincent Gardenia, Peter Falk

Barbara Barrie
Top: Lee Grant, Peter Falk

Phyllis Newman, Hector Elizondo
Top: Barbara Barrie, Art Carney

Robert Morse, Tony Roberts

MAJESTIC THEATRE
Opened Sunday, April 9, 1972.*
David Merrick presents:

SUGAR

Book, Peter Stone; Based on screenplay "Some Like It Hot" by Billy Wilder, I. A. L. Diamond, from a story by Robert Thoeren; Music, Jule Styne; Lyrics, Bob Merrill; Director-Choreographer, Gower Champion; Settings, Robin Wagner; Costumes, Alvin Colt; Lighting, Martin Aronstein; Musical Direction-Vocal Arrangements, Elliot Lawrence; Orchestrations, Philip J. Lang; Dance Music Arranged by John Berkman; Conductor, William Elton; Associate Choreographer, Bert Michaels; Hairstylist, Joe Tubens; Makeup, Joe Cranzano; Production Associate, Lucia Victor; Production Assistant, Regina Lynn; Assistant to Producer, Helen Nickerson; Staff Associates, Shelley Faden, Kim Sellon, Mark Bramble; Sound, Otts Munderloh

CAST

Sweet Sue	Sheila Smith
Society Syncopaters:	
Piano	Harriett Conrad
Drums	Linda Gandell†1
Bass	Nicole Barth†2
Trumpets	Leslie Latham†3, Marylou Sirinek†4
Trombones	Terry Cullen, Kathleen Witmer
Saxophones	Pam Blair, Eileen Casey†5, Debra Lyman, Sally Neal†6, Mary Zahn
Beinstock	Alan Kass
Joe	Tony Roberts
Jerry	Robert Morse
Union Contractor	Gene Cooper
Sugar Kane	Elaine Joyce
Spats Palazzo	Steve Condos
Dude	Gerard Brentte
Spats' Gang	Andy Bew, Roger Bigelow, Gene Cooper, Arthur Faria, Gene GeBauer, Don Percassi, John Mineo†7
Knuckles Norton	Dick Bonelle†8
First Poker Player	Igors Gavon
Knuckles' Gang	Ken Ayers†9, Richard Maxon, Dale Muchmore, Alexander Orfaly†10
Cabdriver	Ken Ayers†11
Olga	Eileen Casey†12
Dolores	Mary Zahn
Rosella	Pam Blair
Marylou	Debra Lyman
Train Conductor	George Blackwell
Bellboy	Andy Bew
Osgood Fielding, Jr.	Cyril Ritchard
"Chicago" Singers	Ken Ayers, George Blackwell, Dick Bonelle, Igors Gavon, Hal Norman, Robert L. Hultman

UNDERSTUDIES: Joe, Igors Gavon; Jerry, Scott Jarvis; Osgood, Fielding, Bienstock, George Blackwell; Sugar, Pam Blair; Sweet Sue, Harriett Conrad; Spats, Gerard Brentte; Swing Dancers, Sandra Brewer, Denny Martin Flinn

MUSICAL NUMBERS: Overture, "Windy City Marmalade," "Penniless Bums," "Tear the Town Apart," "The Beauty That Drives Men Mad," "We Could Be Close," "Sun on My Face," "November Song," "Sugar," "Hey, Why Not!," "Beautiful Through and Through," "What Do You Give to a Man Who's Had Everything?," "Magic Nights," "It's Always Love," "When You Meet a Man in Chicago"

A musical comedy in two acts. The action takes place in 1931 in Chicago, Miami, and in between.

General Manager: Jack Schlissel
Press: Harvey Sabinson, Marilynn LeVine
Stage Managers: Charles Blackwell, Henry Velez, Bob St. Clair, Robert L. Hultman

* Closed June 23, 1973 after 505 performances.
† Succeeded by: 1. Pam Blair, 2. Karen Kristin, 3. Lauren Draper, 4. Lana Sloniger, 5. Lynne Gannaway, 6. Marianne Selbert, 7. Richard Maxon, 8. Dale Muchmore, 9. George Blackwell, 10. Robert L. Hultman, 11. Don Percassi, 12. Lana Sloniger

Martha Swope Photos

Top Left: Tony Roberts, Elaine Joyce, Robert Morse
Below: Sheila Smith and the Society Syncopaters

Steve Condos
Top: Robert Morse, Elaine Joyce

Tony Roberts, Elaine Joyce
Top: Cyril Ritchard, Robert Morse

ST. JAMES THEATRE
Opened Wednesday, December 1, 1971.*
The New York Shakespeare Festival (Joseph Papp, Producer)
presents:

TWO GENTLEMEN OF VERONA

By William Shakespeare; Adapted by John Guare, Mel Shapiro; Lyrics, John Guare; Music, Galt MacDermot; Director, Mel Shapiro; Setting, Ming Cho Lee; Costumes, Theoni V. Aldredge; Lighting, Lawrence Metzler; Choreography, Jean Erdman; Musical Supervision, Harold Wheeler; Additional Musical Staging, Dennis Nahat; Sound, Jack Shearing; Associate Producer, Bernard Gersten; Original Cast Album by ABC/Dunhill Records

CAST

Thurio	Frank O'Brien†1
Speed	Jose Perez
Valentine	Clifton Davis†2
Proteus	Raul Julia†3
Julia	Diana Davila
Lucetta	Alix Elias†4
Launce	John Bottoms
Antonio	Frederick Warriner
Crab	Phineas
Duke of Milan	Norman Matlock†5
Silvia	Jonelle Allen†6
Tavern Host	Frederic Warriner
Eglamour	Alvin Lum
Quartet	Sheila Gibbs, Signa Joy, Kenneth Lowry, Sakinah Mahammud

CITIZENS OF VERONA AND MILAN: Loretta Abbott, Christopher Alden, Roger Briant, Douglas Brickhouse, Stockard Channing, Paul De-John, Nancy Denning, Richard DeRusso, Arthur Erickson, Georgyn Geetlein, Sheila Gibbs, Jeff Goldblum, Edward Henkel, Albert Insinnia, Jane Jaffe, Signa Joy, Kenneth Lowry, Sakinah Mahammud, Otis Sallid, Madeleine Swift, Christopher Cox, Stanton Edghill, Robbee Fian, Larry Giroux, Gregory V. Karliss, Larry Marshall, Craig Richard Nelson, Arnetia Walker

UNDERSTUDIES: Silvia, Signa Joy; Julia, Lucetta, Taro Meyer; Valentine, Dorian Harewood; Proteus, Speed, Rafael de Guzman; Duke, Tiger Haynes; Thurio, Charles Abbott; Lucetta, Carol-Jean Lewis; Eglamour, Ed Linderman; Swing Dancers, Wendy Mansfield, Morton Winston; Swing Singers, Dorian Harewood, Jacqueline Britt

A Musical in two acts.

General Managers: Eugene Wolsk, Emanuel Azenberg
Company Manager: Michael Brandman
Press: Merle Debuskey, Faith Geer
Stage Managers: R. Derek Swire, D. W. Koehler, Anthony Neely

* Closed May 20, 1973 after 614 performances and 20 previews. Received both "Tony" and Drama Critics Circle awards for Best Musical of 1971–72 season, and "Tony" for Best Musical Libretto.
† Succeeded by: 1. Chesley Uxbridge, 2. Samuel E. Wright, Joe Morton, Larry Marshall, 3. Carlos Cestero, Chris Sarandon, 4. Sheila Gibbs, 5. Ellwoodson Williams, 6. Hattie Winston

Friedman-Abeles Photos

Diana Davila, Chris Sarandon

Hattie Winston, Ellwoodson Williams
Top: Raul Julia, Jonelle Allen, Clifton Davis, Diana Davila

Jonelle Allen, Norman Matlock, Frank O'Brien
Above: Phineas, John Bottoms Top: Diana
Davila, Sheila Gibbs

Clifton Davis, Jonelle Allen Top: Jose Perez,
John Bottoms, Raul Julia, Clifton Davis

MUSIC BOX

Opened Thursday, November 12, 1970.*
Helen Bonfils, Morton Gottlieb, Michael White present:

SLEUTH

By Anthony Shaffer; Director, Clifford Williams; Designed by Carl
Toms; Lighting, William Ritman; Production Assistant, E. J. Oshins

CAST

Andrew Wyke .... Anthony Quayle†1
Milo Tindle .... Keith Baxter†2
Inspector Doppler .... Philip Farrar†3
Detective Sergeant Tarrant .... Harold Newman†4
Police Constable Higgs .... Roger Purnell†5

A mystery drama in two acts. The action takes place at the present time
in Andrew Wyke's country home in Wiltshire, England.

General Manager: Ben Rosenberg
Press: Dorothy Ross, Herb Striesfield, Ruth Cage
Stage Managers: Warren Crane, Clint Jakeman, Henry Raymond

* Still playing May 31, 1973. For original production, see THEATRE
  WORLD, Vol. 27. Winner of 1971 "Tony" for Best Play.
† Succeeded by 1. Paul Rogers, Patrick Macnee, George Rose, Patrick
  Macnee, 2. Donal Donnelly, Brian Murray, Jordan Christopher, 3.
  Stanley Rushton, 4. Robin Mayfield, 5. Liam McNulty.

Bert Andrews Photos

Right: Jordan Christopher, Patrick Macnee
(also below)

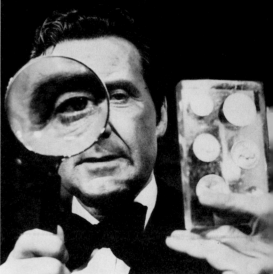

BROADWAY PRODUCTIONS FROM OTHER SEASONS THAT CLOSED THIS SEASON

Title	Opened	Closed	
Fiddler on the Roof	9/22/64	7/2/72	3242
Hair	4/29/66	7/1/72	1758
Oh! Calcutta!	6/17/69	8/12/72	1316
Butterflies Are Free	10/21/69	7/2/72	1128
No, No, Nanette	1/19/71	2/4/73	861
Two Gentlemen of Verona	12/1/71	5/20/73	613
Follies	4/4/71	7/1/72	524
Lenny	5/26/71	6/24/72	453
Ain't Supposed to Die a Natural Death	10/20/71	7/30/72	325
Twigs	11/14/71	7/23/72	312
Sticks and Bones	11/7/71	10/1/72	246
Don't Play Us Cheap	5/16/72	10/1/72	164
A Funny Thing Happened on the Way to the Forum	4/4/72	8/12/72	156
Night Watch	2/28/72	6/11/72	120

OFF BROADWAY PRODUCTIONS

MANHATTAN THEATRE CLUB
Opened Friday, June 2, 1972.*
The Manhattan Theatre Club presents:

SOON JACK NOVEMBER

By Sharon Thie; Director, Don Kvares; Set, Don Kvares; Lighting,
Peter Schneider; Assistant to Director, Linda Brandt Fritzinger

CAST

Soon	Vincent Baggetta
Jack	Ric Mancini
November	Sasha von Scherler
Hostess/Waitress A	Marcia Mohr
Waitress B	Regina Ress
Nun	Lea Scott

A Comedy performed without intermission. The action takes place at
the present time in an Italian-Japanese restaurant.

Stage Manager: Roy Callaway

Closed June 11, 1972 after limited engagement of 6 performances.

**Ric Mancini, Sasha von Scherler, Regina Ress, Vincent
Baggetta**

THEATRE DE LYS
Opened Sunday, June 4, 1972.*
Wits' End presents:

BUY BONDS, BUSTER

Book and Music, Jack Holmes; Lyrics, Bill Conklin, Bob Miller; Origi-
nal Concept by Bill Conklin and Bob Miller; Director, John Bishop;
Musical Numbers Staged by Bick Goss; Designed by William Pitkin;
Lighting, William Strom; Musical Director, Shelly Markham; Technical
Director, Bud Pitman

CAST

Jamie/Joey	William Dalton
J. P./FDR/Sgt. Cracker	Phil Erickson
Bea/Betty	Suellen Estey
Nicholas/Tony	Jay Gregory
Tommy/Harrington/Redcap/	
Washburn/Syracuse	Winston DeWitt Hemsley
Debbie/Trixie	Pamela Hunt
Veronica/Eunice	Virginia Martin
Elmer/Flatbush	Rick Podell
Fannie/Martha	Jane Robertson
Lollie/Eleanor Roosevelt/Sgt. Crisp	Rowena Rollins
Clay/Student	Frank Root

MUSICAL NUMBERS: "Pearl," "So Long for Now," "The Freedom
Choo-Choo," "Tan 'n' Hot," "Dreamboat from Dreamland," "These Are
Worth Fighting For," "The Woogie Boogie," "Canteen Serenade,"
"Donuts for Defense," "Now and Then," "The Master Race Polka," "Us
Two," "Film Flam Flooie," "When the Bluebirds Fly All Over the
World," "Hat Crossover," "Buy Bonds, Buster," "Chico Chico," "My G.
I. Joey," "O Say Can You See"

A Musical in two acts. The action takes place at the present time, and
in the early 1940's.

General Manager: Jordan Hott
Press: Saul Richman
Stage Manager: Robert Buzzell

* Closed June 4, 1972 after one performance.

Finale of "Buy Bonds Buster"
Above: Rowena Rollins, Phil Erickson, Winston DeWitt
Hemsley

PLAZA 9 MUSIC HALL
Opened Thursday, June 6, 1972.*
Costas Omer presents a Timothy Gray and William Justus
production of:

THEY DON'T MAKE 'EM LIKE THAT ANYMORE

Music, Lyrics, and Sketches by Hugh Martin and Timothy Gray;
Director, Timothy Gray; Costumes, E. Huntington Parker, Stephen
Chandler; Decor, Don Gordon; Lighting, Beverly Emmons; Gowns,
Bruno Le Fantastique; Production Coordinator, Carl Thomas Gray; Pia-
nist, Melvin Pahl

CAST

Arthur Blake	Luba Lisa
Phoebe Otis	Kevin Christopher
Dell Hanley	Clay Johns
Gene McCann	Paris Todd

SKETCHES AND MUSICAL NUMBERS: "They Don't Make 'Em
Like that Anymore," "Something Tells Me," "Sorry Wrong Valley,"
"What's His Name," "Once in Love with Amy," "Harvey," "The Architect," "Lili Marlene," "I Lost You," "Mad about the Boy," "Swanis-
lavsky," "Get Me Out of Here," "Buckle Down Winsocki," "Paradise
Lost," "Judy," "Drama Quartet," "Oscar," "Sunset Boulevard," "Frank
and Johnnies," "Invisible Man," "Silence Is Golden," "Show Girl," "Disraeli," "Victoria," "Something Tells Me," "The Party's Over Now"

A Musical Revue in two acts.

General Manager: Susan Roy
Press: Bill Doll & Co.
Stage Manager: Clay Johns

* Closed June 25, 1972 after 24 performances.

Impact Photo

Top Right: **Luba Lisa, Kevin Christopher**

ABBEY THEATRE
Opened Thursday, June 15, 1972.*
Jay Sessa presents·

THE SUNSHINE TRAIN

Conceived and Directed by William E. Hunt; Sets and Lighting, Philip
Gilliam; Musical Directors, Louis Hancock, Howard Nealy; Assistant to
Director, Fred Good; Sound, Gary and Timmy Harris

CAST

The Carl Murray Singers:	The Gospel Starlets:
Carl Murray	Mary Johnson
Ron Horton	Dottie Coley
Ernest McCarroll	Peggie Henry
Joe Ireland	Barbara Davis
Larry Coleman	Gladys Freeman

MUSICAL NUMBERS: "The Sunshine Train," "Near the Cross," "On
My Knees Praying," "Wrapped, Tied, and Tangled," "Thank You,
Lord," "Just Look Where I Come From," "His Eye Is on the Sparrow,"
"Troubled Waters," "Swing Low," "Beams of Heaven," "We Need More
Love," "Jesus Loves Me," "All the World to Me," "Judgement Day,"
"Higher," "Come by Here," "Peace," "Stand Up for Jesus," "God Be
with You"

A joyous gospel musical performed without intermission.

Press: Saul Richman, Sara Altshul

* Closed Dec. 17, 1972 after 280 performances.

The Gospel Starlets
Above: Carl Murray Singers

CIRCLE IN THE SQUARE
Opened Monday, June 19, 1972.*
Theodore Mann (Artistic Director) and Paul Libin (Managing
Director) in association with Seymour Hacker present:

JOAN

Book, Music, Lyrics, and Direction by Al Carmines; Scenery and
Lighting, Earl Eidman; Costumes, Ira Siff, Joan Kilpatrick; Choreography, Gus Solomons, Jr.; Special Choreography, David Vaughan; Production Assistant, Suzanne Kinder.

CAST

Joan	Lee Guilliatt
Mother	Emily Adams
Sandy	Sandy Padilla
Phyllis	Phyllis MacBryde
Ira	Ira Siff
Teresa	Teresa King
Policeman	Tony Clark
Therapist	Margaret Wright
Virgin Mary	Essie Borden
Cardinal	David Vaughan
Bishop	David McCorkle
Rabbi	Jeffrey Apter
Mother Superior	Julie Kurnitz
Tracy	Tracy Moore
Police Matron	Sandy Padilla
Social Worker	David McCorkle
Pianist	Al Carmines

MUSICAL NUMBERS: "Praise the Lord," "Come on Joan," "It's So
Nice," "Go Back," "They Call Me The Virgin Mary," "Salve Madonna,"
"The Woman I Love," "Spoken Aria," "Ira, My Dope Fiend," "A Coun-
try of the Mind," "I Live a Little," "What I Wonder," "The Religious
Establishment," "In My Silent Universe," "Take Courage, Daughter,"
"Rivers of Roses," "I'm Madame Margaret the Therapist," "Look at Me,
Man," "Despair," "Faith Is Such a Simple Thing," "Praise the Lord"

A Musical in two acts.

Production Manager: Martin Herzer
Press: Merle Debuskey, Robert Larkin, Ted Goldsmith
Stage Managers: Martin Herzer, Tony Clark

Closed Aug. 14, 1972 after 64 performances.

Friedman-Abeles Photos

Margaret Wright, Lee Guilliatt
Top: Lee Guilliatt (C) and cast of "Joan"

PLAZA 9 MUSIC HALL
Opened Tuesday, June 26, 1972.*
The Plaza 9 Music Hall presents:

CURLEY McDIMPLE

Book, Mary Boylan, Robert Dahdah; Music and Lyrics, Robert Dahdah; Dance Directors, Don Emmons, George Hillman, Dotty Morgan;
Musical Director, Horace Diaz; Costumes and Hairstyles, Gene D. Gal-
lo; Lighting, April Adams; Director, Robert Dahdah

CAST

Jimmy	Don Emmons
Sarah	Mary Boylan
Alice	Lynn Brossman
Curley McDimple	Robbi Morgan
Bill	George Hillman
Miss Hamilton	Jane Stuart
Mr. Gillingwater	Richard Durham

MUSICAL NUMBERS: "A Cup of Coffee," "I Try," "Curley McDim-
ple," "Love Is the Loveliest Love Song," "Are There Any More Rosie
Gradys?", "Dancing in the Rain," "Be Grateful for What You've Got,"
"At the Playland Jamboree," "I've Got a Little Secret," "You Like
Monkey, You," "Stars and Lovers," "The Meanest Man in Town,"
"Something Nice Is Going to Happen," "Swing-a-Ling," "Hi de hi de hi,
Hi de hi de ho," "Dwarf's Song"

A Musical Comedy in two acts. The action takes place in Sarah's
boarding house in New York City in 1934.

Stage Manager: Charlotte Christman

Closed Aug. 20, 1972 after 96 performances. For original production,
see THEATRE WORLD, Vol. 24.

Tavia Mladinich Photo

Jane Stuart, Richard Durham, Robbi Morgan, Lynn
Brossman, Don Emmons, Mary Boylan, George Hillman

VIVIAN BEAUMONT THEATER
Opened Thursday, June 22, 1972.*
Albert W. Selden and Hal James by arrangement with Lincoln
Center present:

MAN OF LA MANCHA

Book and Musical Staging, Albert Marre; Music, Mitch Leigh; Lyrics,
Joe Darion; Choreography, Jack Cole; Settings and Lighting, Howard
Bay; Costumes, Howard Bay, Patton Campbell; Dance Arrangements,
Neil Warner; Musical Arrangements, Music Makers; Musical Direction,
Joseph Klein; Producers' Surrogate, Walter Fried; Musical Play by Dale
Wasserman; Hairstylist, Henri Chevrier; Technical Adviser, John Hig-
gins; Dance Captain, John Aristides

CAST

Don Quixote/Cervantes	Richard Kiley
	David Atkinson, matinees
Aldonza	Joan Diener
	Gerrianne Raphael, matinees
Sancho	Edmond Varrato
Innkeeper	Jack Dabdoub
Padre	Robert Rounseville
Dr. Carrasco	Lee Bergere
Antonia	Dianne Barton
Barber	Ted Forlow
Pedro, Head Muleteer	Shev Rodgers
Anselmo	Joe Lorden
Housekeeper	Eleanore Knapp
Juan	John Aristides
Tenorio	Fernando Grahal
Paco	Bill Stanton
Jose	Hector Mercado
Dancing Horses	Fernando Grahal, Hector Mercado
Horses	Jeff Killion, Shev Rodgers
Maria, Innkeeper's wife	Rita Metzger
Fermina, Moorish Dancer	Laura Kenyon
Captain of the Inquisition	Renato Cibelli
Guitarist	Stephen Sahlein
Guards and Men of Inquisition	Jeff Killion, David
	Wasson, Robert Cromwell

UNDERSTUDIES: Quixote, Renato Cibelli; Padre, Ronn Carroll; Al-
donza, Laura Kenyon; Inkeeper, Shev Rodgers; Carrasco, Renato Cibelli,
Alfred Leberfeld; Barber, Alfred Leberfeld; Antonia, Fermina, Joyce Mc-
Donald; Housekeeper, Rita Metzger; Maria, Laura Kenyon; Pedro, Jeff
Killion; Captain, David Wasson

MUSICAL NUMBERS: "I Don Quixote, Man of La Mancha," "It's All
the Same," "Dulcinea," "I'm Only Thinking of Him," "I Really Like
Him," "What Does He Want of Me," "Little Bird, Little Bird," "Barber's
Song," "Bolden Helmet of Mambrino," "To Each His Dulcinea," "The
Quest," "The Combat," "The Dubbing," "The Abduction," "Moorish
Dance," "Aldonza," "The Knight of the Mirrors," "A Little Gossip,"
"The Psalm"

A Musical Play performed without intermission. All the characters in
the play are imprisoned in a dungeon in Seville at the end of the sixteenth
century. The entire action takes place there and in various other places
in the imagination of Miguel de Cervantes.

Company Manager: G. Warren McClane
Press: Gifford/Wallace, Violet Welles
Stage Managers: James Gelb, Patrick Horrigan, Al Leberfeld,
Joe Lorden

* Closed Oct. 21, 1972 after 140 performances. For original production,
see THEATRE WORLD, Vol. 22. Irving Jacobson was to have opened
as Sancho, but an accident prevented his rejoining the original cast.

Top Right: Richard Kiley, Irving Jacobson (in previews)
Below: Joan Diener, Richard Kiley

Edmond Varrato

Opened Wednesday, June 28, 1972.*
The John F. Kennedy Center for The Performing Arts and S.
Hurok present:

LEONARD BERNSTEIN'S MASS

Music, Leonard Bernstein; Texts from the Liturgy of the Roman Mass;
English Texts by Stephen Schwartz, Leonard Bernstein; Director, Gor-
don Davidson; Choreography, Alvin Ailey; Settings, Oliver Smith; Cos-
umes, Frank Thompson; Lighting, Gilbert Hemsley, Jr.; Staged by
Gordon Davidson and Alvin Ailey; Musical Director, Maurice Peress;
Production Coordinator, Diana Shumlin; Produced by Roger L. Stevens
and Martin Feinstein; Associate Producer, Schuyler G. Chapin; Sound,
Richard Guy; Associate Conductor, Thomas Pierson; Cast Album by
Columbia Records.

CAST

Celebrant .... Alan Titus or David Cryer

SINGING ENSEMBLE: John D. Anthony, Cheryl Barnes, Jacqueline
Britt, Jane Coleman, David Cryer, Maegaret Cowie, Ed Dixon, Leigh
Dodson, Eugene Edwards, Thom Ellis, Lowell Harris, Lee Hooper, Gary
Lipps, Linda Lloyd, Linda Marks, Larry Marshall, Gina Penn, John
Bennett Perry, Mary Bracken Phillips, Neva Small, David Spangler, Alan
Titus

ALVIN AILEY AMERICAN DANCE THEATRE: Judith Jamison,
Dudley Williams, Clive Thompson, Linda Kent, Kenneth Pearl, Sylvia
Waters, Estelle E. Spurlock, Kelvin Rotardier, Sara Yarborough, Mari
Kajiwara, John Parks, Hector Mercado, Leland Schwantes, Clover Ma-
his, Lynne Dell Walker

NORMAN SCRIBNER CHOIR: Juanita Brown, Carol Gericke, Diane
Higginbotham, Vicki Johnstone, Janet Kenney, Katherine Ray, Cynthia
Richards, Diana Rothman, Sandra Willetts, Barbara Boller, Catherine
Sounds, Alicia Kopfstein-Penk, Patricia George, Suzanne Grant, Raina
Mann, Anne Miller, Janet Sooy, Joy Wood, Barry Butts, David Coon,
Robert Dorsey, Michael Hume, William Jones, Robert Kimball, John
Madden, Robert Stevenson, Robert Whitney, Earl Baker, Glenn Cun-
ingham, Albert deRuiter, Richard Frisch, Arphelius Paul Gatling,
Charles Greenwell, Walter Richardson, Ronald Roxbury, Michael
Bronzo

BERKSHIRE BOYS' CHOIR: David Abell, Ben Borsch, Timothy
Brown, Chris Cole, Sammy Coleman, Peter Coulianos, Thomas Etting-
hausen, Liam Fennelly, Tim Ferrell, Jonathan Gram, Bruce Haynes,
Richard Michael, Michael Miller, Chris Negus, Edward Rosen, Robert
Lough, Miles Smith, Richard Swan, David Voorhees

ANTIPHON: Betty Allen, Karen Altman, Dominic Cossa, Raymond
deVoll

RESPONSORY: Adrienne Albert, Maeretha Stewart, June Magruder,
Charles Magruder, John Manno, William Elliot

MUSICAL NUMBERS: "A Simple Song," "I Don't Know," "Easy,"
"Gloria Tibi," "Thank You," "The Word of the Lord," "God Said,"
"Non Credo," "Hurry," "World without End," "I Believe in God," "Our
Father," "I Go On," "Things Get Broken," "Secret Songs"

A Theatre Piece for singers, players, and dancers performed in 17
scenes without intermission.

Company Manager: Robert I. Goldberg
Press: Sheila Porter, Leo Sullivan, John Gringrich
Stage Managers: Norman A. Grogan, Tom A. Larson, Randall
Brooks, M. Sholar-Taylor

Closed July 22, 1972 after 22 performances and 2 previews. Commis-
sioned for the opening of the John F. Kennedy Center for the Performing Arts on Monday, June 5, 1972 after 2 previews. Closed June 17, and
performed at Philadelphia Academy of Music from June 19 through
June 24, 1972.

Fletcher Drake Photos

Top Right: Judith Jamison

Alan Titus (C), and also above (L)

JONES BEACH THEATRE

Opened Wednesday, June 28, 1972.*
Guy Lombardo presents:

THE KING AND I

Book and Lyrics, Oscar Hammerstein 2nd; Music, Richard Rodgers; Based on novel "Anna and the King of Siam" by Margaret Landon; Director, John Fearnley; Choreography, Yuriko; Based on original choreography by Jerome Robbins; Scenery, James Stewart Morcom; Costumes, Winn Morton; Lighting, Peggy Clark; Orchestrations, Robert Russell Bennett; Choral Arrangements, Trudi Rittman; Musical Direction, Jay Blackton; Entire Production under Supervision of Arnold Spector

CAST

Captain Orton	James Hawthorne
Louis Leonowens	Richard Arnold Beattie
Anna Leonowens	Constance Towers
Interpreter	Paul Flores
Kralahome	Edmund Lyndeck
The King	John Cullum
Phra Alack	Peter Clark
Lun Tha	John Stewart
Tuptim	Patricia Arnell
Lady Thiang	Eileen Schauler
Prince Chululongkorn	Keenan Shimizu
Princess Ying Yaowlak	Cynthia Onrubia
Sir Edward Ramsay	James Hawthorne

PRINCES AND PRINCESSES: June Angela, Barbara Ann Beattie, Charles Beattie, Frank Taofi Fanene, David Mat, Cynthia Onrubia, Gene Profanato, Gary Stevens, Tobe West

SINGERS, ROYAL DANCERS, WIVES, AMAZONS, PRIESTS, SLAVES: Loretta Abbott, Lisa Berg, Renee Binzer, Tisa Chang, Kitty Chen, Lorri Chinn, Gia De Silva, Asha Devi, Doris Galiber, Dale Harimoto, Marina Keijzer, Linda Kettell, Sherry Lambert, Leonore Lanzillotti, Liz Lauter, Mary Ann Rydzeski, Dixie Stewart, Ilene Strickler, Karla Wolfangle, Baruch Blum, Jeff Cahn, David Chase, Peter Clark, Raymond Clay, Gary Dutton, Paul Flores, Nickolas Frank, Sanford Levitt, Robert Monteil, Richard Nieves, Rick Ornellas

UNDERSTUDIES: King, Edmund Lyndeck; Anna, Dixie Stewart; Thiang, Leonore Lanzillotti; Tuptim, Sherry Lambert; Lun Tha, Richard Nieves; Kralahome, Paul Flores; Captain, Ramsay, Peter Clark; Chululongkorn, Nickolas Frank; Louis, Charles Beattie; Eliza, Liz Lauter; Interpreter, Baruch Blum; Phra Alack, Robert Monteil

MUSICAL NUMBERS: "I Whistle a Happy Tune," "My Lord and Master," "Hello, Young Lovers," "March of the Siamese Children," "A Puzzlement," "Royal Bangkok Academy," "Getting to Know You," "We Kiss in a Shadow," "Shall I Tell You What I Think of You?," "Something Wonderful," "Western People Funny," "I Have Dreamed," "Small House of Uncle Thomas," "Shall We Dance?," Finale

Managing Director: Arnold Spector
Company Manager: Sam Pagliaro
Press: Saul Richman, Sara Altschul
Stage Managers: Mortimer Halpern, Bertram Wood, Jeff Cahn

* Closed Sept. 3, 1972 after limited engagement of 55 performances. For original production see THEATRE WORLD, Vol. 7.

Barry Kramer Photos

Richard Beatty, Keenan Shimizu, Patricia Arness, Eileen Schauler, Constance Towers

John Stewart, Patricia Arnell
Top: John Cullum, Constance Towers

NATIONAL BLACK THEATRE

Opened Saturday, July 1, 1972.*
The National Black Theatre (Barbara Ann Teer, Director)
presents:

A REVIVAL

Written by Charlie L. Russell; Director, Barbara Ann Teer; Designers,
Willie Faison, Donald Faison, Harrison Avery, Kurt Lundell, Ademola
Olugebefola; Music, LaReine Hassani LaMar, Ayofemi Folayan, Oseiku,
Earl Smith, Warren Benbow, Donald Faison; Sound, Michael J. Lythcott;
Lighting, Zuri Laini McKie, Al Samuel, Rhonda C. Morman; Costumes,
Ifenu, Evelyn Chisholm, Judy Dearing, Yaa Shepherd, P. M. Bowdwin

CAST

Jason	Willie Faison
Cynthia	Beverly Williams
Robin	William Still
Sonia	Jabulile
Pickwick	Oba Babatunde
Candy	Ntombi
Porky	Ronnie Grant
Beverly	LaVerne Moore
Clarence	Douglas Leslie Dunn
Miss Sylvia	Brenda Thomas Denmark
Sugarfoot	Al Samuel
Bernice	Mary Giles
Virginia	Ifenu
Officer Green	Michael J. Lythcott
Officer Brown	Jingo
Dara	LaVerne Johnson
Mamadou	Akinwole Babatunde
Thembi	Yaa Shepherd
Toussaint	Mathew Bernard Johnson, Jr.
Georgia	Cecilia Talley
Gregory	Steven Tillman
Rita	P. M. Bowdwin
Preacher in Procession	Donald Faison
Ayana	Muhuanda Ali
Njonjo	Charles Wood
Oshun	Zuri Laini McKie
Walt	Jingo
Ancestor	Akinwole Babatunde

* Closed Dec. 10, 1972 after 113 performances.

Cast of "A Revival"

MAYFAIR THEATRE

Opened Wednesday, July 12, 1972.*
Richie Havens presents:

SAFARI 300

A Concept by Tad Truesdale; Director, Hugh Gittens; Dramatic Mate-
rial, Tony Preston; Musical Director, Scat Wilson; Choreography, Larl
Becham; Costumes, Lee Lynn; Sets Bob Olsen; Lighting, David Adams;
Additional Choreography, Phil Black

CAST

Tad Truesdale	Larl Becham
Onike Lee	Earnest Andrews
Joyce Griffen	Holly Hamilton
Fredi Orange	Andre Robinson
Grenna Whitaker	Dorian Williams

MUSICAL NUMBERS: "Dombaye," "Singing Drums," "Adunde,"
"Royal Court Dance," "Little Black Baby," "Slave Auction," "Black
Rape," "Sage," "O Negros Bahianos," "Johnny Too Bad," "World Keeps
Turnin'," "Waiting Song," "Voodoo," "Baron Samedi," "Soon I'll Be
Done," "This Little Light," "Cakewalk," "Song of Sorrow," "Goin' to
Chicago," "Song of Troubles," "Cotton Club Revue," "1950's Singing
Group," "1960's Twist," "Younger Men Grow Older," "My Children
Searching," "Prayer," "Size Places," "Doin' It by the Book," "Get It
Together," "Oratorio," "The Man and His Message," "What Have We
Done," "Hallucinations," "It's Rainin'," "Rock 1975," "Return to
Africa," "Akiwawa"

A Musical Revue in two acts.

Press: Saul Richman, Sara Altshul
Stage Manager: Kevin Breslin

* Closed Aug. 1, 1972 after 29 performances.

Tad Truesdale

SHERIDAN SQUARE PLAYHOUSE

Opened Tuesday, July 18, 1972.*
TDJ Productions, Inc. presents:

PRESENT TENSE

By Frank D. Gilroy; Director, Curt Dempster; Set and Lighting,
Charles Cosler; Costume Coordinator, Leslie Gifford

CAST

"Come Next Tuesday"
Louise Harper .... Lois Smith
Harvey Harper .... Biff McGuire

"Twas Brillig" in two scenes
Edna .... Sarah Cunningham
Bob Kalmus .... Stanley Beck
Mr. Vogel .... Biff McGuire
Judith Kalmus .... Lois Smith

"So Please Be Kind" in two scenes
A Man .... Biff McGuire
A Woman .... Lois Smith
Bellboy .... Gary Nebiol

"Present Tense" in three scenes
Father .... Biff McGuire
Mother .... Lois Smith

Four one-act plays performed with one intermission.

General Managers: Bob MacDonald, Maribeth Gilbert
Press: Samuel J. Friedman, Louise Weiner Ment
Stage Managers: William Yaggy, Gary Nebiol

* Closed July 23, 1972 after 8 performances.

Bert Andrews Photo

Lois Smith, Biff McGuire

MERCER-BRECHT THEATRE
Opened Tuesday, July 25, 1972.*
Daffodil Productions presents:

SPEED GETS THE POPPYS

Book, Lila Levant; Music, Lorenzo Fuller; Lyrics, Lorenzo Fuller, L
Levant; Directed and Choreographed by Charles Abbott; Musical Dir
tion and Arrangements, Robert Estey; Sets, Costumes, Lighting, Mil
Duke; Production Associate, Bill Tabor; Production Assistant, Mich
Anderson

CAST

T. J. Worthyman .... Robin Fi
Pendleton Poppy .... Edward Pe
Priscilla Poppy .... Anita K
Polly Poppy .... Randi Kal
Pandy Poppy .... Joanna My
Smedley V. Speed .... Robert Brown
Sheriff .... Raymond Cerab

MUSICAL NUMBERS: "What Is A Melodrama?," "Living Next D
to the Sun," "Instant Magic," "Caught," "Whatever Happened to
morrow?," "Take It from a Pal," "I'll Bring the Roses," "Speed Wo
Get Me," "What Real True Friends Are For," "Try, Try Again," "
Moustache Is Twitchin'," "An Old-Fashioned Chase," "Good Trium
over Evil"

A Melodrama in two acts. The action takes place on the Poppys' fa

Company Manager: Henry Avery
Press: Alan Eichler, Mary Ann Koegler
Stage Managers: Jeffrey Dunn, Raymond Cerabone

* Closed July 30, 1972 after 7 performances.

Bert Andrews Photo

Joanna Myers, Anita Keal, Randi Kallan, Ed
Penn, Robin Field

NYC PARKS & PLAYGROUNDS
Opened Monday, August 7, 1972.*
Puerto Rican Traveling Theatre presents:

THE PASSION OF ANTIGONA PEREZ

By Luis Rafael Sanchez; Translated by Charles Pilditch; Director, Pablo Cabrera; Set and Lighting, Karl Eigsti; Costumes, A. Christina Giannini; Administrator, Allen Davis III; Technical Director, Pat Hanley

CAST

Antigona Perez	Miriam Colon
Press	Tomy Vargas, Luis Cadiz, Jose Rodriguez, Eddie Velez
Aurora	Mary Bell
Creon Molina	Manu Tupou
Pilar	June Adams
Monsignor Bernardo Escudero	Fred Cook
Irene	Irene De Bari
Waiter	George Bergeron
Guards	Jose Olivero, Philip Alperson, Wilfredo Hernandez, Henry Gonzales

UNDERSTUDIES: Antigona, Irene De Bari; Creon Molina, Jose Rodriguez; Aurora, Pilar, Irene, Iris Martinez

A Drama performed without intermission. The action takes place in the Republic of Molina, somewhere in the Americas at the present time.

Company Manager: C. George Willard
Press: Alan Eichler, James J. O'Rourke
Stage Managers: C. D. Creasap, Allen Davis III

Closed Aug. 26, 1972 after limited engagement of 20 performances.

Friedman-Abeles Photo

June Adams, Manu Tupou, Miriam Colon

MERCER-BRECHT THEATRE
Opened Thursday, August 17, 1972.*
The Performing Ensemble of The Chicago Free Theater presents:

AESOP'S FABLES

By William Russo; Text, Jon Swan; Produced and Directed by William Russo; Staged by Don Sanders; Designed by Vanessa James; Choral Director, Joseph Reiser; Associate Music Director, Frank Shaney; Technical Staff, Nancy Campbell, Thom Drewke, Richard Kravets, Frank Yancey

CAST

Mike Shacochis	Bill Williams
Trisha Long	Frank Shaney
John Davenport	Richard Kravets
Denise Walther	Ken Hayden

FABLES: "The Lion and the Mouse," "The Fox and the Stork," "The Mice in Council," "The Lion and the Boar," "The Wolves and the Jackal," "The Donkey and the Grasshoppers," "The Frog and the Ox," "The Trees and the Ax," "The Cat and the Rooster," "The Ants and the Cocoon," "The Crow and the Fox"

Production Manager: Linda Corby
Press: Alan Eichler, Connie Zonka
Stage Manager: Gary Porto

* Closed Sept. 17, 1972 after 57 performances.

Friedman-Abeles Photo

Left: Bill Williams and cast

EDEN THEATRE
Opened Sunday, September 10, 1972.*
B. F. Concerts presents:

CRAZY NOW

Book and Lyrics, Richard Smithies, Maura Cavanagh; Music, Norman Sus; Directed and Choreographed by Voigt Kempson; Costumes, Margret Tobin; Lighting, Wilson King; Musical Director, Jim Litt; Consultant Director, Richard Smithies

CAST

Carla Benjamin
William Buell
Glenn Mure
Rosalie
John Scoullar

MUSICAL NUMBERS: "Crazy Now," "Shaftway Danger," "Marginal People," "Toll Basket," "Tears," "Great Connection," "Algae," "Beautiful," "Hard Times," "Get Naked," "Dirty Mind," "Regulation Purple," "Sherman's Mom," "Something to Do with My Hands," "Highway Narrows"

Musical Revue performed without intermission.

Production Manager: Peace Chick
Press: Alan Eichler
Stage Manager: Charles Embry

Closed Sept. 10, 1972 after one performance.

Friedman-Abeles Photo

**Carla Benjamin, Glenn Mure, William Buell,
John Scoullar, Rosalie**

95

BROOKLYN ACADEMY
Opened Tuesday, September 19, 1972.*
Brooklyn Academy of Music in association with Kazuko
Hillyer presents JEWISH STATE THEATRE OF BUCHAR-
EST in:

THE DYBBUK

By S. Ansky; Based on Jewish folklore; Artistic Director, S. Franz-Iosif
Auerbach; Technical Director, I. Iosif Bolteansky

CAST

Reb Sender	Benno Popliker
Leah	Leonie Waldman Eliad
Frade	Seidy Gluek
Gittle	Marieta Neuman
Bassia	Mihaela Kreutzer
Manasse	Rudy Rosenfeld
Nakhman	Mano Rippel
Reb Mendel	Ozy Segaly
Messenger	Carol Marcovici
Reb Azrielke	Samuel Fischler
Mikhol	Abraham Naimark
Reb Simschen	Isac Cassvan
Meyer	Isac Cassvan
Khonnon	Adrian Lupo
Hennakh	Mano Rippel
Asher	Ozy Segaly
Batlons	Bebe Berkowitch, Abraham Naimark, Samuel Fischler
Elderly Woman	Nusa Grup Stoian
Wedding Guest	Samuel Godrich
Blind Woman	Trisy Abramovitch
Hassidians	Mano Rippel, Bebe Bercovica, Samuel Godrich
Students	Schapira Ruhale, Sonia Fischler
Paupers	Bertrice Naimarck, Beatrice Radu, Cristina Pongratz, Rudy Bolteansky, Rudy Rosenfeld, Albert Kitzl

A Drama in three acts.
Opened Thursday, September 21, 1972.*

THE PEARL NECKLACE

A Musical by Israel Berkovici; Conductor, Haim Schwartzman; Based
on Jewish folk songs; Performed by the company in sixteen scenes.

Company Manager: Mircea Ciobanu
Press: Jan Hash, Beverly Willis

* Closed Oct. 1, 1972 after 14 performances in repertory in Yiddish.

"The Pearl Necklace"
Above: "The Dybbuk"

John Wardwell, Steven Keats, Raina Barrett,
J. R. Marks, James Doerr

CIRCLE IN THE SQUARE
Opened Sunday, September 24, 1972.*
The Bomb Haven Company presents:

WE BOMBED IN NEW HAVEN

By Joseph Heller; A New Interpretation Conceived and Directed
Peter John Bailey; Scenery, Robert U. Taylor; Lighting, Thomas Skel
Sound, Gary Harris; Associate Producer, Joan Rowe

CAST

Captain Starkey	James D
The Major	John Wardw
Sgt. Henderson	Steven K
Cpl. Bailey	Richard K
Cpl. Sinclair	Christopher Lo
Pfc. Joe Carson	William Pres
Private Fisher	John Kuh
Idiots	Rory Kelly, Robert Shea, Gary Sprin
Ruth	Raina Bar
The Hunter	J. R. M
The Golfer	Frank
Young Fisher	Brian Brow
Starkey's Son	Carter

A Drama in two acts. The action takes place "Always the present,
exact day and hour which the play is being performed, in the theatre,
and country in which the play is presented."

General Managers: Dorthy Olim Associates
Press: John Springer Associates, Ruth Cage, Ted Goldsmith
Stage Manager: Cleveland Morris

* Closed Sept. 24, 1972 after one performance.

Bert Andrews Photo

THEATRE DE LYS
Opened Sunday, October 1, 1972.*
Hank Kaufman and Gene Lerner in association with Michael
Arthur Film Productions present:

BERLIN TO BROADWAY
WITH KURT WEILL

Music, Kurt Weill; Lyrics, Maxwell Anderson, Marc Blitzstein, Bertolt
Brecht, Jacques Deval, Michael Feingold, Ira Gershwin, Paul Green,
Langston Hughes, Alan Jay Lerner, Ogden Nash, George Tabori, Arnold
Weinstein; Staged by Donald Saddler; Musical Direction and Arrange-
ments, Newton Wayland; Text and Format, Gene Lerner; Designed by
Herbert Senn and Helen Pond; Costumes, Frank Thompson; Lighting,
Thomas Skelton; Sound, Gary Harris; Projections, Lester Polakov; Con-
ductor, Robert Rogers; Production Assistant, Mark Kruger; Presented by
special arrangement with Lucille Lortel Productions, Inc.

CAST

Margery Cohen
Ken Kercheval
Judy Lander
Jerry Lanning
Hal Watters

MUSICAL NUMBERS: "Threepenny Opera": "Morning Anthem,"
"Mack the Knife," "Jealousy Duet," "Tango Ballad," "Love Duet,"
"Barbara Song," "Useless Song," "How to Survive," "Pirate Jenny,"
"Happy Ending"; "Happy End": "Bilboa Song," "Surabaya Johnny,"
"Sailor Tango"; "The Rise and Fall of the City of Mahagonny": "Ala-
bama Song," "Deep in Alaska," "Oh, Heavenly Salvation," "As You
Make Your Bed"; "Marie Galante": "I Wait for a Ship"; "Johnny John-
son": "Songs of Peace and War," "Song of the Guns," "Hymn to Peace,"
"Johnny's Song"; "Knickerbocker Holiday": "How Can You Tell An
American?," "September Song"; "Lady in the Dark": "My Ship," "Girl
of the Moment," "The Saga of Jenny"; "One Touch of Venus": "That's
Him," "Speak Low," "Love Life": "Progress," "Love Song"; "Street
Scene": "Moon-Faced, Starry-Eyed," "Ain't It Awful, the Heat?,"
"Lonely House," "Lullaby"; "Lost in the Stars": "Train to Johannesburg,"
"Trouble Man," "Cry the Beloved Country," "Lost in the Stars"

Musical Voyage performed in two parts.

General Manager: Paul B. Berkowsky
Press: Saul Richman, Sara Altshul
Stage Managers: Fred Seagraves, Gregory Porter

Closed Feb. 11, 1972 after 152 performances.

Friedman-Abeles Photo

Hal Watters, Judy Lander, Margery Cohen,
Jerry Lanning, Ken Kercheval

EASTSIDE PLAYHOUSE
Opened Tuesday, October 3, 1972.*
Haila Stoddard and Arnold H. Levy present:

LADY AUDLEY'S SECRET

Adapted by Douglas Seale from novel by Mary Elizabeth Braddon;
Music, George Goehring; Lyrics, John Kuntz; Director, Douglas Seale;
Settings and Costumes, Alicia Finkel; Lighting, Lawrence Metzler; Musi-
cal Direction and Arrangments, John Cina; Musical Staging, George
Bunt

CAST

Phoebe	Lu Ann Post
Luke	Danny Sewell
Lady Audley	Donna Curtis
Sir Michael Audley	Douglas Seale
Alicia	June Gable
Capt. Robert Audley	Russell Nype
George Talboys	Richard Curnock
Butler	Rick Atwell
Parlour Maid	Rosalin Ricci
Policeman	Michael Serrecchia
Shepherd	Jonathan Miele
Barmaid	Virginia Pulos
Game Keeper	Dennis Roberts
Shepherdess	Joyce Maret

UNDERSTUDIES: Sir Michael, Leonardo Cimino; Lady Audley, Alicia,
Virginia Pulos; Phoebe, Barmaid, Joyce Maret; Luke, Michael Serrecchia;
Robert, Dennis Roberts; George, Rick Atwell; Butler, Jonathan Miele

MUSICAL NUMBERS: "The English Country Life," "A Mother's Wish
Is A Daughter's Duty," "The Winter Rose," "Comes a Time," "That
Lady in Eng-a-land," "Civilized," "Dead Men Tell No Tales," "Pas de
Deux," "An Old Maid," "Repose," "The Audley Family Honour," "La-
de-da-da," "I Knows What I Knows," "How? What? Why?," "Firemen's
Quartet," "Forgive Her, Forgive Her"

A Musical in two acts and six scenes.

General Managers: NR Productions, Norman E. Rothstein,
Patricia Carney, Bob MacDonald
Company Manager: Robert Frissell
Press: Betty Lee Hunt, Henry Luhrman, Harriett Trachtenberg,
Abner D. Klipstein
Stage Members: Jan Moerel, Peter Von Mayrhauser

* Closed Oct. 8, 1972 after 8 performances.

Friedman-Abeles Photo

Russell Nype, Donna Curtis

THE NEW THEATRE

Opened Wednesday, October 4, 1972.*
Wroderick Productions present:

OH COWARD!

Words and Music by Noel Coward; Devised and Directed by Roderick Cook; Settings, Helen Pond and Herbert Senn; Musical Direction and Arrangements, Rene Wiegert; Additional Musical Arrangements, Herbert Helbig, Nicholas Deutsch; Production Assistant, William Martis; Pianists, Rene Wiegert, Uel Wade; Drums, Bernard Karl

CAST

Barbara Cason
Roderick Cook†
Jamie Ross†

MUSICAL NUMBERS: "Something to Do with Spring," "Bright Young People," "Poor Little Rich Girl," "Ziegeuner," "Let's Say Goodbye," "This Is a Changing World," "We Were Dancing," "Dance Little Lady," "Room with a View," "Sail Away," "London Pastoral," "The End of the News," "Stately Homes of England," "London Pride," "What Happened to Him?," "Auntie Jessie," "Uncle Harry," "Chase Me Charlie," "Saturday Night at the Rose and Crown," "Island of Bolamazoo," "What Ho Mrs Brisket!," "Has Anybody Seen Our Ship?," "Men about Town," "If Love Were All," "Too Early or Too Late," "Why Do the Wrong People Travel?," "The Passenger's Always Right," "Mrs. Worthington," "Mad Dogs and Englishmen," "The Party's Over Now," "You Were There," "Three White Feathers," "The Star," "The Critic," "The Elderly Actress," "Gertie," "Loving," "I Am No Good at Love," "Sex Talk," "A Question of Lighting," "Mad about the Boy," "Ina," "Alice," "World Weary," "Let's Do It," "Where Are the Songs We Sung?," "Someday I'll Find You," "I'll Follow My Secret Heart," "If Love Were All," "Play Orchestra Play," "I'll See You Again"

A Musical Revue in two acts and 18 scenes.

General Managers: Lily Turner, Bill Levine
Press: Seymour Krawitz
Stage Manager: Jay Leo Colt

* Closed June 17, 1973 to tour before re-opening in the fall.
† Succeeded by Christian Grey during vacations

Friedman-Abeles Photo

Roderick Cook, Jamie Ross, Barbara Cason

Pesach Burstein

MAYFAIR THEATRE

Opened Tuesday, October 10, 1972.*
Moishe Baruch presents:

THE REBBITZEN FROM ISRAEL

Adapted and Staged by Pesach Burstein; Based on play by L. F Musical Director, Elliot Finkel; Music and Lyrics, Lili Amber; Peter Achilles, Choreography, Yona Aloni

CAST

Alice Goldenthal	Janece
Abraham Goldenthal	Pesach E
Shimon	Bernar
Robert Goldenthal	Gene
Edna Goldenthal	Ri
Mirele Shapiro	Lilli
Moishele Shapiro	David
Voice of Art Raymond	

MUSICAL NUMBERS: "Yeverechecha," "Yehi Rutzoin," "Oy sach Pesach," "Where Were You?," "I'm in Love," "Traditiona "I Should Live So," "Love Is International," "Ladies Should Be ful," "I Wish It Was Over," "Tel-Aviv," Finale

A Musical Comedy in two acts.

General Manager: Charlotte Zaltzberg
Press: Max Eisen, Milly Schoenbaum
* Closed Mar. 4, 1973 after 168 performances.

Nuria Espert (L), Jose Luis Pellicena

BROOKLYN ACADEMY OF MUSIC

Opened Wednesday, October 18, 1972.*

The Brooklyn Academy of Music (Harvey Lichtenstein, Executive Director; Courtney Callender, Associate Director) and Madame Ninon T. Karlweis present the Nuria Espert Company of Spain (Armando Moreno, Administrator) in:

YERMA

y Federico Garcia Lorca; Director, Victor Garcia; Set and Costumes, or Garcia, Fabian Puigserver; Lighting, Polo Villasenor; Administra-Ramon Moix; Technician, Antonio Perez; Stage Director, Jose Maria ra

CAST

ma	Nuria Espert
1	Jose Luis Pellicena
or	Daniel Dicenta
Pagan Woman	Amparo Valle
ores	Paloma Lorena
ia	Rosa Vicente
herwomen	Rosa Vicente, Paloma Lorena,
Conchita Leza, Gloria Berrocal, Nuria Moreno, Amparo Valle	
dren	Conchita Leza, Paloma Lorena
e	Enrique Majo
ale	Alicia Day
ale Voice	Gloria Berrocal
ers-in-Law	Enrique Majo, Eduardo Bea
l	Antonio Correncia, Angel Sempere,
Juan Antonio Hormigon, Javier Macua, Eduardo Bea	

Drama in two acts.

Company and Stage Manager: Tennent McDaniel
Press: Jan Hash, Carol Lawhon, Beverly Willis

osed Oct. 29, 1972 after limited engagement of 13 performances in anish.

EDEN THEATRE

Opened Sunday, October 22, 1972.*

H. Rothpearl & S. Ehrenfeld & Associates, The Jewish Nostalgic Productions, Inc. present:

YOSHE KALB

By I. J. Singer; Adapted and Directed by David Licht; Music, Maurice Rauch; Lyrics, Isaac Dogim; Choreography, Lillian Shapero; Musical Director, Renee Solomon; Lighting, Tom Meleck; Scenic Artist, Donald DuVall; Costumes, Sylvia Friedlander; Sets, Jorday Barry; Technical Director, Herbert Rach

CAST

Narrator	Warren Pincus
Psachye	Elia Patron
Moishe Chossed	Jaime Lewin
Mechala	Shmulik Goldstein
Motye Godle	Mordechai Yachson
Isroel Avigdor	Jacob Zanger
Rabbi Reb Ezre	Isaac Dogim
Leah	Miriam Kressyn
Rabbi Reb Melech	David Opatoshu
Nachum (Yoshe Kalb)	David Ellis
Gittel	Reizl Bozyk
Feige	Helen Blay
Serele	Ruth Vool
Aydele	Shifra Lerer
Malkele	Raquel Yossiffon
Tsivye	Miriam Kressyn
Zanvil	Jaime Lewin
Kune	Elia Patron
Abish	Jack Rechtzeit
Bayle-Dobe	Shifra Lerer
Bashe-Dviore	Helen Blay
Schachne	Mordechai Yachson
Rabbi Mayerel	Isaac Dogim
Rabbi from Krakow	Jacob Ben-Ami
Rabbi from Lejane	Jack Rechtzeit

CHASSIDIM AND TOWNSPEOPLE: Dale Carter, Jack Dyville, Susan Griss, Claire Hash, James Vaughan, Robert Yarri, Keith Driggs, Shanna Kanter

MUSICAL NUMBERS: "Ein Koloheinu," "Song of Joy," "The Three Good Deeds," "Wedding Procession," "Chosen Doime le Meilech and Rikodle," "Malkele's Song," "Wedding Dance," "Trio," "Tsivye's Song," "Badchen," "Bwis Iolem Tantz," "Rosh Hashono"

A Musical Drama in two acts and 13 scenes. The action takes place in Russia in 1860 and 1875.

General Manager: Seymour Rexite
Company Manager: Jerry Cohen
Press: Benjamin Rothman, Max Eisen, Milly Schoenbaum
Stage Manager: Bryna Wasserman

* Closed Jan. 7, 1973 after 95 performances.

David Opatoshu, Ruth Vool

Tom Clancy, Stephen D. Newman, Margaret Linn,
Francis Bethencourt
(Martha Swope Photo)

Emlyn Williams

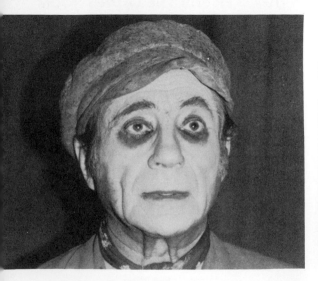

Joseph Buloff

QUEENS PLAYHOUSE
Opened Wednesday, October 25, 1972.*
Queens Playhouse Inc. (Joseph S. Kutrzeba, Founder-Pr
ducer) presents:

PYGMALION

By George Bernard Shaw; Director, Paul Shyre; Scenery and Proje
tions, Eldon Elder; Costumes, Sara Brook; Lighting, David F. Seg
Artistic Director, Joseph S. Kutrzeba; Technical Director, Lary Opi
Production Associate, Michael Mantel

CAST

Workmen	Everett Mays, Jr., James Ciacc
Tea Seller	Lois Liberty Jon
Flower Peddler	Sheila D
Newsboy	Alan K. Sieg
Operagoers	Anne Spinner, Gail Shemchen
Henry Higgins	Stephen D. Newm
Bystander	Bernard Frawley
Mrs. Eynsford-Hill	Virginia Downi
Clara Eynsford-Hill	Susan Hickers
Freddy Eynsford-Hill	Noel Cra
Eliza Doolittle	Margaret Li
Colonel Pickering	Francis Bethencou
Taxi Driver	Robert Wooll
Mrs. Pearce	Paddy Cr
Alfred Doolittle	Tom Clancy
Mrs. Higgins	Edith Meis
Parlourmaid	Alice Lip

UNDERSTUDIES: Eliza, Susan Hickerson; Higgins, Jack Betts; Doo
tle, Pickering, Bernard Frawley; Clara, Alice Lipitz; Bystander, Rob
Woolley

A Comedy in three acts and five scenes. The action takes place
London.

Company Manager: Ian Edward
Press: Robert Ganshaw, Seymour Krawitz, Paul Bernabeo
Stage Manager: David Sell

* Closed Nov. 18, 1972 after 30 performances.
† Succeeded by: 1. Ian Edward, 2. Bernard Frawley

KAUFMANN CONCERT HALL
Opened Tuesday, October 31, 1972.*
Hurok Concerts presents:

EMLYN WILLIAMS

"As Dylan Thomas Growing Up"
A one-man show with Mr. Williams reading from the works of Dy
Thomas.

* Repeated on Thursday, Nov. 2, and Saturday, Nov. 4, 1972 for to
of three performances.

FOLKSBIENE PLAYHOUSE
Opened Saturday, November 4, 1972.*
The Folksbiene Ensemble presents:

YOSHKE MUSIKANT

Based on Ossip Dimow; Director, Joseph Buloff; Music, Z. Mlo
Scenery and Lighting, Harry Baum; Costumes, H. Kulyk; Assistant
rector, Luba Kadison

CAST

Sheyne/Yoshke	Joseph Bu
Royzele	Marilyn G
Sheyne	Diane Cyp
Mendel	David Ro
Hodish	Zipporah Spaizn
Shayke	Menashe Oppenhe
Berl	Morris Ad
Madam Luria	Mina K
Semionchik	Norman Kru
Mekhutn	Harry Gr
Bride	Paul Teitelba
Baker's Wife	Sara Sta
Butcher	Max Po
Kaliputa	Moishe Rosen
Rich Men	Albert Jacobs, Harry Frei
Rabbi	William Men
Shames	Marvin Schwa
Police Chief	Chaim Zaidenwo
Yoshke's Mother	Pauly Rosenblo

A Comedy in two acts.

Stage Managers: Harry Freifeld, Marvin Schwartz
* Closed Apr. 1, 1973.

GHBORHOOD HOUSE
Opened Friday, November 10, 1972.*
Riverdale Community Theatre presents:

FIRST IMPRESSIONS

ok, Abe Burrows; Based on Jane Austen's novel "Pride and Preju-
and the play by Helen Jerome; Music and Lyrics, Robert Goldman,
n Paxton, George Weiss; Directed and Choreographed by Jeffery K.
; Musical Direction and Special Arrangements, Wendell Kindberg;
uction and Costumes Designed by Charles W. Roeder; Producer,
rt Alan Resnik; Production Assistant, Harry Levy; Lighting,
les Sachs, Pat Brooks, Judy Walsh; Props, Tom Lee; Piano, Wendell
berg; Bass, David Perlman

CAST

Wickham	Carmen Pecchio
Denny	Thomas Sheehan
William Lucas	Charles Sachs
Lucas	Eileen Ronaldes
lotte Lucas	Deborah Savadge
Rockingham	Michael J. Walsh
beth Bennet	Meredith Kelly
Bennet	Kirsten Sonstegard
a Bennet	Kathleen Connelly
Bennet	Lila Koven
Bennet	Ann Travolta
Bennet	Doris Balin Bianchi
Bennet	Fred Ponger
aret	Dolores Francis
Darcy	Ward Smith
Bingley	Iris Cohen
Bingley	Edwin A. Folts
ams	Thomas Sheehan
Catherine de Bourgh	Janet Booth
de Bourgh	Dolores Francis
Collins	Robert D. Kane
of Butler	Robert D. Kane

ICAL NUMBERS: "Five Daughters," "I'm Me," "Have You
d the News," "Assembly Dance," "A Perfect Evening," "It's the
to Do,"* "As Long as There's a Mother," "Jane," "Love Will Find
,"* "Gentlemen Don't Fall Wildly in Love," "Fragrant Flowers,"
el Sorry for the Girl," "I Suddenly Find You Agreeable," "This
Isn't Me," "So This Is How It Is,"* "Wasn't It a Simply Lovely
ing," "A House in Town," "The Heart Has Won the Game," "Not
Me,"* "Let's Fetch the Carriage," Finale

Musical in 2 acts and 12 scenes. The action takes place in the village
ryton, England, in 1813.

Press: Celia Kornfeld
Stage Managers: Louis Graff, Thomas A. Buckner, IV

sed Nov. 25, 1972 after limited engagement of 6 performances.
gs with asterisk were omitted from Broadway production.

Meredith Kelly, Ward Smith, Doris Balin Bianchi

(Robert Kornfeld Photo)

Norma Donaldson, Benay Venuta, Helon Blount,
Judy MacMurdo, Paula Cinko

VILLAGE GATE
Opened Sunday, November 12, 1972.*
Phillip R Productions, Inc. presents:

A QUARTER FOR THE LADIES ROOM

Lyrics, Ruth Batchelor; Music, John Clifton, Arthur Siegel; Director,
Darwin Knight; Setting, David R. Ballou; Costumes, Miles White; Light-
ing, Lee Watson; Arrangements, Bill Brohn; Musical Director, Karen
Gustafson; Production Assistant, Cleveland Morris; Hairstylist, Nino
Raffaello

CAST

The Attendant	Helon Blount
The Angel	Paula Cinko
The Harlot	Norma Donaldson
The Mistress	Judy MacMurdo
The Wife	Benay Venuta

Standby: Evelyn Page

MUSICAL NUMBERS: "First Quarter," "Turn Around," "Incom-
plete," "Married Man," "Gemini," "Number One Man," "My Hero's
Grenades," "Talk about the Men," "Feel at Home," "My Lover and His
Wife," "Incest and Apples," "Baby Dolls," "The Princess," "Nice La-
dies," "Woman Power," "Whatshisname," "Butterfly's Lament," "When
Will the Music Be Gone," "The Kind of Guy," "Epitaph," "When the
Time Comes," "Why Don't I Leave Him," "Talk to Me," "Last Quarter"
"A Musical Eyeview" performed without intermission. The action
takes place in "an imaginary ladies room as time is standing still."

General Management: Dorothy Olim Associates
Press: Seymour Krawitz, Patricia Krawitz
Stage Manager: Robert Bruyr

* Closed Nov. 12, 1972 after one performance and 7 previews.

Friedman-Abeles Photo

101

VANDAM THEATRE
Opened Wednesday, November 15, 1972.*
Wayne Clark presents:

TWANGER

Book, Music, Lyrics, Ronnie Britton; Director, Walter Ash; Musical Direction, Lee Gillespie; Musical Arrangements, Gordon Harrell; Lighting, Peter Anderson; Costumes, Owen H. Goldstein; Dance and Overture Arrangements, David Wahler; Musical Numbers and Dances Staged by Ronnie Britton; Additional Arrangements, Lee Gillespie; Production Coordinator, Patricia Smiesko; Puppets, Bill and Harriet Scherer

CAST

Garbage Ella	Andrea Noel
Magician	Nevil Martyn
Twanger	Glenn M. Castello
Phyllis Frog	Sue Renee Bernstein
The Queen	Michelle Roberts
Francis	Jess Peterson
Rhoda	Becky Thatcher McSpadden
Velva	Susane Press
Nikki	Leslie Welles
Wolff	George Heusinger
Arthur	Charles Stuart
Kurt	Charles Flanagan

Standbys: Joe Young, Michael Feinman

MUSICAL NUMBERS: "Prologue," "The Frogs Perform," "Wanna Get Married," "Five Minutes Ago," "Magic Licorice," "Phyllis Frog," "Have You Seen the Princess?," "Sneaky, Creepy Fellows," "Impossibility," "A Sister and Brother," "Obey, Abide," "To Win a Prince," "Big, Big Contest," "Twanger!," "A Potion," "Normal, Normal, Normal," "Garbage-Ella," "Tiny Light," "Forest of Silver," "But, I Love You," "Francis' Feast"

A musical in two acts.

Press: Kurt Nielson
Stage Manager: Bonnie Castle

* Closed Dec. 10, 1972 after 24 performances and 2 previews.

Sue Renee Bernstein, Charles Stuart, Andrea Noel, George Heusinger, Glen M. Castello, Charles Flanagan *(F. Tocco Photo)*

PLAYHOUSE THEATRE
Opened Thursday, November 16, 1972.*
Mary W. John presents:

DEAR OSCAR

Book and Lyrics, Caryl Gabrielle Young; Music, Addy O. F▯ Setting, William Pitkin; Costumes, Mary McKinley; Lighting, Da▯ Segal; Musical Director, Arnold Gross; Musical Sequences, Margery ▯dow; Assistant to the Producer, C. George Willard; Musical Super▯ and Arrangements, Harold Hastings; Production Supervised by ▯ Allen; Hairstylist, Nino Raffaello; Production Assistant, Carrie R▯

CAST

Oscar Wilde	Richard Kne▯
Speranza, Lady Wilde	Nancy Cush▯
Lady Mount-Temple	Jane Hof▯
Frank Harris	Len Goch▯
Charles Brookfield	Garnett S▯
Charles Hawtry	Edward ▯
Bootles	Tinker Gill▯
Comtesse	Sylvia O'▯
Her Son	Roger Leo▯
Frederick	Jack Hoffr▯
Constance Lloyd	Kimberly Va▯
Lord de Grey	Grant W▯
Robert Ross	Gary Krav▯
Vicar	Richard ▯
Marquess of Queensberry	Jack Bi▯
Arthur	Edward McPh▯
Nellie	Lynn Br▯
Clibburn	Tommy B▯
Atkins	Bruce Hei▯
Al Taylor	Garnett S▯
Alfred Wood	Edward ▯
Edward Shelly	James Ho▯
Sidney Mavor	Roger Leo▯
Bosie, Lord Alfred Douglas	Russ Tha▯
Scotland Yard Detective	Roger Leo▯
Theatre Attendant	Edward McPh▯
Sir Edward Clark	Richard ▯
Sir Edward Carson	Grant W▯

UNDERSTUDIES: Bosie, Jack Hoffman; Marquess, Len Gochman ▯ranza, Sylvia O'Brien; Clibburn, Atkins, James Hosbein; Ross, B▯field, Taylor, Roger Leonard; Harris, Grey, Edward Penn; Vicar, ▯ Edward McPhillips; Constance, Gretchen Walther

MUSICAL NUMBERS: "We Like Things the Way They Are," ▯ Street," "Oscar Wilde Has Said It," "Wot's 'Is Name," "Poor B▯ "The Perfect Understanding," "Swan and Edgar's," "We're Only ▯ers," "If I Could," "How Dare He," "We'll Have a Party," "The A▯ "When Did You Leave Me," "Good, Good Times," "There Wher▯ Young Men Go"

A Musical in two acts. The action takes place in London in 188▯ 1894.

General Manager: Paul B. Berkowsky
Company Manager: William Orton
Press: Saul Richman, Sara Altshul
Stage Managers: Ben Janney, William Dolive, James Hosb▯

* Closed Nov. 19, 1972 after 5 performances and 14 previews.

Friedman-Abeles Photo

Richard Kneeland, Gretchen Walther, Tinker Gillespie, Len Gochman, Sylvia O'Brien

ERIDAN SQUARE PLAYHOUSE
Opened Thursday, November 16, 1972.*
Dina and Alexander E. Racolin present:

GREEN JULIA

y Paul Abelman; Directed by William E. Hunt; Set and Lighting,
d F. Segal; Technical Director, Steve Loew

CAST

ert 'Bradshaw' Lacey .... Fred Grandy
b 'Carruthers' Perew .... James Woods†

Comedy-Drama in two acts. The action takes place in the untidy
* in a university town in England shared by Perew and Lacey at the
ent time in late spring.

Press: Max Eisen, Milly Shoenbaum

osed Mar. 25, 1973 after 147 performances.
cceeded by: John Pleshette

Right: Fred Grandy, James Woods

RCER–O'CASEY THEATRE
Opened Thursday, November 23, 1972.*
Lyn Austin and Oliver Smith present the Lenox Art Center
production of:

DOCTOR SELAVY'S MAGIC THEATRE

nceived, Staged, and Designed by Richard Foreman; Music, Stanley
rman; Lyrics, Tom Hendry; Vocal Director, Cathy MacDonald; As-
t Producer, Michael Frazier; Associate Producer, Mary Silverman;
ction Associate, Stephanie Wehle; Sound, Gary and Timmy Harris

CAST

ne Teller .... Denise Delapenha
le Pirate .... Mary Delson
nt ....,,, Ron Faber
Singer ....,,,,,,,,,,.............. Jessica Harper
st Doctor .... George McGrath
or with Most Hair .... Steve Menken
Girl .... Jackie Paris
est Doctor .... Robert Schlee
est Female Doctor .... Amy Taubin

ICAL NUMBERS: "I Live by My Wits," "Three Menu Songs,"
krupt Blues," "Future for Sale," "Life on the Inside," "Strawberry-
erry," "The More You Get," "Money in the Bank," "Life on the
," "Long Live Free Enterprise," "Doesn't It Bug You," "Dusky
ws," "Poor Boy," "Dearest Man," "Where You Been Hiding Till
" "Fireman's Song," "What Are You Proposing," "Party's Gonna
"Requiem," "Let's Hear It for Daddy Moola," "Life on the In-

Musical performed without intermission. The action takes place in
ital.

General Manager: Gil Adler
Company Manager: William Orton
Press: Michael Alpert, Gifford/Wallace
Stage Managers: Duane Mazey, Ron Carrier

ed Mar. 25, 1973 after 144 performances.

Right: Jessica Harper, George McGrath, Ron Faber

Clemens Kalischer Photo

CER-BRECHT THEATRE
pened Friday, November 24, 1972.*
el Weinsarden presents:

F.O.B.

eff Weiss; Director, Gaby Rodgers; Designed by Lewis Rosen

CAST

n Penn Woods .... Jeff Weiss
Speek .... William Finley
medy in two acts and three scenes. The action takes place in 1994
partment in the Polish Belt on the Lower East Side of New York

General Manager: Mark Durand
Press: Samuel J. Friedman
Stage Manager: Lewis Rosen

d Nov. 16, 1972 after 3 performances.

Jeff Weiss, William Finley
Andrew Greenhut Photo

GUGGENHEIM MUSEUM

Opened Sunday, November 26, 1972.*
Lyn Austin, Orin Lehman, Hale Matthews, and Oliver Smith present:

THE MOTHER OF US ALL

Text, Gertrude Stein; Music, Virgil Thomson; Directors, Elizabeth Keen, Roland Gagnon; Musical Director, Roland Gagnon; Designer, Oliver Smith; Costumes, Patricia Zipprodt; Lighting, Richard Nelson; Associate Producer, Mary Silverman; Scenario, Maurice Grosser; Pianist, Conductor, Roland Gagnon; Guest Conductor, Ainslee Cox; Entire production under the artistic direction of Virgil Thomson; A Lenox Arts Center Production; Production Assistant, Stephanie Wehle

CAST

Susan B. Anthony	Judith Erickson or Phyllis Worthington
Anne	Lynne Wickenden
Gertrude A	Olivia Buckley
Virgil T.	Wayne Turnage
Daniel Webster	David Wilder
Jo the Loiterer	Gene West
Chris the Citizen	Wayne Turnage
Indiana Elliot	Lynne Wickenden
Angel Moore	Olivia Buckley
John Adams	Jon Garrison
Thaddeus Stevens	Wayne Turnage
Constance Fletcher	Kate Hurney
Lillian Russell	Olivia Buckley
Jenny Reefer	Kate Hurney
Ulysses S. Grant	Wayne Turnage
Andrew Johnson	Gene West
Indiana Elliot's brother	Wayne Turnage

A Musical in two acts and eight scenes.

General Manager: Brooke Lappin
Press: Michael Alpert
Stage Managers: Jonathan Stuart, Brian Meister

* Closed Dec. 10, 1972 after 17 performances.

Friedman-Abeles Photo

Top Right: Judith Erickson, Phyllis Worthington

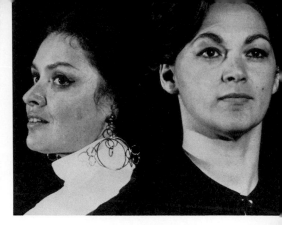

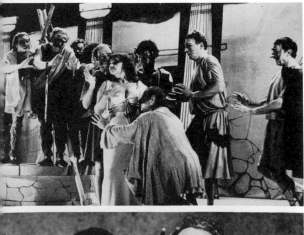

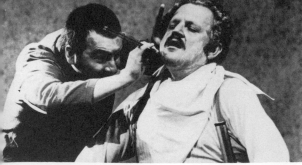

"Woyzeck" Above: "Der Frieden"

(Hilde Zemann Photos)

BARBIZON-PLAZA THEATRE

Opened Tuesday, November 28, 1972.*
The Goethe Insititute Munich and the Gert von Gontard For
dation of New York present Die Brucke German Theatre I
semble in:

DER FRIEDEN

By Aristophanes; Adapted by Peter Hacks; Director, Gunther Fleck
stein; Scenery and Costumes, Hans-Walter Lenneweit; Music, Eric T
Makeup and Wigs, Ursula Esch; Technical Director, Holger Ch
tiansen; Assistant, Imme Siedhoff

CAST

Trygaios	Hans P
Chorus Leader	Dieter Bramr
First Slave	Wolfgang Reinbac
Second Slave	Joost Siedh
Trygaios' First Daughter	Eva Botto
Trygaios' Second Daughter	Claudia L
Hermes	Gerhard Friedr
War	Harald D
Tumult	Klaus Muns
Herbstfleiss	Gudrun M
Lenzwonne	Elisabeth End
Helmschmied	Klaus Muns
Waffenkramer	Wolfgang Reinbac
Kierokles	Dieter Bramr
Boy	Gudrun M

CHORUS: Siegfried Fetscher, Michael Hoffmann, Dieter Steinbrink,
phan Bastian, Klaus Munster, Joost Siedhoff, Harald Dietl, Gerh
Friedrich, Claudia Lobe

A Comedy performed in two acts.

Opened Tuesday, December 5, 1972.*

WOYZECK

By Georg Buchner; Director, Hans Joachim Heyse; Scenery and C
tumes, Christian Bussmann; Music, Dieter Schonbach; Makeup
Wigs, Ursula Esch; Technical Director, Holger Christiansen; Assista
Imme Siedhoff

CAST

Captain	Dieter Bramr
Woyzeck	Wolfgang Reinbac
Andres	Joost Siedh
Marie	Elisabeth End
Margret	Eva Botto
Old Man	Klaus Mun
Girl	Gudrun M
Charlatan	Hans P
His Wife	Claudia L
Drum Major	Harald D
Sergeant	Siegfried Fetsc
Doctor	Gerhard Friedr
Apprentices	Klaus Munster, Michael Hoffm
Innkeeper	Siegfried Fetsc
Students	Dieter Steinbrink, Michael Hoffma
	Siegfried Fetscher, Stephan Bas
Kathe	Claudia L
Jew	Joost Sied
Town Idiot	Michael Hoffm
Grandmother	Eva Botto

A Drama performed without intermission.

* Closed Dec. 10, 1972 after limited engagement of 16 performanc

EASTSIDE PLAYHOUSE
Opened Monday, November 27, 1972.*
Peter Cookson presents:

THE CONTRAST

Adapted by Anthony Stimas from play by Royall Tyler; Music, Don Pippin; Lyrics, Steve Brown; Director, Anthony Stimac; Scenery, David Chapman; Lighting, C. Murawski; Costumes, Robert Pusilo; Musical Director, Dorothea Freitag; Musical Arrangements, Don Pippin; Choreography, Bill Guske

CAST

Charlotte	Connie Danese
Letitia	Elaine Kerr
Frank	Gene Kelton
Maria	Patti Perkins
Van Rough	Gene Kelton
Jenny	Pamela Adams
Dimple	Ty McConnell
Colonel Manly	Robert G. Denison
Jessamy	Grady Clarkson
Jonathan	Philip MacKenzie

Standbys: Merrill Leighton, Jim Brochu

MUSICAL NUMBERS: Prologue, "A Woman Rarely Ever," "A House Full of People," "Keep Your Little Eye upon the Main Chance, Mary," "So They Call It New York," "Dear Lord Chesterfield," "A Sort of Courting Song," "So Far," "She Can't Really Be," "That Little Monosyllable," "It's Too Much," "Wouldn't I," "A Hundred Thousand Ways," "I Was in the Closet"

A Musical in two acts and ten scenes.

General Management: Gatchell & Neufeld
Press: Howard Atlee, Clarence J. Allsopp, Jr.
Stage Managers: Ted Harris, Rick Ladson

* Closed Dec. 17, 1972 after 24 performances.

Martha Swope Photo

**Top Right: Philip MacKenzie, Robert Denison,
Ty McConnell, Grady Clarkson**

MARTINIQUE THEATRE
Opened Wednesday, November 29, 1972.*
Michael Carson presents:

BLUE BOYS

By Allan Knee; Director, Neal Kenyon; Scenery and Lighting, Tom Munn; Costumes, Joan E. Thiel; A Korsunsky Production; Assistants to Producer, Barbara De Rosa, Phil Saltz

CAST

Correspondent/Rebel/Barker	Ray Thorne
Simpson/Papa	Tom Lee Jones
Jenkins	Allan Knee
Cooper	Robert Stattel
Wiggins	Jerry Dodge
Brooks/Mother/Dearie	Diane Kagan
Forest/Samantha/Lucy	Ann Sweeny

UNDERSTUDIES: For Messrs. Stattel, Jones, Thorne, James Rebhorn

A Drama in two acts. The action takes place in April 1861.

General Management: Gatchell & Neufeld
Press: Seymour Krawitz, Patricia Krawitz
Stage Managers: John Hagan, James Rebhorn

* Closed Nov. 29, 1972 after one performance.

QUEENS PLAYHOUSE
Opened Sunday, December 3, 1972.*
Queens Playhouse (Joseph S. Kutrzeba, Founder-Producer) presents:

TWELVE ANGRY MEN

By Reginald Rose; Director, Martin Fried; Design and Lighting, Wolfgang Roth; Costumes, Ruth Morley; Artistic Director, Joseph S. Kutrzeba; Theatre Consultant, Pete Howard; Presented In cooperation with the Parks, Recreation, and Cultural Affairs Administration of the City of New York; Administrative Assistant, Hedy Ewert; Technical Director, Larry Opitz

CAST

Guard	Vincent Duke Milana
Janitor	Simon Deckard

The Jury (in alphabetical order): Rudy Bond, Robert Forster, Howard Green, Constantine Katsanos, Richard Lynch, Peter Maloney, Lazaro Perez, John P. Ryan, John D. Seymour, Joseph Sullivan, James Tolkan, Jack Waltzer

Understudy: Simon Deckard

A Drama performed without intermission. The action takes place in the jury room of a New York Court of Law in the Summer of 1957.

Company Manager: Ian Edward
Press: Robert Ganshaw, Seymour Krawitz, Paul Bernabeo
Stage Manager; Michael Gorelick

Closed Dec. 17, 1972 after 32 performances. (No photos available)

**Ray Thorne, Tom Lee Jones, Diane Kagan, Allan Knee
Robert Stattel, Jerry Dodge, Ann Sweeny**
(Meryl Joseph Photo)

ASTOR PLACE THEATRE
Opened Sunday, December 3, 1972.*
Albert Poland and Bruce Mailman present:

THE BAR THAT NEVER CLOSES

Book, Louisa Rose; Sketches, Marco Vassi; Lyrics, Louisa Rose, John Braswell, Tom Mandel; Music, Tom Mandel; Musical Direction and Arrangements, Cathy MacDonald, Tom Mandel; Associate Producer, Ina Lea Meibach; Director, John Braswell; Production Conceived by John Braswell and Louisa Rose; Bar Drop Painting and Logo, Susan Haskins

CAST

Anybody	Jennie Mortimer
Mistaken Man	Susan Haviland
Old Woman	Nancy Schwartz
Michael	Richard Westlein
Mr. and Mrs. Dear	Mary Jo Kaplan, Kyle Andersen
Girl	Lane Binkley
God	Bill Eddy
The Lovers	Ralph Smith, Kyle Andersen
Anybody's Friend	Sara Parker
Anybody's Friend's Friend	Mary Jo Kaplan
Homosexual	Barbara Greca
Singing Bar	Jean Andalman
Nurse	Raina Hefner
Mrs. Schneider	Susan Haviland
Doctor	Christopher Lamal
The Libidoes	Barbara Greca, Bill Eddy
Table and Spigot	Richard Westlein
Little Woman	Jennie Mortimer
Mad People	Ensemble
Riddle's Woman	Kyle Andersen
Harry	Raina Hefner
Elevator Girl/Debutante	Barbara Greca
Butch Medusa	Camille Tibaldeo

MUSICAL NUMBERS: "Walking with You, Two by Two," "Do It," "Recipe for Love," "Kaleidoscope," "I Don't Think I'll Ever Love You," "Dear Dear," "Tears of Ice," "Circus of Jade," "Precious Little Darkness"

A Musical in two acts and 12 scenes.

General Manager: Jay Kingwill
Press: Saul Richman, Sara Altshul
Stage Manager: Gary Weathersbee

* Closed Dec. 31, 1972 after 33 performances

Cast of "The Bar That Never Closes"

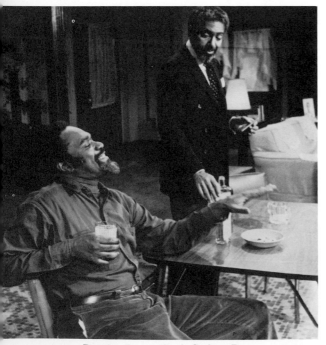

Douglas Turner Ward, Graham Brown

ST. MARK'S PLAYHOUSE
Opened Tuesday, December 5, 1972.*
The Negro Ensemble Company Inc. presents:

THE RIVER NIGER

By Joseph A. Walker; Director, Douglas Turner Ward; Lightin[g] ley Prendergast; Sets, Gary James Wheeler; Costumes, Edna [W] Incidental Music, Dorothy Dinroe; Technical Director, Michael

CAST

Grandma Wilhelmina Brown	Frances
Johnny Williams	Douglas Turner
Dr. Dudley Stanton	Graham
Ann Vanderguild	Grenna Wh
Mattie Williams	Roxie
Chips	Lennal Wain
Mo	Neville
Gail	Saundra M
Skeeter	Charles
Al	Dea
Jeff Williams	Les
Voice of Lt. Staples	Morley M

UNDERSTUDIES: Taurean Blacque, Barbara Clarke, Arthur Louise Heath

A Drama in three acts. The action takes place at the present early February in the Williams' brownstone on 133 St. in Harle[m]

Company Manager: Frederick Garrett
Press: Howard Atlee, Clarence Allsopp, Victoria Luc[a]
Associates
Stage Manager: Wyatt Davis

* Closed March 18, 1973 after 118 performances; moved to Br[o] March 27, 1973 and still playing May 31, 1973.

Bert Andrews Photo

CIRCLE IN THE SQUARE
Opened Wednesday, December 6, 1972.*
Sally Sears and Primavera Productions, Ltd. present:

PLEASE DON'T CRY AND SAY NO

By Townsend Brewster; Director, Philip Taylor; Scenery and Lighting, al Tine; Costumes, Jon Haggins; Original Music, Dorothy A. Dinroe; uitarist, Leon Atkinson; Assistant to Producer, Rose Smith; Assistant Director, Susan Merril-Taylor

CAST

"The Brown Overcoat" by Victor Sejour;
ranslated by Townsend Brewster

ountess	Janet League
nna	Lee Kirk
alet	Michael Brassfield
aron	Tyrone Browne

The action takes place in 1859 in the drawing room of the Countess in Paris.

"The Botany Lesson" by Joaquim Maria Machado de Assis; ranslated by Townsend Brewster

ona Leonor	Vanessa K. Gilder
ona Helena	Ethel Ayler
ona Cecilia	Janet League
aron	David Downing

The action takes place in 1906 in a room in Dona Leonor's house in Rio de Janeiro.

"Please Don't Cry and Say No" by Townsend Brewster

d	David Downing
dina	Vanessa K. Gilder
odiva	Ethel Ayler
ike	Charles Turner
rst Teenager	Ronald Dennis
cond Teenager	Joseph Mydell
ird Teenager	B. Henry Douglass
nloe	Janet League

The action takes place at the present time in New York City during the summer.

USICAL NUMBERS: "She Needs a Good Cry," "The Man Who Plays Alto Flute," "The Bossa Nova," "Conscience Is a Coward," "The in of Summer"

General Manager: David Wyler
Company Manager: Jean Rocco
Press: Dorothy Ross, Herb Striesfield
Stage Managers: Jerry Laws, Michael Brassfield

Closed Dec. 17, 1972 after 15 performances.

Kay Cole, Gregory V. Karliss, Janet Powell

David Downing, Vanessa K. Gilder
(Bert Andrews Photo)

ORPHEUM THEATRE
Opened Monday, December 18, 1972.*
James Rado and Ted Rado present:

RAINBOW

Book, James and Ted Rado; Music and Lyrics, James Rado; Music Supervised, Arranged, and Directed by Steven Margoshes; Sets and Lights, James Tilton; Costumes, Nancy Potts; Sound, Abe Jacob; Associate Producer, Richard Osorio; Directed and Staged by Joe Donovan; Technical Director, John McGraw;

CAST

Man	Gregory V. Karliss
Jesus	Philip A. D.
Ms. Friendstrangle/Stripper	Patricia Gaul
Dr. Banana	Rudy Brown
Mother	Camille
Father	Michael D. Arian
Buddha	Meat Loaf
Opera	Elinor Frye
President	Dean Compton
First Lady	Marie Santell
President's Child	Stephen Scharf
President's Child	Marcia McClain
Wizard	Bobby C. Ferguson
Girl	Kay Cole
Twin Girl	Janet Powell

MUSICAL NUMBERS: "Who Are We," "Love Me Love Me Dorothy Lamour La Sarong," "Fruits and Vegetables," "Welcome Banana," "Questions Questions," "Song to Sing," "My Lungs," "You Got to Be Clever," "Tangled Tangents," "What Can I Do for You," "Oh I Am a Fork," "People Stink," "Guinea Pig," "Give Your Heart to Jesus," "Joke a Cola," "Mama Loves You," "I Want to Make You Cry," "I Am a Cloud," "A Garden for Two," "Starry Old Night," "Bathroom," "O.K. Goodbye," "Deep in the Dark," "You Live in Flowers," "I Don't Hope for Great Things," "Globligated," "Be Not Afraid," "Obedience," "Ten Days Ago," "Oh, Oh, Oh," "Moosh, Moosh," "The Man," "The World Is Round," "Stars and Bars," "Cacophony," "Groovy Green Man Groovy," "Heliopolis," "I Am Not Free," "We Are the Clouds," "How Dreamlike," "Somewhere under the Rainbow," "Star Song"

A Musical in two acts.

General Manager: Richard Osorio
Press: Solters/Sabinson/Roskin, Marilynn LeVine
Stage Managers: Ronald Schaeffer, Meat Loaf

* Closed Jan. 28, 1973 after 48 performances.

Martha Swope Photo

ANDERSON THEATRE

Opened Tuesday, December 19, 1972.*
Richard Scanga presents The Friends of Van Wolf Production
(Ivor David Balding, Executive Producer) of:

THE TRIALS OF OZ

By Geoff Robertson; Songs, Buzzy Linhart, Mick Jagger, John Lennon/Yoko Ono; Director, Jim Sharman; Lighting, Jules Fisher; Costumes, Joseph G. Aulisi; Sets, Mark Ravitz; Music Arranged and Conducted by Bill Cunningham; Associate Producer, Cathy Cochran

CAST

Narrator/Vivien Berger	Harry Gold

Defendants:

Richard Neville	Cliff De Young
James Anderson	Dan Leach
Felix Dennis	Greg Antonacci

Witnesses:

Dr. Schofield	Peter Kybart
George Melly	Dallas Alinder
Dr. Josephine Klein	Myra Carter
Professor Dworkin	Gabor Morea
Caroline Coon	Ginny Russell
Dr. Haward	Peter Kybart
Mrs. Berger	Myra Carter
Marty Feldman	Alek Primrose

Prosecution:

Detective Inspector Luff	Alek Primrose
Brian Leary	Richard Clark
Defense John Mortimer	Graham Jarvis
Judge Michael Argyle	William Roerick
Foreman of the Jury	Gabor Morea
Court Officers	Leata Galloway, Myra Carter
Rupert Bear	Dallas Alinder

UNDERSTUDIES: Judge, Alek Primrose; Neville, Greg Antonacci; Mortimer, Dallas Alinder; Dr. Klein, Mrs. Berger, Feldman, Harry Gold; Dworkin, Haward, Schofield, Melly, Rupert, Gabor Morea; Caroline, Leata Galloway

MUSICAL NUMBERS: "Oranges and Lemons," "Rupert Bear Song," "If You Can't Join 'Em, Beat 'Em," "Dirty Is the Funniest Thing I Know," "Masquerade Ball," "The Love's Still Growing," "Give Me Excess of It," "Schoolboy Blues," "The Justice Game," "God Save Us"

A Play with Music set at the Old Bailey in London in 1971. Each courtroom scene actually took place during the trial. The text has been edited from the actual transcript. Performed in two acts.

General Manager: James E. Walsh
Press: Gifford/Wallace, Merle Frimark
Stage Managers: Rick Thayer, Gabor Morea

* Closed Dec. 31, 1972 after 15 performances.

Greg Antonacci, Cliff DeYoung, Dan Leach
Above: Dallas Alinder

(Martha Swope Photos)

ABBEY THEATRE

Opened Tuesday, January 2, 1973.*
Signature Productions presents:

SHAY DUFFIN
as
Brendan Behan

A one-man performance of excerpts from the works of Brendan Beh Written and Adapted by Shay Duffin; Director, Dennis Hayes; New Y Production Director, Marvin Gordon; Executive Producer, Les We stein; Lighting, Joe Behan; Sets, Shay Duffin, Joe Behan.

General Manager: Mark Cosmedy
Press: Bill Doll & Co., Cindy Reagan
Stage Manager: Joe Behan

* Closed March 18, 1973 after 89 performances.

Shay Duffin

Shenyang Acrobatic Troupe members

Opened Tuesday, January 2, 1973.*
The City Center of Music and Drama in association with National Committee on United States—China Relations, Inc. presents from The People's Republic of China:

SHENYANG ACROBATIC TROUPE

PROGRAM: "Lion Dance," "Plate Spinning," "Long Pole Trick," "Diabolo," "Bicycle Stabilizing Feats on a Raised Stand," "Conjuring," "Pagoda of Bowls," "Trick Cycling," "National Wu Shu," "Balancing on a Roller," "Foot Dexterity," "Balancing on Chairs," "Hoop-Diving," "Flowers of Friendship"

Presented in two parts.

Company Manager: David Bines
Press: Meg Gordean, Ruth D. Smuckler
Stage Manager: Jeffrey Chambers

* Closed Jan. 6, 1973 after limited engagement of 6 performances.

HERRY LANE THEATRE
Opened Wednesday, January 3, 1973.*
J. Craig Owens presents:

MYSTERY PLAY

By Jean-Claude Van Itallie; Director, Jacques Levy; Scenery, Philip lliam; Lighting, Judy Rasmuson; Costumes, Patricia McGourty; Song, chard Peaslee; Assistant to Producer, Valerie Norusis

CAST

e Senator	Judd Hirsch
e Senator's Wife	Cynthia Harris
ward	Rick Friesen
ward	Donald Warfield
e Professor	Tom Brannum
ura	Nancy Charney
e Butler	Rod Browning
ystery Writer	Shami Chaikin
anist	Fred Goldrich

Standby: Jane Marla Robbins

A Farce in two acts. The action takes place at the present time in the nator's home.

General Managers: NR Productions; Norman E. Rothstein, Patricia Carney, Bob MacDonald
Company Managers: Geoffrey R. Horlick, Robert Frissell
Press: David Roggensack
Stage Manager: Robert J. Bruyr

Closed Jan. 7, 1973 after 7 performances.

Bert Andrews Photo

Shami Chaikin, Rod Browning stabs Tom Brannum,
Cynthia Harris, Judd Hirsch, Rick Friesen,
Donald Warfield, Nancy Charney

Karmon Israeli Dancers

FELT FORUM
Opened Thursday, January 4, 1973.*
Madison Square Garden Productions and Hy Einhorn present:

THE GRAND MUSIC HALL OF ISRAEL

Created, Directed, and Choreographed by Jonathon Karmon; Assistant Director, Gavri Levi; Musical Director, Rafi Paz; Costumes, Lydia Punkus Ganay

CAST

Shoshana Damari
Ron Eliran
Myron Cohen
Ariela
The Marganiot
The Tal U'Matar
Karmon Israeli Dancers and Singers

PROGRAM: "Israeli Rhapsody," "The Marganiot," "The Fishermen of Kineret," "The Tal U'Matar," "A Night on the Gilboa Mountains," "Ron Eliran," "A Panorama of Hassidic Life," "The Mediterranean Flavor," "Ariela," "Fire on the Mountains," "Shoshana Damari," "Holiday in the Kibbutz"

Presented in two parts.

Press: Max Eisen, Milly Schoenbaum

* Closed Jan. 14, 1973 after limited engagement of 15 performances.

Geraldine Page, Maya Angelou

PLAYHOUSE THEATRE
Opened Sunday, January 7, 1973.*
Charles B. Bloch in association with Burry Fredrik presen

LOOK AWAY

By Jerome Kilty; Based on book "Mary Todd Lincoln: Her Life a
Letters" by Justin G. Turner and Linda Levitt Turner; Director, I
Torn; Setting and Lighting, Ben Edwards; Costumes, Jane Greenwo
Assistant to Producers, Zita Bloch

CAST

Mary Todd Lincoln .... Geraldine P.
Elizabeth Keckley .... Maya Ange

A Drama in two acts. The action takes place in the Bellevue Hosp
for Insane Persons in Batavia, Illinois, during the last night of Mary T
Lincoln's stay there in 1876.

General Manager: William Craver
Company Manager: Maurice Schaded
Press: Shirley Herz
Stage Managers: Bernard Pollack, Garland Lee Thompson

* Closed Jan. 7, 1973 after one performance and 24 previews.

BIJOU THEATRE
Opened Sunday, January 14, 1973.*
Lee Schumer and Morton Wolkowitz present:

THE ENEMY IS DEAD

By Don Petersen; Director, Arthur Sherman; Setting, Kert Lundell;
Lighting, Roger Morgan; Costumes, Joseph G. Aulisi; Technical Director, Jack Magnifico; Production Assistant, John Banon

CAST

Leah .... Linda Lavin
Emmett .... Arthur Storch
Mr. Wolfe .... Addison Powell

A Comedy in two acts. The action takes place at the present time in
a rented summer cottage.

General Manager: Paul B. Berkowsky
Company Manager: Edward A. Blatt
Press: Saul Richman, Sara Altshul
Stage Manager: Elizabeth Stearns

* Closed Jan. 14, 1973 after one performance and six previews.

Friedman-Abeles Photo

Linda Lavin, Arthur Storch, Addison Powell

HUNTER COLLEGE PLAYHOUSE
Opened Saturday, January 20, 1973.
Hunter College Concert Bureau presents:

THE PAPER BAG PLAYERS

Artistic Director, Judith Martin; Created and Directed by Judith Ma
tin; Assistant Director, Irving Burton; Original Music, Donald Ashwa
der; Technical Supervisor, Daniel Rosenfels; Assistant Administrat
Michele Brustin

COMPANY

Irving Burton
Judith Martin
Donald Ashwander
John Armstrong
Jeanne Michels
Daniel Rosenfels
Gary Gilbert

PRODUCTIONS: "Group Soup" performed Jan. 20 through Feb.
1973 on weekends only; "Dandelion" performed Feb. 17 through Mar
11, 1973 on weekends only; "To the Rescue" performed March
through April 8, 1973 on weekends only.

Administrator: Judith Liss
Press: Edith Harnik
Stage Manager: Gary Gilbert

Jill Krementz Photo

John Armstrong, Judith Martin, Don Ashwander,
Irving Burton, Jeanne Michels

VILLAGE GATE
Opened Thursday, January 25, 1973.*
Tony Hendra presents:

NATIONAL LAMPOON'S LEMMINGS

Director, Tony Hendra; Words and Lyrics, David Axelrod, Anne Beatts, Henry Beard, John Boni, Tony Hendra, Sean Kelly, Doug Kenney, P. J. O'Rourke; Music Composed and Arranged by Paul Jacobs, Christopher Guest; Directed by Paul Jacobs; Lighting, Beverly Emmons; Sound, Abe Jacob; Production Supervisor, Peter Lavery; Production Coordinators, Louise Gikow, Dale Anglund; Production Assistant, Chip Largman; Sound, Alisa Jill Adler.

CAST

John Belushi
Chevy Chase
Garry Goodrow
Christopher Guest
Paul Jacobs
Mary-Jenifer Mitchell
Alice Playten

A Satirical Revue in two acts.

Press: Lenny Traube, Irving Zussman, Harriet Vidal, David Powers, Jeffrey Richards

* Still playing May 31, 1973.

Top Left: Paul Jacobs, Chevy Chase, Garry Goodrow, Christopher Guest, Alice Playten, John Belushi, Mary-Jenifer Mitchell

:W FEDERAL THEATRE
Opened Friday, January 26, 1973.*
Woodie King, Jr. and Dick Williams present:

A RECENT KILLING

3y Imamu Amiri Baraka (LeRoi Jones); Director, Irving Vincent; Set, ry James Wheeler; Lighting, Mark Kruger; Costumes, Judy Dearing; ind, Pete Erskine, Louis Shapiro; Production Coordinator, Mayme cham; Technical Director, C. Richard Mills

CAST

ınie Pearson	Gary Bolling
ırkers from San Loca	Frank Diaz, Felipe Aguayo, Elliot Perez
neral Comb	Gil Rogers
nthia	Sharon Devonish
T. Jackson	Carl Willis Crudup
. Milton Butler	Mba Acaz
ınski	Robert McLane
. Clay	John Blanda
Pyle	Keith Perry
pold Bloom	Elisha Ignatoff
nley Laffkowitz	Stephen Alan Itkin
poral of the Guard	Rick Livert
bara Butler	Marcella Lowery
ores	E. Jaye Tracey, Millie Rudin
astian Flyte	Bruce Thomson
ite Faggot	Rick Livert
sted Sergeant	Obako Adedunyo
ck Faggot	A. B. Grant
geant in latrine	Del Willard
oner	Ed Wheeler
ckade Lieutenant	Alexander Paul
ckade Sergeant	Joseph A. Bosco

. Drama in 3 acts and 22 scenes. The action takes place in the mid-)'s at a Strategic Air Command Base on the Caribbean Island of San ca.

Press: Howard Atlee, Clarence J. Allsopp, Jr.
Stage Manager: Clinton Turner Davis

losed Feb. 11, 1973 after limited engagement of 10 performances.

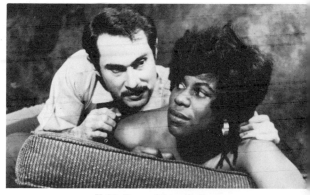

Keith Perry, Marcella Lowery

(Bert Andrews Photo)

CHERRY LANE THEATRE
Opened Monday, February 12, 1973.*
Ruth Kalkstein and Patricia Gray present:

WELCOME TO ANDROMEDA
and
VARIETY OBIT

By Ron Whyte; Director, Tom Moore; Sets, Peter Harvey; Lighting, Roger Morgan; Costumes, Bruce Harrow; Music, Mel Marvin; Words, Ron Whyte, Bob Satuloff; Associate Producer, Sidney Annis; Production Assistant, Richard D. Flagg

CAST

"Welcome to Andromeda"

The Boy	David Clemmon
The Nurse	Bella Jarrett

INTERMISSION

"Variety Obit"

Singers	Andrea Marcovicci, Richard Cox
Narrator	David Clennon
Musicians	Mel Marvin, Gary Mure

General Manager: Al Isaacs
Press: David Lipsky
Stage Manager: Robert Keegan

* Closed Mar. 4, 1973 after 21 performances.

Andrea Marcovicci, Richard Cox

Friedman-Abeles Photo

MERCER/ OSCAR WILDE ROOM
Opened Tuesday, February 13, 1973.*
Jack Temchin, Gil Adler, John A. Vaccaro present:

EL COCA-COLA GRANDE

Title changed to "El Grande de Coca-Cola" Feb. 21, 1973; Conceived by Ron House and Diz White; Written by the cast; Designed by Mischa Petrow; Choreography, Anna Nygh; Musical Arrangements, Alan Shearman, John Neville-Andrews; Special Lighting, Andrew Borden; A Low Moan Spectacular Production.

CAST

Senor Don Pepe Hernandez	Ron House
Miguel Hernandez	Alan Shearman
Juan Rodriguez	John Neville-Andrews
Consuela Hernandez	Diz White
Maria Hernandez	Sally Willis

A Revue performed without intermission. The action takes place at the present time in a nightclub in a run-down section of Trujillo, Honduras.

Press: Lawrence N. Belling
Stage Manager: Lary Opitz

* Still playing May 31, 1973.

Terence Le Goubin Photo

Top Right: Sally Willis, Ron House, Diz White in "El Coca-Cola Grande"

Right: Kay Gillian, Harvey Solin, Robert Fitzsimmons in "Penthouse Legend"

McALPIN ROOFTOP THEATRE
Opened Wednesday, February 21, 1973.*
P. J. and K. Smith present:

PENTHOUSE LEGEND

By Ayn Rand; Formerly "The Night of January 16"; Director, Phillip J. Smith; Scenery and Lighting, David Houston; Assistant to the Producers, Arline Mann

CAST

Bailiff	Edwin Fenton
Judge Heath	Don Lochner
District Attorney Flint	Michael Thompson
Defense Attorney Stevens	Robert Fitzsimmons
Clerk	Waller Thomas Burns
Karen Andre	Kay Gillian
Dr. Kirkland	Gerard McLaughlin
John Hutchins	Merrill E. Joels
Homer Van Fleet	Douglas Fisher
Elmer Sweeney	Joseph O'Sullivan
Magda Svenson	Ruth McCormick
Nancy Lee Faulkner	Holly Hill
John Graham Whitfield	Bob Allen
James Chandler	Douglas Fisher
Siegurd Jungquist	Robert Keiper
"Guts" Regan	Harvey Solin

UNDERSTUDIES: Karen, Nancy, Magda, Charmian Sorbello; Stevens, Flint, Whitfield, Don Lochner; General Understudies, Waller Thomas Burns, Edwin Fenton, Gerard McLaughlin, Richard Yarnell.

A Drama in three acts. The action takes place during the three days of Karen Andre's trial.

General Manager: Gloria Alter
Company Manager: Robert Cherin
Press: Meg Gordean, Tomorrow Today
Stage Manager: Arthur Silber, Charmian Sorbello

* Closed March 18, 1973 after 30 performances.

WEST SIDE YMCA
Opened Saturday, March 3, 1973.*
Hunter College Playwrights (Stuart Baker, Producer: Edwi
Wilson, Director) present:

PLAYS AND COUNTERPLAYS

Directed by Ralph DiFiore; Set, Henry Canter; Lighting, Saul Bosha Cinematic Effects, Marlene Friedman; YMCA Program Director, Kare Bruett; Production Assistant, Debbie McCann

CAST

"Lovers" by Francis M. Chesleigh

Meg	Rebecca Lawren
Jack	Don Marlett

"Clown Alley" by Robert McHaffey

Irene	Susan Ge
Clem	Dennis Per
Margaret	Ivy Spiegle
Wardrobe Woman	Fran Reichi

"Open School Night" by Rudy Gray

Teacher	Frank Vo
Mother	Fran Reich
Son	Grover Kemb

Press: Patricia Molino
Stage Managers: Eve Brandstein, Dorothy Krasiker

* Closed Mar. 11, 1973 after limited engagement of 4 performances. (N photos available)

AYHOUSE THEATRE
Opened Sunday, March 11, 1973.*
Arthur Cantor presents:

42 SECONDS FROM BROADWAY

y Louis Del Grande; Director, Arthur Storch; Scenery, William Pit-
Lighting, Roger Morgan; Costumes, Glenda Miller; Assistant to
ucer, Geraldine Duryea; Hairstylist, John Quaglia; Production As-
nt, Judi Silverman.

CAST

Green	Martin Garner
in	Regina Baff
	Henry Winkler
. Murino	Antonia Rey
Murino	Billy Longo
y	Bob Dermer
Stein	Michael Vale
Marrow	James Tolkan
da	Judith Cohen
	Susan Peretz
ard	Bob Dermer
	Anthony Spina
Marveltine	Edward Kovens
y	Patti Costa
very Boy	John Branon

DERSTUDIES: Robin, Judith Cohen; John, Bob Dermer; Mrs.
ino, Susan Peretz; Green, Stein, Murino, Marrow, Marveltine, An-
y Spina; Joey, Richard, John Branon; Brenda, Liza, Myra Siegel

Comedy in two acts and eight scenes. The action takes place in New
k City and Hoboken, N.J., in 1957.

Company Manager: David Hedges
Press: Beth Trier, C. George Willard
Stage Managers: Ted Harris, John Branon

osed March 11, 1973 after one performance and one preview.

YFAIR THEATRE
Opened Wednesday, March 14, 1973.*
Moishe Baruch presents:

TRY IT, YOU'LL LIKE IT

ook, Max Zalotoff, Jacob Jacobs; Music, Alexander Olshenetsky;
cs, Jacob Jacobs; Director, Jacob Jacobs; Musical Arrangements,
a Kreizberg; Musical Director, Michael Richardone; Scenery, Peter
lles; Lighting, Peter Xantho.

CAST

ele, Usher's daughter	Gerri-Ann Frank
y, Usher's nephew	Bernardo Hiller
ris, Shloime's son	Baruch Blum
er Zeligman	Jaime Lewin
a, his wife	Thelma Mintz
ime	Jacob Jacobs
na Pessel, housekeeper	Nellie Casman

SICAL NUMBERS: "Hient viel eich vu tzi Zingen," "Oy ses git,"
g Dein," "Ven sis du Liebe," "Macht a Lehaim," "Du Zelbege Zah,"
Shain Shulem Zine," "Senior Citizens," "A Nier Tzeit," "Mirele,"
It, You'll Like It"

Musical in two acts and three scenes. The action takes place at the
nt time in the Zeligman house and Dr. Goldman's office.

Press: Max Eisen, Ruth D. Smuckler, Barbara Eisen

osed May 27, 1973 after 87 performances.

Regina Baff, Henry Winkler

EASTSIDE PLAYHOUSE
Opened Monday, March 12, 1973.*
Stanley H. Handman presents:

YOU NEVER KNOW

Music and Lyrics, Cole Porter; Based on play "By Candlelight" by
Siegfried Geyer, Robert Katscher; Adaptation, Rowland Leigh; Musical
Director, Walter Geismar; Hairstylist, Charles of the Ritz; Production
Staged and Designed by Robert Troie; Pianists, Walter Geismar, Kenneth
W. Hirsch; Percussion, Edward Zacko.

CAST

Baron Romer	Dan Held
Gaston	Esteban Chalbaud
Ida Courtney	Grace Theveny
Maria	Lynn Fitzpatrick
Lord Baltin	Rod Loomis
Lady Baltin	Jamie Thomas

MUSICAL NUMBERS: "By Candlelight," "Maria," "I'm Going in for
Love," "I'm Back in Circulation," "From Alpha to Omega," "You've
Got That Thing," "What Shall I Do," "For No Rhyme or Reason," "At
Long Last Love," "Greek to You," "You Never Know," "Ridin' High,"
"They All Fall in Love."

A Musical Comedy in two acts and three scenes. The action takes place
during one night in 1938 in Baron Romer's drawing room.

General Management: Dorothy Olim Associates
Press: Betty Lee Hunt, Harriett Trachtenberg, Henry Luhrman,
Maria C. Pucci
Stage Managers: Robert J. Bruyr, Blair Kersten

* Closed Mar. 18, 1973 after 8 performances.

Kenn Duncan Photo

**Left Center: Jamie Thomas, Dan Held, Lynn Fitzpatrick,
Esteban Chalbaud, Grace Theveny, Rod Loomis**

Nellie Casman, Jacob Jacobs

THEATRE DE LYS
Opened Sunday, March 19, 1973.*
Arthur Whitelaw, Seth Harrison, Dallas Alinder present:

THOUGHTS

By Lamar Alford; Additional Lyrics, Megan Terry, Jose Tapla; Director, Michael Schultz; Musical Staging, Jan Mickens; Musical Consultant, Joyce Brown; Music Arranged by David Horowitz; Lighting, Ken Billington; Scenery, Stuart Wurtzel; Costumes, Joseph Thomas; Supervised by Stanley Simmons; Produced in association with Peter Kean; Presented by special arrangement with Lucille Lortel Productions; Assistant to Producers, Richard Dulaney, Bill Wilson; Production Assistant, Liz Grant; Sound, Gary Harris.

CAST

Mary Alice	Barbara Montgomery
Jean Andalman	Jeffrey Mylett
Martha Flowers	Howard Porter
Robin Lamont	Sarallen
Baruk Levi	E. H. Wright
Bob Molock	

MUSICAL NUMBERS: "Opening," "Blues Was a Pastime," "At the Bottom of Your Heart," "Ain't That Something," "Accepting the Tolls," "One of the Boys," "Trying Hard," "Separate but Equal," "Gone," "Jesus Is My Main Man," "Bad Whitey," "Thoughts," "Strange Fruit," "I Can Do It to Myself," "Walking in Strange and New Places," "Music in the Air," "Sunshine," "Many Men Like You," "Roofs," "Day oh Day"

A "Musical Celebration" presented without intermission.

General Manager: Marvin A. Krauss
Company Manager: Jean Rocco
Press: Max Eisen, Maurice Turet, Barbara Eisen
Stage Managers: Martin Herzer, Kenn Hill, Jean Andalman

* Closed Apr. 8, 1973 after 24 performances.

Amnon Ben Nomis Photo

Top Right: E. H. Wright, Martha Flowers, Barbara Montgomery, Howard Porter in "Thoughts"

Right: Thomas A. Stewart, David Margulies in "An Evening with the Poet-Senator"

ASTOR PLACE THEATRE
Opened Thursday, March 15, 1973.*
The Brother Gorski Company presents:

BROTHER GORSKI

By Emanuel Fried; Director, Salem Ludwig; Settings, Don Jensen; Lighting, Bob Brand; Costumes, Sonia Lowenstein; Assistant to Director, Leonardo Cimino; "Theme from Brother Gorski" by Johnny Brandon

CAST

Stanley Gorski	Ken Chapin
Kewpie	Albert M. Ottenheimer
Carl Morgan	Louis Quinones
Howard Schmeichel	Richard Sisk
Gene Smoyer	John Leighton
Willie Clifford	Richard Triggs
Dave Sigmund	Clinton Allman
Tom Tuttle	Clarence P. Jones, Jr.
Paul Scioli	Larry Gordon
Lennie Doyle	Dennis McMahon
Tim Baker	Leroy Gray
Francine Lovely DeLovely	Bari Michaels
Martha Wlodarczyk	Iris Claire Braun
Irene Gorski	Jean Alexander
Connie Schnell	Nell Burnside
Father James Hogan	Robert Riesel

A comedy drama in two acts.

Stage Manager: G. Allison Elmer

* Closed March 18, 1973 after 6 performances. (No photos available)

PLAYHOUSE 2
Opened Wednesday, March 21, 1973.*
Joel W. Schenker presents:

AN EVENING WITH THE POET-SENATOR

By Leslie Weiner; Director, Isaiah Sheffer; Sets and Lighting, Tom Munn; Costumes, Anne de Velder; Production Assistants, Vincent Nucc, Stephen Brown.

CAST

Norris Cummings	Henderson Forsyth
Aaron Silver	David Margulie
Tom Borden	Thomas A. Stewar
Ed Grabowski	Peter Brando
Margaret Hoyt	Margaret Lin
Jo Munson	Tandy Crony
Robert Hoyt	Donald Symington

A Drama in two acts and eleven scenes. The action takes place in 1944 and at the present time.

General Managers: Robert S. Fishko, John A. Prescott
Press: Solters/Sabinson/Roskin, Milly Schoenbaum
Stage Manager: David Taylor

* Closed Apr. 1, 1973 after 14 performances.

CIRCLE IN THE SQUARE

Opened Thursday, March 22, 1973.*
Kermit Bloomgarden and Roger Ailes present the Circle Theatre Company production of:

THE HOT L BALTIMORE

By Lanford Wilson; Director, Marshall W. Mason; Setting, Ronald Radice; Costume Coordination, Dina Costa; Lighting, Marshall W. Mason

CAST

Bill	Judd Hirsch
Girl	Trish Hawkins
Millie	Helen Stenborg
Mrs. Billotti	Henrietta Bagley
April	Conchata Ferrell
Mr. Morse	Rob Thirkield
Jackie	Mari Gorman
Jamie	Zane Lasky
Mr. Katz	Antony Tenuta
Suzy	Stephanie Gordon
Suzy's John	Burke Pearson
Paul Granger III	Jonathan Hogan
Mrs. Oxenham	Louise Clay
Cab Man	Peter Tripp
Delivery Boy	Marcial Gonzales

UNDERSTUDIES: Girl, Jackie, Suzy, Patricia Carey; Millie, April, Mrs. Oxenham, Henrietta Bagley; Bill, Mr. Katz, Mr. Morse, Burke Pearson; Jamie, Paul, Delivery Boy, Suzy's John, Peter Tripp

A Comedy in three acts. The action takes place at the present time on Memorial Day in the lobby of the Hotel Baltimore in Baltimore, Md.

General Manager: Robert P. Cohen
Press: Dorothy Ross, Herbert Striesfield, Sandra Manley, Cheryl Dolby
Stage Managers: Andie Wilson Kingwill, Burke Pearson

Still playing May 31, 1973. Winner of 1973 Drama Critics Circle Award for Best American Play, Outer Critics Circle Award as Best New Play, and an "Obie" Award as Best New Play. Opened Feb. 4, 1973 at the Circle Theatre and played 17 performances and 7 previews before moving to Circle in the Square.

Mari Gorman, Antony Tenuta, Zane Lasky, Jonathan Hogan, Trish Hawkins, Rob Thirkield, Helen Stenborg

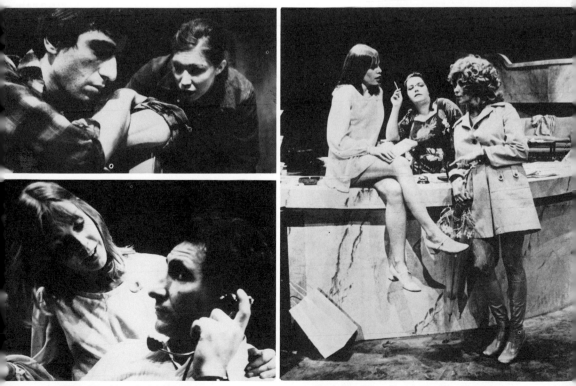

Trish Hawkins, Judd Hirsch
Above: Zane Lasky, Mari Gorman

Trish Hawkins, Conchatta Ferrell, Stephanie Gordon

David Selby, Lynn Milgrim

UPSTAGE AT JIMMY'S
Opened Monday, April 2, 1973.*
Budd Friedman presents:

WHAT'S A NICE COUNTRY LIKE YOU DOING IN A STATE LIKE THIS?

Music, Cary Hoffman; Lyrics, Ira Gasman; Based on an original concept by Ira Gasman, Cary Hoffman, Bernie Travis; Musical Direction-Vocal Arrangements, Arnold Gross; Directed and Choreographed by Miriam Fond; Orchestrations, Hubert Arnold; Set, Billy Puzo; Costumes, Danny Morgan; Design Consultant, Paul Zalon; Lighting, Richard Delahanty; Technical Director, Hugo Napier

CAST

Betty Lynn Buckley†
Sam Freed
Bill LaVallee
Priscilla Lopez
Barry Michlin

MUSICAL NUMBERS: "It's a Political-Satirical Revue," "Liberal's Lament," "I'm in Love with . . . ," "Massage a Trois," "Changing Partners," "Crime in the Streets," "Street People," "It's Getting Better," "I Like Me," "Male Chauvinist," "Primary Tango," "Johannesburg," "But I Love New York," "Why Do I Keep Going to the Theatre?," "I Found the Girl in My Dreams on Broadway," "A Mugger's Work Is Never Done," "Kissinger und Kleindeinst und Klein," "Farewell First Amendment," "Why Johnny?," "The Right Place at the Right Time," "Love Story," "I'm not Myself Anymore," "People Are Like Porcupines," "On a Scale of One to Ten," "Threesome," "Come on, Daisy," "Whatever Happened to the Communist Menace?," Finale.

A "Red, White and Blue Revue" in two acts.

Press: Merlin Group
Stage Manager: Richard Delahanty

* Still playing May 31, 1973.
† Succeeded by Mary Nealie

Bert Andrews Photo

Classic Bunraku "Tsuri Onna"

BIJOU THEATRE
Opened Monday, March 26, 1973.*
Orin Lehman presents:

ECHOES

By N. Richard Nash; Director, Melvin Bernhardt; Setting, Ed Wittstein; Costumes, Sara Brook; Lighting, Martin Aronstein; Assistants Producer, Laurel Ann Wilson, Nancy Ertag

CAST

Tilda	Lynn Milgrim
Sam	David Selby
The Person	Paul Trip

Standbys: Dennis Cooney, Gisela Caldwell

A Drama in two acts. The action takes place at the present time.

General Managers: Joseph Harris, Ira Bernstein
Press: Solters/Sabinson/Roskin, Ellen Levene
Stage Managers: Allan Leicht, Gisela Caldwell

* Closed March 26, 1973 after one performance and 11 previews.

Martha Swope Photo

Priscilla Lopez, Barry Michlin, Sam Freed, Mary Nealie, Bill LaVallee

CITY CENTER
Opened Tuesday, April 3, 1973.*
Kazuko Hillyer presents The National Puppet Theatre of Japan:

BUNRAKU

Executive Director, Masahiko Imai; Simultaneous Translation, Faubion Bowers.

CAST

Tsudaiyu Takemoto, Tokudaiyo Toyotake, Oritayu Takemoto, Redaiyu Toyotake, Aiodayu Takemoto, Shimadayu Toyotake, Katsutara Nozawa, Juzo Tsuruzawa, Dohachi Tsuruzawa, Katsuhei Nozawa, Juzo Tsuruzawa, Katsuhei Nozawa, Danjiro Takezawa, Kamematsu Kiritake, Kanjuro Kiritake, Seijuro Toyomatsu, Minosuke Yoshida, Bunjaku Yoshida, Tomasho Yoshida, Bunsho Yoshida, Tamamatsu Yoshida, Mon Kiritake, Icho Kiritake, Komon Kiritake, Kanju Kiritake, Shojiro Yoshida, Minotaro Yoshida, Haruo Mochizuzi, Kazuo Kawaradani, Mitsuru Ito, Shoji Nagoshi, Kisaku Shinzo, Takami Ikoma.

PROGRAM

Heike Nyogogashima (The Priest in Exile), Sonezaki Shinju (The Double Suicide at Sonezaki).

Company Manager: Alfred Fisher
Press: Bill Doll & Co., Dick Williams
Stage Manager: George Braun

* Closed Apr. 15, 1973 after 16 performances.

Opened Wednesday, April 4, 1973.*
Stuart Duncan presents:

SMILE, SMILE, SMILE

By Hugo Peretti, Luigi Creatore, George David Weiss; Staged by Rob-
Simpson; Scenery, Philip Gilliam; Lighting, Barry Arnold; Costumes,
tricia McGourty; Orchestrations, Jack Andrews; Sound, Astral Acous-
s; Dance Arrangements, Bob Tartaglia; Musical Supervisor, Joseph
ecko; Original Cast Album on Bell Records; Production Coordinator,
net Sonenberg.

CAST

rlie	Bobby Lee
ockalorum	Rudy Tronto
bette	Carole Joan Macho
anny	Diane J. Findlay
ofessor	William Pierson
tch	Chip Zien
mple	Casey Craig
na	Marilyn Saunders
orgio	Joseph Neal
onora	Suellen Estey
renzo	Gary Beach
linda	Virginia Pulos
land	J. Richard Beneville
af	Geoff Leon
rrinna	Donna Liggitt Forbes

NDERSTUDIES: Arlie, Cockalorum, Letch, Professor, J. Richard
neville; Bibette, Leonora, Donna Liggitt Forbes; Lorenzo, Giorgio,
off Leon; Simple, Gina, Virginia Pulos; Franny, Marilyn Saunders

USICAL NUMBERS: "Haven't I Seen You Somewhere Before?,"
aradise," "To Find True Love," "I'm the Cockalorum," "A Good
d-Fashioned Revolutionary," "Open Your Heart," "Adios,"
riends," "God Bless the Fig Tree," "Garland of Roses," "Buttercup,"
mile, Smile, Smile," "It's All for the Good of the People," "Magnetic,"
ove Is a Fragile Thing," "Love Is a Pain," "Breakin' the Spell"

A Musical in two acts. The action takes place at various locales on the
nd of Paradise.

Company Managers: Al J. Isaac, Gail Bell
Press: Max Eisen, Maurice Turet
Stage Managers: Michael Massee, Allan Sobek

Closed Apr. 8, 1973 after 7 performances.

Diane J. Findlay, Casey Craig, Chip Zien, William
Pierson

Opened Wednesday, April 18, 1973.*
Ronald A. Wilford Associates Inc. in association with City
Center of Music and Drama, Inc. presents:

MARCEL MARCEAU

Pantomimes created and performed by Marcel Marceau; Presentation
cards by Pierre Verry; Administrative Director, Alain Mangel; Tour
ection by Columbia Artists Management.

REPERTOIRE

RT I: Walking, Walking against the Wind, The 1500 Meter, The
ircase, The Tightrope Walker, The Side Show, The Public Garden, The
Poster, The Kite, The Man and His Boat, The Magician, The Sculp-
, The Painter, The Cage, Remembrances, A Sunday Walk, The Bu-
ucrats, Luna Park, The Hands, Contrasts, The Maskmaker, The Seven
adly Sins, Youth-Maturity-Old Age-Death, The Japanese Pan-
imes, The Duel in Darkness, The Tango Dancer, The Small Cafe, The
e Players, The Dream, The Creation of the World, The Four Seasons,
dow and Light, The Dress Dealer, The Trial

RT II: BIP Pantomimes: With a Bumble Bee, In the Subway, Travel
Train, Travel by Sea, As a Skater, Hunting Butterflies, Playing David
Goliath, At the Ballroom, Committing Suicide, As a Soldier, At a
iety Party, As a Street Musician, As a China Salesman, As a Fireman,
a Baby Sitter, As a Jeweler Apprentice, As a Professor of Botany, As
ailor in Love, As a Matador, Dreams of Being Don Juan, In an
dition, With Dynamite, As a Lion Tamer, As an Illusionist, Looking
a Job, In the Modern and Future Life, As a Pastry Cook, As Don
xote, As the Bank Employee Who Dreams of a Better World

Company Manager: John Scott
ress: Herbert H. Breslin, Marvin R. Jenkins, Marvin Schofer
Stage Managers: Antoine Casanova, Bruno Clementin

Closed May 6, 1973 after a limited engagement of 24 performances.

Marcel Marceau

PROVINCETOWN PLAYHOUSE
Opened Monday, April 9, 1973.*
Margaret Barker presents:

L'ETE
(Summer)

By Romain Weingarten; Translated by Shepperd Strudwick III; Director, Wendell Phillips; Set and Lighting, William Strom; Sound, Susan Ain; Production Assistants, James Selby, Nelson Ferlita.

CAST

Simon	Michael Mullins
Half Cherry	Michael Higgins
Lorette	Maureen Mooney
Lord Garlic	Jerry Mayer

A Play in two acts. The action takes place during summer in a garden and house outside a small French town at the present time.

General Managers: NR Productions
Company Managers: Geoffrey R. Horlick, Robert Frissell
Press: M. J. Boyer

Stage Manager: Peter von Mayrhauser

* Closed Apr. 18, 1973 after 10 performances.

(Bert Andrews Photo)

Michael Higgins, Jerry Mayer, Michael Mullins, Maureen Mooney

McALPIN ROOFTOP THEATRE
Opened Monday, April 23, 1973.*
Sheila Conlon presents:

CRYSTAL AND FOX

By Brian Friel; Director, Patrick Conlon; Scenery, Philip Gilliam; Lighting, Judy Rasmuson; Costumes, Philip Gilliam, Jennifer von Mayrhauser; Incidental Music, Ted Auletta; Associate Producer, Carmel Quinn.

CAST

Fox Melarkey	Will Hare
Tanya	Jo Anne Belanger
El Cid	Chet Carlin
Crystal	Rue McClanahan
Papa	Joseph Boley
Pedro	Walt Gorney
Irish Policeman	Pat McNamara
Gabriel	Brad Davis
Detectives	Chet Carlin, Barry Corbin

A Drama in two acts and six scenes. The action takes place backstage during a performance of the Fox Melarkey Show, Ballybeg, Ireland.

General Manager: NR Productions
Press: Seymour Krawitz, Robert Larkin
Company Managers: Geoff Horlick, Robert Frissell
Stage Manager: Ginny Freedman

* Closed May 13, 1973 after 24 performances.

118   *Bert Andrews Photo*

PROVINCETOWN PLAYHOUSE
Opened Tuesday, April 10, 1973.*
The DiApeiron Company presents:

THE SOLDIER

By Nick Bellitto; Director, Eleanore Chapin; Set, Richard Ferru Lighting, O. B. Lewis; Sound, George Jacobs.

CAST

Johnny DiCeaser, The Soldier	Tom Kir
Mrs. DiCeaser	Megan H
Mr. DiCeaser	Sam Loca
Harry	Richard Ferru
Wayne DiCeaser	Gregory Tig
Susan	Paula Malia
Trophies, Medics	Frank Girardeau, Steve Simp

A Drama in three acts and seven scenes. The action takes place in living room of the DiCeaser home.

Press: David Lipsky
Stage Managers: Robert Kerman, Richard Ferrugio

* Closed Apr. 15, 1973 after 8 performances.

Friedman-Abeles Photo

Left: Gregory Tigani, Paula Maliandi, Tom Kindle

Rue McClanahan, Jo Anne Belanger, Chet Carlin, Hare

Opened Tuesday, April 24, 1973.*
The Committee for the Theatre of the Riverside Church
presents The Everyman Players in:

PILGRIM'S PROGRESS

By John Bunyan; Director-Adapter, Orlin Corey; Assistant Director-
horeographer, Wren Terry; Designer, Irene Corey; Technical Director,
en Holamon; Coordinator of Special Effects, Merlin Fahey; Composer,
han Franco; Sound, Bob French; An Orlin and Irene Corey Production.

CAST

hristian	Hal Proske
hn Bunyan-Evangelist	Orlin Corey
bstinate, Formalist, Lord Hategood, Atheist	Clay Harris
iable, Clerk of Court, Ignorance	Michael Zipperlin
elpful, Terrified Man, Demon	Ron Foreman
eath, Porter	Charles Merritt
orldly Wiseman, Passion, Presumption, Timorous,	
Vain Confidence	Gary Ballard
oodwill, Hypocrisy, Prudence	Marilee Hebert
terpreter, Shining One, Piety, Town Crier, Envy,	
Punishing Angel	Wren Terry
rvant, Mistrust, Maid	Kathy Parsons
veeper, Charity, Superstition	Anna Antaramian
tience, Sloth, False One	James R. Ray
mple, Discretion	Brenda Musgrove
ining One, Faithful, Gardener	Richard Barker
entleman, Giant	Ken Holamon
entleman, Hopeful	Stewart Slater

A Miracle Play presented without intermission.
Company Manager: Ken Holamon
ress: Betty Lee Hunt, Henry Luhrman, Harriett Trachtenberg,
Maria Pucci

Closed May 6, 1973 after limited engagement of 13 performances.

Opened Saturday, April 28, 1973.*
Hunter College Playwrights present:

I CAN'T GO ON WITHOUT YOU, MINNA MANDELBAUM!

By Alex Byron; Director, Eve Brandstein; Set, Nick Colovos, Eve
andstein; Lighting, Bill Hendricks; Costumes, Edward and Anne Ruth
Cann; Production Assistant, Debbie McCann

CAST

lerie/Stagehand/Minna	Beth Alyson
uglas/Stagehand/Phillie as boy	Billy Natbony
illie Mandelbaum/El Nova	Gregory Lehane
a Greentree/Mamma/Princess Christina	H. E. Wales
rol Rabinowitz/Mourner/Debbie Schlosser/Nasha	Lucy Re
. Ravenal Nadel/Uncle Rudy/Lanevar	Roger Fawcett

A Play in two acts.
Press: Patricia Molino
Stage Managers: Lori Styler, Roy Dorfman

Closed May 6, 1973 after limited engagement of 4 performances. (no
photos available)

TRUCK & WAREHOUSE THEATRE
Opened Tuesday, April 24, 1973.*
Vaslin Productions present:

A PHANTASMAGORIA HISTORIA OF D. JOHANN FAUSTEN MAGISTER, PHD, MD, DD, DL, ETC.

Director, Vasek Simek; Scenery, Clarke Dunham; Lighting, David F.
Segal; Costumes, Patricia Quinn Stuart; Electronic Sound, John Watts;
Technical Assistant, Bill Blackwell.

CAST

Faust	Jack Hollander
Mephistopheles	Barton Heyman
Luce	Lilly Noycs
Euphcrion	Dennis Tate
Lilith as Margaret	Molly McKasson
Kasperlino	Jara Kohout
Goungoune A	Henry L. Baker
Ashtoroth A	Danny DeVito
Harlequin	Mark Siegel
Goungoune B	Muriel Miguel
Ashtoroth B	Ann Miles
Ashtoroth C	Jane Culley
Goungoune C	Natalie Gray
Columbine	Rhea Perlman

A Drama in two acts.
General Manager: Lily Turner
Press: Max Eisen, Maurice Turet
Stage Managers: Richard Husson, Mark Siegel

* Closed Apr. 24, 1973 after one performance.

Top Left: Molly McKasson, Barton Keyman

**Anna Antaramian, Kathy Parsons Above: Stewart
Slater in "Pilgrim's Progress"**

STAGE 73

Opened Monday, April 30, 1973.*
The Spoon River Company presents:

SPOON RIVER ANTHOLOGY

Poems by Edgar Lee Masters; Adapted and Arranged by Charles Aidman; Director, Peter John Bailey; Music, Naomi Caryl Hirshhorn; Lyrics, Charles Aidman; Set, Henry Scott III; Lighting, Barry Arnold; Costumes, Vel Riberto; Associate Producer, Joan Rowe

CAST

Robert Elston
Barbara Gilbert
Paul Larson
Diane Tarleton
Lori Hillman
Ralph Penner

Selections from Edgar Lee Masters' "Spoon River Anthology" presented in two acts.

General Manager: NR Productions
Company Managers: Geoffrey R. Horlick, Robert Frissell
Press: Seymour Krawitz, Robert Larkin
Stage Manager: Cleveland Morris

* Closed May 27, 1973 after 32 performances.

Paul Larson, Barbara Gilbert, Diane Tarleton, Rober Elston

THIRTEENTH STREET THEATRE

Opened Wednesday, May 2, 1973.*
The Ridiculous Theatrical Company presents:

CAMILLE

Written and Directed by Charles Ludlam; Freely adapted from D "La Dame aux Camelias"; Set, Bobjack Callejo; Costumes, Mary B Lighting, Richard Currie; Sound, Jeffrey Selby

CAST

Baron de Varville	John D. Brockr
Nanine	Jack M.
Marguerite Gautier	Charles Lu
Nichette	George Oste
Butler	Stephen S
Olympe de Taverney	Black-Eyed
Saint Gaudens	Robert R
Prudence Duvernoy	Lola Pasha
Gaston Roue	Robert
Armand Duval	Bill
Duval Senior	Richard (

A drama in three acts and four scenes. The action takes place in and Auteuil in 1848.

Press: Alan Eichler
Stage Managers: Richard Gibbs, Virgil Young

* Still playing May 31, 1973.

Left: Bill Vehr, Charles Ludlam

EASTSIDE PLAYHOUSE

Opened Thursday, May 3, 1973.*
Max Brown and Robert Victor by arrangement with The Royal Court Theatre present:

ALPHA BETA

By E. A. Whitehead; Director, John Berry; Scenery, David Chapman; Lighting, David F. Segal; Production Supervisor, Stone Widney

CAST

Frank Elliot	Laurence Luckinbill
Norma Elliot	Kathryn Walker

A Drama in three acts. The action takes place in the lounge of the Elliot's home in Liverpool, England, from the winter of 1962 to the summer of 1971.

Manager: Maurice Turet
Press: Max Eisen, Ruth Smuckler
Stage Managers: Patrick Horrigan, Michael Andrews

* Closed May 13, 1973 after 14 performances.

Kathryn Walker, Laurence Luckinbill

THIRTEENTH STREET THEATRE
Opened Wednesday, May 9, 1973.*
Mama Hare's Tree presents:

HOT AND COLD HEROS

Music and Lyrics, Islish Baldwin, George Bamford, Ronnie Britton, Arnold Borget, Jehan Clements, Tom Hawkins, Johnny Mann, Lance Mulcahy, Robert W. Preston; Special Material, Jehan Clements, Joe Jakubowitz, Larry Meyers, Albert Poland, Joel Schapira, Ivan Todd, Vi Weiner, Ron Zarro, and the company; Musical Direction and Arrangements, Lee Gillespie, Mark Weiner; Choreography, Ivan Todd; Additional Staging, Gary Weathersbee; Conceived by Joe Jakubowitz; Production Adviser, Errol Selsby; Costumes, Fran Caruso; Settings, R. Thomas Finch; Lighting, Nancy Golladlay

CAST

Jehan Clements	Helena Reis
Susan Conderman	Murray Shactman
Damien Leake	Monica Grignon
Melanie Michelle	Ron Zarro

MUSICAL NUMBERS: "Intro," "New Gun in Town," "Subway," "Ode to Willie," "No Dessert," "He Is an Animal," "Name Dropping," "Ballad of Castle Maiden," "Anna Lee," "And Freedom," "Don't Tell Me Too Many Lies," "Man from Glad," "Rape," "Rock and Roll Critic," "N.E.T. and This Is Remote," "Four Eyes," "Mary Alice, Don't Say Shit," "Masks"

A "musical sandwich" in two parts.

Press: Alan Eichler
Stage Managers: Joel Schapira, Diane Mamolou

Still playing May 31, 1973

MERCER-SHAW THEATRE
Opened Tuesday, May 15, 1973.*
Terese Hayden presents:

OWNERS

By Caryl Churchill; Director, Terese Hayden; Designed by Fred Kolouch; Assistant to the Director, Vernon Joyee

CAST

Clegg	Stefan Gierasch
Worsely	Martin Shakar
Marion	Jacqueline Brookes
Lisa	Alix Elias
Alec	Sam Schacht

A Drama in two acts and 14 scenes. The action takes place in a developing bit of North London.

Press: Max Eisen, Maurice Turet
Stage Manager: John Branon
Closed May 16, 1973 after two performances.

(Carl Samrock Photo)

THEATRE DE LYS
Opened Wednesday, May 16, 1973.*
Sal Mineo and Robin Archer Moles in association with Serpentine Productions Ltd. present:

THE CHILDREN'S MASS

By Frederick Combs; Director, Richard Altman; Set and Costumes, Peter Harvey; Lighting, Roger Morgan; Associate Producer, Robert M. Renard; Hairstylist, Carlisle Wilson; Assistant to the Producers, Elaine Holt

CAST

Jimmy	Kipp Osborne
Geoffrey	Gary Sandy
Michael	Bruce Howard
Elizabeth	Shelley Bruce
Butchie	Courtney Burr
Millie	Elizabeth Farley
Young Man	Donald Warfield

A Drama in two acts and four scenes. The action takes place in a loft in the SoHo district of New York City at the present time.

General Manager: Edward H. Davis
Company Manager: Robb Lady
Press: Betty Lee Hunt, Henry Luhrman, Harriett Trachtenberg, Maria Pucci

Closed May 20, 1973 after 7 performances.

Top Right: Melanie Michelle in "Hot and Cold Heroes"

(Joseph W. Neumayer Photo) Below: Alix Elias,

Sam Schacht, Martin Shaker in "Owners"

Courtney Burr, Donald Warfield
Friedman-Abeles Photos

GUGGENHEIM MUSEUM

Opened Wednesday, May 16, 1973.*
The Solomon R. Guggenheim Museum presents:

COUCOU BAZAR

By Jean Dubuffet; Music Composed and Realized by Ilhan Mimaroglu; Managing Director, Brooke Lappin; Artistic Director, Jean E. McFaddin; Technical Director and Lighting, Bruce Bassman; Curator, Margit Rowell; Costumes conceived and executed by Jean Dubuffet and his assistants Richard Dhoedt, Annie Hochart, Marie-Francoise Leger, Mme. Sandoval, Gustav Hohl, Ettore Guggenbuhl

ANIMATORS

Douglas Bentz
Michelle Boston
Carrotte
Jamie Edlin
Kathy Gargan
Jeffrey M. Jeffreys
Dick Jones
Alice Lipitz
Gabriel Oshen
Michael Reeder

* Closed July 29, 1973 after limited engagement of 87 performances.

Robert E. Mates-Susan Lazarus Photo

"Coucou Bazar" (Le Bal de l'Hourloupe)

EDEN THEATRE

Opened Saturday, May 19, 1973.*
Jordan Hott with Robert Anglund, Jack Millstein, Iris Ke lan, Alexander Bedrosian present:

SMITH

Music and Lyrics, Matt Dubey, Dean Fuller; Book, Dean Fuller, T Hendra, Matt Dubey; Director, Neal Kenyon; Choreography, Mic Shawn; Musical Director, Richard Parrinello; Scenery, Fred Voe Costumes, Winn Morton; Lighting, Martin Aronstein; Orchestrati Jonathan Tunick; Dance Arrangements, John Berkman; Choral Arra ments, Dean Fuller; Sound and Effects, Peter J. Fitzgerald; Hairsty Henri Chevrier; Assistant Choreographer, Bonnie Walker; Produc Coordinator, Philip Seldis; Production Assistants, John Italiano, We Nessel

CAST

Melody Hazleton	Virginia Sand
Walter Smith	Don Mu
Ed Baggett	Mort Mars
Mrs. Smith, Irish Maid	Carol Mc
Pilot, Prompter	David Hor
Ralph	Louis Crisc
Island Beauties	Renee Baughman, Patricia Garl
	Penelope Richards, Bonnie Wa
Jacques	Michael T
Policemen	William James, David Vosb
Chief Punitana	Guy Sp
Servant, Herbie	Don Pr
Ernie	William Ja
Bruce	David Vosb
Dancing Melody	Bonnie Wa
Sinclair Firestone	Ted Thurs
Hangers On	Nicholas Dante, Aurelio Pao
Doublemint	Kenneth He
Sydney James	Patricia Garl

SINGERS: Bonnie Hinson, Jacqueline Johnson, Betsy Ann Leadbe Shirley Lemmon, David Horwitz, William James, Don Prieur, D Vosburgh

DANCERS: Renee Baughman, Patricia Garland, Penelope Richa Bonnie Walker, John Cashman, Nicholas Dante, Kenneth Henley, relio Padron

MUSICAL NUMBERS: "Boy Meets Girl," "There's a Big Job Wa for You," "To the Ends of the Earth," "Balinasia," "Onh-Honh-Ho "Police Song," "You Need a Song," "How Beautiful It Was," "Is Ritual," "People Don't Do That," "You're in New York Now," "It ! Be Love," "Song of the Frog," "G'bye," "Melody," Finale.

A Musical Comedy in two acts. The action takes place at Ba Nitrates, Tenafly, N.J., at the present time.

General Manager: Victor Samrock
Company Manager: Malcolm Allen
Press: Saul Richman, Sara Altshul
Stage Managers: William Dodds, Marnel Sumner, Bonnie Walker

* Closed June 2, 1973 after 18 performances.

Abner Symons Photo

Don Murray (top), Ted Thurston, Mort Marshall

Opened Monday, May 21, 1973.*
Performing Arts Repertory Theatre Foundation and NYU's
Town Hall present The Fanfare Ensemble (John Clifton, Joan
Shepard, Evan Thompson, Directors) in:

TREASURE ISLAND

Book, Tom Tippett; Adapted from Robert Louis Stevenson; Music and
yrics, John Clifton; Director, Evan Thompson; Settings, John Nelson;
ostumes, Jennie Cleaver; Pianist, John Clifton

CAST

m Hawkins .... Joan Shepard
illy Bones/Israel Hands/Dr. Livesey .... Evan Thompson
lack Dog/Dick Johnston/Ben Gunn .... Jon Stevens
ind Pew/Tom Morgan/Capt. Smollett .... Bill Steele
quire Trelawny/George Merry .... David Burrow
ong John Silver .... Chester Thornhill

IUSICAL NUMBERS: "Treasure Island," "I'll Buy Me a Ship,"
Gold," "That's What I Would Do," "Honest Sailors, "Yo-Ho," "Let's
e Friends"

Opened Wednesday May 23, 1973.*

RUMPLESTILTSKIN

Book, Joan Shepard; Lyrics, Evan Thompson; Music, Philip
eishman, Joan Shepard; Director, Evan Thompson; Settings, John Nel-
n; Costumes, Jennie Cleaver; Pianist, John Clifton

CAST

roubadour .... David Burrow
latilda Muller .... Nancy Temple
n Muller .... Bill Steele
ing Leopold .... Evan Thompson
oltan Lepescu .... Chester Thornhill
umplestiltskin .... Joan Shepard

IUSICAL NUMBERS: "Travelling Troubadour," "Killer-Diller
iller," "Never," "Down by the Mill," "A Woman in the Palace,"
traw into Gold," "What Will You Give Me?," "A Love Match,"
Guess My Name"

Press: Bill Steele
Stage Manager: Cedric Flower

Closed May 24, 1973 after limited engagement of 4 performances.

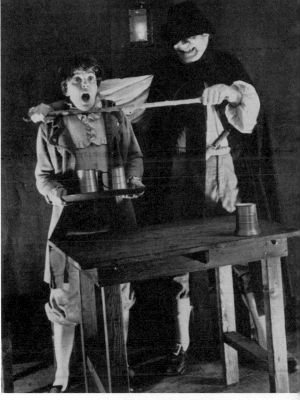

Joan Shepard, Evan Thompson
in "Treasure Island"

OUR LADY OF POMPEII CHURCH
Opened Friday, May 25, 1973.*
Italian Theatre Today presents:

THE JAR
and
L'ADORABILE ZITELLA

Director, Joseph della Sorte; Selection and Organization, Mario Fratti;
Sets and Costumes, George Berechet; Lighting, Tony Giovanetti; Choreography, Alexis Hoff; Sound, Terry Alexander

CAST

"The Jar" by Luigi Pirandello
Doro .... Amelia Romano
Nociarello .... Johnny Biancamano
Friend Pe .... Michael Enserro
Trisuzza .... Roz Valero
Tana .... Gloria Lanbert
Cariminella .... Michele Peruzzi
Don Lolo Zirafa .... Michael Vale
Manure Man .... Frank Piazza
Scime .... Bernie Passeltiner
Fillico .... Robert Caluntino
Tarara .... Richard DeSena
Uncle Dima .... Carlo Grasso

"L'Adorabile Zitella" by Giovanni Mina
Francesca .... Josephine Buscaglia
Marco .... Maurizio Morzelli
Renato .... Pasquale Guardi

STANDBYS: Joe Sorbello, Frank Biancamano, Frank Piazza, Susan
Sparling

Production Managers: Frank Biancamano, Sal Carollo
Stage Managers: Susan Sparling, Gina Macchiarulo

* Closed June 2, 1973 after limited engagement of 7 performances.

Richard DeSena (top), Michele Peruzzi, Robert
Coluntino, Michael Enserro, Amelia Romano,
Gloria Lambert, Roz Valero in "The Jar"

ACTORS STUDIO THEATRE

Opened Thursday, June 8, 1972.*
The Actors Studio presents:

SIAMESE CONNECTIONS

By Dennis J. Reardon; Director, Peter Masterson; Scenery, Donald Crawford; Costumes, Terry Leong; Music, Chris Allport; Lighting, Ray Dooley, Beverly Emmons; Artistic Director, Lee Strasberg; Executive Producer, Arthur Penn; Producers, Elizabeth Stearns, Marilyn Fried; Technical Director, John Branon; Production Assistant, Susan Hammond; Choreography, Julie Arenal

CAST

Grandmother Kroner	Bryarly Lee
Tom Jensen	Clinton Allmon
Minister	Lowell Fink
Frank Kroner, Sr.	James Noble
Kate Kroner	Sandra Seacat
James Kroner	James Woods
Franklin Kroner, Jr.	J. J. Quinn
Gretchen	Margaret Ladd
Auctioneer	Martin Priest

A Play in two acts and four scenes. The action takes place at the present time on an American farm.

Press: Alan Eichler
Stage Managers: Brent Peek, Lowell Fink, John Meyer, Lee Marsh

* Closed June 18, 1972 after limited engagement of 12 performances.

Bert Andrews Photo

Margaret Ladd, James Woods

ACTORS STUDIO THEATRE

Opened Thursday, October 19, 1972.*
The Actors Studio (Lee Strasberg, Artistic Director) pres(

THE BIRDS

By Aristophanes; Modern Translation by William Arrowsmith; D(
tor, George Christodulakes; Producer, Elaine Aiken; Associate Prod(
Michael Tillen; Executive Producer, Arthur Penn; Scenery, Don C(
ford; Costumes and Makeup, Mano; Lighting, James Hardy; Chore(
pher, Emery Hermans; Musical Director, William Garbi(
Improvisational Music, Free Life Communications; Technical Dire(
John Branon; Sound Engineers, David Baker, Peter Burling

CAST

Birds	Janet Katzanberg, Kostantino Tzou(Donald Blumer(
Euelpides	Antony Po(
Pisthetairos	Jack A(
Herald	Douglas Her(
Sandpiper	Kostantino Tzou(
Hoopoe	Burt Y(
Koryphaios	Hy A(
Peacock	Susan P(
Nightingale	Jacqueline H(
Priest	Vincent Duke M(
Prophet	Henry Sta(
Inspector/Informer	Vincent Duke M(
Legislator/Triballos	Rudy E(
Sentry	Donald Blumer(
Iris	Mary A(
Prometheus	Harvey S(
Poseidon	Wendell Ph(
Herakles	Joe R(
Miss Universe	Birgit Win(

BIRDS: Susan Acton, Donald Blumenfeld, Aprille Briggs, Diane E(
Mark Esposito, Kathleen Heath, Amy Karash, Janet Katzenberg, J(
Konopacki, Phillip Little, Sheila A. Mason, Jessica Sayre, Konsta(
Tzoumas, Bonnie Ziegler

A Comedy in two acts. The action takes place in a desolate wilder(

Press: Alan Eichler
Stage Managers: Lee Marsh, David Lyman, Lawrence Eich(

* Closed Oct. 29, 1972 after limited engagement of 12 performan(

David Stanley Lyman Photo

Jessica Sayre, Jack Aaron, Antony Ponzini

THE MASQUE OF ST. GEORGE AND THE DRAGON

An old English Mummers Play originally presented by Fred Stewart;
⎣ector, Anna Strasberg; Producer, Michael Tillem; Executive Pro-
⎣er, Arthur Penn; Musical Director, Paul Grier; Technical Directors,
⎣n Branon, Douglas Kerr; Artistic Director, Lee Strasberg

CAST

⎣ol	Lucy Saroyan
⎣ther Christmas	Joseph Hardy
⎣ng Alfred	Chris Strang
⎣de	Dede Knott
⎣ng Cole	Kim Novick
⎣ng William	Harvey Goldman
⎣ant Blunderbore	Ralph Roberts
⎣ George	Clint Allmon
⎣ng of Egypt	Jay Fletcher
⎣ncess Sabra	Julie Newmar
⎣een Elfreda	Lynne Hardy
⎣rkish Knight	Norman Ornellas
⎣ Ball	Delos V. Smith, Jr.
⎣e Dragon	Richard Sisk

⎣NSTRELS: Julie Blaustein, Karen Green, Karen Kahn, Lydia Reeds,
⎣olann Mary

⎣RRYMEN: Carol Belinkie, Rick Buell, Bill Cotter, Orin Hein, Gail
⎣rber, Greta Kaufman, Bill Parker, Lance Rettig, Norman Roth, Carl
⎣oote, Joan Schoote, Lynn Stephan, Bill Unger, Connie Washburn

⎣losed Dec. 29, 1972 after limited engagement of 10 performances.

Julie Newmar, Clinton Allmon (C)

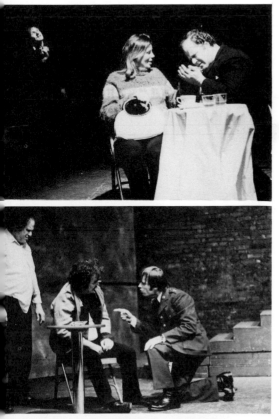

VIRILITY

Written and Directed by Ed Setrakian; Producers, Dennis McMullen,
James Glenn; Sets and Lighting, Jim Hardy; Costumes, Margradel Hicks;
Technical Directors, John Branon, Douglas Kerr, Eric Cowley; Sound,
Saul Spangenberg

CAST

"The Best Secretary He Ever Had"

Customer	J. J. Quinn
Al	Tom Signorelli
Eileen	Sandra Seacat
Booker	Ahmed Nurradin
Lance Lusk	Bob Murdock
Madam	Susan Peretz
Buck Crosley	Jack Hollander
Prof. Clarence McKenna	Sam Schacht
Waitresses	Milo Knott, Carol Belenkie

"I Want to Go to Vietnam"

George	Jack Hollander
Florence	Susan Peretz
Perry Wilson	Will Hare
Booker	Ahmed Nurradin
Mack	J. J. Quinn
Eloise	Marcia Pearsin
Jeannie	Natasha Ebert

A play in two acts. The action takes place in 1965 in an industrial area
in Southern Appalachia.

Press: Alan Eichler, Jack Longhi
Stage Managers: Steven Schachter, John Breslin

* Closed Jan. 21, 1973 after limited engagement of 10 performances.

David Stanley Lyman Photos

Jack Hollander, Will Hare, J. J. Quinn
⎣bove: Sam Schact, Sandra Seacat, Jack Hollander

THEATRE AT ACTORS STUDIO
Opened Thursday, February 8, 1973.*
The Actors Studio presents:

OTHELLO

By William Shakespeare; Director, Gene Frankel; Costumes, Patricia Quinn Stuart; Set, Donald Crawford, David Ballou; Lighting, Jim Hardy; Music, Michael Tschudin; Duels, Chris Tanner; Producer, Patrick Baldauff

CAST

Roderigo	Harvey Solin/Ronald Hale
Iago	John Devlin
Brabantio	Frederic Major
Othello	Manu Tupou
Cassio	Dan Hamilton
Messenger	David Braucher
Duke of Venice	John Straub
First Senator	F. R. McCall
Gratiano	Vincent Duke Milana/Earl Trussell
Desdemona	Stephanie Braxton
Montano	Ronald Hale/Vincent Duke Milana
Emilia	Margaret Hall/Lenka Peterson
Bianca	Marie Puma
Lodovico	John Straub

SOLDIERS, MUSICIANS, ETC: David Braucher, John Kelly, Marc Prensky, Doug Sowell, Dennis Stafford, Earl Trussell

A drama presented in two acts.

Press: Alan Eichler, Jack Longhi
Stage Managers: Andie Wilson Kingwill, F. R. McCall, Ron Vaad

* Closed Feb. 18, 1973 after limited engagement of 10 performances. (No photos available)

Maureen Silliman, Shelley Winters, Margaret Ladd
in "The Effect of Gamma Rays. . . ."

(Albert J. Robbins Photo)

THEATRE AT ACTORS STUDIO
Friday May 18, 1973.*
The Actors Studio presents:

THE EFFECT OF GAMMA RAYS (
MAN-IN-THE-MOON MARIGOLD

By Paul Zindel; Director, Robert H. Livingston; Producer, Aiken; Set, Don Crawford; Production Staff, John Branon, Eric C Kim Novick, Cliff Collings, John Perkins

CAST

Tilly	Maureen Si
Beatrice	Shelley W
Ruth	Margaret
Nanny	Helen
Janice Vickery	Carol

Press: Alan Eichler
Stage Manager: Gretchen Scarry

* Limited to two performances.

THEATRE AT ACTORS STUDIO
Opened Monday, May 28, 1973.*
The Actors Studio presents:

A BREAK IN THE SKIN

By Ronald Ribman; Director, Arthur Sherman; Scenery, Kert L Costumes, Sylvia Woods; Lighting, Roger Morgan; Technical Di John Branon; Producers, Marilyn Fried, Elizabeth Stearns

CAST

Dr. Murray Zeller	Michael
Paul Holliman	James Bro
Mr. Crow	Charles
Julie Holliman	Salom
Dr. Karamanos	Simon De
Chrissy Holliman	Casandra (
Mr. Hum	Lane
Engine	David G
Mission Control Voice	Lois

A play in three acts and seven scenes. The action takes place in east Texas from one night to the following afternoon at the presen
Press: Alan Eichler, Emile Boucian
Stage Managers: Richard Lombard, Rob O'Rourke, Casa Cowles, Sean Nolan

* Closed June 9, 1973 after a limited engagement of 12 perform

James Broderick, David Garfield

Bert Andrews Photo

AMAS REPERTORY THEATRE

Rosetta LeNoire, President-Artistic Director
Margaret Hamilton, Vice President
First Season

EAUMONT HALL
Opened Friday, January 5, 1973.*
The Amas Showcase presents:

AN EVENING WITH THE BOURGEOISIE

CAST

"The Straphangers" by Robert Somerfeld
Director, Hal DeWindt

e	Russ Costen
ie	Dale Hodges
ie	Saundra Kelly
e	Dan DeMott

"Soul Gone Home" by Langston Hughes
Director, Jerry Jarrett

other	Tisa Chang
on	Russ Costen

"A Delicate Question" by Frank Duane
Director, Seymour Penzner
(in 3 acts and 6 scenes)

audia Montroy	June Squibb
lexander Frisby	Conrad McLaren
inston Montroy	John Burstein
ester Plumly	Frolic Taylor
o Montroy	Glenn Johnson
r. London	Sab Shimono
rna Plumly	Diana Penzner
ghway Patrolman	Russ Costen

Closed Jan. 21, 1973 after limited engagement of 9 performances. (No photos available)

EAUMONT HALL
Opened Friday, February 9, 1973.*
The Amas Showcase presents:

OTHELLO

By William Shakespeare; Director, Seymour Penzner; Sets and Light-
g, Conrad McLaren; Costumes, Diana Penzner; Administrative Assis-
nt, Virginia M. Lynch; Stage Manager, Gina Stahl

CAST

derigo	Robert Dinner
go	Gus Fleming
abantio	Sab Shimono
hello	Russ Costen
ssio	John Mitchell
ke of Venice	Arthur Zigouras
esdemona	Rebecca Strum
ontano	Bill O'Boyle
erald	Larry Nabritt
nilia	Tisa Chang
own	Sab Shimono
anca	Michele Mais
dovico	John Burstein
atiano	Arthur Zigouras
tendants	Larry Nabritt, Gary Klyvert

Closed Feb. 25, 1973 after limited engagement of 9 performances.

Mervyn Nelson, Jason, Calvin Jung, Gina Stahl, John
nahan, Prudence Wright Holmes, Manny Cavaco, Jr.,
Frank Emerson, F. Craig Pierce of "House Party"

John Mitchell, Tisa Chang, Guss Fleming, Russ
Costen, Rebecca Strum, Bill O'Boyle in "Othello"

BEAUMONT HALL
Opened Friday, March 9, 1973.*
The Amas Showcase presents:

THE THREE SISTERS

By Anton Chekhov; Director, Charles Kakatsakis; Set, John Mitchell,
Conrad McLaren; Costumes, Linda DeRosa; Sound and Lights, Manny
Cavaco; Administrative Assistant, Virginia M. Lynch; Stage Manager,
Christy Risska

CAST

Olga	June Squibb
Masha	Petronia
Irina	Frances Higgins
Tuzenbach	Peter Brooks
Chebutykin	Laurence Watson
Solyony	Castulo Guerra
Anfisa	Sally Birckhead
Ferapont	Ken Tigar
Virshinin	Richard Bowden
Andrei	Samuel Barton
Kulygin	George K. Emch
Natasha	Christy Risska
Fedotik	John Mitchell
Roday	Larry Nabritt

* Closed Mar. 25, 1973 after limited engagement of 9 performances.

BEAUMONT HALL
Opened Friday, April 13, 1973.*
The Amas Showcase presents:

HOUSE PARTY
"A Musical Memory"

Idea conceived by Rosetta Lenoire; Directed and Staged by Mervyn
Nelson; Set, Conrad McLaren; Lighting, Adrian Durlester; Costumes,
Richard Bexfield; Choreography, Bil Jamis; Administrative Assistant,
Virginia M. Lynch; Vocal Direction, Seymour Penzner.

CAST

Miriam Burton†1	Barrey Smith
Joy Todd	Bernie Rachelle
John Lenehan	Marcia O'Brien
Gina Stahl	Lori Chinn
Frank Emerson	Calvin Jung
Manny Cavaco, Jr.	Jerry McGee
Gerta Grunen	Jim Mosbey
Charles Craig	Clarke Salonist†2
Bob Rapson	Prudence Wright Holmes

Press: Virginia M. Lynch
Stage Manager: Michael Wieben

* Closed May 13, 1973 after limited engagement of 15 performances on weekends only.

† Succeeded by: 1. Rita Madero, 2. Leonard Hayward   **127**

AMERICAN PLACE THEATRE
Wynn Handman, Director
Julia Miles, Associate Director

AMERICAN PLACE THEATRE
Opened Wednesday, November 15, 1972.*
The American Place Theatre presents:

THE KID

By Robert Coover; Director, Jack Gelber; Music Composed and Directed by Stanley Walden; Scenery, Kert Lundell; Costumes, Joe Aulisi; Lighting, Roger Morgan; Movement, Edward Roll; Associate Director, Julia Miles; Technical Director, Steve Crowley; Sound, Gary Harris

CAST

Sheriff	Beeson Carroll
Cowpoke	Albert M. Ottenheimer
Cowpoke	George Bamford
Cowpoke	Bob Gunton
Belle	Alice Beardsley
Belle	Jenny O'Hara
Deputy	John Coe
Cowpoke	David Ramsey
Cowpoke	James Richardson
Cowpoke	Don Plumley
Belle	Cherry Davis
Cowpoke	Sy Johnson
Cowpoke	Neil Portnow
The Kid	Dale Robinette

A Comedy in two acts. The action takes place in a bar in the "Wild West."

Press: David Roggensack
Stage Managers: Franklin Keysar, Grania M. Hoskins
* Closed Dec. 2, 1972 after 34 performances.

Martha Holmes Photos

Right: Jenny O'Hara, Alice Beardsley, Beeson Carroll, Cherry Davis Top: Beeson Carroll, Dale Robinette

Marjorie Barnes, Bill Cobbs, J. A. Preston, Estelle Evans, Dotts Johnson

AMERICAN PLACE THEATRE
Opened Monday, February 5, 1973.*
The American Place Theatre presents:

FREEMAN

By Phillip Hayes Dean; Director, Lloyd Richards; Scenery, [
Higgins; Costumes, Bernard Johnson; Lighting, Shirley Prenderga
sic, William S. Fischer; Associate Director, Julia Miles; Technical
tor, Steve Crowley; Production Assistant, David A. Butler

CAST

Teresa Aquila	Estelle
Ned Aquila	Dotts J
Osa Lee Aquila	Marjorie
Freeman Aquila	Bill
Rex Coleman	J. A.

A Drama in two acts. The action takes place in a small indust
in Michigan during the recent past.

Press: David Roggensack
Stage Managers: Franklin Keysar, Grania M. Hoskin

* Closed Mar. 4, 1973 after 57 performances.

Martha Holmes Photo

128

THE KARL MARX PLAY

By Rochelle Owens; Director, Mel Shapiro; Music, Galt MacDermot;
rics, Rochelle Owens; Scenery, Karl Eigsti; Costumes, Linda Fisher;
hting, Roger Morgan; Associate Director, Julia Miles; Technical Di-
tor, Steve Crowley; Production Assistant, David A. Butler.

CAST

rlee (Clarinet)	Linda Mulrean
ista (Violin)	Deborah Loomis
y (Cello)	Louie Piday
nka (Guitar)	Zenobia Conkerite
urie (Autoharp/Baritone)	Linda Swenson
adbelly	Norman Matlock
rl Marx	Leonard Jackson
ederick Engels	Randy Kim
ny von Westphalen	Katherine Helmond
nchen	Lizabeth Pritchett
by Johann	Ralph Carter

Understudy for Baby Johann, Paul Carrington

A Play with music in two acts. The action takes place during the
d-nineteenth century in London.

Press: David Roggensack
Stage Managers: Franklin Keysar, Grania M. Hoskins
Closed Apr. 14, 1973 after 31 performances.

Top Right: Louie
Piday, Leonard Jackson, Linda Mulrean,
Linda Swenson, Deborah Loomis, Katherine
Helmond, Lizabeth Pritchett, Zenobia
Conkerite, Ralph Carter (foreground)

John Randolph, Olympia Dukakis, R. A. Dow
Right Center: Lou Gilbert, Peggy Whitton

BABA GOYA

By Steve Tesich; Director, Edwin Sherin; Scenery, Karl Eigsti; Lighting, Roger Morgan; Costumes, Whitney Blausen; Technical Director,
Steve Crowley; Production Assistant, David A. Butler; Associate Director, Julia Miles

CAST

Goya	Olympia Dukakis
Mario	John Randolph
Old Man	Lou Gilbert
Bruno	R. A. Dow
Sylvia	Peggy Whitton
Adolf	Ken Tigar
Criminal	Randy Kim
Studly	David A. Butler
Client	James Greene

A Comedy in two acts. The action takes place at the present time in
a house in Queens, New York City.

Press: David Roggensack
Stage Managers: Franklin Keysar, Grania M. Hoskins

* Closed June 2, 1973 after 26 performances.

Martha Holmes Photos

ANTA MATINEE SERIES

Lucille Lortel, Artistic Director
Seventeenth Season

THEATRE DE LYS

Monday, October 30, 1972
and Tuesday matinee, October 31, 1972
MADAME DE SADE A drama in 3 acts by Yukio Mishima; Translated by Donald Keene; Director, Herbert Machiz; Costume-Setting Coordinator, Frank Julian Boros; with Ruth Ford (Comtesse de Saint-Fond), Cavada Humphrey (Baroness de Simiane), Florence Anglin (Charlotte), Lucille Patton (Renee's Mother), Diane Kagan (Renee, the Marquise de Sade), Avra Petrides (Renee's Younger Sister)

Monday, December 4, 1972
and Tuesday matinee December 5, 1972
WILDE! A drama without intermission by Frederick Gaines; Director, John J. Desmond; with Albert Stratton (Oscar Wilde), Charles Siebert (O'Flahertie), Barbara Caruso (Wills), Carol Williard (Fingal)

Monday, January 8, 1973
and Tuesday matinee, January 9, 1973
LOVE GOTTA COME BY SATURDAY NIGHT by Ronnie Paris; Director, Donald Buka; with Ellyn Rudolf (Woman Customer), Kipp Osborne (W. S., the Salesman), Janet Ward (Thalassa Carussa)
ORRIN by Don Evans; Director, Earle Hyman; with Sid Morgan, Jr. (Kenny), Frances Foster (Wilma), Tony Thomas (Orrin), Earle Hyman (Alex)

General Manager: Paul B. Berkowsky
Press: Jean Dalrymple
Series Coordinator: Ken Richards
Stage Managers: Alec Murphy, Leslie Robinson

(no photos available)

Carol Williard
Above: Frances Foster

Charles Siebert
Above: Ruth For[d]

BIL BAIRD THEATER
Opened Sunday, October 29, 1972.
The American Puppet Arts Council (Arthur Cantor, Exec[utive] Producer) presents:

BIL BAIRD'S MARIONETTES

Executive Director, Bil Baird; Artistic Associate, Frank Sullivan[; Cos]tumes, Props, Fania Sullivan, Marianne Harms; Scenery, Jennifer [Provi]dence; Chauffage Central, Erasmo Romero; Majeure Domo, Cha[rles] Dancy

COMPANY

Bil Baird, Peter Baird, Pady Blackwood, Olga Felgemacher, [Marianne] Harms, The Simon Sisters, Frank Sullivan, William Tost, Byron W[hiting]

PRODUCTIONS

WINNIE THE POOH by A. A. Milne; Adapted by A. J. Russell; [Music] Jack Brooks; Lyrics, A. A. Milne, Jack Brooks; Musical Directo[r and] Arranger, Alvy West; Director, Lee Theodore; Opened Oct. 29, 197[2 and] closed Dec. 17, 1972 after 44 performances

DAVY JONES' LOCKER with Book by Arthur Birnkrant and [Waldo] Salt; Music and Lyrics, Mary Rodgers; Musical Director and Arra[nger,] Alvy West; Director, Lee Theodore; Opened Dec. 24, 1972 and [closed] March 11, 1973 after 79 performances

BAND WAGON—a variety revue directed by Lee Theodore; Li[ghting] by Peggy Clark; Opened Mar. 16, 1973 and closed May 20, 1973 af[ter] performances

Nat Messik Photo

"Davy Jones Locker"
Above: "Winnie the Pooh"

130

CENTRAL ARTS CABARET

Albert L. DuBose, Director
Second Season

NTRAL PRESBYTERIAN CHURCH
October 20—November 12, 1972
(weekends only)
ELICATE BALANCE by Edward Albee; Director, Randal Hoey;
ng, Jeremy Unger; Lighting, Gary Grossman; Stage Manager, Cath-
e Foster; with Herman O. Arbeit (Harry), Marian Baer (Agnes), Nina
a (Claire), Verna Hillie (Edna), Pamela Lincoln (Julia), Robert Dale
tin (Tobias), Maggie Rogers (Edna), Judy Stone (Julia)

January 12—February 4, 1973
(weekends only)
MON SKY by Lanford Wilson; Director, Rae Tattenbaum; Set, Philip
iam; Lighting, Dan Bartlett; Stage Manager, Annie Rech; Production
rdinator, Mark Burman; Original Music, Marty Fulton; with Robert
ds (Douglas), James Canada (Alan), Terry Colisino (Penny), Edward
ner (Jack), Mark Rimmer (Jerry), Charmian Sorbello (Ronnie),
hia Woll (Carol)

February 16—March 4, 1973
(weekends only)
HTNIN' BUGS 'N' GOD 'N' THINGS by Bruce Peyton; Music,
r Berinstein; Lyrics, Bruce Peyton; Director, Nyla Lyon; Set, Maxine
Klein; Lighting, Edward M. Greenberg; Associate Producer, Joel
on; Musical Director, James Seymour; Stage Managers, Charles P.
nick, Kathy Baker, Sari Weisman; with Connie Van Ess (Susan),
lyn Cope (Becky), James Seymour (Billy), Joel Simon (David), My-
e Smiley (Mammy), and Samantha Doane, Faith Catlin, Malcolm
ome (Understudies)

March 23—April 9, 1973
(weekends only)
ODBYE TOMORROW with Book and Lyrics by Sue Brock; Music,
Friberg; Director, Anthony Stimac; Set Elements, Plasticity; Light-
C. Murawski; Costumes, Robert Pusillo; Musical Director, Carl Fri-
, Stage Manager, Pat Moesser; with Patti Perkins (Mary), Bob
cer (Joe), Raymond Thorne (The Man), Carl Friberg, Clive Ken-
, Barbara Wheeler (Chorus)

General Manager: Mark Burman
Press: Susan Weeks, Ann Wyant

Barbara J. Ellis Photos

**Right: Robert Dale Martin, Herman O. Arbeit in "A
Delicate Balance" Right: Terry Colisino, Charmian
rbello, James Canada, Cynthia Woll in "Lemon Sky"**

es Seymour, Carolyn Cope in "Lightnin' Bugs . . ."

Patti Perkins, Bob Spencer in "Goodbye Tomorrow"

CHELSEA THEATER CENTER

Robert Kalfin, Artistic Director
Michael David, Executive Director
Burl Hash, Productions Director

BROOKLYN ACADEMY OF MUSIC
Opened Wednesday, October 25, 1972.*
The Chelsea Theater Center of Brooklyn presents:

LADY DAY: A MUSICAL TRAGEDY

By Aishah Rahman; Music, Archie Shepp; Additional Music, Stanley Cowell, Cal Massey; Director, Paul Carter Harrison; Set, Robert U. Taylor; Costumes, Randy Barcelo; Lighting, William Mintzer, Sound, Gary Harris; Musical Director, Stanley Cowell

CAST

Ronnie/Vi-Tone/Wino/Reporter/Guard .... R. T. Vessels
Ricky/Vi-Tone/Wino/Buttercup/Waiter .... Don Jay
Sonny/Vi-Tone/Wino/Beware Scat/Reporter .... Joe Lee Wilson
Bullfrog/Vi-Tone/Wino/Cameraman/Shelly .... Eugene Riley
Flim Flam/Preacher/Freddie Freedom .... Roger Robinson
Mother Horn/ Mom .... Rosetta LeNoire
Billie .... Cecelia Norfleet
Piano Player/White Club Owner/
Judge/Cop/Newsboy .... Frank Adu
Lester .... Clifford Jordan, Jr.
Fanny/Flo .... Madge Sinclair
Anonymous White Woman/Gilly .... Signa Joy
Mort Shazer/Gangster .... Maxwell Glanville
Dan/Levitt/Unknown Lover .... Al Kirk
Cellmate/Nurse .... Onike Lee

UNDERSTUDIES: Billie, Fanny, Flo, Dee Dee Bridgewater; Flim Flam, Freddie, Eugene Riley; Mom, Madge Sinclair; Levitt, Frank Adu; Cellmate, Nurse, Signa Joy; General Understudy, Neville Richen; Lester, Charles Rouse

MUSICAL NUMBERS: "No My Darling," "Lover Man," "In the Spring of the Year 1915," "Song of Fate," "Looking for Someone to Love," "Billie's Blues," "He's Gone," "Strange Fruit," "Beware Scat Song," "Blues for the Lady," "America on Her Back," "Enough," "God Bless the Child," "A Year and a Day," "I Know 'Bout the Life," "What Would It Be without You," "Professional Friends Duet," "I Cried Like a Baby," "Song to a Loved One"

A Musical Tragedy in two acts. The action takes place yesterday, today, but not tomorrow in the eye of the Black Nation.

Press: Penny Peters
Stage Managers: James Doolan, Errol Selsby, Randolph Barron

* Closed Nov. 5, 1972 after 32 performances.

BROOKLYN ACADEMY OF MUSIC
Opened Tuesday, November 28, 1972.*
The Chelsea Theater Center of Brooklyn presents:

SUNSET

By Isaac Babel; Translated from Russian by Mirra Ginsburg an~
mond Rosenthal; Director, Robert Kalfin; Music Composed and ar~
by Ryan Edwards; Set, Santo Loquasto; Costumes, Carrie Fishbei~
bins; Lighting, William Mintzer; Production Assistant, Gail Felto~
Effects, Gary Harris; Technical Director, Mark Twery

CAST

Senka Topun .... Frank An~
Boy .... Fabian ~
Mme. Popyatnik/Tavern Woman/Neighbor .... Blanc~
Potapovna ....
Marusia .... Ellie ~
Arye-Leib .... Martin ~
Benya Krick .... Andrew Jark~
Levka Krick .... Zitto K~
Ourussov/Semen/Cattle Merchant .... K. Lype~
Nikifor, Ryabtsov .... Jerome ~
Flute Player/Major Myron Popyatnik .... Al S~
Fedya .... Martin ~
Pyatirubel .... Ben~
Mitya/Jew/Neighbor/Mr. Weiner .... Paul ~
Blind Singer, Young Peasant .... Sean St~
Tavern Woman/Mme. Weiner/Neighbor .... Ronica~
Dvoira .... Shirley ~
Russian Sailor .... Christopher T~
Boyarski .... Michae~
Fomin, Bobrinetz .... Arn ~
Tavern Woman/Klasha .... Louise W~
Cantor/Blind Singer/Rabbi .... Jerrold ~
Nichama Krick .... Sonia Z~
Mendel Krick .... Louis ~

A Drama in eight scenes. The action takes place in Odessa i~

Press: Penny Peters, Leslie Gifford
Stage Managers: Richard Frankel, Peggy Peckham

* Closed Dec. 24, 1972 after limited engagement of 32 performa~

Sonia Zomina, Louis Zorich (seated), Andrew Jarkowsky, Shirley Stoler, Zitto Kazann

Top: Roger Robinson, Cecelia Norfleet Below: Ros~
LeNoire, Al Kirk, Cecelia Norfleet in "Lady Da~

BROOKLYN ACADEMY OF MUSIC

Opened Tuesday, February 6, 1973.*
The Chelsea Theater Center of Brooklyn (Robert Kalfin, Artistic Director; Michael David, Executive Director; Burl Hash, Productions Director) presents:

KASPAR

By Peter Handke; English Version by Michael Roloff; Director, Carl Weber; Video Conceived and Executed by Arthur Ginsberg, Sip Sweeney, Video Free America; Designed by Wolfgang Roth; Technical Director, Mark Twery; Production Assistants, Ben Dreese, Karin Shearer

CAST

Kaspar	Christopher Lloyd
The Prompters	Randy Chicoine, Veronica Castang, Robert Einenkel, Guy Boyd
The Other Kaspars	Robert Einenkel, Randy Chicoine, Guy Boyd, Veronica Castang
Understudy	Craig Bovia

A Drama in two acts. The action takes place in a barely furnished room.

Press: Penny Peters, Leslie Gifford
Stage Managers: Errol Selsby, Craig Bovia

Closed March 18, 1973 after 48 performances.

Right: Christopher Lloyd

(Amnon Ben Nomis Photo)

"La Carpa de los Rasquachis"
Above: Paul E. Richards, Gerald Hiken

BROOKLYN ACADEMY OF MUSIC

Opened Tuesday, March 20, 1973.*
The Chelsea Theater Center of Brooklyn presents:

THE NEW THEATER

Gerald Hiken and Paul E. Richards are the entire acting company, design staff, promotion department, and playwrights-in-residence. They perform with no sets and house lights on, in a repertory of their own short plays.

* Closed Apr. 1, 1973 after limited engagement of 16 performances.

BROOKLYN ACADEMY OF MUSIC

Opened Tuesday, April 3, 1973.*
The Chelsea Theater Center of Brooklyn presents the Iowa Theatre Lab in:

THE NAMING

Director, Ric Zank; Administrative Director, Gillian Richards

COMPANY

Kim Allen Bent
Harold Goodman
Deborah Gwinn
George Kon

* Closed Apr. 18, 1973 after limited engagement of 18 performances.

BROOKLYN ACADEMY OF MUSIC

Opened Thursday, April 19, 1973.*
The Chelsea Theater Center of Brooklyn presents El Teatro Campesino in:

LA CARPA DE LOS RASQUACHIS

("The Tent of the Underdogs") by the company; Director, Luis Valdez

COMPANY

Phil Esparza, Felix Alvarez, Alan Cruz, Roberta Esparza, Jesus Padron, Olivia Chumacero, Francis Romero, Carlos Acosta, Lily Mejia, Rogelio Rojas, Jose Delgado, Edward Robledo, Rosemary Apodaca

* Closed Apr. 29, 1973 after limited engagement of 10 performances.

CITY CENTER ACTING COMPANY

John Houseman, Artistic Director

Producing Directors, John Houseman, Margot Harley, Stephen Aaron; General Manager, John Bos; Production Manager, Joe Pacitti; Voice Consultant, Elizabeth Smith; Costumes Supervisor, John David Ridge; Press, Sol Jacobson, Lewis Harmon; Stage Manager, Tom Warner.

GOOD SHEPHERD—FAITH CHURCH
Opened Thursday, September 28, 1972.*
The City Center Acting Company presents in repertory:

THE SCHOOL FOR SCANDAL

By Richard Brinsley Sheridan; Director, Gerald Freedman; Settings, Douglas W. Schmidt; Lighting, Joe Pacitti; Music, Robert Waldman

CAST

Lady Sneerwell	Mary Lou Rosato
Snake	Sam Tsoutsouvas
Joseph Surface	David Ogden Stiers
Maria	Leah Chandler/Cindia Huppeler
Mrs. Candour	Cynthia Herman
Lady Crabtree	Anne McNaughton
Sir Benjamin Backbite	Gerald Shaw
Sir Peter Teazle	David Schramm
Rowley	Benjamin Hendrickson
Lady Teazle	Patti LuPone
Sir Oliver Surface	Norman Snow/Dakin Matthews
Moses	Jared Sakren
Charles Surface	Kevin Kline
Careless	Sam Tsoutsouvas
Servants	Leah Chandler, Cindia Huppeler, Dakin Matthews, James Moody, Mary Joan Negro

A Comedy in three acts and eight scenes.

GOOD SHEPHERD—FAITH CHURCH
Opened Sunday, October 1, 1972.*
The City Center Acting Company presents in repertory:

"U. S. A."

Adapted by Paul Shyre from the John Dos Passos novel of the same title; Director, Anne McNaughton; Costumes, John David Ridge; Lighting, Joe Pacitti

CAST

Player A	Norman Snow
Player B	Benjamin Hendrickson
Player C	James Moody
Player D	Mary Joan Negro
Player E	Leah Chandler
Player F	Mary Lou Rosato
Player G/Piano Player	Gerald Shaw

A Dramatic Revue in two acts.

GOOD SHEPHERD—FAITH CHURCH
Opened Tuesday, October 10, 1972.*
The City Center Acting Company presents in repertory:

THE HOSTAGE

By Brendan Behan; Director, Gene Lesser; Settings, Douglas W. Schmidt; Costumes, Carrie F. Robbins; Lighting, Joe Pacitti; Musical Director, Roland Gagnon; Dance Consultant, Elizabeth Keen

CAST

Pat	Dakin Matthews
Meg Dillon	Mary Lou Rosato/Anne McNaughton
Monsewer	David Ogden Stiers
Colette	Anne McNaughton/Patti LuPone
Ropeen	Cindia Huppeler
Princess Grace	Benjamin Hendrickson
Rio Rita	James Moody
Mr. Mulleady	Sam Tsoutsouvas
Miss Gilchrist	Cynthia Herman
Leslie	Norman Snow
Theresa	Mary Joan Negro
Volunteer	Jared Sakren
I.R.A. Officer	Kevin Kline
Piano Player	Gerald Shaw
Kathleen	Patti LuPone
Police Officer	David Schramm

A Comedy in two acts. The action takes place in a lodging house in Dublin.

Diane Gorodnitzki Photos

134

David Ogden Stiers, Patti LuPone in "School for Scandal"
Below: Leah Chandler, Norman Snow, Mary Lou Rosa in "U.S.A."

Mary Lou Rosato, Cynthia Herman, Dakin Matthew David Ogden Stiers in "The Hostage"

OD SHEPHERD—FAITH CHURCH
Opened Tuesday, October 17, 1972.*
The City Center Acting Company presents in repertory:

WOMEN BEWARE WOMEN

By Thomas Middleton; Director, Michael Kahn; Settings, Douglas W.
hmidt; Costumes, John David Ridge; Lighting, Joe Pacitti; Musical
pervision, Martin Verdrager; Choreography, William Burdick

CAST

e Widow	Anne McNaughton
antio	David Schramm
anca	Mary Joan Negro/Patti LuPone
uardiano	Kevin Kline
britio	Dakin Matthews
via	Mary Lou Rosato
ppolito	Sam Tsoutsouvas
bella	Leah Chandler
e Ward	Norman Snow/Gerald Shaw
rdido	Jared Sakren
ke of Florence	David Ogden Stiers
rd Cardinal	Benjamin Hendrickson
diers, Attendants	Cynthia Herman, Patti LuPone, James Moody, Gerald Shaw

A Drama in three acts. The action takes place in Florence.

OD SHEPHERD—FAITH CHURCH
Opened Tuesday, October 24, 1972.*
The City Center Acting Company presents in repertory:

THE LOWER DEPTHS

By Maxim Gorky; Adapted by Alex Szogyi; Director, Boris Tumarin;
ting, Douglas W. Schmidt; Costumes, John David Ridge; Lighting, Joe
citti; Musical Direction, Gerald Shaw; Accordion, William Schimmel

CAST

stilyov	Jared Sakren
silissa	Cynthia Herman
tasha	Patti LuPone
dvedyev	Tom Henschel
ska Pepel	Kevin Kline
eshch	Benjamin Hendrickson
na	Leah Chandler
stya	Mary Joan Negro
ashnya	Mary Lou Rosato
bnov	Dakin Matthews
ron	David Ogden Stiers
in	Sam Tsoutsouvas
tor	Norman Snow
ka	David Schramm
yoshka	Gerald Shaw
rtar	James Moody

A Drama in two acts. The action takes place in a flophouse in a
vincial town in Russia at the turn of the century.

OD SHEPHERD—FAITH CHURCH
Opened Sunday, October 22, 1972.*
The City Center Acting Company presents in repertory:

NEXT TIME I'LL SING TO YOU

By James Saunders; Director, Marian Seldes; Costumes, John David
dge; Lighting, Joe Pacitti

CAST

ff	Benjamin Hendrickson
st	Norman Snow
zie	Patti LuPone
dge	David Schramm
rmit	Jared Sakren

A Comedy in two acts.
Closed Nov. 4, 1972 after limited engagement of 39 performances in
epertory for a national tour.

(no photos available)

**David Schramm, Mary Jane Negro
in "Women Beware Women"**
(Diane Gorodnitzki Photo)

**Leah Chandler, Ben Hendrickson
in "The Lower Depths"**
(Stephen Aaron Photo)

THE CUBICULO

Philip Meister, Artistic Director
Elaine Sulka, Managing Director
Maurice Edwards, Program Director

August 10—19, 1972
(12 performances)
AFTER WE EAT THE APPLE, WE WHAT? by Henry C. Fanelli; Directors, Marcia Rodd, Keith Charles; Set and Costumes, Danny Morgan; Lighting, R. S. Winkler; Stage Managers, Keith Robinson, Diana Buckhantz. CAST: Will Sharpe Marshall or John Bennet Perry (Neil), William Wise (Alex), John Towey (Wes), Jeanne Lucas (Angela), Rei Golenor (Fiona)

THE CUBICULO
October 18—November 4, 1972
(12 performances)
A PHOENIX TOO FREQUENT by Christopher Fry; Director, Gail Kellstrom; Producers, Kate Webster, Gail Kellstrom. CAST: Kate Webster, Grant Sheehan, Susan Walker

October 19—November 4, 1972
(12 performances)
TWO RARE COMEDIES by George Bernard Shaw; Director, Maurice Edwards; Producer, Nicholas John Stathis; Set, Herb Kaufman; Costumes, Jennifer von Mayrhauser, Sue A. Robbins; Music Adviser, George Prideaux; Stage Managers, James O'Leary, Charles Tyndall; English Consultant, Moira Hodgson. THE MUSIC-CURE with Jim Blanton (Doctor), Alan Howard (Reginald), Dorothy Opalach (Lady), PRESS CUTTINGS with Gerald E. McGonagill (Mitchener), Saylor Creswell (Orderly), John LeGrand (Balsquith), Eda Reiss Merin (Mrs. Farrell), Gretel Cummings (Mrs. Banger), Joan Langue (Lady Corinthia)

November 8—11, 1972
(4 performances)
"OH" translated from Swedish by Goran Printz-Pahlson and Brian Rothwell; Speakies by Sandro Key-Aberg; Director, Bob Horen; Designed by Jay B. Keene; Choreography, Cecilia Rice; Lighting, Richard Tsukada; Audio, Jeff Palmer, Ramon Martinez; Presented by The Gold Mask of Adelphi University; Executive Producers, Marilyn Murphy, Barbara Dempsey. CAST: Sean Britt, Barbara Goldberg, Susan Harbour, Martha Heenan, Jay Schildhaus, Richard Sorenson

November 9—25, 1972
(12 performances)
THE ENTREPRENEURS OF AVENUE B by Jack Gilhooley; Director, Clinton J. Atkinson; Set, Richard Williams; Lighting, Peter Casanave; Stage Manager, Michael McMahon. CAST: Alex Colon (Jose), Linda Robbins (Catharine), Jay Hargrove (Sammy)

November 15—25, 1972
(9 performances)
DEATH WISH by T. Frank Gutswa; Director, James Howe; Lighting, Daniel Adams; Stage Manager, Joan Ceriello; Slides, Peter Rockwell; Songs, Penny Hess. CAST: Nancy J. Yost (Grandmother), Charles McKenna (Billy), Penny Hess (Mary), Yusef Bulos (Analyst), Carolyn Michel (Teacher), Bobby Farrell (Young Billy), Deborah Franklin (Barbara)

November 29—December 2, 1972
(4 performances)
THE HUMAN VOICE by Jean Cocteau, with Deborah Jowitt; LA VOIX HUMAINE an opera by Francis Poulenc and Jean Cocteau, with Sheryl King; Musical Director, Judith Houchins; Director, Clinton J. Atkinson; Sets and Lighting, James Singelis; Stage Manager, Richard S. Viola

John Towey, William Wise, John Bennett Perry
in "After We Eat the Apple. . . ."
Below: Gretel Cummings,
Gerald E. McGonagill in "Press Cuttings"

January 12—28, 1973
(10 performances)
NIGHTBIRDS by Andy Milligan; Director, Andy Milligan; Lighting, William Lambert; Stage Manager, Eddie Elias. CAST: Michael Chioc (Dink), Luanne Rohrbacher (Dee), Sharita Hunt (Waitress), Joe Dow ing (Bernie), Laurell Brodie (Mabel), Carol Silverstein (Girl 1), Dav Plummer (Tom), Marian Swan (Mother), Anthony Bertolino (Boy)

January 18—February 4, 1973
(12 performances)
THE GARBAGE COLLECTORS by Frank Steinkellner; Directo Chris Thomas; Sets, Tom Williams; Lighting, Daniel Flannery; Co tumes, Dorothy Bitetto. CAST: Fran Reichin (Lois), Ray Barry (Bob Walter Mantani (Furniture Mover/National Guardsman), Jack Cornwe (Furniture Mover/National Guardsman/Policeman), Pinocchio Madr (Announcer/National Guardsman), Greg Langdon (Announcer/N tional Guardsman)

February 3—18, 1973
(16 performances)
BRIDEGROOM OF DEATH–A CEREMONY OF REMEMBRANC based upon and freely adapted from a play of the same title by Roc Kenyon; Director, Richard A. Rubin; Lighting, Deborah Ann Gorelic Costumes, Felipe Gorostiza; Set, Marc Rosenfeld; Audio, D. Raich Assistant to Director, Joseph Ruben; Stage Manager, James O'Lear Choreographer, Stafford Lyons. CAST: Christopher Ballant (Blind Mus cian), Billy Casper (Death), Christopher Claremont (Stranger), George Coates (King of the Netherworld), Ron Duda (Man), Pete Emo (Farmer), Frank Fabbricatore (Boy), Dean Haglin (Father), Job Hic (Warrior), Jonathan Luria (Thief), Brian Lynner (Poet), Stafford Lyo (Weaver), Edward Malley (Soldier), Lynne Moss (Old Lady), Pa McCarren (Monk), Carolee Palmiotto (Geisha), Martha Rand (Gir Douglas Simes (Priest), Salvatore Trapani (Politician), Linda Var (Bride), Katherine Wright (Mother)

Alan Howard, Dorothy Opalach
in "The Music Cure"

136

Conrad Ward Photos

THE CUBICULO

February 9—25, 1973
(9 performances)
CASSANDRA AND AARON by Abigail Quart; Director, Arthur Pellman; Set, Kathi Kennedy; Costumes, Sara Quart; Statues, Sue Kaplan; Lighting, Jeremy Lewis; Props and Stage Manager, Henrie Benin. CAST: Ann Stanchfield (Cassandra), Tennessee Baywaters (Aaron), Neal Poole (Paris)

March 2—4, 1973
(3 performances)
WHAT IS MIME AND IF YOU KNOW WHAT MIME IS, WHAT IS PANTOMIME? with Gabriel Oshen and Dan Kamin; Lighting, Richard Tsukada

March 8—11, 1973
(4 performances)
CONDITION OF SHADOW conceived and performed by Jerry Rockwood; A characterization of Edgar Allan Poe; Music Composed and Performed by Thomas Wilt; Lights, Marian Z. Murphy, Voice, Barnard Hughes; Stage Manager, Bob Steiger

March 15—April 1, 1973
(12 performances)
PIGEONS by Edward Friedman; Director, Alfred Gingold; Set and Lighting, Will Owen; Assistant Director, Amy Brill. CAST: John Broglio (Bobby), Brenda Currin (Alice)

March 9—April 1, 1973
(12 performances)
THE SWEET ENEMY by Joyce Carol Oates; Director, Maurice Edwards; Producer, Nicholas John Stathis; Music, Jacob Stern; Set, Richard Hoover; Lighting, Peter M. Ehrhardt; Costumes, Nancy Baron; Props, Sue Kaplan. CAST: Robert Judd, Toni Kalem, Rich Partlow, Norman Temple, Gary Baker, Lynne Moss, Anthony Neat

April 19—28, 1973
(7 performances)
TWO BY STANLEY NELSON directed by Larry Nadell; Designed by Diane DiMartino; Production Supervisor, Jim Woolley; Choreography, Carole Schweid; Lighting, Bill Lambert; Stage Manager, Jimmy Salvato. THE POETRY READING with Tom Eleopoulos (Douglas), Arva Holt (Fargo), Rebecca Keen (Mrs. Ganch), Gail Osiecki (Susan), Molly Scole (Barbara) SHUFFLE OFF with William Hunter (Husband), Rebecca Keen (Wife)

May 3—12, 1973
(6 performances)
SONG OF SARA with Book and Music by Daniel Jahn; Based on "Sara Teasdale, A Biography" by Margaret Harley Carpenter, and poems of Sara Teasdale; Director, Anthony Ristoff; Choreography, John Carbone; Accompanist, Daniel Jahn; Production Coordinator, Ronald K. Searcy; Lighting Assistant, Orrin Jay Hill; Stage Manager, Mark Smith. CAST: Anne Beauvais, Dorothy Pietracatella, Nancy Szabo (Singers), Jennifer Low, Anthony Ristoff (Narrators)

May 10—19, 1973
(6 performances)
I'M NOT JEWISH AND I DON'T KNOW WHY I'M SCREAMING by Stan Lachow; Director, Quinton Raines; Set, Hirotsugu Aoki; Lighting, Charles Tyndall; Stage Manager, Jim O'Leary; Production Crew Manager, William Covan. CAST: Stan Lachow (Gerald Lefko), Julia Pongret or Peggy Lettier (Carol Lefko), Tedra Klein (Mother), Liz Getty (Aunt Fanny), Brenda J. Scott (Avon Lady)

May 17—June 2, 1973
(12 performances)
TONTO by Guy Gauthier; Director, Frederick Bailey; with Tom Donaldson (Lone Ranger), Elmo Laurence Clark (Tonto), Chip Brenner (Harvey Miller), Robert Ari (Dutch), Steve Sacco (Doc Morrison), Jack Gilbert (Willy)

MAGIC TIME by William Kushner; Director, Frederick Bailey; with William Kushner (Miss Victoria)

OARSHOCK by Christopher Mathewson; Director, James Gara; Sets, Victor Poleri; Sound, Marc Howard; Costumes, Richard Rice; Lights and Stage Manager, Cynthia Urban; with James Gara (Speaker), Shan Willson (Fifelet), Robert Ari (Hubbie), Kathleen Seward (Model)

May 25—June 9, 1973
(11 performances)
HONOR by Richard Foreman; Director, Mr. Forman; with Jessica Harper, Bill Madden, Amy Taubin

TO CHILDREN SLOWLY by Arthur Sainer; Director, Marjorie Melnick; Music, David Tice; Lyrics, Arthur Sainer; Masks, Ralph Lee; Lights, Charles Tyndall; with Faith Greenfield (Dansity), Lisa Carling (Hot Corners)

April 30 & May 1, 1973
(2 performances)
THE MASK AND MIME THEATRE with Jack Hill and Graciela Daraghi; Lighting, Richard Tsukada; Stage Manager, Anthony Policella

Top Right: Ann Stanchfield, Neal Poole in "Cassandra and Aaron" *(Bob Burns Photo)*

Below: John Broglio, Brenda Currin in "Pigeons"
(Edward Friedman Photo)

Robert Judd, Rick Partlow, Toni Kalem in "The Sweet Enemy"
(Conrad Ward Photo)

137

EQUITY LIBRARY THEATRE PRODUCTIONS

George Wojtasik, Managing Director
Thirtieth Season

NEW YORK PUBLIC LIBRARY AT LINCOLN CENTER
October 16, 17, 18, 1973
Equity Library Theatre Informal presents:

THE WRONG SIDE OF THE MOON

By Ron McLarty; Director, Patrick Reaves; Sets and Lights, Satoshi Ono

CAST

Jack	Brendan Fay
Anne	Pat Disbrow
Howey	Greg Doucette
Ginny	Sarah Harris
Norm	Richard Bowden

(No photos available)

MASTER THEATRE
Opened Thursday, December 7, 1972.*
Equity Library Theatre presents:

IN WHITE AMERICA

By Martin Duberman; Director, Russell Treyz; Musical Director, William Boswell; Sets, Richard Williams; Lighting, Terry Gilbertson; Costumes, Karen Eifert, Robert Anderson; Percussionist, Babafumi Akunyun

CAST

Anthony Call
Yolanda Karr
Gail Kellstrom
Leonard Parker
Casper Roos
Count Stovall
Toby Tompkins

Press: Lewis Harmon, Sol Jacobson
Stage Managers: Ray Parker, Zoya A. Khachadourian

* Closed Dec. 17, 1972 after limited engagement of 12 performances.

MASTER THEATRE
Opened Thursday, October 19, 1972.*
Equity Library Theatre presents:

THE MAID'S TRAGEDY

By Francis Beaumont and John Fletcher; Director, Clinton J. A son; Masque Staged and Choreographed by Deborah Jowitt; Set, Brown; Costumes, Karen Eifert; Lighting, Phyllis Mortimer; Props Soner; Masque Costumes, Dean Brown; Duel Staged by Erick U Sound, Sanda Kayden; Production Director, Lynn Montgomery; Te cal Director, George Turski

CAST

Cleon	Wayne Shar
Lysippus	Barry Je
Diphilus	Kerry W
Strato	Mitchell Edm
Melantius	Richard
Amintor	Ronald Kuhl
Diagoras	Dennis Sou
Calianax	Seamus O'
King	Micheal Du
Evadne	Susan Sar
Aspatia	Tiffany He
Dula	Anne Ash
Vittoria Corombona	Kitty
Pompiona	Haes
Bel-Imperia	Carol
Antiphila	Barbara Lee Go
Olimpias	Lynn MacG
Gentlemen	J. H. Sharp, Craig K
Servant to Melantius	Rod
"The Masque"	
Night	Linnea
Cynthia	Lynn MacG
Neptune	Kerry W
Aeolus	Rod
Winds	Kitty Chen, Haes Hill, Carol K
Lutenist	Marc Pre

A Drama in two acts. The action takes place at the Court of Rh

Press: Sol Jacobson, Lewis Harmon
Stage Manager: Bernard Uhlfelder

* Closed Oct. 29, 1972 after limited engagement of 12 performan

**Top: Richard Kuss, Ron Kuhlman in "The Maid
Tragedy"**
**Left Center: Leonard Parker, Gail Kellstrom in "
America" White**

(Gene Coleman Photos)

Opened Thursday, November 9, 1972.*
Equity Library Theatre (George Wojtasik, Managing Director)
presents:

HOW TO SUCCEED IN BUSINESS WITHOUT REALLY TRYING

Book, Abe Burrows, Jack Weinstock, Willie Gilbert; Based on book by
Shepherd Mead; Music and Lyrics, Frank Loesser; Directed and Choreo-
graphed by Joe Davis; Musical Director, Fred Goldrich; Scenery, Jim
Stewart; Lighting, Gregg Marriner; Costumes, Audrey Arnsdorf; Sound,
David Fleisher; Pianist, John R. Williams; Percussionist, Edward G.
Zacko; Technical Director, George Turski

CAST

Finch	Chip Zien
Gatch	Hal Blankenship
Jenkins	Paul Geier
Tackaberry	Ted Theoharous
Peterson	James Galvin
J. B. Biggley	Bob Allen
Rosemary	Jacquie Ullendorf
Bratt	Raf Michaels
Smitty	Carole Schweid
Frump	Michael Sklar
Miss Jones	Eleanore Knapp
Mr. Twimble	George Emch
Hedy	Joy Claussen
Scrubwomen	Nita Novy, Marsha Warner
Miss Krumholtz	Karen Good
Ovington	Stanley Debel
Policeman	Robert Anderson
Womper	George Emch
Voice of the Book	George Emch

DANCERS: Robert Anderson, Jerry Brian, Elayne Kulaya, Virginia
MacColl, Nita Novy, Gail Oscar, William Pironti, Marsha Warner

MUSICAL NUMBERS: "How To," "Happy to Keep His Dinner
Warm," "Coffee Break," "The Company Way," "A Secretary Is Not a
Toy," "Been a Long Day," "Grand Old Ivy," "Paris Original," "Rose-
mary," "Cinderella, Darling," "Love from a Heart of Gold," "I Believe
You," "Brotherhood of Man," Finale

A Musical Comedy in two acts. The action takes place in the new Park
Avenue office building of World Wide Wicket Co., Inc.

Production Director: Lynn Montgomery
Press: Lewis Harmon, Sol Jacobson
Stage Managers: Robert Charles, Richard Neville, Jim Woolley,
Ellen Faison, Larry Costa

Closed Nov. 26, 1972 after limited engagement of 19 performances.

Gene Coleman Photo

Top Right: Joy Claussen, Michael Sklar

Matthew Tobin, Tracy Phelps, Laura Dean

Opened Thursday, January 11, 1973.*
Equity Library Theatre presents:

THE SECRET LIFE OF WALTER MITTY

Book, Joe Manchester; Based on Story by James Thurber; Lyrics, Earl
Shuman; Music, Leon Carr; Director, Jerry Grant; Musical Director,
John R. Williams; Choreography, John Montgomery; Sets, Jimmy
Cuomo; Lighting, Steve Loew; Costumes, Linda De Rosa; Props, Susan
Kaplan; Pianist, John R. Williams; Percussionist, Edward G. Zacko

CAST

Tenor	Dan Kruger
MacMillan	Joel Eagon
Walter Mitty	Matthew Tobin
Agnes Mitty	Tracey Phelps
Peninnah Mitty	Laura Dean
Head Nurse	Nancy Trumbo
Dr. Renshaw	Don Croll
Dr. Benbow	Dan Kruger
Prof. Remington	Daniel Brown
Dr. Pritchard-Mitford	Glen McClaskey
Harry	Stewart Craig Wood
Ruthie	Barbara Erwin
Willa	Jo Ann Lehmann
Irving	Doug Jeffers
Fred Gorman	Frank Moon
Hazel	Marsha Warner
Crepe Suzette	Marsha Zamoida
Tortoni	Donna Maria Sorbello
Apple Turnover	Nancy Trumbo
Fortune Cookie	Lori Chinn
Juvenile Delinquent	Don Croll
Nymphomaniac	Marsha Zamoida
Sylvia	Lori Chinn

MUSICAL NUMBERS: "The Secret Life," "Walter Mitty March,"
"Walking with Pininnah," "Drip, Drop, Tapocketa," "Aggie," "Don't
Forget," "Marriage Is for Old Folks," "Hello, I Love You, Goodbye,"
"Strip Number," "Willa," "Confidence," "Telephone Number," "The
New Walter Mitty," "Two Little Pussycats," "Fan the Flame," "Now
that I'm Forty," "She's Talking out Her Problems," "You're Not,"
"Lonely Ones," Finale

A Musical in two acts. The action takes place at the present time in
Waterbury, Conn., in the everyday and secret life of Walter Mitty.

Press: Sol Jacobson, Lewis Harmon
Stage Managers: Eve Sorel, Peter Cambariere, Barbara Gorman

* Closed Jan. 28, 1973 after limited engagement of 19 performances.

NEW YORK PUBLIC LIBRARY AT LINCOLN CENTER
December 11, 12, 13, 1973
Equity Library Theatre Informal presents:

THE APPLE TREE

Music, Jerry Bock; Lyrics, Sheldon Harnick; Book, Messers Harnick, Boch, Jerome Coopersmith; Director, Al Settimio; Musical Direction, Don Mannon; Set and Costumes, Margaret Tobin; "Forbidden Fruit" staged by Judith Haskell; Stage Manager, Blair Kersten; Props, Laurie Hudson

CAST

Adam	Michael Petro
Eve	Pamela Hall
Snake	Paul Keith

MUSICAL NUMBERS: "Beautiful, Beautiful World," "Here in Eden," "Feelings," "This Eve," "Friends," "Forbidden Fruit," "It's a Fish," "Go to Sleep Whatever You Are," "What Makes Me Love Him?" (No photos available)

MASTER THEATRE
Opened Thursday, February 8, 1973.*
Equity Library Theatre presents:

THUNDER ROCK

By Robert Ardrey; Director, Stephen Book; Set, T. Winberry; Costumes, Lorie Watson; Props, Jody Steiger; Sound, Bill O'Dell; Hairstylist, Larry Costa

CAST

Streeter	Arlen Dean Snyder
Nonny	Ron Paul Little
Inspector Flanning	Peter Carew
Charleston	Dempster Leech
Capt. Joshua	Benjamin H. Slack
Briggs	Ken Tigar
Dr. Stefan Kurtz	Bruce Hall
Melanie	Ellin Ruskin
Miss Kirby	Virginia Downing
Anne Marie	Eunice Anderson
Chang	John Batson
Cassidy	Ed Oster

A Drama in three acts. The action takes place before the Second World War in a lighthouse on Thunder Rock, a speck of an island in northern Lake Michigan.

Press: Lewis Harmon, Sol Jacobson
Stage Managers: Ed Oster, John Batson

* Closed Feb. 18, 1973 after limited engagement of 12 performances.

Ellin Ruskin, Ben Slack, Eunice Anderson
in "Thunder Rock"

(Gene Coleman Photo)

NEW YORK PUBLIC LIBRARY AT LINCOLN CENTER
February 26, 27, 28, 1973
Equity Library Theatre Informal presents:

TWO ONE-ACT PLAYS

By A. R. Gurney, Jr.; Director, Saylor Creswell; Designer, Jennifer Von Mayrhauser; Stage Manager, Douglas Drew

CAST

"The Golden Fleece"

Betty	Carolee Campbell
Bill	Jay Bell

"The Love Course"

Sally	Susan Harney
Prof. Burgess	Ray Thorne
Mike	Tom Smink
Prof. Carroway	Sue Lawless

(No photos available)

MASTER THEATRE
Opened Thursday, March 8, 1973.*
Equity Library Theatre presents:

OUT OF THIS WORLD

Music and Lyrics, Cole Porter; Book, George Oppenheimer; Based on a Libretto by Dwight Taylor and Reginald Lawrence; Director, Richard Michaels; Chorography, Carole Schweid; Setting, Ken Lewis; Costumes, Gerry Leahy; Lighting, George Turski; Hairstylist, Larry Costa; Pianist, Lee Gillespie; Harpist, Patricia A. Scott; Percussionist, Mark Owen

CAST

Mercury	Joel Craig
Venus/Night	Barbara Monte-Britton
Mars/Mr. Ward	Michael Serrecchia
Minerva/Leda	Lana Caradima
Baccus/Strephon	Paul Latchaw
Ceres/Chloe	Gail Johnston
Diana/Helen	Marsha Kramer
Apollo/Jeff	Ward Smith
Jupiter	Kenneth Cory
Juno	Joy Franz

MUSICAL NUMBERS: "High Flyin' Wings on My Shoes," "I, Jupiter I, Rex," "A Woman's Career," "Time-Passage," "Cherry Pies Ought to Be You," "From This Moment On," "Where Oh Where," "The Couldn't Compare to You," "No Lover," "You're the Prize Guy of Guys," "When Your Troubles Have Started," "I Could Kick Myself, "Night Ballet," "Nobody's Chasing Me," "I Am Loved," "Climb up the Mountain," "You Don't Remind Me," "Use Your Imagination," Finale

A Musical Comedy in two acts. The action takes place Then and Now on Heaven and Earth.

Press: Sol Jacobson, Lewis Harmon
Stage Managers: Susan K. Robison, Sally Hassenfelt, Jimmy Salvato, Jeffrey Campbell

* Closed Mar. 25, 1973 after limited engagement of 19 performances.

Ward Smith, Kenneth Cory, Marsha Kramer
in "Out of This World" *(Gene Coleman Photo)*

DINNER AT THE AMBASSADOR'S

By Michael O'Reilly; Director, Charles Maggiore; Set, Ara Soner; Lighting, Guy Smith, Frank Verocca; Stage Managers, R. V. Pivirotto, Rebecca Reed

CAST

Deirdre Collins	Katherine Bruce
Margo	Uta Hofmann
Ambassador	Bryant Simms
Aunt Dolly	Carolyn Chrisman
Jacky	Alex Molina
Walter	Francis Barnard
Milton O'Brien	Jay Fletcher
Freddie Simmons	Tony Thomas

(No photos available)

MASTER THEATRE
Opened Thursday, April 5, 1973.*
Equity Library Theatre presents:

SUMMER BRAVE

By William Inge; Originally presented as "Picnic"; Director, Ian Wilder; Scenery, Robert Joyner; Costumes, Joyce Aysta; Lighting, Jerold Richland; Sound, Bill O'Dell; Millinery, Vivian Kraft; Production Assistants, Dennis Haber, Eileen Schneider, David Tambini, Marla Freedman, Myra French, Gregory Pellitteri; Hairstylist, Larry Costa; Technical Director, George Turski

CAST

Millie Owens	Faith Catlin
Bomber McCullough, newsboy	Bill Cwikowski
Bomber	Jon Banks
Geano	Ron Paul Little
Madge Owens	Judy Fields
Alan Seymour	Rod Gibbons
Flo Owens	Dolores Kenan
Hal Carter	Edward Easton
Rosemary Sydney	Fran Anthony
Helen Potts	Ruth Russell
Irma Kronkite	Barbara Boyle
Christine Schoenwalder	Mary Cass
Howard Bevans	Mordecai Lawner
Baker	Steve Scott

A Play in three acts. The action takes place in a small Kansas town, few years ago, around the Owens' home.

Press: Lewis Harmon, Sol Jacobson
Stage Managers: Donald Walters, John J. D. Sheehan, Steve Scott

Closed Apr. 16, 1973 after limited engagement of 14 performances.

REFLECTIONS OF PORGY AND BESS AND CARMEN JONES

Music, George Gershwin, George Bizet; Lyrics, Dubose Heyward and Ira Gershwin, Oscar Hammerstein II; Accompanist, Shirley Seguin; Narrated by Karl Gipson

CAST

Dolores Bauer
Karl Gipson

(No photos available)

Top Right: Mordecai Lawner, Edward Easton, Rod Gibbons in "Summer Brave"
Below: Renee Orin, Randy Phillips,
Greg Macosko, Helon Blount in "Riverwind"

Gene Coleman Photos

MASTER THEATRE
Opened Thursday, May 3, 1973.*
Equity Library Theatre presents:

RIVERWIND

Book, Music, and Lyrics by John Jennings; Director, Jeff Hamlin; Musical Director, Danny Troob; Additional Choreography, Lynne Gannaway; Set, Bill Stabile; Lighting, Cheryl Thacker; Costumes, Cheryl Lovett; Pianist, John R. Williams; Percussionist, Edward G. Zacko; Sound, Cliff Nicholas

CAST

Mrs. Farrell	Helon Blount
Jenny Farrell	Marty Morris
Virginia	Lynn Grossman
Burt	Stephan Mark Weyte
John Stone	Greg Macosko
Louise Sumner	Renee Orin
Dr. Fred Sumner	Randy Phillips

A Musical in two acts. The action takes place at the present time at Riverwind, a "Tourist Rest" on the banks of the Wabash River in Indiana.

Press: Sol Jacobson, Lewis Harmon
Stage Managers: Jeffrey Dunn, Bill Ownbey, Lesley Barthell

* Closed May 20, 1973 after limited engagement of 19 performances.

ROOMERS

By Peter Gorman; Director, Eve Sorel; Sets and Costumes, Pat Gorman; Lighting, H. Gabriel Kuivila II; Stage Managers, John J. D. Sheehan, Barbara Gorman

CAST

Young Man	Gregory Lehane
Young Woman	Clare Waugh
Old Woman	Janine Cooper
Old Man	Everett Jacobson

(no photos available)

THE NEW DRAMATISTS INC.

September 21–23, 1972 (3 performances)
RITES OF PASSAGE by Rose Leiman Goldemberg; Director, Ted Weiant; Set, Stephen Askinazay; Assistant Stage Manager, Steven Dubey; Props, Ellen Foloy. CAST: Richard Fancy (Charles), Davida Manning (Louisa), Jane Ranzman (Looey), Edith Greenfield (Crys), Jane Marla Robbins (Louisa at 31), Susan Rockower (Louisa at 24), Debbie White (Louisa at 19), Lorelle Brownell (Ideal Louisa), Lisa Schiller (Looey at 5)

September 28–30, 1972 (3 performances)
HEYDAY by Herbert Appleman; Based on Ring Lardner's "I Can't Breathe"; Director, Herbert Appleman; Choreographer, Carole Schweid; Musical Direction, Fred Goldrich; Set, William Stabile; Lighting, William Dreisbach; Stage Manager, Jeanne Fornadel. CAST: Tandy Cronyn (Alva), Michael Sklar (Dr. Walter Barnes), Nancy Franklin (Julia), Jess Adkins (Nat), George Guidall (Merle), Rick Seer (Young Caswell), David Christmas (Gordon), Lorry Goldman (Frank), Mark Schaffnit (Clerk), Jeremy Lawrence (Page), Dana Kyle, Jackie Muth, Shary Seltzer,

Melinda Tanner (Girls), James Hackett, Jeremy Lawrence, Mark Schaffnit, Rick Seer (Boys)

October 5–7, 1972 (3 performances)
SKIPPING by David Trainer; Director, Fritz Holt. CAST: Audre Johnston (Stephanie), Corinne Niox-Chateau (Daisy), Helen Noyes (Miss Dow), Joseph Boley (Stanley), Michael Sacks (Samuel), Paul Lipson (Max), Clay Watkins (Mike)

THE ELIZABETHANS by Sidney Michaels; Directed by the author; Songs, Sandy Rapp; Choreography, Bert Michaels; Lighting, David Manning; Stage Managers, Edward Strum, Ed Moran; Masks, Shozo Nagano; Lighting, Mark J. Kurlansky; Sound, Jeff Peters. CAST: John Cullum (Shakespeare), Delphi Lawrence (Queen Elizabeth), Jack Hollander (Ben Johnson), Audre Johnston (Anne Hathaway), John Costopoulos (Earl of Southampton), Peter Brouwer (Earl of Essex), Gordon Hammett (Dr. Lopez), Charles Maggiore (Burleigh/Burbage), Steven Dubey (Christopher Marlowe/Cecil), Berlinda Tolbert (Lucy Morgan), Jacqueline Bertrand (Countess of Southampton), Eileen Dietz (Judith/Hamnet), Connie Forslund (Susanna), Erin Connor (Mary Fitton), Michael Donaghue (Greene/Poley), Sharon Shayne (Penny/Wench), Roger Howell (Sir Walter Raleigh), Clay Watkins (Drayton), Chris Anastasio (Ingram/Singer), Kevin Corbett (Nicolas), Frank Rohrbach (Dick Field), Michael Toles (Cock Fighter/Young Poet), Stephen Deghelder (Cock Fighter), Jeff Peters (Walsingham), Candia Michaels (Orange Girl), Cotter Michaels (Young Prince/Drummer Boy), John Forster (Actor/Soldier), Sandy Rapp (Troubadour)

November 24–25, 1972 (2 performances)
THE FORTUNE HUNTERS by Herbert Appleman; Directed by the author; Lighting, David Manning. CAST: Nancy Pinkerton (Roe), Sharon Shayne (Sandy), Peter Brouwer (David), Ruth Baker (Mrs. Hall), Mark J. Kurlansky (Burt), Philip Sterling (Mr. Hall), Edith Greenfield (Florence), James Secrest (Ralph)

November 30, December 1–2, 1972 (3 performances)
TODAY WE KILLED MOLLY BLOOM by Eric Thompson; Director, Roger Hendricks Simon; Associate Director, John Beary; Lighting, Scott Johnson; Stage Managers, Anita Siegel, Howard Kuperberg. CAST: Matthew Joplin (James), Jeanne Ruskin (Sharon), Roger Hendricks Simon (Joseph), Arnold Johnson (Peter), Gil Rogers (William), Eva Lawrence (Oona), Joan Shepard (A Woman), Edward A. Dowling (Various Newsmakers)

Philip Bruns, Dick Pardy in "In the Beginning"
Top Right: Barbara McMahon, Humbert Allen Astredo,
Tom Sawyer in "Ghost Dance" *(Eugene Netzer Photos)*

142

Friday, December 8, 1972 (1 performance)
THE RABINOWITZ GAMBIT by Rose Leiman Goldemberg; Director, Richard Fancy. CAST: Reuben Schafer (Irfing Rabinowitz), Jeff Pe (Blitz), Jeremy Lawrence (Jerry), Audre Johnston (Niele), Barry Mic (Etcetera)

Monday, December 11, 1972 (1 performance)
THE RED BLUE-GRASS WESTERN FLYER SHOW by Conn Fl ing; Music by Richard Foltz. CAST: John Leighton (Big Emmit), Ei Lawlor (Emma Lou), Dolph Armstrong (Scotty), Virginia Down (Hattie) Polly Holiday (Dolly), Rex Robbins (Arlen), John Canema (Stage Directions), Carol Watkins (guitar)

Monday, December 18, 1972 (1 performance)
TOUSSAINT by Barry Berg; Director, Aldo Bonura. CAST: J McCurry (Black Narrator), Romola Robb Allrud (Mama Leger), Sha Shayne (Pamela), Janice Kent (Suzanne), David Beckman (Father cent), Stephen Hotchner (White Narrator), Laurence Watson (Raymo /Telemaque), L. Basil Gray (Gen. Christophe), Paul Knowles (C LaPlume), Palmer Deane (Toussaint), Leonard Parker (Gen. Dessalir Anthony Call (Gen. LeClerc), Maxine Boreau (Pauline), Art Vasil (C Rochambeau), Fields Curtis (Placide), Joseph Mydell (Isaac)

Friday, January 19, 1973 (1 performance)
WORLDS by Frieda Lipp; Director, Peter Weil; Lighting, Step Harty. CAST: Audre Johnston (Gloria), Palmer Deane (Lewis), D Berrings (Art), Susan Gilliss (Joan), Leslie Rivers (Brenda) Charlet O ley (Mrs. Stillman), Eli Levine (Mrs. Stillman), Saundra Sharp (Syl Anita Sorels (Ruth), Jeff Peters (Larry)

February 1–5, 1973 (5 performances)
IN THE BEGINNING by Edward Freenberg; Director, Seymour V Lighting, Stephen Harty; Stage Managers, Dennis Drew, Helene Ka Liatsos; Props, Carol Frederick, Lighting, Dean Agrivides. CAST: Ph Bruns (Harry), Adelle Reel (Clara), Dick Pardy (Lenny), John Herz (Rafe), Sarah Harris (Debbie), Berlinda Tolbert (Tina), Corinne N Chateau (Mildred), Roger Howell (Michael/Louis), Richard N (Ben/Joe), Jerry McGee (George/Irwin)

Thursday, February 8, 1973 (1 performance)
THE OFF SEASON by Harding Lemay. CAST: Roy Shuman (Bi Eileen Dietz (Sharon), Constance Ford (Caroline), Richard Niles (Cle Marian Seldes (Arline), Addison Powell (Kingsley)

March 13–17, 1973 (5 performances)
KINDLY OBSERVE THE PEOPLE by Barry Berg; Director, C Anderson; Lighting, Michael Farrell; Stage Managers, John Bat Carol Frederick; Costume Consultant, David James; Scenic Consult M. Imhof. CAST: Lisa Schiller (Lisa), Peter Brouwer (Ben), Lo Brownell (Girl/Lucy), Gayle Kelly Landers (Girl/Tiffany Lady), De White (Allison), Susan Sullivan (Leslie), Joe Jamrog (Walter), J McGee (IRS Man/Army Doctor/Minister), Ingrid Sonnichsen (Ma Gene Parseghian (Freddy/Chuck/Roger), Jeff Peters (Mailman/In tee/Mugger/Hard Hat), I. W. Klein (Dr. Kessler/Psychiatrist/Doct Lawyer), Norm Garon (Army sergeant/Bert), John Batson (Induct

May 15–19, 1973 (5 performances)
GHOST DANCE by Stuart Vaughan; Directed by the author; Scer and Lighting, Harry Silverglat; Costumes, B. J. Myers; Choreograp Carole Schweid; Props, M. Imhof; Musical Director, Doe Lang; Pro tion Associates, Andre Bishop, Vincent Curcio; Stage Managers, J Batson, Louie Stancari; Sound, Christy Risska; Costumes, Anne Ha way, Donna Meyer, Sally Smith, Frank Cox. CAST: Gregory Abels Eastman), Howard Green (Kicking Bear), Richard Council (Porcup Thomas Dickman (Sgt. Bullhead), Sam Gray (Sitting Bull), Hum Allen Astredo (Maj. McLaughlin), John Wardwell (Gen. Miles), Ro Sevra (Col. Drum), Jeff Peters (Ralph), Barbara McMahon (I McLaughlin), Anne Thompson (Catherine), Tom Sawyer ("Buffalo I Cody), Jennifer Flood, Cheri Couture, Bonnie Gondell, Castulo Gue Michael Kemmerling, Tom Mahon, Joseph Noah, Lucy Sweeney

PUBLIC/OTHER THEATER
Opened Thursday, June 22, 1972.*
The New York Shakespeare Festival (Joseph Papp, Producer) presents:

THE CORNER

(Three One-Act Plays)

Associate Producer, Bernard Gersten; Settings, Marsha L. Eck; Clothes, Theoni V. Aldredge; Lighting, Ian Calderon

CAST

"Andrew" by Clay Goss
Directed by Carl Taylor

Andrew	Rafic Bey (Carl Taylor)
Paul	Frankie Russell Faison
Billy	Alfred Dean Irby

The action takes place in North Philadelphia: Was, Is and Will Be.

"His First Step" by Oyamo
Directed by Ktid Keiser

Pritchard	Michael Coleman
Country	Ilunga Adell
Mary	Yolanda Karr
Tim	Cornelius Suares

The action takes place on a street in Harlem at the present time.

"The Corner" by Ed Bullins
Directed by Sonny Jim Gaines

Jack	Willard Reece, Jr.
Sammie	Basil A. Wallace
Stella	Petronia
Sue	Hampton Clanton
Silly Willy Clark	Michael Coleman
Cliff	Bob Delegall

The action in three scenes takes place in The Ghetto in the '50's during the summer.

Closed July 23, 1972 after 87 performances. Originally previewed as "4 for 1" with "The Corner," "You Gonna Let Me Take You Out Tonight, Baby?" "His First Step," "One: The Two of Us."

Friedman-Abeles Photos

Top Right: Bob Delegall, Petronia in "The Corner"

PUBLIC/NEWMAN THEATER
Opened Thursday, October 26, 1972.*
The New York Shakespeare Festival Public Theater (Joseph Papp, Producer) presents:

WEDDING BAND

By Alice Childress; Directors, Alice Childress, Joseph Papp; Setting, Ming Cho Lee; Costumes, Theoni V. Aldredge; Lighting, Martin Aronstein; Associate Producer, Bernard Gersten; Assistant Director, Meir Zvi Barlow

CAST

Julia Augustine	Ruby Dee
Teeta	Calisse Dinwiddie
Mattie	Juanita Clark
Lula Green	Hilda Haynes
Fanny Johnson	Clarice Taylor†1
Nelson Green	Albert Hall
Bell Man	Brandon Maggart†2
Princess	Vicky Geyer
Herman	James Broderick†3
Annabelle	Polly Holliday
Herman's Mother	Jean David

UNDERSTUDIES: Mattie, Lula, Mildred Hassel; Nelson, David Petaha; Teeta, Deedee Hall; Fanny, Betty Haynes; Princess, Kristen Vigard

A Drama in three acts and four scenes. The action takes place in 1918 in a South Carolina city by the sea.

Press: Merle Debuskey, Norman L. Berman
Stage Managers: Ron Dozier, David Petaha

Closed Feb. 25, 1973 after 175 performances.
Succeeded by: 1. Barbara Montgomery, 2. Anthony Palmer, 3. Robert Loggia

Ruby Dee, Hilda Haynes
Above: James Broderick, Ruby Dee 143

PUBLIC/NEWMAN THEATER
Opened Sunday, December 17, 1972.*
The New York Shakespeare Festival (Joseph Papp, Producer)
presents:

THE CHILDREN

By Michael McGuire; Director, Paul Schneider; Setting, Marsha Eck;
Costumes, Theoni V. Aldredge; Lighting, Arden Fingerhut; Associate
Producer, Bernard Gersten

CAST

Kathleen	Fern Sloan
Christopher	Bob Balaban
Dan	Kevin McCarthy
Alexander	Terry Kiser

Understudy: Molly McKasson

A Drama in two acts. The action takes place in the American Midwest
farm country in 19-?.

Press: Merle Debuskey, Norman L. Berman
Stage Managers: Dyanne Hochman, Molly McKasson

* Closed Jan 21, 1973 after 64 performances.

Friedman-Abeles Photo

**Top Right: Fern Sloan, Bob Balaban, Kevin McCarthy,
Terry Kiser**

PUBLIC/ANSPACHER THEATER
Opened Thursday, January 11, 1973.*
The New York Shakespeare Festival Public Theater (Joseph
Papp, Producer) presents:

THE CHERRY ORCHARD

By Anton Chekhov; Production Conceived by James Earl Jones; Director, Michael Schultz; Setting, David Mitchell; Costumes, Theoni V. Aldredge; Lighting, Ian Calderon; Music, John Morris; Choreography, Eliot
Feld; Associate Producer, Bernard Gersten; Production Supervisor, David Eidenberg; Production Assistant, Peggy Fogarty

CAST

Lubov Andreyevna Ranevskaya	Gloria Foster
Anya	Suzanne Johnson
Varya	Ellen Holly
Leonid Andreyevich Gayev	Earle Hyman
Yermolay Alexeyevich Lopahin	James Earl Jones
Pyotr Sergeyevich Trofimov	Robert Jackson
Simeonov-Pishchik	Clark Morgan
Charlotta Ivanovna	Josephine Premice
Semyon Yepihodov	Dennis Tate
Dunyasha	Verona Barnes
Firs	Zakes Mokae
Yasha	Leon Morenzie
Wayfarer	Paul Benjamin
Another Wayfarer	Paul Makgoba
Stationmaster	Clifford Mason
Post Office Clerk	Paul Makgoba
Police Chief	Paul Benjamin
Guests	Zaida Coles, Phylicia Ayers-Allen
Violinist	Noel Pointer

SINGING CHORUS: Verona Barnes, Zaida Coles, Deloris Gaskins,
Paul Makgoba, Leon Morenzie, Clark Morgan, Dennis Tate

UNDERSTUDIES: Ranevskaya, Zaida Coles; Gayev, Clifford Mason;
Charlotta, Dunyasha, Deloris Gaskins; Trofimov, Conrad Roberts;
Yepihodov, Paul Makgoba; Pishchick, Paul Benjamin; Varya, Anya, Phy-
licia Ayers-Allen

A Drama in four acts. The action takes place in 1900 on Mme. Ranevskaya's estate in Russia.

Press: Merle Debuskey, Norman L. Berman
Stage Managers: Lou Rogers, Deloris Gaskins

* Closed Feb. 18, 1973 after 86 performances.

Friedman-Abeles Photos

**James Earl Jones, Earle Hyman, Robert Jackson, Glo-
Foster, Zakes Mokae Above: Josephine Premice**

Opened Thursday, January 25, 1973.*
The New York Shakespeare Festival Public Theater presents:

SIAMESE CONNECTIONS

Dennis J. Reardon; Director, David Schweizer; Setting, Santo Lo-
:o; Costumes, Nancy Adzima, Richard Graziano; Lighting, Ian
ron; Music, Cathy MacDonald; Associate Producer, Bernard Gers-
'roduction Assistant, Eric Blasenheim; Sound, Gary Harris

CAST

k Kroner, Sr	Roberts Blossom
Kroner	Cathryn Damon
lin "Junior" Kroner	David Selby
dmother Kroner	William Hickey
Jensen	Ralph Roberts
:hen	Mary Hamill

Understudy: Dale Soules

Drama in two acts and four scenes. The action takes place at the
t time on an American farm.

General Manager: David Black
Press: Merle Debuskey, Norman L. Berman

sed March 4, 1973 after 64 performances.

Friedman-Abeles Photo

ow: William Hickey, David Selby, Cathryn Damon,
Roberts Blossom, James Staley, Ralph Roberts

IC/ANSPACHER THEATER
pened Wednesday, April 18, 1973.*
he New York Shakespeare Festival Public Theater presents:

THE ORPHAN

David Rabe; Director, Jeff Bleckner; Setting, Santo Loquasto; Cos-
Theoni V. Aldredge; Music, Peter Link; Associate Producer, Ber-
Gersten; Hairstylist, Dorman Allison; Production Manager,
w Mihok.

CAST

peaker	Jeanne Hepple
s	Cliff DeYoung
nnestra 1	Marcia Jean Kurtz
nnestra 2	Rae Allen
a	Carol Williard
nia	Laurie Heineman
emnon	W. B. Brydon
hus	John Harkins
irl	Mariclare Costello
....	Richard Lynch
s	Tom Aldredge
s	Peter Maloney
amily .... Laurie Heineman, Peter Maloney,	

Joanne Nail, Janet Sarno, Carol Williard, Annemarie Zinn

RSTUDIES: Agamemnon, Aegisthus, Apollo, Frederick Coffin;
s, Peter Maloney; Clytemnestra 2, Speaker, Janet Sarno; Girl,
lia, Carol Williard; Electra, Laurie Heineman; Clytemnestra 1,
arie Zinn

rama in two acts.

General Manager: David Black
Press: Merle Debuskey, Norman Berman
Stage Managers: David Eidenberg, Helaine Head

d May 13, 1973 after 53 performances.

Friedman-Abeles Photo

PHOENIX THEATRE SIDESHOWS

T. Edward Hambleton, Managing Director

EDISON THEATRE
Monday, December 18, 1972
The New Phoenix Repertory Company (Harold Prince, Ste-
phen Porter, Michael Montel, Artistic Directors) present:
A MEETING BY THE RIVER by Christopher Isherwood and Don
Bachardy; Director, Michael Montel; Lighting, Ken Billington; Produc-
tion Manager, Val Mayer; Production Coordinator, Karen Hendel; Pro-
duction Assistant, Mary Hambleton; with Jacqueline Brookes (Mother),
Sam Waterston (Oliver), Laurence Luckinbill (Patrick), Robin Strasser
(Penelope), Gordon Hoban (Tom), Anthony Mainionis, Charles Turner
(Passport Officials), Stephen Macht (Rafferty), Tom Tarpey, Anthony
Mainionis, Charles Turner (Swamis)

Sunday & Monday, January 14 & 15, 1973
STRIKE HEAVEN ON THE FACE! by Richard Wesley; Director,
Israel Hicks; Lighting, Ken Billington; Production Manager, Val Mayer;
Stage Manager, Karen Hendel; Production Assistant, Mary Hambleton;
with Nathan George (Hollis Jackson), Beatrice Winde (Mrs. Jackson),
Yvette Hawkins (Toni), Les Roberts (Hammer), William Mooney (Schu-
macker)

Monday, January 22, 1973
GAMES/AFTER LIVERPOOL by James Saunders; Director, Michael
Montel; Lighting, Ken Billington; Production Manager, Val Mayer; Pro-
duction Coordinator, Karen Hendel; Production Assistant, Mary Ham-
bleton; with Charlotte Moore, Thomas A. Stewart, Clyde Burton, Bonnie
Gallup

Sunday & Monday, January 28 & 29, 1973
THE GOVERNMENT INSPECTOR by Nikolai V. Gogol; Adapted by
Peter Raby; Director, Daniel Freudenberger; Visual Conception, James
Tilton; Costumes, Clifford Capone; Lighting, Ken Billington; Stage Man-
agers, Ellen Barry, Rufus Botzow; Production Coordinator, Carol Freu-
denberger; Technical Director, Neil Louison; Production Assistants,
Karen Hendel, Wylie Hunt; with David Dukes (The Judge), Robert
Phelps (Director of Charities), Rufus Botzow; (The Doctor), Thomas A.
Stewart (Director of Education), Curt Karibalis (The Mayor), James
Greene (The Postmaster), Peter Friedman, David Garfield (Landowners),
Robert Ginty (Policeman), Ellen Tovatt (Mayor's Wife), Gretchen Cor-
bett (Mayor's Daughter), Bonnie Gallup (Mayor's Servant), Bill McIn-
tyre (Osip), John Glover (Government Clerk), Frederic Major
(Merchant), Charlotte Moore (Locksmith's Wife), Rufus Botzow (Korob-
kin)

General Manager: Marilyn S. Miller
Company Manager: Gintare Sileika
Press: Daniel Langan

(No photos available)

Rae Allen, John Harkins in "The Orphan"

145

PLAYWRIGHTS HORIZONS

Westside YWCA-Clark Center
Robert Moss, Director

WESTSIDE YWCA-CLARK CENTER

June 17—24, 1972
(9 performances)
THREE ONE ACT PLAYS BY PHILIP MAGDALANY; Directors, Philip Magdalany, Michael Flanagan; Designer, Steve Duffy; Lighting, Laura Lowrie; Costumes, Lorie Watson; Stage Manager, Richard Flagg. IDYLLIC with Kathleen Miller (She), Michael Sacks (He), Ruth Manning (Mother), James Hand (Stranger); ON THE BRINK with Geraldine Court (Diane), Gina Collens (Susan), Saul Fredericks (Man); BOO HOO directed by Michael Flanagan, with Holland Taylor (Minerva), Elaine Kerr (Melanie), Anna Shaler (Sally)

July 12, 13, 1972
(2 performances)
TWO PLAYS BY CRAIG CLINTON; Director, Al Settimio; Stage Manager, Margaret Tobin. A SHARED THING with Daniel Keyes (Man), Naomi Riseman (Woman); LUNCH HOUR with Daniel Keyes (Piebald), Naomi Riseman (Miss Gross), Berney Shepard (Miss Buns), I. W. Klein (Maxwell)

July 20, 21, 1972
(2 performances)
THE LAST OF THE KINGS OF IRELAND by Thomas Conklin; Director, Joe Guadagni; with Thomas Conklin (St. Joseph), Georgia Curtan (Peggy), Max Cole or Michael d'Forrest (Father Savage), Saul Fredericks (Smoke), Michael Shannon (Paul)

Sept. 14—23, 1972
(9 performances)
FOUR ONE ACT PLAYS Lighting Designer, Laura Lowrie; Stage Managers, Richard Flagg, Ira Hayes Fuchs, Melanie Ray, Barbara Stanley. MONKEY PLAY by Jonathan Levy; Director, J. Kevin Hanlon; with Tom Bade (Male), Abbie Morris (Female One), Julia Willis (Female Two); CHARLIE THE CHICKEN by Jonathan Levy; Director, Charles Karchmer; with Bill Cwikowski (Charlie), Donald Marcus (Ferenc), Beatrice Colen (Dorthea); MEMORIAL by Harvey Zuckerman; Director, John Merensky; with Gabrielle Strasun (Tessie), Parker McCormick (Marie); THE DAY OF THE PAINTER by Tom Topor; Director, Peter Schneider; with Art Vasil (Painter), Michael Durrell (First Messenger), Charlene Stegman (Clerk), Peter Simpson (Second Messenger), Mark Curran (Manager), Lynn Oliver (Typist), Ed Clein (Cop), William Robertson (Doctor), Mark Weston (Broker), Perry Katz (Musician), L. R. (Candy Lady), Paul Knowles (Lt.).

Sept. 30—Oct. 9, 1972
(10 performances)
EMPEROR AND GALILEAN, PART I by Henrik Ibsen; Adapted and Directed by Barnet Kellman; Associate Director, David Rosengarten; Produced in association with Quarry Theatre Corps; Settings, Holmes Easley; Associate Designer, Marty Henderson; Costumes, Rosemary Kelly; Masks, Dennis Kear; Music, Martin Siegel, Dan Padnos; Stage Manager, David Rubin; with Arnold Meyer (Constantius), Roy London (Julian), Rosemary Kelly (Eusabia), Paul Zegler (Hecebolius), Dennis Kear (Gregory), Maurice Blanc (Libanius/Maximus), Stephen Clarke (Gallus), Mark French (Basil), Gene Farseglian (Leontes), Ed Hooks (Oribases), Chase Williams (Coreopsis), John Colon (Eutherius), Karen Ludwig (Helena), Gail Hayden (Myrrha), Raymond Singer (Decentius), Tom Dawber (Sintula), Alex Schub (Soldier), Chuck Jones (Sallust)

Anna Shaler, Holland Taylor, Elaine Kerr in "Boo Hoo"
Below: "Emperor and Galilean"
(Ted Yaple Photos)

Oct. 12—22, 1972
(12 performances)
MAN OUT OF DARKNESS written and directed by William Gill; Malcolm Drummond; Lighting, Laura Lowrie, with Stanley Greene (Josie), Yvonne Warden or Sundra J. Williams (Lorean), Lockie Edwards Milledge Mosley, Jr. (Willie), Mary Carter (Betty), Bernice Frazier Jessie Hill (Dee Dee), Bernard Washington (Child), Lee Kimble (Jan Sylvia Soares (Gwen)

Oct. 19—28, 1972
(9 performances)
CINDERS by Michael Carton; Director, Joseph Cali; with Gil Ro (John), Margaret Hall (Virginia) Julia Willis (Ginnie); LECTURE W SINGING written and delivered by Tom Johnson; THE MARRIA PROPOSAL an opera based on play by Anton Chekhov; Music, Jerem Murray; Director, Louis Galterio; Sets and Costumes, Phil Grazi with Ray Harrell (Stepan), Henry Grossman (Ivan), Kate Hurney (N lya); Stage Managers, Charles Richetelle, Neftali Melendez

Oct. 31—Nov. 6, 1972
(6 performances)
THE CHILDREN'S CRUSADE by William M. Hoffman; Directed Choreographed by William A. Dunas; Music, John H. Smead; Light Edward R. Effron; Produced in association with Ambrose Arts Fou tion and The Wolf Co.; with Robert Kubera (Boy), Linn Va (Mother), Walter Leyden Brown (Father), Skye Vermont (Girl with C Cup), Charles Stanley (Schoolmaster), Anthony Brazina (Murde Cathy Heinrich (Victim), Giulio Sorrentino (Friar), Robert Taylor (I key), Barbara Clay (Saint), J. Kevin Hanlon and Lucy Silvay (Lov Jacques Brouwers (Naked Flagellant), Richard Pinter (Slave Dri Carolyn Lord (Witch), Robert Patrick (Black King)

Nov. 30—Dec. 9, 1972
(10 performances)
TISSUE PAPER LIES by Maurice Noel; Songs, Jeremiah Murray; ics, Maurice Noel; Director, Henry Velez; Designer, Andre St. Jean; S Managers, Barry Lenner, Gretchen Brinckerhoff; with Donovan Sy (Jonathan), Bonnie Barton (Annabel), Eleanor Cody Gould (Grand Dolores Kenan (Charlene/Rose), Ed Kuczewski (Reverend/Ignat Marlena Lustik (Letty/Gale), John O'Leary (Preacher/Jesse), John rensky (Nick/Gavin), Parker McCormick (Valerie), Priscilla McPhe (Myrna), Frank Verroca (Jake), Greg Doucette, Paula Heringhi, B Kryder, Frank Verroca (Radio Choir)

Marlena Lustik, Donovan-Sylvest (on floor), Priscilla MacPherson, Ed Kuczewski, Dolores Kenan, Frank Verroca, Bryan Kryder, Paula Heringhi in "Tissue Paper Lies"

Ted Yaple Photo

Dec. 6—7, 1972
(2 performances)
NE WAY NON STOP by Thomas C. Rosica; Director, Michael
Varner; with Andrew Winner (Joey), Duncan Hoxworth (Man), Jane
anford (Marie), Leonard DiSesa (Martin)

Dec. 16—23, 1972
(9 performances)
HE SECRET PLACE by Garrett Morris; Director, Bill Duke; Choreog-
apher, Harold Pierson; Lighting, Shirley Prendergast; Musical Director,
eopoldo Fleming; Costumes, Judy Dearing; Set, Jokolo Cooper; Stage
Manager, Yaa Shepherd; Props, R. M. Bowdwin; with Frank Adu (Alex),
bba Babatunde (Ralph), Akinwole Babatunde (Kwami), Lettie Battle
Dancer-spirit), Taurean Blacque (Jason), Mathew Bernard Johnson
Caesar), Charles Leipart (Abraham), Elouise Loftin (Sara), Robbie
cCauley (Femi), Jim Murtagh (Kluzewski), Irwin Rosen (Coffee), Jessie
aunders (Gert), Seret Scott (Dancer-spirit), Terrie Taylor (Dancer-
pirit), Chase Williams (Jimmy), Bernard Wyatt (Vagrant)

Jan. 12—20, 1973
(2 performances)
WO ONE ACT PLAYS by Walter Turney; Director, Anthony DeVito;
ighting, Todd Lichtenstein; Stage Manager, Margaret Soricelli; THE
UCCESSORS with Tom Cuff or Leonard DiSesa (Mr. Ho), Ted Ulmer
Digger), Alan Koss (Ironfish), Bill Cwikowski (Billy), Rich Petrucelli
Horse), Jeff Rubin (Joe); DAWN with Don Parker (Archy, Sr.), Con
oche (Archy, Jr.), Bill Cwikowski (Moony), Ted Ulmer (Sonny), Tom
uff (Pledge John), Connie Morrill (Corie), John O'Leary (Smith)

Jan. 18—19, 1973
(2 performances)
HREE PLAYS BY EVE FRIEDMAN directed by Kent Wood;
OODNIGHT with Sarah Harris (Lise), Henrietta Valor (Marie);
HREE LITTLE KITTENS with Sarah Harris (Trina), Alice Elliott
Bitsy), Adelle Reel (Rusty), David Laundra (Ivan); PREMIERE with
avid Kerry Hefener (Father), Alice Elliott (Bobbie), Don Dolan (Super-
tendent) David Laundra (Louis)

Feb. 14—24, 1973
(11 performances)
NDER MACDOUGAL by James Prideaux; Director, Robert Moss;
et and Lights, Robert W. Perkins; Costumes, Lorie Watson; Stage Man-
ers, Ira Hayes Fuchs, Melanie Ray; with Marjorie Erdreich (Elizabeth),
hilip MacKenzie (Teddy), Jim Hillgartner (Grady), Jack Bannon (Bill),
itchell Edmonds (Harry), John O'Leary (Harris)

Feb. 21—23, 1973
(3 performances)
HE CONDITIONING OF CHARLIE ONE by Robert Karmon; Di-
ctor, A. Kent Gravett; with Bruce Weitz (Roland), Mimi Kennedy
Alpha), Richard Kline (Cicero), Chip Lucia (Chip), Donnis Honeycutt
Flip), Richert Easley (Investigator), Dolores Kenan (Mom), Robert
arger (Dad), Monica Smith (Amy), Bruce McInnes and Ken Tesoriere
Death Squadron)

) Eleanor Cody Gould, Rose Lischner, Mary
Boylan, William Robertson in "Girls Most
kely..." Above: Sudy Bond (C), Malcolm
Groome in "Billy"
(Nathaniel Tileston Photos)

**James Hillgartner, Jack Bannon, Philip MacKenzie,
Mitchell Edmonds in "Under MacDougal"**
(Ted Yaple Photo)

Below: Barbara Lee GoVan, Alice Elliott, Robert Burgos
in "Bloodsport"

WESTSIDE YWCA-CLARK CENTER
March 7—22, 1973
(14 performances)
BLOODSPORT by Milburn Smith; Director, Russell Treyz; Lighting,
Jim Miller; Set, Richard Williams; Stage Managers, Suzanne Gedance,
Valerie Ceriano; with Robert Burgos (Michael), Alice Elliott (Ann), Bar-
bara Lee GoVan (Janet), Anne Shropshire (Mrs. Young)

March 14—15, 1973
(2 performances)
GETTING THROUGH by Carl Tiktin; Director, Peter Schneider; with
Mark Weston (Mike), Donna Hodge (Alma), Bob Ghent (Harry), Rich-
ard Canter (Sol), John Eldridge (Ken), Fran Dorsey (Marigold), Mike
Zelenko (Giovanni), Robert Heine (Shelley), Paige Massman (Elissa),
Michael Krauss (Mac), Nancy Franklin (Lottie)

March 28—30, 1973
(3 performances)
PIECE OF RESISTANCE by Charles Leipart; Director, Gary Weist;
with Joel Tropper (Chuck), Barry Kael (Barney), Renee Orin (Dorothy),
Beatrice Winner (Virginia), Rod Houts (Mr. J)

April 5—6, 1973
(2 performances)
ANY WOMAN CAN'T by Wendy Wasserstein; Director, Charles
Karchmer; with Ann Sachs (Christina), David Kagen (Charles), Polly
Adams (Hilda/Nancy), Bill Cwikowski (Irv/Bob), Sarah Adams (Nata-
lie/Pat/Amy), Marjorie Lovett (Old Woman/Bag Lady), Tom McKit-
terick (Boy), David Rimmer (Newsman), Leigh Woods (George/Mark)

April 18—29, 1973
(12 performances)
BILLY by Frederick Kirwin; Produced in association with Quarry Theatre Corps; Director, Barnet Kellman; Settings, Marty Henderson; Lighting, David MacWilliams; Associate Producer, David Rosengarten; Stage
Managers, David Rubin, Gerry Weinstein; with Malcolm Groome
(Jeeter), John Seidman (Dakota), Sudie Bond (Old Lady Phipps), Marjorie Lynne Feiner (Melody), Jayne Haynes (Mrs. Jones), Stephen Mendillo
(Sam), Phillip Schopper (Billy), Dale McIntosh (Batter), Marty Henderson (First Baseman), Michael St. John (Priest), Sudie Bond (Mrs. Phipps)

April 25—27, 1973
(3 performances)
STORKWOOD by Mark Dunster; Directed and designed by Christopher
Cox; Stage Manager, Kristian Kirsch; with Craig Richard Nelson (Reed),
Donald Snell (Rin), Don Parker (Claude), Norman Thomas Marshall
(Goff), Willy Switkes (Aycrig), Marjorie Lovett (Mrs. Jowers), Alix Elias
(Claire), Mary Boylan (Alicia), Margaret Miller (Laetitia), Tom Cuff
(Clarke)

May 9—20, 1973
(12 performances)
THE GIRLS MOST LIKELY TO SUCCEED by Dennis Andersen;
Director, Russell Treyz; Set, Richard Williams; Lighting, Jim Miller;
Stage Managers, Ira Hayes Fuchs, Valerie Ceriano; with Margaret Impert
(Molly), Larry C. Lott (Andy), Phoebe Dorin (Kathy), John Washbrook
(Paul), Robert Hitt (Ted), Polly Holliday (Lee), Robert McFarland
(Mike), Alice Elliott (Jane), Tom Cuff (Howard), Rose Lischner (Kate),
Eleanor Cody Gould (Effie), Mary Boylan (Edna), William Robertson
(Charlie)

147

THE REPERTORY THEATER OF LINCOLN CENTER
Jules Irving, Director

VIVIAN BEAUMONT THEATER
Opened Thursday, November 9, 1972.*
The Repertory Theater of Lincoln Center presents:

ENEMIES

By Maxim Gorky; English Version, Jeremy Brooks, Kitty Hunter-Blair; Director, Ellis Rabb; Settings, Douglas W. Schmidt; Lighting, John Gleason; Costumes, Ann Roth; Music, Cathy MacDonald; Production Assistant, Bill Conway; Hairstyles and Makeup, Jim Sullivan

CAST

Zakhar Bardin	Robert Symonds
Paulina	Frances Sternhagen
Yakov Bardin	Joseph Wiseman
Tatiana	Nancy Marchand
Nadya	Susan Sharkey
General Pechenegov	Stefan Schnabel
Kon	Will Lee
Mikhail Skrobotov	Philip Bosco
Kleopatra	Barbara Cook
Nikolai Skrobotov	Josef Sommer
Agrafena	Jane Rose
Pologgy	George Pentecost
Sintsov	Christopher Walken
Grekov	Robert Phalen
Levshin	Sydney Walker
Yagodin	Fred Morsell
Ryabtsov	Everett McGill
Yakimov	Dan Sullivan
Vyripaev	Frank Dwyer
Peasant Women	Penelope Allen, Murrell Gehman, Carole Ocwieja
Capt. Boboyedov	Tom Lacy
Kvach	Ray Fry
Lt. Strepetov	George Taylor
District Police Inspector	Louis Turenne
Policeman	James Ray Weeks

UNDERSTUDIES: Zakhar, Ray Fry; Paulina, Kleopatra, Murrell Gehman; Yakov, Fred Morsell; Tatiana, Agrafena, Penelope Allen; Nadya, Carole Ocwieja; Pechenegov, Mikhail, Louis Turenne; Nikolai, Robert Phalen; Boboyedov, Kvach, Yagodin, Frank Dwyer; Pologgy, Levshi, George Taylor; Sintsov, Ryabtsov, Lt., James Ray Weeks; Grekov, Everett McGill

A Drama in three acts. The action takes place on the Bardin estate in Provincial Russia in 1905.

General Manager: Alan Mandell
Press: Susan Bloch, William Schelble, Norman Lombino
Stage Managers: Craig Anderson, Robert Lowe, Barbara-Mae Phillips, Robert Walter

* Closed Dec. 16, 1972 after 44 performances and 13 previews.

Martha Swope Photos

Right: First Act curtain Above: Philip Bosco, Barbara Cook

Joseph Wiseman, Susan Sharkey, Christopher Walken, Nancy Marchand

Nancy Marchand, Barbara Cook, Frances Sternhage Joseph Wiseman

148

Opened Monday, November 20, 1972.*
The Repertory Theater of Lincoln Center (Jules Irving, Director) presents:

SAMUEL BECKETT FESTIVAL

Plays by Samuel Beckett: Director, Alan Schneider; Settings, Douglas Schmidt; Lighting, John Gleason; Costumes, Sara Brook; Assistant ector, Susan Einhorn; Hairstylist, Jim Sullivan; Production Assistants, ly Larner, Lillah McCarthy; Production Supervisor, Frank Bayer; duction Manager, Bruce Hoover

CAST

PPY DAYS
nie .... Jessica Tandy
lie .... Hume Cronyn

T WITHOUT WORDS 1
Player .... Hume Cronyn

Opened Wednesday, November 22, 1972.**

APP'S LAST TAPE
app .... Hume Cronyn

T I (World Premiere)
Mouth .... Jessica Tandy
Auditor .... Henderson Forsythe

STANDBYS: Pauline Flanagan, Henderson Forsythe
Press: Susan Bloch, William Schelble
Stage Managers: Barbara-Mae Phillips, Robert Walter

losed Dec. 17, 1972 after 16 performances and 17 previews.
losed Dec. 16, 1972 after 15 performances and 19 previews.

Martha Swope Photos

Right: Hume Cronyn, Jessica Tandy in "Happy Days"
Above: Hume Cronyn in "Krapp's Last Tape"

**Hume Cronyn in
"Act without Words 1"**

**Jessica Tandy
in "Happy Days"**

VIVIAN BEAUMONT THEATER
Opened Thursday, January 4, 1973.*
The Repertory Theater of Lincoln Center (Jules Irving, Dire
tor) presents:

THE PLOUGH AND THE STARS

By Sean O'Casey; Director, Dan Sullivan; Settings, Douglas V
Schmidt; Lighting, John Gleason; Costumes, Carrie F. Robbins; Origin
Music, John Duffy; Vocal Director, Cathy MacDonald; Sound Gary Ha
ris; Production Assistants, Jane E. Neufield, Elliott Vizansky; Hairstyl
and Makeup, Jim Sullivan; Dialogue Consultant, Michael Clarke-La
rence

CAST

Jack Clitheroe	Christopher Walke
Nora Clitheroe	Roberta Maxwe
Peter Flynn	Leo Leyde
Young Covey	Kevin Conwa
Bessie Burgess	Pauline Flanaga
Mrs. Gogan	Nancy Marchar
Mollser	Susan Sharke
Fluther Good	Jack MacGowran*
Lt. Langon	Peter Roga
Capt. Brennan	Robert Phal
Cpl. Stoddart	Philip Bos
Sgt. Tinley	David H. Lea
Rosie Redmond	Lee Laws
Bartender	Sydney Walk
A Woman	Paddy Croft
Figure in the Window	Michael Clarke-Lauren

UNDERSTUDIES: Fluther, Robert Symonds; Nora, Caroline Kav
Mrs. Gogan, Bessie, Paddy Croft; Peter, Ray Fry; Young Covey, Robe
Phalen; Rosie, Woman, Murrell Gehman; Brennan, Everett McGi
Stoddart, Frank Dwyer; Langon, Tinley, James Ray Weeks; Jack, Dav
H. Leary

A Drama in four acts presented with one intermission. The action tak
place in Dublin from November 1915 to Easter Week of 1916.

Press: Susan Bloch, William Schelble
Stage Managers: Patrick Horrigan, Barbara-Mae Phillips

* Closed Feb. 10, 1973 after limited engagement of 44 performances a
13 previews.
†Succeeded by: 1. Robert Symonds, 2. Maureen Quinn

Martha Swope Photos

**Left: Roberta Maxwell, Christopher Walken Top: Jack
MacGowran, Kevin Conway, Leo Leyden, Sydney
Walker, Lee Lawson**

Nancy Marchand, Leo Leyden, Jack MacGowran

Pauline Flanagan, Jack MacGowran, Christopher Walk

IVIAN BEAUMONT THEATER
Opened Thursday, March 1, 1973.*
The Repertory Theater of Lincoln Center (Jules Irving, Director) presents:

THE MERCHANT OF VENICE

By William Shakespeare; Director, Ellis Rabb; Setting, Lighting, Productions, James Tilton; Costumes, Ann Roth; Musical Supervision, Cathy MacDonald; Production Supervisor, Frank Bayer; Hairstylist, Jim Sullivan

CAST

ntonio	Josef Sommer
alarino	Gastone Rossilli
eonardo	Robert Phalen
alaria	Caroline Kava
assanio	Christopher Walken
ratiano	Philip Bosco
orenzo	Peter Coffield
ortia	Rosemary Harris
erissa	Olivia Cole
tephano	Michael Clarke-Laurence
rince of Morocco	Fred Morsell
hylock	Sydney Walker
auncelot Gobbo	Dan Sullivan
essica	Roberta Maxwell
rince of Arragon	Alan Mandell
ubal	Ray Fry
uke of Venice	Robert Symonds
ourt Clerk	Frank Dwyer

and Richard Council, Calvin Culver, Joseph Lambie, Robert LaTourneaux, Amy Levitt, Evertt McGill, Ellen Newman, Casper Roos, Sterling St. Jacques, James Ray Weeks, Peter Weller, James Whittle, William Wright

A Drama presented in two acts. The action takes place in Venice and the Belmont.

General Manager: Alan Mandell
Production Manager: Bruce Hoover
Press: Susan Bloch, William Schelble, Norman J-F. Lombino
Stage Managers: Patrick Horrigan, Barbara-Mae Phillips

Closed Apr. 7, 1973 after limited engagement of 44 performances and 12 previews.

Martha Swope Photos

ight: Christopher Walken, Peter Coffield, Josef Sommer, Amy Levitt, Philip Bosco Top: Rosemary Harris

Christopher Walken, Sydney Walker

Robert Phalen, Caroline Kava, Gastone Rossilli, Josef Sommer

VIVIAN BEAUMONT THEATER

Opened Thursday, April 26, 1973.*
The Repertory Theater of Lincoln Center presents:

A STREETCAR NAMED DESIRE

By Tennessee Williams; Director, Ellis Rabb; Setting, Douglas W. Schmidt; Lighting, John Gleason; Costumes, Nancy Potts; Music, Cathy MacDonald; Hairstylist, Jim Sullivan; Production Assistants, Bill Conway, Alexander Donaldson, Susan Sobel-Feldman

CAST

A Woman	Rosetta LeNoire
Stanley Kowalski	James Farentino†1
Harold Mitchell	Philip Bosco
Stella Kowalski	Patricia Conolly†2
Eunice Hubbel	Priscilla Pointer
Blanche Du Bois	Rosemary Harris†3
Steve Hubbel	Robert Symonds†4
Pablo Gonzales	Dan Sullivan
Young Collector	Brian Brownlee
Mexican Man	Sydney Walker†5
Doctor	Ray Fry
Nurse	Penelope Allen

HABITUES OF THE QUARTER: Frank Dwyer, Donald M. Griffith, Everett McGill, Ellen Newman†6, John Newton, Robert Phalen, Alyce E. Webb, James Ray Weeks
UNDERSTUDIES: Blanche, Penelope Allen; Stanley, Dan Sullivan; Stella, Eunice, Nurse, Ellen Newman; Harold, John Newton; Steve, Pablo, Robert Phalen; Woman, Alyce E. Webb; Collector, Everett McGill; Pablo, Mexican, Donald M. Griffith; Doctor, Frank Dwyer

A Drama in two acts. The action takes place in the Spring, Summer, and early Fall in New Orleans.

Press: Susan Bloch, William Schelble
Stage Managers: Barbara-Mae Phillips, Patrick Horrigan

* Closed July 29, 1973 after 110 performances and 13 previews.
† Succeeded by: 1. Rudy Solari, 2. Barbara eda-Young, 3. Lois Nettleton, 4. Tom Rosqui, 5. Antonia Rey, 6. Sandra Seacat

Martha Swope Photos

Rosemary Harris, James Farentino
Below: Philip Bosco, Rosemary Harris

Robert Forster, Barbara eda-Young, Lois Nettleton

Patricia Conolly, Rosemary Harris, Priscilla Pointer

152

ROUNDABOUT THEATRE

Gene Feist, Producing Director
Michael Fried, Executive Director

ROUNDABOUT THEATRE
Opened Wednesday, October 11, 1972.*
The Roundabout Theatre Company presents:

RIGHT YOU ARE

By Luigi Pirandello; English Version, Eric Bentley; Director, Gene
[Fe]ist; Set and Lighting, Holmes Easley; Costumes, Mimi Maxmen;
[So]und, Karen Kantor; Production Coordinator, Philip Campanella;
[Te]chnical Director, Roger Cunningham

CAST

[La]mberto Laudisi .... William Shust
[Ame]nalia Agazzi .... Elizabeth Owens
[Di]na Agazzi .... Ellen Newman
[Ni]na .... Madeleine Wallack
[Sig]nora Sirelli .... Charlotte Lane
[Sig]nor Sirelli .... Lance Brilliantine
[Co]uncillor Agazzi .... Fred Stuthman
[Sig]nora Frola .... Dorothy Sands
[Sig]nor Frola .... John LaGioia
[Es]ther Centuri .... Philip Campanella
[Go]vernor .... Sterling Jensen
[Sig]nora Ponza .... Susan Johnson

A Comedy in two acts. The action takes place in the reception room
[of] the Agazzi apartment in an Italian provincial capital in 1912.

General Manager: Michael Maso
Press: Michael Fried
Stage Manager: Jeff Schecter

[C]losed Nov. 5, 1972 after limited engagement of 64 performances.

Martha Swope Photo

William Shust, John LaGioia, Dorothy Sands
in "Right You Are"

ROUNDABOUT THEATRE
Opened Sunday, November 19, 1972.*
The Roundabout Theatre Company presents:

AMERICAN GOTHICS

By Donald Kvares; Set, Victor Poleri; Lighting, Robert Murphy; Cos-
[tum]es, Evelyn Thompson; Associate Producer, Roger Cunningham;
[Tec]hnical Director, Philip Campanella

CAST

["A Piece of Fog" directed by Frank Errante
[B]oby .... Matthew Barry
[Mo]ther .... Elizabeth Owens
[Fa]ther .... Dennis Helfend

[T]he action takes place in the near future in a living room in a small
[Am]erican town.

["M]odern Statuary" directed by Nancy Rhodes
[Mr]s. Gelb .... Lorraine Serabian
[An]na .... Susan Peretz
[Te]ddy .... Tracey Walter
[Be]tty .... Alice Elliott
[Le]nny .... Robert Burgos
[Mr]. Gelb .... Dennis Helfend

[T]he action takes place at the present time in the Gelb home in
[sub]urban Long Island.

INTERMISSION

["Fil]ling the Hole" directed by Nancy Rubin
[Be]lla .... Alice Elliott
[Al] .... Robert Burgos
[Mo]ther .... Susan Peretz

[T]he action takes place on a day in spring in Central Park, New
[Yor]k City.

["T]rangulation" directed by Frank Errante
[Rut]h .... Lorraine Serabian
[.........] .... Alice Elliott

[T]he action takes place in the recent past.

Press: Michael Fried
Stage Manager: Jeff Schecter

[C]losed Nov. 26, 1972 after limited engagement of 15 performances.

Elizabeth Owens, Donald Kvares, Lorraine Serabian
("American Gothics")

ROUNDABOUT THEATRE
Opened Friday, November 24, 1972*
The Roundabout Theatre Company presents:

ANTON CHEKHOV'S GARDEN PARTY

An Entertainment devised and adapted from the works of Anton Chekhov by Elihu Winer; Production Coordinator, Philip Campanella; Technical Director, Roger Cunningham

CAST

Anton Chekhov .... William Shust

Presented in two parts.

Stage Manager: Jeff Schecter

* Closed Dec. 10, 1972 after limited engagement of 21 performances.
Three additional performances were given Feb. 28, March 1 & 2, 1973
at the Lambs Club. (no photos available)

Monday, December 4, 1972*
The Roundabout Theatre Company presents:

HAMLET

By William Shakespeare; Conceived and Staged by Gene Feist; S
tings, Holmes Easley; Costumes, Mimi Maxmen; Lighting, R. S. Winkl
Stage Manager, Curtiss W. Sayblack

CAST

Lance Brilliantine
Fred Stuthman
Philip Campanella
Lou Trapani
Sterling Jensen
John Guerrasio
Daryl Croxton
Mel Johnson
Robert Stocking
Michael Tolaydo

* Closed Dec. 8, 1972 after limited engagement of 35 performances.

Top Left : Fred Stuthman, Philip Campanella, Sterling
Jensen

ROUNDABOUT THEATRE
Opened Tuesday, January 9, 1973.*
The Roundabout Theatre Company presents:

THE PLAY'S THE THING

By Ferenc Molnar; Adapted by P. G. Wodehouse; Director, Gene
Feist; Set, Holmes Easley; Costumes, Mimi Maxmen; Lighting, R. S.
Winkler; Original Score, Philip Campanella; Production Assistants, Harley Hackett, Janet Orentzel, Paul Sudds; Technical Director, Roger Cunningham

CAST

Sandor Turai .... Hugh Franklin†
Mansky .... Humphrey Davis
Albert Adam .... Richard Larson
Ilona Szabo .... Elizabeth Owens
Almady .... Neil Flanagan
Johann Dwornitschek .... Fred Stuthman
Mell .... Philip Campanella

A Comedy in three acts. The action takes place in a room in a villa on
the Italian Riviera on a Saturday in the summer of 1926.

General Manager: Michael Maso
Press: Michael Fried
Stage Manager: David Petersen

*Closed Mar. 4, 1973 after limited engagement of 64 performances, and
re-opened on Broadway May 1, 1973 for 23 performances and 14 previews. (See Broadway Calendar)
† Succeeded by Winston May for one week.

Elizabeth Owens, Hugh Franklin
in "The Play's the Thing"

Wesley Addy, Victor Garber, Beatrice
Straight in "Ghosts"

ROUNDABOUT THEATRE
Opened Tuesday, March 13, 1973.*
The Roundabout Theatre Company presents:

GHOSTS

By Henrik Ibsen; Adapted and Directed by Gene Feist; Set, Holm
Easley; Costumes, Sue A. Robbins; Lighting, R. S. Winkler; Music, Phi
Campanella; Production Assistants, John Guyot, Harley Hackett, De
rah Robins, James Roman; Technical Director, Roger Cunningham

CAST

Mrs. Helene Alving .... Beatrice Strai
Osvald Alving .... Victor Garber
Pastor Manders .... Wesley Ad
Jacob Engstrand .... Fred Stuthman
Regina Engstrand .... Laura Esterm

A Drama in two acts and three scenes. The action takes place in M
Alving's country home on one of the larger fjords of western Norw
during spring in the late nineteenth century.

General Manager: Michael Maso
Press: Michael Fried
Stage Manager: Nancy Rhodes

* Closed May 27, 1973 after 89 performances.
† Succeeded by: 1. W. T. Martin, 2. William Shust

SPANISH THEATRE REPERTORY COMPANY

Gilberto Zaldiver, Producer

RAMERCY ARTS THEATRE
Opened Friday, October 13, 1972.*
The Spanish Theatre Repertory Company presents in Spanish:

WHO'S AFRAID OF VIRGINIA WOOLF?

By Edward Albee; Director, Rene Buch; Designed by Robert Federico;
ghting, Tony Quintavalla; Production Assistant, Harlan Villegas; Tech-
ians, Bill Barclay, James Soto; Assistant to the Director, Marco San-
go

CAST

artha	Silvia Brito
orge	Raul Davila
ney	Miriam Cruz
k	Jean Paul Delgado

A drama in three acts. The action takes place at the present time in the
ne of Martha and George in a university town.

Press: Marian Graham

Closed Jan. 14, 1973 after 37 performances.

Bert Andrews Photo

Jean Paul Delgado, Miriam Cruz, Raul Davila, Silvia
Brito in "Who's Afraid of Virginia Woolf?"

RAMERCY ARTS THEATRE
Opened Wednesday, November 15, 1972*
The Spanish Theatre Repertory Company presents:

DON JUAN TENORIO

By Jose Zorrilla; Director, Rene Buch; Set, Robert Federico; Cos-
es, Maria Ferreira; Lighting, Tony Quintavalla; Assistant Director,
n Paul Delgado; Production Assistant, Harlan Villegas

CAST

ot, Centellas	Sadel Alamo
n Luis	Esteban Chalbaud
mendador	George Dal Lago
cia y Mujer	Idalia Diaz
na Ana	Maria Dolores
tarelli	Enrique Gomez
gida	Lolina Gutierrez
tti	Alfonso Manosalvas
n Juan	Jose Rodriguez
ultor	Marco Santiago
llaneda	Juan Carlos Sawage
na Ines	Isabel Segovia
dre Abades	Conchita Vargas
n Juan	Jean Paul Delgado

Press: Marian Graham

losed Feb. 18, 1973 after 41 performances.

Bert Andrews Photo

RAMERCY ARTS THEATRE
Opened Saturday, December 2, 1972.*
The Spanish Theatre Repertory Company presents:

LIFE IS A DREAM

By Pedro Calderon de la Barca; Director, Rene Buch; Designed by
ert Troie; Musical Director, Juan Viccini

CAST

aura	Idalia Diaz
rin	Esteban Chalbaud
smundo	Jose Rodriguez
taldo	Alberto Beraldo
olfo	Jean Paul Delgado
ella	Maria Dolores
lio	George Dal Lago
ier	Mauricio Villar

Press: Marian Graham

losed Dec. 14, 1972 after limited engagement of 3 performances.

Esteban Chalbaud, Jose Rodriguez, Idalia Diaz
in "Don Juan"

GRAMERCY ARTS THEATRE
Opened Sunday, March 11, 1973*
The Spanish Theatre Repertory Company presents:

BLOOD WEDDING

By Federico Garcia Lorca; Director, Rene Buch; Musical Director, Juan Viccini; Designed by Robert Federico, Tony Quintavalla; Coordinator, Chris Munoz; Assistant to the Director, Pedro Vega; Technical Director, Leonard Simoncek; Production Assistant, Harlan Villegas

CAST

Novio	Jorge Lopez Pondal
Madre	Carmen Montejo
Vecina	Conchita Vargas
Suegra	Fini Moreno
Mujer	Idalia Diaz
Leonardo	Jean Paul Delgado
Nina	Gabrielle Gazon
Criada	Lolina Gutierrez
Padre	Alfonso Manosalvas
Novia	Ilka Tanya Payan
Muchacha	Iris Diaz
Lenador #1	Pedro Vego
Lenador #2	Mauricio Villar
Luna	Sadel Alamo
Mendiga	Enrique Gomez

Understudies: Eduardo Aranco, Marco Santiago

Press: Marian Graham

* Closed May 24, 1973 after 55 performances.

Bert Andrews Photo

Ilka Tanya Payan, Jorge Lopez Pondal in "Blood Wedding"

Iris Diaz, Carmen Montejo in "The Effect of Gamma Rays. . . ."

GRAMERCY ARTS THEATRE
Opened Sunday, April 29, 1973*
The Spanish Theatre Repertory Company presents:

NADA QUE VER

By Griselda Gambaro; Director, George Dal Lago; English tran Charles Pilditch; Designed by Tony Quintavalla; Coordinator Amud

CAST

Manolo	Roberto Antonio or Eduardo
Toni	George Da
Brigita Maria	Alicia
La Abuela	Near
Hombre #1	Eduardo Aranco or Roberto
Hombre #2	Mauricio

Press: Marian Graham

* Closed May 16, 1973 after 9 performances.

GRAMERCY ARTS THEATRE
Opened Saturday, May 12, 1973*
The Spanish Theatre Repertory Company presents:

THE EFFECT OF GAMMA RAYS MAN-IN-THE-MOON MARIGOLD

By Paul Zindel; Director, Nancy Cardenas; Translation, Nar denas, Emma Cevallos; Set, Robert Federico; Lighting, Ray McC Coordinator, Chris Munoz; Assistant Director, Silvia Brito; T Director, Leonard Simoncek; Production Assistants, Tony Mon Woertendyke

CAST

Tillie	I
Beatriz	Carmen
Ruth	Ilka Tanya
Nanny	Fini
Janice Vickery	Irene

Understudy: Haydee Zambrana

Press: Marian Graham

* Closed May 27, 1973 after limited engagement of 13 perform

Bert Andrews Photo

156

THEATRE AT NOON

Miriam Fond, Artistic Director

. PETER'S GATE
October 16—27, 1973
(20 performances)
HAT'S A NICE COUNTRY LIKE YOU DOING IN A STATE
KE THIS? (or, who got America in trouble?) based on an original
ncept by Bernie Travis, Ira Gasman, Cary Hoffman; Music, Cary Hoff-
n; Lyrics, Ira Gasman; Musical Direction and Arrangements, William
ster McDaniel; Associate Musical Director, Michael D. Neville; Set,
b Hartmann; Lighting, Richard Delahanty; Stage Managers, Richard
lahanty, Kathryn Baumann; Entire Production Directed and Choreo-
aphed by Miriam Fond; with Paul Hodes, Bill LaVallee, Wendy Les-
k, Barry Michlin, Jane Robertson

his production was moved to the American Place Theatre Jan. 10—
b. 3, 1973 for 12 additional performances)

December 11—22, 1973
(20 performances)
E BLUE MAGI by Sally Dixon Wiener; Based on "The Gift of the
agi" by O. Henry; Music and Lyrics by Sally Dixon Wiener; Director,
riam Fond; Musical Direction and Arrangements, William Foster
Daniel; Set, Billy Puzo; Costumes, Danny Morgan; Lighting, Richard
lahanty; Stage Managers, Diane Ertmoed, Richard Delahanty; Pro-
ction Assistants, Pinocchio Madrid, Ann Wiener; with Sy Travers
ssie), Ruth Brisbane (Mme. Sophronie), Ross Gifford (Gaspard),
ger Woodson (Jim), Leilani Johnson (Della), Bill LaVallee (Clarinet-

January 15—18, 1973
(8 performances)
MP AT MIDNIGHT by Barrie Stavis; Director, Miriam Fond; Sets
Lighting, Richard Delahanty; Costumes, Danny Morgan; Stage Man-
rs, Richard Delahanty, Joel Bergman; with Neil Flanagan (Sagredo),
Lype O'Dell (Galileo), Brian Hartigan (Gepe), Marcia Bennett (Polis-
a), Patrick L. Farrelly (Barberini), Charles Maggiore (Bellarmin),
rman Beim (Carlo), Brian Hartigan (Francesco), Jack Axelrod (Firen-
la), Charles Maggiore (Riccardi)

February 5—16, 1973
(20 performances)
RFARINI'S DYING by Stan Cornyn; Director, Miriam Fond; Set
Lighting, Richard Delahanty; Costumes, Danny Morgan; Stage Man-
rs, Richard Delhanty, Diane Ertmoed; House Manager, Barbara Cer-
; with Lou Rodgers (Madame Jermaile), Joe Vaccarella (Farfarini),
da Ivey (Desrelda) Bernie Passeltiner (Semprino)

February 19—March 2, 1973
(20 performances)
PRISE! excerpts from past musical productions with Jim Horn as
st; and performers Miriam Fond, Roger Woodson, Leilani Johnson,
LaVallee, Arne Gundersen, Suzanne Oberjat, Ross Gifford; excerpts
n "The Marriage Broker," "A Lady Named Jo," "Telemachus,
end," "The Blue Magi," and "What's a Nice Country like You. . . ."

Top Right: Ross Gifford, Leilani Johnson in "Blue
Magi" Below: Arne Gunderson, Suzanne Oberjat,
Bill LaVallee in "Telemachus, Friend"

Paul Hodes, Wendy Lesniak, Barry Michlin, Jane
rtson, Bill LaVallee in "What's a Nice Country. . . ."

Bill LaVallee

157

THEATRE AT ST. CLEMENT'S

Artistic Director, Kevin O'Connor
Production Manager, Lewis Rosen
Coordinator, Jean Halbert

ST. CLEMENT'S CHURCH
Opened Wednesday, June 7, 1972.*
Theatre at Saint Clements presents:

EYES OF CHALK

By Toné Brulin; Directed and Adapted from the French by David Villaire; Music, Paul Alan Levi; Sets and Lighting, Scott Johnson; Costumes, James Berton Harris; Sound Collage, Lewis Rosen; Projections, Sally Sullivan; Production Assistant, Alexa Penzner; Photography, Polly Bennell, William Curtis, Scott Johnson, Robert Sevra, Edward Willard; Presented by special arrangement with the Hamm and Clov Stage Co. and Universal Movement Theatre Repertory prior to European tour.

CAST

Abe	Kevin O'Connor
A Woman	Hollin Hood
Zake	Megan Sullivan

A Drama performed without intermission. The action takes place at the present time.

Stage Manager: Lewis Rosen
Press: Alan Eichler, Jean Halbert

* Closed June 25, 1972 after limited engagement of 15 performances and 3 previews.

Kevin O'Connor in "Eyes of Chalk"

THEATRE AT ST. CLEMENT'S

Opened Thursday, September 21, 1972*
Theatre at St. Clement's presents:

OF MICE AND MEN

By John Steinbeck; Director, Charles Briggs; Decor, Carl W Lighting, Gary Grossman; Sound, Lewis Rosen; Harmonica, Jack lente

CAST

George	Gary Michael F
Lennie	Joe F
Candy	Stanley Sied
The Boss	Ken A
Curley	Jerry Co
Curley's Wife	Phyllis Somme
Slim	Anthony Chis
Carlson	Rai-M
Whit	Norman Orn
Crooks	Jimmy Hay

A drama in two acts and six scenes. The action takes place on a on the banks of the Salinas River.

Press: Alan Eichler
Stage Managers: Rick Ralston, Shelly Pryor

* Closed Oct. 15, 1972 after limited run of 16 performances. (no p available)

THEATRE AT ST. CLEMENT'S

Opened Thursday, November 9, 1972.*
Theatre at St. Clement's presents a Theatre of Latin Am (TOLA) production of:

CEREMONY FOR A MURDERED BLACK

By Arrabal; Director, Castulo Guerra; Assistant Director, Cost and Lighting, Esther Williams; Production Assistant, Christy R Technical Staff, Lewis Rosen, Dale Mosher

CAST

Vincent	Ray
Jerome	Tom L
Lucy	Patric E
St. Francis of Assisi	Castulo Guerra/John Henry Red

Performed without intermission.

Press: Alan Eichler
Stage Manager: Stanley Schnur

* Closed Dec. 30, 1972 after limited engagement of 11 performa

John Henry Redwood in "Ceremony for a Murdered Black"

Helio Oiticica Photo

TWO BY PAUL AUSTIN

Director, Louis Turenne; Lighting Designed by Dan Blaszuk; Press,
an Eichler

CAST

"The Funny Men Are in Trouble"
performed by Kevin O'Connor

"Quietus"
h Philip R. Allen, Maury Cooper, Eddie Jones, Bruce
Kornbluth, Betsy Redfield

Closed Dec. 7, 1972 after limited engagement of 12 performances.

Right: Eddie Jones, Betsy Redfield in "Quietus"

**Andrea Stark, Lee McClelland, Ed Henkel Above:
Jean Erdman in "Moon Mysteries"**

THEATRE AT ST. CLEMENT'S
Opened Sunday, November 26, 1972.*
The Theatre at St. Clement's presents the Open Eye Production
of:

MOON MYSTERIES

By W. B. Yeats; Director, Jean Erdman; Sets and Lighting, Scott
Johnson; Costumes and Masks, Ralph Lee; Songs, Teiji Ito, Wendy Erdman, John Fitzgibbon

CAST

"A Full Moon in March"
Attendant Entertainers .... Dana Alexis Zeller, John FitzGibbon
Queen .... Lee McClelland (masked), Jane Roseman,
Andrea Stark
Swineherd .... John Genke (masked), Edward Henkel
Queen .... Jean Erdman, Jane Roseman, Andrea Stark
Alternates: Elizabeth Lage, Diana Byer

"The Cat and the Moon"
A Blind Beggar .... John Genke
A Lame Beggar .... John FitzGibbon
The Singer .... Ralph Lee
Musicians .... Teijo Ito, Wendy Erdman, Dan Erkkila, Genji Ito

"Calvary"
Singers .... Wendy Erdman, Lee McClelland, Dana Alexis Zeller
Christ .... Theodore Sorel
Lazarus .... John Genke
Judas .... John FitzGibbon
Roman Soldiers .... Charles Dinsthul, Jamey Gurman,
Ralph Lee

Press: Alan Eichler, Marcia Sherman
Stage Managers: Tony Davis, Wendy Erdman

* Closed Jan. 28, 1973 after limited engagement of 25 performances.

Cherel Winett Photo

Ruth Hermine

(Anna-Maria Friedinger Photo)

THEATRE AT ST. CLEMENT'S
Opened Friday, February 2, 1973.*
The Theatre at St. Clement's presents in Spanish and English
the Duo Theatre's production of:

THE WHITE WHORE AND THE BIT PLAYER

By Tom Eyen; Director, Manuel Martin; Choreography, Tony Can-
tanese; Assistant to the Director, Martha Chavez; Lighting, Lewis Rosen,
Dale Mosher; Technical Assistants, Antonio Candolfi, Martha Chavez;
Scenery, Jose Erasto Ramirez; Costumes, Van Labriola; Sound, Felipe
Napoles; Hairstylist, Carlos Noceda

CAST

Whore .... Candy Darling
                          or Magaly Alabau (in Spanish)
Nun .... Hortensia Colorado
                          or Graciela Mas (in Spanish)

LOS LOCOS: Edwing Avila, Antonio Candolfi, Rafael Delgado, Ken
Evans, Arturo Gines, Roberto Lopez, Pedro Lorca, Carlos Noceda, Rene
Troche

A play in one act.

Press: Alan Eichler

* Closed Feb. 18, 1973 after limited engagement of 22 performances.

**Michael Sacks, Susan Browning, Tom Rosqui,
Charlotte Rae, Beeson Carroll**

THEATRE AT ST. CLEMENT'S
Opened Thursday, January 4, 1973.*
Theatre at St. Clement's presents:

THE GOLDEN DAFFODIL DWARF

By Daniela Gioseffi; Directed and Choreographed by Nancy Rub
Costumes, Danny Morgan; Sound, George Prideaux; Lighting, R. S. W
kler; Technical Adviser, Richard Kearney; Costumes, Projections, a
song for the "Sea Hag" composed and sung by Daniela Gioseffi; Produ
tion Assistant Irene Wiley; Assistant Producer, Joseph Morella

CAST

"The Golden Daffodil Dwarf"
Young Woman .... Susanne Marl
Dwarf .... Ruth Hermi

"Care of the Body"
First Man .... Evan Thomps
Second Man .... Bob Murr
First Woman .... Mary Mo
Second Woman .... Susanne Marl

"The Sea Hag in the Cave of Sleep"
Old Woman .... Tessa Ka
Middle-aged Woman .... Ingrid Sonnichs
Young Woman .... Mary Mo

"Violets and Violins"
The Company

Presented in two parts.

Press: Alan Eichler
Stage Manager: Robert Ellowitz

* Closed Jan. 14, 1973 after limited engagement of 12 performances

Candy Darling

(Amnon Ben Nomis Photo)

THEATRE AT ST. CLEMENT'S
Opened Sunday, April 29, 1973.*
Theatre at Saint Clement's presents:

WHISKEY

By Terrence McNally; Director, Kevin O'Connor; Sets, Kert Lun
Lighting, Charles Cosler; Costumes, Lorie Watson; Sound, Lewis Ro
Organist, Jeff Sweet; Co-ordinator, Jean Halbert; Production Assista
Shelley Mitchell, Dan Crugnale, Patrick McCord

CAST

Announcer .... Kelly Fitzpa
I. W. Harper .... Tom Ro
Tia Maria .... Charlotte
Johnny Walker .... Beeson Ca
Southern Comfort .... Susan Brow
Jack Daniels .... Michael S

A Comedy in two acts and four scenes. The action takes place a
present time in the Houston Astrodome, and a large suite in a very sw
hotel in Downtown Houston.

Administrative Director: Lawrence Goossen
Press: Alan Eichler
Stage Manager: Jimmy Cuomo

* Closed May 6, 1973 after limited engagement of 17 performance

Henry Grossman Photo

LLIVAN STREET PLAYHOUSE
Opened Tuesday, May 3, 1960.*
Lore Noto presents:

THE FANTASTICKS

ook and Lyrics, Tom Jones; Suggested by Edmond Rostand's play
s Romantiques"; Music, Harvey Schmidt; Director, Word Baker;
sical Direction-Arrangements, Julian Stein; Designed by Ed Wittstein;
oelate Producers, Sheldon Baron, Dorothy Olim, Robert Alan Gold;
inal Cast Album by MGM Records.

CAST

Narrator	Martin Vidnovic†1
Girl	Marty Morris†2
Boy	Phil Killian†3
's Father	Donald Babcock†4
's Father	Gonzalo Madurga†5
Actor	Ron Prather†6
Who Dies	Bill McIntyre†7
Mute	Robert Schrock†8
he piano	William F. McDaniel
he harp	Sally Foster†9

SICAL NUMBERS: Overture, "Try to Remember," "Much More,"
taphor," "Never Say No," "It Depends on What You Pay," "Soon
Gonna Rain," "Rape Ballet," "Happy Ending," "This Plum Is Too
," "I Can See It," "Plant a Radish," "Round and Round," "They
e You"

Musical in two acts.

General Manager: Bob MacDonald
Press: Solters/Sabinson/Roskin, Marilyn LeVine
Stage Managers: Jonathan Penzner, Geoffrey Brown

ll playing May 31, 1973. For original production, see THEATRE
ORLD, Vol. 16.
cceeded by: 1. Joe Bellomo, 2. Sharon Werner, 3. Michael Glenn-
ith, 4. Lore Noto, 5. John High, 6. Seamus O'Brien, 7. James Cook,
Robert Brigham, 9. Pattee Cohen

Van Williams Photos

Lore Noto, Michael Glenn-Smith

Joe Bellomo (top), Sharon Werner, Michael Glenn-Smith

PLAYHOUSE THEATRE
Opened Wednesday, April 19, 1972.*
(Moved June 13, 1972 to Edison Theatre)
Edward Padula and Arch Lustberg present Vinette Carroll's
Urban Arts Corps production of:

DON'T BOTHER ME, I CAN'T COPE

Conceived a. ┤ Directed by Vinnette Carroll; Written by Micki Grant;
Music and Lyrics Micki Grant; Scenery, Richard A. Miller; Costumes,
Edna Watson; Lighting, B. J. Sammler; Musical Direction and Arrangements, Danny Holgate; Associate Producer, Gordon Gray, Jr.; Production Supervisor, Sam Ellis; Choreography, George Faison; Scenery
supervised by Neil Peter Jampolis; Costumes, supervised by Sara Brook;
Lighting supervised by Ken Billington; Assistant to Producers, Robert

Moeser; Presented in association with Ford's Theatre Society of Washington, D.C.; Original Cast Album by Polydor Records.

CAST

Alex Bradford
Hope Clarke†1
Micki Grant†2
Bobby Hill†3
Arnold Wilkerson †4

SINGERS: Alberta Bradford, Charles Campbell, Marie Thomas, Pat
Lundy, D. Morris Brown

DANCERS: Thommie Bush, Gerald G. Francis, Ben Harney, Leona
Johnson

UNDERSTUDIES: Alex Bradford, Alberta Bradford; Bobby Hill, Ben
Harney; Micki Grant, Marie Thomas; Arnold Wilkerson, Ben Harney;
Hope Clarke, Arlene Rolant; Arlene Rolant, Leona Johnson

MUSICAL NUMBERS: "I Gotta Keep Movin'," "Harlem Streets,"
"Lookin' over from Your Side," "Don't Bother Me, I Can't Cope,"
"When I Feel Like Movin'," "Help," "Fighting for Pharoah," "Good
Vibrations," "Love Power," "You Think I Got Rhythm?," "They Keep
Coming," "My Name Is Man," "Questions," "It Takes a Whole Lot of
Human Feeling," "Time Brings about a Change," "So Little Time,"
"Thank Heaven for You," "Show Me That Special Gene," "So Long
Sammy," "All I Need"

A Musical Entertainment in two acts.

General Manager: Norman Kean
Company Manager: Jay Kingwill
Press: Betty Lee Hunt, Harriett Trachtenberg, Henry Luhrman,
Maria C. Pucci
Stage Managers: Robert Moeser, Marie Thomas

* Still playing May 31, 1973.
† Succeeded during vacations by: 1. Arlene Rolant, 2. Vivian Reed, 3.
Andy Torres, 4. Damon Evans

Friedman-Abeles Photo

Bobby Hill, Micki Grant

CHERRY LANE THEATRE
Opened Monday, May 17, 1971.*
(Moved August 10, 1971 to Promenade Theatre)
Edgar Lansbury, Stuart Duncan, Joseph Beruh present:

GODSPELL

Music and Lyrics, Stephen Schwartz; Conceived and Directed by Jo┤
Michael Tebelak; Based on "The Gospel according to St. Matthe┤
Lighting, Lowell D. Achsinger; Costumes, Susan Tsu; Production Supe┤
sor, Nina Faso; Musical Director, David Lewis; Associate Produc┤
Charles Haid; Musical Arrangement and Direction, Stephen Schwa┤
Assistant to Producers, Darrell Jonas; Musical Supervision, Steve R┤
hardt; Production Assistant, Jan Allred; Original Cast Album by ┤
Records.

CAST

Lamar Alford†	Sonia Manzan┤
Peggy Gordon	Gilmer McCormic┤
David Haskell	Jeffrey Mylet┤
Joanne Jonas	Stephen Natha┤
Robin Lamont	Herb Simo┤

MUSICAL NUMBERS: "Tower of Babble," "Prepare Ye the Way┤
the Lord," "Save the People," "Day by Day," "Learn Your Less┤
Well," "Bless the Lord," "All for the Best," "All Good Gifts," "Ligh┤
the World," "Turn Back, O Man," "Alas for You," "By My Side," "┤
Beseech Thee," "On the Willows"

A Musical in two acts and sixteen scenes.

General Manager: Al Isaac
Company Managers: Gary Gunas, Bob Skerry
Press: Gifford/Wallace, Merle Frimark, Tom Trenkle
Stage Managers: Peter Kean, Judy Schoen, Clint Spencer

* Still playing May 31, 1973. For original NY production, see T┤
ATRE WORLD, Vol. 28.
† During the season the following appeared in the cast: Herb Braha,┤
Braverman, Delores Hall, Judy Kahan, Jeanne Lange, Elizabeth┤
thram, Bobby Lee, Andy Rohrer, Marley Sims, Howard L. Sponse┤
Jr., William Thomas, Jr., Mark Baker, Enid Edelman, Paul Krep┤
Don Scardino, Debbie Weems, with alternates Carter Cole, Judy ┤
gress, Bob Garrett, Barbara Lail, Linda Sherwood, Dan Stone┤

Don Scardino, Mark Baker and company

William L. Smith Photo

MERCER-HANSBERRY THEATRE
Opened Tuesday, March 23, 1971.*
Sankowich/Golyn Productions presents:

ONE FLEW OVER THE CUCKOO'S NEST

By Dale Wasserman; From novel by Ken Kesey; Director, Lee D.
Sankowich; Producer, Rudi Golyn; Designed by Neil Peter Jampolis;
Production Supervisor, Harvey Medlinsky; Sound, Gary and Timmy
Morris; Costumes, Carolyn Klay

CAST

Chief Bromden	William Burns†1
Aide Williams	William Paterson, Jr.†2
Aide Washington	John Henry Redwood†3
Nurse Ratched	Janet Ward†4
Nurse Flinn	Eve Packer†5
Dale Harding	James J. Sloyan†6
Billy Bibbitt	Lawrie Driscoll†7
Charles Atkins Cheswick III	Williams Duff-Griffin†8
Frank Scanlon	Jon Richards†9
Anthony Martini	Danny DeVito†10
Ruckly	Joseph Napoli†11
Randle Patrick McMurphy	William Devane†12
Dr. Spivey	Jack Aaron†13
Aide Turkle	Jeffrey Miller†14
Candy	Louie Piday†15
Technician	Kelly Monaghan†16
Sandy	Sydney Adreani†17

A Drama in two acts. The action takes place at the present time in a
ward in a state mental hospital.

General Manager: William Craver
Company Manager: Harry Chittenden
Press: Gifford/Wallace, Tom Trenkle, Merle Frimark
Stage Managers: Philip Cusack, James Himelsbach, Scott Bruno

Still playing May 31, 1973. For original NY production, see THEA-
TRE WORLD, Vol. 20.

Succeeded by: 1. Donn Whyte, Maxwell Gail, Jr., 2. James Dickson,
Michael Mitchell, 3. Earl Ferguson, Charles Kashi, John Henry Red-
wood, 4. Jane Cronin, 5. Carolyn Cunningham, Wendy Lee, Andrea
Skolnick, 6. Arthur Berwick, 7. Jerry Dodge, Kelly Monaghan, Bruce
Bouchard, 8. John D. Gowans, 9. Sherman Lloyd, 10. Larry Spinelli,
11. Lee Cotterell, 12. Lane Smith, George Welbes, Kevin Conway, 13.
Lou Bullock, James B. Spann, 14. Charles Kashi, Earl Ferguson, David
Stewart, 15. Marlena Lustik, 16. Thomas Barrett, James Himelsbach,
Scott Bruno, Peter Boyden, Frank Hall, 17. Jeannie Teller

Yapa Photo

Arthur Berwick, Louie Piday, Lane Smith, Sydney
Andreani

GRAMERCY ARTS THEATRE
Opened Wednesday, March 24, 1971*
(Moved April 28, 1971 to Mercer-Shaw Arena)
Manon Enterprises Ltd. and Propositions Inc. present:

THE PROPOSITION

Conceived and Directed by Allan Albert; Designed by Allan Albert,
Ron Ginsberg, Clint Helvey; Musical Director and Pianist, Danny Troob;
Costumes, Arthur McGee; Musical Director, Raphael Crystal

CAST

Paul Kreppel	Ray Baker
Judy Kahan	Ginny Russell
Gerri Librandi	John Monteith
David Brezniak	John Jutkowitz
David Brezniak	John Jutkowitz
Fred Grandy	Jane Ranallo
Shelly Burns	Judith Cohen
Sam Jory	Jim Cyrus
Sam Freed	

An Improvisational Musical Revue in two acts.

General Manager: Cynthia Parker
Press: Alan Eichler

* Still playing May 31, 1973

Sam Freed, Judith Cohen Right Center: Ray Baker,
Gerri Librandi, Jim Cyrus, John Monteith

Friedman-Abeles Photos

THEATRE FOUR

Opened Sunday, April 23, 1972*
Susan Richardson, Lawrence Goossen and Seth Schapiro present:

THE REAL INSPECTOR HOUND
and
AFTER MAGRITTE

By Tom Stoppard; Director, Joseph Hardy; Scenery, William Ritman; Lighting, Richard Nelson; Costumes, Joseph G. Aulisi; Hairstylist, Joe Tubens; Choreography, Patricia Birch; Technical Assistant, Archie Gresham; Production Assistant, Jonathan Sand

CAST

"After Magritte"
In a room during early evening
Harris .... Konrad Matthaei[1]
Thelma .... Carrie Nye[2]
Mother .... Jane Connell[3]
Foot .... Remak Ramsay[4]
Holmes .... Edmond Genest

"The Real Inspector Hound"
Opening night in a theatre
Moon .... David Rounds[5]
Birdboot .... Tom Lacy[6]
Mrs. Drudge .... Jane Connell[3]
Simon .... Konrad Matthaei[1]
Felicity .... Boni Enten[7]
Cynthia .... Carrie Nye[2]
Magnus .... Remak Ramsay[4]
Inspector Hound .... Edmond Genest
BBC Voice .... Brian Murray
Body .... Abe de la Houssaye[8]
Standbys: Ted Danson, Bruce Kornbluth, Lynn Milgrim, George Blackman

Company Managers: Dorothy Olim, Phyllis Restaino
Press: Alan Eichler, James J. O'Rourke
Stage Managers: Suzanne Egan, Katherine McGrath

* Closed June 3, 1973 after 465 performances. For original production see THEATRE WORLD, Vol. 28.
† Succeeded by: 1. Christopher Bernau, Donegan Smith, Ted Danson, 2. Lynn Milgrim, Katherine McGrath, 3. Georgia Heaslip, Katherine McGrath, Lizabeth Pritchett, Kate Wilkinson, 4. William Bogert, John-David Keller, 5. Lenny Baker, 6. Michael Egan, 7. Randy Danson, Mary Denham, 8. Jonathan Sand

Martha Swope Photos

Right: Mary Denham, Edmond Genest Top: Katherine McGrath, John-David Keller, Edmond Genest, Lizabeth Pritchett, Lenny Baker, Michael Egan, Donegan Smith, Mary Denham

OFF-BROADWAY PRODUCTIONS FROM OTHER SEASONS THAT CLOSED THIS SEASO

Title	Opened	Closed	
Jacques Brel Is Alive and Well and Living in Paris	1/22/68	7/2/72	1847
Small Craft Warnings	4/2/72	9/17/72	201
Anna K	5/7/72	12/10/72	196
Walk Together Children	3/16/72	7/2/72	89
The Hunter	5/23/72	7/16/72	96
Older People	5/14/72	6/25/72	70
Jamimma	3/16/72	6/25/72	49
The Crucible	4/27/72	6/3/72	44
Frederick Douglas through His Own Words	5/9/72	6/4/72	32

PRODUCTIONS THAT OPENED AND CLOSED BEFORE SCHEDULED BROADWAY PREMIERES

COMEDY

Book, Lawrence Carra; Music and Lyrics, Hugo Peretti, Luigi Crea-
re, George David Weiss; Director, Lawrence Carra; Musical Numbers
[sta]ged by Stephen Reinhardt; Scenery and Costumes, William Pitkin;
[Li]ghting, Roger Morgan; Orchestrations, Jack Andrews; Musical Direc-
[to]r, Joseph Stecko; Musical Arrangements, Mel Marvin; Sound, Astral
[A]coustics; Producers, Edgar Lansbury, Stuart Duncan, Joseph Beruh;
[Pr]oducers Assistants, Gary Gunas, Bob Skerry; Production Assistants,
[Ja]net Sonenberg, Ron Bunker; Based on commedia dell'arte "The Great
[M]agician"; Opened at the Colonial Theatre in Boston on Monday, Nov.
[13,] 1972 and closed there Nov. 18, 1972.

CAST

[Th]e Great Magician of Arcadia	Merwin Goldsmith
[Ca]pitano Cockalorum	George S. Irving
[Z]oviello	Joseph Bova
[Pa]ntalone	Joseph R. Sicari
[Pu]lcinella	Bill McCutcheon
[D]octor Gratiano	Jerry Sroka
[Fr]anceschina	Diane J. Findlay
[Za]nni	Frank Vohs
[M]elbi	Marty Morris
[Cl]eno	George Lee Andrews
[Cl]ori	Suellen Estey
[Es]pino	John Witham
[Ba]cchus	Marc Jordan
[Ba]cchantes	Marilyn Saunders, Lana Shaw
Country Fellow	Thom Christoph
[So]undman	Bobby Lee

[U]NDERSTUDIES: Franceschina, Clori, Marilyn Saunders; Melbi, Lana
[Sh]aw; Capitano, Cockalorum, Gratiano, Pantalone, Marc Jordan; Co-
[vie]llo, Pulcinella, Zanni, Magician, Bacchus, Soundman, Frank Gior-
[da]no; Elpino, Sireno, Thom Christoph

[M]USICAL NUMBERS: "Comedy," "Open Your Heart," "I'm the
[Co]ckalorum," "Gotta Hang My Wash out to Dry," "A Friend Is a
[Fri]end," "Where Is My Love," "Scarifice," "God Bless the Fig Tree,"
[T]arantella," "Buttercup," "Smile, Smile, Smile," "Magnetic," "Love Is
[Su]ch a Fragile Thing," "Breakin' the Spell," "Whirlwind Circle," Finale

A Musical Comedy in two acts. The action takes place on the island
[of] Arcadia.

General Manager: Marvin A. Krauss
Press: Gifford/Wallace
Company Managers: Al Isaac, Gail Bell
Stage Managers: Gigi Cascio, Peter Kean, Marc Jordan

William L. Smith Photo

Joseph R. Sicari, Frank Vohs, Diane J. Findlay,
Thom Christoph, Joseph Bova

DETECTIVE STORY

By Sidney Kingsley; Director, Harold J. Kennedy; Setting and Lighting, William Ritman; Costumes, Nancy Potts; Associate Producer, Michael Kasdan; Hairstylist, Steve Atha; Producers Assistant, Ray
Cerabone; Associate Producer, Harold Endicott; Presented by Theater
1973 (Richard Barr, Charles Woodward); Opened Saturday, March 10,
1973 at the Shubert in Philadelphia, and closed there Mar. 24, 1973.

CAST

Detective Dakis	Michael Beirne
Shoplifter	Rita Moreno
Detective Gallagher	Walter Flanagan
Patrolman Keogh	Eddie Jones
Mrs. Farragut	Doro Merande
Joe Feinson	Marty Brill
Detective Callahan	Jack Collard
Detective O'Brien	Sam J. Coppola
Detective Brody	Paul Lipson
Endicott Sims	Harold J. Kennedy
Detective McLeod	Barry Nelson
Arthur Kindred	Allen Williams†
Patrolman Barnes	Freeman Roberts
Charlie (1st burglar)	Marc Alaimo
Lewis (2nd Burgler)	Philip Larson
Mrs. Bagatelle	Helen Noyes
Dr. Schneider	Robert Strauss
Lt. Monoghan	James Pritchett
Susan Carmichael	Maureen Anderman
Miss Hatch	Rita Gam
Mr. Gallantz	Macon McCalman
Patrolman Baker	Neil Alan
Mr. Pritchett	Charles White
Mary McLeod	Nancy Dussault
Tami Giacoppetti	Charles Siebert
Photographer	J. Patric Flynn
Lady	Erica Yohn
Indignant Citizen	Marilyn Brodnick

UNDERSTUDIES: Sims, Schneider, Richard Woods; Joe Feinson, Macon McCalman; Susan, Shoplifter, Marilynn Brodnick

A Drama in three acts. The action takes place in 1949 in the detective
squad room of a New York City precinct police station.

General Manager: Michael Kasdan
Press: Betty Lee Hunt, Henry Luhrman, Harriett Trachtenberg,
Maria C. Pucci
Stage Managers: Bruce Blaine, Allen Williams

† Succeeded by Kipp Osborne. For original New York production, see
THEATRE WORLD, Vol. 5.

Friedman-Abeles Photo

**Paul Lipson, Rita Moreno, Marty Brill, Barry
Nelson, Robert Strauss**

AND MISS REARDON DRINKS A LITTLE

By Paul Zindel; Director, Melvin Bernhardt; Scenery, Fred Voelpel; Lighting, Martin Aronstein; Costumes, Sara Brook; Presented by James B. McKenzie, Spofford J. Beadle, Seth L. Schapiro, Kenneth Waissman, Maxine Fox, in association with Gordon Crowe; Tour Direction, American Theatre Productions; Assistant to Producers, Linda D. Ford; Opened Thursday, Jan. 25, 1973 in Powers Auditorium, Youngstown, Ohio, and closed Apr. 8, 1973 in Masonic Auditorium, Scranton, Pa.

CAST

Catherine Reardon	Lillian Roth†1
Mrs. Pentrano	Victoria Zussin
Delivery Boy	William Spencer Reilly
Ceil Adams	Avril Gentles†2
Anna Reardon	Gretchen Wyler
Fleur Stein	Marilyn Cooper
Bob Stein	Stan Edelman

A Drama in three acts. The action takes place at the present time in the apartment of Catherine and Anna Reardon.

Company Manager: Donald Tirabassi
Press: Harvey B. Sabinson, Lee Solters
Stage Managers: Heinz Hohenwald, William Spencer Reilly

† Succeeded by: 1. Avril Gentles, 2. Jeannette Leahy
For original NY Production, See THEATRE WORLD, Vol. 27.

Right: Lillian Roth, Gretchen Wyler, Avril Gentles

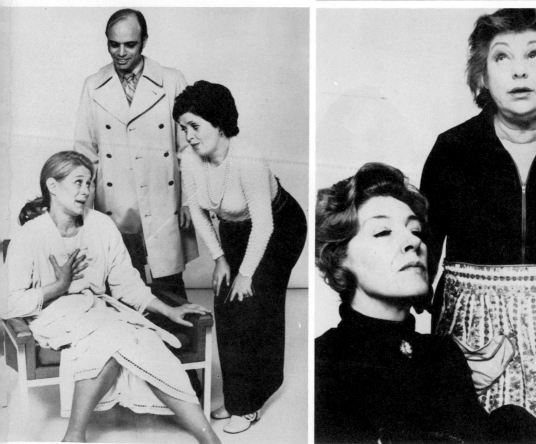

Gretchen Wyler, Stan Edelman, Marilyn Cooper

Avril Gentles, Lillian Roth

APPLAUSE

Book, Betty Comden, Adolph Green; Music, Charles Strouse; Lyrics,
ee Adams; Based on film "All about Eve," and original story by Mary
rr; Director-Choreographer, Ron Field; Original Choreography re-
aged by Ed Nolfi; Scenery, Robert Randolph; Costumes, Ray Aghayan;
ighting, Tharon Musser; Vocal Arrangements, Donald Pippin; Orches-
ations, Philip J. Lang; Dance and Incidental Music arranged by Mel
1arvin; Musical Direction, Michael Rose; Original cast album by ABC
ecords; Presented by William Court Cohen, Edward H. Davis, and
olumbia Artists Theatrical Corp.; Costume Coordinator, Orrin Reiley;
roduction Associate, Charlotte Wilcox; Production Assistant, Robb
ady; Hairstylist, Louis Guzman; Presented in association with Robert
. Schuler; Opened Friday Sept. 22, 1972 in the Masonic Auditorium,
cranton, Pa., and closed May 5, 1973 in Veterans Memorial Auditorium,
rovidence, R. I.

CAST

1argo Channing	Patrice Munsel
ve Harrington	Diane McAfee
oward Benedict	Ed Fuller
ert	Alan Jordan†1
uzz Richards	Stephen Everett
ill Sampson	Virgil Curry
uane Fox	Bryan Spencer†2
aren Richards	Lisa Carroll†3
artender	Brandt Edwards
ancer in bar	Scott David†4
eter	Jay Bonnell
an Harding	Brandt Edwards
anny	David Kresser
ia	Pia Zadora
arol	Zuzane Knycht†5
ey	Scott David†6
usicians	Jay Grimes †7, Alan Jordan, David Westphal
V Director	J. Curtis Crimp
utograph Seeker	B. J. Hanford

NGERS: Cynthia Cobey, Bobbie Franklin, Jay Bonnell, Alan Jordan,
ephen Wright
ANCERS: Carole Banninger, B. J. Hanford, Jane Karel, Zuzane
nych, Jodie McDowell, Heidi Schuler, J. Curtis Crimp, Scott David, Jay
rimes, Louis Guzman, Marius Hanford, David Kresser, Dennis Stew-
t, David Westphal

NDERSTUDIES: Margo, Lisa Carroll; Bill, Alan Jordan; Howard,
uzz, Jay Bonnell; Karen, Pia, Bobbie Franklin; Eve, Cynthia Cobey;
eter, Stan, Marius Hanford; Bert, David Kresser

1USICAL NUMBERS: "Backstage Babble," "Think How It's Gonna
e," "But Alive," "The Best Night of My Life," "Who's That Girl?,"
Applause," "Hurry Back," "Fasten Your Seat Belts," "Welcome to the
heatre," "Inner Thoughts," "Good Friends," "She's No Longer a
ypsy," "One of a Kind," "One Halloween," "Something Greater"

A Musical in 2 acts and 16 scenes. The action takes place at the present
ne in and around New York City.

Company Manager: Donald Antonelli, Johanna Pool
Press: Robert W. Jennings
NY Promotion Manager: Bernard Simon
Stage Managers: John Holly, Peter B. Mumford, Jay Crimes,
Marius Hanford

Succeeded by: 1. Brad Tyrrell, 2. Stephen Wright, Scott David, 3. Ann
Gardner, 4. Patrick McCann, Dennis Stewart, 5. Wendy Worth, 6.
Patrick McCann, 7. Fabian Stuart
or original NY production, see THEATRE WORLD Vol. 26.

**Top Right: Pia Zadora Below: Stephen Everett, Ed
Fuller, Lisa Carroll, Patrice Munsel, Virgil Curry**

Patrice Munsel (also above), Bryan Spencer, Diane
McAfee

THE EFFECT OF GAMMA RAYS ON MAN-IN-THE-MOON MARIGOLDS

By Paul Zindel; Director, Leland Ball; Music and Sound, James Reichert; Setting, Fred Voelpel; Lighting, Martin Aronstein; Costumes, Sara Brook; Associate Producer, Julie Hughes; Production Supervisor, Paul Bengsten; Tour Coordinator, Jane B. Friedlander; Production Associate, Charlotte W. Wilcox; An Orin Lehman Production; Presented by Theatre Now, Inc.; Opened Friday, Oct. 13, 1972 in Masonic Temple, Scranton, Pa., and closed Jan. 11, 1973 in Castleton, Vt.

CAST

Tillie	Alexandra Stoddart
Beatrice	Teresa Wright
Ruth	Robin Nolan
Nanny	Helen Ross
Janice Vickery	Carol Potter

STANDBYS: Beatrice, Mary Hara; Tillie, Ruth, Carol Potter; Janice, Christie Virtue

A Play in two acts. The action takes place at the present time in Beatrice's home: a room of wood which was once a vegetable store, and a point of debarkation for a horse-drawn wagon to bring its wares to a small town.

Company Manager: Robb Lady
Press: Fred Weterick
Stage Managers: Jack Hines, Christie Virtue
For original New York production, see THEATRE WORLD, Vol. 26.

Robin Nolan, Helen Ross, Teresa Wright, Alexandra Stoddart
Top Right: Robin Nolan, Alexandra Stoddart, Teresa Wright

FOLLIES

Book, James Goldman; Music and Lyrics, Stephen Sondheim; Direc-
[to]rs, Harold Prince, Michael Bennett; Choreography, Michael Bennett;
[Sce]nery, Boris Aronson; Costumes, Florence Klotz; Lighting, Tharon
[Mu]sser; Musical Direction, Paul Gemignani; Orchestrations, Jonathan
[Tu]nick; Dance Music Arrangements, John Berkman; Hairstylist, Joe
[Tub]ens; Original Cast Album by Capitol Records; Associate Choreogra-
[phe]r, Bob Avian; Production Supervisor, Ruth Mitchell; Production As-
[sist]ant, Ted Chapin; Presented by Harold Prince in association with Ruth
[Mit]chell; Opened new Shubert Theatre, Century City, Calif., Saturday,
[July] 22, 1972, and closed there Oct. 1 1972.

CAST

[Ma]jor-Domo	Joseph Nelson
[Sal]ly Durant Plummer	Dorothy Collins†1
[Yo]ung Sally	Marti Rolph
[Ch]ristine Crane	Jan Clayton
[Wil]ly Wheeler	Joel Craig
[Stel]la Deems	Mary McCarty
[Ma]x Deems	Keith Kaldenberg
[He]di Schiller	Justine Johnston
[Ch]auffeur	John Grigas
[Me]ridith Lane	Terry Saunders
[Ro]et Richards	Peter Walker
[Ro]scoe	Michael Bartlett
[Ro]scoe's Daughter	Candace Cooke
[De]edee West	Helon Blount
[San]dra Donovan	Sonja Levkova
[Hat]tie Walker	Ethel Shutta
[You]ng Hattie	Jacqueline Payne
[Em]ily Whitman	Camila Ashland
[The]odore Whitman	Ted Lawrie
[Vin]cent	Patrick Spohn
[Van]essa	Jayne Turner
[You]ng Vincent	David Evans
[You]ng Vanessa	Margot Travers
[Sol]ange LaFitte	Fifi D'Orsay
[Car]lotta Campion	Yvonne De Carlo
[Phyl]lis Rogers Stone	Alexis Smith
[Ben]jamin Stone	John McMartin†2
[You]ng Phyllis	Suzanne Rogers
[You]ng Ben	Kurt Peterson
[Bud]dy Plummer	Gene Nelson
[You]ng Buddy	Harvey Evans
[Dmi]tri Weismann	Edwin Steffe
[You]ng Heidi	Marti Rolph
[Ka]in	Roy Barry
[Part]y Musicians	Arthur Wagner and Friends
[Sho]wgirls	Suzanne Briggs, Ursula Maschmeyer, Margot Travers, Sandahl Bergman

[SIN]GERS AND DANCERS: Susanna Clemm, Candace Cooke, Patricia
[Gar]land, Sonia Haney, Trish Maloney, Jacqueline Payne, Pamela Serpe,
[Roy] Barry, Steve Boockvor, Joel Craig, David Evans, Joseph Nelson, Ken
[Urmst]s, Ken Urmston

[STA]NDBYS AND UNDERSTUDIES: Phyllis, Carlotta, Terry Saun-
[ders]; Sally, Jan Clayton; Buddy, Ted Lawrie; Benjamin, Peter Walker;
[You]ng Phyllis, Candace Cooke; Young Ben, Ken Urmston; Vincent, Joel
[Crai]g; Solange, Sonja Levkova

[MU]SICAL NUMBERS: "Beautiful Girls," "Don't Look at Me," "Wait-
[ing] for the Girls Upstairs," "Listen to the Rain on the Roof," "Ah!
[Paris]!," "Broadway Baby," "The Road You Didn't Take," "Bolero d'A-
[mou]r," "In Buddy's Eyes," "Who's That Woman?," "I'm Still Here,"
[Too] Many Mornings," "The Right Girl," "One More Kiss," "Could I
[Lea]ve You?," "Loveland," "You're Gonna Love Tomorrow," "Love Will
[See] Us Through," "The God-Why-Don't-You-Love-Me-Blues," "Losing
[My] Mind," "The Story of Lucy and Jessie," "Live, Laugh, Love"

[A] Musical performed without intermission. The action takes place
[toni]ght on the stage of the Weismann Theatre.

General Manager: Carl Fisher
Company Manager: John Caruso
Press: Mary Bryant, Stanley F. Kaminsky
Stage Managers: Fritz Holt, George Martin, John Grigas

[Su]cceeded by: 1. Janet Blair, 2 Edward Winter
[For o]riginal New York production, see THEATRE WORLD, Vol. 27.

Martha Swope, Van Williams Photos

[T]op Right: Kurt Peterson, Virginia Sandifur, Harvey
Evans, Marti Rolph
[Bel]ow: Alexis Smith, John McMartin, Dorothy Collins,
Gene Nelson

**Alexis Smith, Mary McCarty, Dorothy Collins, Helon
Blount**

GODSPELL

Conceived by John-Michael Tebelak; Music and Lyrics, Stephen Schwartz; Based on The Gospel According to St. Matthew; Director, Nina Faso; Lighting, Spencer Mosse; Costumes, Susan Tsu; Musical Director, Steve Reinhardt; Associate Producer, Charles Haid; Musical Arrangement and Direction, Stephen Schwartz; Original Cast Album by Bell Records; Assistant to Producers, Gary Gunas; Production Coordinator, Gail Bell; Production Assistants, Ronald Bunker, Ellen Katz, Kathe Baar; Presented by Edgar Lansbury, Stuart Duncan, Joseph Beruh; Opened in the Wilbur Theatre, Boston, Dec. 11, 1971 and still playing May 31, 1973.

CAST

Lee Anthony	Barbara Allen Lail
Lloyd Bremseth	Carla Meyer
Lillian Cataldi	Maureen Moore
Wendie Cohen	Mark Shera
Kathie Covette	Kathy Sillaway
Peter Covette	Mark Syers
Helen Gelzer	Dan Stone
Lee Anthony Genesis	Evelyn Weller
Gary Imhoff	Jeffrey F. Weller
Rosanne Katon	

MUSICAL NUMBERS: "Tower of Babble," "Prepare Ye the Way of the Lord," "Save the People," "Day by Day," "Learn Your Lesson Well," "Bless the Lord," "All for the Best," "All Good Gifts," "Light of the World," "Turn Back, O Man," "Alas for You," "By My Side," "We Beseech You," "On the Willows," Finale.

A Musical in two acts.

General Manager: Marvin A. Krauss
Company Manager: Janice Stanton, Patt Dale
Press: Gifford/Wallace, Horace Greeley McNab, Stanley Kaminsky
Stage Manager: Clint Spencer, Steve Zweigbaum

Jeffrey F. Weller and company
(William L. Smith Photo)

Gordon Thomson, Gerry Salsberg

GODSPELL

Credits same as listed above, except: Musical Conductor, Paul Shaff Production Supervised by Howard L. Sponseller, Jr.; Opened at the Roy Alexandra Theatre, Toronto, Canada, Thursday, June 1, 1972, a moved to Playhouse Theatre, Sept. 8, 1972 where it is still playing M 31, 1973.

CAST

Valda Aviks	Victor Garber
Avril Chown	Gilda Radner
Jayne Eastwood	Gerry Salsberg
Eugene Levy	Don Scardino
Andrea Martin	Martin Short
Maryann McDonald	Rudy Webb
Derek McGrath	Gordon Thomson
Patti Elsasser	Nancy Dolman, Robin White

Company Manager: Marlene Smith
Press: Folio Creative
Stage Managers: Don Thomas, Derek McGrath, Robin White

GODSPELL

Credits same as listed above; Opened in Geary Theatre, San Francisco, Cal., July 18, 1972, and still playing May 31, 1973.

CAST

Jon Buffington	Stephen Nathan
Angela Ruth Elliott	Kitty Rea
Laurie Faso	Tom Rolfing
Lois Foraker	Craig Schaefer
Patti Mariano	Cle Thompson

Alternates: Emil Borelli, Faye Butler, Roger Kozol, Tina Chappel

General Manager: Marvin A. Krauss
Company Manager: Reginald S. Tonry
Press: Gifford/Wallace, Cheryle Elliott, Merle Frimark
Stage Manager: Stan Page

Stephen Nathan (R) and company

GODSPELL

Credits same as listed above; Opened at the Nixon Theatre, Pittsburgh, , Oct. 27, 1972 and still touring May 31, 1973.

CAST

Cheryl Barnes   Barbara Lauren
Barbara Deutsch   Danny Lipman
Mark Ganzel   Mark Shera
Kathleen Gordon   Rich Vairetta
Peter Jurasik   Valerie Williams
Alternates: Scott Burns, Philip Casnoff, Catherine Cox, Naomi Wexler

General Manager: Marvin A. Krauss
Company Manager: Harold Kusell
Press: Gifford/Wallace, Horace Greeley McNab, Ellen Chenoweth
Stage Manager: Herbert Vogler

Mark Ganzel, Mark Shera and company

GODSPELL

Credits same as listed above; Opened Sept. 21, 1972 in Toledo, Ohio, and still touring May 31, 1973.

CAST

Tom DeMastri   Sid Marshall
Kate Draper   Melanie Mayron
Mary-Pat Green   Susan Morse
Michael Hoit   Jeremy Sage
Sherry Landrum   Jeffrey Winner
Alternates: Graham Hubbel, Rex Knowles, Anne O'Donnell, Dale Rehfeld

General Manager: Marvin A. Krauss
Company Manager: Mario DeMaria
Press: Gifford/Wallace, Stanley Brody
Stage Managers: William Falkner, Donald Hinde

Susan Morse (C) and company

GODSPELL

Credits same as listed above; Opened Sept. 18, 1972 at the Studebaker Theatre in Chicago, and still playing there May 31, 1973.

CAST

Jo-Ann Brown-El   Joe Mantegna
Sammy Chester   Carol McGill
Karla Jayne DeVito   Jim Parks
Richard Gilliland   Karole Selmon
Merrell Jackson   Fran Uditsky
Alternates: Pat Lavery, Nancy McCall, Ed Trotta, Gigi Williams

General Manager: Marvin A. Krauss
Company Manager: Douglas Helgeson
Press: Gifford/Wallace, William P. Wilson Associates
Stage Manager: Cynthia Gricus

Karole Selmon, Jo-Ann Brown-El and company

GREASE

Book, Music, and Lyrics, Jim Jacobs, Warren Casey; Director, Tom Moore; Musical Numbers and Dances Staged by Patricia Birch; Musical Director, Mack Schlefer; Sets, Douglas W. Schmidt; Costumes, Carrie F. Robbins; Lighting, Karl Eigsti; Orchestrations, Michael Leonard; Musical Supervision-Vocal and Dance Arrangements, Louis St. Louis; Sound, Jack Shearing; Hairstylist, Nino Raffaello; General Management, Theatre Now, Inc.; General Manager, Edward H. Davis; Production Supervisor, T. Schuyler Smith; Opened Saturday, Dec. 23, 1972 at Shubert Theatre, Boston, and still touring May 31, 1973.

CAST

Miss Lynch	Lesslie Nicol
Patty Simcox	Carol Culver
Eugene Florczyk	Stephen Van Benschoten
Jan	Rebecca Gilchrist
Marty	Marilu Henner
Betty Rizzo	Judy Kaye
Doody	John Travolta
Roger	Ray DeMattis
Kenickie	Jerry Zaks
Sonny LaTierri	Michael Lembeck†1
Frenchy	Ellen March
Sandy Dumbrowski	Pamela Adams†2
Danny Zuko	Jeffrey Conaway†3
Vince Fontaine	Walter Charles
Johnny Casino	Mike Clifford
Cha-Cha DiGregorio	Judith Sullivan†4
Teen Angel	Mike Clifford

UNDERSTUDIES: Susan Pomeranze, Ann Travolta, Tommy Gerard, John Lansing

For musical numbers, see Broadway production.

A musical in two acts and 12 scenes. The action takes place at the reunion of the Class of 1959 of Rydell High School.

Company Manager: Donald Antonelli
Press: Betty Lee Hunt, Fred Weterick
Stage Managers: M. William Lettich, Frank Marino, John Weeks, Hal Halvorsen, Tommy Gerard

† Succeeded by: 1. Tommy Gerard, Michael Lembeck, 2. Candice Earley, 3. Barry Bostwick, 4. Vivian Fineman, Judith Sullivan

Top Right: Entire Cast Below: Marilu Henner, Rebecca Gilchrist, Ellen March, Judy Kaye

Michael Lembeck, Ray DeMattis, Jeffrey Conaway, Jerry Zaks, John Travolta

Ellen March, Mike Clifford

HAIR

Book and Lyrics, Gerome Ragni, James Rado; Music, Galt MacDer-
ot; Director, Tom O'Horgan; Executive Producer, Bertrand Castelli;
oreographer, Julie Arenal; Costumes, Nancy Potts; Scenery, Robin
agner; Lighting, Jules Fisher; Sound, Abe Jacob; Musical Direction,
ed Waring, Jr.; Conductor, Ken Yovicson; Presented by Michael But-
; Restaged by Robert Farley; Opened in Hanna Theatre, Cleveland,
io, Mar. 9, 1971, and closed in Latham, N.Y., Sept. 3, 1972.

CAST

aude	William Swiggard†1
rger	Rick Spiegel†2
oof	Randy Keys†3
d	Gerry Combs†4
eila	Linda Gaines
nie	Gayle Riffle
issy	Lynn Pitney
others	Jeanie, Arnold McCuller, Kalani Molina†5
thers	Lynn Humphrey†6, Betty Lloyd†7, David Hunt†8
ncipals	Anita Krpan, Kalani Molina, Sue Marn†9
urist Couple	David Lasley†10, Steve Scharf†11
ung Recruit	George Mansour, Jr.†12
neral Grant	Meatloaf
e Lincoln	Betty Lloyd†13
cruit Parents	Kathleen Shearer, John David Yarbrough†14
oth	Sue Marn†15
olidge	Naomi Wexler†16
ble	Lynn Humphrey†17
arlet	Zora Rasmussen†18
tterfly McQueen	Yvette Williams
etha Franklin	Nedra Dixon
nda	Linda Compton
rlynne	Verlynne Hutson
w	L. Llewellyn Lafford
b	Robert Golden

NDERSTUDIES: Claude, Randy Keys, L. Llewellyn Lafford; Berger,
orge Mansour, Jr., Robert Golden; Woof, L. Llewellyn Lafford; Hud,
vid Hunt, Bobby C. Ferguson; Sheila, Anita Krpan, Linda Compton,
ria Goldman; Jeanie, Zora Rasmussen, Linda Compton; Crissy, Linda
mpton, Yvette Williams

JSICAL NUMBERS: "Aquarius," "Donna," "Hashish," "Sodomy,"
olored Spade," "Manchester," "Ain't Got No," "Dead End," "I Be-
e in Love," "Air," "Initials," "I Got Life," "Going Down," "Hair,"
y Conviction," "Easy to Be Hard," "Don't Put It Down," "Frank
ls," "Be-In," "Where Do I Go," "Electric Blues," "Black Boys,"
hite Boys," "Walking in Space," "Abie Baby," "Three-Five-Zero-
o," "What a Piece of Work Is Man," "Good Morning Starshine,"
ne Bed," "The Flesh Failures," "Let the Sun Shine In"

The American tribal-love rock musical in two acts.

Company Manager: Richard Osorio
Press: Gifford/Wallace
tage Managers: Fred Reinglass, Barry Kearsley, John Weeks

For Original NY production, see THEATRE WORLD, Vol. 24.

ucceeded by: 1. John David Yarbrough, 2. Doug Rowell, 3. Steve
charf, Michael Danso, 4. Stan Shaw, 5. Meatloaf, 6. Gloria Goldman,
. Nedra Dison, 8. Anita Krpan, 9. Bobby C. Ferguson, 10. Patrick
Carlock, 11. Meatloaf, 12. Meatloaf, Bobby C. Ferguson, 13. Verlynne
Hutson, 14. Meatloaf, 15. Linda Compton, Kathleen Shearer, 16.
Gloria Goldman, 17. Anita Krpan, 18. Linda Compton, Kathleen
hearer

William L. Smith Photos

Betty Lloyd, Arnold McCuller, Naomi Wexler, David
Lasley (front)

Top: Gayle Riffle (C) and Mercury Hair Tribe

Mark Harlik, Paul Baker, Dede Washburn, Shashi
Musso

JACQUES BREL IS ALIVE AND WELL AND LIVING IN PARIS

Music by Jacques Brel; Original Production Conception by Eric Blau
and Mort Shuman; This production conception by the entire company;
Entire production put together by Wayne Adams, Paul Plumadore; Musi-
cal Director, Mark Harlik; Musical Arrangers, Mark Harlik, Bill
Schneider; Vocal Co-Directors, Paul Baker, Dede Washburn; Lighting,
Ken Graham; Sound, Ed Maier; Presented by Wayne Adams through
special arrangement with Music Theatre International; Opened Sunday,
Oct. 29, 1972 in Greenville, Pa., and closed Apr. 26, 1973 in Nashville,
Tenn.

CAST

Paul Baker
Mark Harlik
Shashi Musso
Dede Washburn

MUSICAL NUMBERS: "Marathon," "Alone," "Madeleine," "I
Loved," "Mathilde," "Bachelor's Dance," "Timid Frieda," "My Death,"
"Girls and Dogs," "Jackie," "The Statue," "Desperate Ones," "Sons of,"
"Amsterdam," "The Bulls," "Old Folks," "Marieke," "Brussels," "Fa-
nette," "Funeral Tango," "Middle Class," "No Love," "Next," "Carou-
sel," "If We Only Have Love"

A Musical Entertainment in two parts.

NY Promotion Manager: Bernard Simon
Stage Managers: Ken Graham, Ed Maier

For original NY production, see THEATRE WORLD, Vol. 24.

LORELEI

Book, Kenny Solms, Gail Parent; Music, Jule Styne; Lyrics, Be[tty]
Comden, Adolph Green; Based on "Gentlemen Prefer Blondes" w[ith]
Book by Anita Loos, Joseph Fields; Music, Jule Styne; Lyrics, Leo Rob[in];
Staged by Joe Layton; Assistant Director, Evelyn Russell; Scenery, Jo[hn]
Conklin; Costumes, Alvin Colt; Lighting, John Gleason; Miss Channin[g's]
Costumes, Ray Aghayan, Bob Mackie; Musical Direction, Milton Rose[n-]
stock; Dance Music Arrangements, Jay Thompson; Orchestrations, P[hi-]
lip J. Lang, Don Walker; Vocal Arrangements, Hugh Martin, Bus[ter]
Davis; Hairstylist, Ernest Adler; Original Cast Album by MGM/Ver[ve]
Records; Presented by Lee Guber and Shelly Gross; Opened Monda[y,]
Feb. 26, 1973 at Civic Center Music Hall in Oklahoma City, and s[tarted]
touring May 31, 1973.

CAST

Minister	Ray C[ ]
Lorelei Lee	Carol Channi[ng]
Gus Esmond	Peter Palm[er]
Dorothy	Tamara Lo[ ]
Tapsters	Joyce Chapman, Bob Fitch, John Mineo, Ken Plo[ ]
Bartender	Ray C[ ]
Henry Spofford	Lee Roy Rear[ ]
Mrs. Ella Spofford	Dody Goodm[an]
Lord Francis Beekman	Brooks Mort[ ]
Lady Phyllis Beekman	Jean Bru[ ]
Josephus Gage	Brandon Magga[ ]
Frank	David Rom[ ]
George	Bob Dal[ ]
Pierre	Ray C[ ]
Charles	Ken Plo[ ]
Robert Lemanteur	Bob Fit[ch]
Louis Lemanteur	John Min[eo]
Tenor	Ken Plo[ ]
Lobster	Gia De Sil[va]
Caviar	Angela Mar[ ]
Pheasant	Aniko Farr[ell]
Salad	Donna Monr[oe]
Dessert	Carol Channi[ng]
Maitre D'	David Rom[ ]
Zizi	Katherine Hull Min[ ]
Fifi	Maureen Crock[ett]
Master of Ceremonies	Robert Rik[er]
Announcer	Ray C[ ]
Engineer	Ken Sher[ ]
Mr. Esmond	David Neum[an]
Bridesmaids	Gia DeSilva, Aniko Farrell, Angela Mart[ ] Donna Monr[oe]

PASSENGERS, TOURISTS, WAITERS, GUESTS, ETC.: Joyce Cha[p-]
man, Maureen Crockett, Georgia Dell, Gia De Silva, Aniko Farr[ell,]
Peggy Marie Haug, Linda Lee MacArthur, Angela Martin, Kather[ine]
Hull Mineo, Donna Monroe, Penny Pritchard, Chris Bartlett, Ray C[ ]
Bob Daley, Bob Fitch, Casey Jones, Howard Leonard, Jonathan Mie[ ]
John Mineo, Richard Natkowski, Ken Ploss, Robert Riker, David R[ ]
man, Ken Sherber

UNDERSTUDIES: Lorelei, Donna Monroe; Dorothy, Angela Mart[ ]
Ella, Phyllis, Georgia Dell; Gus, Gage, David Roman; Henry, Ken Plo[ ]
Beekman, David Neuman

MUSICAL NUMBERS: "Looking Back," "Bye Bye Baby," "It's Hi[gh]
Time," "Little Rock," "I'm A-Tingle, I'm A-Glow," "Olympic Cal[is-]
thenics," "I Love What I'm Doing," "A Girl Like I," "Paris," "I Wo[n't]
Let You Get Away," "Keeping Cool with Coolidge," "Coquette," "M[am-]
mie Is Mimi," "Lorelei," "Homesick," "We're Just a Kiss Apart," "B[ut-]
ton up with Esmond," "Diamonds Are a Girl's Best Friend"

A Musical Comedy in two acts and ten scenes. The action takes pla[ce]
aboard the Ile de France, in Paris, and in New York.

General Managers: Joseph Harris, Ira Bernstein
Company Manager: Milton M. Pollack
Press: Solters/Sabinson/Roskin, Sy Freedman
Stage Managers: Ben D. Kranz, Maxine Sholar-Taylor, David[ ]
Neuman

For Original New York production of "Gentlemen Prefer Blondes," s[ee]
THEATRE WORLD, Vol. 7.

Peter Palmer, Carol Channing (also above), John
Mineo, Bob Fitch *(Martha Swope Photos)*

NATIONAL SHAKESPEARE COMPANY

Artistic Director, Philip Meister; Managing Director, Elaine Sulka; General Manager, Albert Schoemann; Tour Director, Mildred Torffield; Directors, Philip Meister (King Lear), William Francisco (Midsummer Night's Dream), Louis Criss (Antigone); Set, Philip Meister; Scenery, Carl Eigsti; Costumes, James Berton Harris; Lighting, Richard Ronald Beebe; Production Assistant, Mitchell Eil; Stage Managers, Cynthia Darlow, Grade Woodard, Richard Ronald Beebe; Music, Arnold Black; Opened Oct. 2, 1972 in Riverdale, N.Y., and closed May 3, 1973 in Virginia Beach, Va.

CAST

KING LEAR

Lear	John Hostetter
Goneril	Grace Woodard
Cordelia	Megan McTavish
Regan	Mary Noel
Earl of Kent	Richard LeVene
Duke of Albany	Richard Boddy
Duke of Cornwall	Charles Davis
Earl of Gloucester	Richard Ronald Beebe
Duke of Burgundy	Antonino Pandolfo
King of France	Jere O'Donnell
Edmund	Jeffrey DeMunn
Edgar	James Lavin
Oswald	Antonino Pandolfo
The Fool	Aidn Jaro
Gentleman and Servant	Jere O'Donnell

MIDSUMMER NIGHT'S DREAM

Wrestlers	John Hostetter, Richard LeVene
Theseus/Oberon	Charles Davis
Hippolyta/Titania	Mary Noel
Puck/Philostrate	Jere O'Donnell
Egeus	Richard Boddy
Lysander	James Lavin
Demetrius	Jeffrey DeMunn
Hermia	Cynthia Darlow
Helena	Megan McTavish
Nick Bottom	Richard Ronald Beebe
Peter Quince	Richard Boddy
Francis Flute	Antonino Pandolfo
Tom Snout	John Hostetter
Snug	Richard LeVene
Robin Starveling	Aidn Jaro

ANTIGONE by Sophocles

Antigone	Megan McTavish
Ismene	Cynthia Darlow
Chorus	Charles Davis, Jeffrey DeMunn, Jere O'Donnell
Chorus Leader	Richard LeVene
Creon	Richard Boddy
Sentry	Antonino Pandolfo
Haimon	James Lavin
Tiresias	John Hostetter
Girl	Mary Noel
Messenger	Aidn Jaro
Eurydice	Grace Woodard

Richard Boddy, Megan McTavish in "Antigone"
Right: John Hostetter, Megan McTavish in "King Lear"

Mary Noel, Jere O'Donnell, Richard Ronald Beebe in "Midsummer Night's Dream"

NO, NO, NANETTE

Book, Otto Harbach, Frank Mandel; Music, Vincent Youmans; Lyr
Irving Caesar, Otto Harbach; Adapted and Directed by Burt Shevelc
Dances and Musical Numbers Staged by Donald Saddler; Product
Supervised by Busby Berkeley; Designed by Raoul Pene du Bois; Lig
ing, Jules Fisher; Musical Direction-Vocal Arrangements, Buster Da
Orchestrations, Ralph Burns; Dance Music Arranged and Incidental N
sic Composed by Luther Henderson; Conductor, Jack Holmes; Sou
Jack Shearing; Original Cast Album by Columbia Records; Presented
Pyxidium Ltd. (Cyma Rubin, Producer) and Theatre Now, Inc.; Ope
Friday, Oct. 6, 1972 in Music Hall, Dallas, Tex., and closed Aug. 4, 1
at Garden State Arts Center, Woodbridge, N.J.

CAST

Pauline	Ruth Donnel
Lucille Early	Lainie Nel
Sue Smith	Evelyn Ke
Jimmy Smith	Don Ame
Billy Early	Swen Swen
Tom Trainor	Tim Heathm
Nanette	Darlene And
Flora Latham	Charlene Math
Betty Brown	Elisabeth Kov
Winnie Winslow	Jeannine Mo

NANETTE'S FRIENDS: Rita Abrams, Linda Andrus, Naomi Bo
Sharon Bruce, Dolly Colby, Jo Ela Flood, Jessica Lee, Mary Ac
Marsh, Kathy McFadden, Cardi O'Connor, Jane Owens, Carole Phill
Joy Robertson, Diane Ryan, Marilyn Seven, Douglas Allen, Rich
Cooper Bayne, Steven Belin, Sonny Carl, Christopher Howard, Te
Kennedy, Paul McConnell, Larry McMillian, Tom Miller, Dennis So
Ralph Stenwall

MUSICAL NUMBERS: "Too Many Rings around Rosie," "I've C
fessed to the Breeze," "Call of the Sea," "I Want to Be Happy," "No,
Nanette," "Peach on the Beach," "Tea for Two," "You Can Dance v
Any Girl," "Telephone Girlie," "Where-Has-My-Hubby-Gone Blu
"Waiting for You," "Take a Little One-Step," Finale.

A musical in three acts. The action takes place on a weekend in e
summer of 1925 in the Smiths' New York City home, and Chicka
Cottage in Atlantic City.

Company Manager: James Preston
Press: Merle Debuskey, Paul G. Anglim
Stage Managers: Charles Durand, Eugene Stuckmann

† Succeeded by Ann B. Davis. For original NY production, see Tl
ATRE WORLD, Vol. 27.

Friedman-Abeles Photos

Swen Swenson
Above: Tim Heathman, Darlene Anders

Top: (L) Elisabeth Kovacs, Jeanine Moore, Don Amech
Charlene Mathies (R) Evelyn Keyes

ONE FLEW OVER THE CUCKOO'S NEST

By Dale Wasserman; Based on novel by Ken Kesey; Director, Lee D. Sankowich; Producer, Rudi Golyn; Designer, John Scheffler; Music, James Barnett, John Blakeley; Sound, Gary and Timmy Harris; Assistant Director, Danny Hild; Assistant Lighting Designer, Judith Rasmussen; Presented by Sankowich/Golyn Productions in association with William Craver; Opened Thursday, Nov. 16, 1972 at the Charles Playhouse, Boston, and still playing May 31, 1973.

CAST

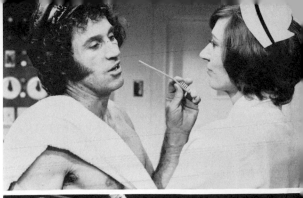

Chief Bromden	Frank Savino[1]
Aide Williams	Marc Frasier
Aide Washington	Charles Kashi
Nurse Ratched	DeAnn Mears[2]
Nurse Flinn	Sheila Coren[3]
Dale Harding	Roger Harkenrider
Billy Bibbitt	Lawrason Driscoll[4]
Charles Atkins Cheswick III	John Aylward[5]
Frank Scanlon	Jon Richards[6]
Anthony Martini	William Preston[7]
Ruckly	David McNair[8]
Randle Patrick McMurphy	George Welbes[9]
Dr. Spivey	James Kiernan[10]
Aide Turkle	William Hart
Candy	Maureen Byrnes[11]
Technician	Danny Hild
Sandy	Sheila Coren[3]

UNDERSTUDIES: Bromden, McMurphy, Harding, James Kiernan; Scanlon, William Preston; Spivey, Cheswick, Turkle, Martini, Billy, Danny Hild; Ronald Hunter, Mary Jane Wells, William Lyman

A Drama in two acts. The action takes place in a ward in a state mental hospital at the present time.

General Manager: William Craver
Company Manager: Peter Henderson
Press: Gifford/Wallace, Edwin Gifford, Bonnie Jacob
Stage Managers: Mark Healy, Danny Hild

Succeeded by: 1. Christopher Taaj, 2. Josephine Lane, 3. Carol Anne Young, 4. Danny Hild, 5. Frank McCarthy, 6. James O'Connell for vacation, 7. David S. Howard, 8. Mark B. R. Liebert, 9. Michael Cavanaugh, 10. Jon Terry, 11. Binky Wood

William L. Smith Photos

Right: Michael Cavanaugh, Charles Kashi, DeAnn Mears
Above: Jon Richards, George Welbes, John Aylward,
William Hart, Sheila Coren, Roger Harkenrider
Top: George Welbes, DeAnn Mears

June Travis, Robert Anthony, Douglas Fairbanks, Jr.,
Fawne Harriman

THE PLEASURE OF HIS COMPANY

By Samuel Taylor and Cornelia Otis Skinner; Director, Neal Kenyon; Setting, Donald G. Beaman; Lighting, John Doepp; Produced by Roger L. Stevens and J. Charles Gilbert for the John F. Kennedy Center for the Performing Arts; Opened Monday, July 10, 1972 at the Eisenhower Theatre, Washington, D.C., and closed at the Huntington Hartford Theatre in Los Angeles on Sept. 9, 1972.

CAST

Toy	Arsenio Trinidad
Biddeforde Poole	Douglas Fairbanks, Jr.
Jessica Poole	Fawne Harriman
Katharine Dougherty	June Travis
Jim Dougherty	Alan Manson
Mackenzie Savage	Wallace Rooney
Roger Henderson	Robert Anthony

A Comedy in two acts and four scenes. The action takes place at the present time in the living room of a house high on a hill in San Francisco overlooking the Golden Gate.

Press: Leo Sullivan
Stage Managers: Bud Coffey, Bryon Predika

For original New York Production, see THEATRE WORLD, Vol. 15.

Hans Trebor Photo

THE PRISONER OF SECOND AVENUE

By Neil Simon; Director, Mike Nichols; Setting, Richard Sylbert; Lighting, Tharon Musser; Costumes, Anthea Sylbert; Hairstylist, John Mincieli; Produced by Nancy Enterprises; Presented by Saint-Subber; Opened at the Ahmanson Theatre, Los Angeles, Oct. 17, 1972, and still touring May 31, 1973.

CAST

Mel Edison	Art Carney†1
Edna Edison	Barbara Barrie†2
Harry Edison	Jack Somack†3
Pearl	Ruth Jaroslow
Jessie	Jean Barker
Pauline	Roslyn Alexander

STANDBYS: Edna, Barbara Carney; Harry, Joel Wolfe; Pearl, Jessie, Pauline, Elsa Raven

A Comedy in two acts. The action takes place at the present time in a New York City apartment building.

General Manager: C. Edwin Knill
Company Manager: Morry Efron
Press: Harvey Sabinson, Robert Reud, Marilyn LeVine
Stage Managers: Wally Peterson, Elsa Raven

For original NY production, see THEATRE WORLD, Vol. 28.

† Succeeded by: 1. Jack Somack during Mr. Carney's illness, 2. Harry Goz, Bill Morev, 3. Rosemary Prinz

Martha Swope Photos

Right: Art Carney, Barbara Barrie
(also below)

David Haviland, George Rose

SLEUTH

By Anthony Shaffer; Director, Warren Crane; Designed by Will Ritman; Tour Direction, Columbia Artists Theatricals Corp.; Presen by Helen Bonfils, Morton Gottlieb, Michael White; Opened Friday, S 22, 1972 in Community Theatre, Scranton, Pa., and closed Mar. 24, 1 in Veterans Memorial Auditorium, Providence, R.I.

CAST

Andrew Wyke	George R
Milo Tindle	David Havil
Inspector Doppler	Herbert F
Detective Sgt. Tarrant	Frank Sturtev
Police Constable Higgs	Martin K. Pagli

STANDBYS AND UNDERSTUDIES: Andrew, Donald Silber; M Henry Raymond; Doppler, Henry Raymond; Tarrant, Higgs, John phen

A Suspense Drama in two acts. The action takes place in And Wyke's country home in Wiltshire on a summer evening at the pres time.

General Manager: Ben Rosenberg
Company Manager: L. Liberatore
Press: Mae S. Hong
NY Promotion Manager: Bernard Simon
Stage Managers: Clint Jakeman, Mark LaMura

For original NY production, see THEATRE WORLD, Vol. 27. Win of 1971 "Tony" for best play.

Bert Andrews Photo

TWIGS

By George Furth; Director, Michael Bennett; Incidental Music, Stephen Sondheim; Settings, Peter Larkin; Costumes, Sara Brook; Lighting, David F. Segal; Hairstylist, Joe Tubens; Make-up, Joe Cranzano; Assistant to Producers, Fred Hebert; Production Assistant, Bob Avian; Production Supervisor, Jeff Chambers; Presented by Frederick Brisson in association with Plum Productions, Inc.; Opened Wednesday, Sept. 6, 1972 in the Fisher Theatre, Detroit, and closed March 18, 1973 at the Shubert in Los Angeles.

CAST

Emily	Sada Thompson
Frank	Dan Travanty
Celia	Sada Thompson
Phil	Mark Dawson
Swede	Joe Mantell
Lou	Jack Murdock
Dorothy	Sada Thompson
Ned	Joseph Boland
Pa	Herbert Nelson
Ma	Sada Thompson
Priest	Stacy McAdams

Standbys: Carol Gustafson, Lloyd Harris

A Comedy in two acts and four scenes. The action takes place at the present time in a variety of kitchens, on the outskirts of a major city, on the day before Thanksgiving. The time is continuous from 9 A.M. to 9 P.M.

General Manager: Ben Rosenberg
Company Manager: James Awe
Press: Harvey Sabinson, Lee Solters, Willard Keefe
Stage Manager: Bud Coffey

For original New York production, see THEATRE WORLD, Vol. 28.

**Right: Mark Dawson, Sada Thompson, Joe Mantell
Top: Sada Thompson, Dan Travanty**

TWO BY TWO

Book, Peter Stone; Music, Richard Rodgers; Lyrics, Martin Charnin; Based on "The Flowering Peach" by Clifford Odets; Staged by Richard Michaels; Choreography, Rick Atwell; Musical Director, Albert L. Fiorillo, Jr.; Scenery, David Hays; Lighting, John Harvy; Assistant Conductor, Josef Stopak; Assistant to Producer, Ann Levack; Presented by Tom Mallow; Opened Monday, Sept. 11, 1972 in Dupont Theatre, Wilmington, Del., and closed March 11, 1973 in Memorial Hall, Dayton, Ohio.

CAST

Noah	Shelley Berman
Esther	Taina Elg
Japheth	Miche Priaulx
Shem	William Countryman
Leah	Mary Jo Gillis
Ham	Roger Brown
Rachel	Leslie Miller
Goldie	Marcia King

STANDBYS: Ham, Japheth, James Wilson; Esther, Mary Jo Gillis; Leah, Goldie, Rachel, Jane Ann Sargia; Shem, Roger Brown

MUSICAL NUMBERS: "Why Me?," "Put Him Away," "The Gitka's Song," "Something, Somewhere," "You Have Got to Have a Rudder on the Ark," "Something Doesn't Happen'" "An Old Man," "Ninety Again!," "Two by Two," "I Do Not Know a Day I Did Not Love You,"

"When It Dries," "You," "The Golden Ram," "Poppa Knows Best," "As Far as I'm Concerned," "Hey, Girlie," "The Covenant"

A Musical in two acts. The action takes place before, during, and after The Flood.

General Manager: James Janek
Company Manager: Horace Wright
Press: Bev Kelley, Joseph Felician
Stage Managers: Bert Wood, Jeff Cahn, James Wilson

For original New York production, see THEATRE WORLD, Vol. 27.

**Leslie Miller, Mary Jo Gillis, William Countryman,
Taina Elg, Shelley Berman, Miche Priaulx
Above: Shelley Berman**

TWO GENTLEMEN OF VERONA

Based on play by William Shakespeare; Adapted by John Guare; Shapiro; Lyrics, John Guare; Music, Galt MacDermot; Director, Shapiro; Setting, Ming Cho Lee; Costumes, Theoni V. Aldredge; L ing, Lawrence Metzler; Choreography, Dennis Nahat; Musical Direc Richard Kaufman; Orchestrations, Galt MacDermot, Harold Whe Sound, Jack Shearing; Associate Producer, Bernard Gersten; Ori Cast Album, ABC/Dunhill Records; Presented by The New York Sh speare Festival (Joseph Papp, Producer); Opened Jan. 20, 1973 in O'K Theatre, Toronto, Can., and still touring May 31, 1973.

CAST

Thurio	Frank O'B
Speed	Charlie J. Rodrig
Valentine	Clifton D
Proteus	Larry
Julia	Edith D
Lucetta	Jacque Lynn Co
Launce	Phil L
Antonio	David Tho
Crab	W
Duke of Milan	John McC
Silvia	Jonelle A
Tavern Host	David Tho
Eglamour	Alvin

CITIZENS OF VERONA AND MILAN: Billy Abernathy, Ynez thony, Larry G. Bailey, Jai Cee Calloway, David Curtis, Joanna Varona, Edloe, Michael Eha, Leopoldo Fernandez, Damita Jo Free Aaron Hale, Sherrill Harper, Bonnie Hawkins, Randall Keys, McGill, Joshua Michaels, Maris O'Neill, A. William Perkins, B Pierovich, Katie Sagal, Carl Scott, Gayle White

UNDERSTUDIES: Silvia, Edloe; Valentine, Carol Scott; Pro Charlie J. Rodriguez; Julia, Sherrie Harper; Lucetta, Katie Sagal; D Billy Abernathy; Thurio, Antonio, Host, Joshua Michaels; Launce, D Thomas; Eglamour, David Curtis; Speed, Randall Keys

A Musical in two acts. The action takes place in Verona, Milan, the forest.

General Managers: Eugene Wolsk, Emanuel Azenberg
Company Manager: Charles Willard
Press: Merle Debuskey, Faith Geer, Harry Davies
Stage Managers: Kathleen A. Sullivan, Moose Peting, Lou

Rogers, III

For original NY production, see THEATRE WORLD, Vol. 2

Friedman-Abeles Photo

Top Left: Clifton Davis, Jonelle Allen, Edith Diaz, La Kert

WILL ROGERS' U.S.A.

Adapted and Directed by Paul Shyre; Designed by Eldon Elder; A ciate Producer, Bryan Sterling; Original Cast Album by Colun Records; Booking Direction, Kolmar-Luth Entertainment; A Ge Spota Production; Opened Friday, Jan. 26, 1973 in Fullerton, Calif., closed Feb. 9, 1973 in Sheepshead Bay, Brooklyn, NY.

CAST

PAUL TRIPP

A one-man show in two parts, using the words of Will Rogers.

General Manager: Seth Schapiro
NY Promotion Manager: Bernard Simon

Paul Tripp

ANNUAL SHAKESPEARE FESTIVALS

AMERICAN SHAKESPEARE FESTIVAL

Stratford, Conn.
June 20—September 3, 1972
Eighteenth Season

Executive Producer, Joseph Verner Reed; Managing Producer, Berenice Weiler; Artistic Director, Michael Kahn; Director of Educational Projects, Mary Hunter Wolf; Production Manager, Lo Hardin; Music Director and Conductor, Allan Lewis; Directors, Michael Kahn, Edwin Sherin; Assistant Director, Marc Jacobs; Stage Managers, Walter W. Boyer, Stephen Nasuta; Scenery, Robin Wagner, William Ritman; Costumes, Jane Greenwood; Lighting, Marc B. Weiss; Music, John Morris; Battles Staged by Patrick Crean; Choreography, Lee Theodore; Associate Director, Garland Wright; Press, Reginald Denenholz

COMPANY

Jane Alexander, Frank Alford, John Arnone, Jeanne Bartlett, Robert Blumenfeld, David Darlow, Peter DeMaio, Ronald Frazier, Rosalind Harris, Paul Hecht, Edward Herrmann, Ruby Holbrook, Salome Jens, Steve Karp, Bernard Kates, Philip Kerr, Joseph Lambie, William Larsen, Sharon Laughlin, David Leary, Michael Levin, Larry C. Lott, Joseph Maher, Edwin J. McDonough, Martha Miller, Jan Miner, Gene Nye, Ruman Pendleton, James Ray, Lee Richardson, John Schak, Stephen Stenzer, Jack Schultz, Josef Sommer, Madelon Thomas, Peter Thompson, John Tillinger, Bryan Utman, J. Steven White

Dennis Creaghan, David Duhaime, Charles T. Harper, Peter Harris, Joseph Horvath, Peter Kingsley, Daniel Landon, Michael R. Murphy, Joseph F. Muzikar, Sidney Shaw, Douglas W. Simes, Stanleigh Williams

PRODUCTIONS

"Julius Caesar" (Michael Kahn, Director), "Antony and Cleopatra" (Michael Kahn, Director), "Major Barbara" by George Bernard Shaw (Edwin Sherin, Director)

Martha Swope Photos

Right: Paul Hecht, Salome Jens in "Antony and Cleopatra" Below: Rosalind Harris, Jane Alexander, Peter Thompson, Lee Richardson in "Major Barbara"

Jane Alexander, Jan Miner, Lee Richardson, Peter Thompson in "Major Barbara"

Paul Hecht, Bernard Kates in "Julius Caesar"

NATIONAL SHAKESPEARE FESTIVAL

San Diego, California
June 6—September 17, 1972
Twenty-third Season

Producing Director, Craig Noel; Art Director, Peggy Kellner; Stage Managers, Tom Corcoran, Randy Carter, William R. Franklin; Technical Director, Gene Reilly; Sound, Nathan Haas; Props, Steve Carmack; Wardrobe, Anne Armatis; Designers, Edguard Johnson, Douglas Russell, John McLain, Dan Dugan; Composer, Conrad Susa; Directors, Craig Noel, Jack O'Brien, Eric Christmas, Edward Payson Call

COMPANY

Marjorie Battles, Joseph Bird, Mary Doyle, Wayne Grace, Elizabeth Huddle, Michael Keenan, Barry Kraft, Sandy McCallum, Tom McCorry, Peter Nyberg, Carl Reggiardo, Christopher Reeve, Paul Rudd, Marilee Sennett, G. Wood, Anthony Zerbe

C. Wayland Capwell, Robert Cooke, Marley Days, Roger Kern, Carla Kirkwood, R. Bruce McLean, Michael Molloy, Jenny Mosiev, Paul Perkins, Joel Story, Robert Hartmann, Robert Hays, Michael Horton, Don Jenkins, Michael Miller, James Owsley, Armin Shimerman, Ralph Steadman, Tina Dean, Lorna Eshenbaugh, Christine Hulter, Michael Jankowski, Lisabeth Johnson, Tyler Ochoa, Carol Roche

PRODUCTIONS

"The Merry Wives of Windsor," "Love's Labour's Lost,.' "King Richard III," and "Beyond the Fringe" that opened May 23, 1972 for 123 performances, closing Sept. 17, 1972, with Herbert Foster, Michael Byers, Wayne B. Smith, Don Sparks

Bill Reid Photos

Right: Michael Byers, Herbert Foster, Wayne B. Smith, Don Sparks in "Beyond the Fringe"

Marjorie Battles, Paul Rudd in "Love's Labour's Lost"
Above: Elizabeth Huddle, Michael Keenan, Marjorie Battles in "Merry Wives of Windsor"

Carl Reggiardo, Anthony Zerbe Above:
Sandy McCallum, Anthony Zerbe (L) in "Richard II

NEW JERSEY SHAKESPEARE FESTIVAL

Madison, N.J.
June 27—September 10, 1972
Eighth Season

Artistic Director, Paul Barry; Press, Ellen Barry, Steven Bunnell; Costumes, Bambi Jeanne Stoll; Lighting, William J. Plachy; Stage Managers, ...eslie Robinson, E. Reiss; Technical Supervisor, Jared Snyder; Sound, ...bert C. Santy, Jr.; Original Music, Hescal Brisman; Visual Effects, ...alter Wood

COMPANY

Paul Barry, Brendan Burke, Catherine Byers, Howland Chamber-..., Clarence Felder, Christian Grant, Philip Hanson, Peter Mac-...n, Frederic Major, Kendall March, Alex Panas, Ellen Reiss, Leslie ...obinson, Jack Ryland, Margery Shaw, Albert Sanders

Adele Ahronheim, Elizabeth Bady, Marvin Barrett, Carol Cassella, ...argaret Cowling, Richard Crater, James Dembowski, Nicholas Dur-...m, Edith Louise Knauf, Alice Langer, Christopher McCann, Kathleen ...cCutcheon, Ellyn Meade, David Misner, Kestal Phillips, Jr., Ron ...etti, Jane Roeder, Rita Rofe, Wally Rubin, Carolyn Shelby, Susan ...colowski, Gloria Steffenburg, Lois Steinberg, Deborah Townell, Debo-...h Tompkins, Jerome Turner, Kurt VonWier, G. Douglas Wagner, Rob-...; Yahner

PRODUCTIONS

"The Taming of the Shrew," "The Hostage," "Beyond the Fringe," ...roilus and Cressida," "The Bourgeois Gentleman"

Right: Peter MacLean, Catherine Byers in "Taming of the Shrew"

...rgery Shaw, Jack Ryland (C) in "The Hostage"
Above: Brendan Burke, Clarence Felder, Paul ...arry, Albert Sanders in "Beyond the Fringe"

Kendall March, Albert Sanders in "Bourgeois Gentleman" Above: Kendall March, Jack Ryland, Alex Panas in "Troilus and Cressida"

NEW YORK SHAKESPEARE FESTIVAL

Delacorte Theater, Central Park
June 20—September 7, 1972
Sixteenth Season
Producer, Joseph Papp; Associate Producer, Bernard Gersten; Gene
Manager, David Black; Press, Merle Debuskey, Faith Geer; Producti
Manager, Andrew Mihok; Assistant to Producer, Gail Merrifield; Tech
cal Director, Mervyn Haines, Jr.; Music Coordinator, Herbert Harr
Setting, Ming Cho Lee; Costumes, Theoni V. Aldredge; Lighting, Mar
Aronstein; Stage Managers, John Beven, Dan Sedgwick, Ron Dozi
John Margulis; Production Supervisor, David Eidenberg; Technical C
ordinator, Michael Hopper

June 20—July 16, 1972
(21 performances)

HAMLET

Director, Gerald Freedman; Music, John Morris; Duels Staged
James J. Sloyan.

CAST

John Michalski (Bernardo), Roger Brown (Francisco), Robert Sta
(Horatio), Michael Goodwin (Marcellus), James Earl Jones (Claudiu
James McGill (Cornelius), Sam Waterston (Laertes), Barnard Hugl
(Polonius), Stacy Keach (Hamlet), Colleen Dewhurst (Gertrude), Ki
Winn (Ophelia), Frank Dwyer (Reynaldo), George Taylor (Playe
Linda Hunt (Player Queen), Frank Dwyer (Lucianus), Michael Goodw
(Fortinbras), Greg Wnorowski (Captain), William Robertson (Lord), N
thaniel Robinson, Charles Dinstuhl (Sailors), Anna Brennen (Lad
Charles Durning, Tom Aldredge (Gravediggers), Mel Cobb (Priest), R.
Julia (Osric), Roger Brown, Gerald Finnegan, James McGill, Jim W
(Lords), Christine Baranski, Bonnie Gallup (Ladies), Mel Cobb, Char
Dinstuhl, John Nichols, Nathaniel Robinson, Frank Seales, Alan To
gret, Greg Wnorowski, Richard Yarnell, Mark Zeray

July 19, 1972—August 5, 1972
(15 performances)

TI-JEAN AND HIS BROTHERS

By Derek Walcott; Music, Andre Tanker; Lyrics, Derek Walcott, A
dre Tanker; Director, Derek Walcott; Choreography and Musical St
ing, George Faison; Setting, Edward Burbridge; Musical Direction a
Arrangements, Patti Brown; Additional Dance Music, Patti Brov
George Butcher; Associate Director, Paul Schneider

CAST

Madge Sinclair (Mother), Dennis Hines (Ti-Jean), Hamilton Pa
(Frog), Elaine R. Graham (Cricket), Diane Bivens (Bird), Deborah Al
(Firefly), Clebert Ford (Gros-Jean), Leon Morenzie (Mi-Jean), Alb
Laveau (Devil, Papa Bois and Planter), Stephannie Hampton Howa
(Bolom), Renee Rose (Goat), Dancers: Deborah Allen, Gary Deloat
Dyane Harvey, Eugene Little, Edward Love, Renee Rose, Jason Tayl
Evelyn Thomas (George Faison Universal Dance Experience), Singe
Margie Barnes, John Barracuda, Gail Boggs, Sharon Redd

August 16—September 3, 1972*
(20 performances)

MUCH ADO ABOUT NOTHING

By William Shakespeare; Director, A. J. Antoon; Music, Pet r Li
Dances, Donald Saddler; Musical Director, Henry "Bootsie" Norma

CAST

Mark Hammer (Leonato), Charles Bartlett (Reporter), Kathl
Widdoes (Beatrice), April Shawhan (Hero), Sam Waterston (Benedi
Glenn Walken (Claudio), Douglass Watson (Don Pedro), Jerry Ma
(Don John), Lou Gilbert (Antonio), Jack Gianino (Conrade), Freder
Coffin (Borachio), Jeanne Hepple (Margaret), Marshall Efron (Balt
sar), Bette Henritze (Ursula), Barnard Hughes (Dogberry), Will Mack
zie (Verges), George Gugleotti (First Watch), David Lenthall (Seco
Watch), David Anderson, James McGill, John Michalski (Ot
Watches), Tom McDermott (Friar Francis), Charles Bartlett (Sexto
Townspeople: David Anderson, Anna Brennen, J. J. Lewis, Jar
McGill, John Michalski, Lynne Taylor, Nina Jordan

* Re-opened on Broadway at the Winter Garden on Nov. 11, 1972
Broadway calendar)

Friedman-Abeles Photos

Top Left: Raul Julia, James Earl Jones, Anna
Brennen, Colleen Dewhurst, Stacy Keach in "Hamlet"
Below: Stacy Keach, Kitty Winn

Leon Morenzie, Dennis Hines, Madge Sinclair, Clebert Ford in
"Ti-Jean" Above: Stacy Keach, Colleen Dewhurst in "Hamlet"

OREGON SHAKESPEARE FESTIVAL

Ashland, Oregon
March 9—September 9, 1972
Thirty-second Season

Founder-Development Consultant, Dr. Angus L. Bowmer; Producing Director, Dr. Jerry Turner; General Manager, William W. Patton; Production Coordinator, Pat Patton; Directors, Robert L. Benedetti, Laird Williamson, Jerry Turner, Larry Oliver, Pat Patton, William Roberts; Education Coordinator, Forbes W. Rogers; Designers, Richard L. Hay, Jean Schultz Davidson; Press, Robert F. Knoll, Stan Grindstaff; Music Director and Composer, W. Bernard Windt; Choreographers, Judith Kennedy, Sally Chaney; Technical Director, Skip Hubbard; Lighting, Steven A. Maze, Jerry Glenn

COMPANY

Janie E. Atkins, Diana Bellamy, Powers Boothe, Jeffrey Brooks, Kent Christman, Elizabeth Cole, Joel Colodner, Rebecca Colodner, Timothy D'Arcy, Philip Davidson, David C. deBerry, Joseph DeSalvio, Tom Donaldson, Diane Dimeo, Jim Edmondson, Richard Allan Edwards, Miriam Espeseth, Kent Fillmore, Lockhart Fryer, Jo Goff, Daniel Gundich, Jeff Hanley, James Barton Hill, Will Huddleston, Byron Jennings, Merril Kannasto, Brian Edward Keith, Ron Lagomarsino, Dick Leonard, Julian Lopez-Morillas, Robert Lowry, Elizabeth McAninch, Randall Merrifield, Ken McGanty, Terry Mills, Laurie Monahan, Tim Monich, Larry Moore, Paul Myrvold, Saundra Nelson, David Ohannesian, Krista Anne Patton, Shirley Patton, Matt Pearl, Dave Richardt, Richard Riehle, William Roberts, Alice Rorvik, Neil Savage, Douglas Scherer, Karen Seal, Edna Sterling, Dave Studach, Alan Tilson, Mary Turner, Stephanie Voss, Chan Walker, Laird Williamson, Mike Winters

PRODUCTIONS

"The Taming of the Shrew," "Love's Labour's Lost," "Troilus and Cressida," "Henry IV, Part II," "Uncle Vanya," "The Crucible," "Room Service," "The Playboy of the Western World," "The Importance of Being Earnest," "Our Town," "The Alchemist," "Othello"

Hank Kranzler, Carolyn Mason Jones Photos

Right: le Clanche du Rand, Denene von Glan, Peter Silbert, Garry Moore, Elizabeth Cole in "The Importance of Being Earnest" Top: Alice Rorvik, Garry Moore, Diana Bellamy, Richard Riehle in "Henry IV, Part II"

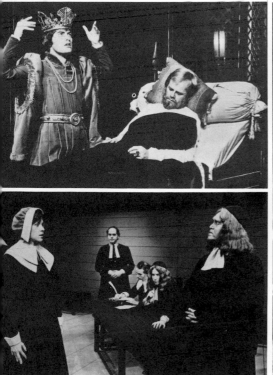

Elizabeth Cole, Garry Moore in "The Crucible" Above: Powers Boothe, Jim Edmondson in "Henry IV, Part II"

Laird Williamson, Ernie Stewart in "Othello"

STRATFORD FESTIVAL OF CANADA

Stratford, Ontario
June 5—October 21, 1972
Twentieth Season

General Manager, William Wylie; Artistic Director, Jean Gascon; Associate Director, William Hutt; Production Director, John Hayes; Assistant to Artistic Director, Michael Bawtree; Comptroller, Bruce Swerdfager; Production Manager, Jack Hutt; Technical Directors, Robert Scales, Robert Hall; Music Administrator, Andree Gingras; Director of Operations, Cedric Fresco; Press, Anne Selby, Mary Webb, Sandra Fresco; Company Manager, Max Helpmann; Stage Managers, Thomas Hooker, Ron Francis, Paddy McEntee, Gilbert Fournier, Elspeth Gaylor, Brian Longstaff, Nora Polley, Michael Tabbit; Directors, Michael Bawtree, Andre Brassard, Jean Gascon, William Hutt, Albert Millaire, David William, John Wood; Designers, Michael Annals, Alan Barlow, John Ferguson, Desmond Heeley, Mark Negin, Art Penson, Robert Prevost, Eoin Sprott, Annena Stubbs; Lighting, Gil Wechsler, F. Mitchell Dana

COMPANY

Edward Atienza, Mary Barton, Christine Bennett, Colin Bernhardt, Mervyn Blake, Theodore Britton, Pamela Brook, Michael Burgess, Leo Burns, Trudy Cameron, J. Kenneth Campbell, Richard Cohen, Stanley Coles, Vincent Cole, Giuseppe Condello, Dan Conley, Suzette Couture, Jack Creley, Daniel Davis, Eric Donkin, Bernerd Engel, Denise Fergusson, Michael Fletcher, Christine Foster, Roy Frady, Carl Gall, Pat Galloway, Marilyn Gardner, Lewis Gordon, Edward Henry, Roland Hewgill, Eric Hutt, William Hutt, John Innes, Jeff Jones, Lila Kedrova, Joel Kenyon, Jean Leclerc, Veronique Leflaguais, Maureen Lee, Monique Leyrac, Anne Linden, Michael Liscinsky, Barry MacGregor, Iris MacGregor, Phyllis Mailing, Stephen Markle, Robin Marshall, Doug McGrath, Monique Mercure, Allan Migicovsky, William Needles, Stephen Nesrallah, Blaine Parker, Antony Parr, Nicole Pelletier, Nicholas Pennell, Henry Ramer, Krysia Read, Roland Richard, Jack Roberts, Anton Rodgers, Pam Rogers, Joseph Rutten, Mary Savidge, Elsie Sawchuk, Alan Scarfe, David Schurmann, Errol Slue, Carole Shelley, Elizabeth Sheperd, Sylvia Shore, Thomas Stebing, Sean Sullivan, Don Sutherland, Anni Lee Taylor, Powys Thomas, Joseph Totaro, Tony van Bridge, William Webster, David Wells, Jonathan Welsh, Kenneth Welsh, Tim Whelan, Kenneth Wickes
GUEST ARTISTS: Le Theatre du Nouveau Monde

PRODUCTIONS

"King Lear," "As You Like It," "Lorenzaccio," "She Stoops to Conquer," "The Threepenny Opera," "La Guerre, Yes Sir!," "Orpheus," "Mark," "Pinocchio," "Patria II: Requiems for the Party Girl:"
Robert C. Ragsdale Photos

**Right: Carole Shelley, Powys Thomas, Barry MacGregor, Alan Scarfe, Tony Van Bridge in "She Stoops to Conquer"
Top: Nicholas Pennell, Carole Shelley in "As You Like It"**

William Hutt, Elizabeth Shepherd in "King Lear"

Lila Kedrova, Jack Creley, Monique Leyrac in "Threepenny Opera"

THEATRE VENTURE '73

Beverly, Massachusetts
April 2—June 2, 1973

Formerly North Shore Shakespeare Festival; Produced by North Shore Community Arts Foundation; C. Henry Glovsky, President; Managing Director, Stephen Slane; Directors, Edward Roll, Ben Shaktman; Sets ve Lyon; Costumes, Betsy Potter; Lighting, Theda Taylor; Stage Managers, William Bond, Robert J. Bruyr; Press, Peter Downs, Eve Slane

PRODUCTIONS AND CASTS

KING LEAR with Jeff Corey, Barbara Andres, Carol Mayo Jenkins, Laurie Kennedy, Peter Lombard, Barry Ford, Michael Kermoyan, Tom Toner, Jack Ryland, Stephen Collins, Will Mackenzie, Howard Meadow, Douglas Simes, Cliff Alvey, Peter Doe, Christopher Claremont, Jonathan Hall, Robert Boardman, Phillip Hecht, Cliff Alvey, John Butman, Richard Kurtzman, Robert Ladanyi, Brian Muehl, Robert Stone, Peter Van Wagner, Robert Wilkins

GREAT SCENES FROM SHAKESPEARE with Eileen Barnett, Peter Lombard, Dick Latessa, Brian Farrell

A DOLL'S HOUSE with Betsy Palmer, Dick Latessa, Carol Mayo Jenkins, Tom Toner, Mary Tiffany, Linda Russell

Peter Downs Photos

Below Left: Peter Lombard, Barbara Andres, Stephen Collins
Right: Dick Latessa, Brian Farrell, Eileen Barnett

Jeff Corey, Will Mackenzie in "King Lear"

Stephen D. Newman, Betsy Palmer in "A Doll's House"
Above: Eileen Barnett, Brian Farrell in "Great Scenes"

ACTORS THEATRE OF LOUISVILLE

Louisville, Ky.
October 19, 1972–May 13, 1973

Producing Director, Jon Jory; Administrative Director, Alexander Speer; Associate Director and Press, Trish Pugh; Company Manager, Vaughn McBride; Business Manager, Janet Levy; Directors, Jon Jory, Victor Jory, Frank Wicks, Patrick Tovatt, John Wylie, Charles E. Kerr, Vaughn McBride; Designers, Paul Owen, Kurt Wilhelm, Diann Fay, Geoffrey T. Cunningham, Grady Larkins, Judy Haskell, Ron Antone, Carol Canavan, Jan Kastendieck; Costumiere, Mary Lou Owen; Stage Managers, David Semonin, Charles Traeger, Charles E. Kerr, Jack Wann; Technical Director, Mark Luking; Technical Staff, Ron Antone, Warren Camhi, Richard Lukaszewicz

COMPANY

G. W. Bailey, Leslie Barrett, Fran Brill, David Byrd, David Canary, Dale Carter Cooper, Peggy Cowles, Donna Curtis, Daniel Davis, Ed Dixon, Ronnie Claire Edwards, Lee Anne Fahey, James Glenn, Patrick Gorman, Max Gulack, Pamela Hall, Max Howard, Jean Inness, Jim Jansen, Victor Jory, Marion Killinger, Susan Cardwell Kingsley, Mark Lenard, David MacEnulty, Carmen Mathews, Vaughn McBride, Sandy McCallum, Michael McCarty, Jon Oak, Stephen Pearlman, Garrison Phillips, Lu Ann Post, Dennis Predovic, Jo Rowan, Rhonda Saunders, Linda Selman, Danny Sewell, Anne Shropshire, Tom Sinclair, Jennifer Stock, Gina Swain, Carol Teitel, Katherine Thompson, Ian Thomson, Toby Tompkins, Patrick Tovatt, Charles Traeger, Anne Wakefield, Bruce Weitz, Angela Wood, John Wylie

PRODUCTIONS

"A Man for All Seasons," "You Can't Take It with You," "The Pirates of Penzance," "Kentucky," "In Fashion," "Macbeth," "What the Butler Saw," "Just between Us," "Adaptation/Next," "Old Times"
David S. Talbott Photos

Right: Sandy McCallum, Anne Wakefield, Ed Dixon in "Pirates of Penzance" Above: Garrison Phillips, David Canary, Carol Teitel in "Macbeth"

Daniel Davis
in "In Fashion"

Sandy McCallum, Jean Inness, Fran Brill in
"You Can't Take It with You"

ALLEY THEATRE

Houston, Texas
October 19, 1972—July 1, 1973

Producing Director, Nina Vance; Managing Director, Iris Siff; Press,
Feingold; Administrative Assistant, Toni Simon; Merry-Go-Round
ministrative Director, Bettye Gardner; Producing Associate, H. Wilk-
d; Directors, William Hardy, Robert E. Leonard, Beth Sanford, Jack
in; Production Manager, Bettye Fitzpatrick; Company Manager,
rt E. Leonard; Stage Managers, George Anderson, Henry Westin;
gners, Jerry Williams, William Troutman; Technical Director, Wil-
C. Lindstrom; Lighting, Jonathan Duff

COMPANY

avid Adamson, Lee Burnett, Rutherford Cravens, Woody Eney, Phi-
isher, Lauren Frost, John Green, Michael Hall, William Hardy,
r Hatch, I. M. Hobson, Gary Hubbard, William Hutson, Rick Lieb-
n, Joseph Maher, Laurie Main, John Napierala, Jennifer Reed,
dy Skaggs, Lee Smith

PRODUCTIONS

Pantagleize," "Happy Birthday, Wanda June," "Life with Father,"
Hostage," "All Over," "Colette," "School for Wives," "Jacques
Is Alive and Well and Living in Paris"

Bill Thompson, Dome, David Adamson Photos

ight: Judy Rice, J.T. Cromwell, Denise LeBrun,
eldon Epps in "Jacques Brel Is Alive..." Below
eft: Barbara Barnett, Woody Skaggs, Woody
Eney in "Happy Birthday, Wanda June"

avid Cindric, Anthony Auer, Bettye Fitzpatrick (top),
ottom) David Folwell, William Trotman, Christopher
Newlin in "Life with Father"

Woody Skaggs, Glynis Bell, William Hansen in "All Over"
Above: Jeannette Clift, Jonathan Kidd in "Colette"

189

AMERICAN CONSERVATORY THEATRE

San Francisco, California
October 1972—May 1973

General Director, William Ball; Executive Producer, James B. M
zie; Executive Director, Edward Hastings; Development Director,
Markson; Conservatory Director, Allen Fletcher; Directors, W
Ball, Bonaventura, Allen Fletcher, Edward Hastings, Nagle Jackson
O'Brien, Eugene Barcone, Paul Blake; Composer, Lee Hoiby; Prod
Director, Benjamin Moore; Designers, Robert Blackman, F. M
Dana, Arthur Dinsmore, Ralph Funicello, Fred Kopp, Walter W
Les Kane, James Edmund Brady, Robert Fletcher, Robert Morgan
Managers, James Haire, James L. Burke, Diana Clarke, Raymond S
General Manager, Charles Dillingham; Press, Cheryle Elliott, Jin
ber, Jane Harada

COMPANY

Janie Atkins, Andy Backer, Ramon Bieri, Joseph Bird, R.
Brown, Joy Carlin, Robert Chapline, Barbara Colby, Jim Corti, K
Crosby, Peter Donat, Dana Elcar, Donald Ewer, Ed Flanders,
Gilliam, Sarina C. Grant, Charles Hallahan, John Hancock, Henry
man, Elizabeth Huddle, Judith Knaiz, Anne Lawder, Marsha M
Deborah May, Robert Mooney, Frank Ottiwell, William Paters
Kerrigan Prescott, Ray Reinhardt, Ken Ruta, Paul Shenar, Howard
man, Marc Singer, Shirley Slater, Mary Wickes, J. Steven Whit
Winter, G. Wood

Phoebe Alexander, Christopher Cara, Katherine Conklin, J
Dawson, Robert Dicken, Barbara Dirickson, Bobby Ellerbee, Jerry
patrick, Ross Graham, Barbara Herring, Michael Hume, Robe
sabella, Daniel Kern, Roger Kern, Victor Pappas, Carole Payot, R
Poe, John Rue, Rebecca Sand, Donovan Scott, Warner Shook,
Timpson, Francy Walsh, Kathleen Worley, Stephen Yates

PRODUCTIONS

"Cyrano de Bergerac," "The House of Blue Leaves," "The Me
of Venice," "The Mystery Cycle," "You Can't Take It with You
Doll's House," "Godspell," "A Midsummer Night's Dream,"
Championship Season," "The Crucible"

William Douglas Ganslen, Ken Howard Photos

**Top Left: Marsha Mason, Peter Donat in "A D
House" Below: Henry Hoffman, Joy Carlin, Ju
Knaiz, E. Kerrigan Prescott, Ray Reinhard
William Paterson, Donald Ewer in "You Ca
Take it with You"**

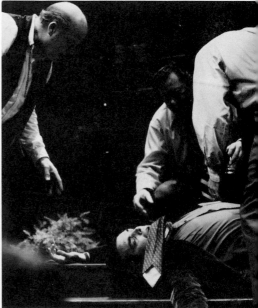

J. Steven White, Marsha Mason in "Merchant of
Venice" Above: Barbara Colby, Joy Carlin, Ed
Flanders in "House of Blue Leaves"

Dana Elcar, Paul Shenar, Ramon Bieri, Ed Flande
in "That Championship Season"

Lee Shallat, Jean Burch, Wayne Hudgins in "Butterflies Are Free" Top: Lee Shallat, Jessie [Nore]s-Haas, Ann McCaffray, Jean David in "Effect [of] Gamma Rays. . . ." Right: "The Me Nobody [Kno]ws" Below: Ben Tone, Gisela Caldwell, Stanley Anderson, in "Echoes"

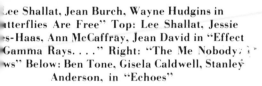

A CONTEMPORARY THEATRE

Seattle, Washington
June 27, 1972—April 28, 1973

Artistic Director, Gregory A. Falls; General Manager, Terence C. [M]urphy; Press, Edna K. Hanna; Directors, Gregory A. Falls, Pirie Mac-[D]onald, William F. West, Allie Woods, Tunc Yalman, Clayton Corzatte; [M]usical Director, Stan Keen; Designers, Bill Raoul, S. Toff Muffatti, [Ja]mes R. Crider, Phil Schermer; Technical Director, Dick Montgomery, [St]age Manager, Don Correll; Props, Shelley Schermer

COMPANY

Cathy Jamerson, Diane DeFunis, Rene Laigo, Cecilia Cordova, David [Be]rry, Joe Ginza, Donna Uno, Annette Ensley, Lloyd Hardy, Tom Tang-[le]y, Kelly Walters, Eileen Ramsey, William Swan, Bonnie Hurren, Anne [M]urray, Robert Cornthwaite, Charles Layne, Lee Shallat, Jean David, [An]n McCaffray, Jessie Nores-Haas, Gisela Caldwell, Stanley Anderson, [Be]n Tone, Jack Axelrod, Sid Conrad, Wayne Hudgins, Matt Pelto, [B]rian Speaks, Dori Warren, Toby Andersen, Hershey Parady, William [N]ewman, D. Quinton, B. Inga Douglas, Adrian Sparks, Anne Etue, [Pa]trick G. Duffy, Deborah Hedwall, Don Bearden, Glen Buttkus, Russell [W]oodbury, Gary Thomsen, Jean Burch, Patricia Hodges, John Kauff-[m]an, Martin LaPlatney, Jo Leffingwell, Jim Royce, Deems Urquhart

PRODUCTIONS

"The Me Nobody Knows," "What the Butler Saw," "The Effect of [Ga]mma Rays on Man-in-the-moon Marigolds," "Echoes" (Premiere by [N.] Richard Nash), "Trial of the Catonsville Nine," "Moonchildren," ["B]utterflies Are Free," "The Christmas Show," "Gilgamesh," "Wunder [Mi]lk Wood," "Oboade"

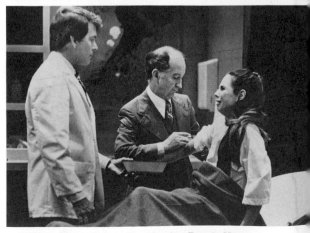

William Swan, Robert Cornthwaite, Bonnie Hurren in "What the Butler Saw" Above: Adrian Sparks, Lee Shallat, Kelly Walters, Wayne Hudgins in "Moonchildren" 191

AMERICAN MIME THEATRE

New York, N.Y.
Twenty-first Year

Director, Paul J. Curtis; Assistant to the Director, Rick Wessler; F
Jean Barbour; Stage Managers, Charles Barney, Joel S. Charleston

COMPANY

Jean Barbour
Charles Barney
Paul Curtis
Kender Jones
Marion Knox

Marc Mais
Nina Petruce
Rick Wessl
Arthur Yorin
Mr. Bon

REPERTOIRE

"The Lovers," "The Scarecrow," "Dreams," "Burlyburly," and
miere of "Evolution" Feb. 1, 1973 with music by Tod Dockstader
James Reichert

Jim Moore Photos

Left: Rick Wessler, Paul J. Curtis, Charles Barne
(bottom) in "Hurlyburly"

ARENA STAGE

Washington, D.C.
October 1972—June 1973

Producing Director, Zelda Fichandler; Executive Director, Thom
Fichandler; Associate Director, Lan Schneider; Associate Prod
Hugh Lester; Technical Director, Henry R. Gorfein; Stage Mana
Elizabeth Darr, Julia Gillett, Sidney McLain, Jimmy Cuomo; Sets, I
ert U. Taylor, Howard Anderson; Costumes, Marjorie Slaiman; Ligh
William Mintzer, Nora Pepper; Business Manager, JoAnn M. Over
Press, Alton Miller, Susanne Roschwalb, Suzanne Heard; Musical D
tor, Susan Romann; For Living Stage: Director, Robert Alexander; M
cal Director, Tom Pile; Stage Manager, James Devney

PRODUCTIONS AND CASTS

American Premiere of THE FOURSOME by E. A. Whitehead; Dire
Alan Schneider; Costumes, Gwynne Clark; Lighting, Hugh Lester; T
nical Director, Henry R. Gorfein; Set, Robert U. Taylor. CAST:
Horn (Harry), Munson Hicks (Tim), Lynn Ann Leveridge (Marie),
bara Dana (Bela)

American Premiere of A PUBLIC PROSECUTOR IS SICK OF IT
by Max Frisch; Director, Zelda Fichandler; Sets, Santo Loquasto;
tumes, Linda Fisher; Lighting, William Mintzer; Original Score, D
Horowitz; Translation, Michael Bullock; Presented by arrangement
Suhrkamp Verlag. CAST: Shepperd Strudwick (Public Prosecu
Dorothea Hammond (Elsa), Dianne Wiest (Hilde/Inge/Coco),
Wright (Murderer), Stanley Anderson (Dr. Hahn), Gene Gross ("
der/Gendarme), Richard Sanders (Asst. Hotel Manager), Leslie
(Inge's Mother), George Ebeling (Inge's Father/Police Inspector), F
ard Bauer (Signor Mario), Jan Freenfield, Bruce Kaiden (Bellhops),
rence Currier (Cab Driver), William Myers (Director of Bank
Howard Witt (Interior Minister), Glenn Taylor (General of the Ar
Gary Bayer (Student), Wendell Wright (Convict 112), Halo Wines (
Hofmeier), Robert Pastene (Aged President)

A LOOK AT THE FIFTIES with Book, Music, and Lyrics by Al
mines; Director, Lawrence Kornfeld; Choreographer, Dan Wagoner;
sical Director, Susan Romann. CAST: Boni Enten (Nan), Stuart S
(Paul), Maureen Sadusk (Sandy), Margaret Wright (Auntie), Julie
nitz (Mother), Don Nute (Ned), Emily Adams (Grandmother) F
Coppola (Referee), Reathel Bean (Coach), Essie Borden (Lane), L
Franigam (Terry), Dorian Barth (Carol), Kristi Tucker (Timn
Semina De Laurentis (Betsy), Michael Petro (Bobby), Roger O
(Charlie), Scott Stevenson (Kevin), John Kuhner (Clovis), Edn
Gaynes (Tommy), Scott Mansfield (Scoop), Tom Everett (Tony),
Podell (Ken), Jeff Dalton (Jim), Michael Mullins (Moon), Bruce Ho
(Drum Major), Lee Guilliatt (Sister Mary), and Ira Siff, Innis Ande
E. L. James, Judith Long, Bill Reynolds, Phyllis MacBryde, Marion

RAISIN by Robert Nemiroff and Charlotte Zaltzberg; Based on pla
Raisin in the Sun" by Lorraine Hansberry; Music, Judd Woldin; Ly
Robert Brittan; Directed and Choreographed by Donald McKayle; M
cal Director, Joyce Brown; Dance Music, Dorothea Freitag; Orche
tions, Al Cohn; Costumes, Bernard Johnson; Assistant Choreogra
Dorene Richardson. CAST: Ernestine Jackson (Ruth), Ralph C
(Travis), Helen Martin (Mrs. Johnson), Joe Morton (Walter Lee), S
wae Powell (Beneatha), Virginia Capers (Lena), Ted Ross (Bobo),
Burbridge (Travis' Friend), Robert Jackson (Joseph), Aristeed Po
(Drummer), Norman Matlock (Willie/Pastor), Herb Downer
bra/Orator/George), Richard Sanders (Karl), Al Peryman, Ch
Thorpes (Moving Men)

(No other material available)

Don Nute, Julie Kurnitz, Maureen Sadusk, Boni Enten,
Margaret Wright, Stuart Silver in "A Look at the Fifties"

ARLINGTON PARK THEATRE

Arlington Heights, Illinois
June 1, 1972—May 31, 1973

Managing Director, David Lonn; Press, Karen Alton; An Enterprise of Rannoch Productions; Designers, William B. Fosser, Rick Paul, Jeanne Sinclaire, Sandro La Ferla, Sean Roark, Andrea Kalish, Alan Steiner

PRODUCTIONS

DEATH OF A SALESMAN directed by Harvey Medlinsky, with Jack Warden, Jo Van Fleet, Robert H. Harris, John Randolph, Ben Hayes, Scott Marlowe, Patrick Mulvihill, Sandy Lipton, Don Stroup, Edith Wilson, Joe Shea, Nora Wells, Rebecca Phillips

LAST OF THE RED HOT LOVERS directed by James Burrows, with Don Knotts, Pamela Britton

THE ONLY GAME IN TOWN directed by Harvey Medlinsky, with Peter Marshall and Lois Nettleton

GOODBYE, CHARLIE directed by James Burrows, with Jo Anne Worley and Roger Perry

CHARLEY'S AUNT directed by James Burrows, with Louis Nye

ANGEL STREET directed by Shepard Traube, with Margaret Phillips, Joseph Campanella

THE FANTASTICKS directed by Lee Theodore, with Richard Chamberlain, John Carradine, Barney Martin, Art Kassul, Edward Garrabrandt, Rob Bowers, Indira Danks, Michael Byers

ONE FLEW OVER THE CUCKOO'S NEST directed by Harvey Medlinsky, with James Farentino, Albert Salmi, Jo de Winter, Alexander Courtney, Mike Nussbaum, Delos V. Smith, Jr., Mel Haynes, Joe Greco, Norman Rice, Barbara Muir, Ruben Anderson, J. J. Johnston, David Whitaker, James O. McCloden, Judith Ann Jonassen, Mark Thomas, Sharon Repking

THE DESPERATE HOURS directed by Harvey Medlinsky with Hugh O'Brian and Constance Towers

PRIVATE LIVES directed by Basil Langton, with Louis Jourdan, Barbara Rush, Francis Bethencourt, Elizabeth Swain, Edith Wilson

YOU NEVER CAN TELL directed by Peter Levin, with David Birney, John Carradine, Nancy Wickwire, Cara Duff-MacCormick, Robert Gerringer, Rebecca Balding, Cliff Osmond, John Carpenter, Michael Wayne Phillips, Ira Kahn

Lane, Sam Photos

Left: Louis Jourdan, Barbara Rush in "Private Lives"
Top: David Birney, Cara Duff-MacCormick in "You Never Can Tell"

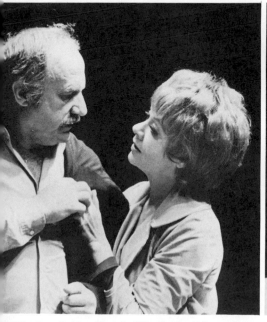

:k Warden, Jo Van Fleet in "Death of a Salesman"

John Carradine, Richard Chamberlain in "The Fantasticks"

Penelope Willis, Patrick Egan in "Philadelphia Story"
Top: Isa Thomas, Penelope Willis, Susan Goff, Corie
Sims in "Effect of Gamma Rays. . . ." Right: Patrick
Egan, Barbara Reid McIntyre in "Angel Street"

ASOLO STATE THEATRE

Sarasota, Florida
June 1, 1972—May 31, 1973

Executive Director, Richard G. Fallon; Managing Director, Howard
J. Millman; Artistic Directors, Robert Strane, Eberle Thomas; Director
of Education, Jon Spelman; Director of Children's Theatre, Visiting Di-
rectors, Richard D. Meyer, Peter J. Saputo; Press, Edith N. Anson;
Technical Director, Victor Meyric; Designers, Henry Swanson, John
Ezell, James Tilton, Rich Pike, Catherine King, Martin Petlock, James
Meade; Stage Managers, Marian Wallace, Stephanie Moss; Special
Projects Designer, Bob Naismith; Costume Supervisor, Flozanne John

COMPANY

Bradford Wallace, Polly Holliday, Walter Rhodes, Barbara Redmond,
Robert Lanchester, Kathleen O'Meara Noone, William Leach, Bill E.
Noone, Kathleen Klein, Philip LeStrange, Richard Hopkins, B. G. Ross,
Penelope Willis, Justin T. Deas, Robert Strane, Eberle Thomas, Jon Spel-
man, Jim Wrynn, Rita Grossberg, Charles Davis, Irene Ballinger, John
Moskal, Jr., Elizabeth Brincklow, Isa Thomas, Patrick Egan, Barbara
Reid McIntyre, Corie Sims, Nona M. Pipes, Vicki Casarett, Burton
Clarke, Richard Jacobs, Doug Kaye, Henson Keys, Morris Mathews,
Kerry Shanklin

PRODUCTIONS

"The Front Page," "Twelfth Night," "The Best Man," "Hay Fever,"
"Dracula," "The House of Blue Leaves," "The Matchmaker," "War and
Peace," "The Time of Your Life," "The Yellow Laugh," "The Legend of
Sleepy Hollow," "The King Stag," "Pygmalion," "Angel Street," "The
Philadelphia Story," "The Crucible," "Hotel Paradiso," "The Effect of
Gamma Rays on Man-in-the-moon Marigolds," "Little Mary Sunshine,"
"The Rose Tattoo," "The Merchant of Venice," "Big Klaus and Little
Klaus," "Aladdin," "The Canterville Ghost," "The Wind in the Wil-
lows"

Kathleen O'Meara Noone, Philip LeStrange, Justin D
Penelope Willis in "Matchmaker" Above: Robert Str
Bradford Wallace, William Leach, Walter Rhodes
"Front Page"

BARTER THEATRE

Abingdon, Virginia
April 1972—November 1972

Producing Director, Rex Partington; Business Manager, Pearl P. ...er; Designers, Bennet Averyt, Ann Colby Brady, Edward V. Re-...anni, Richard Davis, Evelyn Lea Moricle, Marvin Roark; Technical ...ctor, Thomas Brady; Stage Managers, Cindy Ann Kite, John Olson, ...iss Sayblack; Lighting, Stuart M. Richman; Directors, Rae Allen, ...ina Callahan, Kenneth Frankel, John Edward Going, George ...iatos

COMPANY

...slie Barrett, Jay Bell, Marcia Lou Bennett, Richard Bowden, Sarah ...Burke, Caryll Coan, Robert J. Foley, James W. Gillespie, Mary Jo ...derson, Edward Holmes, Susan Kingsley, David Laden, Ellen March, ...ael Medeiros, John Milligan, Dorothy Marie Robinson, Joseph Al-...Russo, Richard Sanders, James Sargent, Milton Tarver, Beth Dixon, ...leen Doyle, Jennifer Warren, Frederick W. Burrell

...ST ARTISTS: Robert Blackburn, Ann Buckles, Nancy Coleman, ...on Dearborn, Haskell Gordon, Michaele Myers, George Nahoon, ...dy Romoff, Sheila Russell

PRODUCTIONS

...luch Ado about Nothing," "Our Town," "Dracula," "Butterflies ...Free," "Last of the Red Hot Lovers," "The Country Girl," "Har-...Summer and Smoke," "Dear Liar," "You Know I Can't Hear You ...the Water's Running," "Gammer Gurton's Needle," "Apple Pie," ...cht on Brecht," "Magical Musical Mountain," "A Thurber Carni-

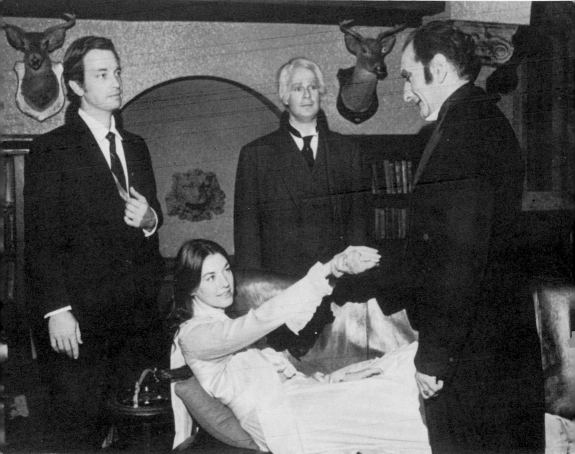

Milton Tarver, Sarah Burke, John Milligan, Woody Romoff in "Dracula"
Top Right: Jay Bird Porterfield, Kristina Callahan, Susan Kingsley in "Our Town"

195

BUCKS COUNTY PLAYHOUSE

New Hope, Pennsylvania
June 1, 1972—May 31, 1972

Managing and Artistic Director, Lee R. Yopp; Assistant Ma~
Director, Carol J. Gilbert; Sets, Paul Hoffman; Technical Director
Baun; Costumes, Betsey Roberts; Lighting, Rick Belzer; Production
ager, Don Yopp; Stage Managers, Marcy Gamzon, Charles Ha
Press, Gerry Cortese

COMPANY

Gloria Willis, Dennis M. Fitzpatrick, Jack Washburn, Joe
Marcia Mahon, William Simington, Ed Dennehy, Phil Kellmen, W
Parent, John Favorite, Gennady Komkov

GUEST ARTISTS: Tom Poston, Dana Andrews, Joan Bennett
Shawn, John Svar, David Wayne, Jay Barney, Ruth Ford, Robert I
Scott McKay, Richard Mathews, Lloyd Harris, Wesley Addy, Cara
MacCormick, Lewis J. Stadlen

PRODUCTIONS

"The Crucible," "The Odd Couple," "Anything Goes," "T
Night," "The Fantasticks," "The Glass Menagerie," "Butterflie
Free," "Our Town," "The Rivals," "1776," "The King and I,"
Subject Was Roses," "Cactus Flower," "The Lion in Winter," "M
All Seasons," "Play It Again, Sam," "Forty Carats," "Last of th
Hot Lovers"

WORLD PREMIERS: "Halloween" by Mitch Leigh directed by
Marre, "A Breeze from the Gulf" by Mart Crowley directed by
Going," "Smile, Smile, Smile" by Hugo Peretti, Luigi Creato
George David Weiss, "The Girl Who Has Everything" by Harry I

Dana Andrews and the cast of "Our Town" performed at the 1
dike Theatre in Surrey, England while the Thorndike actors pre
"The Rivals" at Bucks County Playhouse.

Left: Tom Poston, Mary Louise, Merv Deskins i
"Anything Goes"

Dick Shawn
in "Halloween"

Robert Drivas, Ruth Ford in "A Breeze from the G
Above: Jaqui-Ann Carr, Isla Blair in "The Rival

CENTER STAGE

Baltimore, Maryland
October 24, 1972—May 13, 1973

Producing Director, Peter W. Culman; Artistic Director, John Stix; Assistant Artistic Director, Carl Shurr; General Manager, David L. Dannenbaum; Directors, Larry Arrick, Robert H. Livingston, Mitchell Nestor, John Stix; Musical Directors and Staging, Gerri Dean, John Sichina; Scenery, Bennet Averyt, John Boyt, Raymond C. Recht; Costumes, John Boyt, Raymond C. Recht, Mary Strieff, Juliellen Weiss; Lighting, Bennet Averyt, Raymond C. Recht; Music, Barbara Damashek, Thom Shovestull, John Sichina; Choreography, Bert Houle, Sophie Wibaux; Technical Directors, Thomas Brady, Sichina; Stage Managers, Peter Murray, Margaret Stuart-Ramsey, Shana Sullivan, Hamp Watson; Press, Flo Harbold, Suzanne Wade, Wayne Woodward; Director of Special Projects, Joseph Patterson; Workshop Director, Vivienne Shrub; Touring Administrator, Jack Deisler.

COMPANY

Jack Deisler, Richard Dix, Carol DuPont, Stephen Fleagle, Bert Houle, Wil Love, Dale McIntosh, Peter Murray, Jan Rothman, Carl Schurr, Henry Strozier, Margaret Stuart-Ramsey, Shana Sullivan, Ann Ulvestad, Alan Wade, Sophie Wibaux

GUEST ARTISTS: Melba L. Alston, Kathryn Baumann, Edward Bell, Chad Burton, Tipper Steve Burton, Cheryl Lynn Brown, Robert Chamberlain, C. David Colson, Mark Dallas, Barbara Damashek, Ronnie Duncan, Bob DeFrank, Michael Ebert, Jon L. Feather, Sarah Felder, Nancy Franklin, David Freeman, Bonnie Gondell, Marcia Haufrecht, Brucke Hawkins, Liz Kemp, Charlotte Y. Johnson, Kila Kitu, Bobby London, Jack McClure, Troy McQuaige, Hector Mercado, Alexander Panas, Dennis Patella, Steve Railsback, Anthony Richburg, George Shannon, Betty Sinclair, Millie Slavin, Lane Smith, Gilbert Loren Stafford, James Tolkan, Manu Tupou

PRODUCTIONS

"One Flew over the Cuckoo's Nest," "Dandy Dick," "Two Saints," "Julius Caesar," "The Petrified Forest," "The Me Nobody Knows," "Mimes and Pantomimes," "Children's Story Telling," "Christmas—Center Stage," "A Poetic Patchwork," "The Clinic"

C. B. Nieberding Photos

Left: Richard Dix, Henry Strozier in "Dandy Dick"
Above: Margaret Stuart-Ramsey, George Shannon, Ann Ulvestad in "One Flew over the Cuckoo's Nest" Top: Bert Houle, Sophie Wibaux, Alan Wade in "Two Saints"

Liz Kemp, Edward Bell in "The Petrified Forest"

"The Me Nobody Knows"

CENTER THEATRE GROUP
AHMANSON THEATRE

Music Center of Los Angeles
October 17, 1972—April 28, 1973

Managing Director, Robert Fryer; Manager, Charles Mooney; Assistant Manager, Barbara Stocks; Press, Allan/Ingersoll (Rupert Allan), Farrar Cobb; Technical Supervisor, H. R. Poindexter; Production Associate, Robert Linden; Production Coordinator, Michael Grossman; Stage Managers, Bill Holland, David Barber

PRODUCTIONS AND CASTS

THE PRISONER OF SECOND AVENUE by Neil Simon; Director, Mike Nichols; Setting, Richard Sylbert; Lighting, Tharon Musser; Costumes, Anthea Sylbert; with Art Carney, Barbara Barrie, Jack Somack, Ruth Jaroslow, Jean Barker, Roslyn Alexander

THE CRUCIBLE by Arthur Miller; Director, Joseph Hardy; Settings and Lighting, H. R. Poindexter; Costumes, Noel Taylor; with Charlton Heston, Inga Swenson, James Olson, Beah Richards, Donald Moffat, Gale Sondergaard, Ford Rainey, Robert Cornthwaite, Sandra Morgan, Norma Connolly, Linda Kelsey, Philip Kenneally, Brendan Dillon, John Ragin, Frederic Downs, Phil Chambers, Renee Tetro, Sylvia Sage Lane, Alpha Blair

A MIDSUMMER NIGHT'S DREAM by William Shakespeare with the Royal Shakespeare Company; Director, Peter Brook; Designed by Sally Jacobs; Music, Richard Peaslee; Assistant Director, Michael Bogdanov; with Doyne Byrd, Denis Carey, Ralph Cotterill, Patricia Doyle, Alan Howard, Gemma Jones, Gillian Joyce, Hugh Keays Byrne, Robert Lloyd, Phillip Manikum, David Meyer, Pauline Munro, Malcolm Rennie, Zhivila Roche, Philip Sayer, Roshan Seth, Barry Stanton, Jennie Stroller, George Sweeney, Terence Taplin, Tony McVey, Robin Weatherall, John Zaradin

A STREETCAR NAMED DESIRE by Tennessee Williams; Director, James Bridges; Setting, Robert Tyler Lee; Costumes, Theodora Van Runkle; Lighting, H. R. Poindexter; Music, Fred Werner; Music Supervisor, Gerhard Samuel; with Jon Voight, Faye Dunaway, Earl Holliman, Lee McCain, Peggy Rea, Jerome Guardino, Paul Zayas, Betty Harford, Nelson Welch, Scott Colomby, Ella Mae Brown, Margarita Garcia, Paul Factor, Keven Dobson

Top Right: Ford Rainey, Inga Swenson, Charlton Heston in "The Crucible"

Jon Voight, Faye Dunaway in "A Streetcar Named Desire"

Lee McCain, Earl Holliman in "A Streetcar Named Desire" Above: Royal Shakespeare Co. in "Midsummer Night's Dream"

McMartin, Charlotte Moore, Betsy Slade, Bud
Cort in "Forget-Me-Not Lane" Right: Victor
Buono, Kristoffer Tabori in "Henry IV, Part I"

CENTER THEATRE GROUP
MARK TAPER FORUM

Music Center of Los Angeles
June 1, 1972—May 31, 1973

Artistic Director, Gordon Davidson; General Manager, Francis von
Brneck; Press, Richard Kitzrow, Thomas Brocato, Dennis Hammer,
Ronald Warden; Design Consultant, Peter Wexler; Staff Lighting De-
signer, Tharon Musser; Technical Supervisor, H. R. Poindexter; Produc-
tion Manager, John DeSantis; Stage Managers, Tom A. Larson, Don
Winton, David Barber, Madeline Puzo, Lawrence K. Pool, Bethe Ward;
Staff Directors, Wallace Chappell, Robert Greenwald, John Dennis

PRODUCTIONS AND CASTS

DON'T BOTHER ME, I CAN'T COPE by Micki Grant; Director, Vin-
nette Carroll; Choreographer, Claude Thompson; Musical Director, H. B.
Barnum; Designers, H. R. Poindexter, Noel Taylor, Ken Billington;
CAST; Amanda Ambrose, Hannah Dean, Marguerite DeLain, Jacquelyn
DuBois, Winston DeWitt Hemsley, Isaiah Jones, Jr., Juliet Jones, Paula
Kelly, Billy King, Bobby King, Brad Manuel, Avery Sommers, George
Turner, Alan Weeks, Myrna White, Emily Yancy

HENRY IV, PART I by William Shakespeare; Director, Gordon David-
son; Designers, Ming Cho Lee, Lewis Brown, Martin Aronstein; Music,
Shelly Manne; Assistant Director, Diana Maddox; Battles and Fights
staged by Patrick Crean; CAST: Al Alu, Toby Andersen, Harry Basch,
Michael Baseleon, Jack Bender, Rand Bridges, Victor Buono, Timothy
Burns, Frank Cady, J. Kenneth Campbell, Charles Cyphers, William
Devane, Dan Ferrone, Penny Fuller, Peggy Gordon, Michael Graves, Ed
Hall, Ben Hammer, Jerry Hardin, J. S. Johnson, Darrell Larson, James
Rosi, David Nash, Thor Nielsen, Harold Oblong, Ted Pejovich, Jackson
Zippin, V. Phipps-Wilson, John Stefano, Kristoffer Tabori, Peter Virgo,
John Voldstad, Ronald Warden

MASS by Leonard Bernstein; Director, Gordon Davidson; Additional
Texts, Stephen Schwartz, Leonard Bernstein; Musical Director, Maurice
Peress; Choreographer, Donald McKayle; Designers, Peter Wexler,
Frank Thompson, Gilbert V. Hemsley, Jr.; Conductor and Assistant
Music Director, Earl Rivers; Assistant Director, Gordon Hunt; CAST:
Gilbert Price, Michael Hume, Lawrence N. Bond, Robert Corff, Carolyn
Baker, Bruce Heath, Lee Hooper, Tip Kelley, Jennifer Ann Lee, Linda
Boyd, Georgelton McClain, Kim Milford, Cleveland Pennington, Mi-
chael Rupert, Holly Sherwood, Michele Simmons, Eron Tabor, Emily
Yancy, Leslie Watanabe, Oren Waters, Barbara Williams

THE MIND WITH THE DIRTY MAN by Jules Tasca; Director, Ed-
ward Parone; Designers, Robert O'Hearn, Noel Taylor, Donald Harris;
CAST; Jane Dulo, James Flavin, Joe Flynn, Barra Grant, Ann Morgan
Guilbert, Allyn Ann McLerie, Peter Ratray, Peter Strauss

FORGET-ME-NOT LANE by Peter Nichols; Director, Arvin Brown;
Designers, Elmon Webb, Virginia Dancy, Pete Menefee, Tharon Musser;
CAST; Jill Cook, Bud Cort, Beulah Garrick, Bruce Kimmel, John
McMartin, Donald Moffat, Charlotte Moore, Betsy Slade, John Trayne

Steven Keull Photos

**Right Center: Paula Kelly, Winston DeWitt
Hemsley, Emily Yancy, Alan Weeks, Amanda
Ambrose, George Turner in "Don't Bother Me, I
Can't Cope"**

Allyn Ann McLerie, Peter Strauss, Joe Flynn
in "The Mind with the Dirty Man"

CENTER THEATRE GROUP
NEW THEATRE FOR NOW

Music Center of Los Angeles

Director, Edward Parone; Manager, William P. Wingate; Desig
Marianna Elliott, Donald Harris, Russell Pyle, Terence Tam Soo
Ted Shell

PRODUCTIONS AND CASTS

THE MIND WITH THE DIRTY MAN by Jules Tasca; Director
ward Parone; CAST: Timothy Blake, Helen Page Camp, John Fi
Kathleen Freeman, Allyn Ann McLerie, William Schallert, Peter St

REVOLUTION by Eric Monte; Director, Robert Greenwald; C
Margaret Avery, Brunetta Barnett, Paul Carr, Lee Corrigan,
DuBois, Danny Goldman, Gloria Jones, Jim Millsap, Eric Monte, C
Turman, Spence Wil-Dee, Bill Woodard

A BOOTH CALLED WAR by Leonard Horowitz; Director, Wa
Chappell; CAST: Mary Ann Beck, John D. Garfield, Barra Grant, D
Redfield, Rudy Solari, Ellen Sommers

FORUM LABORATORY
Robert Greenwald, Director

HELP by Michael McGuire; Director, Robert Greenwald; CAST
Bang, Kenneth Mars, Nan Martin

WHAT ARE YOU DOING AFTER THE WAR? by Merrick Ta
Director, Wallace Chappell; Designer, Jackson Phippin; CAST; C
Arner, Frank Cady, Anthony Costello, Tyne Daly, Jo de Winter, R
Legionaire, Robert Pratt, Davis Roberts, Joseph Ruskin, William Zu

HERE I AM by Ted Graham; Director, Ted Lange, Designers, R
Pyle, Billy Griffin; Choreographer, Sheryl Thompson; CAST: Tom
ner, Arthur M. Blythe, Everett A. Brown, Jr., David S. Bryant, Sa
Ego, Susan Gelb, Angela E. Gibbs, Beverly Kushida, Frank Liu, G
Mitchell, Michael Rhone, Bettie Ross, Fred C. Stofflet, Horace Tap
Della Thomas, Raymond Vago, Ronald Warden, Steven Wells, R
Williams, Bill Woodard

SOON by Scott Fagan; Director, Robert Greenwald; Music, Scott F
Joe Kookolis; Musical Director, Will "Rusty" Graham; Designer, R
Pyle; CAST: Indira Danks, Scott Fagan, Gar MacRae, Susan McA
Alan Martin, David Talisman, Robin Tapp, Freda Eilene Walker

HARVEY PERR'S SCANDALOUS MEMORIES by Harvey Pe
collaboration with Jack Rowe; Director, Harvey Perr; Designers, D
Harris, Ron Rudolph, John Sefick; CAST: Cynthia Adler, Nira B
Judith Chaikin, Naomi Pollack, Ron Rifkin, JoAnne Strauss, Clyde
tura, Joe Warfield

RAINBOWS FOR SALE by John Ford Noonan; Director, Gc
Hunt; Designer, John Sefick; CAST: Dennis Dugan, Will Geer

SUPERMAN IN THE BONES II by John Dennis; Director, John
nis; Designer, John Sefick; CAST: Dean Anderson, Rene Assa, I
Campbell, Michael Graves, John Koch, Michael Prichard, Robert R
John Stefano, Patrecia Wynand

THE WOMEN OF TRACHIS by Sophocles; Translated by Ezra Pe
Director, Robert Greenwald; Designer, Russell Pyle; CAST: John C
ford, Charles Cyphers, Nedra Deen, Jane Elliot, Michael Lerner,
Mannix, Nan Martin, Melissa Murphy, Michael J. Prichard, Edith V

TALES OF ONCLE JO by Harold Oblong; Director, Harold Ol
Designers, Kitty Vallacher, Goshen Gilbert, James Gaine; CAST:
can Gamble, Collandis Gibson, Archie Hahn, Toni Lawrence, H
Oblong, Whitney Rydbeck, Kitty Vallacher, John Voldstad

IMPROVISATIONAL THEATRE

Director, Wallace Chappell; Supervising Producer, Ditta Oliker; De
ers, N. Ted Shell, Ken Fryer, Terence Tam Soon, Nancy Norris

COMPANY

Chris Callan, Bob Delegall, K. Lawrence Dunham, Haunani M
Timothy Near, Dennis Redfield, Jack Rowe, Pepe Serna, Ray Bukte
Kathy Gackle, Raphael Grinage, Ernest Harada, Mary Kay Pass, I
Pickford, Mabel Robinson, Oren Waters

Steven Keull Photos

Top Left: Allyn Ann McLerie, William Schallert, Joh
Fiedler, Helen Page Camp, Kathleen Freeman, Pete
Strauss in "The Mind with the Dirty Man" Below:
Ja'net DuBois, Glynn Turman in "Revolution"

Dennis Redfield, Barra Grant, Ellen Sommers, John D.
Garfield, Rudy Solari in "A Booth Called War"

CINCINNATI PLAYHOUSE

Eden Park, Cincinnati, Ohio
June 1, 1972—May 31, 1973

Artistic Directors, Word Baker, Harold Scott; Managing Director, Sara O'Connor; Business Manager, Audrey Teljeur; Assistants to Artistic Director, Philip Kraus, David Juaire; Assistants to Managing Director, Jane Krause, Nathleen Norris; Press, Will Gray, Lanni Johnston Brengel, Frankie Banta; Technical Director, John Saalfeld; Sets, Stuart Wurtzel; Costumes, Caley Summers; Associate Designer, Tom Oldendick; Guest Director, Glenn Jordan.

COMPANY

Adrian Berwick, Flair Bogan, George Brengel, Thomas Burke, Dorothy Chace, Debby DeGuire, Dan Early, Laura Edwards, Jonathan Fairbanks, Tony Gaetano, Sally Gensler, Jack Gwillim, Dana Hibbard, Philip Kraus, Richard Loder, David Mack, T. Richard Mason, Paul Milikin, Georgia New, Charlotte Patton, Frank Raiter, Patty Romito, Marja Scheers, Oliver Schwab, Anita Trotta, David Wiles, Gene Wolters, Edward Zang

GUEST ARTISTS: Carolyn Coates, James Noble, Carrie Nye

PRODUCTIONS

"The Play's the Thing," "The Rivals," "The Crucible," and world premieres of "Sensations of the Bitten Partner," and "Baboon!!!"
Walt Burton Photos

Left: Carrie Nye (also below) in "A Streetcar Named Desire" Below Right: Paul Milikin, Debby Deguire, George Brengel, Richard Loder, Dorothy Chace in "Baboon!!!"

Frank Raiter, Paul Milikin in "The Rivals"

Paul Milikin, George Brengel, T. Richard Mason in "The Crucible"

Edmund Lyndeck, Jonathan Farwell, John Buck,
Jr., Brenda Curtis in "A Yard of Sun" Right:
Richard Oberlin, Douglas Jones, Richard Halver-
son in "Johnny No-Trump"

CLEVELAND PLAY HOUSE

Cleveland, Ohio
Fifty-seventh Season

Director, Richard Oberlin; General Manager, Nelson Isekeit; Business Manager, James Sweeney; Associate Director, Larry Tarrant; Press, Dennis Brown; Directors, Jonathan Bolt, Jonathan Farwell, Jose Ferrer, Edmund Lyndeck, Evie McElroy, Richard Morse, J Ranelli, Dennis Rosa, Larry Tarrant, George Touliatos; Designers, Richard Gould, Barbara Leatherman; Costumes, Harriet Cone, Bernadette O'Brien, Estelle Painter, Joe Dale Lunday; Lighting, Larry Jameson, William J. Plachy, John Rolland, Properties, David Smith

COMPANY

Robert Allman, John Bergstrom, Norm Berman, Sharon Berridge, Jonathan Bolt, John Buck, Jr., Eric Conger, Candace Corr, Brenda Curtis, John David, Jo Farwell, Jonathan Farwell, Richard Halverson, Eugene Hare, Bill Jones, Douglas Jones, Allen Leatherman, Evie McElroy, Bob Moak, Daniel Morris, Richard Morse, Christine Mower, Ralph Neeley, Richard Oberlin, Edith Owen, Dale Place, Michelle Reilley, Peggy Roeder, Mary Shelley, Marcus Smythe, Robert Snook, Lavinia Whitworth

GUEST ARTISTS: Jean Barret, Victor Caroli, Pilar Garcia, June Gibbons, Jana Gibson, Ibby Hardies, Margaret Hilton, Myrna Kaye, Viveca Lindfors, Edmund Lyndeck, Dorothy Paxton, Richard Sewell, Kenny Slattery, George Touliatos, Don White, Carolyn Younger

PRODUCTIONS

"I Am a Woman," "Forty Carats," "The Show-Off," "The Richard Morse Mime Theatre," "Johnny No-Trump," "Old Times," "The Caretaker," "Butterflies Are Free," "Sherlock Holmes," "One Flew over the Cuckoo's Nest," "The Loves of Cass McGuire," "Last of the Red Hot Lovers," "Romeo and Juliet"

PREMIERES: "A Yard of Sun" (national), "The Short Magical Ministry of the Reverend Doctor John Faust," "The Rabinowitz Gambit" (world)

James Fry Photos

Jonathan Farwell, Robert Snook in "Sherlock Holm
Above: Robert Allman, June Gibbons, Margaret Hi
in "The Loves of Cass McGuire"

COMPANY THEATRE

Los Angeles, California
October 2, 1972—June 8, 1973

Executive Director, Peter Chernack; Press, Lance Larsen; Directors,
~~hen~~ Bellon, Gar Campbell, Lance Larsen, Marcina Motter, Dennis
~~field~~; Children's Theatre Directors, Roger Barnes, Marcina Motter;
~~and~~ Lighting, Russell Pyle; Technical Director, Charles E. Hurley
Lighting, Donald Harris; Costumes, Marcina Motter; Music, Michael
~~e~~, Walter Kennon, Stan Levine, Lynn Murray; Associates, Caryl
~~ch~~, Tim Bloch, Laurence D. Cohen, Myrna Gawryn, Gail Kaplan,
~~issa~~ Hubbert, Michael Hubbert, Susan Levy, Carol Marie, Kent
~~ergall~~, Marsha Polekoff, Robyn Rice, Michael Sheehan, Steve
~~mpe~~, Lisa Wujnovich

COMPANY

~~rthur~~ Allen, Roger Barnes, Polita Marnes, Stephen Bellon, Lyn
~~wn~~, Gar Campbell, Vincent Cresciman, William Dannevik, Barbara
~~ver~~, Donald Harris, Nancy Hickey, Jerry Hoffman, Lori Landrin,
~~ce~~ Larsen, Sandra Morgan, Marcina Motter, Roxann Pyle, Russell
~~e~~, Dennis Redfield, Jack Rowe, Trish Soodik, Michael Stefani
~~ES~~T ARTISTS: Tom Baker, Oren Curtis, John Carlyle, Louise Dun-
~~John~~ Fletcher, Mark Johnson, Harvey Kahn, David Man, Kres
~~sky~~, Robert Redding, Beverly Ross, Patsy Sabline, Judy Taylor, Ste-
~~n~~ Vaughan, Ray Vitte

PRODUCTIONS

~~Endgame,~~" "Michael McClure on Toast," "Mary Stuart," "The
~~hish~~ Club," and children's productions "The Beast and the Rose,"
~~phne,~~ The Stuck-up Princess"

John Rose Photos

**Right: Jack Rowe, Gar Cambell, Lance Larsen,
Dennis Redfield, Michael Stefani in "The
Hashish Club"**

Brown, Jerry Hoffman, Trish Soodik in "The Button"
Above: Arthur Allen, Nancy Hickey in "Endgame"

Nancy Hickey in "Mary Stuart"

Director, Paul Baker; Assistant Director, Mary Sue Jones; Adminis-
tive Director, Gary Moore; Press, Lynn Trammell; Directors; Paul Bal
Sally Netzel, Ryland Merkey, Michael Dendy, David Pursley, Mary
Jones, Ken Latimer; Sets, John Henson, Yoichi Aoki, David Purs
Kathy Latimer; Costumes, David Pursley, Kathy Latimer, Patricia Lc
John Henson, Yoichi Aoki, Margaret Tallman, Bonnie Stroup; Light
Allen Hibbard, Robyn Flatt, John Henson, Linda Blase, Sam Na
Randy Moore, Sally Netzel

COMPANY

Judith Davis, Michael Dendy, John Figlmiller, Robyn Flatt, J
Henson, Mary Sue Jones, Preston Jones, Kathleen Latimer, Ken Latir
John Logan, Steven Mackenroth, Ryland Merkey, Reginald Montg
ery, Gary Moore, Randy Moore, Louise Mosley, Sally Netzel, Da
Pursley, Mona Pursley, Bryant J. Reynolds, Synthia Rogers, Marg
Tallman, Randolph Tallman, Jacque Thomas, Lynn Trammell

GUEST ARTISTS: John Reich, Carol Teitel, Jerome Lawrence, Na
Levinson

PRODUCTIONS

"The House of Blue Leaves," "The Effect of Gamma Rays on Mar
the-moon Marigolds," "Life with Father," "Summer and Smoke," "F
the Other Half Loves"

AMERICAN PREMIERES: "Wind in the Branches of the Sassafras'
Rene de Obaldia, translated by Joseph Foster; "The Happy Hunter"
Georges Feydeau, translated by Barnett Shaw; "Jabberwock" by Jer
Lawrence and Robert E. Lee

Andy Hanson Photos

**Left: Ken Latimer, Ryland Merkey, Synthia
Rogers, Mona Pursley in "House of Blue Leave
Below: American premiere of "Jabberwock"**

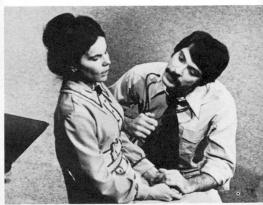

Randy Moore, Carol Teitel
in "The Happy Hunter"

Sally Netzel, Margaret Tallman, Ellen Lynsky
in "Effect of Gamma Rays. . . ." Above: Robyn Flat
John Figlmiller in "Summer and Smoke"

DETROIT REPERTORY THEATRE
Detroit, Michigan
October 26, 1972—June 30, 1973

rtistic Director, Bruce E. Millan; Community Coordinator, Robert
ms; Directors, Dolores Andrus, Barbara Busby, Bruce E. Millan,
.. A. Smith; Sets, Bruce E. Millan; Lighting, Richard Smith; Cos-
, Dolores Andrus

COMPANY

nk Monico, Tom Clark, Council Cargle, Marvin Jones, Robert
ms, Cliff Roquemore, W. Paul Unger, Barbara Busby, Lee O'Con-
David Hopson, Barbara Jacobs, Ruth Palmer, Richard Ian Berk,
o Milani, Jesse Newton, Dolores Porter, Dee Andrus, Charles
orough, Mark Z. Segal, John C. Bryson, Patrick Halley, Phillip W.
artin, Ronald S. Merkin, Jeff Nahan, Dennis Holly, Kent Martin,
Dickerson, Barbara Molson

PRODUCTIONS

hildren of Darkness," "What the Butler Saw," "The Hairy Ape,"
man Is That You?"

p: (L) David Hopson, Ruth Palmer in "What
e Butler Saw" (R) Robert Williams, Ruth
er in "Capricious Crump" Center: (R) Bar-
Busby, W. Paul Unger, Frank Monico, Coun-
l Cargle, Cliff Roquemore in "Children of
Darkness"

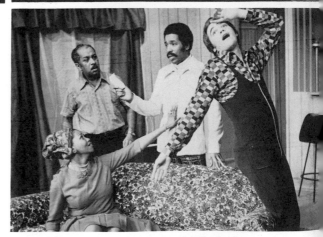

Barbara Molson, Kent Martin, Council Cargle, Dennis Holly
in "Norman Is That You?" Above: Jesse Newton,
W. Paul Unger in "The Hairy Ape"

FIRST REPERTORY COMPANY

San Antonio, Texas
September 1, 1972—August 31, 1973

Managing Director, J. Robert Swain; General Manager, Donald S. Bayne; Stage Directors, J. Robert Swain, Donald S. Bayne, David McKenna, Tracy Thornell; Sets, Tracy Thornell, Karl Schneider, Sean Keating, O'Neill Ford, Ken Graves, Allen Galli; Costumes, Catherine Brewer, Nancy Nichols; Press, David McKenna

COMPANY

Linda Ford, Allen Galli, David McKenna, Nancy Nichols, Arnaldo Santana-Zuniga, Carol Sowa, James Williams, Michael Wright, Louis Botto, Ronn Walker, Linda Conway, Rebecca Ballard, Tracy Thornell, Carroll Rue, Charles W. Gregory (Guest Artist)

PRODUCTIONS

"Hamlet," "Boy Meets Girl," "The Balcony," "Canterbury Tales," "Desire under the Elms," "The Roar of the Greasepaint, the Smell of the Crowd," "Aesop's Fables," and World Premiere of "The Troublemaker" by Charles W. Gregory

Top Right: Arnaldo Santana-Zuniga in "The Balcony"
Below: (L) James Williams, Linda Ford, Rebecca Ballard,
Linda Conway, Allen Galli in "Aesop's Fables"
(R) Tracy Thornell, Rebecca Ballard, Arnaldo
Santana-Zuniga, James Williams in "The Troublemaker"

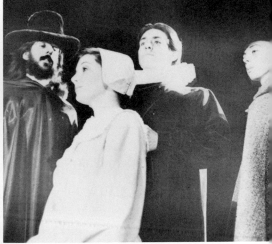

Dean Pitchford (C) and company in "Godspell"

FORD'S THEATRE

Washington, D.C.
April 6, 1972—September 16, 1973

Executive Producer, Frankie Hewitt; Press, Jan DuPlain; Administrative Assistant, Maury Sutter; Business Manager, Linda Lachowicz; Technical Director, Tom Berra; Stage Managers, Larry Whiteley, Mich Makman

COMPANY

Kerin Blair, Scotch Byerley, George-Paul Fortuna, Baillie Gerste Tony Hoty, Maggie Hyatt, D. Jamin-Bartlett, Gus Kaikkonen, R Kaptur, Irving Lee, Mike Makman, Dean Pitchford, Berlinda Tolb John-Ann Washington, Lynn Zidanic, Carol Anne McCarthy, Na Robin, James Zubiena

PRODUCTION
"Godspell"

GOODMAN THEATRE CENTER

Chicago, Illinois
October 8, 1972—June 17, 1973

Executive Director, Kenneth Myers; Resident Manager, John Econo-
~s; Press, Joanne Unkovsky, Rhona Schultz; Business Manager, Janet
~telleau; Stage Managers, Joseph DePauw, Greg Nash, Donna Lyn-
~ite; Technical Director, Lorenzo Gentile; Scenic Artist, Robert
~ody; Props, James Swank; Costumes, John Fitzpatrick; Administra-
~ Assistant, Joseph Baltz; Directors, Michael Kahn, Harold Stone,
~ne Lesser, William Woodman, Stephen Porter, Melvin Bernhardt; Mu-
~al Directors, Bill McCauley, Daryl Wagner; Sets, Marjorie Kellogg,
~vid Jenkins, Robert U. Taylor, Clarke Dunham, Alicia Finkel; Cos-
~nes, Alicia Finkel, Virgil Johnson; Lighting, G. E. Naselius, William
~ntzer; Choreography, Joyce Trisler, Betsy Haug

PRODUCTIONS AND CASTS

~LD TIMES" with Donald Madden, Sharon Laughlin, and Tudi Wig-
~s

~CENES FROM AMERICAN LIFE" with Chet Carlin, Susan Mer-
~a, Anthony Mockus, Gretchen Oehler, Roy K. Stevens, Marcy Vos-
~gh, Tudi Wiggins, Jerry Zafer

~N THE MATTER OF J. ROBERT OPPENHEIMER" with William
~nce, Maurice D. Copeland, J. Kent More, Otto L. Schlesinger, Charles
~ndall, Bruce Weitz, Ray Rayner, Roy K. Stevens, Paul Larson, Bob
~kin, Jerome Dempsey, Joseph Leon, George Womack, Michael
~anger, Rai Kristan, Douglas L. Lieberman

~WENTIETH CENTURY" with Lorry Young, Marty Zagon, Adele
~lis, Mitch Maurer, Joseph Rodgers, Duane Archie, Charles Youmans,
~eph Baltz, Robert McCord, Merwin Goldsmith, Ken Parker, Robert
~rgan, Joseph Leon, Neil Crainie, Paul Tomasello, Otto Schlesinger,
~ome Dempsey, Joseph Rodgers, Mary B. Best, Jan Farrand, Peter
~ompson, Clair Nelson, Frank Miller, Douglas Mellor

~HE LADY'S NOT FOR BURNING" with David Whitaker, John
~llum, Marcy Vosburgh, Curt Karibalis, Beatrice Fredman, William
~Cauley, Merwin Goldsmith, Tudi Wiggins, Roy K. Stevens, Will
~ary, Otto L. Schlesinger

~AL JOEY" with Anthony S. Teague, Nancy Marchand, Dave Shelley,
~san Lubeck, Barbara Erwin, Betsy Haug, Cheryl Benish, Susanne Car-
~, Jeanie Irvine, Richay Winters, Marti Rolph, David Reed Staller,
~chael Fisher, Gary Giocomo, Ann Hodges, P. J. Benjamin, Merwin
~ldsmith, Jim Carey, Clair Nelson

David H. Fishman Photos

~ght: Nancy Marchand, Anthony Teague in "Pal Joey"

~Top: Donald Madden, Tudi Wiggins in "Old Times"

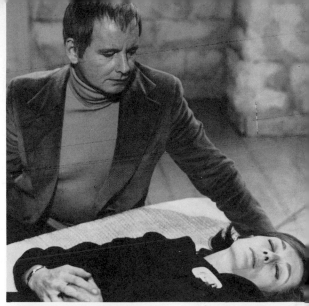

Jerome Dempsey, Jan Farrand
in "Twentieth Century"

Tudi Wiggins, John Cullum in "The Lady's
not for Burning"

GUTHRIE THEATER COMPANY

Minneapolis/St. Paul, Minn.
July 7, 1972—January 6, 1973

Artistic Director, Michael Langham; Associate Directors, Len Cariou, David Feldshuh; Managing Director, Don Schoenbaum; Press, Craig Scherfenberg, Charlotte Solomon; Production Manager, Denny Spence; Directors, Michael Langham, David Feldshuh, Len Cariou, John Hirsch; Designers, John Jensen, Desmond Heeley, Carl Toms, Hal George; Composers, Stanley Silverman, Henry Mollicone, John Duffy, Dick Whitbeck; Stage Managers, Ron Brucati, J. Warren Johnson, John Cranney; Lighting, Gil Wechsler; Choreography, Fran Bennett

COMPANY

Len Cariou, Frank Langella, Richard McKenzie, Peter Michael Goetz, Paul Ballantyne, Ken Pogue, Erik Fredricksen, Michele Shay, Bernard Behrens, James J. Lawless, Lance Davis, Fred Pinkard, Roberta Maxwell, Edward Zang, Robert Pastene, Diane Wiest, Gastone Rossilli, Leon Pownall, Linda Carlson, James Blendick, Ivar Brogger, Tovah Feldshuh, David Monasch, Carey Connell, Robert John Metcalf, Katherine Ferrand, Katherine Lenel

PRODUCTIONS

"A Midsummer Night's Dream," "Of Mice and Men," "The Relapse," "An Italian Straw Hat," "Oedipus the King" (world premiere of translation and adaptation by Anthony Burgess), "A Christmas Carol"

Top: (L) Patricia Conolly, Len Cariou in "Oedipus"

(R) Barbara Bryne, Len Cariou in "Midsummer Night's Dream" Left Center: Frank Langella, Katherine Ferrand, Roberta Maxwell in "The Relapse"

Peter Michael Goetz, Katherine Ferrand in "T Italian Straw Hat" Above: Richard McKenzi Peter Michael Goetz in "Of Mice and Men"

HARTFORD STAGE COMPANY

Hartford, Connecticut
October 6, 1972—June 24, 1973

Producing Director, Paul Weidner; Managing Director, William Stewart; Business Manager, Jessica Andrews; Press, Thomas O'Connor; Stage Managers, Fred Hoskins, Gary Lamagna; Directors, Paul Weidner, Jacques Cartier, Paul Shyre; Sets, John Conklin, Santo Loquasto, Lawrence King; Costumes, Victoria Zussin, Linda Fisher, Kathleen Ankers, Carola Meleck; Lighting, Larry Crimmins, Peter Hunt

COMPANY

Ray Aranha, Evalyn Baron, Jack Betts, Jani Brenn, James Broderick, Barbara Caruso, Eve Collyer, Paddy Croft, John Dignan, Bernard Frawley, John Frey, Tom Fuccello, Alan Gifford, Pamela Gilbreath, Ted Graeber, Richard Greene, Paul Haggard, Tana Hicken, Jay Higgins, Ruth Maynard, Eda Reiss Merin, Lynn Milgrim, Robert Moberly, Peg Murray, Tony Musante, Virginia Payne, Larry Pertilla, David O. Petersen, Richard Pilcher, Maureen Quinn, Chris Sarandon, Daniel Snyder, Arthur Stedman, Henry Thomas, Angela Thornton

PRODUCTIONS

"The Misanthrope," "A Streetcar Named Desire," "You Can't Take It With You," "Old Times," "Juno and the Paycock," and world premiere of "Nightlight" by Kenneth H. Brown

David Robbins Photos

Left: Angela Thornton, Tony Musante in "A Streetcar Named Desire" Below: "You Can't Take It with You"

ana Hicken, Chris Sarandon in "The Misanthrope"

Alan Gifford in "Nightlight" Above: Barbara Caruso, Maureen Quinn, James Broderick in "Old Times"

INNER CITY REPERTORY THEATR

Los Angeles, California
June 1, 1972—June 30, 1973

Executive Director, C. Bernard Jackson; General Manager, Josie
son; Executive Assistant, Jeanne Joe; Assistant to Executive Dir
Elaine Kashiki; Press, Norse Gaines, Bruce Feldman; Sets, Rae Cr
Juan Lotero; Costumes, Terence Tam Soon; Lighting, Rae Creevey
Lotero; Stage Managers, Annette Ensley, Elaine Kashiki; Prod
Coordinator, Beulah Quo

COMPANY

Gloria Calomee, Michael Cameron, Jesse Dixon, Shizuko
Mimosa Iwamatsu, Elaine Kashiki, Richard Kato, Clyde Ku
Joanne Lee, John Mamo, Serrena McCarthy, Irvin Paik, Th
Rasulala, Bill Shinkai, Bette Treadville, Glynn Turman, Momo Ya
GUEST ARTISTS: Mako, Nobu McCarthy, Beah Richards

PRODUCTIONS

"Gold Watch," "There Is No Place for a Tired Ghost," "One Is a C

Left: Jesse Dizon, Bill Shinkai, Irvin Paik,
John Mamo in "There Is no Place for a Tired Gho

Thalmus Rasulala, Beah Richards Above: Thalmus
Rasulala, Bette Treadville in "One Is a Crowd"

Mako, Joann Lee, Nobu McCarthy, and above with J
Dizon in "Gold Watch"

LONG WHARF THEATRE

New Haven, Connecticut
October 15, 1972—June 2, 1973

Artistic Director, Arvin Brown; Executive Director, M. Edgar Rosen-
am; Press, Lorraine Osborne; Directors, Arvin Brown, Kent Paul, Aus-
Pendleton, Michael Rudman, Max Stafford-Clark; Designers,
hitney Blausen, John Conklin, Virginia Dancy, Linda Fisher, David
kins, Marjorie Kellogg, Judy Rasmuson, Steven Rubin, Bill Walker,
nald Wallace, Elmon Webb; Stage Managers, Anne Keefe, Nina See-
, Simon Siegl

COMPANY

Tom Atkins, Emery Battis, Louis Beachner, John Braden, Shirley
yan, Clyde Burton, Alan Castner, Chuck Cioffi, Katina Commings,
er DeMaio, Jake Dengel, Ralph Drischell, Mildred Dunnock, Joyce
ert, George Ede, Geraldine Fitzgerald, John Glover, Sean Griffin,
orge Hearn, Ruby Holbrook, James Hummert, Linda Hunt, David H.
ary, Suzanne Lederer, Thomas Leopold, John Lithgow, Roberta Max-
l, Linda McGuire, Joseph Maher, Richard D. Masur, Richard Mat-
ws, Robert Murch, Joseph F. Muzicar, David Parker, Christina
kles, Bill Rhys, Rex Robbins, Paul Rudd, Jack Schultz, Michael Shan-
, Ronald Siebert, Douglas Stender, William Swetland, Henry Thomas,
n Tillinger, Christopher Walken, Mark Winkworth

PRODUCTIONS

"The Lady's Not For Burning," "What Price Glory?," "Trelawny of
'Wells'," "Juno and the Paycock," "Forget-Me-Not Lane," "Dance
Death," "Miss Julie," and American premiere of "The Changing
om"

William L. Smith Photos

Top: (L) Emery Battis, Joseph Maher in "Juno
d the Paycock" (R) Suzanne Lederer, William
etland in "Trelawny of the Wells" Center (L)
ul Rudd, Charles Cioffi in "What Price Glory?"

Joseph Maher, Joyce Ebert in "Forget-Me-Not Lane"
Above: "The Changing Room" (American premiere)

Mark Lenard, Lauri Peters
in "Rosmersholm"

Frank Langella in U.S. premiere
of "The Tooth of Crime"

Francesca Norsa, Mark Metcalf in "The Tempest"
Above: Cara Duff-MacCormick, Dolph Sweet, Nan
Martin in "Agamemnon"

McCARTER THEATRE

Princeton, N.J.
October 26, 1972—April 8, 1973

Artistic Director, Louis Criss; Productions Director, Leon Lea.
Press, Valerie B. Morris; Stage Director, Edward Payson Call; Admi
trative Assistant, Edward A. Martensen; Sets, John Conklin, David
kins, Philip Gilliam; Costumes, Elizabeth Covey, Linda Fisher; Light
John McLain; Stage Managers, Steve McCorkle, Robert Farley, S
Covey; Sound, Cathy MacDonald, Abe Jacobs, Patsy Rodgers; Chore
rapher, Geulah Abrahams

COMPANY

Wanda Bimson, Peter Blaxill, Andrew Bloch, Tom Brannum, Al C
bin, Louis Criss, Clifford David, Jerome Dempsey, MacIntyre Dix
Cara Duff-MacCormick, David Duhaime, Clarence Felder, Gray Ga
James Gallery, Franklin Getchell, Gene Gross, Dale Helward, I.
Hobson, Anne Louise Hoffmann, Nicholas Kepros, Jeanette Lan
Frank Langella, Mark Lenard, Joseph Leon, Karl Light, Julian Lo
Morillas, Gloria Maddox, Nan Martin, Mark Metcalf, William My
Fracesca Norsa, Judy Parton, Lauri Peters, Jess Richards, John Scan
Dwight Schultz, Daniel Seltzer, Anne Sheldon, Dolph Sweet, Dor
Warfield, Edward Zang

PRODUCTIONS

World premiere of "Agamemnon" by William Alfred, American
miere of "The Tooth of the Crime" by Sam Shepard, "The Tempe
"Loot," "Rosmersholm"

Boris Bohun-Chudyniv Photos

**Right Center: Donald Warfield, Jeanette Landis, Jam
Gallery in "Loot"**

212

Debra Mooney, Robert Casper, William LeMassena in "Doctor in spite of Himself"

Bill Moor, Elisabeth Orion in "The Country Girl"

MEADOW BROOK THEATRE

Rochester, Michigan
October 12, 1972—May 20, 1973

Artistic Director, Terence Kilburn; Managing Director, David Robert Kanter; Scenery and Lighting, Richard Davis; Costumes, Mary Schakel; Lighting, Dan T. Willoughby; Stage Manager, Robert Mooney; Press, Rose Marie McClain; Community Relations, Jane Mosher

COMPANY

Richard Baylis, Mark Bennett, Dorothy Blackburn, John Brandon, Ivar Brogger, Leonard Brotzman, Ealine Browne, Jaime Carriere, Renee Clare, J. L. Dahlmann, Robert Englund, Steven Greenstein, Frika Gray, Demene Hall, Sadie M. Hawkins, Doug Hill, David Himes, LeRoy Kalbas, Don Konrad, David Kroll, Francis Loud, Anne M. Lynas, Philip Mallet, Anthony McKay, Fred Michaels, Carolyn Miller, Jack Curtis Miller, Ted Moniak, Debra Mooney, Kristin Mooney, Cheryl Munson, Charles Nolte, James D. O'Reilly, Elisabeth Orion, Jan Owen, Julia Quiroz, Richard Riehle, Harold Roe, Fred Thompson, Ronald Wendschuh, LeRoy Williams

GUEST ARTISTS: Robert Casper, Margaret Christopher, Booth Colman, Jennifer Harmon, Celia Howard, Judith Jordan, Louise Kirtland, Lynn Ann Leveridge, William LeMassena, Kerri LuBell, Bill Moor, Jim Oyster, David Sabin, Katherine Squire, Jean-Pierre Stewart, Eric Tavaris, Dee Victor

PRODUCTIONS

"Front Page," "Inherit the Wind," "The Torch-Bearers," "The Miracle Worker," "Right You Are!," "The Country Girl," "Bedtime Story," "A Doctor in spite of Himself," "Count Dracula"

Right Center: James D. O'Reilly, Dee Victor, Phillip Mallet, Louise Kirtland, Debra Mooney in "The Torch-Bearers"

Jennifer Harmon, Kerri Lubell in "The Miracle Worker" Above: James Oyster, William LeMassena, James O'Reilly, LeRoy Kalbas in "Front Page"

MILWAUKEE REPERTORY THEATER

Milwaukee, Wisconsin
October 6, 1972—July 21, 1973

Artistic Director, Nagle Jackson; Managing Director, Charles R. McCallum; Press, Michael Krawczyk; Directors, Rod Alexander, Nagle Jackson, Charles Kimbrough, Richard Risso, Raye Birk; Sets, Christopher M. Idoine, Grady Larkins, Stuart Wurtzel, Michael F. Hottois; Costumes, James Edmund Brady, Pamela Scofield; Lighting, Christopher M. Idoine, Ken Billington; Stage Manager, Merry Tigar

COMPANY

Jim Baker, Candace Barrett, Raye Birk, Jerry Brown, Montgomery Davis, Robert Ground, Ric Hamilton, Charles Kimbrough, Mary Jane Kimbrough, William McKereghan, Josephine Nichols, Fredi Olster, Penelope Reed, Jack Swanson, Jeffery Tambor, Martha J. Tippin, G. Wood
GUEST ARTISTS: Elizabeth Franz, Davis Hall, Judith Light, Mary Wright

PRODUCTIONS

"Two Gentlemen of Verona," "Scenes from American Life," "The Play's the Thing," "The Cherry Orchard," "Sticks and Bones," "The Diaries of Adam and Eve," "Adaptation," "The Golden Fleece," "The Brute," and world premiere of "All Together Now . . ."

Jack Hamilton Photos

Right: Raye Birk in "Two Gentlemen of Verona"
Below: (L) Jack Swanson, Charles Kimbrough, William McKereghan in "The Play's the Thing" (R) Candace Barrett, G. Wood in "The Cherry Orchard"

Mary Jane Kimbrough, William McKereghan in "Sticks and Bones"

Candace Barrett, Ric Hamilton in "Scenes from American Life"

214

PAF PLAYHOUSE
Huntington Station, N.Y.
July 1, 1972—May 26, 1973

Executive Director, Clint Marantz; Directors, Richard Jamieson, ly Patton; Sets, William Gensel, David Jenkins, Robert Kaiser, Vic er, John W. Shane; Lighting, William Gensel, Vic Leder, Guy Lock- od, John W. Shane; Stage Managers, Mary Ann Carlin, William Gen- Technical Directors, Vic Leder, John W. Shane; Costumes, Elizabeth her; Press, Ruth H. Stone; Wardrobe, Molly Conant, Lois Singer

COMPANY

ack Axelrod, Donald Casey, Frank Converse, Virginia Drake, Will no, Clement Fowler, Donald Gantry, Minnie G. Gaster, Sean G. ffin, Howard Honig, Richmond Hoxie, Richard Jamieson, Vera Lock- od, Heidi Mefford, William Pardue, Louis Plante, Leslie Ann Rivers, n Rudner, Ben Seligsohn, Raymond Singer, Liam Smith, Henry mas, Joan Welles

ich Baron, Ronn Kistler, Eric Marantz, James Nichols, Jim Palmer, n Sly, Betsy Wood, Steve Marantz, Jamie Oliviero, Ann Schifrin, ole Weiner

PRODUCTIONS

"Little Murders," "Barefoot in the Park," "The Glass Menagerie," artuffe," "Charley's Aunt," "Hedda Gabler," "The Show-Off," "Wait- for Godot," "Circus," "Westward Movements," "Walt Whitman," aply Your Eye Shall Light Upon Some Toy"

Joan James Photos

elow: Richard Jamieson, Virginia Drake, Will Fenno, Heidi Mefford, Vera Lockwood in "The Show-Off"
Right:
Heidi Mefford, Vera Lockwood in "Glass Menagerie"

Joan Welles, Liam Smith
in "Hedda Gabler"

Will Fenno, Jack Axelrod, Richmond Hoxie
in "Waiting for Godot"

PHILADELPHIA DRAMA GUILD

Philadelphia, Pennsylvania
November 28, 1972—April 29, 1973

Producer, Sidney S. Bloom; Artistic Director, William Ross; Art
Consultant, John Randolph; Scenery and Lighting, Clarke Dunham; C
tumes, Joseph F. Bella; Stage Managers, Gerald Nobles, Jeanna Be
Press, McClelland & Carter Associates; Administrative Director, M
Gregg; Assistant to the Producer, Lillian Steinberg; Chairman of
Board, Robert Morgan

PRODUCTIONS AND CASTS

TARTUFFE by Moliere; Adapted by Richard Wilbur; Director, Mic
Kahn. CAST: Veronica Castang (Flipote), Edith Meiser (Mme. Perne
Jan Farrand (Elmire), Bernadette Peters (Dorine), Jobeth Williams (M
ianne), Dennis Higgins (Damis), James Ray (Cleante), Kurt Kasz
(Orgon), David Huffman (Valere), Richard Kiley (Tartuffe), Ro
Frazier (M. Loyal), Nick Smith (Emissary)

THE WALTZ OF THE TOREADORS by Jean Anouilh; Director, B
Murray. CAST: Anne Jackson (Mme. St. Pe), Eli Wallach (Genera
Pe), Victor Garber (Gaston), Laura Esterman (Sidonia), Karen John
(Estelle), John Randolph (Dr. Bonfant), Anne Freeman (Leonti
Louise Troy (Mlle. de Ste-Euverte), Miriam Burton (Mme. Dup
Fredaine), Charles Hudson (Father Ambrose), Charon Lee Co
(Pamela)

CEREMONIES IN DARK OLD MEN by Lonne Elder III; Direc
Shauneille Perry. CAST: Carl Willis Crudup (Voice of Announc
Douglas Turner Ward (Russell B. Parker), Bill Cobbs (William Jenk
Peter DeAnda (Theopolis Parker), Roger Hill (Bobby Parker), Rosa
Cash (Adele Eloise Parker), Nathan George (Blue Haven), Judy N
(Young Girl)

JUNO AND THE PAYCOCK by Sean O'Casey; Director, Dou
Campbell. CAST: Tom Ewell ("Captain" Jack Boyle), Kate Reid (J
Boyle), Curt Williams (Johnny Boyle), Janice Ehrlich (Mary Boy
Leonardo Cimino ("Joxer" Daly), Beulah Garrick (Mrs. Madigan),
Kressen ("Needle" Nugent), Virginia Downing (Mrs. Tancred), P
Rogan (Jerry Devine), Bruce Gray (Charlie Bentham), Douglas W
(Charlie Bentham), Joy Dobbs (An Irregular), Milt Commons (C
Block Vendor), Douglas Wing (Sewing Machine Man), Odysseus L
well (Furniture Removal Man), Veronica Castang, Melanie F
(Neighbors)

Peter Lester Photos

**Left: Eli Wallach, Anne Jackson in "Waltz of the
Toreadors" Above: Leonardo Cimino, Tom Ewell, Beul
Garrick, Kate Reid, Janice Ehrlich, Bruce Gray in
"Juno and the Paycock"**

Kurt Kasznar, Bernadette Peters in "Tartuffe"

Roger Hill, Peter De Anda in "Ceremonies
in Dark Old Men"

Barbara Lynn Block, Ken Costigan, Sylvia Miles
in "Who's Afraid of Virginia Woolf?"

Barbara Lynn Block, Kurt Kasznar
in "Fiddler on the Roof"

PITTSBURGH PLAYHOUSE

Pittsburgh, Pennsylvania
September 9, 1972—June 24, 1973
Thirty-ninth Season

xecutive Producer, S. Joseph Nassif; Artistic Director, Ken Costigan;
s, Thom Toney; Production Manager, James Yeiser; Technical Direc-
Robert Kuiper; Stage Manager, Walter A. Hess; Designers, Mary
n Kennedy, Leonard Feldman, Eric Head, Pat Simmons, Frank
ds; Musical Director, James Reed Lawlor; Assistant Production
ager, Wayne Brinda; Sound, Bonnie Davies; Stage Directors, Ken
tigan, Joseph Nassif, John Pasquin, Maria Piscator, Tom Thomas;
irman of the Board, Arthur M. Blum

COMPANY

arl Boen, David Emge, Alan Clarey, Helen Wayne Rauh, Ken Costi-
Barbara Lynn Block, Daniel Mooney, Betty Gillett, Lynn Archer,
Bruce, Glen McClaskey, David Tompkins, Ben Gillespie, Kathy
bo, Art Pingree, Anderson Matthews, Donna Pelc, Celia Howard,
Endes, Ted Chapman, Ann Muffly, Rosalie Half, Jo Stuhr, Sally
n, Elynn Shapiro, Henry Luba, Fred McCarren, Gregory Lehane,
ara Orwid, Carol DePaul, Florence Lacy, Elizabeth Austin, Sherry
e, Doug Sortino, Larry Dykeman, Lenora Nemetz, Lee Ann Moffett,
Greeno, Richard Fox

EST ARTISTS: Kurt Kasznar, Marc Scott, Sylvia Miles, Ted Chap-
, Anna Strasberg, Norman Ornellas, Hal Robinson, Angela Wood

PRODUCTIONS

Fiddler on the Roof," "How the Other Half Loves," "Enter a Free
," "Who's Afraid of Virginia Woolf?," "Last of the Red Hot Lovers,"
rty Carats," "You Can't Take It with You," "A Streetcar Named
re," "The Prime of Miss Jean Brodie," "Gilgamesh," "Carousel,"
World Premiere of "Alfred the Great" by Israel Horovitz on March
1973.

Michael Friedlander Photos

enter: (L) Barbara Lynn Block, Kathy Rubbo, Ann
ffly, Ted Chapman in "Last of the Red Hot Lovers"

(R) Hal Robinson, Florence Lacy in "Carousel"

Anna Strasberg, Norman Ornellas in "A Streetcar
Named Desire"

217

THE PROFESSIONAL PERFORMIN
COMPANY

Chicago, Illinois
January 1,—May 6, 1973

Producer, H. Adrian Rehner; Artistic Coordinator, Haller Lau
Designer, Jack Montgomery; Coordinator, Frank Hayashida; Cost
Patricia Foerster; Sound and Lighting, Jerome Gorrell, James High
Stage Managers, Mary Cobb, Jesse Wooden, Jr.; Props, Neshan Kres
Business Manager, Thomas Dillon; Assistant to the Producer, M
Holly; Production Assistants, Carole McKay, Toimiken Threet; I
tors, Patricia Carmichael, Judy Haskell, Lenard Norris, Gennaro
tanino, Haller Laughlin

COMPANY

Tara Bidwell, Paul Butler, Thelma Carter, Patricia Cruz, Bryan H
Mary Anne McGarry, Hall Middleton, Lenard Norris, Terrence Ph
Frank Rice, Timothy Staton, Toni Trimble

Alberta Bachelor, Phill Billington, Gigi Binns, Denise Bowman
cille Brown, Rita Cristiani, Earlene Coleman, Bronnie Davidson, V
Deans, Bruce Edwards, John Gardner, Larry Holmes, Robert G
Joann Jones, Thomas Jones, Jr., Donald Lane, Carole McKay, C
Maybry, John Macon, Patricia McDowell, Alvanor Mitchell, Sl
Murff, Patrice Patton, Creed Rawls, Eleanor Schlesinger, Deborah
man, Howard Spaulding, Cheryl Stennis, Ronald Turner, Sylvia V
ington, Henry Watson, Sandrell Whitaker, Phillip Williams

PRODUCTIONS

"Allegro," "She Stoops to Conquer," "In White America," "
Back, Little Sheba," "Dracula," "Mr. Herman and the Cave Comp

Bob Zay, Bryan Harris in "Dracula"
Above: Florence Hayle, Frank Rice, Mary Ann McGarry
in "Come Back, Little Sheba"

Top: Pat Cruz in "In White America"
Right Center: Hall Middleton, Toni Trimble, Timo
Staton, Tari Bidwell in "In White America"

Don Perkins, Arthur A. Rosenberg in "Of Mice and Men" Left: Vance Sorrells, Robert Darnell, Brendan Burke, Don Perkins, Lewis Arlt, Mike Genovese in "One Flew over the Cuckoo's Nest" Top: Michele Gianinni, Kate Harper in "Twelfth Night"

THE REPERTORY THEATRE

At Loretta Hilton Center
St. Louis, Missouri
November 14, 1972—April 24, 1973

Managing Director, David Frank; Business Manager, M. Rose Jonas; Stage Directors, Davey Marlin-Jones, John Olon-Scrymgeour, Charles Werner Moore, Frederick Rolf; Sets and Costumes, Grady Larkins, Lawrence Miller; Lighting, Peter E. Sargent, Grady Larkins; Stage Manager, John E. Peters; Company Manager, Nelson D. Sheeley; Press, Susan H. Curry, Colleen Finnegan

COMPANY

Lewis Arlt, Brendan Burke, J. Robert Dietz, Mike Fenovese, Michelle Giannini, Lilene Mansell, Arthur A. Rosenberg

GUEST ARTISTS: Humbert Allen Astrada, Robert Darnell, Roni Dengel, Kate Harper, Duane L. Jones, Joneal Joplin, Myron Kozman, Jackie Parker, Don Perkins, Jan Ross, James Scott, Vance Sorrells

PRODUCTIONS

"Of Mice and Men," "Twelfth Night," "One Flew over the Cuckoo's Nest," "The Mousetrap," "A Flea in Her Ear"

Bill Patterson Photos

Lilene Mansell, J. Robert Dietz in "The Mousetrap"

SEATTLE REPERTORY THEATRE

Seattle, Washington
October 25, 1972—March 25, 1973
Tenth Season

Artistic Director, Duncan Ross; Producing Director, Peter Donn[...]
Directors, Duncan Ross, Mario Siletti, Edward Payson Call, Cla[...]
Corzatte; Scenery, Jason Phillips; Costumes, Lewis D. Rampino; S[...]
Manager, Marc Rush; Lighting, Bennet Averyt, Steven A. Maze, Ric[...]
Nelson; Press, Shirley Dennis

COMPANY

John Abajian, Gwen Arner, David Burrow, Tom Carson, Sid Con[...]
Clayton Corzatte, Ted D'Arms, Wayne Hudgins, James Jansen, Mic[...]
Keenan, Charles Lanyer, Michael Lewis, Judith Light, Robert Lo[...]
Susan Ludlow, Gun-Marie Nilsson, Eve Roberts, Lee Shallat, M[...]
Siletti, Eric Sinclair, Adrian Sparks, James Tripp, Kelly Walters, [...]
West

GUEST ARTISTS: Susan Clark, Peter Coffield, Rita Gam, Laur[...]
Hugo, Robert Moberly, June Gibbons, Donald Woods, James Ca[...]
Nina Foch, Pippa Scott, Donald Moffat, Hume Cronyn, Jessica Ta[...]
Biff McGuire, Russ Thacker

PRODUCTIONS

"Macbeth," "Camino Real," "Charley's Aunt," "Child's Play," [...]
Over," "The Tavern," "Promenade All!"

Left: James Cahill, Don West in "Child's Play"

Pippa Scott, Nina Foch in "All Over"
Above: Rita Gam in "Camino Real"

Susan Clark, Peter Coffield in "Macbeth"
Above: Ted D'Arms, Donald Moffat in "The Taver[...]

STAGE/WEST

West Springfield, Massachusetts
November 10, 1972—May 6, 1973

Managing Director, Stephen E. Hays; Artistic Director, John Ulmer; Directors, John Ulmer, William Guild; Press, Susan B. Hutton; Designer, Charles G. Stockton; Stage Managers, William Guild, Frenchy Lunning; Technical Director, Stephen Milam; Technical Assistants, Robert Sagerman, Robert Lunning, Joseph Kleban; Costumes, Susan Glenn Harvuot; Lights, Erica Lee Lewis; Props, Terry Burgler, Mark Brandon

PRODUCTIONS AND CASTS

HEDDA GABLER with Edward Holmes, Lucy Martin, Anthony McKay, Shirley Jean Measures, Virginia Payne, Margery Shaw, Curt Williams

TEN LITTLE INDIANS with Peter Blaxill, Ed Bordo, James Caporale, Harry Ellerbe, Ted Graeber, Edward Holmes, Anthony McKay, Shirley Jean Measures, Virginia Payne, Margery Shaw, Stanley Tackney

World Premiere of THE GOOD NEWS by Paul G. Enger, with James Caporale, Edward Clinton, Ted Graeber, Anthony McKay, Virginia Payne, Betty Williams

THE EFFECT OF GAMMA RAYS ON MAN-IN-THE-MOON MARIGOLDS with Olivia Clark, Rosanne Falbo, Mary Gallagher, Michaele Myers, Paula Wagner

THE IMPORTANCE OF BEING EARNEST with Peter Blaxill, Terry Burgler, James Caporale, John Colenback, Mary Gallagher, Charlotte Jones, Michaele Myers, Jeremiah Sullivan, Paula Wagner

OLD TIMES with Ed Bordo, Michaele Myers, Patricia Peardon

BUTTERFLIES ARE FREE with Terry Burgler, Edward Clinton, Joy McConnochie, Michaele Myers

Mort Handler, Willy Ralph Photos

Top Left: Virginia Payne in "The Good News"
Below: John Colenback, Mary Gallagher, Charlotte Jones, Jeremiah Sullivan, Paula Wagner, Michaele Myers, Peter Blaxill in "The Importance of Being Earnest"

Mary Gallagher, Michaele Myers, Paula Wagner in "The Effect of Gamma Rays. . . ."

Edward Holmes, Lucy Martin in "Hedda Gabler"

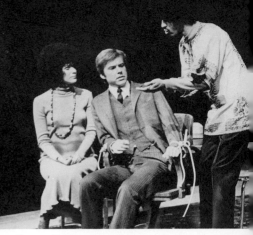

Jeanne DeBaer, Rod Browning, Milton Earl Forre
in "The Saving Grace" Left: Bonnie Franklin, Le
Roy Reams in "Roberta"

STUDIO ARENA THEATRE

Buffalo, N.Y.
October 12, 1972—May 20, 1973
Eighth Season

Executive Producer, Neal Du Brock; General Manager, Robert 7
Assistant Director, Kathryn Kingdon; Press, Blossom Cohan; Bu
Manager, William E. Lurie; Special Services, Eleanor Albertson;

ciate Director, Warren Enters; Director Emeritus, Jane Keeler;
Larry Aumen, Karl Eigsti, Kenneth Foy, David F. Segal, Dougl
brecht; Costumes, Duane Anderson, Evelyn Lea Moricle, Karen I
Rosten, Lorena McDonald, Pearl Smith, Christine Cotter; Dire
William Gile, Neal DuBrock, Leland Ball, Bick Goss, Paul Aaron, ·
beth Caldwell, Warren Enters, Richard Landon; Technical Dir
Dennis Shenk; Stage Managers, Richard Hoge, Patterson Rogers; I
David Webster

PRODUCTIONS AND CASTS

ROBERTA with Lilia Skala, Bonnie Franklin, Tricia O'Neil, M
Beirne, Lee Roy Reams, Michael Prince, Bryan Hull, Guy Spaull, ·
Daly, Carol Culver, Kristina Kelley, Elizabeth Shelle, Kenneth H
Tom Offt, Diana Broderick, Jinny Kordek, Linda Madama

SITTING with John Newton, Dorothy Chace, Winfred William
June Squibb, Ric Mancini, Samuel Barton

THE SAVING GRACE with Samuel Barton, Milton Earl Forres
Mancini, Jeanne DeBaer, Rod Browning, June Squibb

PETER PAN with Bonnie Franklin, Mary Meikleham, Marsha Kr
Todd Dorfman, Rhoda Butler, Tom Smith, Craig Bundy, Stephen ·
Jonathan Miele, Tom Offt, Jane Robertson, John Scherer, Frank N
nez III, Albert B. Simmons, Ted Bouton, Mary Jane Houdina,
Mardirosian, James Kirsch, Sefan Mark Weyte, Tom Patrick Da
Peter Wandel, Linda Andrews, Kevin Daly

World Premiere of RING-A-LEVIO by Donald Ross, Jason Darrov
Lance Mulcahy, with Harvey Evans, Susan Campbell, Camila Ash
Bernard Erhard, Alan Brasington, Paul Farin, Merry Flershem,
Jane Houdina, Erik Robinson, Renee Semes, Mychelle Smiley, Bob
cer

BUTTERFLIES ARE FREE with Celeste Holm, Kipp Osborne,
Connor, Raymond Cole

THE TAMING OF THE SHREW with Richard Greene, Linda Ca
Phillip Clark, Gordon Connell, Kathleen Doyle, Paul Milikin, Alan
ington, Yusef Bulos, Lee Goodman, John Towey, K. C. Wilson,
Adrian, Walter D. Berny, Paul Femia, George Seper, Kevin Ke
Patterson Rogers, Peter Wandel, Bryna Weiss

CHILD'S PLAY with Donald Moffat, Ronald Bishop, Robert Ant
Robert G. Denison, Dale Helward, Richard Kline, Jamie Alexande
Barrett, Steve Bonino, Mike Sisti, Doug Crane, Michael La Rocca,
Osborne, Scott Sherris, Charles Wisnet

BERLIN TO BROADWAY WITH KURT WEILL with Stephen ·
Susan Campbell, Margery Cohen, Dale Helward, Hal Watters

Greenberg-May Photos

Left Center: Richard Kline, Scott Sherris,
Ronald Bishop, Donald Moffat in "Child's Play"

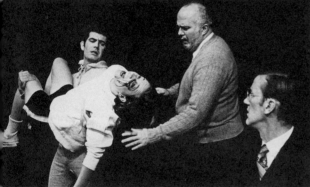

Kipp Osborne, Celeste Holm, Raymond Cole, Erin
Connor in "Butterflies Are Free"

SYRACUSE REPERTORY THEATRE

Syracuse, N.Y.
October 20, 1972—May 12, 1973

Managing Director, Max Henriot; Press, Kittie B. Sine; Sets, Leonard
ansky, Robert Lewis Smith, James Singelis; Costumes, Marilyn Skow,
McGillivray, Jean Levine; Lighting, Robert Lewis Smith, James
etti, James Singelis, Walter Uhrman; Stage Managers, Jane E. Neu-
John Blakemore; Guest Directors, David Gold, Gerard E. Moses;
reographer, Mallory Graham

COMPANY

ephen Keep, Patrick Desmond, Gerald Richards, Jay Lanin, Jack
ard, William Newman, John Thomas Waite, Walter Wood, Gary
, Susan Hunter Harney, Rex Henriot, Anna Kathleen White, Denise
n, Ruth Fenster, Joyce Krempel, Barbara McMahon, Joan Manis-
, Ivan Smith, Richard Blair, Mitchell Edmonds, Betty Lynd, Daniel
ff, Charles Crutchfield, Chuck Nixon, Channing Chase, Edward
n, Marilyn Wassell, Michael Coerver, Gretchen Giel, James Car-
rs, Gerard E. Moses, Kathryn Loder, Adale O'Brien, Rod Loomis,
Heffernan

ST ARTISTS: Carolyn Kirsch, Howard Da Silva

PRODUCTIONS

Child's Play," "Miss Lonelyhearts," "Bye Bye Birdie," "Galileo,"
Secret Life of Walter Mitty," "The Ginderbread Lady," "Dear

J. Greenberger, Butler Photos

Rex Henriot, Barbara McMahon, Stephen Keep
in "Miss Lonelyhearts"

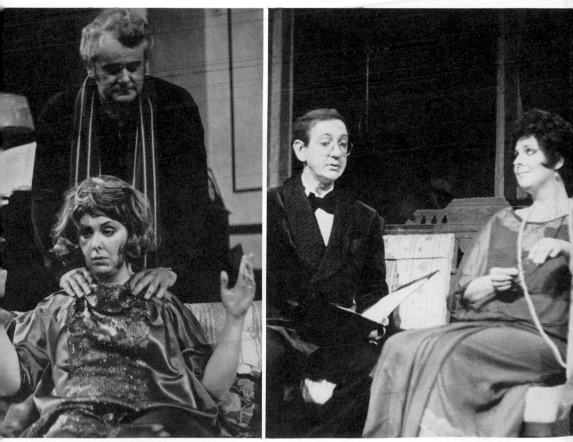

Adale O'Brien, James Carruthers
in "The Gingerbread Lady"

John Heffernan, Adale O'Brien in "Dear Liar"

THEATRE COMPANY OF BOSTON

Boston, Massachusetts
December 5, 1972—April 1, 1973

Producing Director, David Wheeler; Managing Director, Peggy Forbes; Director of School Tour, Andrea Womack; Assistant to Managing Director, Margaret Genovese; Stage Managers, Simon Siegl, Mary Ryan; Directors, David Wheeler, James Kirkup, William Young; Sets and Costumes, Franco Colavecchia, Michael Anania, Betsy Leichliter, Marsha MacDonald, Lance J. Henriksen, Jan Egleson; Lighting, Norton Associates

COMPANY

Penelope Allen, Paul Benedict, DeVeren Bookwalter, Larry Bryggman, Stockard Channing, Roberta Collinge, Jan Egleson, Cathi Frasier, Marcia Haufrecht, Lance J. Henriksen, Ronald Hunter, Gustave Johnson, Josephine Lane, Frank McCarthy, Norman Ornellas, Carolyn Pickman, Harriet Rogers, Linda Selman, James Spruill, William Young

John Barrett, Robin Bartlett, Michael Bofshever, Robert Burke, Dan Carter, Stephen Case, Marc Frasier, Demetri Hadjis, William Hart, John Jellison, Bob McCarthy, David Neill, Andrea Petersen, Claire Rosenberg, Timothy Sawyer, Donald Silva

GUEST ARTIST: Al Pacino

PRODUCTIONS

"Play Strindberg," "Richard II," "Old Times"

Mary Crowe, Cameron Forbes Photos

Top: Larry Bryggman, Stockard Channing, Paul Benedict in "Play Strindberg"

Paul Benedict, Al Pacino in "Richard III"

THIRD EYE THEATRE

Denver, Colorado
November 1, 1972—August 11, 1973

Producer-Director, Jean Favre; Production Coordinator-Director, Ed Baierlein; Associate Directors, David Ode, Robert Breuler; Lighting, David Lewis, Tom Bleecker; Sound, Bob Burnham, Alan Burnham; Visuals, Duffie White, Susan Rember, Jim Valone; Special Effects, Doug Hubbard; Technical Directors, Sean Woodburn, Steve Merle; Musical Direction, Beverly Mango, Nancy Adams, Halka Morrill, Virginia Baldwin; Costumes, Judy Graese, Nancy Yeager, Mary Heller, Elizabeth Pelegrin, Marcia Bishop, Sheila Johnson; Hairstylist, Jim Huffman; Production Manager, Jean Smith; Stage Managers, Connie Hilb, Donna Porter, Nancy Yeager, Ginger Valone, Cathie Robinson; Press, Robert Breuler, Sallie Diamond, June Favre

COMPANY

Jean Favre, Ed Baierlein, David Ode, June Favre, Robert Breuler, Sallie Diamond, Jeannie Marlin, Danny Woods, Lee Gallup, Cathie Robinson, Steve Merle, Jack McKnight, Bob Hayes, John Callas, Dan Phillips, Kenneth Washington, Ginger Valone, Tom Bleecker, Donna Porter, George Dolmas, Lori Ann Toombs, Dino Figueroa, Nancy Satter, Dimitri Cocovinis, Louis de Paemelere, Albert Turner, Joe Switz, Timothy Willson, Ara Marx

PRODUCTIONS

"The School for Wives," "Uncle Vanya," "Where Has Tommy Flowers Gone?," "The Birthday Party," "Orphee," "Tom Paine," "The Thieves' Carnival," "A Touch of the Poet," "Jacques Brel Is Alive and Well and Living in Paris," "The Fantasticks," and World Premiere of "Ferril, Etc."

Tom Bleecker, George Salem Photos

Left: Sallie Diamond, David Ode, Thomas Hornsby Ferril, Robert Breuler, June Favre, Jean Favre in "Ferril, Etc." Top: Ginger Valone, Dan Phillips, David Ode, Sallie Diamond, Jack McKnight, June Favre in "Tom Paine"

Ed Baierlein, Sallie Diamond in "Where Has Tommy Flowers Gone?"

Ed Baierlein, June Favre in "School for Wives"

TRINITY SQUARE REPERTORY COMPANY

Providence, Rhode Island
October 19, 1972—May 19, 1973

Director, Adrian Hall; General Manager, Daniel B. Miller; Ass
to Director, Marion Simon; Press, David Wynne; Musical Director,
ard Cumming; Sets, Eugene Lee, Robert D. Soule; Lighting, Roger
gan, Shirley Prendergast; Costumes, Sunny B. Warner, A. Cha
Giannini, Betsey Potter; Props, Sandra Nathanson; Stage Manage
liam Radka; Directors, Adrian Hall, Word Baker, Jacques Cartie

COMPANY

Robert Black, Robert J. Colonna, Timothy Crowe, William Da
ehler, James Eichelberger, Barbara Jean, Richard Jenkins, Dav
Jones, Richard Kavanaugh, David Kennett, Richard Kneeland,
Mack, Mina Manente, George Martin, T. Richard Mason, Cy
McKay, Barbara Orson, Ben Powers, Margo Skinner, Donald Sc
Daniel Von Bargen, Jobeth Williams
GUEST ARTISTS: Leta Anderson, Gerardine Arthur, Paul Ben
Richard Loder, Georgia Neu, Ann Sachs, Angela Thornton, Kate Y

PRODUCTIONS

"Endgame," "Old Times," "Lady Audley's Secret," "The Royal
of the Sun," "School for Wives," and World Premiere of "Feasting
Panthers" by Adrian Hall and Richard Cumming

William L. Smith Photos

Left: Leta Anderson, Richard Jenkins, David C. Jo
Barbara Orson in "Lady Audley's Secret" Below: A
Thornton, Paul Benedict, Gerardine Arthur in "O
Times" (R) Richard Kneeland, William Damkoehle
"Feasting with Panthers"

Richard Kneeland, Richard Loder, James Eichelberger
in "Royal Hunt of the Sun"

Richard Kavanaugh, George Martin in "School for
Wives"

VIRGINIA MUSEUM THEATRE

Richmond, Virginia
November 10, 1972—April 22, 1973

Producing Director, Keith Fowler; Associate Director, Ken Letner; Stage Directors, Alfred Drake, William Prosser; Costumes, Andre Bruce Ward; Scenery, Robert Franklin, De Teel Patterson Tiller; Lighting, Michael Watson; Stage Manager, Rachael Lindhart; Business Manager, Loraine Slade; Press, Fred Haseltine, Michael P. Hickey

COMPANY

Norman Barrs, Janet Bell, Leta Bonynge, James Buss, Mel Cobb, Keith Fowler, Russell Gold, Colin Hamilton, Marie Goodman Hunter, James Kirkland, Mary Layne, Ken Letner, Jamie MacFarlane, E. G. Marshall, Sam Maupin, Michael Miller, Dick Newdick, Don Pasco, William Prosser, Gene Snow, Sally Sommer, Roxana Stuart, John Wardwell, David Williams

PRODUCTIONS

"Cyrano de Bergerac," "A Christmas Carol," "Loot," "The Night Thoreau Spent in Jail," "Macbeth," "Jacques Brel Is Alive and Well and Living in Paris," and American Premiere of "The Royal Rape of Ruari Macasmunde" by Richard Stockton, based on a story by Richard T. Herd, and directed by Alfred Drake

Ronald Jennings Photos

Left: Ken Letner, E. G. Marshall in "Macbeth"

Below: Jamie Macfarlane (R) in "The Night Thoreau Spent in Jail" (R) Mary Layne, Mel Cobb, Jamie Macfarlane, Marie Goodman Hunter in "Jacques Brel Is Alive. . . ."

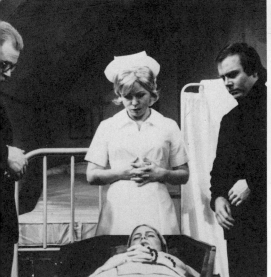

Gene Snow, Janet Bell, James R. Kirkland in "Loot"

Russell Gold as
Cyrano de Bergerac

227

WASHINGTON THEATER CLUB

Washington, D.C.
May 25, 1972—May 27, 1973
Twelfth Season

Executive Director, Hazel H. Wentworth; Producer-Artistic Director, Stephen Aaron; General Manager, Debrah Denemark; Production Manager, E. O. Larson; Communications, Ann Swanson; Press, Charles W. Stevens; Community Relations, Sara B. Kurtz; Designers, John H. Paull, Michael Stauffer; Technical Director, Keith Arnett; Stage Managers, E. O. Larson, Bruce Macdonald; Costumes, Danica Eskind

PRODUCTIONS AND CASTS

LADY AUDLEY'S SECRET directed by Douglas Seale, with Donna Curtis, Russell Nype, Ann Ault, James Carrington, Richard Curnock, Mickey Hartnett, David Long, Lu Ann Post, Ronn Robinson, Douglas Seale, Jack Sevier, Danny Sewell, June Gable

SPREAD EAGLE PAPERS directed by Sue Lawless, with Ann Clements, Lynn Grossman, Mickey Hartnett, William McClary, Ken Olfson, Ronn Robinson, Renny Temple

World Premiere of THE RAPISTS directed by Stephen Book, with Edward Clinton, Robert Dannenberg, Louis Edmonds, Bruce Hall, Robert LaTourneaux, Dempster Leech, William McClary, Lenka Peterson, Mark Robinson, Ronn Robinson, Henry Carter Shaffer

THE BOYS FROM SYRACUSE directed by Pirie MacDonald, with Paul Campbell, Jackie Cronin, Angelina Dahmer, Gary Dontzig, Bruce A. Goldstein, Franz Jones, Tina Kay, Dave Landsberg, Susan Long, Greg Macosko, Cathy Miller, Mary Ellen Nester, Sylvia Nolan, Joe Ostopak, Art Ostrin, Ronn Robinson, Deborah St. Darr, Karen Shallo, Kelly Walters, Michael Zaslow

CEREMONIES IN DARK OLD MEN directed by Bette Howard, with Frank Adu, Jerry Bell, Ensley-Everett, Jimmy Hayeson, Bette Howard, Sheila Johnson, William Newman

World Premiere of THE ENCLAVE directed by Arthur Laurents, with Jack Betts, Don Gantry, Tom Happer, Lawrence Hugo, Hal Linden, Peg Murray, Rochelle Oliver, Ann Sweeny, Charles Turner

SCENES FROM AMERICAN LIFE directed by Stephen Aaron, With Laurinda Barrett, Mickey Hartnett, Oliver Malcolmson, Ronn Robinson, Mimi Norton Salamanca, Karen Shallo, Justin Taylor, Art Vasil

American Premiere of THE ECSTASY OF RITA JOE directed by Harold Stone, with Frances Hyland, Chief Dan George, Henry Bal, Laurinda Barrett, Pat Corley, Richard DeAngelis, Roger DeKoven, Kathy Gittel, Philip Baker Hall, Mike Halsey, John Jackson, Billie Lyon, Bruce Macdonald, Ronn Robinson, Giulia Pagano, John Tiger

Arvil A. Daniels Photos

**Top Right: Peg Murray, Hal Linden
in "The Enclave"**

**June Gable, Russell Nype, Donna Curtis
in "Lady Audley's Secret"**

**Frances Hyland, Chief Dan George
in "The Ecstacy of Rita Joe"**

YALE REPERTORY THEATRE

New Haven, Connecticut
October 4, 1972—May 19, 1973

...stic Director, Alvin Epstein; Managing Director, Sheldon Klein-
...Resident Designer, Steven Rubin; Lighting Director, William War-
...ess, Anne Goodrich; Artistic Administrator, Robert J. Orchard;
...istrative Assistant, Kathryn Stiles; Assistants to Managing Direc-
...arbara Hauptman, William Baker; Artistic Advisers, Allan Miller,
...rie Phillips, Carmen de Lavallade; Stage Managers, Frank Torok,
...M. Waaser, Judith Gorman; Production Supervisor, John Robert
...Technical Director, George Moredock; Props, Hunter Nesbitt
...; Costumer, Gerda Proctor; Directors, Arthur Sherman, Michael
...k, David Giles, Tom Haas, John McAndrew, William Peters, Alvin
...n; Designers, Ming Cho Lee, Jeanne Button, Ian Rodney Calderon,
...Poersch, Nathan L. Drucker, John Beatty, Maura B. Smolover, D.
...nd Thomas, Barbara A. Harris, William Warfel, Steven Rubin,
...el Yeargan

COMPANY

...Balaban, Miles Chapin, Donald Davis, Herb Davis, Carmen de
...ade, Alvin Epstein, Al Freeman, Jr., Leonard Frey, Linda Gates,
...y Geidt, Tom Haas, Stephen Joyce, Marcia Jean Kurtz, John
...drew, Allan Miller, Elizabeth Parrish, Hannibal Penney, Jr., Wil-
...eters, Eugene Troobnick, Richard Venture, Janet Ward

PRODUCTIONS

...e Bourgeois Gentleman," "Baal," AMERICAN PREMIERES of
...ett" by Ionesco, "Lear" by Edward Bond, WORLD PREMIERES
...Break in the Skin" by Ronald Ribman, "Are You Now or Have
...ver Been" by Eric Bentley, "In the Clap Shack" by William Styron,
...The Mirror" by Isaac Bashevis Singer

William Baker Photos

**Right: Carmen de Lavallade, Leonard Frey and
entire company in "The Bourgeois Gentleman"**

Alan Miller in "Are You Now or
Have You Ever Been"

Alvin Epstein in "Macbeth"

229

PULITZER PRIZE PLAYS

1918-Why Marry?, 1919-No award, 1920-Beyond the Horizon, 1921-Miss Lulu Bett, 1922-Anna Christie, 1923-Icebound, 1924-Hell-Bent Fer Heaven, 1925-They Knew What They Wanted, 1926-Craig's Wife, 1927-In Abraham's Bosom, 1928-Strange Interlude, 1929-Street Scene, 1930-The Green Pastures, 1931-Alison's House, 1932-Of Thee I Sing, 1933-Both Your Houses, 1934-Men in White, 1935-The Old Maid, 1936-Idiot's Delight, 1937-You Can't Take It With You, 1938-Our Town, 1939-Abe Lincoln in Illinois, 1940-The Time of Your Life, 1941-There Shall Be No Night, 1942-No award, 1943-The Skin of Our Teeth, 1944-No award, 1945-Harvey, 1946-State of the Union, 1947-No award, 1948-A Streetcar Named Desire, 1949-Death of a Salesman, 1950-South Pacific, 1951-No award, 1952-The Shrike, 1953-Picnic, 1954-The Teahouse of the August Moon, 1955-Cat on a Hot Tin Roof, 1956-The Diary of Anne Frank, 1957-Long Day's Journey into Night, 1958-Look Homeward, Angel, 1959-J. B., 1960-Fiorello!, 1961-All the Way Home, 1962-How to Succeed in Business without Really Trying, 1963-No award, 1964-No award, 1965-The Subject Was Roses, 1966-No award, 1967-A Delicate Balance, 1968-No award, 1969-The Great White Hope, 1970-No Place to Be Somebody, 1971-The Effect of Gamma Rays on Man-in-the-Moon Marigolds, 1972-No award, 1973-That Championship Season

NEW YORK DRAMA CRITICS CIRCLE AWARD PRODUCTIONS

1936-Winterset, 1937-High Tor, 1938-Of Mice and Men, Shadow and Substance, 1939-The White Steed, 1940-The Time of Your Life, 1941-Watch on the Rhine, The Corn is Green, 1942-Blithe Spirit, 1943-The Patriots, 1944-Jacobowsky and the Colonel, 1945-The Glass Menagerie, 1946-Carousel, 1947-All My Sons, No Exit, Brigadoon, 1948-A Streetcar Named Desire, The Winslow Boy, 1949-Death of a Salesman, The Madwoman of Chaillot, South Pacific, 1950-The Member of the Wedding, The Cocktail Party, The Consul, 1951-Darkness at Noon, The Lady's Not for Burning, Guys and Dolls, 1952-I Am a Camera, Venus Observed, Pal Joey, 1953-Picnic, The Love of Four Colonels, Wonderful Town, 1954-Teahouse of the August Moon, Ondine, The Golden Apple, 1955-Cat on a Hot Tin Roof, Witness for the Prosecution, The Saint of Bleecker Street, 1956-The Diary of Anne Frank, Tiger at the Gates, My Fair Lady, 1957-Long Day's Journey into Night, The Waltz of the Toreadors, The Most Happy Fella, 1958-Look Homeward Angel, Look Back in Anger, The Music Man, 1959-A Raisin in the Sun, The Visit, La Plume de Ma Tante, 1960-Toys in the Attic, Five Finger Exercise, Fiorello!, 1961-All the Way Home, A Taste of Honey, Carnival, 1962-Night of the Iguana, A Man for All Seasons, How to Succeed in Business without Really Trying, 1963-Who's Afraid of Virginia Woolf?, 1964-Luther, Hello, Dolly!, 1965-The Subject was Roses, Fiddler on the Roof, 1966-The Persecution and Assassination of Marat as Performed by the Inmates of the Asylum of Charenton under the Direction of the Marquis de Sade, Man of La Mancha, 1967-The Homecoming, Cabaret, 1968-Rosencrantz and Guildenstern Are Dead, Your Own Thing, 1969-The Great White Hope, 1776, 1970-The Effect of Gamma Rays on Man-in-the-Moon Marigolds, Borstal Boy, Company, 1971-Home, Follies, The House of Blue Leaves, 1972-That Championship Season, Two Gentlemen of Verona, 1973-The Hot L Baltimore, The Changing Room, A Little Night Music

AMERICAN THEATRE WING ANTOINETTE PERRY (TONY) AWARD PRODUCTIONS

1948-Mister Roberts, 1949-Death of a Salesman, Kiss Me, Kate, 1950-The Cocktail Party, South Pacific, 1951-The Rose Tattoo, Guys and Dolls, 1952-The Fourposter, The King and I, 1953-The Crucible, Wonderful Town, 1954-The Teahouse of the August Moon, Kismet, 1955-The Desperate Hours, The Pajama Game, 1956-The Diary of Anne Frank, Damn Yankees, 1957-Long Day's Journey into Night, My Fair Lady, 1958-Sunrise at Campobello, The Music Man, 1959-J. B., Redhead, 1960-The Miracle Worker, Fiorello! tied with Sound of Music, 1961-Becket, Bye Bye Birdie, 1962-A Man for All Seasons, How to Succeed in Business without Really Trying, 1963-Who's Afraid of Virginia Woolf?, A Funny Thing Happened on the Way to the Forum, 1964-Luther, Hello, Dolly!, 1965-The Subject Was Roses, Fiddler on the Roof, 1966-The Persecution and Assassination of Marat as Performed by the Inmates of the Asylum of Charenton under the Direction of the Marquis de Sade, Man of La Mancha, 1967-The Homecoming, Cabaret, 1968-Rosencrantz and Guildenstern Are Dead, Hallelujah, Baby!, 1969-The Great White Hope, 1776, 1970-Borstal Boy, Applause, 1971-Sleuth, Company, 1972-Sticks and Bones, Two Gentlemen of Verona, 1973-That Championship Season, A Little Night Music

JASON MILLER
Prize-winning playwright for "That Championship Season"

Harry Belafonte

Carol Burnett

David Carradine

Cloris Leachman

George Mah

PREVIOUS THEATRE WORLD AWARD WINNERS

1944–45: Betty Comden, Richard Davis, Richard Hart, Judy Holliday, Charles Lang, Bambi Linn, John Lund, Donald Murphy, Nancy Noland, Margaret Phillips, John Raitt
1945–46: Barbara Bel Geddes, Marlon Brando, Bill Callahan, Wendell Corey, Paul Douglas, Mary James, Burt Lancaster, Patricia Marshall, Beatrice Pearson
1946–47: Keith Andes, Marion Bell, Peter Cookson, Ann Crowley, Ellen Hanley, John Jordan, George Keane, Dorothea MacFarland, James Mitchell, Patricia Neal, David Wayne
1947–48: Valerie Bettis, Edward Bryce, Whitfield Connor, Mark Dawson, June Lockhart, Estelle Loring, Peggy Maley, Ralph Meeker, Meg Mundy, Douglass Watson, James Whitmore, Patrice Wymore
1948–49: Tod Andrews, Doe Avedon, Jean Carson, Carol Channing, Richard Derr, Julie Harris, Mary McCarty, Allyn Ann McLerie, Cameron Mitchell, Gene Nelson, Byron Palmer, Bob Scheerer
1949–50: Nancy Andrews, Phil Arthur, Barbara Brady, Lydia Clarke, Priscilla Gillette, Don Hanmer, Marcia Henderson, Charlton Heston, Rick Jason, Grace Kelly, Charles Nolte, Roger Price
1950–51: Barbara Ashley, Isabel Bigley, Martin Brooks, Richard Burton, James Daly, Cloris Leachman, Russell Nype, Jack Palance, William Smithers, Maureen Stapleton, Marcia Van Dyke, Eli Wallach
1951–52: Tony Bavaar, Patricia Benoit, Peter Conlow, Virginia de Luce, Ronny Graham, Audrey Hepburn, Diana Herbert, Conrad Janis, Dick Kallman, Charles Proctor, Eric Sinclair, Kim Stanley, Marian Winters, Helen Wood
1952–53: Edie Adams, Rosemary Harris, Eileen Heckart, Peter Kelley, John Kerr, Richard Kiley, Gloria Marlowe, Penelope Munday, Paul Newman, Sheree North, Geraldine Page, John Stewart, Ray Stricklyn, Gwen Verdon
1953–54: Orson Bean, Harry Belafonte, James Dean, Joan Diener, Ben Gazzara, Carol Haney, Jonathan Lucas, Kay Medford, Scott Merrill, Elizabeth Montgomery, Leo Penn, Eva Marie Saint
1954–55: Julie Andrews, Jacqueline Brookes, Shirl Conway, Barbara Cook, David Daniels, Mary Fickett, Page Johnson, Loretta Leversee, Jack Lord, Dennis Patrick, Anthony Perkins, Christopher Plummer
1955–56: Diane Cilento, Dick Davalos, Anthony Franciosa, Andy Griffith, Laurence Harvey, David Hedison, Earle Hyman, Susan Johnson, John Michael King, Jayne Mansfield, Sarah Marshall, Gaby Rodgers, Susan Strasberg, Fritz Weaver
1956–57: Peggy Cass, Sydney Chaplin, Sylvia Daneel, Bradford Dillman, Peter Donat, George Grizzard, Carol Lynley, Peter Palmer, Jason Robards, Cliff Robertson, Pippa Scott, Inga Swenson
1957–58: Anne Bancroft, Warren Berlinger, Colleen Dewhurst, Richard Easton, Tim Everett, Eddie Hodges, Joan Hovis, Carol Lawrence, Jacqueline McKeever, Wynne Miller, Robert Morse, George C. Scott

1958–59: Lou Antonio, Ina Balin, Richard Cross, Tammy Grim Larry Hagman, Dolores Hart, Roger Mollien, France Nuyen, Su Oliver, Ben Piazza, Paul Roebling, William Shatner, Pat Suzuki, Torn
1959–60: Warren Beatty, Eileen Brennan, Carol Burnett, Pa Duke, Jane Fonda, Anita Gillette, Elisa Loti, Donald Madd George Maharis, John McMartin, Lauri Peters, Dick Van Dyk
1960–61: Joyce Bulifant, Dennis Cooney, Nancy Dussault, Rob Goulet, Joan Hackett, June Harding, Ron Husmann, James MacA thur, Bruce Yarnell
1961–62: Elizabeth Ashley, Keith Baxter, Peter Fonda, Don Gal way, Sean Garrison, Barbara Harris, James Earl Jones, Janet Mar lin, Karen Morrow, Robert Redford, John Stride, Brenda Vacca
1962–63: Alan Arkin, Stuart Damon, Melinda Dillon, Rob Drivas, Bob Gentry, Dorothy Loudon, Brandon Maggart, Julier Marie, Liza Minnelli, Estelle Parsons, Diana Sands, Swen Swens
1963–64: Alan Alda, Gloria Bleezarde, Imelda De Martin, Clau Giraud, Ketty Lester, Barbara Loden, Lawrence Pressman, Gilb Price, Philip Proctor, John Tracy, Jennifer West
1964–65: Carolyn Coates, Joyce Jillson, Linda Lavin, Luba Li Michael O'Sullivan, Joanna Pettet, Beah Richards, Jaime Sanch Victor Spinetti, Nicholas Surovy, Robert Walker, Clarence Willia III
1965–66: Zoe Caldwell, David Carradine, John Cullum, John D vidson, Faye Dunaway, Gloria Foster, Robert Hooks, Jerry La ning, Richard Mulligan, April Shawhan, Sandra Smith, Lesley A Warren
1966–67: Bonnie Bedelia, Richard Benjamin, Dustin Hoffma Terry Kiser, Reva Rose, Robert Salvio, Sheila Smith, Connie S vens, Pamela Tiffin, Leslie Uggams, Jon Voight, Christopher Walk
1967–68: Pamela Burrell, Sandy Duncan, Julie Gregg, Bernade Peters, Alice Playten, Brenda Smiley, David Birney, Jordan Chris pher, Jack Crowder, Stephen Joyce, Mike Rupert, Russ Thacke
1968–69: Jane Alexander, David Cryer, Ed Evanko, Blythe Dann Ken Howard, Lauren Jones, Ron Leibman, Marian Mercer, J O'Hara, Ron O'Neal, Al Pacino, Marlene Warfield
1969–70: Susan Browning, Donny Burks, Catherine Burns, L Cariou, Bonnie Franklin, David Holliday, Katharine Houghto Melba Moore, David Rounds, Lewis J. Stadlen, Kristoffer Tabo Fredricka Weber
1970–71: Clifton Davis, Michael Douglas, Julie Garfield, Mart Henry, James Naughton, Tricia O'Neil, Kipp Osborne, Roger Rat burn, Ayn Ruymen, Jennifer Salt, Joan Van Ark, Walter Willis
1971–72: Jonelle Allen, Maureen Anderman, William Atherto Richard Backus, Adrienne Barbeau, Cara Duff-MacCormick, Ro ert Foxworth, Elaine Joyce, Jess Richards, Ben Vereen, Beatri Winde, James Woods

Patricia Neal

Ron O'Neal

Kim Stanley

Robert Redford

Brenda Vacca

1973 THEATRE WORLD AWARD WINNERS

PATRICIA ELLIOTT
of "A Little Night Music"

JAMES FARENTINO
of "A Streetcar Named Desire"

BRIAN FARRELL
of "The Last of Mrs. Lincoln"

KELLY GARRETT
of "Mother Earth"

VICTOR GARBER
of "Ghosts"

MARI GORMAN
of "The Hot 1 Baltimore"

TRISH HAWKINS
of "The Hot 1 Baltimore"

LAURENCE GUITTARD
of "A Little Night Music"

MONTE MARKHAM
of "Irene"

D. JAMIN-BARTLETT
of "A Little Night Music"

JENNIFER WARREN
of "6 Rms Riv Vu"

JOHN RUBINSTEIN
of "Pippin"

1973 THEATRE WORLD AWARD PARTY

(Van Williams Photos)

John Rubinstein, Rosemary Harris

Below: Trish Hawkins, Ken Howard

Brian Farrell, Rosemary Harris

Below: Alexander H. Cohen, John Willis

Patricia Elliott, Laurence Guittard, D. Jamin-Bartlett

James Farrentino, Rosemary Harris

Victor Garber, Rosemary Harris

Monte Markham, Rosemary Harris

Below: Mr. and Mrs. John Ehle and daughter Jennifer

Below: Maureen Stapleton, Victor Garber

Walter Willison, Patricia Elliott,
Keene Curtis, Jacqueline Brookes

Nancy Dussault, Charles White

Herman O. Arbeit	Rae Allen	William Atherton	Patricia Arnell	Richard Backu

BIOGRAPHIES OF THIS SEASON'S CAST

AARON, DAVID. Born Sept. 19, 1947 in Denver, Colo. Attended UDenver. Made NY debut 1969 OB in "You're a Good Man, Charlie Brown," followed by NYSF's "Wars of Roses," "Richard III," and "Macbeth," "Accounting for Murder," "Bubbles."

AARON, JACK. Born May 1, 1933 in NYC. Attended Hunter Col., Actors Workshop. OB in "Swim Low Little Goldfish," "Journey of the Fifth Horse," "The Nest," "One Flew Over the Cuckoo's Nest," "The Birds."

ABRAHAM, F. MURRAY. Born Oct. 24, 1939 in Pittsburgh, Pa. Attended UTex. OB bow 1967 in "The Fantasticks," followed by "An Opening in the Trees," "Fourteenth Dictator," "Young Abe Lincoln," "Tonight in Living Color," "Adaptation," "Survival of St. Joan," "The Dog Ran Away," "Fables," "Richard III," "Little Murders," "Scuba Duba," "Where Has Tommy Flowers Gone?," Bdwy debut "The Man In The Glass Booth" (1968), followed by "6 Rms Riv Vu."

ACKERMAN, LONI ZOE. Born Apr. 10, 1949 in NYC. Attended New School. Bdwy debut 1968 in "George M!," followed by "Dames at Sea" (OB), "No, No, Nannette."

ADDY, WESLEY. Born Aug. 4, 1913 in Omaha, Neb. Attended UCLA. Bdwy debut 1935 in "Panic," followed by "How Beautiful with Shoes," "Hamlet," "Richard II," "Henry IV," "Summer Night," "Romeo and Juliet," "Twelfth Night," "Antigone," "Candida," "Another Part of the Forest," "Galileo," "Leading Lady," "The Traitor," "The Enchanted," "King Lear," "The Strong Are Lonely," "First Gentleman," "South Pacific," OB in "A Month in the Country," "Candida," "Ghosts."

AIMEE, KIRSTEN. Born Feb. 28, 1969 in Plainfield, NJ. Made NY debut 1973 OB in "Medea."

AINSLEY, PAUL. Born Apr. 11, 1945 in Boston. Graduate San Fernando State Col. Bdwy bow 1971 in "Jesus Christ Superstar."

ALBERT, EDDIE. Born Apr. 22, 1908 in Rock Island, Ill. Attended UMinn. Bdwy debut 1936 in "Brother Rat," followed by "Room Service," "Boys from Syracuse," "Miss Liberty," "Say, Darling," "Music Man," "No Hard Feelings."

ALBERTSON, JACK. Born in Revere, Mass. Appeared in vaudeville before Bdwy bow 1941 in "Meet the People," followed by "Strip for Action," "The Lady Says Yes," "Allah Be Praised," "The Red Mill," "The Cradle Will Rock," "Make Mine Manhattan," "High Button Shoes," "Tickets, Please," "Top Banana," "The Subject Was Roses," "Sunshine Boys."

ALDREDGE, TOM. Born Feb. 28, 1928 in Dayton, O. Attended Dayton U., Goodman Theatre. Bdwy bow 1959 in "The Nervous Set," followed by "UTBU," "Slapstick Tragedy," "Everything in the Garden," "Indians," "Engagement Baby," "How the Other Half Loves," "Sticks and Bones." OB in "The Tempest," "Between Two Thieves," "Henry V," "The Premise," "Love's Labour's Lost," "Troilus and Cressida," "Butter and Egg Man," "Ergo," "Boys In The Band," "Twelfth Night," "Colette," "Hamlet" (NYSF), "The Orphan."

ALEXANDER, JANE. Born Oct. 28, 1939 in Boston. Attended Sarah Lawrence, UEdinburgh. Bdwy debut 1968 in "The Great White Hope" for which she received a Theatre World Award, followed by "6 Rms Riv Vu."

ALICE, MARY. Born Dec. 3, 1941 in Indianola, Miss. Studied with NEC, and appeared in its "Trials of Brother Jero" and "The Strong Breed" (1967); Bdwy debut 1971 in "No Place to Be Somebody," followed by "Duplex" (LC), "Thoughts" (OB).

ALLEN, JONELLE. Born July 18, 1944 in NYC. Attended Professional Children's School. Bdwy debut 1949 in "The Wisteria Trees," followed by "Hair," "George M!," "Two Gentlemen of Verona" for which she received a Theatre World Award, OB in "Someone's Coming Hungry," "5 on the Blackhand Side," "Bury the Dead," "Moon on a Rainbow Shawl."

ALLEN, NORMAN. Born Dec. 24, 1939 in London. Bdwy bow 1963 in "Chips with Everything," followed by "Half a Sixpence," "Rockefeller and the Red Indians," "Get Thee to Canterbury" (OB), "Borstal Boy," "Vivat! Vivat Regina!," "Jockey Club Stakes."

ALLEN, RAE. Born July 3, 1926 in Bklyn. Attended Hunter Col., AADA. Bdwy debut 1948 in "Where's Charley?," followed by "Alive and Kicking," "Call Me Madam," "Pajama Game," "Damn Yankees," "I Knock at the Door," "Traveller without Luggage," "On a Clear Day You Can See Forever," "Fiddler on the Roof," "And Miss Reardon Drinks a Little," "Dude," OB in "Pictures in the Hallway," "Cock-a-Doodle Dandy," "U.S.A.," "Drums under the Window," "Death of Bessie Smith," "Ginger Man," "Love's Labour's Lost," APA's "You Can't Take It with You," "School for Scandal," and "Right You Are," "Henry IV," "The Orphan."

ALLEN, SETH. Born July 13, 1941 in Bklyn. Attended Musical Theatre Acad. OB in "Viet Rock," "Futz," "Hair," "Candaules Commissioner," LC in "Mar Stuart" and "Narrow Road to the Deep North," Bdwy debut 1972 in "Jesu Christ Superstar."

ALVAREZ, CARMEN. Born July 2 in Los Angeles. Bdwy debut 1954 i "Pajama Game," followed by "Li'l Abner," "West Side Story," "Bye B Birdie," "Zorba," "Look to the Lilies," "Irene," OB in "That Hat," "Co Porter Revisited."

ANDERMAN, MAUREEN. Born Oct. 26, 1946 in Detroit. Graduate UMich Bdwy debut 1970 in ASF's "Othello," followed by "Moonchildren" for whic she received a Theatre World Award, "An Evening with Richard Nixon an . . . ," "The Last of Mrs. Lincoln."

ANDERSON, THOMAS. Born Nov. 28, 1906 in Pasadena, Cal. Attende Pasadena Jr. Col., Am. Theatre Wing. Bdwy debut 1934 in "4 Saints in 3 Acts, followed by "Roll Sweet Chariot," "Cabin In The Sky," "Native Son," "Set M People Free," "How Long Till Summer," "A Hole In The Head," "The Grea White Hope," "70, Girls, 70," OB in "Conquering Thursday," "The Peddler, "The Dodo Bird," "Don't Play Us Cheap."

ANDREWS, GEORGE LEE. Born Oct. 13, 1942 in Milwaukee, Wisc. Debu OB 1970 in "Jacques Brel Is Alive . . . ," followed by Bdwy debut 1973 in " Little Night Music."

ANTHONY, ROBERT. Born May 10, 1941 in Newark, NJ. Attended Bosto U., AADA. OB in "Jerico-Jim Crow," "Bugs and Veronica," "Dirty Old Man, "Hamlet" and "Othello" (NYSF), "Scuba Duba," Bdwy in "The Man in th Glass Booth" ('68), "Butterflies Are Free."

APLON, BORIS. Born July 14 in Chicago. Attended U. Chicago, Goodma Theatre. OB in "Makrapoulos Secret," "King of the Whole Damn World," C in "Carousel" and "Show Boat," Bdwy in "Candide," "Anya," "Fiddler on th Roof."

ARBEIT, HERMAN. Born Apr. 19, 1925 in Bklyn. Attended CCNY, HE Studio, Neighborhood Playhouse. Debut OB 1959 in "The Golem," followe by "Awake and Sing," "A Delicate Balance."

ARMEN, JOHNNY. Born Jan. 4, 1938 in NYC. Graduate Fordham U. Bdwy debut 1971 in "Lenny."

ARNELL, PATRICIA. Born Oct. 13, 1950 in New Orleans, La. Attended LSU, Loyola U, Bdwy debut 1972 in "The Ambassador."

ATHERTON, WILLIAM. Born July 30, 1947 in New Haven, Conn. Carnegie Tech graduate. Debut 1971 OB in "House of Blue Leaves," followed by "Basic Training of Pavlo Hummel," "Suggs" (LC) for which he received a Theatre World Award; Bdwy bow 1972 in "The Sign in Sidney Brustein's Window."

ATKINS, TOM. Born in Pittsburgh. Graduate Duquesne U., AADA. With LCRep in "Unknown Soldier and His Wife," and "Cyrano," Bdwy 1967 in "Keep It in the Family," "Front Page," "The Changing Room," OB in "Whistle in the Dark," "Nobody Hears a Broken Drum," "Long Day's Journey into Night."

ATKINSON, DAVID. Born in Montreal, Can., Oct. 20, 1921. Attended McGill U., Pasadena Playhouse. Bdwy in "Inside U.S.A.," "Girl In Pink Tights," "The Vamp," CC revivals of "Carousel," "Kiss Me, Kate," "Brigadoon," and "Annie Get Your Gun," "Man of La Mancha."

ATTLE, JOHN C. Born in Tacoma, Wash. Graduate U. Wash. Bdwy bow 1964 in "Fiddler On The Roof," followed by "Jacques Brel Is Alive and Well and Living In Paris" (OB).

ATTLES, JOSEPH. Born Apr. 7, 1903 in Charleston, SC. Attended Harlem Musical Conserv. Bdwy bow in "Blackbirds of 1928," followed by "John Henry," "Porgy and Bess," "Kwamina," "Tambourines to Glory," "The Last of Mrs. Lincoln," OB in "Jerico-Jim Crow," "Cabin in the Sky." "Prodigal Son," "Day of Absence," with LCRep in "Cry of Players," "King Lear," and "Duplex."

AUBERJONOIS, RENE. Born June 1, 1940 in NYC. Graduate Carnegie Inst. With LCRep in "A Cry of Players," "King Lear," and "Twelfth Night," Bdwy in "Fire," "Coco," "Tricks."

AVALOS, LUIS. Born Sept. 2, 1946 in Havana. Graduate NYU. Debut at CC in "Never Jam Today," followed by "Rules for the Running of Trains" (OB), and LC's "Camino Real," "Beggar on Horseback," "Good Woman of Setzuan," and "Kool Aid," "The Architect and the Emperor."

BACKUS, RICHARD. Born Mar. 28, 1945 in Goffstown, NH. Harvard graduate. Bdwy debut 1971 in "Butterflies Are Free," followed by "Promenade, All!!" for which he received a Theatre World Award.

BAER, MARIAN. Born Aug. 18, 1926 in Sedalia, Mo. AADA graduate. Debut 1958 OB in "The Night Is My Enemy," followed by "Glass Menagerie," "Ugly Duckling," "Delicate Balance."

drienne Barbeau   Thomas Barbour   Francine Beers   Lee Bergere   Meg Bennett

AIN, CONRAD. Born Feb. 4, 1923 in Lethbridge, Can. Attended AADA. dwy in "Sixth Finger In A Five Finger Glove," "Candide," "Hot Spot," Advise and Consent," "The Cuban Thing," "Twigs," "Uncle Vanya," OB in The Makropoulous Secret," "The Queen and The Rebels," "Hogan's Goat," The Kitchen," "Scuba Duba," "Nobody Hears A Broken Drum," "Steamath," Play Strindberg"(LC).

AKER, BENNY. Born May 5, 1907 in St. Joseph, Mo. Bdwy debut 1931 in You Said It," followed by "DuBarry Was a Lady," "Let's Face It," "The empest," "No, No, Nanette."

AKER, MARK. Born Oct. 2, 1946 in Cumberland, Md. Attended Wittenberg ., Carnegie-Mellon U., Neighborhood Playhouse, AADA. Debut 1971 OB in Love Me, Love My Children," followed by "Via Galactica."

ALABAN, ROBERT. Born Aug. 16, 1945 in Chicago. Attended Colgate, YU. Debut OB 1967 in "You're a Good Man, Charlie Brown," followed by Plaza Suite" (Bdwy '68), "Up Eden," "White House Murder Case," "Basic raining of Pavlo Hummel," "The Children."

ARBEAU, ADRIENNE. Born June 11, 1945 in Sacramento, Cal. Attended oothill Col. Bdwy debut 1968 in "Fiddler on the Roof," followed by "Stag Movie" (OB), "Grease" for which she received a Theatre World Award.

ARBOUR, THOMAS. Born July 25, 1921 in NYC. Princeton, Harvard graduate. Bdwy in "Portrait of a Queen," "Great White Hope," "Scratch," The Lincoln Mask," OB in "Twelfth Night," "Merchant of Venice," "Admirale Bashville," "River Line," "The Lady's Not for Burning," "The Enchanted," Antony and Cleopatra," "The Saintliness of Margery Kemp," "Dr. Willy illy," "Under the Sycamore Tree," "Epitaph for George Dillon," "Thracian Horse," "Old Glory," "Sjt. Musgrave's Dance."

ARON, SANDY. Born in Bklyn in 1938. Bklyn. Col. grad. Appeared in Second City," "The Premise," "Tchin-Tchin," "One Flew over the Cuckoo's Nest," "Arturo Ui," "Generation," "Muzeeka"(OB), "Lenny."

ARRETT, RAINA. Born Jan. 5, 1941 in Detroit. Graduate Ithaca Col. Debut 968 OB in "Recess," followed by "Oh! Calcutta!," "We Bombed in New Haven."

ARRIE, BARBARA. Born May 23, 1931 in Chicago. Graduate UTex. Bdwy ebut 1955 in "The Wooden Dish" followed by "Happily Never After," "Comany," "Selling of the President," "Prisoner of Second Avenue," OB in "The Crucible," "The Beaux Stratagem," "Taming of The Shrew," "Twelfth Night," and "All's Well That Ends Well"(CP), "Horseman, Pass by."

ARRY, MATTHEW. Born Sept. 5, 1962 in NYC. Debut 1972 OB in "A Piece of Fog," followed by "American Gothics."

BARTLETT, CHARLES. Born Aug. 18, 1941 in San Antonio, Tex. Graduate SUNY. Bdwy debut 1970 in "Story Theatre," followed by "Metamorphosis," "Much Ado about Nothing," OB in "The Screens."

BARTLETT, MICHAEL. Born Aug. 23, 1901 in North Oxford, Mass. Attended Princeton. Bdwy debut 1930 in "Through the Years," followed by "Three Waltzes," "Cat and the Fiddle," "School for Husbands," "Follies."

BASS, EMORY. Born in Ga.; Bdwy bow 1952 in "Kiss Me, Kate," followed by "Teahouse of the August Moon," CC's "Pal Joey" and "Where's Charley?," "1776," "Lysistrata," OB in "Chic," "Bartleby," "Gay Divorce," "Boys from Syracuse," "By Jupiter."

BASSIE, JOAN. Born July 22, 1939 in Chicago. Attended RADA. NY debut 1964 in "Arms and the Man"(OB), followed by Bdwy bow 1967 in "The Imaginary Invalid" and "Tonight at 8:30," "Not Now, Darling," "Taming of the Shrew"(OB), "Jockey Club Stakes."

BATES, ALAN. Born Feb. 17, 1934 in Derbyshire, Eng. Attended RADA. Bdwy debut 1957 in "Look Back in Anger," followed by "The Caretaker," "Poor Richard," "Butley."

BAXTER, KEITH. Born Apr. 29, 1935 in Newport, Wales. Graduate RADA. Bdwy debut 1961 in "A Man for All Seasons" for which he received a Theatre World Award, followed by "The Affair," "Avanti," "Sleuth."

BEACH, GARY. Born Oct. 10, 1947 in Alexandria, Va. Graduate NC School of Arts. Made Bdwy bow 1971 in "1776," followed by "Smile, Smile, Smile"(OB).

BEACHNER, LOUIS. Born June 9, 1923 in Jersey City, NJ. Bdwy bow 1942 in "Junior Miss," followed by "No Time For Sergeants," "Georgy," "The Changing Room," OB in "Time to Burn," "The Hostage."

BEARDSLEY, ALICE. Born Mar. 28, 1927 in Richmond, Va. UIowa graduate. Bdwy debut 1960 in "The Wall," OB in "Eastward in Eden," "In Good King Charles' Golden Days," "Leave It to Jane," "Camino Real," "A Man's a Man," "Cindy," "Boy on a Straight-back Chair," "Things," "The Kid."

BECK, STANLEY. Born June 5, 1936 in NYC. On Bdwy in "Mr. Roberts," OB in "The Balcony," "There Is no End," "Days and Nights of Beebee Fenstermaker," "Present Tense," LC's "Changeling," and "Incident at Vichy."

BEDFORD, BRIAN. Born Feb. 16, 1935 in Morley, Eng. Attended RADA. NY bow 1960 in "Five Finger Exercise," followed by "Lord Pengo," "The Private Ear," "The Knack" (OB). "The Astrakhan Coat," "The Unknown Soldier and His Wife," "Seven Descents of Myrtle," with APA in "Misanthrope," "Cocktail Party," and "Hamlet," "Private Lives," "School for Wives."

BEDFORD, PATRICK. Born May 30, 1932 in Dublin. Appeared with Dublin Gate Theatre before Bdwy bow 1966 in "Philadelphia, Here I Come," followed by "The Mundy Scheme," "Small Craft Warnings"(OB).

BEERS, FRANCINE. Born Nov. 26 in NYC. Attended Hunter Col., CCNY, HB Studio. Debut 1962 OB in "King of the Whole Damned World," followed by "Kiss Mama," "Monopoly," Bdwy in "Cafe Crown," "6 Rms Riv Vu."

BEERY, LEIGH. Born March 20 in Minneapolis, Minn. Attended McPhail School. Debut 1965 OB in "Leonard Bernstein's Theatre Songs," followed by "Pic-a-Number," "Oklahoma!"(LC), Bdwy debut 1973 in "Cyrano."

BEL GEDDES, BARBARA. Born Oct. 31, 1922 in NYC. Bdwy debut 1941 in "Out of the Frying Pan," followed by "Little Darling," "Nine Girls," "Mrs. January and Mr. X," "Deep Are the Roots" for which she received a Theatre World Award, "Burning Bright," "The Moon Is Blue," "The Living Room," "Cat on a Hot Tin Roof," "The Sleeping Prince," "Silent Night, Lonely Night," "Mary, Mary," "The Porcelain Year," "Luv," "Everything in the Garden," "Finishing Touches."

BELL, MARY. Born Nov. 17, 1904 in Austin, Tex. Attended UTex. Many credits include "The Shrike," "Cat on a Hot Tin Roof," "Cloud 7," "Miracle Worker," "Beyond Desire," "Passion of Antigona Perez"(OB).

BELLAVER, HARRY. Born Feb. 12, 1905 in Hillsboro, Ill. Attended Brookwood Col. Bdwy bow 1931 in "House of Connelly," followed by "Night over Taos," "Carry Nation," "We, the People," "Threepenny Opera," "The Sellout," "Page Miss Glory," "Noah," "Black Pit," "How Beautiful with Shoes," "Russet Mantle," "St. Helena," "To Quito and Back," "Tortilla Flat," "Johnny 2 X 4," "Mr. Sycamore," "The World's Full of Girls," "Annie Get Your Gun," "That Championship Season."

BELLOMO, JOE. Born Apr. 12, 1938 in NYC. Attended Manhattan Sch. of Music. Bdwy bow 1960 in "New Girl in Town," followed by CC's "South Pacific" and "Guys and Dolls," OB in "Cindy," "Fantasticks."

BEN-AMI, JACOB. Born Nov. 23, 1890 in Minsk, Russia. Prominent on English and Yiddish stages. Among his many plays are "Samson and Delilah," "Johannes Kreisler," "Idle Inn," "The Failures," "Man and the Masses," "Diplomacy," "Even Song," "A Ship Comes In," "Who Is Who," "Tenth Man," "The Seagull," "Infernal Machine," "The World of Sholom Aleichem," "Walking to Waldheim," "Happiness," "Yoshe Kalb."

BENNETT, MEG. Born Oct. 4, 1948 in Los Angeles. Graduate Northwestern U. Debut OB 1971 in "Godspell," on Bdwy 1972 in "Grease."

BERGERE, LEE. Born in NYC. Attended Columbia U. Bdwy debut 1949 in "Inside U.S.A.," followed by "Mrs. McThing," "Man of La Mancha."

BERRIAN, WILLIAM. Born Feb. 7, 1929 in Bklyn. Bdwy bow 1948 in "My Romance," followed by "Man in the Dog Suit," "Do I Hear a Waltz?," "Auntie Mame," "Maggie Flynn," "Say When" (OB).

BERRY, ERIC. Born Jan. 9, 1913 in London. Graduate RADA. NY debut 1954 in "The Boy Friend," followed by "Family Reunion," "The Power and the Glory," "Beaux Stratagem," "Broken Jug," "Pictures in the Hallway," "Peer Gynt," "Great God Brown," "Henry IV," "The White House," "White Devil," "Charley's Aunt," "The Homecoming"(OB), "Capt. Brassbound's Conversion," "Pippin."

BETHENCOURT, FRANCIS. Born Sept. 5, 1924 in London. Attended Mayfield Col. Bdwy debut 1948 in "Anne of the Thousand Days," followed by "Happy Time," "Dial 'M' for Murder," "Visit to a Small Planet," "Ross," "Right Honourable Gentleman," "Hamp"(OB), "Borstal Boy," "Pygmalion" (OB).

BEY, RAFIC. Born July 19, 1948 in Morocco. Attended NYU. Debut OB 1972 in "3 One Act Plays," followed by "You Gonna Let Me Take You Out Tonight," "Works in Progress," "The Corner."

BINGHAM, BOB. Born Oct 29, 1946 in Seattle, Wash. Attended UWash. Bdwy debut 1971 in "Jesus Christ Superstar."

BIRNEY, DAVID. Born Apr. 23, 1939 in Washington, D.C. Graduate Dartmouth, UCLA. OB with NYSF in "Comedy of Errors," "Titus Andronicus," and "King John," "MacBird," "Crime of Passion," "Ceremony of Innocence," LC's "Summertree" for which he received a Theatre World Award, "The Miser," "Playboy of The Western World," "Good Woman of Setzuan," "An Enemy of The People," and "Antigone"(LC).

BITTNER, JACK. Born in Omaha, Neb. Graduate UNeb. Has appeared in "Nathan the Wise," "Land of Fame," "Beggars' Holiday," "Rip Van Winkle," "Dear Oscar"(OB).

BLACKTON, JACK. Born Mar. 16, 1938 in Colorado Springs. Graduate U. Colo. OB in "The Fantasticks," "Put It In Writing," "Jacques Brel Is Alive . . ." "Hark," Bdwy bow 1966 in "Mame."

Helon Blount

Graham Brown

Jacqueline Brookes

Rod Browning

Jean Bruno

BLANKSHINE, ROBERT. Born Dec. 22, 1948 in Syracuse, NY. Appeared with Joffrey Ballet before Bdwy debut 1972 in "Via Galactica."

BLOCK, CHAD. Born May 1, 1938 in Twin Falls, Ida. Bdwy bow 1954 in "The Vamp," followed by "Li'l Abner," "Destry Rides Again," "Take Me Along," "Do Re Mi," "Come On Strong," "Hello, Dolly!," "Walking Happy," "Hallelujah, Baby!" "Coco," "A Funny Thing Happened on the Way to the Forum."

BLOUNT, HELON. Born Jan. 15 in Big Spring, Tex. Graduate UTex. Bdwy debut 1956 in "Most Happy Fella," followed by "How to Succeed in Business . . . ," "Do I Hear a Waltz?," "Fig Leaves Are Falling," "Follies," OB in "Fly Blackbird," "Riverwind," "My Wife and I," "Curley McDimple," "A Quarter for the Ladies Room."

BLYDEN, LARRY. Born June 23, 1925 in Houston, Tex. Bdwy bow 1949 in "Mr. Roberts," followed by "Wish You Were Here," "Oh, Men! Oh, Women!," "Italian Straw Hat" (OB), "Who Was that Lady I Saw You With?" "Flower Drum Song," "Foxy," "Blues for Mr. Charlie," "Luv," "Apple Tree," "Mother Lover," "You Know I Can't Hear You When the Water's Running," "A Funny Thing Happened on the Way to the Forum."

BOBBIE, WALTER. Born Nov. 18, 1945 in Scranton, Pa. Graduate UScranton, Catholic U. Bdwy bow 1971 in "Frank Merriwell," followed by "Grass Harp," "Grease," "Drat!" (OB), "Tricks."

BOGERT, WILLIAM. Born Jan. 25, 1936 in NYC. Yale graduate. Bdwy in "Man for All Seasons," "Hamlet," "Star Spangled Girl," "Cactus Flower," "Sudden and Accidental Re-education of Horse Johnson," OB in "Country Wife," "Taming of the Shrew," "Henry V," "Love's Labour's Lost," "A Gun Play," "The Real Inspector Hound."

BOGGS, GAIL. Born Aug. 10, 1951 in Glen Ridge, NJ. Attended Seton Hall, AADA. Debut OB 1971 in "Iphigenia," followed by "Ti-Jean and His Brothers," Bdwy bow 1972 in "Mother Earth."

BOND, RUDY. Born Oct. 1, 1915 in Philadelphia. Attended UPa. Bdwy in "Streetcar Named Desire," "Bird Cage," "Two Blind Mice," "Romeo and Juliet," "Glad Tidings," "Golden Boy," "Fiorello," "Illya Darling," "Night Watch," OB in "O'Daniel," LCR's "After the Fall" and "Incident at Vichy," "Big Man," "Match-Play," "Papp," "Twelve Angry Men," "The Birds."

BOND, SUDIE. Born July 13, 1928 in Louisville, Ky. Attended Rollins Col. OB in "Summer and Smoke," "Tovarich," "American Dream," "Sandbox," "Endgame," "Theatre of the Absurd," "Home Movies," "Softly and Consider the Nearness," "Memorandum," "Local Stigmatic," "Billy" Bdwy in "Waltz of the Toreadors," "Auntie Mame," "The Egg," "Harold," "My Mother, My Father and Me," "The Impossible Years," "Keep It in the Family," "Quotations from Chrmn. Mao Tse-Tung," "American Dream," "Forty Carats," "Hay Fever," "Grease."

BONELLE, DICK. Born Apr. 11, 1936 in Houston, Tex. Graduate UHouston. Debut OB 1970 in "Lyle," followed by "Sugar" (Bdwy).

BORRELLI, JIM. Born Apr. 10, 1948 in Lawrence, Mass. Graduate Boston Col. NY debut OB 1971 in "Subject to Fits," followed by "Grease."

BOSCO, PHILIP. Born Sept. 26, 1930 in Jersey City, NJ. Graduate Catholic U. Credits: "Auntie Mame," "Rape of The Belt," "Ticket of Leave Man"(OB), "Donnybrook," "Man For All Seasons," with LCRep in "The Alchemist," "East Wind," "Galileo," "St. Joan," "Tiger At The Gates," "Cyrano," "King Lear," "A Great Career," "In The Matter of J. Robert Oppenheimer," "The Miser," "The Time of Your Life," "Camino Real," "Operation Sidewinder," "Amphitryon," "An Enemy of the People," "Playboy of the Western World," "Good Woman of Setzuan," "Antigone," "Mary Stuart," "Narrow Road to the Deep North," "The Crucible," "Twelfth Night," "Enemies," "Plough and the Stars," "Merchant of Venice," and "A Streetcar Named Desire."

BOSTWICK, BARRY. Born Feb. 24, 1945 in San Mateo, Cal. Graduate Cal-Western, NYU. Bdwy debut with APA in "War and Peace," "Pantagleize," "Misanthrope," "Cock-A-Doodle Dandy," "Hamlet," OB in "Salvation," "Colette," "Soon," "Screens," "Grease" (Bdwy).

BOVA, JOSEPH. Born May 25 in Cleveland, O. Graduate Northwestern U. Debut OB 1959 in "On the Town," followed by "Once upon a Mattress, "House of Blue Leaves," "Comedy," NYSF's "Taming of the Shrew," "Richard III," "Comedy of Errors," "Invitation to a Beheading," on Bdwy in "Rape of the Belt," "Irma La Douce," "Hot Spot," "The Chinese."

BOYLAN, MARY. Born in Plattsburg, NY. Attended Mt. Holyoke Col. Bdwy debut 1938 in "Dance Night," followed by "Susannah and the Elders," "The Walrus and the Carpenter," "Our Town," "Live Life Again," OB in "To Bury a Cousin," "Curley McDimple," "Blood," "Middle of the Night"(ELT), "Girls Most Likely to Succeed."

BRAHA, HERB. (formerly Herb Simon) Born Sept. 18, 1946 in Hyannis, Mass. Attended Carnegie Tech. Debut 1971 OB in "Godspell."

BRANDO, JOCELYN. Born Nov. 18, 1919 in San Francisco. Attended Lake Forest Col., AADA. Bdwy debut 1941 in "The First Crocus," followed by "Mr.

Roberts," "Golden State," "Desire under the Elms," "Mourning Becomes Electra."

BRANDON, PETER. Born July 11, 1926 in Berlin. Attended Neighborhood Playhouse. Bdwy debut 1950 in "Cry of the Peacock," followed by CC's "Come of Age," and "Tovarich," "Ondine," "The Young and Beautiful," "Hidden River," "Infernal Machine," "A Man for All Seasons," "The Investigation," "An Evening with the Poet-Senator" (OB).

BRANNUM, TOM. Born June 17, 1941 in Shawnee, Pa. Bdwy bow 1961 in "Once There Was a Russian," followed by "Take Her, She's Mine," "We Bombed in New Haven," "Room Service," "Mystery Play"(OB).

BRANON, JOHN. Born Oct. 7, 1939 in Chicago. Attended Chicago City Col. Bdwy debut 1968 in "The Guide," OB in "Scuba Duba," "The Glorious Ruler," "42 Seconds from Broadway."

BRAUNSTEIN, ALAN. Born Apr. 30, 1947 in Bklyn. Debut OB 1962 in "Daddy Come Home," followed by Bdwy bow 1970 in "Hair," "Jesus Christ Superstar," "Dude."

BRENNEN, ANNA. Born in Elko, Nev. UCal. graduate. Debut 1972 OB in "Eros and Psyche," followed by "Hamlet."

BRESLIN, TOMMY. Born Mar. 24, 1946 in Norwich, Conn. Attended Iona Col. OB in "For Love or Money," "Freedom Is a Two-Edged Sword," "Who's Who, Baby?," "Beggar on Horseback"(LC), "Moon Walk," "Dear Oscar," Bdwy bow 1971 in "70 Girls 70."

BROCKSMITH, ROY. Born Sept. 15, 1945 in Quincy, Ill. Debut OB 1971 in "Whip Lady," followed by "The Workout," "Beggar's Opera."

BRODERICK, JAMES. Born Mar. 7, 1928 in Charlestown, NH. Attended UNH, Neighborhood Playhouse. Bdwy bow 1953 in "Maggie," followed by "Johnny No Trump," "Let Me Hear You Smile," OB in "A Touch of the Poet," "Two by Saroyan," "Firebugs," LC's "The Time of Your Life," and "Scenes from American Life," "Wedding Band."

BROOKES, JACQUELINE. Born July 24, 1930 in Montclair, NJ. Graduate UIowa, RADA. Bdwy debut 1955 in "Tiger at the Gates," followed by "Watercolor," "Abelard and Heloise," OB in "The Cretan Woman" for which she received a Theatre World Award, "The Clandestine Marriage," "Measure for Measure," "Duches of Malfi," "Ivanov," "Six Characters in Search of an Author," "An Evening's Frost," "Come Slowly, Eden," "The Increased Difficulty of Concentration"(LC), "The Persians," "Sunday Dinner," "House of Blue Leaves," "A Meeting by the River," "Owners."

BROWN, DANIEL. Born June 9, 1947 in Little Rock, Ark. Graduate LSU. Debut OB 1972 in "Absolutely Time!," followed by "The Secret Life of Walter Mitty."

BROWN, GRAHAM. Born Oct. 24, 1924 in NYC. Graduate Howard U. OB in "Widower's Houses," "The Emperor's Clothes," "Time of Storm," "Major Barbara," "Land Beyond the River," "The Blacks," "Firebugs," "God Is a (Guess What?)," "An Evening of One Acts," "Man Better Man," "Behold! Cometh the Vanderkellans," "Ride a Black Horse," on Bdwy in "Weekend," "Man in the Glass Booth," "The River Niger."

BROWN, TALLY. Born Aug. 1, 1934 in NYC. Graduate NYU, Juilliard. Bdwy in "Pajama Game," "Tenderloin," "Mame," OB in "Jackass," "Justice Box," "Medea."

BROWNING, ROBERT. Born Apr. 30, 1942 in Syracuse, NY. Graduate Carnegie Tech, Purdue. Bdwy debut 1970 in "Candida," followed by "Speed Gets the Poppys."

BROWNING, ROD. Born Nov. 25, 1942 in Manhasset, NY. Attended New Morris Col. Debut 1966 OB in NYSF's "All's Well That Ends Well," followed by "Measure for Measure," "Richard III," "Mystery Play."

BROWNING, SUSAN. Born Feb. 25, 1941 in Baldwin, NY. Graduate Penn. State. Bdwy bow 1963 in "Love and Kisses," followed by "Company" for which she received a Theatre World Award, "Shelter," OB in "Jo," "Dime A Dozen," "Seventeen," "Boys from Syracuse," "Collision Course," "Whiskey."

BROWNLEE, BRIAN. Born July 6 in Virginia. Attended UNC, AADA. Debut 1972 OB in "We Bombed in New Haven," followed by "A Streetcar Named Desire"(LCR).

BROWNLEE, DELL. Born in Paris. Attended Marymount, Neighborhood Playhouse. Bdwy debut 1961 in "The Unsinkable Molly Brown," followed by "Carnival," "Here's Love," "Fade Out, Fade In," "Man of La Mancha."

BRUCE, KATHERINE. Born Apr. 25, 1941 in Cleveland, O. Attended AADA. Debut OB 1967 in "The Rimers of Eldritch," followed by "Dinner at the Ambassador's."

BRUNO, JEAN. Born Dec. 7, 1926 in Bklyn. Attended Hofstra Col., Feagin School. Bdwy debut 1960 in "Beg, Borrow or Steal," followed by "Midgie Purvis," "Music Man," "Family Affair," "Minnie's Boys," "The Lincoln Mask," OB in "All That Fall," "Hector," "Hotel Paradiso," "Pidgeons in the Park," "Ergo," "Trelawny of the Wells," "Song for the First of May."

Joseph Buloff

Eileen Burns

Peter Carew

Luz Castanos

James Carruthers

BRUNS, PHILIP. Born May 2, 1931 in Pipestone, Minn. Graduate Augustana Col., Yale. Bdwy bow 1964 in "The Deputy," followed by "Lysistrata," OB in "Mr. Simian," "The Cradle Will Rock," "He Who Gets Slapped," "Dr. Willy Nilly," "Come Play with Me," "Listen to the Mocking Bird," "Bald Soprano," "Jack of the Submission," "Endgame," "Servant of Two Masters," "Pantomania," "Square in the Eye," "Butter and Egg Man," "Spitting Image," "Henry V," "A Dream out of Time."

BRYDON, W. B. Born Sept. 20, 1933 in Newcastle, Eng. NY debut OB 1962 in "The Long, the Short, and the Tall," followed by "Live Like Pigs," "Sjt. Musgrave's Dance," "The Kitchen," "Come Slowly Eden," "The Unknown Soldier and His Wife" (LC and Bdwy), "Moon for the Misbegotten," "The Orphan," "The Lincoln Mask"(Bdwy).

BUCKLEY, BETTY. Born July 3, 1947 in Big Spring, Tex. Graduate TCU. Bdwy debut 1969 in "1776," followed by "Pippin," OB in "Ballad of Johnny Pot," "What's a Nice Country like You Doing in a State Like This?"

BULOFF, JOSEPH. Born Dec. 6, 1907 in Wilno, Lithuania. Bdwy debut 1936 in "Don't Look Now," followed by "Call Me Ziggy," "To Quito and Back," "The Man from Cairo," "Morning Star," "Spring Again," "My Sister Eileen," "Oklahoma!," "The Whole World Over," "Once More with Feeling," "The Fifth Season," "Moonbirds," "The Wall," "Yoshke Musikant"(OB).

BURNS, EILEEN. Born in Hartsdale, NY. Has appeared in "Native Son," "Christopher Blake," "The Small Hours," "American Way," "The Women"(1936), "Merrily We Roll Along," "Daughters of Atreus," "First Lady," "Mourning Becomes Electra."

BURROWS, VINIE. Born Nov. 15, 1928 in NYC. Graduate NYU. On Bdwy in "Wisteria Trees," "Green Pastures," "Mrs. Patterson," "The Skin of Our Teeth," "The Ponder Heart," OB in her one-woman "Walk Together Children."

BYRNE, GAYLEA. Born in Baltimore, Md. Graduate Peabody Conservatory. Debut 1961 OB in "All In Love," followed by "Music Man" (CC), "Man of La Mancha."

BYRNES, MAUREEN. Born May 14, 1944 in Chicago. Bdwy debut 1965 in "La Grosse Valise," followed by "Oh, Calcutta!"

CALDWELL, ZOE. Born Sept. 14, 1933 in Melbourne, Aus. Attended Methodist Ladies Col. Bdwy debut 1965 in "The Devils," followed by "Slapstick Tragedy" for which she received a Theatre World Award, "The Prime of Miss Jean Brodie," "Colette" (OB), "The Creation of the World and Other Business."

CAMPANELLA, PHILIP. Born May 24, 1948 in Jersey City, NJ. Graduate St. Peter's Col., HB Studio. Debut OB 1970 in "Lady from Maxim's," followed by "Hamlet," "Tug of War," "Charles Abbott & Son," "She Stoops to Conquer," "Taming of the Shrew," "Misalliance," "The Play's the Thing."

CANEMAKER, JOHN. Born May 28, 1943 in Waverly, NY. Attended AADA. OB in "Pimpernel," "That Hat," "Route One," "Papers," "The Making of Americans."

CANNING, JAMES J. Born July 2, 1946 in Chicago. Graduate DePaul U. Debut 1972 in "Grease."

CARA, IRENE. Born Mar. 18, 1959 in NYC. Bdwy debut 1968 in "Maggie Flynn," followed by "The Me Nobody Knows," "Via Galactica."

CARADIMAS, LANA. Born Dec. 5, 1945 in NYC. Graduate Hunter Col. Debut OB 1967 in "Shoemaker's Holiday," followed by American Savoyards, "Out of This World," Bdwy in "Lost in the Stars" (1972).

CAREW, PETER. Born Nov. 8, 1922 in Old Forge, Pa. NYU graduate. Debut OB 1948 in "Coffee House," followed by "Street Scene," "Ah, Wilderness," "Antigone," "Waiting for Lefty," "12 Angry Men," "Falling from Heaven," "Go Show Me a Dragon," "A Stage Affair," "King of the Whole Damn World," "Purple Canary," "Kiss Mama," "A View from the Bridge," "He Who Gets Slapped," "Istanboul," "Great White Hope" (Bdwy 1969), "Thunder Rock."

CAREY, FRANK. Born Oct. 12, 1934 in Tarrytown, NY. Attended AADA. Debut OB 1960 in "Nat Turner," followed by "The Brick and the Rose," "Black Quartet," Bdwy bow 1972 in "Don't Play Us Cheap."

CARIOU, LEONARD. Born Sept. 30, 1939 in Winnipeg, Can. Bdwy debut 1968 with Minn. Theatre Co. in "House of Atreus," followed by "Henry V.," "Applause" for which he received a Theatre World Award, "Night Watch," "A Little Night Music."

CARLIN, CHET. Born Feb. 23, 1940 in Malverne, NY. Graduate Ithaca Col., Catholic U. Bdwy bow 1972 in "An Evening with Richard Nixon and . . . ," OB in "Under Gaslight," "Lou Gehrig Did Not Die of Cancer," "Graffiti!," "Crystal and Fox."

CARNEY, ART. Born Nov. 4, 1918 in Mt. Vernon, NY. Bdwy bow 1957 in "Rope Dancers," followed by "Take Her, She's Mine," "Odd Couple," "Lovers," "Prisoner of Second Avenue."

CARROLL, HELENA. Born in Glasgow, Scot. Attended Weber-Douglas School, London. US debut with Dublin Players. Founded, directed, acted with Irish Players Off-Bdwy. Bdwy debut 1956 in "Separate Tables," followed by "Happy as Larry," "A Touch of the Poet," "Little Moon of Alban," "The Hostage," "Oliver!," "Pickwick," "Three Hand Reel" (OB), "Something Different," "Georgy," "Borstal Boy," "Pictures in the Hallway" (LC), "Small Craft Warnings" (OB).

CARRUTHERS, JAMES. Born May 26, 1931 in Morristown, NJ. Attended Lafayette Col., HB Studio. Debut OB 1959 in "Our Town," followed by "Under the Sycamore Tree," "Misalliance," "The Hostage," "Telemachus Clay," "Shadow of a Gunman."

CARTER, MYRA. Born in Chicago Oct. 27, 1930. Attended Glasgow U. Bdwy debut 1957 in "Major Barbara," followed by "Maybe Tuesday," "Trials of Oz" (OB).

CARTER, RALPH. Born June 30, 1961 in NYC. Bdwy debut 1971 in "The Me Nobody Knows," followed by "Tough to Get Help," "Dude," "Via Galactica," "The Karl Marx Play" (OB).

CASON, BARBARA. Born Nov. 15, 1933 in Memphis, Tenn. Graduate Iowa U. Bdwy debut 1967 in "Marat/Sade," followed by "Jimmy Shine," "Night Watch," OB in "Firebugs," "Spitting Image," "Enemy of the People" (LC), "Oh, Coward!"

CASPER, RICHARD. Born Jan. 21, 1949 in Springfield, Ill. Graduate Northwestern U. Bdwy debut 1971 in "Much Ado about Nothing."

CASTANOS, LUZ. Born July 15, 1935 in NYC. Graduate CUNY. Debut OB 1959 in "Last Visit," followed by "Eternal Sabbath," "Finis for Oscar Wilde," "Young and Fair," "La Dama Duende," "A Media Luz Los Tres," "Yerma."

CATLETT, MARY JO. Born Sept. 2, 1938 in Denver, Colo. Graduate Loretto Hts. Col. Has appeared in "Along Came A Spider" (OB), "New Girl In Town," "Fiorello," "Pajama Game," "Hello, Dolly!" "Canterbury Tales," "Promenade" (OB), "Greenwillow" (ELT), "Different Times," "Lysistrata."

CATLIN, FAITH. Born Sept. 19, 1949 in Troy, NY. Graduate Boston U. Debut OB 1969 in "Pequod," followed by "Approaching Simone," "Summer Brave."

CAVANAUGH, MICHAEL. Born in NYC. Attended San Francisco State Col. NY bow 1969 in "Oh! Calcutta!"

CHACE, DOROTHY. Born in North Bergen, NJ. Attended SF State Col., Stanford, Yale. Bdwy debut 1969 in "3 Men on a Horse," followed by LCRep's "Caucasian Chalk Circle," and "Cyrano," "Screens" (OB).

CHAIKIN, SHAMI. Born Apr. 21, 1931 in NYC. Debut OB 1966 in "America Hurrah," followed by "Serpent," "Terminal," "Mutation Show," "Viet Rock," "Mystery Play."

CHALBAUD, ESTEBAN. Born Mar. 7, 1945 in Caracas, Ven. Graduate Boston Conserv. Debut OB 1970 in "Maria Sabina," followed by "Life Is a Dream," Don Juan Tenorio," "You Never Know."

CHANDLER, LEAH. Born Oct. 19, 1950 in Smithville, Mo. Juilliard graduate. Debut OB 1972 in "School for Scandal," followed by "U.S.A.," "Women Beware Women," "Lower Depths."

CHANNING, CAROL. Born Jan. 31, 1921 in Seattle, Wash. Bennington Col. graduate. Bdwy debut 1941 in "No for an Answer," followed by "Let's Face It," "Proof through the Night," "Lend an Ear" for which she received a Theatre World Award," "Gentlemen Prefer Blondes," "Wonderful Town," "The Vamp," "Show Girl," "Hello, Dolly!," "Four on a Garden."

CHARNEY, JORDAN. Born in NYC. Graduate Bklyn Col. Off-Bdwy in "Harry, Noon and Night," "A Place for Chance," "Hang Down Your Head and Die," "The Pinter Plays," "Telemachus Clay," "Zoo Story," "Viet Rock," "MacBird," "Red Cross," "The Glorious Ruler," "Waiting for Godot," "Slow Memories," "One Flew over the Cuckoo's Nest," "The Boy Who Came to Leave," Bdwy in "Slapstick Tragedy," "The Birthday Party."

CHARTOFF, MELANIE. Born Dec. 15, 1948 in New Haven, Conn. Graduate Adelphi U. Debut OB 1971 in "The Proposition," followed by Bdwy bow 1972 in "Via Galactica."

CHINN, LORI. Born in Seattle, Wash. Bdwy debut 1970 in "Lovely Ladies, Kind Gentlemen," followed OB in "Coffins for Butterflies," "Hough in Blazes," "Peer Gynt," "King and I," "Children," "Secret Life of Walter Mitty."

CHRIS, MARILYN. Born May 19, 1939 in NYC. Attended CCNY. Appeared in "The Office," "Birthday Party," "7 Descents of Myrtle," "Lenny," OB in "Nobody Hears a Broken Drum," "Fame," "Judas Applause," "Junebug Graduates Tonight," "Man Is Man," "In the Jungle of Cities," "Good Soldier Schweik," "The Tempest," "Ride a Black Horse," "Screens," "Kaddish."

CHRISMAN, CAROLYN. Born in NYC. Appeared OB in "Games," "Fantastic Gardens," "Home Again," "Something for Kitty Genovese," "Greenwillow," "Dinner at the Ambassador's."

| Thom Christopher | Kay Cole | Peter Coffield | Miriam Colon | Kenneth Cory |

CHRISTIE, JULIE. Born Apr. 14, 1941 in Chukua, Assam, India. Bdwy debut 1973 in "Uncle Vanya."

CHRISTOPHER, JORDAN. Born Oct. 23, 1940 in Youngstown, O. Attended Kent State U. Bdwy debut 1967 in "Black Comedy" for which he received a Theatre World Award, followed by "Sleuth."

CHRISTOPHER, THOM. Born Oct. 5, 1940 in Jackson Heights, NY. Attended Ithaca Col., Neighborhood Playhouse. Debut 1972 OB in "One Flew over the Cuckoo's Nest," followed by Bdwy bow 1973 in "Emperor Henry IV."

CINKO, PAULA. Born Dec. 14, 1950. Debut 1972 OB in "A Quarter for the Ladies Room."

CISSEL, CHUCK. Born Oct. 3, 1948 in Tulsa, Okla. Graduate UOkla. Bdwy debut 1971 in "Purlie," followed by "Lost in the Stars," "Via Galactica."

CLANCY, TOM. Born Oct. 29, 1926 in Ireland. Attended Christian Brothers Col. Has appeared in "King Lear," "Under Milk Wood," "A Touch of the Poet," OB in "Winkelberg," "Ulysses in Nighttown," "Guests of the Nation," "Pygmalion."

CLANTON, RALPH. Born Sept. 11, 1914 in Fresno, Cal. Attended Pasadena Playhouse. Bdwy in "Victory Belles," "Macbeth," "Richard III," "Othello," "Lute Song," "Cyrano," "Antony and Cleopatra," "Design for a Stained Glass Window," "Taming of the Shrew," "Burning Glass," "Vivat! Vivat Regina!," "The Last of Mrs. Lincoln," OB in "Ceremony of Innocence," "Endecott and the Red Cross."

CLARKSON, JOHN. Born Jan. 19, 1932 in London. Graduate Oxford U. NY debut OB 1971 in "Murderous Angels," followed by Bdwy bow 1973 in "No Sex Please, We're British."

CLAY, LOUISE. Born Mar. 3, 1938 in Lafayette, La. LSU graduate. Bdwy debut 1966 in "Marat/deSade," followed by "Mike Downstairs," OB in "Rondelay," "The Hot L Baltimore."

CLAYBURGH, JILL. Born Apr. 30, 1944 in NYC. Sarah Lawrence graduate. Bdwy debut 1968 in "The Sudden and Accidental Re-education of Horse Johnson," followed by "The Rothschilds," "Pippin," OB in "It's Called the Sugar Plum," "Calling in Crazy," "The Nest."

CLAYTON, JAN. Born Aug. 26, 1917 in Almogordo, NM. Attended Gulf Park Col. Bdwy debut 1945 in "Carousel," followed by "Show Boat," "The King and I," "Follies," followed by Bdwy bow 1973 in "No Sex Please, We're British."

COCKERILLE, LILI. Born in Washington, DC. Joined NYC Ballet in 1963, Joffrey Ballet 1969. Bdwy debut 1972 in "Via Galactica."

COE, JOHN. Born Oct. 19, 1925 in Hartford, Conn. Graduate Boston U. Bdwy in "Passion of Josef D," "Man in the Glass Booth," "La Strada," OB in "Marrying Maiden," "Thistle in My Bed," "John," "Wicked Cooks," "June Bug Graduates Tonight," "Drums in the Night," "America Hurrah," "Father Uxbridge Wants to Marry," "Nobody Hears a Broken Drum," "Dylan," "Screens," "The Kid."

COFFIELD, PETER. Born July 17, 1945 in Evanston, Ill. Graduate of Northwestern, UMich. With APA in "The Misanthrope," "Cock-a-Doodle Dandy" and "Hamlet," followed by "Abelard and Heloise," "Vivat! Vivat Regina!," "Merchant of Venice" (LCR).

COFFIN, FREDERICK. Born Jan. 16, 1943 in Detroit. Graduate UMich. Debut 1971 OB in "Basic Training of Pavlo Hummel," followed by "Much Ado about Nothing."

COHEN, MARGERY. Born June 24, 1947 in Chicago. Attended UWisc., UChicago, HB Studio, Bdwy debut 1968 in "Fiddler on the Roof," followed by "Jacques Brel Is Alive and Well ....," OB in "Berlin to Broadway."

COLE, KAY. Born Jan. 13, 1948 in Miami, Fla. Bdwy debut 1961 in "Bye Bye Birdie," followed by "Stop the World I Want to Get Off," "Roar of the Greasepaint . . . ," "Hair," "Jesus Christ Superstar," OB in "The Cradle Will Rock," "Two if by Sea," "Rainbow."

COLES, ZAIDA. Born Sept. 10, 1933 in Lynchburg, Va. OB in "The Father," "Pins and Needles," "The Life and Times of J. Walter Smintheus," "Cherry Orchard," Bdwy in "Weekend," "Zelda."

COLLINS, CHARLES. Born July 24, 1942 in Santa Rosa, Cal. Attended UDallas, TCU, HB Studio. Debut 1970 OB in "The Last Sweet Days of Isaac," followed by "Coming Together," "Soft Core Pornographer," Bdwy bow 1973 in "Shelter."

COLLINS, DOROTHY. Born 1927 in Windsor, Ont., Can. Bdwy debut 1971 in "Follies."

COLLINS, STEPHEN. Born Oct. 1, 1947 in Des Moines, I. Graduate Amherst Col. Bdwy debut 1972 in "Moonchildren," followed by "No Sex Please, We're British," OB in "Twelfth Night."

COLON, MIRIAM. Born 1945 in Ponce, PR. Attended UPR, Actors Studio. Bdwy debut 1953 in "In the Summer House," OB in "Me, Candido," "The Ox Cart," "Passion of Antigona Perez."

COLSON, C. DAVID. Born Dec. 23, 1941 in Detroit. Graduate UMich. Debut 1970 in "The Last Sweet Days of Isaac" (OB), followed by "Masquerade," "Ballet behind the Bridge," Bdwy debut 1970 in "Purlie."

COLTON, CHEVI. Born in NYC. Attended Hunter Col. OB in "Time of Storm," "Insect Comedy" (CC). "The Adding Machine," "O Marry Me," "Penny Change," "The Mad Show," "Jacques Brel Is Alive . . . ," Bdwy in "Cabaret."

CONNELL, DAVID. Born Nov. 24, 1935 in Cleveland, O. Attended Kent State U. Bdwy bow 1968 in "Great White Hope," followed by "Don't Play Us Cheap," OB in "Ballet behind the Bridge."

CONNELL, GORDON. Born Mar. 19, 1923 in Berkeley, Cal. Graduate UCal., NYU. Bdwy bow 1961 in "Subways Are for Sleeping," followed by "Hello, Dolly!," "Lysistrata" OB in "Beggar's Opera."

CONNELL, JANE. Born Oct. 27, 1925 in Berkeley, Cal. Attended UCal. OB in "Shoestring Revue," "Threepenny Opera," "Pieces of Eight," "Demi-Dozen," "She Stoops to Conquer," "Drat!," "The Real Inspector Hound," Bdwy in "New Faces of 1956," "Drat! The Cat!," "Mame," "Dear World," "Lysistrata."

CONNOLLY, GEORGE. Born Oct. 26, 1944 in Boston. Attended Boston U. Bdwy debut 1968 in "The Happy Time," followed by "Up Eden" (OB), "Borstal Boy," "The Last of Mrs. Lincoln."

CONOLLY, PATRICIA. Born Aug. 29, 1933 in Tabora, E. Africa. Attended USydney. With APA in "You Can't Take It with You," "War and Peace," "School for Scandal," "Wild Duck," "Right You Are," "We Comrades Three," "Pantagleize," "Exit the King," "Cherry Orchard," "Misanthrope," "Cocktail Party," and "Cock-a-Doodle Dandy," followed by LCR's "Streetcar Named Desire."

CONWAY, KEVIN. Born May 29, 1942 in NYC. Debut 1968 OB in "Muzeeka," on Bdwy 1969 in "Indians," followed by "Saved" (OB), "Moonchildren," "The Plough and the Stars" (LCR), "One Flew over the Cuckoo's Nest" (OB).

COOK, BARBARA. Born Oct. 25, 1927 in Atlanta, Ga. Bdwy debut 1951 in "Flahooley," followed by "Plain and Fancy" for which she received a Theatre World Award, "Candide," "Music Man," CC's "Carousel" and "The King and I," "The Gay Life," "She Loves Me," "Something More," "Any Wednesday," "Show Boat" (LC), "Little Murders," "Man of La Mancha," "Grass Harp," "Enemies" (LCR).

COOK, JAMES. Born Mar. 7, 1937 in NYC. Attended AADA. OB in "The Fantasticks," "Goa," "Cyrano," "A Cry of Players," "King Lear," "The Miser," "Playboy of the Western World," "Good Woman of Setzuan," "Enemy of the People," "In the Matter of J. Robert Oppenheimer," "The Architect and the Emperor," on Bdwy in "Great White Hope," "Wrong Way Light Bulb."

COOK, RODERICK. Born in 1932 in London. Attended Cambridge U. Bdwy debut 1961 in "Kean," followed by "Roar like a Dove," "The Girl Who Came to Supper," "Noel Coward's Sweet Potato," OB in "A Scent of Flowers," "Oh, Coward!"

COOLEY, DENNIS. Born May 11, 1948 in Huntington Park, Cal. Attended Northwestern U. Bdwy debut 1970 in "Hair," followed by "Jesus Christ Superstar," "Creation of the World and Other Business."

COONEY, DENNIS. Born Sept. 19, 1938 in NYC. Attended Fordham U. OB in "Whisper to Me," "Every Other Girl" for which he received a Theatre World Award, "In a Summer House," LCR's "Tiger at the Gates" and "Cyrano de Bergerac," Bdwy in "Ross," "Love and Kisses," "Lion in Winter," "The Last of Mrs. Lincoln."

COOTE, ROBERT. Born Feb. 4, 1909 in London. Bdwy debut 1953 in "The Love of Four Colonels," followed by "Dear Charles," "My Fair Lady," "Jockey Club Stakes."

COPE, PATRICIA. Born Sept. 3, 1943 in Meridian, Miss. Attended Lon Morris Col. Bdwy debut 1965 in "Roar of the Greasepaint. . . . ," followed by "How to Succeed in Business. . . . ," "Hooray! It's a Glorious Day" (OB), "Wonderful Town" (CC), "How Now Dow Jones," "Hello, Dolly!," "The Lincoln Mask."

COPPOLA, SAM. Born July 31, 1935 in NJ. Attended Actors Studio. Debut 1968 OB in "A Present from Your Old Man," followed by "Things That Almost Happen," "Detective Story."

CORBETT, GRETCHEN. Born Aug. 13, 1947 in Portland, Ore. Attended Carnegie Tech. OB in "Arms and The Man," "The Bench," "Iphigenia In Aulis," "Henry VI," "Survival of St. Joan," "Justice Box," "The Government Inspector," on Bdwy in "After The Rain," "Forty Carats."

CORBIN, BARRY. Born Oct. 16, 1940 in La Mesa, Tex. Attended Tex. Tech. Appeared with ASF's "Othello" on Bdwy in 1969, OB in "Masquerade," "Crystal and Fox."

CORY, KENNETH. Born July 21, 1941 in Hanover, Pa. Studied with Meisner, Adler. Bdwy debut 1971 in "Company," followed by "Out of This World" (OB).

Casey Craig   Joel Craig   Sarah Cunningham   Bill Cwikowski   Connie Danese

COSTELLO, MARICLARE. Born in Peoria, Ill. Appeared OB in "The Hostage," LCR's "After the Fall" and "But for Whom Charlie," "The Orphan," on Bdwy in "Lovers and Other Strangers," "A Patriot for Me," "Harvey."

COSTER, NICOLAS. Born Dec. 3, 1934 in London. Attended Neighborhood Playhouse. Bdwy bow 1960 in "Becket," followed by "90 Day Mistress," "But Seriously," "Twigs," OB in "Epitaph for George Dillon," "Shadow and Substance," "Thracian Horses," "O, Say Can You See," "Happy Birthday, Wanda June."

COURT, GERALDINE. Born July 28, 1942 in Binghamton, NY. Attended AADA. Debut 1968 OB in "Possibilities," followed by "Medea," "Lower Depths."

CRAIG, CASEY. Born Sept. 11 in St. Louis, Mo. Graduate UMo. Debut 1973 OB in "Smile, Smile, Smile."

CRAIG, JOEL. Born Apr. 26, in NYC. Attended Brandeis U. Bdwy debut 1961 in "Subways Are for Sleeping," followed by "Nowhere to Go but Up," "Hello, Dolly!," "Follies," "Out of This World" (OB), "Cyrano."

CRAIG, NOEL. Born Jan. 4 in St. Louis, Mo. Attended Northwestern, Goodman Theatre, Guildhall School London. Bdwy debut 1967 in "Rosencrantz and Guildenstern Are Dead," followed by "A Patriot for Me," "Conduct Unbecoming," "Vivat! Vivat Regina!," "Pygmalion" (OB).

CRISCUOLO, LOUIS. Born Jan. 23, 1934 in NYC. Attended Actors Studio. Debut OB 1964 in "Matty, the Moron, and the Madonna," followed by "Hooray! It's a Glorious Day," "Smith," Bdwy in "Man of La Mancha," "Hurry Harry."

CROFT, PADDY. Born in Worthing, Eng. Attended Avondale Col. Debut OB 1961 in "The Hostage," followed by "Billy Liar," "Live Like Pigs," "Hogan's Goat," "Long Day's Journey into Night," "Shadow of a Gunman," "Pygmalion," "The Plough and the Stars" (LC), Bdwy in "The Killing of Sister George," "The Prime of Miss Jean Brodie."

CROMWELL, ROBERT. Born Jan. 17, 1921 in Kansas City, Mo. Attended UAriz, RADA, HB Studio. Debut 1946 OB in "Othello," followed by "Little Mary Sunshine," "The Boy Friend," "Man of La Mancha" (LC).

CRONIN, JANE. Born Apr. 4, 1936 in Boston, Mass. Attended Boston U. Bdwy debut 1965 in "Postmark Zero," OB in "Bald Soprano," "One Flew over the Cuckoo's Nest."

CRONYN, HUME. Born July 18, 1911 in London, Ont., Can. Attended McGill U., AADA. Bdwy debut 1934 in "Hipper's Holiday," followed by "Boy Meets Girl," "High Tor," "Room Service," "There's Always a Breeze," "Escape This Night," "Off to Buffalo," "Three Sisters," "Weak Link," "Retreat to Pleasure," "Mr. Big," "Survivors," "Four-poster," "Madam, Will You Walk" (OB), "The Honeys," "A Day by the Sea," "Man in the Dog Suit," "Triple Play," "Big Fish, Little Fish," "Hamlet," "Physicists," "Delicate Balance," "Hardrian VII," "Promenade, All!," LC's "Krapp's Last Tape," "Happy Days," and "Act without Words."

CRONYN, TANDY. Born Nov. 27, 1945 in Los Angeles. Attended Central School in London. Bdwy debut 1969 in "Cabaret," followed by LC's "Playboy of the Western World," "Good Woman of Setzuan," "Enemy of the People," and "Antigone," OB in "An Evening with the Poet-Senator."

CRYER, DAVID. Born Mar. 8, 1936 in Evanston, Ill. Attended DePauw U. OB in "The Fantasticks," "Streets of New York," "Now Is The Time For All Good Men," "Whispers on The Wind," "The Making of Americans," on Bdwy in "110 In The Shade." "Come Summer," for which he received a Theatre World Award, "1776," "Ari," "Leonard Bernstein's Mass."

CULLEY, JANE. Born Dec. 3, 1943 in Lawrenceburg, Tenn. Attended Reed Col. Debut 1964 OB in "Of Mice and Men," followed by "Scuba Duba," "Night of the Iguana," "A Phantasmagoria Historia . . ."

CULLUM, JOHN. Born Mar. 2, 1930 in Knoxville, Tenn. Graduate U. Tenn. Bdwy bow 1960 in "Camelot," followed by "Infidel Caesar," "The Rehearsal," "Hamlet," "On A Clear Day You Can See Forever" for which he received a Theatre World Award, "The Hand Reel" (OB), "Man of LaMancha," "1776," "Vivat! Vivat Regina!" "The King and I" (JB), "The Elizabethans" (OB).

CUNNINGHAM, SARAH. Born Sept. 8, 1918 in Greenville, SC. Attended Furman U., Actors Studio. Bdwy debut 1948 in "The Respectful Prostitute," followed by "A Happy Journey," "Blood Wedding," "The Young and Fair," "Fair Game," "The Visit," "Toys in the Attic," "The Zulu and the Zayda," "My Sweet Charlie," OB in "Portrait of the Artist . . . ," "Barroom Monks," "Christy," "Oh, Pioneers," "Present Tense."

CURNOCK, RICHARD. Born May 9, 1922 in London. Bdwy bow 1964 in "Oh! What a Lovely War," followed by "The Cherry Orchard," "There's One in Every Marriage," "Lady Audley's Secret" (OB).

CURTIS, DONNA. Born Jan. 12, 1938 in Ft. Dodge, Iowa. Graduate Northern State Col. OB with American Savoyards, and in "Now Is the Time for All Good Men," "Lady Audley's Secret."

CURTIS, KEENE. Born Feb. 15, 1925 in Salt Lake City. Graduate U. Utah. Bdwy bow 1949 in "Shop At Sly Corner," with APA in "School For Scandal," "The Tavern," "Anatole," "Scapin," "Right You Are," "The Importance of Being Earnest," "Twelfth Night," "King Lear," "The Seagull," "Lower Depths," "Man and Superman," "Judith," "War and Peace," "You Can't Take It With You," "Pantagleize," "The Cherry Orchard," "Misanthrope," "Cocktail Party," "Cock-A-Doodle Dandy," and "Hamlet," followed by "A Patriot for Me," "Colette" (OB), "The Rothschilds," "Ride across Lake Constance" (LC), "Night Watch," "Via Galactica."

CUSHMAN, NANCY. Born Apr. 26, 1913 in Brooklyn. Graduate Rollins Col. Bdwy in "White Man," "Storm over Patsy," "Gloriana," "Janie," "Be Your Age," "J. B.," "Little Me," "Skyscraper," "Harold," OB in "American Dream," "Child Buyer," "Sondra," "Dear Oscar."

CWIKOWSKI, BILL. Born Aug. 5, 1945 in Newark, NJ. Graduate Monmouth, Smith Cols. Debut 1972 OB in "Charlie the Chicken," followed by "Summer Brave."

CYPKIN, DIANE. Born Sept. 10, 1948 in Munich, Ger. Attended Bklyn Col. Bdwy debut 1966 in "Let's Sing Yiddish," followed by "Papa Get Married," "Light, Lively and Yiddish," "Yoshke Musikant" (OB).

DABDOUB, JACK. Born Feb. 5 in New Orleans. Graduate Tulane U. OB in "What's Up," "Time For The Gentle People," "The Peddler," "The Dodo Bird," on Bdwy in "Paint Your Wagon," "My Darlin' Aida," "Happy Hunting," "Hot Spot," "Camelot," "Baker Street," "Anya," "Annie Get Your Gun" (LC), "Her First Roman," "Coco," "Man of La Mancha."

DAMON, CATHRYN. Born Sept. 11 in Seattle, Wash. Bdwy debut 1954 in "By The Beautiful Sea," followed by "The Vamp," "Shinbone Alley," "A Family Affair," "Foxy," "Flora, The Red Menace," "UTBU," "Come Summer," "Criss-Crossing," "A Place for Polly," "Last of the Red Hot Lovers," OB in "Boys from Syracuse," "Secret Life of Walter Mitty," "Show Me Where The Good Times Are," "Effect of Gamma Rays on Man-in-the-Moon Marigolds," "Siamese Connections."

DANA, LEORA. Born Apr. 1, 1923 in NYC. Attended Barnard Col., RADA. Bdwy debut 1947 in "Madwoman of Chaillot," followed by "Happy Time," "Point of No Return," "Sabrina Fair," "Best Man," "Beekman Place," "The Last of Mrs. Lincoln," "The Women," OB in "In the Summer House," "Wilder's Triple Bill," "Collision Course," "Bird of Dawning Singeth All Night Long," "Increased Difficulty of Concentration" (LC), "Place without Mornings."

DANESE, CONNIE. Born in Brooklyn. Debut 1972 OB in "The Contrast."

DANGLER, ANITA. Born Sept. 26 in NYC. Attended NYU. Bdwy debut 1956 in "Affair of Honor," followed by "The Hostage," APA's "Right You Are," "You Can't Take It with You," and "War and Peace," "Hamlet" (NYSF), "Cyrano."

DANIELE, GRACIELA. Born Dec. 8, 1939 in Buenos Aires. Bdwy debut 1964 in "What Makes Sammy Run?" followed by "Here's Where I Belong," "Promises, Promises," "Follies."

DARNELL, ROBERT. Born Sept. 26, 1929 in Los Angeles. Bdwy bow 1962 in "Irma La Douce," followed by "Spoon River," "Luv," "You Know I Can't Hear You . . . ," "Selling of the President," "Hurry Harry," OB in "Threepenny Opera," "Young Abe Lincoln," "Tempest," "On the Town," "In White America," "Who's Happy Now?"

DARRIEUX, DANIELLE. Born May 1, 1917 in Bordeaux, France. Attended Paris Cons. Bdwy debut 1970 in "Coco," followed by "Ambassador."

DAVID, JEAN. Born May 4, 1931 in Denver Colo. Columbia U. graduate. Debut 1963 OB in "Six Characters in Search of an Author," followed by "Miss Julie," "Hobbies," "Jack," "Oedipus," "Epitaph for George Dillon," "Now You See It," "Moondreamers," "Istanboul," "Triple Image," "Beclch," "Finnegan's Wake," "Dark of the Moon," "Subject to Fits," "Wedding Band."

DAVID, THAYER. Born Mar. 4, 1927 in Medford, Mass. Harvard graduate. Bdwy in "The Relapse," "King Lear," "Mr. Johnson," "Protective Custody," "Man for All Seasons," "Andorra," "The Seagull," "The Crucible," "Royal Hunt of the Sun," "Those That Play the Clowns," "Jockey Club Stakes," OB in "Carefree Tree," "White Devil," "Oscar Wilde," "The Bench," "Uncle Vanya."

DAVILA, DIANA. Born Nov. 5, 1947 in NYC. Bdwy debut 1967 in "Song of The Grasshopper," followed by "The Prime of Miss Jean Brodie," OB in "What the Butler Saw," "The Refrigerators," "People Are Living There" (LC), "Two Gentlemen of Verona," "Last Analysis."

DAVIS, CHERRY. Born in Independence, Mo. Attended RADA. OB in "Young Abe Lincoln," "Threepenny Opera," "Corner of the Morning," "As You Like It," "Your Own Thing," "Small Craft Warnings," "The Kid," Bdwy in "Gypsy," "Oliver," "George M!"

DAVIS, CLIFTON. Born Oct. 4 in Chicago. Attended Oakwood Col. Debut OB 1968 in "How to Steal an Election," followed by "Horseman, Pass By," "To Be Young, Gifted and Black," "No Place to Be Somebody," "Do It Again!" for which he received a Theatre World Award, on Bdwy in "Hello, Dolly!" "Jimmy Shine," "Look to the Lilies," "The Engagement Baby," "Two Gentlemen of Verona."

DAWSON, MARK. Born Mar. 23, 1920 in Philadelphia. Studied at Phila. Cons. Bdwy bow 1942 in "By Jupiter," followed by "Dancing in the Streets," "Sweethearts," "High Button Shoes" for which he received a Theatre World Award, "Great to Be Alive," "Me and Juliet," "Ankles Aweigh," "New Girl in Town," "Fiorello," "Riot Act," "Odd Couple," "Twigs."

DeCARLO, YVONNE. Born Sept. 1, 1924 in Vancouver, BC. Attended Vancouver School of Drama. Bdwy debut 1971 in "Follies."

DEE, BLANCHE. Born Jan. 18, 1936 in Wheeling, WVa. Graduate Bklyn Col. Debut 1967 OB in "Rimers of Eldritch," followed by "Tom Paine," "Sunset," Bdwy bow 1970 in "Grin and Bare It."

DEE, RUBY. Born Oct. 27, 1923 in Cleveland, O. Graduate Hunter Col. Bdwy debut 1946 in "Jeb," followed by "Anna Lucasta," "Smile of the World," "Long Way Home," "Raisin in the Sun," "Purlie Victorious," OB in "World of Sholom Aleichem," "Boesman and Lena," "Wedding Band."

DEEBLE, DEBORAH. Born Oct. 27, 1945 in Plainfield, NJ. Attended Carnegie Tech. Debut 1968 in "Up Eden," followed by "Beggar's Opera."

DeMAIO, PETER. Born in Hartford, Conn. Attended New School, Juilliard. Debut OB 1961 in "Threepenny Opera," followed by "Secret Life of Walter Mitty," "Dark of the Moon," Bdwy in "Billy," "Indians," "The Changing Room."

DEMAS, CAROLE. Born May 26, 1940 in Bklyn. Attended UVt., NYU. OB in "Morning Sun," "The Fantasticks," "How to Steal an Election," "Rondelay," Bdwy debut 1965 in "Race of Hairy Men," followed by "Grease."

DENGEL, JAKE. Born June 19, 1933 in Oshkosh, Wis. Graduate Northwestern U. Debut OB in "The Fantasticks," followed by "Red Eye of Love," "Fortuna," "Abe Lincoln in Illinois," "Dr. Faustus," "An Evening with Garcia Lorca," "Shrinking Bride," APA's "Cock-a-Doodle Dandy" and "Hamlet," Bdwy in "Royal Hunt of the Sun," "The Changing Room."

DENISON, ROBERT G. Born Mar. 5, 1937 in Detroit, Mich. UMich. graduate. Debut 1972 OB in "The Contrast."

DENNEN, BARRY. Born Feb. 22, 1938 in Chicago. UCLA graduate. Bdwy debut 1971 in "Jesus Christ Superstar."

DENNIS, RONALD. Born Oct. 2, 1944 in Dayton, O. Has appeared in "Show Boat" (LC'66), OB in "Of Thee I Sing," "Moon Walk," "Please Don't Cry."

DENNIS, SANDY. Born Apr. 27, 1937 in Hastings, Neb. Bdwy debut 1957 in "The Dark at the Top of the Stairs," followed by "Burning Bright" (OB), "Face of a Hero," "Complaisant Lover," "A Thousand Clowns" for which she received a Theatre World Award, "Any Wednesday," "Daphne in Cottage D." "How the Other Half Loves," "Let Me Hear You Smile."

DE RUSSO, RICHARD. Born May 30, 1946 in NYC. Graduate Columbia U. Debut 1971 OB in "The Wanderers," Bdwy bow 1971 in "Two Gentlemen of Verona," followed by "Via Galactica."

DE SHIELDS, ANDRE. Born Jan. 12, 1946 in Baltimore, Md. Graduate UWisc. Bdwy debut 1973 in "Warp."

DE SIMONE, B. J. Born Dec. 7, 1939 in Boston, Mass. Graduate Tufts U. Bdwy bow 1964 in "West Side Story," followed by "Royal Hunt of the Sun," "The Unknown Soldier and His Wife," "Rosencrantz and Guildenstern Are Dead," "Hadrian VII," "Madwoman of Chaillot" (OB), "Oh, Calcutta."

DESPO. Born July 13, 1920 in Piraeus, Greece. Bdwy debut 1967 in "Illya, Darling," followed by "A Little Night Music," OB in "Istanbul," "Screens," "Sunset."

DEVLIN, JOHN. Born Jan. 26, 1937 in Cleveland, O. Carnegie Tech. graduate. Bdwy bow 1964 in "Poor Bitos," followed by "Billy," "Vivat! Vivat Regina!," NYSF's "Richard III," "King Lear" (LC).

DEWHURST, COLLEEN. Born in Montreal, Can. Attended Downer Col., AADA. Bdwy debut 1952 in "Desire under the Elms," followed by "Tamburlaine the Great," "Country Wife," "Caligula," "All the Way Home," "Great Day in the Morning," "Ballad of the Sad Cafe," "More Stately Mansions," "All Over," "Mourning Becomes Electra," OB in "Taming of the Shrew," "The Eagle Has Two Heads," "Camille," "Macbeth," "Children of Darkness" for which she received a Theatre World Award, "Antony and Cleopatra" (CP), "Hello and Goodbye," "Good Woman of Setzuan" (LC), "Hamlet" (NYSF).

DeYOUNG, CLIFF. Born Feb 12, 1945 in Los Angeles. Graduate Cal. State, Ill. U., HB Studio. Bdwy bow 1970 in "Hair," followed by "Sticks and Bones," OB in "Trials of Oz," "The Orphan."

DIAMOND, MICHAEL. Born July 18, 1945 in Bklyn. Attended UNH. Debut 1969 OB in "King Lear," followed by "Henry V," "Heloise," "Capt. Brassbound's Conversion" (Bdwy '72), "Emperor Henry IV."

DIAMOND, NEIL. Born Jan. 24, 1941 in Brooklyn. Attended NYU. Bdwy debut 1972 in his one-man show.

DICKSON, JAMES. Born Jan. 5, 1949 in Akron, O. Attended NYATA. Debut 1971 OB in "One Flew over the Cuckoo's Nest."

DIENER, JOAN. Born Feb. 24, 1934 in Cleveland, O. Attended Sarah Lawrence Col. Bdwy debut 1948 in "Small Wonder," followed by "Season in the Sun," "Kismet" for which she received a Theatre World Award, "Cry for Us All," "Man of La Mancha."

DIETRICH, DENA. Born Dec. 4, 1928 in Pittsburgh. Attended AADA. Debut 1962 OB in "Out of This World," followed by "Cindy," "Rimers of Eldritch," Bdwy in "Funny Girl," "Here's Where I Belong," "Freaking out of Stephanie Blake," "Prisoner of Second Avenue."

DIETZ, EILEEN. Born in NYC; attended Neighborhood Playhouse, AADA. OB in "Come Back, Little Sheba," "Steambath," "Ontological Proof of My Existence," "The Elizabethans."

DIXON, MacINTYRE. Born Dec. 22, 1931 in Everett, Mass. Graduate Emerson Col. OB in "Quare Fellow," "Plays for Bleecker St.," "Stewed Prunes," "Cat's Pajamas," "Three Sisters," "3 X 3," "Second City," "Mad Show," "Meeow!," Bdwy in "Xmas in Las Vegas," "Cop-Out," "Story Theatre," "Metamorphoses," "Twigs."

DMITRI, RICHARD. Born June 27 in NYC. Bdwy bow 1945 in "Dark of the Moon," followed by "The Immoralist" (OB), "The Guide," "Zorba," "Lysistrata."

DODGE, JERRY. Born Feb. 1, 1937 in New Orleans. Graduate Notre Dame. Bdwy bow 1961 in "Bye Bye Birdie," followed by "110 in the Shade," "Hello, Dolly!," "George M!," OB in "Sap of Life," "One Flew over the Cuckoo's Nest," "Blue Boys."

DONNELLY, DONAL. Born July 6, 1931 in Bradford, Eng. Bdwy debut 1966 in "Philadelphia, Here I Come!," followed by "A Day in the Death of Joe Egg," "Sleuth."

DONNELLY, RUTH. Born May 17, 1896 in Trenton, NJ. Bdwy debut 1914 in "A Scrap of Paper," followed by "Going Up," "A Prince There Was," "As You Were," "Meanest Man in the World," "Madeleine and the Movies," "Riot Act," "No, No, Nanette."

DORIN, PHOEBE. Born June 26, 1940 in NYC. Graduate Cooper Union. Bdwy debut 1968 in "Happiness Is a Rolls Royce," OB in "2 by Saroyan," "Burn Me to Ashes," "To Be Young, Gifted and Black," "Awake and Sing," "Girls Most Likely to Succeed."

D'ORSAY, FIFI. Born Apr. 16, 1904 in Montreal, Can. After long and successful film career, made Bdwy debut 1971 in "Follies."

DOUGLASS, B. HENRY. Born Aug. 7, 1951 in Washington, DC. Attended Antioch Col., NYU. Debut 1972 OB in "Please Don't Cry and Say No."

DOVA, NINA. Born Jan. 15, 1926 in London. Attended Neighborhood Playhouse. Debut OB in "I Feel Wonderful," followed by Bdwy in "Zorba," "The Rothschilds," "A Delicate Balance" (OB).

DOW, R. A. Born Aug. 30, 1941 in Cambridge, Mass. Graduate UPa. Debut OB 1970 in "The Dirtiest Show in Town," followed by "Baba Goya."

DOWD, M'EL. Born Feb. 2, in Chicago. Attended Goodman Theatre. OB in "Macbeth," "A Midsummer Night's Dream" "Romeo Juliet," "Julius Caesar," "Royal Gambit," "The Emperor," "Invitation To A Beheading," "Mercy Street," "Gun Play," Bdwy debut 1958 in "Methuselah," followed by "A Case of Libel," "Sweet Bird of Youth," "Camelot," "The Right Honourable Gentleman," "The Sound of Music" (CC), LCRep "Unknown Soldier and His Wife," and "Tiger At The Gates," "Everything In The Garden," "Dear World," "Not Now, Darling," "Ambassador."

DOWNING, DAVID. Born July 21, 1943 in NYC. OB in "Day of Absence," "Happy Ending," "Song of The Lusitanian Bogey," "Ceremonies in Dark Old Men," "Man Better Man," "The Harangues," "Brotherhood," "Perry's Mission," "Rosalee Pritchett," "Dream on Monkey Mt.," "Ride a Black Horse," "Ballet behind the Bridge," "Please Don't Cry and Say No."

DOWNING, VIRGINIA. Born Mar. 7 in Washington, DC. Attended Bryn Mawr. OB in "Juno and the Paycock," "Man with the Golden Arm," "Palm Tree in a Rose Garden," "Play with a Tiger," "The Wives," "The Idiot," "Medea," "Mrs. Warren's Profession," "Mercy Street," "Thunder Rock," "Pygmalion," Bdwy in "Father Malachy's Miracle," "Forward the Heart," "The Cradle Will Rock," "A Gift of Time," "We Have Always Lived in the Castle."

DREMAK, W. P. Born Aug. 2, in Akron, O. Carnegie Tech graduate. Debut OB 1967 in "Jonah," Bdwy bow 1972 in "Jesus Christ Superstar."

DUDA, ANDREA. Born June 1, 1945 in East Douglas, Mass. Attended Boston U., AADA. Bdwy debut 1968 in "The Education of Hyman Kaplan," followed by "George M!," "Jimmy," "Say When" (OB).

Marian Ellis   Joel Eagon   Judith Evans   Richard Ferrugio   Charlotte Fairchild

DUFF-MacCORMICK, CARA. Born Dec. 12 in Woodstock, Can. Attended AADA. Debut 1969 OB in "Love Your Crooked Neighbor," Bdwy 1972 in "Moonchildren" for which she received a Theatre World Award, followed by "Out Cry."

DURRELL, MICHAEL. OB 1961 in "Worm in the Horseradish," "Butterfly Dream," "Phedre," "MacBird," "A Maid's Tragedy," APA's "Cherry Orchard," "Pantagleize," "Misanthrope," "Capt" "Cock-a-Doodle Dandy," and "Hamlet," Bdwy 1973 in "Emperor Henry IV."

DUSSAULT, NANCY. Born June 30, 1936 in Pensacola, Fla. Graduate Northwestern U. Debut OB 1958 in "Diversions," followed by "Street Scene" (CC), "Dr. Willy Nilly," "The Cradle Will Rock," "No for an Answer," "Whispers on the Wind," "Trelawney of the Wells," "Detective Story," Bdwy in "Do Re Mi" for which she received a Theatre World Award, "Sound of Music," "Bajour," CC's "Carousel" and "Finian's Rainbow."

DWYER, FRANK. Born Feb. 1, 1945 in Kansas City, Mo. Graduate NYU, SUNY. Debut 1970 OB in "Moby Dick," followed by "Hamlet" (NYSF), "Bacchai," "The Governor," "Imaginary Invalid," LCR's "Enemies," "Merchant of Venice," and "Streetcar Named Desire."

DYBAS, JAMES. Born Feb. 7, 1944 in Chicago. Bdwy debut 1965 in "Do I Hear a Waltz?," followed by "George M!," "Via Galactica."

EAGON, JOEL. Born July 22, 1941 in Brooklyn. Graduate Fashion Inst. Debut OB 1970 in "Fear," followed by "Harold and Perpetua," "The Secret Life of Walter Mitty," "Buffet."

EASTON, EDWARD. Born Oct. 21, 1942 in Moline, Ill. Graduate Lincoln Col., UIll., Neighborhood Playhouse. Debut 1967 OB in "Party on Greenwich Avenue," followed by "Middle of the Night," "Summer Brave."

eda-YOUNG, BARBARA. Born Jan. 30, 1945 in Detroit, Mich. Bdwy debut 1968 in "Lovers and Other Strangers," OB in "The Hawk," LCRep's "Time of Your Life," "Camino Real," "Operation Sidewinder," "Kool Aid," and "A Streetcar Named Desire."

EDE, GEORGE. Born Dec. 22, 1931 in San Francisco, Cal. Bdwy debut 1969 in "A Flea in Her Ear," followed by "Three Sisters," "The Changing Room."

EDELSTEIN, RAY. Born Sept. 6, 1937 in Roanoke, Va. Debut 1970 in "Candyapple" (OB), followed by "Oh! Calcutta!

EDLOE. Born April 1943 in Baltimore, Md. Attended Neighborhood Playhouse. Bdwy debut 1967 in "Hello, Dolly!," followed by "Salvation" (OB), "Via Galactica."

EDMONDS, MITCHELL. Born Jan. 24, 1940 in Knoxville, Tenn. Bdwy debut 1969 in "Red, White, and Maddox," OB in "Importance of Being Earnest," "Midsummer Night's Dream," "A Maid's Tragedy."

EDWARDS, RONNIE CLAIRE. Born Feb. 9, 1933 in Oklahoma City. Graduate U Okla. Bdwy debut 1963 in "Paint Your Wagon," followed by "Trial of the Catonsville 9," "The Lincoln Mask."

ELIAS, HECTOR. Born Sept. 24 in Buenos Aires. Studied at HB Studio. Debut 1968 OB in "Grab Bag," followed by Puerto Rican Traveling Theatre, Bdwy bow 1972 in "Sticks and Bones."

ELIZONDO, HECTOR. Born Dec. 22, 1936 in NYC. Attended CCNY. Bdwy debut in "Great White Hope," followed by "Prisoner of Second Avenue," OB in "Drums in the Night," "Steambath."

ELLIN, DAVID. Born Jan. 10, 1925 in Montreal, Can. Attended AADA. Bdwy in "Swan Song," "West Side Story," "Education of Hyman Kaplan," "Light, Lively and Yiddish," OB in "The Trees Die Standing," "Mirele Efros," "End of All Things Natural," "Yoshe Kalb."

ELLIOTT, PATRICIA. Born July 21, 1942 in Gunnison, Colo. Graduate U. Colo., London Academy. Debut with LCRep 1968 in "King Lear," and "A Cry of Players," followed OB in "Henry V," "The Persians," "A Doll's House," "Hedda Gabler," "In Case of Accident," "Water Hen.," Bdwy bow 1973 in "A Little Night Music" for which she received a Theatre World Award.

ELLIS, LARRY. Born July 28, 1939 in NYC. Bdwy debut 1966 in "Slapstick Tragedy," followed by "Frank Merriwell," "No, No, Nanette."

ELLIS, MARIAN. Born Apr. 23, 1942 in Davenport, Io. Graduate Ill. State, HB Studio. Bdwy debut 1972 in "Oh! Calcutta!"

ELSTON, ROBERT. Born May 29, 1934 in NYC. Graduate Hunter Col., CCNY. Bdwy debut 1958 in "Maybe Tuesday," followed by "Tall Story," "Golden Fleecing," "Spoon River Anthology," "You Know I Can't Hear You When the Water's Running," "Vivat! Vivat Regina!" OB in "Undercover Man," "Conditioned Reflex," "Spoon River Anthology."

EMCH, GEORGE. Born Oct. 18, 1927 in Poland, O. Attended New School. Debut OB 1957 in "Macbeth," followed by "Redhead." "How to Succeed in Business . . . ," Bdwy bow 1972 in "Capt. Brassbound's Conversion."

ENSERRO, MICHAEL. Born Oct. 5, 1918 in Soldier, Pa. Attended Allegheny Col., Pasadena Playhouse. On Bdwy in "Me and Molly," "Passion of Josef D," "Song of the Grasshopper," "Mike Downstairs," "Camino Real" (LC), OB in "Penny Change," "Fantasticks," "The Miracle," "The Kitchen," "Rome, Rome," "The Jar."

ENTEN, BONI. Born Feb. 20, 1947 in Baltimore, Md. Attended TCU. Bdwy debut 1965 in "The Roar of the Greasepaint," OB in "You're a Good Man, Charlie Brown," "Oh! Calcutta," "Salvation," "The Real Inspector Hound."

ERDMAN, JEAN. Born in Honolulu. Sarah Lawrence graduate. Dance debut 1938 with Martha Graham Co. OB in "Coach with the Six Insides," "Moon Mysteries."

ERWIN, BARBARA. Born June 30, 1937 in Boston, Mass. Soloist with Boston Ballet before debut OB 1973 in "The Secret Life of Walter Mitty."

ESPOSITO, GIANCARLO. Born Apr. 26, 1958 in Copenhagen, Den. Bdwy debut 1968 in "Maggie Flynn," followed by "The Me Nobody Knows," "Lost in the Stars," "Seesaw."

ESTERMAN, LAURA. Born Apr. 12, 1945 in NYC. Attended Radcliffe, London's AMDA. Debut 1969 OB in "The Time of Your Life" (LCR), followed by "Pig Pen," "The Carpenters," "Ghosts."

ESTEY, SUELLEN. Born Nov. 21, in Mason City, Ia. Graduate Stephens Col., Northwestern U. Debut OB 1970 in "Some Other Time," followed by "June Moon," "Buy Bonds Buster," "Smile, Smile, Smile," Bdwy 1972 in "The Selling of the President."

EVANS, DAMON. Born Nov. 24, 1950 in Baltimore, Md. Studied at Boston Cons. Debut 1971 OB in "A Day in the Life of Just about Everyone," followed by "Love Me, Love My Children," "Don't Bother Me, I Can't Cope," Bdwy bow 1971 in "The Me Nobody Knows," followed by "Lost in the Stars," "Via Galactica."

EVANS, DILLON. Born Jan. 2, 1921 in London. Attended RADA. Bdwy bow 1950 in "The Lady's Not for Burning," followed by "School for Scandal," "Hamlet," "Ivanov," "Vivat! Vivat Regina!," "Jockey Club Stakes," OB in "Druid's Rest," "Rondelay," "Little Boxes."

EVANS, HARVEY. Born Jan. 7, 1941 in Cincinnati, O. Bdwy debut 1957 in "New Girl in Town," followed by "West Side Story," "Redhead," "Gypsy," "Anyone Can Whistle," "Hello Dolly!," George M!," "Our Town," "The Boy Friend," "Follies."

EVANS, JUDITH. Born in Pittsburgh, Pa. Graduate Manhattanville Col., AMDA. OB in "Darkness," "Sabrina Fair," "The Lie," "The Crucible," "Miss Lizzie," "Baccae," "The Wanderers," Bdwy debut 1972 in "Lenny."

FABRAY, NANETTE. Born Oct. 27, 1922 in San Diego, Cal. Attended Max Reinhardt School. Bdwy debut 1940 in "Meet the People," followed by "Let's Face It," "By Jupiter," "Jackpot," "My Dear Public," "Bloomer Girl," "High Button Shoes," "Love Life," "Arms and the Girl,""Make a Wish," "Mr. President," "No Hard Feelings."

FAIRCHILD, CHARLOTTE. Born June 3, 1930 in Dayton, O. Attended Western Reserve U., Cleveland Playhouse. Bdwy debut 1957 in "Damn Yankees," followed by "Fiorello," "Mr. President," "Mame," "All the Girls Came out to Play," OB in "Penny Friend.," "Oh Coward!"

FALK, PETER. Born Sept. 16, 1927 in NYC. Graduate New School, Syracuse U. Debut OB 1956 in "Don Juan," followed by "The Changeling," "The Iceman Cometh," "St. Joan," "Diary of a Scoundrel," "The Lady's Nor for Burning," "Purple Dust," "Bonds of Interest," "Comic Strip," Bdwy bow 1964 in "Passion of Josef D," subsequently "Prisoner of Second Avenue."

FARENTINO, JAMES. Born Feb. 24, 1938 in Brooklyn. Attended AADA. Bdwy debut 1961 in "Night of the Iguana," OB in "Days and Nights of Beebee Fenstermaker," "In the Summer House," LC's "Streetcar Named Desire" for which he received a Theatre World Award.

FARIA, ARTHUR. Born Nov. 24, 1944 in Fall River, Mass. Studied at SMTI, Boston Cons. Bdwy bow 1970 in "Georgy," followed by "The Boy Friend," "Sugar."

FARR, KIMBERLY. Born Oct. 16, 1948 in Chicago. UCLA graduate. Bdwy debut 1972 in "Mother Earth."

FARRELL, BRIAN. Born March 22 in Englewood, NJ. Graduate Ind. U. Debut 1971 OB in "Masquerade," followed by "Brothers," Bdwy bow 1972 in "The Last of Mrs. Lincoln" for which he received a Theatre World Award.

FASCIANO, RICHARD. Born Mar. 18, 1943 in Ansonia, Conn. Graduate U Conn. Bdwy debut 1970 in "Butterflies Are Free."

FAY, BRENDAN. Born in NYC; attended Maritime Acad. Bdwy 1959 in "Legend of Lizzie," "First Love," "Borstal Boy," OB in "Heloise," "Threepenny Opera," "Donogoo," "King of the Whole Damned World," "Wretched the Lion-Hearted," "Time of the Key," "Thistle in My Bed," "Posterity for Sale," "Stephen D," LCRep's "King Lear" and "Cry of Players," "Brothers," "Wrong Side of the Moon."

FERRELL, CONCHATA. Born Mar. 28, 1943 in Charleston, WVa. Graduate Marshall U. Debut 1973 OB in "The Hot L Baltimore."

FERRUGIO, RICHARD. Born July 28, 1949 in Brooklyn. Princeton graduate. Debut 1973 OB in "The Soldier."

Judy Fields

Douglas Fisher

Connie Forslund

Gene Foote

Helen Gallagher

FIELD, ROBIN. Born Apr. 13, 1947 in Los Angeles. Attended USCal. Debut 1968 OB in "Your Own Thing," followed by "Look Me Up," "Speed Gets the Poppys."

FIELDS, JUDY. Born. in Louisville, Ky. Graduate Georgetown Col., Northwestern U. Debut 1973 OB in "Summer Brave."

FIRE, RICHARD. Born Nov. 12, 1945 in Paterson, NJ. Graduate Rutgers, UWisc. Bdwy debut 1973 in "Warp!"

FIRESTONE, SCOTT. Born Oct. 26, 1962 in NYC. Bdwy debut 1972 in "Voices," followed by "Dude," "Finishing Touches."

FISHER, DOUGLAS. Born July 9, 1934 in Brooklyn. Attended St. John's U., AADA. Debut 1963 OB in "Best Foot Forward," followed by "Frere Jacques," "Devil's Disciple," "Accent on Youth," "Lost in the Stars," "Say, Darling," "Shoestring Revue," "Penthouse Legend."

FITZPATRICK, LYNN. Born in Philadelphia, Pa. Graduate Ohio Dominican Col. Bdwy debut 1972 in "Ambassador," followed by "You Never Know" (OB)

FLANAGAN, NEIL. Born May 3, 1934 in Springfield, Ill. Debut 1966 OB in "Fortune and Men's Eyes," followed by "Haunted Host," "Madness of Lady Bright," "Dirtiest Show in Town," "The Play's the Thing," Bdwy in "Sheep on the Runway," "Secret Affairs of Mildred Wild."

FLANAGAN, PAULINE. Born June 29, 1925 in Sligo, Ire. Debut OB 1958 in "Ulysses in Nighttown," followed by "Pictures in the Hallway," "Antigone" (LC), Bdwy in "God and Kate Murphy," "The Living Room," "The Crucible" and "The Plough and the Stars" (LC).

FLANAGAN, WALTER. Born Oct 4, 1928 in Ponta, Tex. Graduate Houston U. On Bdwy in "Once for the Asking," "Front Page," OB in "Bedtime Story," "Coffee and Windows," "Opening of a Window," "The Moon Is Blue," "Laughwind," "Dodo Bird."

FLEMING, RHONDA. Born Aug. 10, 1922 in Los Angeles. Bdwy debut 1973 in "The Women."

FLETCHER, JACK. Born Apr. 21, 1921 in Forest Hills, NY. Attended Yale. On Bdwy in "Trial Honeymoon," "She Stoops to Conquer," "Romeo and Juliet," "Ben Franklin in Paris," "Drat! The Cat!," "Lysistrata," OB in "Comic Strip," "Way of the World," "Thieves' Carnival," "Amorous Flea," "American Hamburger League," "The Time of Your Life," CC's "Can-Can," "Cyrano," and "Wonderful Town."

FOOTE, GENE. Born Oct. 30, 1936 in Johnson City, Tenn. Attended ETSU. Bdwy debut 1961 in "Unsinkable Molly Brown," followed by "Bajour," "Sweet Charity," "Golden Rainbow," "Applause," "Pippin."

FORBES, DONNA LIGGITT. Born Sept. 9, 1947 in Wilson, NC. Graduate E. Carolina U. Bdwy debut 1972 in "Hurry Harry," followed by "Smile, Smile, Smile" (OB).

FORD, RUTH. Born July 7, 1915 in Hazelhurst, Miss. Attended UMiss. Bdwy debut 1938 in "Shoemaker's Holiday," followed by "Danton's Death," "Swingin' the Dream," "No Exit," "This Time Tomorrow," "Clutterbuck," "House of Bernarda Alba," "Island of Goats," "Requiem for a Nun," "The Milk Train Doesn't Stop Here Anymore," "Grass Harp," OB in "Glass Slipper," "Miss Julie," "Madame de Sade."

FORLOW, TED. Born Apr. 29, 1931 in Independence, Mo. Attended Baker U. Bdwy debut 1957 in "New Girl in Town," followed by "Juno," "Destry Rides Again," "Subways Are for Sleeping," "Can-Can," "Wonderful Town" (CC), "A Funny Thing Happened on the Way to the Forum," "Milk and Honey," "Carnival" (CC), "Man of La Mancha."

FORSLUND, CONNIE. Born June 19, 1950 in San Diego, Cal. Graduate NYU. Debut OB 1972 in "The Divorce of Judy and Jane," Bdwy 1973 in "The Women."

FORSTER, ROBERT. Born July 13, 1941 in Rochester, NY. Attended URochester. Bdwy debut 1965 in "Mrs. Dally," followed by "12 Angry Men" (OB), "A Streetcar Named Desire" (LC).

FORSYTHE, HENDERSON. Born Sept. 11, 1917 in Macon, Mo. Attended UIowa. OB in "The Iceman Cometh," "The Collection," "The Room," "A Slight Ache," "Happiness Cage," "Waiting for Godot," "In Case of Accident," "Not I" (LC), "An Evening with the Poet-Senator," Bdwy in "The Cellar and the Well," "Miss Lonelyhearts," "Who's Afraid of Virginia Woolf?," "Malcolm," "Right Honourable Gentleman," "Delicate Balance," "Birthday Party," "Harvey," "Engagement Baby."

FOSTER, FRANCES. Born June 11 in Yonkers, NY. Bdwy debut 1955 in "The Wisteria Trees," followed by "Nobody Loves an Albatross," "Raisin in the Sun," "The River Niger." OB in "Take a Giant Step," "Edge of the City," "Tammy and the Doctor," "The Crucible," "Happy Ending," "Day of Absence," "An Evening of One Acts," "Man Better Man," "Brotherhood," "Akokawe," "Rosalee Pritchett," "Sty of the Blind Pig," "Ballet behind the Bridge," "Good Woman of Setzuan" (LC) "Behold! Cometh the Vanderkellans," "Orrin."

FOSTER, GLORIA. Born Nov. 15, 1936 in Chicago. Attended Ill. State U., Goodman Theatre. OB "In White America," "Medea" for which she received a Theatre World Award, "Yerma" (LC), "A Hand Is on the Gate," "Black Visions," "The Cherry Orchard."

FRANCIS, GERALD G. Born Mar. 22, 1950 in NYC. CCNY graduate. Bdwy debut 1972 in "Don't Bother Me I Can't Cope."

FRANKLIN, BONNIE. Born Jan. 6, 1944 in Santa Monica, Cal. Attended Smith Col. UCLA. Debut OB 1968 in "Your Own Thing," followed by "Dames at Sea," "Drat!," "Carousel" (JB), Bdwy bow 1970 in "Applause" for which she received a Theatre World Award.

FRANKLIN, HUGH. Born Aug. 24, 1916 in Muskogee, Okla. Attended Northwestern U. Bdwy bow 1938 in "Gloriana," followed by "Harriet," "Alice in Wonderland," "Medea," "Best Man," "Luther," "A Shot in the Dark," "Arturo Ui," "The Devils," "What Did We Do Wrong?," OB in "How Much, How Much?," "Misalliance," "The Play's the Thing."

FRANZ, JOY. Born in 1944 in Modesto, Cal. Graduate UMo. Debut OB 1969 in "Of Thee I Sing," followed by "Jacques Brel Is Alive. . . . ," "Out of This World," on Bdwy in "Sweet Charity," "Lysistrata."

FREEMAN, AL, JR. Born in 1934 in San Antonio, Tex. Attended CCLA. On Bdwy in "The Long Dream," "Tiger, Tiger, Burning Bright," "Living Premise," "Blues for Mr. Charlie," "Dozens," "Look to the Lilies," OB in "Slave," "Dutchman," "Trumpets of the Lord," "Medea."

FREEMAN, ARNY. Born Aug. 28, 1908 in Chicago. Bdwy bow 1949 in "Streetcar Named Desire," followed by "Great Sebastians," "Tall Story," "Hot Spot," "What Makes Sammy Run?," "Cactus Flower," "Minnie's Boys," "Much Ado about Nothing," OB in "Gay Divorce," CC's "Dream Girl" and "The Shrike," "A Gun Play."

FRENCH, ARTHUR. Born in NYC. Attended Bklyn Col. OB 1962 in "Raisin' Hell In the Sun," "Ballad of Bimshire," "Day of Absence," "Happy Ending," "Jonah," "Black Girl," "Ceremonies In Dark Old Men," "An Evening of One Acts," "Man Better Man," "Brotherhood," "Perry's Mission," "Rosalee Pritchett." Bdwy 1971 in "Ain't Supposed to Die a Natural Death."

FRY, RAY. Born Feb. 22, 1923 in Hebron, Ind. Graduate SF State Col., Northwestern. Bdwy bow 1944 in "Hickory Stick," followed by "Cyrano," "The Cradle Will Rock," LCRep's "Danton's Death," "Country Wife," "Caucasian Chalk Circle," "Alchemist," "Galileo," "St. Joan," "Tiger At The Gates," "Cyrano," "A Cry of Players," "Bananas," "The Miser," "Operation Sidewinder," "Beggar on Horseback," "Playboy of the Western World," "Good Woman of Setzuan," "Birthday Party," "Antigone," "Mary Stuart," "Twelfth Night," "Enemies," "Merchant of Venice," and "Streetcar Named Desire."

FUCHS, DICK. Born Feb. 23, 1944 in St. Louis, Mo. Graduate UMo. Debut 1972 OB in "Anna K."

GABLE, JUNE. Born June 5, 1945 in NY. Graduate Carnegie Tech. OB in "MacBird," "Jacques Brel Is Alive and Well and Living In Paris," "A Day in the Life of Just about Everyone," "Mod Donna," "Wanted," "Lady Audley's Secret."

GALIK, DENISE. Born Dec. 4, 1951 in Cleveland, O. Attended Neighborhood Playhouse. Bdwy debut 1973 in "Finishing Touches."

GALLAGHER, HELEN. Born in Brooklyn, 1926. Bdwy debut 1947 in "Seven Lively Arts," followed by "Mr. Strauss Goes to Boston," "Billion Dollar Baby," "Brigadoon," "High Button Shoes," "Touch and Go," "Make a Wish," "Pal Joey," "Hazel Flagg," CC's "Guys and Dolls," "Finian's Rainbow," and "Oklahoma," "Pajama Game," "Bus Stop," "Portofino," "Sweet Charity," "Mame," "Cry For Us All," "No, No, Nanette."

GALLUP, BONNIE. Born Nov. 17, 1945 in Long Beach, Cal. Attended CSU, Juilliard. Bdwy debut 1972 in "Great God Brown," followed by "Don Juan."

GALVIN, JAMES. Born Jan. 15, 1933 in NYC. Debut OB 1966 in "The Employment Agency," followed by "How to Succeed in Business . . ." (ELT).

GAM, RITA. Born Apr. 2, 1928 in Pittsburgh, Pa. Attended Columbia, Actors Studio. Bdwy debut 1946 in "A Flag Is Born," followed by "Temporary Island," "Insect Comedy" (CC), "The Young and the Fair," "Montserrat," "There's a Girl in My Soup."

GARBER, VICTOR. Born Mar. 16, 1949 in London, Ont., Can. Debut 1973 OB in "Ghosts" for which he received a Theatre World Award.

GARDENIA, VINCENT. Born Jan. 7 in Italy. Debut OB 1956 in "Man With The Golden Arm," followed by "Brothers Karamazov," "Power of Darkness," "Machinal," "Gallows Humor," "Endgame," "Little Murders," "Passing through from Exotic Places," "Carpenters," Bdwy in "The Visit," "The Cold Wind and the Warm," "Rashomon," "Only in America," "The Wall," "Daughters of Silence," "Siedman and Son," "Dr. Fish," "Prisoner of Second Avenue."

GARFIELD, DAVID. Born Feb. 6, 1941 in Brooklyn. Graduate Columbia, Cornell. OB in "Hang Down Your Head and Die," "The Government Inspector," Bdwy bow 1967 in "Fiddler on the Roof," followed by "The Rothschilds."

Frank Geraci   Livia Genise   Allen Ginsberg   Sheila Gibbs   Michael Goodwin

GARLAND, GEOFF. Born June 10, 1932 in Warrington, Eng. Debut OB 1961 in "The Hostage," followed by "Trelawney of the Wells," "Timon of Athens" (NYSF), "Waiting for Godot." Bdwy in "Hamlet," "The Imaginary Invalid," "A Touch of The Poet," "Tonight At 8:30," "Front Page," "Capt. Brassbound's Conversion," "Cyrano."

GARRETT, BOB. Born Mar. 2, 1947 in NYC. Graduate Adelphi U. Debut OB 1971 in "Godspell."

GARRETT, KELLY. Born Mar. 25, 1948 in Chester, Pa. Attended Cincinnati Cons. Bdwy debut 1972 in "Mother Earth" for which she received a Theatre World Award.

GARY, HAROLD. Born May 7, 1910 in NYC. Bdwy bow 1928 in "Diamond Lil," followed by "Crazy with the Heat," "A Flag Is Born," "Guys and Dolls," "Oklahoma!," "Arsenic and Old Lace," "Billion Dollar Baby," "Fiesta," "The World We Make," "Born Yesterday," "Will Success Spoil Rock Hunter?," "Let It Ride," "Counting House," "Arturo Ui," "A Thousand Clowns," "Enter Laughing," Illya, Darling," "The Price," "Rosebloom" (OB), "The Sunshine Boys."

GAUL, PATRICIA. Born Oct. 31 in Philadelphia Pa. Debut 1972 OB in "And They Put Handcuffs on Flowers," followed by "Rainbow."

GAVON, IGORS. Born Nov. 14, 1937 in Latvia. Bdwy bow 1961 in "Carnival," followed by "Hello Dolly!" "Marat/deSade," "Billy," "Sugar," OB in "Your Own Thing," "Promenade," "Exchange," "Nevertheless, They Laugh."

GeBAUER, GENE. Born June 28, 1934 in Ord, Neb. NY Bow OB 1960 in "Machinal," followed by "Once Upon a Mattress," "Stag Movie," Bdwy in "Camelot," "No Strings," "Hello, Dolly!," "Oh! Calcutta!," "Sugar."

GENEST, EDMOND. Born Oct. 27, 1943 in Boston. Attended Suffolk U. Debut 1972 OB in "The Real Inspector Hound."

GENISE, LIVIA. Born Oct. 15, 1949 in Brooklyn. Attended UIll. Bdwy debut 1972 in "Via Galactica."

GENTLES, AVRIL. Born Apr. 2, 1929 in Upper Montclair, NJ. Graduate UNC. Bdwy debut 1955 in "The Great Sebastians," followed by "Nude with Violin," "Present Laughter," "My Mother, My Father, and Me," "Jimmy Shine," "Grin and Bare It," "Lysistrata," OB in "Dinny and the Witches," "The Wives," "Now Is the Time."

GERACI, FRANK. Born Sept, 8, 1939 in Bklyn. Attended Yale, HB Studio. Debut 1961 OB in "Color of Darkness," followed by "Mr. Grossman," "Balm in Gilead," "Fantasticks," "Tom Paine," "End of All Things Natural," "Union Street," Bdwy bow 1972 in "Love Suicide at Schofield Barracks."

GIBBONS, ROD. Born June 25, 1949 in Seattle, Wash. Attended UWash. Bdwy debut 1970 in "Child's Play," followed by OB's "Summer Brave."

GIBBS, SHEILA. Born Feb. 16, 1947 in NYC. Graduate NYU. Bdwy debut 1971 in "Two Gentlemen of Verona."

GIBSON, JUDY. Born Sept. 11, 1947 in Trenton, NJ. Graduate Rider Col. Bdwy debut 1970 in "Purlie," followed by "Seesaw," OB in "Sensations," "Manhattan Arrangement," "Two if by Sea."

GIERASCH, STEFAN. Born Feb. 5, 1926 in NYC. On Bdwy in "Kiss and Tell," "Snafu," "Billion Dollar Baby," "Montserrat," "Night Music," "Hatful of Rain," "Compulsion," "Shadow of a Gunman," "War and Peace" (APA), OB in "7 Days of Mourning," "AC/DC," "Owners."

GILBERT, BARBARA. Born July 20 in Brooklyn. Attended AADA, HB Studio. Bdwy debut 1956 in "Pajama Game," followed by "Fiorello!," "Cop-Out," OB in "Threepenny Opera," "Spoon River Anthology."

GILBERT, LOU. Born Aug. 1, 1909 in Sycamore, Ill. Bdwy debut 1945 in "Common Ground," followed by "Beggars Are Coming to Town," "Truckline Cafe," "Dream Girl," "The Whole World Over," "Volpone," "Hope Is a Thing with Feathers," "Sundown Beach," "Detective Story," "Enemy of the People," "Anna Christie," "The Victim," "Whistler's Grandmother," "His and Hers," "Abie's Irish Rose," "Highway Robbery," "Streetcar Named Desire," "Good as Gold," "Diary of Anne Frank," "The Egg," "In the Counting House," "Great White Hope," "Creation of the World and Other Business," "Much Ado about Nothing," OB in "A Month in the Country," "Dig Man," "Dynamite Tonight," "Good Woman of Setzuan," "The Three Sisters," "The Tempest," "King Lear," "Baba Goya."

GILFORD, JACK. Born July 25 in NYC. Bdwy bow 1940 in "Meet the People," followed by "They Should Have Stood in Bed," "Count Me In," "The Live Wire," "Alive and Kicking," "Once Over Lightly," "Diary of Anne Frank," "Romanoff and Juliet," "The Tenth Man," "A Funny Thing Happened . . . ," "Cabaret," "3 Men on a Horse," "No, No, Nanette."

GILLIAN, KAY. Born July 4, 1932 in Evelyn, Minn. Graduate UMinn., UUtah. Debut 1973 OB in "Penthouse Legend."

GIM, ASA. Born May 30, 1945 in Korea. NYU graduate. Debut 1971 OB in "Basic Training of Pavlo Hummel," followed by "Sticks and Bones."

GINGOLD, HERMIONE. Born Dec. 9, 1897 in London. Bdwy debut 1953 in "John Murray Anderson's Almanac," followed by "Sleeping Prince," "First Impressions," "From A to Z," "Milk and Honey," "Oh, Dad, Poor Dad, Mama's Hung You . . . ," "A Little Night Music."

GINSBERG, ALLEN. Born June 3, 1926 in Newark, NJ. Attended Columbia. Debut 1972 OB in "Kaddish."

GINTY, ROBERT. Born Nov. 14, 1948 in Brooklyn. Attended CUNY, Neighborhood Playhouse. Debut 1972 OB in "Three in One," followed by "Silent Partner," Bdwy bow 1972 in "Great God Brown," "Don Juan."

GIRARDEAU, FRANK. Born Oct. 19, 1942 in Beaumont, Tex. Attended Rider Col., HB Studio. Debut 1972 in "22 Years," followed by "The Soldier."

GISH, LILLIAN. Born Oct. 14, 1896 in Springfield, O. Bdwy debut 1930 in "Uncle Vanya," followed by "Camille," "9 Pine Street," "Joyous Season," "Hamlet," "Star Wagon," "Dear Octopus," "Life with Father," "Mr. Sycamore," "Crime and Punishment," "Curious Savage," "Trip to Bountiful," "Family Reunion," (OB), "All the Way Home," "Too True to Be Good," "Anya," "I Never Sang for My Father," "Uncle Vanya" (1973).

GLANVILLE, MAXWELL. Born Feb. 11, 1918 in Antigua, BWI. Attended New School. Bdwy debut 1946 in "Walk Hard," followed by "Anna Lucasta," "How Long Till Summer," "Freight," "Autumn Garden," "Take a Giant Step," "Cat on a Hot Tin Roof," "Simply Heavenly," "Interlock," "Cool World," "The Shrike," "Golden Boy," "We Bombed in New Haven," "Zelda," OB in over 250 plays, including "The Blacks," "Nat Turner," "Simple," "Lady Day."

GLOVER, JOHN. Born Aug. 7, 1944 in Kingston, NY. Attended Towson State Col. Debut OB 1969 in "A Scent of Flowers," followed by "Subject to Fits," "House of Blue Leaves," "Government Inspector," Bdwy in "The Selling of the President," "Great God Brown," "Don Juan."

GOLDRICH, FRED. Born Jan. 20, 1947 in NYC. Graduate NYU, Princeton. Debut OB 1972 in "How to Succeed in Business . . ." (ELT), followed by "Mystery Play."

GOLDSMITH, MERWIN. Born Aug. 7, 1937 in Detroit, Mich. Graduate UCLA. Studied at Old Vic. Bdwy debut 1970 in "Minnie's Boys," OB in "Hamlet as a Happening," "The Chickencoop Chinaman," "Wanted," "Comedy."

GOOD, KAREN. Born Dec. 28, 1948 in Buffalo, NY. Attended AADA. Debut 1972 OB in "How to Succeed in Business . . ." (ELT).

GOODMAN, DODY. Born Oct. 28 in Columbus, O. Bdwy debut 1947 in "High Button Shoes," followed by "Miss Liberty," "Call Me Madam," "Wonderful Town," "Fiorello," "A Rainy Day in Newark," "My Daughter, Your Son," "Front Page," OB in "Shoestring Revue," "Shoestring '57," "Parade," "New Cole Porter Revue."

GOODROW, GARRY. Born Nov. 5, 1938 in Malone, NY. Debut OB 1960 in "Many Loves," followed by "The Connection," "Tonight We Improvise," "In the Jungle of Cities," "National Lampoon's Lemmings," Bdwy in "The Committee," "Story Theatre."

GOODWIN, MICHAEL. Born in Virginia, Minn. Bdwy debut 1969 in "A Patriot for Me," followed by "Charley's Aunt," "Ambassador," "Cyrano," OB in "Colette," "Hamlet" (NYSF).

GORDON, CARL. Born Jan. 20, 1932 in Richmond, Va. Bdwy bow 1966 in "Great White Hope," followed by "Ain't Supposed to Die a Natural Death," OB in "Day of Absence," "Happy Ending," "Strong Breed," "Trials of Brother Jero," "Kongi's Harvest."

GORDON, PEGGY. Born Dec. 26, 1949 in NYC. Attended Carnegie Tech. Debut OB 1971 in "Godspell."

GORMAN, CLIFF. Born Oct. 13, 1936 in NYC. Attended UCLA. OB in "Hogan's Goat," "Boys in the Band," "Ergo," Bdwy bow 1971 in "Lenny."

GORMAN, MARI. Born Sept. 1, 1944 in NYC. Debut 1966 OB in "The Kitchen," followed by "Walking to Waldheim," "The Memorandum," "Hot L Baltimore" for which she received a Theatre World Award.

GOZ, HARRY G. Born June 23, 1932 in St. Louis. Attended St. Louis Inst. Debut 1957 in "Utopia Limited," followed by "Bajour," "Fiddler on the Roof," "Two by Two," "Prisoner of Second Avenue."

GRANDY, FRED. Born June 29, 1948 in Sioux City, Io. Harvard graduate. Debut OB 1971 in "The Proposition," followed by "Green Julia," "The Boy Who Came to Leave."

GRANT, LEE. Born Oct. 31, 1927 in NYC. Attended Neighborhood Playhouse. Bdwy debut 1948 in "Joy to the World," followed by "Detective Story," "Arms and the Man," "Lo and Behold!," "Wedding Breakfast," "A Hole in the Head," "Two for the Seesaw," "The Captains and the Kings," "The Maids" (OB), "Electra" (NYSF), "Prisoner of Second Avenue."

Christian Grey

Karen Grassle

Donald M. Griffith

Carol Hanzel

Ron Harper

GRANT, MICKI. Born June 30 in Chicago. Attended U. Ill., Geller School. Bdwy debut 1963 in "Tambourines to Glory," OB in "Fly Blackbird," "The Blacks," "Brecht on Brecht," "Jerico-Jim Crow," "The Cradle Will Rock," "Leonard Bernstein's Theatre Songs," "To Be Young, Gifted and Black," "Don't Bother Me, I Can't Cope."

GRASSLE, KAREN. Born in Albany, Cal. Graduate UCal., London Acad., Pasadena Playhouse. Bdwy debut 1969 in "The Gingham Dog," followed by "Cymbeline" (NYSF), "Butterflies Are Free."

GREEN, HOWARD. Born March 9 in Detroit, Mich. Graduate UMich. OB in "Darkness at Noon," "Cyrano de Bergerac," "Ceremony of Innocence," NYSF's "Henry VI" and "Richard III," "Anna K," "12 Angry Men."

GREENE, JAMES. Born Dec. 1, 1926 in Lawrence, Mass. Graduate Emerson Col. OB in "The Iceman Cometh," "American Gothic," "The King and the Duke," "The Hostage," "Plays for Bleecker St.," "Moon in the Yellow River," "Misalliance," "The Government Inspector," "Baba Goya," with LCRep 2 years, with APA in "You Can't Take It with You," "School for Scandal," "Wild Duck," "Right You Are," "The Show-Off" and "Pantagleize." Bdwy in "Romeo and Juliet," "Girl on Via Flaminia," "Compulsion," "Inherit the Wind," "Shadow of a Gunman," "Andersonville Trial," "Night Life," "School for Wives," "Ring Round the Bathtub," "Great God Brown," "Don Juan."

GREENHOUSE, MARTHA. Born June 14 in Omaha, Neb. Attended Hunter Col., Theatre Wing. On Bdwy 1942 in "Sons and Soldiers," followed by "Dear Me, the Sky Is Falling," "Family Way," "Woman Is My Idea," OB in "Clerambard," "Our Town," "3 by Ferlinghetti," "No Strings," "Cackle."

GREY, CHRISTIAN. Born Mar. 31, 1938 in Pittsburgh, Pa. Attended Pittsburgh Playhouse. Bdwy debut in "How to Succeed in Business . . . ," followed by "Skyscraper," OB in "Secret Life of Walter Mitty," "Oh Coward!"

GRIFFITH, DONALD M. Born Feb. 2, 1947 in Chicago, Graduate Loyola U. Debut OB 1971 in "Contributions," followed by "The Me Nobody Knows," "Clara's Ol' Man," LCR's "Merchant of Venice" and "A Streetcar Named Desire."

GRIGAS, JOHN. Born Feb. 16, 1930 in Shenandoah, Pa. Bdwy debut 1956 in "Plain and Fancy," followed by "My Fair Lady," and "Milk and Honey," "Baker Street," "It's Superman," "Man of La Mancha," "Dear World," "Follies."

GRIZZARD, GEORGE. Born Apr. 1, 1928 in Roanoke Rapids, Va. Graduate UNC. Bdwy bow 1954 in "All Summer Long," followed by "Desperate Hours," "Happiest Millionaire" for which he received a Theatre World Award, "Disenchanted," "Big Fish Little Fish," with APA 1961–62, "Who's Afraid of Virginia Woolf?," "Glass Menagerie," "You Know I Can't Hear You When the Water's Running," "Noel Coward's Sweet Potato," "Gingham Dog," "Inquest," "The Country Girl," "Creation of the World and Other Business."

GUERRERO, DANNY. Born Oct. 14, 1945 in Tucson, Ariz. Attended UCLA, Pasadena Playhouse. OB in "Hello, Tourista," "Two Gentlemen of Verona," "Devil's Disciple," "Who's Who, Baby," "Manhattan Arrangement," "Hark!"

GUEST, CHRISTOPHER. Born Feb. 5, 1948 in NYC. Attended Bard Col., NYU. Bdwy bow 1970 in "Room Service," followed by "Moonchildren," OB in "Little Murders," "National Lampoon's Lemmings."

GUILLAUME, ROBERT. Born Nov. 30, 1937 in St. Louis, Mo. Bdwy debut 1961 in "Kwamina," followed by "Finian's Rainbow," "Tambourines to Glory," "Porgy and Bess," "Golden Boy," "Purlie," OB in "Charlie Was Here and Now He Is Gone," "Life and Times of J. Walter Smintheus," "Jacques Brel Is Alive. . . ."

GUITTARD, LAURENCE. Born July 16, 1939 in San Francisco, Cal. Graduate Stanford U. Bdwy debut 1965 in "Baker Street," followed by "Anya," "Man of La Mancha," "A Little Night Music" for which he received a Theatre World Award.

GUNN, VINCENETTA. Born Mar. 3, 1944 in Seattle, Wash. Attended SFCC, HB Studio. Bdwy debut 1971 in "Love Suicide at Schofield Barracks," OB in "Rain," "Foul Movement."

GWYNNE, FRED. Born July 10, 1926 in NYC. Harvard graduate. Bdwy debut 1952 in "Mrs. McThing," followed by "Love's Labour's Lost," "Frogs of Spring," "Irma La Douce," "Here's Love," "The Lincoln Mask."

HACKETT, JOAN. Born Mar. 1 in NYC. Attended Actors Studio. OB debut 1959 in "A Clearing in the Woods," followed by "Call Me by My Rightful Name" for which she received a Theatre World Award, Bdwy bow 1959 in "Much Ado about Nothing," followed by "Peterpat," "Park," "Night Watch."

HADGE, MICHAEL. Born June 6, 1932 in Greensboro, NC. Bdwy bow 1958 in "The Cold Wind and the Warm," followed by "Lady of the Camellias," "Impossible Years," OB in "Local Stigmatic," "The Hunter."

HAILEY, MARIAN. Born Feb. 1, 1941 in Portland Ore. U. Wash graduate. Bdwy debut 1965 in "Mating Dance," followed by "Any Wednesday," "Best Laid Plans," "Keep It In The Family," "Harvey," "Company," "The Women,"

OB in "Under the Yum Yum Tree," "Thornton Wilder's Triple Bill," "Castro Complex."

HAINES, A. LARRY. Born Aug. 3, 1917 in Mt. Vernon, NY. Attended CCNY. Bdwy bow 1962 in "A Thousand Clowns," followed by "Generation," "Promises, Promises," "Last of the Red Hot Lovers," "Twigs," "No Hard Feelings."

HALL, ALBERT. Born Nov. 10, 1937 in Boothton, Ala. Columbia graduate. Debut 1971 OB in "Basic Training of Pavlo Hummel," followed by "Duplex" (LC), "Wedding Band," Bdwy in "Ain't Supposed to Die a Natural Death."

HALL, BRUCE. Born Dec. 7, 1919 in NYC. Attended Pasadena Playhouse. On Bdwy in "Joan of Lorraine," "Song of Bernadette," "Seagulls over Sorrento," "Barefoot in Athens," "Southern Exposure," "Traveling Lady," OB in "To Be Young, Gifted and Black," "Thunder Rock."

HALL, PAMELA. Born Oct. 16, 1947 in Champaign, Ill. Attended UIll. OB in "Harold Arlen Songbook," "Frere Jacques," "A Month of Sundays," "Promenade," "Diary of Adam and Eve," Bdwy in "Dear World," "1776," "A Funny Thing Happened on the Way to the Forum."

HALLER, TOBIAS. Born in Baltimore, Md. Graduate Towson State Col. Debut 1971 OB in "Now There's Just the Three of Us," followed by "The Screens," Bdwy bow 1972 in "The Last of Mrs. Lincoln."

HAMILL, MARY. Born Dec. 29, 1943 in Flushing, NY. Graduate UDallas. Debut OB 1969 in "Spiro Who?," followed by "What the Butler Saw," "Siamese Connections," "The Boy Who Came To Leave," Bdwy in "4 on a Garden."

HAMILTON, ROGER. Born in San Diego, Cal., May 2, 1928. Attended San Diego Col., RADA. OB in "Merchant of Venice," "Hamlet," "Live Like Pigs," "Hotel Passionato," "Sjt. Musgrave's Dance," Bdwy in "Someone Waiting," "Separate Tables," "Little Moon of Alban," "Luther," The Deputy," "Rosencrantz and Guildenstern Are Dead," "The Rothschilds," "Pippin."

HAMMER, MARK. Born Apr. 28, 1937 in San Jose, Cal. Graduate Stanford, Catholic U. Debut OB 1966 in "Journey of the Fifth Horse," followed by "Witness for the Prosecution," NYSF's "Cymbeline," Bdwy 1972 in "Much Ado about Nothing."

HANEY, SONJA. Born May 24, 1943 in Portsmouth, Va. Attended LACC. Bdwy debut 1972 in "A Funny Thing Happened on the Way to the Forum."

HANLEY, KATIE. Born Jan. 17, 1949 in Evanston, Ill. Attended Carnegie-Mellon U. Debut 1971 OB in "Godspell," followed by "Grease."

HANZEL, CAROL. Born Dec. 17, 1945 in Brooklyn. Debut 1966 in LC's "Show Boat," followed by "West Side Story" (LC), Bdwy in "Sherry," "Cabaret," "Promises, Promises," OB in "Beggar's Opera."

HARE, WILL. Born Mar. 30, 1919 in Elkins, WVa. Attended Am. Actors Theatre. Credits: "The Eternal Road," "The Moon Is Down," "Suds in Your Eye," "Only the Heart," "The Visitor," "Trip to Bountiful," "Witness for the Prosecution," "Marathon '33," OB in "The Viewing," "Winter Journey," "Dylan," "Older People," "Crystal and Fox."

HARMON, JILL. Born in NYC, Apr. 25, 1949. Attended Northwestern Debut 1962 OB in "Black Monday," followed by "Rate of Exchange," Bdwy in "Fiddler on the Roof."

HARNEY, BEN. Born Aug. 29, 1952 in Bklyn. Bdwy debut 1971 in "Purlie," OB in "Don't Bother Me, I Can't Cope."

HARPER, RON. Born Jan. 12, 1936 in Turtle Creek, Pa. Princeton graduate. Debut OB 1955 in "3 by Dylan Thomas," followed by "A Palm Tree in a Rose Garden," Bdwy in "Sweet Bird of Youth," "Night Circus," "6 Rms Riv Vu."

HARRIS, CYNTHIA. Born in NYC. Graduate Smith Col. Bdwy debut 1963 in "Natural Affection," followed by "Any Wednesday," "Best Laid Plans," "Company," OB in "The Premise," "Three by Wilder," "America Hurrah," "White House Murder Case," "Mystery Play."

HARRIS, JULIE. Born Dec. 2, 1925 in Grosse Point, Mich. Attended Yale, Bdwy debut 1945 in "It's a Gift," followed by "Henry V," "Oedipus," "The Playboy of the Western World, "Alice in Wonderland," "Macbeth," "Sundown Beach" for which she received a Theatre World Award, "The Young and The Fair," "Magnolia Alley," "Montserrat," "The Member of the Wedding." "I Am a Camera," "Mlle. Colombe," "The Lark," "Country Wife," "Warm Peninsula," "Little Moon of Alban," "A Shot in the Dark," "Marathon '33," "Ready When You Are, C.B," "Hamlet" (CP), "Skyscraper," "40 Carats," "And Miss Reardon Drinks A Little," "Voices," "The Last of Mrs. Lincoln."

HARRIS, ROSEMARY. Born Sept. 19, 1930 in Ashby, Eng. Attended RADA. Bdwy debut 1952 in "Climate of Eden" for which she received a Theatre World Award, followed by "Troilus and Cressida," "Interlock," "The Disenchanted," "The Tumbler," APA's "The Tavern, "School for Scandal," "Seagull," "Importance of Being Earnest," "War and Peace" "Man and Superman," "Judith" and "You Can't Take It with You," "Lion in Winter," "Old Times," LC's "Merchant of Venice" and "Streetcar Named Desire."

Hilda Haynes   Bob Heath   Barbara Heuman   Randy Herron   Joy Hodges

HARRISON, REX. Born Mar. 5, 1908 in Huyten, Eng. Attended Liverpool Col. Bdwy debut 1936 in "Sweet Aloes," followed by "Anne of a Thousand Days," "Bell, Book, and Candle," "Venus Observed," "The Love of Four Colonels," "My Fair Lady," "Fighting Cock," "Emperor Henry IV."

HAWKINS, TRISH. Born Oct. 30, 1945 in Hartford, Conn. Attended Radcliffe, Neighborhood Playhouse. Debut OB 1970 in "Oh! Calcutta!" followed by "Iphigenia," "The Hot L Baltimore" for which she received a Theatre World Award.

HAYESON, JIMMY. Born June 27, 1924 in Carthage, NC. Graduate NC Col. Debut 1969 OB in "Black Quartet," followed by "Black Girl," Bdwy 1971 in "Ain't Supposed to Die a Natural Death."

HAYNES, HILDA. Born in NYC. Attended Braithwaite Col. Bdwy debut 1948 in "A Streetcar Names Desire," followed by "Anna Lucasta," "King of Hearts," "Wisteria Trees," "Lost in the Stars," "The Long Dream," "Irregular Verb to Love," "Blues for Mr. Charlie," "Golden Boy," "Great White Hope," OB in "Monday Heroes," "Trouble in Mind," "Take a Giant Step," "Wedding Band."

HEARN, GEORGE. Born June 18, 1934 in St. Louis. Graduate Southwestern Col. In NYSF's "Macbeth," "Antony and Cleopatra," "As You Like It," "Richard III," and "Henry IV," OB in "Horseman, Pass By," Bdwy in "A Time for Singing," "Changing Room."

HEATH, BOB. Born Dec. 30, 1948 in Arlington, Tex. Graduate UOkla, SMU. Bdwy debut 1973 in "Cyrano."

HECHT, PAUL. Born Aug. 16, 1941 in London. Attended McGill U. OB in "Sjt. Musgrave's Dance" and "MacBird," Bdwy in "Rosencrantz and Guildenstern Are Dead," "1776," "The Rothschilds," "The Ride Across Lake Constance" (LC), "Great God Brown," "Don Juan," "Emperor Henry IV."

HEFFERNAN, JOHN. Born May 30, 1934 in NYC. Attended CCNY, Columbia, Boston U. OB in "The Judge," "Julius Caesar," "Great God Brown," "Lysistrata," "Peer Gynt," "Henry IV," "Taming of the Shrew," "She Stoops to Conquer," "The Plough and the Stars," "Octoroon," "Hamlet," "Androcles and the Lion," "A Man's a Man," "Winter's Tale," "Arms and the Man," "St. Joan" (LCR), "Peer Gynt" (CP), "Memorandum," "Invitation to a Beheading," "Shadow of a Gunman," Bdwy in "Luther," "Tiny Alice," "Postmark Zero," "Woman Is My Idea," "Morning, Noon and Night," "Purlie."

HEFLIN, MARTA. Born Mar. 29, 1945 in Washington, DC. Attended Northwestern, Carnegie Tech. Debut 1967 in "Life With Father" (CC), followed OB in "Salvation," "Soon," "Wedding of Iphigenia," Bdwy debut 1972 in "Jesus Christ Superstar."

HEIGHLEY, BRUCE. Born May 7, 1939 in Liverpool, Eng. Attended St. Anselms Col. Bdwy debut 1970 in "Borstal Boy," followed by "Dear Oscar" (OB).

HELD, DAN. Born May 20, 1948 in NYC. Graduate Hofstra U. Debut 1973 OB in "You Never Know."

HELFEND, DENNIS. Born Mar. 15, 1939 in Los Angeles. Attended UCLA. Debut 1968 OB in "The Mad Show," followed by "American Gothics," Bdwy in "Man in the Glass Booth."

HELMERS, JUNE. Born Oct. 21, 1941 in Middletown, O. Attended Carnegie Tech. Bdwy debut 1967 in "Hello, Dolly!," followed by "Oklahoma!" (LC), OB in "Johnny Johnson," "Beggar's Opera."

HELMOND, KATHERINE. Born in Galveston, Tex. OB 1959 in "Orpheus Descending," followed by "Trip to Bountiful," "The Time of Your Life," "Another Part of the Forest," "Mousetrap," "House of Blue Leaves," "Karl Marx Play," Bdwy debut 1972 in "Great God Brown," "Don Juan."

HEMSLEY, SHERMAN. Born Feb. 1, 1938 in Philadelphia. Attended Phila. Academy of Dramatic Arts. Debut 1968 OB in "The People vs. Ranchman," Bdwy in "Purlie."

HENDRY, TIFFANY Born Oct. 13, 1942 in Waterbury, Conn. Attended Boston U., Neighborhood Playhouse. Debut OB 1963 in "The Trojan Women," followed by "Getting Married," "Brotherhood," "A Maid's Tragedy."

HENREID, PAUL. Born Jan. 10, 1908 in Trieste, Italy. Bdwy debut 1940 in "Flight to the West," followed by "Festival," "Don Juan in Hell."

HENRITZE, BETTE. Born May 3 in Betsy Layne, Ky. Graduate U. Tenn. OB in "Lion in Love," "Abe Lincoln in Illinois," "Othello," "Baal," "Long Christmas Dinner," "Queens of France," "Rimers of Eldritch," "Displaced Person," "Acquisition," "Crime of Passion," "Happiness Cage," NYSF's "Henry VI," "Richard III," "Older People," Bdwy debut 1948 in "Jenny Kissed Me," followed by "Pictures in the Hallway," "Giants, Sons of Giants," "Ballad of the Sad Cafe," "The White House," "Dr. Cook's Garden," "Here's Where I Belong," "Much Ado about Nothing."

HEPPLE, JEANNE. Born in London; attended ULondon. Bdwy debut 1965 in "Inadmissible Evidence," followed by "A Touch of the Poet," "Tonight at 8:30," "Imaginary Invalid," NYSF's "Henry VI," and "Richard III," "How the Other Half Loves," "Night Watch," "Much Ado about Nothing," OB in "Sjt. Musgrave's Dance," "Early Morning," "Reliquary of Mr. and Mrs. Potterfield," "The Orphan."

HERLIE, EILEEN. Born Mar. 8, 1920 in Glasgow, Scot. Bdwy debut 1955 in "The Matchmaker," followed by "Makropoulos Secret" (OB), "Epitaph for George Dillon," "Take Me Along," "All American," "Photo Finish," "Hamlet," "Halfway up the Tree," "Emperor Henry IV."

HERRON, RANDY. Born Apr. 26, 1946 in Los Angeles, Cal. Attended Neighborhood Playhouse. Debut 1969 OB in "Your Own Thing," Bdwy bow 1972 in "Tricks."

HEUMAN, BARBARA. Born Feb. 24, 1944 in Montrose, Pa. Graduate UWash. Debut 1970 OB in "Dames at Sea," Bdwy 1971 in "No, No, Nanette."

HEYMAN, BARTON. Born Jan. 24, 1937 in Washington, DC. Attended UCLA. Bdwy debut 1969 in "Indians," followed by "Trial of Catonsville 9," OB in "Midsummer Night's Dream," "Sleep," "Phantasmagoria Historia . . ."

HICKEY, WILLIAM. Born in Bklyn. Studied at HB Studio, Bdwy bow 1951 in "St. Joan," followed by "Tovarich," "Miss Lonelyhearts," "Body Beautiful," "Make a Million," "Not Enough Rope," "Happy Birthday, Wanda June," "Small Craft Warnings," "Mourning Becomes Electra," "Siamese Connections."

HIGGINS, MICHAEL. Born Jan. 20, in Bklyn. Attended Theatre Wing. Bdwy bow 1946 in "Antigone," followed by "Our Lan'," "Romeo and Juliet," "The Crucible," "The Lark," OB in "White Devil," "Carefree Tree," "Easter," "The Queen and the Rebels," "Sally, George and Martha," "L'Ete," "Uncle Vanya."

HIKEN, GERALD. Born May 23, 1927 in Milwaukee, Wis. Attended UWis. OB in "Cherry Orchard," "Seagull," "Good Woman of Setzuan," "The Misanthrope," "The Iceman Cometh," "The New Theatre," Bdwy in "Lovers," "Cave Dwellers," "Nervous Set," "Fighting Cock," "49th Cousin," "Gideon," "Foxy," "Three Sisters."

HILLMAN, LORI. Born Sept. 15, 1951 in NYC. Attended NYU, HB Studio. Debut 1973 OB in "Spoon River Anthology."

HINES, PATRICK. Born Mar. 17, 1930 in Burkesville, Tex. Graduate Tex.U. Debut OB in "Duchess of Malfi," followed by "Lysistrata," "Peer Gynt," "Henry IV," Bdwy bow 1959 in "Great God Brown," subsequently "Passage to India," "The Devils," "Cyrano."

HINNANT, BILL. Born Aug. 28, 1935 on Chincoteague Island, Va. Yale Graduate. Bdwy in "No Time for Sergeants," followed by "Here's Love," "Frank Merriwell," "Hurry Harry," OB in "All Kinds of Giants," "Put It in Writing," "You're A Good Man, Charlie Brown," "American Hamburger League," "God Bless Coney."

HIRSCH, JUDD. Born Mar. 15, 1935 in NYC. Attended AADA. Bdwy debut 1966 in "Barefoot in the Park," followed OB in "On the Necessity of Being Polygamous," "Scuba Duba," "Mystery Play," "Hot L Baltimore."

HOCTOR, ROBIN. Born Oct. 6, 1953 in NYC. Bdwy debut 1972 in "Sugar."

HODAPP, ANN. Born May 6, 1946 in Louisville, Ky. Attended Hunter, NYU. Debut OB 1968 in "You're A Good Man, Charlie Brown," followed by "A Round with Ring," "House of Leather," "Shoestring Revue" "God Bless Coney," "What's a Nice Country like You . . ."

HODGES, JOY. Born in Des Moines, Io. Bdwy debut 1937 in "I'd Rather Be Right," followed by "Best Foot Forward," "Something for the Boys," "Dream with Music," "The Odds on Mrs. Oakley," "Nellie Bly," "No, No, Nanette."

HOFFMAN, JANE. Born July 24 in Seattle, Wash. Attended U. Cal. Bdwy debut 1940 in "Tis of Thee," followed by "Crazy with the Heat," "Something for the Boys," "One Touch of Venus," "Calico Wedding," "Mermaids Singing," "A Temporary Island," "Story for Strangers," "Two Blind Mice," "The Rose Tattoo," "The Crucible," "Witness for the Prosecution," "Third Best Sport," "Rhinoceros," "Mother Courage and Her Children," "Fair Game for Lovers," "A Murderer among Us," OB in "American Dream," "Sandbox," "Picnic on the Battlefield," "Theatre of The Absurd," "Child Buyer," "A Corner of The Bed," "Someone's Comin' Hungry," "Increased Difficulty of Concentration" (LC), "American Hamburger League," "Slow Memories," "Last Analysis," "Dear Oscar."

HOGAN, JONATHAN. Born June 13, 1951 in Chicago, Ill. Graduate Goodman Theatre. Debut OB 1972 in "The Hot L Baltimore."

David Huffman   Tresa Hughes   Robert L. Hultman   Bella Jarrett   William James

HOLLANDER, JACK. Born Jan. 29, 1918 in Chicago. Graduate Goodman Theatre. Bdwy debut 1959 in "Miracle Worker," followed by "All the Way Home," "Gideon," "Impossible Years," "Man in the Glass Booth," "Inquest," OB in "Girl of the Golden West," "Dybbuk," "Journey to the Day," NYSF's "Titus Andronicus" and "Comedy of Errors," "Ergo," "Phantasmagoria Historia . . ."

HOLLIDAY, POLLY. Born in Jasper, Ala. Attended Ala. Col., Fla. State U. Debut OB 1964 in "Orphee," followed by "Dinner on the Ground," "Wedding Band," "Girls Most Likely to Succeed."

HOLLY, ELLEN. Born Jan. 17, 1931 in NYC. Graduate Hunter Col. Debut OB 1955 in "2 for Fun," followed by "Salome," "A Florentine Tragedy," "Tevya and His Daughters," "Othello," "Moon on a Rainbow Shawl," "Antony and Cleopatra," "Funny House of a Negro," "Midsummer Night's Dream," "Cherry Orchard," Bdwy in "Too Late the Phalarope," "Face of a Hero," "Tiger, Tiger Burning Bright," NYSF's "Henry V," and "Taming of the Shrew," "A Hand Is on the Gate."

HOOKS, DAVID. Born Jan. 9, 1920 in Smithfield, NC. Graduate UNC. Bdwy deput 1950 in "Pride's Crossing," followed by "Golden Apple," "Gideon," "Gantry," OB in "Ardele," "Antigone," "Zoo Story," "American Dream," "Corruption in the Palace of Justice," "Medea," APA's "Seagull," "Tavern," "School for Scandal," NYSF's "Antony and Cleopatra," and "Henry IV," "Small Craft Warnings."

HOUSE, JANE. Born in 1946 in Panama City, Pan. Attended Stanford U. Bdwy debut 1971 in "Lenny."

HOUSE, RON. Born in Chicago. Attended Wilson Col., Roosevelt U. Debut OB 1973 in "El Grande de Coca Cola."

HOWARD, KEN. Born Mar. 28, 1944 in El Centro, Cal. Yale graduate. Bdwy debut 1968 in "Promises, Promises," followed by "1776" for which he received a Theatre World Award, "Child's Play," "Seesaw."

HUFFMAN, DAVID. Born May 10, 1945 in Berwin, Ill. Bdwy debut 1971 in "Butterflies Are Free," followed by OB's "Small Craft Warnings."

HUGHES, BARNARD. Born July 16, 1915 in Bedford Hills, N.Y. Attended Manhattan Col. OB in "Rosmersholm," "A Doll's House," "Hogan's Goat," "Line," "Older People," "Hamlet" (NYSF), Bdwy in "The Ivy Green," "Dinosaur Wharf," "Teahouse of The August Moon" (CC), "A Majority of One," "Advise and Consent," "The Advocate," "Hamlet," "I Was Dancing," "Generation," "How Now, Dow Jones?," "Wrong Way Light Bulb," "Sheep On The Runway," "Abelard and Heloise," "Much Ado about Nothing," "Uncle Vanya."

HUGHES, TRESA. Born Sept. 17, 1929 in Washington, DC. Attended Wayne U. OB in "Electra," "The Crucible," "Hogan's Goat," "Party On Greenwich Avenue," "Fragments," "Passing Through from Exotic Places," "Beggar On Horseback" (LC), "Early Morning," Bdwy in "Miracle Worker," "Devil's Advocate," "Dear Me, The Sky Is Falling," "Last Analysis," "Spofford," "Man In The Glass Booth," "Prisoner of Second Avenue."

HULTMAN, ROBERT L. Born Nov. 15, 1927 in East Grand Rapids, Mich. Attended Chicago Cons. Bdwy debut 1963 in "Luther," followed by "Kelly," "Hello, Dolly!," "Carnival" (CC), "Ambassador."

HUMMERT, JAMES. Born June 30, 1944 in USA. Graduate UConn. Debut OB 1969 in "Three Cuckolds," followed by "Murder in the Cathedral," "Restoration of Arnold Middleton," Bdwy in "The Changing Room."

HUMPHREY, CAVADA. Born June 17, in Atlantic City, NJ. Smith Col. Graduate. Debut OB 1943 in "A Man's House," followed by "Moon in Capricorn," "Girl of the Golden West," "Dear Liar," "Life Is a Dream," "Madame de Sade," Bdwy in "House in Paris," "Song of Bernadette," "As the Girls Go," "Time Remembered," CC's "Devil's Disciple," "Richard III," "Othello," and "Henry IV," "You Can't Take It with You" (APA), "Candida."

HUNTER, KIM. Born Nov. 12, 1922 in Detroit, Mich. Attended Actors Studio. Bdwy debut 1947 in "A Streetcar Named Desire," followed by "Darkness at Noon," "The Chase," "The Children's Hour," "Tender Trap," "Come Slowly, Eden" (OB), "Write Me a Murder," "Weekend," "Penny Wars," "The Women."

HUPPELER, CINDIA. Born Jan. 29, 1951 in Boston, Mass. Juilliard graduate. Debut OB 1972 in "School for Scandal," followed by "The Hostage," "Women Beware Women."

HURNEY, KATE. Born in Quincey, Mass. Graduate Tufts U. Debut OB 1960 in "Beautiful Dreamer," followed by "Galileo" (LC), "Mother of Us All."

HUSMANN, RON. Born June 30, 1937 in Rockford, Ill. Attended Northwestern, On Bdwy in "Fiorello!" "Greenwillow," "Tenderloin" for which he received a Theatre World Award, "Ali American," "Lovely Ladies, Kind Gentlemen," "Look Where I'm At" (OB). "On the Town," "Irene."

HYDE-WHITE, WILFRID. Born May 12, 1903 in Glouestershire, Eng. Attended RADA. Bdwy debut 1947 in "Under The Counter," followed by "Antony and Cleopatra," "Reluctant Debutante," "Caesar and Cleopatra," "Jockey Club Stakes."

HYMAN, EARLE. Born Oct. 11, 1926 in Rocky Mount, NC. Attended New School, Theatre Wing. Bdwy debut 1943 in "Run, Little Chillun," followed by "Anna Lucasta," "Climate of Eden," "Merchant of Venice," "Othello," "Julius Caesar," "The Tempest," "No Time for Sergeants," "Mr. Johnson" for which he received a Theatre World Award, "St. Joan," "Hamlet," "Waiting for Godot," "Duchess of Malfi," "Les Blancs," OB in "The White Rose and the Red," "Worlds of Shakespeare," "Jonah," "Life and Times of J. Walter Smintheus," "Orrin," "Cherry Orchard."

IRVING, GEORGE S. Born Nov. 1, 1922 in Springfield, Mass. Attended Leland Powers Sch. Bdwy bow 1943 in "Oklahoma!," followed by "Call Me Mister," "Along Fifth Avenue," "Two's Company," "Me and Juliet," "Can-Can," "Shinbone Alley," "Bells are Ringing," "The Good Soup," "Tovarich," "A Murderer Among Us," "Alfie," "Anya," "Galileo" (LC), "The Happy Time," "Up Eden" (OB), "4 on a Garden," "An Evening with Richard Nixon and . . ." "Irene."

IVES, ANNE. Born in Providence, RI. Attended Sargent's School, Am. Th. Wing. Bdwy debut 1906 in "The Chorus Lady," after many years in London returned in 1952 to Bdwy in "Point of No Return," followed by "Masquerade," "The Crucible" (OB), "Effect of Gamma Rays on Man-in-the-Moon Marigolds," (OB), "Good Woman of Setzuan" (LC).

JACKSON, LEONARD. (formerly L. Errol Jaye) Born Feb. 7, 1928 in Jacksonville, Fla. Graduate Fisk U. Debut 1965 OB in "Troilus and Cressida" (NYSF), followed by "Henry V," "Happy Ending," "Day of Absence," "Who's Got His Own?," "Electronic Nigger and Others," "Black Quartet," "Five on the Blackhand Side," "Boesman and Lena," "Murderous Angels," "Chickencoop Chinaman," "The Karl Marx Play," Bdwy in "Great White Hope," "Lost in the Stars."

JACOBS, WILL. Born July 14, 1945 in Center, Tex. Graduate Lamar U., UCLA. Debut OB 1969 in "Your Own Thing," followed by "National Lampoon's Lemmings," Bdwy 1972 in "Mother Earth."

JAMES, WILLIAM. Born Apr. 29, 1938 in Jersey City, NJ. Graduate NJ State Teachers Col. Bdwy debut 1962 in "Camelot," followed by "Maggie Flynn," "Coco," CC's "Where's Charley?," and "My Fair Lady," OB in "Anything Goes," "Smith."

JAMIN-BARTLETT, D. Born May 21, 1948 in NYC. Attended AADA. Bdwy debut 1973 in "A Little Night Music" for which she received a Theatre World Award.

JANIS, CONRAD. Born Feb. 11, 1928 in NYC. Bdwy debut 1942 in "Junior Miss," followed by "Dark of the Moon," "The Next Half Hour," "Brass Ring" for which he received a Theatre World Award, "Time Out for Ginger," "Terrible Swift Sword," "Visit to a Small Planet," "Make a Million," "Sunday in New York," "Marathon '33," "Front Page," "No Hard Feelings."

JARRETT, BELLA. Born Feb. 9, 1931 in Adairsville, Ga. Graduate Wesleyan Col. Debut OB 1958 in "Waltz of the Toreadors," followed by "Hedda Gabler," "The Browning Version," "Cicero," "Pequod," "Welcome to Andromeda."

JARRETT, JERRY. Born Sept. 9, 1918 in Brooklyn. Attended New Theatre School. OB in "Waiting for Lefty," "Nat Turner," "Me Candido," "That 5 A.M. Jazz," Bdwy bow 1948 in "At War with the Army," followed by "Gentlemen Prefer Blondes," "Stalag 17," "Fiorello," "Fiddler on the Roof."

JEFFERS, DOUG. Born Apr. 15, 1942 in Denver, Colo. Graduate UColo. Debut OB 1973 in "The Secret Life of Walter Mitty."

JEFFERSON, HERBERT, JR. Born Sept. 28, 1946 in Sandersville, Ga. Attended Rutgers U., AADA. Debut OB in "Damn Yankees," followed by "Black Electra," "Murderous Angels," "The Blacks," "Dream on Monkey Mountain," Bdwy in "Great White Hope," "Last of Mrs. Lincoln."

JETHRO, PHIL. Born Sept. 10, 1947 in Minneapolis, Minn. Attended UCLA. Bdwy debut 1971 in "Jesus Christ Superstar."

JOHANN, JOHN. Born Dec. 23, 1942 in Madison, Wisc. Attended LA State Col. Debut OB 1966 in "Autumn's Here," followed by "My Fair Lady" (CC), "Me and Juliet" (ELT), Bdwy in "Come Summer," "Follies."

JOHNS, GLYNIS. Born Oct. 5, 1923 in Pretoria, S.Af. Bdwy debut 1952 in "Gertie," followed by "Major Barbara," "Too True to Be Good," "A Little Night Music."

JOHNSON, BOBBY. Born Oct. 26, 1946 in San Francisco, Cal. Bdwy debut 1968 in "Hello, Dolly!," followed by "Seesaw."

JOHNSON, DOTTS. Born Feb. 3 in Baltimore, Md. Bdwy debut 1950 in "Freight," followed by "Anna Lucasta," OB in " Freeman."

| Suzanne Johnson | Page Johnson | Judy Kahan | Curt Karibalis | Anita Keal |

JOHNSON, ONNI. Born Mar. 16, 1949 in NYC. Graduate Brandeis U. Debut 1964 in "Unfinished Business," followed by "She Stoops to Conquer," "22 Years," Bdwy in "Oh! Calcutta!"

JOHNSON, PAGE. Born Aug. 25, 1930 in Welch, W. Va. Graduate Ithaca Col. Bdwy bow 1951 in "Romeo and Juliet," followed by "Electra," "Oedipus," "Camino Real," "In April Once" for which he received a Theatre World Award, "Red Roses for Me," "The Lovers," OB in "The Enchanted," "Guitar," " 4 in 1," "Journey of the Fifth Horse," APA's "School for Scandal," "The Tavern" and "The Seagull," "Odd Couple," "Boys In The Band," "Medea."

JOHNSON, SUZANNE. Born Sept. 29 in Washington, DC. Graduate Beloit Col. Debut OB 1973 in "The Cherry Orchard."

JOHNSTON, AUDRE. Born July 22, 1939 in Chicago. Attended Northwestern U. Debut OB 1962 in "Half Past Wednesday," followed by "The Elizabethans."

JOHNSTON, GAIL. Born Aug. 8, 1943 in Far Rockaway, NY. Attended Hofstra, Hunter Col. Bdwy debut 1959 in "Juno," followed by "Tenderloin," "Do Re Mi," OB in "Streets of NY," "Shoemaker's Holiday," "Out of This World."

JOHNSTON, JUSTINE. Born June 13 in Evanston, Ill. OB debut 1959 in "Little Mary Sunshine," followed by "The Time of Your Life" (LC), Bdwy in "Pajama Game," "Milk and Honey," "Follies," "Irene."

JONES, CHARLOTTE. Born Jan. 1 in Chicago. Attended Loyola, DePaul U. OB in "False Confessions," "Sign of Jonah," "Girl on the Via Flaminia," "Red Roses for Me," "Night Is Black Bottles," "Camino Real," "Plays for Bleecker St.," "Pigeons," "Great Scot!" "Sjt. Musgrave's Dance," "Papers," "Johnny Johnson," "Beggar's Opera," Bdwy in "Camino Real," "Buttrio Square," "Mame," "How Now Dow Jones."

JONES, JAMES EARL. Born Jan. 17, 1931 in Arkabutla, Miss. Graduate Mich U. OB in "The Pretender," "The Blacks," "Clandestine on the Morning Line," "The Apple," "A Midsummer Night's Dream," "Moon on a Rainbow Shawl" for which he received a Theatre World Award. "PS 193," "Last Minstrel," "Love Nest," "Bloodknot," "Othello," "Baal," "Danton's Death" (LC), "Boesman and Lena," "Hamlet" (NYSF) "Cherry Orchard," Bdwy in "The Egghead," "Sunrise at Campobello," "The Cool World," " A Hand is on the Gate," "Great White Hope," "Les Blancs."

JONES, TOM LEE. Born Sept. 15, 1946 in San Saba, Tex. Harvard graduate. Bdwy debut 1969 in "A Patriot for Me," followed by "4 on a Garden," "Blue Boys" (OB).

JORDAN, CLIFFORD, JR. Born Sept. 2, 1931 in Chicago, Ill. Debut OB 1972 in "Lady Day."

JOY, SIGNA. Born Sept. 18, 1947 in Springfield, Ill. Bdwy debut 1971 in "Hair," followed by "Two Gentlemen of Verona," "Lady Day" (OB).

JOYCE, ELAINE. Born Dec. 19, 1945 in Cleveland, O. Attended UCLA. Bdwy debut 1972 in "Sugar" for which she received a Theatre World Award.

JUDE, PATRICK. Born Feb. 25, 1951 in Jersey City, NJ. Bdwy debut 1972 in "Jesus Christ Superstar."

JULIA, RAUL. Born Mar. 9, 1940 in San Juan, PR. Graduate UPR. OB in "Macbeth," "Titus Andronicus" (CP), "Theatre in the Streets," "Life Is A dream" "Blood Wedding," "Ox Cart," "No Exit," "Memorandum," "Frank Gagliano's City Scene," "Your Own Thing," "Persians," "Castro Complex," "Pinkville," "Hamlet" (NYSF), Bdwy bow 1968 in "The Cuban Thing," followed by "Indians," "Two Gentlemen of Verona," "Via Galactica."

JUNDELIN, ROBERT. Born March 8 in NYC. Attended Boston U., Neighborhood Playhouse. Debut OB 1964 in "Midsummer Night's Dream," followed by "Iphigenia in Aulis," "Foreplay," Bdwy in "The Impossible Years," "No Sex Please, We're British."

KAGAN, DIANE. Born in Maplewood, NJ. Graduate Fla. State U. Debut OB 1963 in "Asylum," followed by "Days and Nights of Beebee Fenstermaker," "Death of the Well-Loved Boy," "Madame de Sade," "Blue Boys," Bdwy in "Chinese Prime Minister," "Never Too Late," "Any Wednesday," "Venus Is," "Tiger at the Gates" (LC).

KAHAN, JUDY. Born May 24, 1948 in NYC. Graduate Boston U. Debut OB 1971 in "The Proposition," followed by "Godspell," Bdwy in "A Little Night Music,"

KALLAN, RANDI. Born Oct. 9, 1950 in Chicago. Attended LACC, HB Studio. Debut OB 1972 in "Speed Gets the Poppys."

KARIBALIS, CURT. Born Feb. 24, 1947 in Superior, Wis. Graduate UWis. Debut OB 1971 in "Woyzeck," Bdwy in "Great God Brown," "Don Juan."

KARR, PATTI. Born July 10 in St. Paul, Minn. Attended TCU. Bdwy debut 1953 in "Maggie," followed by "Carnival in Flanders," "Pipe Dream," "Bells Are Ringing," "New Girl in Town," "Body Beautiful," "Bye Bye Birdie," "New Faces of 1962," "Come on Strong," "Look to the Lilies," "Different Times," "Lysistrata," OB in "A Month of Sundays," "Up Eden."

KASON, CORINNE. Born Mar. 10 in San Francisco. Attended San Jose State Col. Debut 1968 OB in "Futz" followed by "By Jupiter," "Unfair to Goliath," Bdwy bow 1969 in "Fiddler on the Roof."

KASS, ALAN. Born Apr. 23, 1928 in Chicago. Graduate CCNY. Bdwy bow 1968 in "Golden Rainbow," followed by "Sugar," OB in "Guitar."

KEAL, ANITA. Born in Philadelphia. Graduate Syracuse U. Debut OB 1956 in "Private Life of the Master Race," followed by "Brothers Karamazov," "Hedda Gabler," "Witches' Sabbath," "Six Characters in Search of an Author," "Yes, My Darling Daughter," "Speed Gets the Poppys."

KEEL, HOWARD. Born Apr. 13, 1919 in Gillespie, Ill. Bdwy debut 1945 in "Carousel," followed by "Oklahoma!," "Saratoga," "No Strings," "Ambassador."

KEELER, RUBY. Born Aug. 25, 1910 in Halifax, N.S., Can. Bdwy debut 1923 in "The Rise of Rosie O'Reilly," followed by "Show Girl," "Bye Bye, Bonnie," "Lucky," "Sidewalks of New York" "Hold on to Your Hats," films, retirement, and "No, No, Nanette" in 1970.

KEES, JOHN DAVID. Born in Brookhaven, Miss. Graduate La. State U., Columbia. Debut 1972 OB in "Small Craft Warnings."

KEIPER, ROBERT. Born Sept. 18, 1935 in Akron, O. Attended Ohio State U. Debut OB 1973 in "Penthouse Legend."

KELLOGG, RILEY. Born May 5, 1961 in NYC. Debut 1972 OB in "And They Put Handcuffs on the Flowers."

KELLSTROM, GAIL. Born June 24, 1944 in Newark, NJ. Graduate Rutgers, Penn State. Debut OB 1970 in "Second Cummings," followed by "Yerma," "In White America."

KELLY, PATSY. Born Jan. 12, 1910 in Bklyn. Bdwy debut 1928 in "Three Cheers," followed by "Earl Carroll's Sketch Book," "Vanities," "Wonder Bar," "Flying Colors," "Dear Charles," "No, No, Nanette," "Irene."

KELTON, GENE. Born Oct. 21, 1938 in Flagstaff, Ariz. Bdwy in "Once upon a Mattress," "Destry Rides Again," "Subways Are for Sleeping," "Here's Love," "Fade Out-Fade In," "Skyscraper," "Mame," "Dear World," "Applause," "Contrast" (OB)

KERCHEVAL, KEN. Born July 15, 1935 in Indiana. Attended Pacific U., Neighborhood Playhouse. OB in "Dead End," "Young Abe Lincoln," "Black Monday," "A Man's a Man," "23 Pat O'Brien Movies," "Father Uxbridge Wants to Marry," "Horseman, Pass By," "Who's Happy Now?," "Berlin to Broadway," Bdwy in "Something about a Soldier," "Fiddler on the Roof," "Happily Never After," "The Apple Tree," "Cabaret," "Father's Day."

KERR, ELAINE. Born Apr. 20, 1942 in Indianapolis, Ind. Graduate Ind. U. Bdwy debut 1971 in "No Place to Be Somebody," followed by "Night Watch," OB in "Trojan Women," "Contrast."

KERR, PHILIP. Born Apr. 9, 1940 in NYC. Attended Harvard, London's AMDA. Bdwy debut 1969 in "Tiny Alice," followed by "A Flea in Her Ear," "Three Sisters," "Hamlet" (OB), "Jockey Club Stakes."

KERT, LARRY. Born Dec. 5, 1934 in Los Angeles. Attended LACC. Bdwy bow 1953 in "John Murray Anderson's Almanac," followed by "Ziegfeld Follies," "Mr. Wonderful," "Walk Tall," "Look Ma, I'm Dancin'," "Tickets, Please," "West Side Story," "A Family Affair," "Breakfast at Tiffany's," "Cabaret," "La Strada," "Company," "Two Gentlemen of Verona."

KEYES, DANIEL. Born Mar. 6, 1914 in Concord, Mass. Attended Harvard. Bdwy debut 1954 in "The Remarkable Mr. Pennypacker," followed by "Bus Stop," "Only in America," "Christine," "First Love," "Take Her, She's Mine," "Baker Street," "Dinner at 8," "I Never Sang for My Father," "Wrong Way Light Bulb," "A Place for Polly," "Scratch," OB in "Our Town," "Epitaph for George Dillon," "Plays for Bleecker Street," "Hooray! It's a Glorious Day!," "Six Characters in Search of an Author," "Sjt. Musgrave's Dance," "Arms and the Man," "Mourning Becomes Electra."

KILEY, RICHARD. Born Mar. 31, 1922 in Chicago. Attended Loyola U. Bdwy debut 1953 in "Misalliance" for which he received a Theatre World Award, followed by "Kismet," "Sing Me No Lullaby," "Time Limit!" "Redhead," "Advise and Consent," "No Strings," "Here's Love," "I Had a Ball," "Man of La Mancha" (also LC), "Her First Roman," "The Incomparable Max," "Voices."

KILLIAN, PHIL. Born July 30 in Charlotte, NC. Graduate Northwestern U. Debut OB 1972 in "The Fantasticks."

| Kenneth Kimmins | Marcia Jean Kurtz | Paul Larson | Lucie Lancaster | Will Lee |

KILLINGER, MARION. Born July 12, 1941 in Corbin, Ky. Bdwy debut 1972 in "Via Galactica."

KIMMINS, KENNETH. Born Sept. 4, 1941 in Bklyn. Graduate Catholic U. Debut 1966 OB in "The Fantasticks," followed by "Adaptation," Bdwy in "Fig Leaves Are Falling," "Gingerbread Lady," "Company," "Status Quo Vadis."

KINDLE, TOM. Born Dec. 30, 1948 in St. Louis, Mo. Attended UNC. Debut OB 1973 in "The Soldier."

KISER, TERRY. Born Aug. 1, 1939 in Omaha, Neb. Graduate U. Kan. Debut 1966 in "Night of the Dunce," followed by "Fortune and Men's Eyes" for which he received a Theatre World Award, "Horseman, Pass By," "Frank Gagliano's City Scene," "The Ofay Watcher," "Castro Complex," "In Case of Accident," "The Children," Bdwy in "Paris Is Out," "Shelter."

KLAVUN, WALTER. Born May 8, 1906 in NYC. Yale graduate. Bdwy debut 1928 in "Say When," followed by "No More Ladies," "Arms for Venus," "Annie Get Your Gun," "Twelfth Night," "Dream Girl," "Auntie Mame," "Say, Darling," "Desert Incident," "How to Succeed in Business. . . . ," "What Makes Sammy Run," "Twigs," OB in "Mornings at 7," "Dandy Dick."

KLINE, KEVIN. Born Oct. 24, 1947 in St. Louis, Mo. Graduate Ind. U., Juilliard. Debut OB 1970 in NYSF's "Wars of the Roses," followed OB by "School for Scandal," "Lower Depths," "The Hostage," "Women Beware Women."

KLINE, RICHARD. Born Apr. 29, 1944 in NYC. Graduate Queen's Col., Northwestern U. Debut 1971 in LCRep's "Mary Stuart," "Narrow Road to the Deep North," "Twelfth Night," and "The Crucible," OB in "We Bombed in New Haven."

KLING, IRENE FRANCES. Born Mar. 25, 1947 in Bklyn. Graduate NYU, AADA. Debut 1966 OB in "Miss Julie," followed by "The Stronger," "Death of Bessie Smith," "Don Juan in Hell," "Hands of God," "Beggar's Opera."

KLUNIS, TOM. Bdwy debut 1961 in "Gideon," followed by "The Devils," "Henry V," OB in "The Immoralist," "Hamlet," "Arms and the Man," "Potting Shed," "Measure for Measure," "Romeo and Juliet," "The Balcony," "Our Town," "Man Who Never Died," "Gos Is My Ram," "Rise, Marlowe," "Iphigenia in Aulis," "Still Life."

KNAPP, ELEANORE. Born in Passaic, NY. Graduate Western Reserve U. Career in opera before Bdwy debut 1965 in "Man of La Mancha."

KOVENS, EDWARD. Born June 26, 1934 in NYC. Attended NY Inst. of Arts. Bdwy debut 1964 in "Three Sisters," OB in "Modern Statuary," "Never Ending Rain," "Waiting for Godot," "Dirty Hands," "Country Girl," "Deer Park," "Fortune and Men's Eyes," "42 Seconds from Broadway."

KRAMER, MARSHA. Born June 19, 1945 in Chicago. Graduate UCLA. Debut OB 1973 in "Out of This World."

KRAUS, PHILIP. Born May 10, 1949 in Springville, NY. Graduate Carnegie Tech. Bdwy debut 1973 in "Shelter."

KRAWFORD, GARY. Born Mar. 23, 1941 in Kitchener, Can. Debut OB 1968 in "The Fantasticks," followed by "Manhattan Arrangement," "Dear Oscar," Bdwy in "Pousse Cafe," "Education of Hyman Kaplan."

KUHNER, JOHN. Born Dec. 27, 1942 in Cleveland, O. Graduate Denison U. Debut 1968 OB in "Your Own Thing," followed by "House of Leather," "Tarot," "Wanted," "We Bombed in New Haven."

KURTZ, MARCIA JEAN. Born in The Bronx. Juilliard graduate. Debut 1966 OB in "Jonah," followed by "America Hurrah," "Red Cross," "Muzeeka," "Effects of Gamma Rays on. . . . ," "The Year Boston Won the Pennant" (LCR), "The Mirror," "The Orphan," Bdwy in "The Chinese and Dr. Fish."

KUSS, RICHARD. Born July 17, 1927 in Astoria, NY. Attended Ithaca Col. Debut OB 1951 in "Mother Said No," followed by "A Maid's Tragedy," Bdwy in "J.B.," "Wait until Dark," "Solitaire/Double Solitaire."

KUSSACK, ELAINE. Born Dec. 30 in Brooklyn. Graduate Hunter, Col., Columbia. Bdwy debut 1969 in "Fiddler on the Roof."

LACY, TOM. Born Aug. 30, 1933 in NYC. Debut OB 1965 in "The Fourth Pig," followed by "Fantasticks," "Shoemaker's Holiday," "Love and Let Love," "Millionairess," "Crimes of Passion," "The Real Inspector Hound," "Enemies" (LC).

LAGERFELT, CAROLYN. Born Sept. 23 in Paris. Attended AADA. Bdwy debut 1971 in "The Philanthropist," followed by "4 on a Garden," "Jockey Club Stakes."

LAMONT, ROBIN. Born June 2, 1950 in Boston, Attended Carnegie-Mellon U. Debut OB 1971 in "Godspell," followed by "Thoughts."

LAMOS, MARK. Born Mar. 10, 1946 in Chicago. Attended Northwestern U. Bdwy debut 1972 in "The Love Suicide at Schofield Barracks," followed by "Creation of the World and Other Business," "Cyrano."

LANCASTER, LUCIE. Born Oct. 15, 1907 in Chicago. Bdwy debut 1947 in "Heads or Tails," followed by "Mr. Pickwick," "The Girl Who Came to Supper," "Bajour," "How Now, Dow Jones," "Little Boxes" (OB), "70 girls 70," "Pippin."

LANNING, JERRY. Born May 17, 1943 in Miami, Fla. Graduate USCal. Bdwy debut 1966 in "Mame" for which he received a Theatre World Award, followed by "1776," OB in "Memphis Store Bought Teeth," "Berlin to Broadway."

LANSING, ROBERT. Born June 5 in San Diego, Cal. Bdwy debut 1951 in "Stalag 17," followed by "Cyrano de Bergerac," "Richard III," "Charley's Aunt" (CC), "The Lovers," "Cue for Passion," "Great God Brown," "Cut of the Axe," "Finishing Touches."

LARSEN, WILLIAM. Born Nov. 20, 1927 in Lake Charles, La. Attended UTex. On Bdwy in "Ballad of the Sad Cafe," "Half A Sixpence," "Funny Girl," "Halfway up a Tree," "There's a Girl in My Soup," "Dear World," OB in "The Crucible," "Fantasticks," "Legend of Lovers," "Twelfth Night," APA's "Tavern," "Lower Depths," and "School for Scandal," "Troilus and Cressida," "Murderous Angels."

LARSON, PAUL. Born Dec. 22, 1918 in Detroit, Mich. Attended St. Francis Col. Bdwy debut 1949 in "The Father," followed by "Dylan," "The Investigation," "Spoon River Anthology" (OB).

LASKY, ZANE. Born Apr. 23, 1953 in NYC. Attended Manhattan Com. Col., HB Studio. Debut OB 1973 in "The Hot L Baltimore."

LASLEY, DAVID. Born Aug. 20, 1947 in Sault-St.-Marie, Mich. Bdwy debut 1972 in "Dude."

LATCHAW, PAUL. Born Jan. 3, 1945 in Pittsburgh, Pa. Graduate Princeton. Debut OB 1972 in "Yoshe Kalb," followed by "Out of This World."

LATHRAM, ELIZABETH. Born Apr. 23, 1947 in Washington, DC. Graduate UOre. Debut OB 1971 in "Godspell."

LaVALLEE, BILL. Born June 13, 1943 in Baton Rouge, La. Attended LSU. Debut OB 1968 in "Redhead," followed by "God Bless You, Harold Fineberg," "Shoestring Revue," "The Web," "What's a Nice Country like you . . ."

LAVIN, LINDA. Born Oct. 15, 1939 in Portland, Me. Graduate Wm. & Mary Col. Bdwy bow 1962 in "A Family Affair," followed by "Riot Act," "The Game Is Up," "Hotel Passionato," "It's Superman!," "On a Clear Day You Can See Forever," "Something Different," "Cop-Out," "Last of the Red Hot Lovers," "Story Theatre," "The Enemy Is Dead," OB in "Wet Paint" for which she received a Theatre World Award, "Mad Show," "Little Murders."

LAWLESS, SUE. Born Sept. 26 in Freeport, Ill. Graduate DePaul U. Debut OB 1961 in "The Sudden End of Anne Cinquefoil," followed by "Shoemaker's Holiday," "In the Nick of Time," "Don't Shoot, Mable, It's Your Husband," "Now," "Love Course."

LAWRENCE, DELPHI. Born Mar. 23, 1932 in London. Attended RADA. Debut 1972 OB in "The Divorce of Judy and Jane," followed by "Dylan." "The Elizabethans."

LAWSON, LEE. Born Oct. 14, 1941 in NYC. Attended Boston U. Columbia. OB in "Firebugs," "The Knack," "Birthday Party" (LC), "Scenes from American Life" (LC), Bdwy in "Agatha Sue, I Love You," "Cactus Flower," "My Daughter, Your Son," "Suggs" and "The Plough and the Stars" (LC).

LAWSON, ROGER. Born Oct. 11, 1942 in Tarrytown, NY. Attended Fredonia Col. Bdwy debut 1967 in "Hello, Dolly!," followed OB by "Pins and Needles," "Billy Noname," "Dinner at the Ambassador's."

LEA, BRUCE. Born Mar. 9, 1949 in New Orleans, La. Graduate Tex.CU. Bdwy debut 1971 in "On the Town," followed by "DuBarry Was a Lady" (OB), "Irene."

LEARY, DAVID. Born Aug. 8, 1939 in Brooklyn. Attended CCNY. Debut OB 1969 in "Shoot Anything That Moves," followed by "Macbeth," "The Plough and the Stars" (LC).

LEBOWSKY, STANLEY. Born Nov. 29, 1926 in Minneapolis, Minn. Graduate. UCLA. Bdwy debut 1959 in "Whoop-Up," followed by "Irma La Douce," "Family Affair," "Tovarich," "Half a Sixpence," "Breakfast at Tiffany's," "Gantry," "Ari," "Jesus Christ Superstar."

LEE, MICHELE. Born June 24, 1942 in Los Angeles. Attended LACC. Bdwy debut 1960 in "Vintage '60," followed by "How to Succeed in Business. . . . ," "Bravo Giovanni," "Seesaw."

LEE, WILL. Born Aug. 6, 1908 in Brooklyn. Bdwy debut 1935 in "Young Can Go First," followed by "Boy Meets Girl," "Family Portrait," "The Strings, My Lord, Are False," "The Shrike," "The Time of Your Life," "Johnny Johnson," "Night Music," "Heavenly Express," "Golden Boy," "Once upon a Mattress," "Carnival," "Last Analysis," "Deer Park" (OB), LC's "Incident at Vichy," and "Enemies."

LEECH, DEMPSTER. Born Mar. 31, 1942 in Chicago. Graduate Adelphi U. Debut OB 1972 in "Thunder Rock."

LEEDS, PHIL. Born in NYC. Bdwy bow 1942 in "Of V We Sing," followed by "Make a Wish," "Let Freedom Ring," "Can-Can," "Romano and Juliet," "Girls against the Boys," "Christine," "Banker's Daughter" (OB), "Nowhere to Go but Up," "Sophie," "Nobody Loves an Albatross," "Dinner at 8," "Little Murders," "Inquest," "Hurry Harry."

Betty Lester   Ed Linderman   Deborah Loomis   Paul Lipson   Marcella Lowery

LEIGHTON, BETTY. Born July 8, 1920 in London. Debut 1961 OB in "One Way Pendulum," Bdwy in "Cyrano."

LeNOIRE, ROSETTA. Born Aug. 8, 1911 in NYC. Attended Theatre Wing. Bdwy debut 1936 in "Macbeth," followed by "Bassa Moona," "Hot Mikado," "Marching with Johnny," "Janie," "Decision," "Three's a Family," "Destry Rides Again," "Finian's Rainbow," "South Pacific," "Sophie," "Tambourines to Glory," "Blues for Mr. Charlie," "Great Indoors," "Show Boat" (LC), "Lost in the Stars," "A Cry of Players" (LC), OB in "Bible Salesman," "Double Entry," "Clandestine on the Morning Line," "Cabin in the Sky," "Lady Day," "Streetcar Named Desire" (LC).

LENS, PATRICIA. Born May 3, 1947 in Philadelphia. Attended Northwestern. Bdwy debut 1969 in "Celebration," followed by "Man of LaMancha."

LENTHALL, DAVID. Born Nov. 9, 1948 in Scranton, Pa. Attended Parsons Col., AADA. Debut OB 1971 in "Basic Training of Pavlo Hummel," Bdwy bow 1972 in "Much Ado about Nothing."

LEON, GEOFF. Born in Long Beach, Cal. Graduate UCal. Bdwy debut 1970 in "Georgy," OB in "Gertrude Stein's First Reader," "One for the Money," "Smile, Smile, Smile."

LEONTOVICH, EUGENIE. Born in Moscow in 1894. Bdwy debut 1928 in "And So to Bed," followed by "Grand Hotel," "Twentieth Century," "Dark Eyes," "Obsession," "Anastasia," "Cave Dwellers," OB in "Anna K."

LeROUX, MADELEINE. Born May 28, 1946 in Laramie, Wyo. Graduate Cape Town. Debut OB 1969 in "The Moondreamers," followed by "Dirtiest Show in Town," "Rain," Bdwy 1972 in "Lysistrata."

LeROY, KEN. Born Aug. 17, 1927 in Detroit. Attended Neighborhood Playhouse. Bdwy in "The American Way," "Morning Star," "Anne of England," "Oklahoma!," "Carousel," "Brigadoon," "Call Me Madam," "Pajama Game," "West Side Story," "Fiddler on the Roof."

LESTER, BARBARA. Born Dec. 27, 1928 in London. Graduate Columbia U. Bdwy debut 1956 in "Protective Custody," followed by "Legend of Lizzie," "Luther," "Inadmissible Evidence," "Johnny No-Trump," "Grin and Bare It," "Butley," OB in "Electra," "Queen after Death," "Summer of the 17th Doll," "Richard II" and "Much Ado About Nothing" (NYSF), "One Way Pendulum," "Abelard and Heloise," "There's One in Every Marriage."

LESTER, BETTY. Born Dec. 1 in Grand Island, Neb. Graduate UNeb., Columbia. Debut OB 1952 in "Merry-Go-Round," followed by "3 in 1," "Streetcar Named Desire," "Medea."

LEVENE, SAM. Born Aug. 28, 1905 in NYC. Graduate AADA. Bdwy debut 1927 in "Wall Street," followed by "3 Men on a Horse," "Dinner at 8," "Room Service," "Margin for Error," "Sound of Hunting," "Light up the Sky," "Guys and Dolls," "Hot Corner," "Fair Game," "Make a Million," "Heartbreak House," "Good Soup," "Devil's Advocate," "Let It Ride," "Seidman & Son," "Cafe Crown," "Last Analysis," "Nathan Weinstein, Mystic, Conn.," "The Impossible Years," "Paris Is Out," "A Dream out of Time" (OB), "The Sunshine Boys."

LEVERIDGE, LYNN ANN. Born Mar. 16, 1948 in NYC. Attended Hofstra U. Debut 1970 in "Saved," followed by "Beggar's Opera."

LEVI, BARUK. Born June 14, 1947 in Bklyn. Graduate Bklyn Col. Debut 1972 OB in "And They Put Handcuffs on the Flowers," followed by "Thoughts."

LEWIS, MARCIA. Born Aug. 18, 1938 in Melrose, Mass. Graduate UCinn. OB in "Impudent Wolf," "Who's Who, Baby?," "The Time of Your Life" (LC), "God Bless Coney," "Let Yourself Go," Bdwy in "Hello, Dolly!"

LEYDEN, LEO. Born Jan. 28 1929 in Dublin, Ire. Attended Abbey Theatre School. Bdwy debut 1960 in "Love and Libel," followed by "Darling of the Day," "The Mundy Scheme," "The Rothschilds," "Capt. Brassbound's Conversion," "The Plough and the Stars" (LC).

LINDERMAN, ED. Born May 21, 1947 in Chicago. Attended Northwestern, DePaul, UIll., AMDA. Debut 1969 OB in "Weigh-In, Weigh-Out!," followed by "June Moon," "Some Other Time," Bdwy 1971 in "Fiddler on the Roof."

LINDSTROM, CARL. Born Dec. 9, 1938 in Portland, Ore. Bdwy debut 1972 in "A Funny Thing Happened on the Way to the Forum."

LINN, MARGARET. Born Aug. 21, 1934 in Richmond, Ind. Attended Northwestern U., Denver U. OB in "Pale Horse Pale Rider," "The Room," "Billy Liar," "Huui, Huui," "Disintegration of James Cherry" (LC), "House of Blue Leaves," "Pygmalion," "An Evening with the Poet-Senator," Bdwy in "How's the World Treating You?," "Halfway Up the Tree," "Ring Round the Bathtub."

LIPSON, CLIFFORD. Born Feb. 10, 1947 in Providence, RI. Attended Neighborhood Playhouse, AMDA. OB in "Great Scot!," "Hooray, It's A Glorious Day," "The Indian Wants the Bronx," "Salvation," Bdwy in "Hair," followed by "Jesus Christ Superstar."

LIPSON, PAUL. Born Dec. 23, 1913 in Brooklyn. Attended Ohio State, Theatre Wing. Bdwy bow 1942 in "Lily of the Valley," followed by "Heads or Tails," "Detective Story," "Remains to Be Seen," "Carnival in Flanders," "I've Got Sixpence," "The Vamp," "Bells Are Ringing," "Fiorello" (CC), "Sound of Music," "Fiddler on the Roof."

LITTLE, RON PAUL. Born Apr. 2, 1949 in New Haven, Conn. UConn. graduate. Debut OB 1973 in "Thunder Rock," followed by "Summer Brave."

LOGGIA, ROBERT. Born Jan. 3, 1930 in Staten Island, NY. Attended UMo., Actors Studio. Debut OB 1956 in "Man with the Golden Arm," followed by "Three Sisters," "World War 2 1/2," "Passing through from Exotic Places," "Wedding Band."

LOMBARD, PETER. Born Oct. 12, 1935 in Spokane, Wash. Graduate UAriz. Bdwy debut 1960 in "Conquering Hero," followed by "Carnival," "Generation," "Sweet Charity," "Promises Promises," "1776," OB in "Will the Mail Train Run Tonight?," "Wanted," "Beggar's Opera."

LONG, AVON. Born June, 18, 1910 in Baltimore, Md. Studied at New Eng. Cons. Bdwy debut 1942 in "Porgy and Bess," followed by "Memphis Bound," "Carib Song," "Beggar's Holiday," "Don't Play Us Cheap," OB in "Ballad of Jazz Street."

LONG, TAMARA. Born Nov. 7, 1941 in Oklahoma City. Graduate Okla.U. Debut OB 1968 in "Dames at Sea."

LONGO, PEGGY. Born Oct. 1, 1943 in Brooklyn. Graduate Ithaca Col. With NYC Opera before 1967 Bdwy debut in "Fiddler on the Roof."

LOOMIS, DEBORAH. Born July 2, 1945 in NYC. Attended New Eng. Cons., AADA. Debut OB 1973 in "The Karl Marx Play."

LOOMIS, ROD. Born Apr. 21, 1942 in St. Albans, Vt. Graduate Boston U, Brandeis U. Debut 1972 OB in "Two if by Sea," followed by "You Never Know," "Uncle Vanya."

LOROS, GEORGE. Born Jan. 9, 1944 in NYC. Attended Neighborhood Playhouse. Debut OB 1967 in "Nighthawks," followed by "Happiness Cage," "Danton's Death," "Eddie and Susanna in Love."

LOWERY, MARCELLA. Born Apr. 27, 1946 in Jamaica, NY. Graduate Hunter Col. Debut 1967 OB in "Day of Absence," followed by "American Pastoral," "Ballet behind the Bridge," "Jamimma," "A Recent Killing."

LOY, MYRNA. Born Aug. 2, 1905 in Helena, Mont. Bdwy debut 1966 in "Barefoot in the Park," followed by "The Women."

LUCKINBILL, LAURENCE. Born Nov. 21, 1938 in St. Smith, Ark. Graduate UArk., Catholic U. Bdwy debut in "A Man for All Season," followed by "Beekman Place," OB in "Oedipus Rex," "There Is a Play Tonight," "Fantasticks," "Tartuffe," "Boys in the Band," "Horseman, Pass By," "Memory Bank," "What the Butler Saw," "A Meeting by the River," "Alpha Beta."

LUM, ALVIN. Born May 28, 1931 in Honolulu. Attended U. Hawaii. Debut 1969 OB in "In the Bar of a Tokyo Hotel," followed by Bdwy in "Lovely Ladies, Kind Gentlemen," "Two Gentlemen of Verona."

LuPONE, PATTI. Born Apr. 21, 1949 in Northport, NY. Juilliard graduate. Debut 1972 OB in "School for Scandal," followed by "Women Beware Women," "Next Time I'll Sing to You," "Lower Depths."

LYMAN, DEBRA. Born July 17, 1940 in Philadelphia. Graduate Phil. Col. Debut 1967 OB in "By Jupiter," followed by Bdwy bow 1972 in "Sugar."

LYMAN, PEGGY. Born June 28, 1950 in Cincinnati, O. Attended UCinn. Bdwy debut 1972 in "Sugar."

LYNCH, RICHARD. Born Feb. 12, 1940 in Brooklyn. Attended Actors Studio. Bdwy debut 1965 in "The Devils," followed OB in "Live Like Pigs," "One Night Stands of a Noisy Passenger," "Things That Almost Happen," "12 Angry Men," "The Orphan."

LYNDE, JANICE. Born Mar. 28, 1947 in Houston, Tex. Attended UInd. Bdwy debut 1971 in "The Me Nobody Knows," followed by "Applause," "Butterflies Are Free," OB in "Sambo."

LYNDECK, EDMUND. Born Oct. 4, 1925 in Baton Rouge, La. Graduate Montclair State Col., Fordham U. Bdwy debut 1969 in "1776," followed by "The King and I" (JB).

MacCAULEY, MARK. Born Dec. 11, 1948 in NYC. Attended UInd. Debut 1969 OB in "Crimes of Passion," followed by "Anna K," "Godspell."

MacCOLL, VIRGINIA LENORE. Born Oct. 31, 1951 in Bridgeport, Conn. Attended UGa., Conn. Col. Debut OB 1972 in "How to Succeed in Business . . ." (ELT), followed by "Ruddigore."

MacGREGOR, LYNN. Born Oct. 24, 1945 in NYC. Graduate SFSC. Debut OB 1971 in "Late for Oblivion," followed by "Maid's Tragedy."

MACHRAY, ROBERT. Born May 4, 1945 in San Diego, Cal. Attended Yale, NYU. Debut OB 1972 in "Servant of Two Masters."

MACKENZIE, WILL. Born July 24, 1938 in Providence, RI. Graduate Brown U. Bdwy debut 1965 in "Half a Sixpence," followed by "Hello, Dolly!," "Sheep on the Runway," "Scratch," "Much Ado about Nothing," OB in "Wonderful Town," "Put It in Writing," "Morning Sun," "Brigadoon" (CC).

MACNEE, PATRICK. Born Feb. 1922 in London. Attended Eton. Bdwy debut 1972 in "Sleuth."

MAGGART, BRANDON. Born Dec. 12, 1933 in Carthage, Tenn. Graduate U. Tenn. OB in "Sing, Muse!," "Like Other People," "Put It In Writing" for which he received a Theatre World Award, "Wedding Band," Bdwy in "Kelly," "New Faces of 1968," "Applause."

MAGGIORE, CHARLES. Born Mar. 19, 1936 in Valley Stream, NY. Attended Bates Col., Adelphi U., Neighborhood Playhouse. OB in "Six Characters in Search of an Author," "Rivals," "Iceman Cometh," "Othello," "The Elizabethans," Bdwy 1967 in "Spofford."

MAHONEY, TRISH. Born Feb. 1, 1946 in Cairo, Egy. Attended Long Beach City Col. Bdwy debut 1972 in "A Funny Thing Happened on the Way to the Forum."

MAITLAND, RUTH. Born Apr. 16, 1926 in NYC. Bdwy debut 1940 in "Walk with Music," followed by "Johnny 2X4," "Junior Miss," "Burlesque," "No, No, Nanette," OB in "Solid Gold Cadillac," "Pullman Car Hiawatha," "Spiral Staircase."

MALIANDI, PAULA. Born Apr. 21, 1949 in Brooklyn. Graduate Bklyn Col. Debut OB 1973 in "The Soldier."

MALLORY, VICTORIA. Born Sept. 20, 1948 in Virginia. Graduate AMDA. Debut 1968 in "West Side Story" (LC), followed by "Carnival" (CC'68), "Follies," "A Little Night Music."

MANSON, ALAN. Born in NYC. Bdwy debut 1940 in "Journey to Jerusalem," followed by "This Is the Army," "Call Me Mister," "Southern Exposure," "Angels Kiss Me," "Ponder Heart," "Maybe Tuesday," "Tenth Man," "Gideon," "Nobody Loves an Albatross," "Funny Girl," "A Place for Polly," "40 Carats," "No Hard Feelings," OB in "Dr. Jekyll and Mr. Hyde," "Midsummer Night's Dream," "Oh Say Can You See L.A.?," "The Other Man."

MANSOUR, GEORGE P., JR. Born Apr. 16, 1949 in Youngstown, O. Attended Juilliard. Bdwy debut 1972 in "Jesus Christ Superstar."

MARCHAND, NANCY. Born June 19, 1928 in Buffalo, NY. Graduate Carnegie Tech. Debut in "The Taming of the Shrew" (CC), followed by "Merchant of Venice," "Much Ado About Nothing," "The Balcony," (OB) "Three Bags Full," "After The Rain," LCRep's "The Alchemist," "Yerma," "Cyrano," "Mary Stuart," "Enemies," and "The Plough and the Stars," "Forty Carats," "And Miss Reardon Drinks A Little."

MARKHAM, MONTE. Born June 21, 1935 in Manatee, Fla. Graduate UGa. Bdwy debut 1973 in "Irene," for which he received a Theatre World Award.

MARKLIN, PETER. Born Dec. 22, 1939 in Buffalo, NY. Graduate Northwestern U. Appeared in "The Brig" (OB), "Fiddler on the Roof."

MARLOW, DAVID. Born Feb. 26, 1945 in NYC. Graduate NYU. Bdwy debut 1973 in "No Hard Feelings."

MARR, RICHARD. Born May 12, 1928 in Baltimore, Md. Graduate UPa. On Bdwy in "Baker Street," "How to Succeed in Business . . . ," "Here's Where I Belong," "Coco," OB in "Sappho," "Pilgrim's Progress," "Pimpernel," "Witness," "Dear Oscar."

MARSHALL, E. G. Born June 18, 1910 in Owatonna, Minn. Attended UMinn. Bdwy debut 1938 in "Prelude to Glory," followed by "Jason," "Skin of Our Teeth," "Petrified Forest," "Jacobowsky and the Colonel," "The Iceman Cometh," "Hope's the Thing," "Survivors," "The Crucible," "Red Roses for Me," "Waiting for Godot," "The Gang's All Here," "Little Foxes," "Plaza Suite," "Nash at 9."

MARSHALL, MORT. Born Aug. 17, 1918, in NYC. Graduate Rollins Col., Yale. Bdwy bow 1947 in "Crime and Punishment," followed by "Gentlemen Prefer Blondes," "Of Thee I Sing," "Best House in Naples," "Men of Distinction," "Ziegfeld Follies," "All American," "Little Me," "Gypsy," "Music Man," "Minnie's Boys," "A Funny Thing Happened on the Way to the Forum."

MARSHALL, WILL SHARPE. Born Jan. 12, 1947 in East Chicago, Ind. Graduate Brown U. Debut OB 1969 in "The Drunkard," Bdwy in "Butterflies Are Free," "A Little Night Music."

MARTIN, HELEN. Born in St. Louis, Mo. Attended Paul Mann Workshop. Bdwy debut 1941 in "Native Son," followed by "Take a Giant Step," "Long Dream," "Deep Are the Roots," "Amen Corner," "Period of Adjustment," "Purlie Victorious," "My Mother, My Father and Me," "Purlie," OB in "Major Barbara," "Juno and the Paycock," "Land Beyond the River," "Ballad of Jazz Street," "The Blacks," "Stevedore," "The Cat and the Canary."

MARTIN, IAN. Born Apr. 29, 1912 in Glasgow, Scot. Attended Harvard. On Bdwy in "Finian's Rainbow," "Devil's Disciple," "Capt. Brassbound's Conversion," "Cock-a-Doodle Dandy," "King of Friday's Men," "Victoria Regina," "All Men Are Alike," "Spofford," "Lost in the Stars," "The Changing Room."

MARTIN, LEILA. Born Aug. 22, 1932 in NYC. Bdwy debut 1944 in "Peep show," followed by "Two on the Aisle," "Wish You Were Here," "Guys an Dolls" (CC), "Best House in Naples," "Ernest in Love" (OB), "Henry Swe Henry," "The Wall," "Visit to a Small Planet," "The Rothschilds," "Begga Opera" (OB).

MARTIN, RON. Born June 23, 1947 in NYC. Attended Queens Col. Bdw debut 1968 in "Red, White and Maddox," followed by "Child's Play," OB "Sensations," "Small Craft Warnings."

MARTIN, W. T. Born Jan. 17, 1947 in Providence, RI. Attended Lafayette Co Debut OB 1972 in "Basic Training of Pavlo Hummel," followed by "Ghosts

MASCOLO, JOSEPH. Born Mar. 13, 1935 in Hartford. Conn. Bdwy "Night Life," "A View from the Bridge," "Dinner at 8," "To Clothe t Naked" (OB), LCRep's "The Time of Your Life," "Camino Real," and "Go Woman of Setzuan," "Murderous Angels" (OB), "The Championship Season

MASIELL, JOE. Born Oct. 27, 1939 in Bklyn. Studied at HB Studio. Deb 1964 OB in "Cindy," followed by "Jacques Brel Is Alive . . . ," "Sensations "Leaves of Grass," Bdwy in "Dear World," "Different Times," "Jacques B is Alive . . ."

MASUR, RICHARD. Born Nov. 20, 1948 in NYC. Attended SUNY, Ya Bdwy debut 1973 in "The Changing Room."

MATHEWS, CARMEN. Born May 8, 1918 in Philadelphia. Graduate RAD, Bdwy debut 1938 in "Henry IV," followed by "Hamlet," "Richard II," "Ha riet," "Cherry Orchard," "The Assassin," "Man and Superman," "Ivy Green "Courtin' Time," "My Three Angels," "Holiday for Lovers," "Night Life "Lorenzo," "The Yearling," "Delicate Balance," "I'm Solomon," "De World," "Ring Round the Bathtub," "Ambassador."

MATHIS, SHERRY. Born Feb. 2, 1949 in Memphis, Tenn. Attended Mer phis State U. Bdwy debut 1973 in "A Little Night Music."

MATTHAEI, KONRAD. Born in Detroit; Yale graduate. Debut 1961 OB "She Stoops to Conquer," followed by "Thracian Horses," "Trelawney of t Wells," "King of the Dark Chamber," "Don Carlos," "A Man's a Mar "Riverwind," "Boys in the Band," "The Real Inspector Hound," Bdwy in ". Daughters," "The Milk Train Doesn't Stop Here Anymore," "A Place f Polly."

MATTHEWS, DAKIN. Born Nov. 7, 1940 in Oakland, Cal. Graduate S Patrick's Col., Cal. State, NYU. Debut OB 1972 in "School for Scandal followed by "The Hostage," "Women Beware Women," "Lower Depths."

MAY, WINSTON. Born Feb. 3, 1937 in Mammoth Spring, Ark. Gradua Ark. State U., Am. Th. Wing. Debut OB 1967 in "Man Who Washed H Hands," followed by "King Lear," "Candida," "Trumpets and Drums," "Oth the Great," "Uncle Vanya," "Servant of Two Masters" (ELT), "The Play's t Thing."

MAYER, JERRY. Born May 12, 1941 in NYC. Graduate NYU. Debut C 1968 in "Alice in Wonderland," NYSF and Bdwy 1972 in "Much Ado abo Nothing," followed by "L'Ete" (OB).

McADAMS, STACY. Born Aug. 23, 1938 in Memphis, Tenn. Attended UBru sels, Georgetown U. Debut 1968 OB in "Up Eden," followed by "Blind Guy

McCALL, JANET. Born June 26, 1935 in Washington, DC. Graduate Pen State. Debut 1960 OB in "Golden Apple," followed by "Life Is a Dream "Tatooed Countess," "The Bacchantes," "Jacques Brel is Alive . . . ," Bdwy "Camelot," "1776," "Two by Two," "Jacques Brel Is Alive . . ."

McCARTHY, KEVIN. Born Feb. 15, 1914 in Seattle, Wash. Attended UMin Bdwy debut 1938 in "Abe Lincoln in Illinois," followed by "Flight to the West "Winged Victory," "Truckline Cafe," "Joan of Lorraine," "Death of a Sale man," "Anna Christie," "Deep Blue Sea," "Red Roses for Me," "Day th Money Stopped," "Two for the Seesaw," "Advise and Consent," "Somethir about a Soldier," "Three Sisters," "Warm Body," "Cactus Flower," "Happ Birthday, Wanda June," "The Children" (OB).

McCARTY, MARY. Born 1923 in Kan. Bdwy debut 1948 in "Sleepy Hollow for which she received a Theatre World Award, followed by "Small Wonder "Miss Liberty," "Bless You All," "A Rainy Day in Newark," "Follies."

McCAULEY, JUDITH. Born Dec. 14, in Marietta, O. Graduate Cincinna Cons. Debut OB 1964 in "Jo," followed by "Oklahoma!" (LC), Bdwy in "A plause," "Seesaw."

McCLANAHAN, RUE. Born Feb. 21 in Healdton, Okla. Bdwy debut 1965 "Best Laid Plans," followed by "Jimmy Shine," "Father's Day," "Sticks an Bones," OB in "Secret Life of Walter Mitty," "Big Man," "Macbird!," "Tonig in Living Color," "Who's Happy Now?," "Dark of the Moon," "God Sa There Is No Peter Ott," "Dylan," "Crystal and Fox."

McCONNELL, TY. Born Jan. 13, 1940 in Coldwater, Mich. Graduate UMic Debut OB 1962 in "The Fantasticks," followed by "Promenade," "Contrast Bdwy in "Lion in Winter," "Dear World."

Ruth McCormick   Richard McKenzie   Laura Michaels   Raf Michaels   Shirley Monroe

McCORMICK, RUTH: Born Mar. 27, 1913 in Wichita, Kan. Graduate UOkla., UDenver. Debut 1973 OB in "Penthouse Legend."

McDONALD, JAMES. Born June 23 in Jersey City. NJ. Attended Rutgers U. OB in "The Trojan Women," "White Devil," "Fortune and Men's Eyes," Bdwy "Fiddler on the Roof."

McDONALD, TANNY. Born Feb. 13, 1939 in Princeton, Ind. Vassar graduate. Debut OB with Am. Savoyards, followed by "All in Love," "To Broadway with Love," "Carricknabauna," "Beggar's Opera," "Brand," "Goodbye, Dan Bailey," Bdwy in "Fiddler on the Roof," "Come Summer," "The Lincoln Mask."

McGILL, EVERETT. Born Oct. 21, 1945 in Miami Beach, Fla. Graduate UMo., RADA. Debut OB 1971 in "Brothers," followed by "Father," "Enemies" (LC).

McGRATH, KATHERINE. Born Dec. 11, 1944 in Winchester, Mass. Attended Boston Cons., RADA. Debut OB in "The Bacchants," followed by "Perry's Mission," "The Real Inspector Hound."

McGUIRE, BIFF. Born Oct. 25, 1926 in New Haven, Conn. Attended Mass. State Col. Bdwy in "Make Mine Manhattan," "South Pacific," "Dance Me a Long," "The Time of Your Life" (CC&LC), "A View from the Bridge," "Greatest Man Alive," "The Egghead," "Triple Play," "Happy Town," "Beg, Borrow or Steal," "Finian's Rainbow" (CC), "Beggar on Horseback" (LC), "Father's Day," "Trial of the Catonsville 9," "Present Tense" (OB).

McGUIRE, MITCHELL. Born Dec. 26, 1936 in Chicago. Attended Goodman Th. Schools, Santa Monica City Col. OB in "The Rapists," "Go, Go, Go, God Is Dead," "Waiting for Lefty," "The Bond," "The Guns of Carrar," "Oh, Calcutta."

McHATTIE, STEPHEN. Born Feb. 3 in Antigonish, N.S. Graduate Acadia U, AADA. With NYSF in "Henry IV," on Bdwy in "The American Dream" (68), OB in "Richard III," "The Persians," "Pictures in the Hallway" (LC), "Now There's Just the Three of Us," "Anna K.," "Twelfth Night" (LC), "Mourning Becomes Electra."

McINTYRE, BILL. Born Sept. 2, 1935 in Rochester, NY. Debut OB 1970 in "The Fantasticks," Bdwy 1972 in "Secret Affairs of Mildred Wild."

McKENNA, SIOBHAN. Born May 24, 1922 in Belfast, Ire. Graduate UDublin. Bdwy debut 1955 in "Chalk Garden," followed by "St. Joan," "Rope Dancers," OB in "Hamlet" (title role), "Here Are Ladies."

McKENZIE, RICHARD. Born June 2, 1930 in Chattanooga, Tenn. Attended UTenn, UMo, RADA. Bdwy debut 1969 in "Indians," followed by "That Championship Season," OB in "Whistle in the Dark," "Nobody Hears a Broken Drum."

McLANE, ROBERT. Born Aug. 4, 1944 in Macon, Ga. Attended AMDA. Bdwy debut 1969 in "Indians," OB in "Antigone," "Madonna in the Orchard," "A Recent Killing."

McMARTIN, JOHN. Born in Warsaw, Ind. Attended Columbia. Debut OB 1959 in "Little Mary Sunshine" for which he received a Theatre World Award, followed by Bdwy in "The Conquering Hero," (1968) "Blood, Sweat and Stanley Poole," "Children from Their Games," "Rainy Day in Newark," "Too Much Johnson" (OB), "Sweet Charity," "Follies," "Great God Brown," "Don Juan."

McNAUGHTON, ANNE. Born Aug. 19, 1943 in Pasadena, Cal. Juilliard graduate. Debut OB 1972 in "School for Scandal," followed by "U.S.A.," "Women Beware Women," "The Hostage."

McPHILLIPS, EDWARD. Born July 23, 1925 in Eng. Debut OB 1967 in "Stephen D," followed by "The Victims," "Happy Hypocrite," "Dear Oscar."

MEISER, EDITH. Born May 9, 1898 in Detroit, Mich. Vassar graduate. Bdwy debut 1923 in "The New Way," followed by "Fata Morgana," "The Guardsman," "Garrick Gaieties," "The Chief Thing," "Peggy-Ann," "Greater Love," "He," "Strangler Fig," "Let's Face It," "Mexican Hayride," "Round Trip," "Rich Full Life," "I Gotta Get Out," "Getting Married," "Sabrina Fair," "The Magic and the Loss," "Happy Hunting," "Unsinkable Molly Brown," OB in Airways Inc.," "Carefree Tree," "Pygmalion."

MENKEN, FAYE. Born Feb. 19, 1947 in NYC. Graduate NYU. Bdwy debut 1969 in "Fiddler on the Roof."

MERANDE, DORO. Born in Columbia, Kan. Bdwy debut 1935 in "Loose Moments," followed by "One Good Year," "Fulton of Oak Falls," "Red Harvest," "Angel Island," "Our Town," "Love's Old Sweet Song," "Beverly Hills," "The More the Merrier," "Junior Miss," "Hope for a Harvest," "Three's a Family," "Naked Genius," "Pickup Girl," "Violet," "Hope for the Best," "Apple of His Eye," "Silver Whistle," "Rat Race," "4 Twelves Are 48," "Lo and Behold," "Diary of a Scoundrel" (OB), "Front Page."

MERCOURI, MELINA. Born in Athens, Greece. Bdwy debut 1967 in "Illya, Darling," followed by "Lysistrata."

MEREDITH, LEE. Born Oct. 22, 1947 in River Edge, NJ. Graduate AADA. Bdwy debut 1969 in "A Teaspoon Every Four Hours," followed by "The Sunshine Boys."

MEYERS, MARSHA. Born Sept. 20, 1946 in Brooklyn. Attended AMDA. Debut OB 1969 in "Lend an Ear," followed by "Medea."

MICHAELS, LAURA. Born Nov. 17, 1953 in NYC. Attended HB Studio. Bdwy debut 1962 in "Sound of Music," followed by "Roar of the Greasepaint ...," "A Time For Singing," "The Me Nobody Knows," "Jesus Christ Superstar," "Mother Earth."

MICHAELS, RAF. Born Oct. 24, 1928 in Whitewater, Wis. Attended UWis. Bdwy debut 1955 in "Inherit the Wind," followed by "Deadfall," OB in "Faith of an Immigrant," "The Power and the Glory," "And the Wind Blows," "Matchmaker," "Kiss Me, Kate," "Hamlet," "Welded," "Taming of the Shrew," "Abe Lincoln in Illinois," "How to Succeed in Business ..."

MILANA, VINCENT DUKE. Born Apr. 11, 1939 in Newark, NJ. Graduate Carroll U., Neighborhood Playhouse. With APA, OB in "Abe Lincoln in Illinois," "Taming of the Shrew," "Color of Darkness," "Cannibals," "Now Is the Time," "The Birds," "12 Angry Men."

MILES, SYLVIA. Born Sept. 9, 1934 in NYC. Attended Pratt Inst., Actors Studio. Debut 1954 OB in "A Stone for Danny Fisher," followed by "Iceman Cometh," "The Balcony," "Chekhov Sketch Book," "Matty, Moron, Madonna," "The Kitchen," "Rosebloom," Bdwy "The Riot Act" (1963).

MILGRIM, LYNN. Born Mar. 17, 1944 in Philadelphia, Pa. Graduate Swarthmore, Harvard. Debut OB 1969 in "Frank Gagliano's City Scene," followed by "Crimes of Passion," "Macbeth," "Charley's Aunt," "Real Inspector Hound."

MILLER, BETTY. Born Mar. 27, 1925 in Boston. Attended UCLA. OB in "Summer and Smoke," "Cradle Song," "La Ronde," "Plays for Bleecker St.," "Desire under the Elms," "The Balcony," "The Power and the Glory," "Beaux Stratagem," "Gandhi," "Girl on the Via Flaminia," NYSF's "Hamlet," with APA in "You Can't Take It with You," "Right You Are," "Wild Duck," and "Cherry Orchard."

MILLER, JASON. Born in 1939 in Long Island City, NY. Graduate UScranton, CatholicU. Appeared OB in "Subject to Fits," "That Championship Season" which he wrote.

MILLER, KATHLEEN. Born July 1, 1945 in Los Angeles. Attended U Cal., AADA Debut OB in "House of Leather," followed by Bdwy bow (1970) in "Butterflies Are Free."

MILLER, MICHAEL. Born Sept. 1, 1931 in Los Angeles. Attended Bard Col. OB debut 1961 in "Under Milk Wood," followed by "The Lesson," "A Memory of 2 Mondays," "Little Murders," "Tom Paine," "Morning, Noon and Night," "Enemy of the People" (LC), "Whitsuntide," "Say When," Bdwy in "Ivanov," "Black Comedy," "Trial of Lee Harvey Oswald."

MILLER, SHARRON. Born in 1948 in Montclair, NJ. Attended Juilliard. On Bdwy in "A Funny Thing Happened on the Way ...," "How to Succeed in Business ...," "West Side Story," OB in "Love Me, Love My Children," "Hark!"

MINER, JAN. Born Oct. 15, 1917 in Boston. Debut 1958 OB in "Obligato," followed by "Decameron," "Dumbbell People," "Autograph Hound," Bdwy in "Viva Madison Avenue," "Lady of the Camellias," "Freaking out of Stephanie Blake," "Othello," "Milk Train Doesn't Stop Here Anymore," "Butterflies Are Free," "The Women."

MISISA, MICHAEL. Born Jan. 10, 1947 aboard HMS Queen Mary. Graduate Boston Cons. Bdwy debut 1968 in "Fig Leaves Are Falling," followed by "Mame," "Applause," "Follies," "Say When" (OB).

MITCHELL, ANN. Born Oct. 23 in Providence, RI. Bdwy debut 1958 in "Make a Million," OB in "Threepenny Opera," "Once upon a Mattress," "Amorous Flea," "Anna K."

MIXON, ALAN. Born Mar. 15, 1933 in Miami, Fla. Attended UMiami. Bdwy bow 1962 in "Something about a Soldier," followed by "Sign in Sidney Brustein's Window," "The Devils," "Unknown Soldier and His Wife," "Love Suicide at Schofield Barracks," OB in "Suddenly Last Summer," "Desire under the Elms," "Trojan Women," "Alchemist," "Child Buyer," "Mr. and Mrs. Lyman," "A Whitman Portrait," "Iphigenia in Aulis," "Small Craft Warnings," "Mourning Becomes Electra."

MONROE, SHIRLEY. Born Aug. 2 in North Carolina. Bdwy debut 1971 in "Purlie."

MONTALBAN, RICARDO. Born Nov. 25, 1920 in Mexico City. Bdwy debut 1956 in "Seventh Heaven," followed by "Jamaica," "Don Juan in Hell."

MOONEY, WILLIAM. Born in Bernie, Mo. Attended UColo. Bdwy debut 1961 in "A Man for All Seasons," followed by "A Place for Polly," OB in "Half Horse, Half Alligator," "Strike Heaven on the Face."

| Marty Morris | Nat Morris | Mary Ann Niles | John Newton | Lilly Noyes |

MOOR, BILL. Born July 13, 1931 in Toledo, O. Attended Northwestern, Denison U. Bdwy debut 1964 in "Blues for Mr. Charlie," followed by "Great God Brown," "Don Juan," OB in "Dandy Dick," "Love Nest," "Days and Nights of Beebee Fenstermaker," "The Collection," "The Owl Answers," "Long Christmas Dinner," "Fortune and Men's Eyes," LC's "King Lear" and "Cry of Players," "Boys in the Band."

MOOREHEAD, AGNES. Born Dec. 6, 1906 in Boston, Mass. Attended UWis., AADA. Bdwy debut 1929 in "Scarlet Pages," followed by "Soldiers and Women," Mercury Theatre productions, "Lord Pengo," "Don Juan in Hell."

MORDEN, ROGER. Born Mar. 21, 1939 in Iowa City, Io. Graduate Coe Col., Neighborhood Playhouse. Debut OB 1964 in "Old Glory," followed by "3 by Ferlinghetti," "Big Broadcast," Bdwy in "Man of La Mancha."

MORENO, RITA. Born Dec. 11, 1931 in Humacao, PR. Bdwy debut 1945 in "Skydrift," followed by "West Side Story," "Sign in Sidney Brustein's Window," "Last of the Red Hot Lovers."

MORRIS, GARRETT. Born Feb. 1, 1944 in New Orleans. Graduate Dillard U. OB in "Bible Salesman," "Slave Ship," "Transfers," "Operation Sidewinder" (LC), "In New England Winter," "Basic Training of Pavlo Hummel," Bdwy in "Porgy and Bess," "Hallelujah, Baby," "I'm Solomon," "The Great White Hope," "Ain't Supposed to Die a Natural Death."

MORRIS, MARTY. Born June 8, 1949 in Clarksburg, WVa. Graduate UWVa. Debut 1972 OB in "Riverwind," followed by "Riverwind" (ELT).

MORRIS, NAT. Born Mar. 13, 1951 in Richmond, Va. Attended Howard U. Bdwy debut 1972 in "Hair," followed by "Jesus Christ Superstar," "Dude."

MORSE, HAYWARD. Born Sept. 13, 1947 in London. Attended Upper Canada Col., RADA. Bdwy debut 1972 in "Butley."

MORSE, RICHARD. Born May 31 in Brookline, Mass. Attended Principia Col., Neighborhood Playhouse. Debut 1955 OB in "Teach Me How to Cry," followed by "Thor With Angels," "Makropoulos Secret," "All Kinds of Giants," "Mime Theatre," on Bdwy in "Mother Courage," "Fiddler on the Roof."

MORSE, ROBERT. Born May 18, 1931 in Newton, Mass. Bdwy debut 1955 in "The Matchmaker," followed by "Say, Darling" for which he received a Theatre World Award, "Take Me Along," "How to Succeed in Business . . ." "Sugar."

MORSELL, FRED. Born Aug. 3, 1940 in NYC. Graduate Dickinson Col. Debut OB 1971 in "Any Resemblance to Persons Living or Dead," followed by LC's "Enemies" and "Merchant of Venice."

MORTON, BROOKS. Born Oct. 5, 1932 in Ky. Attended Northwestern U. Debut OB 1962 in "Riverwind," followed by "Sunday Dinner," "Beyond the Fringe," CC's "West Side Story" and "Say, Darling," Bdwy in "Marathon '33," "Three Sisters," "Ivanov," "Prime of Miss Jean Brodie," "Her First Roman."

MOSS, ARNOLD. Born Jan. 28, 1910 in Bklyn. Attended CCNY, Columbia. With LeGallienne's Repertory Co., Bdwy in "Fifth Column," "Hold on to Your Hats," "Journey to Jerusalem," "Flight to the West," "The Land Is Bright," "The Tempest," "Front Page," "Twelfth Night," "King Lear," "Measure for Measure," "Follies."

MULHARE, EDWARD. Born in 1923 in Ireland. Bdwy debut 1957 in "My Fair Lady," followed by "Devil's Advocate," "Mary, Mary," "Don Juan in Hell."

MURCH, ROBERT G. Born Apr. 17, 1935 in Jefferson Barracks, Mo. Graduate Wash. U. Bdwy bow 1966 in "Hostile Witness," followed by "The Harangues" (NEC), "Conduct Unbecoming," "The Changing Room," OB in "Charles Abbott & Son," "She Stoops to Conquer."

MURRAY, BRIAN. Born Oct. 9, 1939 in Johannesburg, SA. Debut 1964 OB in "The Knack," followed by "King Lear" (LC), Bdwy in "All in Good Time," "Rosencrantz and Guildenstern Are Dead," "Sleuth."

MURRAY, PEG. Born in Denver, Colo. Attended Western Reserve U. OB in "Children of Darkness," "A Midsummer Night's Dream," "Oh, Dad, Poor Dad . . . ," "Small Craft Warnings," Bdwy in "Great Sebastians," "Gypsy," "Blood, Sweat and Stanley Poole," "She Loves Me," "Anyone Can Whistle," "The Subject Was Roses," "Something More," "Cabaret," "Fiddler on the Roof."

MYDELL, JOSEPH. Born June 30, 1945 in Savannah, Ga. Graduate NYU. Debut OB 1969 in "Ofay Watcher," followed by NYSF's "Volpone," and "Henry IV," "Please Don't Cry and Say No."

NAIL, JOANNE. Born June 3, 1947 in Spokane, Wash. Graduate Wash. State Col. Bdwy debut 1971 in "Scratch," followed by "Lysistrata," "The Orphan" (OB).

NAPOLI, JOSEPH. Born Aug. 1940 in New Orleans. Attended Fordham, Tulane, Sorbonne. Debut OB 1971 in "One Flew Over the Cuckoo's Nest."

NEBIOL, GARY. Born Aug. 27, 1943 in NYC. Debut OB 1972 in "Present Tense."

NELSON, BARRY. Born in 1925 in Oakland, Cal. Graduate UCal. Bdwy debut 1943 in "Winged Victory," followed by "Light up the Sky," "The Moon Is Blue," "Wake Up Darling," "Rat Race," "Mary, Mary," "Nobody Loves Albatross," "Cactus Flower," "Everything in the Graden," "Only Game in Town," "Fig Leaves Are Falling," "Engagement Baby."

NELSON, CHRISTOPHER. Born Apr. 29, 1944 in Duluth, Minn. Bdwy debut 1968 in "Cabaret," followed by "Promises, Promises," "Follies."

NELSON, GENE. Born Mar. 24, 1920 in Seattle, Wash. Bdwy debut 1942 "This is the Army," followed by "Lend an Ear" for which he won a Theatre World Award, "Follies."

NELSON, HERBERT. Born Dec. 17, 1913 in Stillwater, Min. Attended UMn. On Bdwy in "Night Before Christmas," "First Crocus," "His and Hers," "Twigs," OB in "Abe Lincoln in Illinois," "Baal," "Othello," "Comma-Performance."

NELSON, JOAN. Born June 7, 1943 in LaGrande, Ore. Graduate Redlands U. Bdwy debut 1968 in "Here's Where I Belong," followed by "Wonderful Town" (CC), "Lovely Ladies, Kind Gentlemen," OB in "Beggar's Opera."

NESBITT, CATHLEEN. Born Nov. 24, 1889 in Cheshire, Eng. Attended Victoria Col. Bdwy debut 1911 in "Well of the Saints," followed by "Justice," "Hush," "Such Is Life," "Magic," "Garden of Paradise," "General Post," "Saving Grace," "Diversion," "Cocktail Party," "Gigi," "Sabrina Fair," "Portrait of a Lady," "Anastasia," "My Fair Lady," "The Sleeping Prince," "Second String," "Romulus," "Uncle Vanya."

NETTLETON, LOIS. Born in Oak Park, Ill. Attended Goodman Theatre, Actors Studio. Bdwy debut 1949 in "Biggest Thief in Town," followed by "Darkness at Noon," "Cat on a Hot Tin Roof," "God and Kate Murphy," "Silent Night, Lonely Night," "A Streetcar Named Desire" (LCR).

NEWMAN, ELLEN. Born Sept. 5, 1950 in NYC. Attended San Diego State U., Central School in London. Debut 1972 OB in "Right You Are," followed by LCR's "Merchant of Venice" and "Streetcar Named Desire."

NEWMAN, PHYLLIS. Born Mar. 19, 1935 in Jersey City, NJ. Attended Western Reserve U. Bdwy debut 1953 in "Wish You Were Here," followed by "Bells Are Ringing," "I Feel Wonderful" (OB), "First Impressions," "Subways Are for Sleeping," "Apple Tree," "On the Town," "Prisoner of Second Avenue."

NEWMAN, STEPHEN D. Born Jan. 20, 1943 in Seattle, Wash. Stanford Graduate. Debut 1971 OB in Judith Anderson's "Hamlet," followed by "School for Wives," "Beggar's Opera," "Pygmalion," Bdwy in "An Evening with Richard Nixon and . . . ," "Emperor Henry IV."

NEWTON, JOHN. Born Nov. 2, 1925 in Grand Junction, Colo. Graduate UWash. Debut 1951 OB in "Othello," followed by "As You Like It," "Candida," "Candaules Commissioner," LCR'S "The Crucible" and "Streetcar Named Desire," Bdwy in "Weekend" (1968).

NICHOLLS, ALLAN. Born Apr. 8, 1945 in Montreal, Can. Bdwy debut 1968 in "Hair," followed by "Inner City," "Dude."

NICKERSON, SHANE. Born Jan. 29, 1964 in Miami, Fla. Bdwy debut 1972 in "Pippin."

NILES, MARY ANN. Born May 2, 1933 in NYC. Attended Miss Finchley's Ballet Acad. Bdwy debut in "Girl from Nantucket," followed by "Beggar's a Song," "Call Me Mister," "Make Mine Manhattan," "La Plume de Ma Tante," "Carnival," "Flora the Red Menace," "Sweet Charity," "George M!," "No, No, Nanette," "Irene," OB in "The Boys from Syracuse," CC's "Wonderful Town" and "Carnival."

NISSEN, PETER. Born Aug. 23, 1964 in St. Louis, Mo. Bdwy debut 1972 in "Via Galactica."

NOONE, BILL E. Born May 1, 1944 in Montgomery, WVa. Graduate SMU. Debut OB 1973 in "Medea."

NORFLEET, CECELIA. Born Sept. 18, 1949 in Chicago. Graduate Roosevelt U. Bdwy debut 1969 in "Hair," followed by "Jesus Christ Superstar," "Ain't Supposed to Die a Natural Death," "Lady Day" (OB), "Seesaw."

NORWICK, DOUGLAS. Born Oct. 27 in NYC. Graduate UMich. Bdwy debut 1967 in "Rosencrantz and Guildenstern Are Dead," followed by "Purlie."

NOVY, NITA. Born June 13, 1950 in Wilkes-Barre, Pa. Graduate Duke U. Bdwy debut 1960 in "Gypsy," followed by "Sound of Music," ELT's "How to Succeed in Business . . ."

NOYES, LILLY. Born July 27, 1944 in San Francisco, Cal. Attended Sarah Lawrence Col. Debut OB 1967 in "The Wicked Cooks," followed by "The Retreat," "Harold and Sondra," "As You Like It," "The Phantasmagoria Historia . . . ."

| Don Nute | Renee Orin | Seamus O'Brien | Lucille Patton | Anthony Palmer |

UTE, DON. Born Mar. 13, in Connellsville, Pa. Attended UDenver. Debut 1965 in "The Trojan Women," followed by "Boys in the Band," "Mad eatre for Madmen," "The Eleventh Dynasty," "About Time," "The Urban risis," "Christmas Rappings," "The Life of Man," "A Look at the Fifties."

YE, CARRIE. Attended Stephens Col., Yale. Bdwy debut 1960 in "A Second ring," followed by "Mary, Mary," "Half a Sixpence," "A Very Rich oman," "Cop-out," OB in "Ondine," "Ghosts," "Importance of Being Earst," "Trojan Women," "The Real Inspector Hound."

YPE, RUSSELL. Born Apr. 26, 1924 in Zion, Ill. Attended Lake Forest Col. wy debut 1949 in "Regina," followed by "Call Me Madam" for which he ceived a Theatre World Award, "Tender Trap," "Tunnel of Love," "Wake , Darling," CC's "Carousel" and "Brigadoon," "The Owl and the Pussycat," irl in the Freudian Slip," "Hello, Dolly!," OB in "Brouhaha," "Private ves," "Lady Audley's Secret."

AKLAND, SIMON. Born Aug. 28, 1920 in Bklyn. Attended Columbia. wy in "Skipper Next to God," "Light up the Sky," "Caesar and Cleopatra," arvey," "The Shrike," "Sands of Negev," "The Great Sebastians," "Angela," wigs."

'BRIEN, FRANK. Born Apr. 28 in NYC. Graduate Georgetown U. Bdwy but 1971 in "Two Gentlemen of Verona."

'BRIEN, MARCIA. Born Mar. 17, 1934 in Indiana. Graduate Ind.U. Bdwy but 1970 in "Man of La Mancha," followed OB in "Now Is the Time for All ood Men," "House Party."

'BRIEN, SEAMUS. Born July 14, 1932 in London. Graduate UDetroit. ebut OB 1971 in "The Eagle with Two Heads," followed by "Salome," "The antasticks," Bdwy in "Vivat! Vivat Regina!"

'BRIEN, SYLVIA. Born May 4, 1924 in Dublin, Ire. Debut OB 1961 in "O arry Me," followed by "Red Roses for Me," "Every Other Evil," "3 by Casey," "Essence of Women," "Dear Oscar," Bdwy in "Passion of Josef D.," ight Honourable Gentleman," "Loves of Cass McGuire," "Hadrian VII," onduct Unbecoming."

CASIO, JOSE. Born July 13, 1938 in Morovis, PR. Attended UPR, Theatre ing. Debut OB 1965 with NYSF, followed by "Ox Cart," Bdwy in "Plaza ite," "6 Rms Riv Vu."

CONNOR, KEVIN. Born May 7, 1938 in Honolulu. Attended UHawaii, eighborhood Playhouse. Debut 1964 OB in "Up to Thursday," followed by ix from LaMama," "Rimers of Eldritch," "Tom Paine," "Boy on the raight-back Chair," "Dear Janet Rosenberg," "Eyes of Chalk," Bdwy (1970) loria and Esperanza," "Kool Aid" (LC).

HARA, JENNY. Born Feb. 24 in Sonora, Cal. Attended Carnegie Tech. dwy debut 1964 in "Dylan," followed by "Fig Leaves Are Falling," "Crissrossing," "Promises, Promises," OB in "Hang Down Your Head and Die," lay with a Tiger," "Arms and the Man," "Sambo," "My House Is Your ouse," "The Kid."

LEARY, JOHN. Born May 5, 1926 in Newton, Mass. Graduate Northwest-n U. Bdwy debut 1962 in "General Seeger," OB in "Picture of Dorian Gray," Rimers of Eldritch," "Big Broadcast."

LIVER, JODY. Born Aug. 6, 1954 in Forest Hills, N.Y. Bdwy debut in "The lappy Time," followed by "Lenny."

PATOSHU, DAVID. Born Jan. 30, 1918 in The Bronx. Attended CCNY. dwy debut 1940 in "Night Music," followed by "Clinton Street," "Man of omorrow," "Me and Molly," "Flight into Egypt," "Reclining Figure," "Silk tockings," "Once More with Feeling," "The Wall," "Bravo Giovanni," Lorenzo," "Does a Tiger Wear a Necktie," OB in "Yoshe Kalb."

RBACH, JERRY. Born Oct. 20, 1935 in NYC. Attended Northwestern, UIll. dwy debut 1961 in "Carnival," followed by "Guys and Dolls" (CC), LC's Carousel" and "Annie Get Your Gun," "The Natural Look," "Promises, romises," "6 Rms Riv Vu," OB in "Threepenny Opera," "Fantasticks," "Cra-le Will Rock," "Scuba Duba."

RFALY, ALEXANDER. Born Oct. 10, 1935 in Brooklyn. Appeared in South Pacific" (LC), "How Now, Dow Jones," "Ari," "Sugar," "Cyrano," OB "The End of All Things Natural," "Mahagonny," "Johnny Johnson."

RIN, RENEE. Born Oct. 25 in Slatington, Pa. Attended Carnegie Tech. ebut 1951 OB in "Good News," followed by "The Great Magician," "River-ind," Bdwy in "Plain and Fancy," "Cafe Crown," "Slapstick Tragedy," Show Me Where the Good Times Are," "Plaza Suite."

SBORNE, KIPP. Born Oct. 17, 1944 in Jersey City, N.J. Attended UMich., eighborhood Playhouse. Bdwy debut 1970 in "Butterflies Are Free" for which e received a Theatre World Award, followed (OB) by "The Children's Mass," Love Gotta Come by Saturday Night."

O'SULLIVAN, MAUREEN. Born May 17, 1911 in Roscommon, Ire. Bdwy debut 1962 in "Never Too Late," followed by "The Subject Was Roses," "Keep It in the Family," "Front Page," "Charley's Aunt," "No Sex Please, We're British."

OTTENHEIMER, ALBERT M. Born Sept. 6, 1904 in Tacoma, Wash. Graduate UWash. Bdwy debut 1946 in "Affair of Honor," followed by "West Side Story," "Deputy," OB in "Monday's Heroes," "Tiger," "Mother Riba," "A Christmas Carol," "Juno and the Paycock," "Italian Straw Hat," "Iceman Cometh," "Call It Virtue," "Immoralist," "Cat and the Canary," "Exhaustion of Our Son's Love," "Deadly Game," "Brother Gorski," "The Kid."

OWENS, ELIZABETH. Born Feb. 26, 1938 in NYC. Attended New School, Neighborhood Playhouse. Debut 1955 OB in "Dr. Faustus Lights the Lights," followed by "The Lovers" (Bdwy), "Chit Chat on a Rat," "The Miser," "The Father," "The Importance of Being Earnest," "Candida," "Trumpets and Drums," "Oedipus," "Macbeth," "Not Now Darling" (Bdwy), "Uncle Vanya," "Misalliance," "Master Builder," "American Gothics," "The Play's the Thing."

PAGE, GERALDINE. Born Nov. 22, 1924 in Kirksville, Mo. Attended Goodman Theatre. OB in "7 Mirrors," "Summer and Smoke" for which she received a Theatre World Award, "Macbeth," "Look Away," Bdwy debut 1953 in "Midsummer," followed by "The Immoralist," "Rainmaker," "Innkeepers," "Separate Tables," "Sweet Bird of Youth," "Strange Interlude," "Three Sisters," "P.S. I Love You," "The Great Indoors," "White Lies," "Black Comedy," "Little Foxes," "Angela."

PAISNER, DINA. Born in Brooklyn. Bdwy debut 1963 in "Andorra," OB in "Cretan Women," "Pullman Car Hiawatha," "Lysistrata," "If 5 Years Pass," "Troubled Waters," "Sap of Life," "Cave at Machpelah," "Threepenny Opera," "Montserrat," "Blood Wedding," "Gandhi," "Medea."

PALMER, ANTHONY. Born July 19, 1934 in Eagle Pass, Tex. Bdwy debut 1964 in "Passion of Josef D," followed by "Traveller without Luggage," OB in "Antony and Cleopatra," "Macbeth," "Winter's Tale," "Whistle in the Dark," "Nobody Hears a Broken Drum," "Wedding Band."

PALMER, LELAND. Born June 16, 1945 in Port Washington, NY. Bdwy debut 1966 in "Joyful Noise," followed by "Applause," "Pippin," OB in "Your Own Thing."

PALMER, PETER. Born Sept. 20, 1931 in Milwaukee, Wis. Attended UIll. Bdwy debut 1956 in "Li'l Abner" for which he received a Theatre World Award, followed by "Brigadoon" (CC), "Lorelei."

PALMIERI, JOSEPH. Born Aug. 1, 1939 in Bklyn. Attended Catholic U. With NYSF 1965–6, "Cyrano de Bergerac" (LCR), OB in "Butter and Egg Man," "Boys in the Band," "Beggar's Opera," Bdwy in "Lysistrata."

PANKIN, STUART. Born Apr. 8, 1946 in Philadelphia, Pa. Graduate Dickinson Col., Columbia. With NYSF (1968–71) in "Wars of the Roses," "Richard III," "Timon of Athens," "Cymbeline," LCR's "Mary Stuart," "Narrow Road to the Deep North," "Twelfth Night," and "The Crucible."

PAPAS, IRENE. Born Sept. 3, 1929 in Chiliomodion, Greece. Bdwy debut 1967 in "That Summer, That Fall," followed OB by "Iphigenia in Aulis," "Medea."

PAPE, JOAN. Born Jan. 23, 1944 in Detroit, Mich. Graduate Purdue U., Yale. Debut 1972 in "Suggs" (LC), Bdwy in "The Secret Affairs of Mildred Wild."

PARIS, JACKIE. Born Sept. 11, 1961 in Jersey City, NJ. Debut OB in "A Cry of Players" (LC), followed by "Dr. Selavy's Magic Theatre."

PARKER, LEONARD. Born July 22, 1932 in Cleveland, O. Graduate Western Reserve U. Debut OB 1958 in "Dark of the Moon," followed by "The Apple," "The Connection," "In White America," Bdwy in "Porgy and Bess," "Fly Blackbird," "The Physicists," "The Long Dream," "One Flew over the Cuckoo's Nest."

PASSELTINER, BERNIE. Born Nov. 21, 1931 in NYC. Graduate Catholic U. OB in "Square in the Eye," "Sourball," "As Virtuously Given," "Now Is the Time for All Good Men," "Rain," "Kaddish," on Bdwy in "The Office," "The Jar."

PATTERSON, WILBUR, JR. Born May 25, 1946 in NYC. Attended AMDA. Debut OB 1971 in "One Flew over the Cuckoo's Nest."

PATTON, LUCILLE. Born in NYC; attended Neighborhood Playhouse. Bdwy debut 1946 in "Winter's Tale," followed by "Topaze," "Arms and the Man," "Joy to the World," "All You Need Is One Good Break," "Fifth Season," "Heavenly Twins," "Rhinoceros," "Marathon '33," "Last Analysis," "Dinner at 8," "La Strada," "Unlikely Heroes," "Love Suicide at Schofield Barracks," OB in "Ulysses in Nighttown," "Failures," "Three Sisters," "Yes, Yes, No, No," "Tango," "Mme. de Sade."

Lou Polan   Marylou Perhacs   Tom Poston   Lu Ann Post   Barry Primus

PAYTON-WRIGHT, PAMELA. Born Nov. 1, 1941 in Pittsburgh. Graduate Birmingham Southern Col. RADA. Bdwy debut 1967 with APA in "The Show-Off," "Exit The King," and "The Cherry Orchard," "Jimmy Shine," OB in "The Effect of Gama Rays on Man-in-the-Moon Marigolds," "Crucible" (LC), "Mourning Becomes Electra."

PEERCE, JAN. Born June 3 in NYC. Studied at NY Col. of Music. Leading opera and concert tenor before Bdwy debut Dec. 14, 1971 in "Fiddler on the Roof."

PENN, EDWARD. Born in Washington, DC. Studied at HB Studio. Debut 1965 OB in "The Queen and the Rebels," followed by "My Wife and I," "Invitation to a March," "Of Thee I Sing," "Fantasticks," "Greenwillow," "One for the Money," "Dear Oscar," "Speed Gets the Poppys."

PENNER, RALPH. Born Dec. 9, 1947 in NYC. Graduate Yale. Debut OB 1973 in "Spoon River Anthology."

PENTECOST, GEORGE. Born July 15, 1939 in Detroit. Graduate Wayne State, UMich. With APA in "Scapin," "Lower Depths," "The Tavern," "School for Scandal," "Right You Are," "War and Peace," "The Wild Duck," "The Show-Off," "Pantagleize," and "The Cherry Orchard," "The Boys in the Band" (OB), "School for Wives," "Twelfth Night" and "Enemies" at LC.

PENZNER, SEYMOUR. Born July 29, 1915 in Yonkers, NY. Attended CCNY. OB in "Crystal Heart," "Guitar," Bdwy in "Oklahoma," "Finian's Rainbow," "Call Me Madam," "Paint Your Wagon," "Can-Can," "Kean," "Baker Street," "Man of La Mancha."

PEREZ, LAZARO. Born Dec. 17, 1945 in Havana, Cuba. Bdwy debut 1969 in "Does a Tiger Wear a Necktie?," OB in "Romeo and Juliet," "12 Angry Men," "Wonderful Years," "Alive."

PERHACS, MARYLOU. Born June 15, 1944 in Teaneck, NJ. Juilliard graduate. Bdwy debut 1969 in "Promises, Promises," followed by "Sugar," "Lysistrata."

PERRY, JOHN BENNETT. Born Jan. 4, 1941 in Williamston, Mass. Graduate St. Lawrence U. Debut OB 1967 in "Now Is the Time for All Good Men," followed by "A Month of Sundays," "Ballad of Johnny Pot," Bdwy in "Mother Earth."

PETERSON, KURT. Born Feb. 12, 1948 in Stevens Point, Wisc. Attended AMDA. Appeared in "An Ordinary Miracle" (OB), "West Side Story" (LC'68), Bdwy debut 1969 in "Dear World," followed by "Dames at Sea" (OB), "Follies"

PETRICOFF, ELAINE. Born in Cincinnati, O. Graduate Syracuse U. Bdwy debut 1971 in "The Me Nobody Knows," OB in "Hark!"

PETRO, MICHAEL. Born July 1, 1944 in Westfield, NY. Graduate Slippery Rock Col., HB Studio. Bdwy debut 1971 in "Fiddler on the Roof," followed by "Diary of Adam and Eve" (ELT).

PHALEN, ROBERT. Born May 10, 1937 in San Francisco. Attended CCSF. UCal. With LCRep in "Danton's Death," "Country Wife," "Caucasian Chalk Circle," "Alchemist," "Yerma," "Galileo," "St. Joan," "Tiger at the Gates," "Cyrano," "King Lear," "Cry of Players," "In the Matter of J. Robert Oppenheimer," "Operation Sidewinder," "Beggar on Horseback," "Good Woman of Setzuan," "Birthday Party," "Silence," "Mary Stuart," "Narrow Road to the Deep North," "Twelfth Night," "The Crucible," "Enemies," "The Plough and the Stars," "Merchant of Venice," and "Streetcar Named Desire."

PHILLIPS, MARY BRACKEN. Born Aug. 15, 1946 in Kansas City, Mo. Attended Kansas U. Debut 1969 OB in "Perfect Party," Bdwy bow in "1776," followed by "Look Where I'm At" (OB), "Different Times," "Hurry Harry."

PHILLIPS, RANDY. Born Jan. 22, 1926 in NYC. Attended Juilliard. Bdwy debut in "How to Succeed in Business . . .," followed by "Hello, Dolly!," "Mame," OB in "Pinafore," "Riverwind."

PHILLIPS, WENDELL K. Born Nov. 27, 1907 in Bladinsville, Ill. Attended UWisc. Bdwy bow 1931 in "Incubator," followed by "Mother Sings," "Many Mansions," "Abe Lincoln in Illinois," "Fifth Column," "Anne of the Thousand Days," "Solid Gold Cadillac," "The Investigation," OB in "Death of J. K." "The Birds."

PINCUS, WARREN. Born Apr. 13, 1938 in Bklyn. Attended CCNY. OB in "Miss Nepertiti Regrets," "Circus," "Magician," "Boxcars," "Demented World," "Give My Regards," "Electronic Nigger," "Last Pad," "Waiting for Godot," "In the Time of Harry Harass," "Yoshe Kalb."

PINZA, CARLA. Born Feb. 2, 1942 in Puerto Rico. Attended Hunter Col. OB in "The Ox Cart," "House of Flowers," Bdwy debut 1968 in "The Cuban Thing," followed by "Two Gentlemen of Verona."

PLAYTEN, ALICE. Born Aug. 28, 1947 in NYC. Attended NYU. Bdwy debut 1960 in "Gypsy," followed by "Oliver," "Hello, Dolly!," "Henry, Sweet Henry" for which she received a Theatre World Award, "George M!," OB in "Promenade," "Last Sweet Days of Isaac," "National Lampoon's Lemmings."

PLESHETTE, JOHN. Born July 27, 1942 in NYC. Attended Brown U. Bdwy debut 1966 in "The Zulu and the Zayda," followed by "Jimmy Shine," OB in "Sound of Silence," NYSF, "Macbird," "It's Called the Sugar Plum," "Shrinking Bride," "Green Julia."

PLUMLEY, DON. Born Feb. 11, 1934 in Los Angeles. Graduate Pepperdine Col. Debut OB 1961 in "The Cage," followed by NYSF's "Midsummer Night Dream," "Richard II," "Cymbeline," and "Much Ado about Nothing," "Saving Grace," "A Whistle in the Dark," "Operation Sidewinder" and "Enemy of The People" (LC), "Back Bog Beast Bait," "The Kid."

PLUMMER, CHRISTOPHER. Born Dec. 13, 1929 in Toronto, Can. Bdwy debut 1954 in "Starcross Story," followed by "Home Is the Hero," "The Dark Is Light Enough" for which he received a Threatre World Award, "Medea," "The Lark," "Night of the Auk," "J.B.," "Arturo Ui," "Royal Hunt of the Sun," "Cyrano."

PODELL, RICK. Born Nov. 16, 1946 in Los Angeles. Attended San Francisco State. Debut 1972 OB in "Two if by Sea," followed by "Buy Bonds Buster," Bdwy in "Mother Earth."

POINTER, PRISCILLA. Born in NYC. With LCRep from 1965, in "Summertree," "An Evening for Merlin Finch," "Inner Journey," "Disintergration of James Cherry," "Time of Your Life," "Camino Real," "Amphitryon," "Good Woman of Setzuan," "Scenes from American Life," "Play Strindberg," "Ride Across Lake Constance," and "Streetcar Named Desire."

POLAN, LOU. Born June 15, 1904 in Russia. Attended Neighborhood Playhouse. Bdwy debut 1922 in "R.U.R.," followed by "Bootleggers," "Jolly Roger," "Cyrano," "Othello," "Hamlet," "Goat Song," "Immortal Thief," "Electra," "Henry V," "Light of Asia," "Enemy of the People," "Bonds of Interest," "Merchant of Venice," "Firebird," "Yoshe Kalb," "The Young Generation First," "Sweet Mystery of Life," "Hymn to the Rising Sun," "Haiti," "All the Living," "Golden Boy," "Night Music," "Liberty Jones," "Walk into My Parlor," "Cafe Crown," "Whole World Over," "Gentleman from Athens," "Golden State," "Desire under the Elms," "Bus Stop," "Seagull," "Drink to Me Only," "Legend of Lizzie," "Tenth Man," "Creation of the World and Other Business."

POST, LU ANN. Born July 18, 1947 in Oak Park, Ill. Attended Purdue U. Goodman Theatre. Debut OB 1972 in "Lady Audley's Secret."

POSTON, TOM. Born Oct. 17, 1921 in Columbus, O. Attended Bethany Col. AADA. Bdwy debut 1947 in "Cyrano," followed by "Insect Comedy" (CC), "King Lear," "Stockade," "Grand Prize," "Will Success Spoil Rock Hunter?," "Goodbye Again," "Romanoff and Juliet," "Drink to Me Only," "Golden Fleecing," "Come Play with Me" (OB), "The Conquering Hero," "Come Blow Your Horn," "Mary, Mary," "But Seriously," "40 Carats," "A Funny Thing Happened on the Way to the Forum."

PREMICE, JOSEPHINE. Born July 21, 1926 in Brooklyn. Graduate Columbia, Cornell. Bdwy debut 1945 in "Blue Holiday," followed by "Caribbean Carnival," "Mister Johnson," "Jamaica," "A Hand Is on the Gate," OB in "House of Flowers," "Cherry Orchard."

PRICE, PAUL B. Born Oct. 7, 1933 in Carteret, NJ. Attended Pasadena Playhouse. Debut OB 1960 in "Dead End," followed by "Banquet for the Moon," "O Say Can You See," "Dumbwaiter," "Live Like Pigs," "Medea," "4H Club," "Waiting for Godot," Bdwy in "A Cook for Mr. General," "Let Me Hear You Smile."

PRIMROSE, ALEK. Born Aug. 20, 1934 in San Joaquin, Cal. Attended Col. of the Pacific. OB in "In Good King Charles' Golden Days," "Golem," "Leave It to Jane," "The Balcony," "Rules of the Game," "A Man's a Man," "In White America," "Kitchen," "Trials of Oz," LCRep's "Incident at Vichy" and "Tartuffe," Bdwy in "A Cook for Mr. General," "House of Atreus," "Arturo Ui," "Room Service," "Ring Round the Bathtub," "The Lincoln Mask."

PRIMUS, BARRY. Born Feb. 16, 1938 in NYC. Attended CCNY. Bdwy debut 1960 in "The Nervous Set," followed by "Oh, Dad, Poor Dad . . .," "Creation of the World and Other Business," OB in "Henry IV," "Huui, Huui," "The Criminals."

PRITCHETT, LIZABETH. Born Mar. 12, 1920 in Dallas, Tex. Attended SMU. Bdwy debut 1959 in "Happy Town," followed by "Sound of Music," "Maria Golovin," "The Yearling," "A Funny Thing Happened on the Way to the Forum," OB in "Cindy," "The Real Inespctor Hound," "The Karl Marx Play."

PUGH, TED. Born Apr. 24, 1937 in Anadarko, Okla. Graduate UOkla. OB in "In the Nick of Time," "Have I Got One for You," "Don't Shoot, Mable, It's Your Husband," "Now," "Lend an Ear," Bdwy in "Irene."

258

Virginia Pulos   Richard Quarry   Mimi Randolph   Orrin Reiley   Regina Ress

PULOS, VIRGINIA. Born Oct. 12, 1947 in Dayton, O. Graduate Cincinnati Cons. Debut OB 1972 in "Lady Audley's Secret," followed by "Smile, Smile, Smile."

QUARRY, RICHARD. Born Aug. 9, 1944 in Akron, O. Graduate UAkron, NYU. Bdwy bow 1970 in "Georgy," followed by "Oh! Calcutta!," "Grease."

QUAYLE, ANTHONY. Born Sept. 7, 1913 in Ainsdale, Eng. Attended RADA. Bdwy debut 1936 in "Country Wife," followed by "Tamburlaine the Great," "The Firstborn," "Galileo" (LC) "Halfway up the Tree," "Sleuth."

RACHELLE, BERNIE. Born Oct. 7, 1939 in NYC. Graduate Yeshiva U., Hunter Col. OB in "Winterset," "Golden Boy," "Street Scene," "World of Scholom Aleichem," "Diary of Anne Frank," "Electra," "Nighthawks," "House Party."

RACHINS, ALAN. Born Oct. 3, 1942 in Brookline, Mass. Attended U. Pa. Bdwy debut 1967 in "After The Rain," followed by "Hadrian VII," "Oh! Calcutta!"

RAE, CHARLOTTE. Born Apr. 22, 1926 in Milwaukee, Wis. Northwestern Graduate. Bdwy debut 1952 in "3 Wishes for Jamie," followed by "Li'l Abner," "The Beauty Part," "Pickwick," "Morning, Noon and Night," "The Chinese," "B in "Threepenny Opera," "Littlest Revue," "Beggar's Opera," "New Tenant," "Victims of Duty," "Henry IV," "Whiskey."

RAGNO, JOSEPH. Born Mar. 11, 1936 in Bklyn. Attended Allegheny Col. Debut 1960 OB in "Worm in the Horseradish," followed by "Elizabeth the Queen," "A Country Scandal," "The Shrike," "Cymbeline," "Love Me, Love My Children," "Interrogation of Havana," "The Birds," Bdwy bow 1969 in "Indians."

RALSTON, TERI. Born Feb. 16, 1943 in Holyoke, Colo. Graduate SF State Col. Debut 1969 OB in "Jacques Brel Is Alive . . . ," Bdwy 1970 in "Company," followed by "A Little Night Music."

RAMSAY, REMAK. Born Feb. 2, 1937 in Baltimore, Md. Princeton graudate. OB in "Hang Down Your Head and Die," "The Real Inspector Hound," Bdwy in "Half a Sixpence," "Sheep on the Runway," "Lovely Ladies, Kind Gentlemen," "On the Town."

RANDOLPH, JOHN. Born June 1, 1915 in the Bronx. Attended CCNY, Actors Studio. Bdwy debut 1937 in "Revolt of the Beavers," followed by "The Emperor's New Clothes," "Capt. Jinks," "No More Peace," "Coriolanus," "Medicine Show," "Hold on to Your Hats," "Native Son," "Command Decision," "Come Back, Little Sheba," "Golden State," "Peer Gynt," "Paint Your Wagon," "Seagulls over Sorrento," "Grey-Eyed People," "Room Service," "All Summer Long," "House of Flowers," "The Visit," "Mother Courage and Her Children," "Sound of Music," "Case of Libel," "Conversation at Midnight," "My Sweet Charlie," OB in "An Evening's Frost," "The Peddler and the Dodo Bird," "Our Town," "Line," "Baba Goya."

RANDOLPH, MIMI. Born Dec. 26, 1922 in Montreal, Can. Debut OB 1962 In "All in Love," followed by "Jo," "Pocketwatch," on Bdwy in "Dear Me, the Sky Is Falling," "Fiddler on the Roof."

RAPHAEL, GERRIANNE. Born Feb. 23, 1935 in NYC. Attended New School, Columbia. On Bdwy in "Solitaire," "Guest in the House," "Violet," "Goodbye, My Fancy," "Seventh Heaven," "Li'l Abner," "Saratoga," "Man of La Mancha," OB in "Threepenny Opera," "The Boy Friend," "Ernest in Love," "Say When."

RATCLIFFE, SAMUEL D. Born Mar. 30, 1945 in Eagle Lake, Fla. Graduate Birmingham Southern Col. Debut 1969 OB in "The Fantasticks," Bdwy in "Fiddler on the Roof," "Hurry Harry."

RATHBURN, ROGER. Born Nov. 11, 1940 in Perrysburg, O. Attended Ohio State, Neighborhood Playhouse. Bdwy debut 1971 in "No, No, Nanette," for which he received a Theatre World Award.

RAYE, MARTHA. Born Aug. 27, 1916 in Butte, Mont. Bdwy debut 1934 in "Calling All Stars," followed by "Earl Carroll's Sketchbook," "Hold on to Your Hats," "Hello, Dolly!," "No, No, Nanette."

RAYSON, BENJAMIN. Born in NYC. Bdwy debut 1953 in "Can-Can," followed by "Silk Stockings," "Bells Are Ringing," "A Little Night Music."

REAMS, LEE ROY. Born Aug. 23, 1942 in Covington, Ky. Graduate U. Cinn. Cons. Bdwy debut 1966 in "Sweet Charity," followed by "Oklahoma!" (LC), "Applause."

REDFIELD, WILLIAM. Born Jan. 26, 1927 in NYC. Bdwy bow 1936 in "Swing Your Lady," followed by "Excursion," "Virginia," "Stop-over," "Our Town," "Second Helping," "Junior Miss," "Snafu," "Barefoot Boy with Cheek," "Montserrat," "Miss Liberty," "Out of This World," "Misalliance," "Double in Hearts," "Man for All Seasons," "Minor Adjustment," "Love Suicide at Schofield Barracks," "Dude," OB in "Making of Moo."

REILEY, ORRIN. Born Aug. 12, 1946 in Santa Monica, Cal. Graduate UCLA. Bdwy debut 1969 in "Dear World," followed by "Man of La Mancha," "Applause," "On the Town," "Seesaw."

RESS, REGINA. Born in Pittsburgh; graduate Carnegie-Mellon, and Villanova U. Debut OB 1971 in "Ubu Roi," followed by "Servant of Two Masters," "Soon Jack November," Bdwy 1973 in "The Women."

REY, ANTONIA. Born Oct. 12, 1927 in Havana, Cuba. Graduate Havana U. Bdwy debut 1964 in "Bajour," followed by "Mike Downstairs," "Engagement Baby," OB in "Yerma," "Fiesta in Madrid" (CC), "Camino Real" (LC), "Back Bog Beast Bait," "Rain," "42 Seconds from Broadway."

REYNOLDS, DEBBIE. Born Apr. 1, 1932 in El Paso, Tex. After 40 films, made Bdwy debut 1973 in "Irene."

RHYS, WILLIAM. Born Jan. 2, 1945 in NYC. Graduate Wesleyan U. Bdwy debut 1969 with National Theatre of the Deaf, followed by "The Changing Room."

RICCI, ROSALIN. Born Mar. 3, 1948 in Santa Ana, Cal. Debut OB 1972 in "Lady Audley's Secret."

RICHARDS, JENNIFER. Born June 18, 1948 in Brooklyn. Graduate Bklyn Col. Bdwy debut 1973 in "No Sex Please, We're British."

RICHARDS, JESS. Born Jan. 23, 1943 in Seattle, Wash. Attended UWash. Bdwy debut 1966 in "Walking Happy," followed by "South Pacific" (LC), "Blood Red Roses," "Two by Two," "On the Town" for which he received a Theatre World Award, OB in "One for the Money."

RICHARDS, JON. Born in Wilkes Barre, Pa. Bdwy in "Tobacco Road," "Arsenic and Old Lace," "Love or Money," "Gramercy Ghost," "Bad Seed," "Sunrise at Campobello," "Sail Away," "A Murderer among Us," "A Very Rich Woman," "Roar like a Dove," "Elizabeth the Queen," "3 Bags Full" "Woman Is My Idea," "Does a Tiger Wear a Necktie?," OB in "Leave It to Jane," "One Flew over the Cuckoo's Nest."

RICHARDS, PENELOPE. Born Jan. 16, 1948 in Columbus, O. Debut 1973 OB in "Smith."

RITCHARD, CYRIL. Born Dec. 1, 1897 in Sydney, Austr. Attended Sydney U. Bdwy debut 1947 in "Love for Love," followed by "Make Way for Lucia," "The Relapse," "Peter Pan," "Visit to a Small Planet," "The Pleasure of His Company," "Happiest Girl in the World," "Romulus," "Too True to Be Good," "Irregular Verb to Love," "Roar of the Greasepaint . . . ," "Peter and the Wolf," "Sugar."

ROBBINS, REX. Born in Pierre, SDak. Bdwy debut 1964 in "One Flew over the Cuckoo's Nest," followed by "Scratch," "The Changing Room," OB in "Servant of Two Masters," "The Alchemist," "Arms and the Man," "Boys in the Band."

ROBERTS, ARTHUR. Born Aug. 10, 1938 in NYC. Harvard graduate. Debut 1964 OB in "Hamlet" (NYSF), followed by "Galileo" (LC), "Boys in the Band," "Anna K.," Bdwy bow 1970 in "Borstal Boy."

ROBERTS, DENNIS. Born Nov. 3, 1950 in Chicago. Northwestern graduate. Debut OB 1972 in "Lady Audley's Secret."

ROBERTS, DORIS. Born in St. Louis, Mo. Attended Actors Studio, Neighborhood Playhouse. Bdwy debut 1956 in "The Desk Set," followed by "Have I Got a Girl for You," "Malcolm," "Marathon '33," "Under the Weather," "The Office," "The Natural Look," "Last of the Red Hot Lovers," "Secret Affairs of Mildred Wild," OB in "Death of Bessie Smith," "American Dream," "Color of Darkness," "Don't Call Me By My Rightful Name," "Christy," "Boy in the Straight-back Chair," "A Matter of Position," "Natural Affection," "Time of Your Life" (CC).

ROBERTS, RALPH. Born Aug. 17 in Salisbury, NC. Attended UNC. Debut 1948 in CC's "Angel Street," followed by "4 Chekhov Comedies," "S. S. Glencairn," "Madwoman of Chaillot," "Witness for the Prosecution," "The Lark," "Bells Are Ringing," "The Milk Train Doesn't Stop Here Anymore," "Love Suicide at Schofield Barracks," "Siamese Connections" (OB).

ROBERTS, TONY. Born Oct. 22, 1939 in NYC. Graduate Northwestern. Bdwy bow 1962 in "Something about a Soldier," followed by "Take Her, She's Mine," "Last Analysis," "The Cradle Will Rock" (OB), "Never Too Late," "Barefoot in the Park," "Don't Drink the Water," "How Now, Dow Jones," "Play It Again, Sam," "Promises, Promises," "Sugar."

ROBERTSON, WILLIAM. Born Oct. 9, 1908 in Portsmouth, Va. Graduate Pomona Col. Bdwy debut 1936 in "Tapestry in Grey," followed by "Cup of Trembling," "Liliom," "Our Town," OB in "Uncle Harry," "Shining Hour," "Aspern Papers," "Madame Is Served," "Tragedian in spite of Himself," "Kibosh," "Sun-Up," "The Last Pad," "Hamlet," "Girls Most Likely to Succeed."

Esther Rolle   Peter Rogan   Patricia Roos   Thomas Ruisinger   Evelyn Russe[

ROBINSON, ROGER. Born May 2, 1941 in Seattle, Wash. Attended USCal. Bdwy debut 1969 in "Does a Tiger Wear a Necktie?," OB in "Walk in Darkness," "Jerico-Jim Crow," "Who's Got His Own," "Trials of Brother Jero," "The Miser" (LC), "Interrogation of Havana," "Lady Day."

RODD, MARCIA. Born July 8 in Lyons, Kan. Attended Northwestern, Yale. OB in "Oh Say Can You See," "Cambridge Circus," "Mad Show," "Madame Mousse," "Love and Let Love," "Your Own Thing," Bdwy debut 1964 in "Love in E-Flat," followed by "Last of the Red Hot Lovers," "Shelter."

RODEN, ERIC JOHN. Born Feb. 7, 1966 in NYC. Debut OB 1973 in "Medea."

RODGERS, ENID. Born Apr. 29, 1924 in London. Attended Royal Col. NY debut OB in "Sourball," followed by "Getting Married" (ELT), Bdwy 1973 in "Jockey Club Stakes."

RODGERS, SHEV. Born Apr. 9, 1928 in Holister, Cal. Attended SF State Col. Bdwy bow 1959 in "Redhead," followed by "Music Man," "Man of La Mancha" (also LC), OB in "Get Thee to Canterbury," "War Games."

RODRIGUEZ, CHARLIE J. Born Oct. 15, 1944 in Mayaguez, PR. Bdwy debut 1970 in "Lovely Ladies, Kind Gentlemen," followed by "Mother Earth."

ROGAN, PETER. Born May 11, 1939 in County Leitrim, Ire. Bdwy debut 1966 in "Philadelphia, Here I Come!," OB in "The Kitchen," "Nobody Hears a Broken Drum," "Picture of Dorian Gray," "Macbeth," "Sjt. Musgrave's Dance," "Stephen D.," LC's "People Are Living There," and "The Plough and the Stars."

ROGERS, GIL. Born Feb. 4, 1934 in Lexington, Ky. Attended Harvard. OB in "The Ivory Branch, "Vanity of Nothing," "Warrior's Husband," "Hell Bent fer Heaven," "Gods of Lightning," "Pictures in the Hallway," "Rose," "Memory Bank," "A Recent Killing," Bdwy debut 1968 in "The Great White Hope."

ROGERS, PAUL. Born Mar. 22, 1917 in Plympton, Eng. Attended Chekhov Theatre Sch. Bdwy debut with Old Vic (1956–7) in "Macbeth," "Romeo and Juliet," "Troilus and Cressida," and "Richard II," subsequently in "Photo Finish," "The Homecoming," "Here's Where I Belong," "Sleuth."

ROLLE, ESTHER. Born Nov. 8 in Pompano Beach, Fla. Attended Hunter Col. Bdwy debut 1964 in "Blues for Mr. Charlie," followed by "Purlie Victorious," "Amen Corner," "Don't Play Us Cheap," OB in "The Blacks," "Happy Ending," "Day of Absence," "Evening of One Acts," "Man Better Man," "Brotherhood," "Okakawe," "Rosalee Pritchett," "Dream on Monkey Mt.," "Ride a Black Horse," "Ballet behind the Bridge."

ROOP, RENO. Born Dec. 19 in Narva, Estonia. Graduate Goodman Theatre. Debut OB 1965 in "Medea," followed by NYSF's "Hamlet," "Timon of Athens," Bdwy 1973 in "Emperor Henry IV."

ROOS, PATRICIA. Born May 2, 1945 in New Haven, Conn. Attended AADA. Bdwy debut 1973 in "Cyrano."

ROSE, GEORGE. Born Feb. 19, 1920 in Bicester, Eng. Bdwy debut with Old Vic 1946 in "Henry IV," followed by "Much Ado About Nothing," "A Man For All Seasons," "Hamlet," "Royal Hunt of the Sun," "Walking Happy," "Loot," "My Fair Lady" (CC'68), "Canterbury Tales," "Coco," "Wise Child," "Sleuth."

ROSE, JANE. Born in Spokane, Wash. Bdwy debut 1952 in "Time of the Cuckoo," followed by "Wooden Dish," "Orpheus Descending," "The Gazebo," "Heartbreak House," NYSF 1966–1967, OB in "Arms and the Man," "Enemies" (LC).

ROSQUI, TOM. Born June 12, 1928 in Oakland, Calif. Graduate Col. of Pacific. With LCRep in "Danton's Death," "Condemned of Altona," "Country Wife," "Caucasian Chalk Circle," "Alchemist," "Yerma," "East Wind," and "A Streetcar Named Desire," OB in "Collision Course," "Day of Absence," "Brotherhood," "What the Butler Saw," "Waiting for Godot," "Whiskey," Bdwy in "Unlikely Heroes," "The Lincoln Mask."

ROSS, HELEN. Born Jan. 16, 1914 in NYC. In Federal Theatre productions, Bdwy debut 1967 in "Marat/de Sade," followed by "Our Town," "Effect of Gamma Rays on Man-in-the-moon Marigolds" (OB).

ROSS, JAMIE. Born May 4, 1939 in Markinch, Scot. Attended RADA. Bdwy debut 1962 in "Little Moon of Alban," followed by "Moon Besieged," "Penny Friend" (OB), "Ari," "Different Times," "Oh Coward!" (OB).

ROUNDS, DAVID. Born Oct. 9, 1938 in Bronxville, NY. Attended Denison U. OB in "You Never Can Tell," "Money," "The Real Inspector Hound," Bdwy debut 1965 in "Foxy" followed by "Child's Play" for which he received a Theatre World Award, "The Rothschilds," "The Last of Mrs. Lincoln."

ROUNSEVILLE, ROBERT. Born Mar. 25, 1919 in Attleboro, Mass. Attended Tufts U. Bdwy bow 1937 in "Babes In Arms," followed by "Two Bouquets," "Knickerbocker Holiday," "Higher and Higher," "Up In Central Park," "Show Boat" "Merry Widow," "Candide," "Brigadoon"(CC), "Man of La Mancha" (also LC).

ROWE, HANSFORD. Born May 12, 1924 in Richmond, Va. Graduate URic[mond. Bdwy debut 1968 in "We Bombed in New Haven," OB in "Curl[McDimple," "Fantasticks," "Last Analysis," "God Says There Is No Pet[Ott," "Mourning Becomes Electra."

ROWLES, POLLY. Born Jan. 10, 1914 in Philadelphia, Pa. Carnegie Te[graduate. Bdwy debut 1938 in "Julius Caesar," followed by "Richard III["Anne of the Thousand Days," "Golden State," "Small Hours," "Gertie["Time out for Ginger," "Wooden Dish," "Goodbye Again," "Auntie Mame["Look after Lulu," "A Mighty Man Is He," "No Strings," "The Killing [Sister George," "Forty Carats," "The Women," OB in "Older People."

RUBINSTEIN, JOHN. Born Dec. 8, 1946 in Los Angeles. Attended UCL[Bdwy debut 1972 in "Pippin" for which he received a Theatre World Awar[

RUISINGER, THOMAS. Born May 13, 1930 in Omaha, Neb. Graduate SM[Neighborhood Playhouse. Bdwy debut 1959 in "Warm Peninsula," followed ["The Captains and The Kings," "A Shot in the Dark," "Frank Merriwell," O[in "The Balcony," "Thracian Horses," "Under Milk Wood," "Six Characte[in Search of an Author," "Papers."

RUSSELL, EVELYN. Born Aug. 4 in NYC. Debut 1958 OB in "On t[Town," Bdwy 1961 in "Sail Away," followed by "Nobody Loves an Albatross["A Warm Body," "A Place for Polly," "Lysistrata."

RYAN, CHARLENE. Born in NYC. Bdwy debut 1964 in "Never Live Ov[a Pretzel Factory," followed by "Sweet Charity," "Fig Leaves Are Falling ["Coco," "A Funny Thing Happened on the Way to the Forum."

RYAN, JOHN P. Born July 30, 1938 in NYC. Graduate CCNY. Bdwy deb[1967 in "Daphne in Cottage D," followed by "Love Suicide at Schofield Ba[racks," OB in "Big Man," "Nobody Hears a Broken Drum," "12 Angry Men["Medea."

RYLAND, JACK. Born July 2, 1935 in Lancaster, Pa. Attended AFDA. Bdw[debut 1958 in "The World of Suzie Wong," followed by "A Very Rich Woman["Henry V," OB in "A Palm Tree in a Rose Garden," "Lysistrata," "The Whi[Rose and the Red," "Old Glory," "Cyrano" (LC), "Mourning Becomes Ele[tra."

SABIN, DAVID. Born Apr. 24, 1937 in Washington, DC. Graduate Cathol[U. Debut OB 1965 in "The Fantasticks," followed by "Now Is the Time for A[Good Men," Bdwy in "The Yearling," "Slapstick Tragedy," "Jimmy Shine["Gantry," "Ambassador."

SAINT, EVA MARIE. Born July 4, 1924 in Newark, NJ. Attended Bowlin[Green State U., Actors Studio. Bdwy debut 1953 in "The Trip to Bountiful[for which she received a Theatre World Award, followed by "The Lincol[Mask."

SAKREN, JARED. Born June 18, 1950 in Danbury, Conn. Attended Juilliar[Debut OB 1972 in "School for Scandal," followed by "Lower Depths," "Th[Hostage," "Next Time I'll Sing to You," "Women Beware Women."

SANDERS, ALBERT. Born Feb. 4, 1943 in NYC. Graduate USFla. Debut O[in "Two Gentlemen of Verona," followed by "You're a Good Man, Charli[Brown," Bdwy 1972 in "Jockey Club Stakes."

SANTANGELO, MELODY. Born Jan. 25, 1946 in Chicago. Attended Good[man Theatre, UCLA. Bdwy debut 1970 in "Hair," followed by "Lenny."

SARANDON, CHRIS. Born July 24, 1942 in Beckley, WVa. Graduat[UWVa., Catholic U. Bdwy debut 1970 in "The Rothschilds," followed by "Tw[Gentlemen of Verona."

SARNO, JANET. Born Nov. 18, 1933 in Bridgeport, Conn. Graduate S. Conn[TC, Yale. Bdwy debut 1963 in "Dylan," OB in "Six Characters in Search of a[Author," "Who's Happy Now," "Closing Green," "Fisher," "Survival of S[Joan," "The Orphan."

SAUNDERS, LANNA. Born Dec. 22, 1941 in NYC. Bdwy debut 1957 i["Sunrise at Campobello," followed by "Milk and Honey," "Never Live over [Pretzel Factory," "Philadelphia, Here I Come," OB in "Marcus in the Hig[Grass," LCRep's "After the Fall," and "The Changeling," "Anna K."

SAUNDERS, MARILYN. Born Apr. 28, 1948 in Brooklyn. Attended Bkly[Col. OB in "Dames at Sea," "Smile, Smile, Smile," Bdwy debut 1970 in "Com[pany."

SCHACT, SAM. Born Apr. 19, 1936 in The Bronx. Graduate CCNY. OB i["Fortune and Men's Eyes," "Cannibals," "I Met a Man," "The Increase[Difficulty of Concentration" (LCR), "One Night Stands of a Noisy Passenger,["Owners."

SCHAEFER, LOUIS. Born Sept. 29, 1931 in Oak Park, Ill. Graduat[UChicago. Bdwy debut 1972 in "The Last of Mrs. Lincoln."

SCHINDLER, ELLEN. Born Oct. 26, 1942 in Sioux City, I. Graduate Syra[cuse U. Debut 1969 OB in "The Serpent," followed by "Red Burning Light,["Terminal," "And They Put Handcuffs on the Flowers."

SCHLEE, ROBERT. Born June 13, 1938 in Williamsport, Pa. Graduate L[coming Col. Debut OB 1972 in "Dr. Selavy's Magic Theatre."

Steve Scott   Janie Sell   John D. Seymour   Fern Sloan   Harvey Solin

SCHNABEL, STEFAN. Born Feb. 2, 1912 in Berlin, Ger. Attended UBonn, Old Vic. Bdwy bow 1937 in "Julius Caesar," followed by "Shoemaker's Holiday," "Glamour Preferred," "Land of Fame," "Cherry Orchard," "Around the World," "Now I Lay Me Down to Sleep," "Idiot's Delight" (CC), "Love of Four Colonels," "Plain and Fancy," "Small War on Murray Hill," "A Very Rich Woman," "In the Matter of J. Robert Oppenheimer" (LC), "A Patriot for Me," OB in "Tango," "Older People," Enemies" (LC).

SCHOEN, JUDY. Born Nov. 10, 1941 in Atlanta, Ga. Attended Stratford Col. Bdwy debut 1969 in "Red, White and Maddox," followed by "Godspell" (OB).

SCHULTZ, JACK. Born Feb. 4, 1936 in Gregory, SDak. Graduate ULowa, UWis., AMDA. Bdwy debut 1973 in "The Changing Room."

SCOTT, GEORGE C. Born Oct. 18, 1927 in Wise, Va. OB in "Richard II" for which he received a Theatre World Award, followed by "As You Like It," "Children of Darkness," "Desire under the Elms," Bdwy in "Comes a Day," "Andersonville Trial," "The Wall," "General Seegar," "Little Foxes," "Plaza Suite," "Uncle Vanya."

SCOTT, STEVE. Born Oct. 11, 1949 in Denver, Colo. Graduate UDenver. Debut OB 1970 in "The Drunkard," followed by "Summer Brave" (ELT).

SELL, JANIE. Born Oct. 1 in Detroit, Mich. OB in "Upstairs at the Downstairs," "Dames at Sea," Bdwy debut 1968 in "George M!," followed by "Irene."

SELLERS, ARTHUR. Born Aug. 16, 1945 in Terre Haute, Ind. Graduate NYU. Debut 1969 with LCR in "The Time of Your Life," "Camino Real," "Operation Sidewinder" and "Beggar on Horseback," followed by "The Boy Who Came to Leave" (OB).

SERABIAN, LORRAINE. Born June 12, 1945 in NYC. Graduate Hofstra U. OB in "Sign of Jonah," "Electra," "Othello," "Secret Life of Walter Mitty," "Bugs and Veronica," "Trojan Women," "American Gothics," Bdwy in "Cabaret," "Zorba."

SEYMOUR, JOHN D. Born Oct. 24, 1897 in Boston, Mass. Attended Colgate U. Bdwy debut 1918 in "Out There," followed by "Richard III," "Dearest Enemy," "Blood Money," "Barretts of Wimpole Street," "Sweet Adeline," "Cyrano," "Pride and Prejudice," "Susan and God," "The Moon Is Down," "Eastward in Eden," "The Vigil," "Light up the Sky," "The Sacred Flame," CC's "Pal Joey," "King and I," and "Life with Father," OB in "12 Angry Men."

SHAKAR, MARTIN. Born in Detroit, Jan. 1, 1940. Attended Wayne State U. OB in "Lorenzaccio," "Macbeth," "The Infantry," "Americana Pastoral," "No Place To Be Somebody," "The World of Mrs. Solomon," "And Whose Little Boy Are You?," "Investigation of Havana," "Night Watch," "Owners," Bdwy bow 1969 in "Our Town."

SHALER, ANNA. Born Apr. 8, 1940 in NYC. Graduate Bennington Col. With Martha Graham Co. before Bdwy debut 1965 in "The Devils," followed by "Nathan Weinstein, Mystic, Conn.," "6 Rms Riv Vu," OB in "Trojan Women," "White Devil," "Philosophy in the Boudoir."

SHANNON, MICHAEL. Born Jan. 24, 1943 in Chicago. Graduate Northwestern U. Bdwy bow 1971 in "Butterflies Are Free," followed by "Ambassador," OB in "Orestes," "In Case of Accident."

SHANNON, WAYNE. Born Jan. 16, 1948 in Spokane, Wash. Attended Highline Col., AADA. Debut OB 1972 in "The Maid's Tragedy."

SHARKEY, SUSAN. Born Dec. 12, 1944 in NYC. Graduate U Ariz. Debut OB 1968 in "Guns of Carrar" and "Cuba Si," with LCRep in "Playboy of the Western World," "Good Woman of Setzuan," "Enemy of the People," "People Are Living There," "Narrow Road to the Deep North," "Enemies," and "The Plough and the Stars."

SHAWHAN, APRIL. Born Apr. 10, 1940 in Chicago. Debut OB 1964 in "Jo," followed by "Hamlet," "Oklahoma!" (LC), "Mod Donna," Bdwy in "Race of Hairy Men," "3 Bags Full" for which she received a Theatre World Award, "Dinner at 8," "Cop-Out," "Much Ado about Nothing."

SHELTON, REID. Born Oct. 7, 1924 in Salem, Ore. Graduate UMich. Bdwy bow 1952 in "Wish You Were Here," followed by "Wonderful Town," "By the Beautiful Sea," "Saint of Bleecker St." "My Fair Lady," "Oh! What a Lovely War," "Carousel" (CC), "Canterbury Tales," "The Rothschilds," OB in "Phedre," "Butterfly Dream," "Man with a Load of Mischief," "Beggar's Opera."

SHERMAN, GERALDINE. Born in London. Attended Burlington School. Bdwy debut 1972 in "Butley."

SHERWOOD, MADELEINE. Born Nov. 13, 1926 in Montreal, Can. Attended Yale. OB in "Brecht on Brecht," "Medea," "Hey You, Light Man," "Friends and Relations," "Older People," Bdwy in "The Chase," "The Crucible," "Cat on a Hot Tin Roof," "Invitation to a March," "Camelot," "Arturo ," "Do I Hear a Waltz?," "Inadmissible Evidence," "All Over."

SHUTTA, ETHEL. Born Dec. 1, 1896 in NYC. On Bdwy in "Ziegfeld Follies," "Passing Show of 1923," "Marjorie," "Louis XIV," "Whoopee," "My Dear Public," "Jennie," "Follies."

SICARI, JOSPEH. Born Apr. 29, 1939 in Boston, Mass. Graduate Catholic U. OB in "The Parasite," NYSF's "Comedy of Errors" and "Henry IV," "Love and Let Love," "Dames at Sea," "Comedy."

SIEBERT, CHARLES. Born Mar. 9, 1938 in Kenosha, Wisc. Graduate Marquette U., LAMDA. Appeared in "Richard III" (CP), "Galileo" (LC), on Bdwy in "Jimmy Shine," "Gingerbread Lady," "Sticks and Bones," "Wilde" (OB), "Lysistrata."

SIEBERT, RONALD H. Born in Kenosha, Wis. Graduate UWis., Brandeis U. Bdwy debut 1973 in "The Changing Room."

SIEGEL, MARK. Born Aug. 22, 1947 in Minneapolis, Minn. Graduate UMinn. Debut 1973 OB in "A Phantasmagoria Historia. . . ."

SILVER, STUART. Born June 29, 1947 in Hollywood, Cal. Attended URochester, AADA. Debut 1969 OB in "Little Murders," followed by "Seven Days of Mourning," "Dance Wi' Me," "Wanted," "The Making of Americans."

SILVERS, PHIL. Born May 11, 1911 in Bklyn. In vaudeville before 1939 Bdwy bow in "Yokel Boy," followed by "High Button Shoes," "Top Banana," "Do Re Mi," "How the Other Half Loves," "A Funny Thing Happened on the Way to the Forum."

SIMPSON, DENNIS. Born Nov. 4, 1950 in Jamaica, BWI. Attended York U. Bdwy debut 1972 in "Dude," followed by "Love Me, Love My Children" (OB), "Jesus Christ Superstar."

SIMPSON, STEVE. Born Sept. 3, 1947 in Perryton, Tex. Graduate UOkla., Wake Forest U. Debut OB 1973 in "The Soldier."

SIMS, MARLEY. Born Feb. 23, 1948 in NYC. Graduate NYU. Bdwy debut 1971 in "The Me Nobody Knows," followed by "Godspell" (OB).

SLACK, BEN. Born July 23, 1937 in Baltimore, Md. Graduate Catholic U. Debut 1971 OB in "Oedipus at Colonus," followed by "Interrogation of Havana," "Rain," "Thunder Rock."

SLAUGHTER, HARRIET. Born Apr. 2, 1937 in Ft. Worth, Tex. Graduate U Tex. Bdwy debut 1960 in "The Hostage," followed by "Fiddler on the Roof."

SLOAN, FERN. Born June 2, 1940 in Protection, Kan. Graduate Wichita State U. Debut OB 1972 in "The Children."

SMITH, ALEXIS. Born June 8, 1921 in Penticton, Can. Attended LACC. Bdwy debut 1971 in "Follies," followed by "The Women."

SMITH, GARNETT. Born Sept. 22, 1937 in Richmond, Va. Bdwy debut 1967 in "Rosencrantz and Guildenstern Are Dead," followed by "Canterbury Tales," OB in "Cambridge Circus," "Dear Oscar."

SMITH, LOIS. Born Nov. 3, 1930 in Topeka, Kan. Attended UWash. Bdwy debut 1952 in "Time Out for Ginger," followed by "The Young and Beautiful," "Wisteria Trees," "Glass Menagerie," "Orpheus Descending," OB in "Sunday Dinner," "Present Tense."

SMITH, SHEILA. Born Apr. 3, 1933 in Conneaut, O. Attended Kent State U., Cleveland Playhouse. Bdwy debut 1963 in "Hot Spot," followed by "Mame" for which she received a Theatre World Award, "Follies," "Company," "Sugar," OB in "Taboo Revue," "Anything Goes," "Best Foot Forward," and "Sweet Miani," "Fiorello" (CC'62).

SNYDER, ARLEN DEAN. Born Mar 3, 1933 in Rice, Kan. Graduate U Tulsa, U Iowa. Bdwy bow 1965 in "The Family Way," followed OB in "Benito Cereno," "Hogan's Goat," "Miss Pete," "Open 24 Hours," "Candyapple," "June Moon," "Big Broadcast," "Thunder Rock."

SNYDER, DREW. Born Sept. 25, 1946 in Buffalo, N.Y. Graduate Carnegie Tech. Bdwy debut 1968 with APA in "Pantagleize," "Cocktail Party" "Cock-a-doodle Dandy," and "Hamlet," followed by NYSF's "Henry VI," "Richard III," and "Sticks and Bones."

SOBOLOFF, ARNOLD. Born Nov. 11, 1930 in NYC. Attended Cooper Union. OB in "Threepenny Opera," "Career," "Brothers Karamazov," "Vincent," "Bananas," "Papp," "Camino Real" (LCR), Bdwy in "Mandingo," "The Egg," "Beauty Part," "One Flew over the Cuckoo's Nest," "Anyone Can Whistle," "Bravo Giovanni," "Sweet Charity," "Mike Downstairs," "Cyrano."

SOLEN, PAUL. Born Mar. 27, 1941 in Cincinnati, O. Bdwy debut 1964 in "Hello, Dolly!," followed by "Breakfast at Tiffany's," "Dear World," "Pippin."

SOLIN, HARVEY. Born Oct. 17 in NYC. Attended CCNY, Actors Studio. Debut OB 1960 in "Ring Round the Moon," followed by "Sign of Jonah," "Worm in the Horseradish," "A Man's a Man," "Next Time I'll Sing to You," "Louis and the Elephant," "Penthouse Legend."

SOMMER, JOSEF. Born June 26, 1934 in Greifswald, Ger. Graduate Carnegie Tech. Bdwy bow 1970 with ASF's "Othello," followed by "Children, Children," "Trial of the Catonsville 9," LCR's "Enemies," and "Merchant of Venice."

Zipora Spaisman

James Staley

Lynne Stuart

James Sutorius

Britt Swanson

SPAISMAN, ZIPORA. Born Jan. 2, 1920 in Lublin, Poland. Debut OB 1955 in "Lonesome Ship," followed by "In My Father's Boys," "Thousand and One Nights," "Eleventh Inheritor," "Enchanting Melody," "Fifth Commandment," "Bronx Express," "Melody Lingers On," "Yoshke Muzikant."

SPELMAN, LEON. Born July 29, 1945 in Kingsport, Tenn. Attended CCNY, AADA. Bdwy debut 1972 in "Via Galactica."

SPENCER, BOB. Born May 4, 1938 in Chicago. Bdwy debut 1960 in "Bye Bye Birdie," followed by "Enter Laughing" "Via Galactica," OB in "Sing, Muse," "The Fantasticks," "Manhattan Arrangement."

STADLEN, LEWIS J. Born Mar. 7, 1947 in Brooklyn. Attended Neighborhood Playhouse. Bdwy debut 1970 in "Minnie's Boys" for which he received a Theatre World Award, followed by "Happiness Cage" (OB), "The Sunshine Boys."

STALEY, JAMES. Born May 20, 1948 in Oklahoma City. Graduate Okla. U. Bdwy debut 1972 in "Promenade, All!," followed by "Siamese Connections" (OB).

STANLEY, FLORENCE. Born July 1 in Chicago. Graduate Northwestern. OB in "Machinal," "Electra," Bdwy debut 1965 in "Glass Menagerie," followed by "Fiddler on the Roof," "Prisoner of Second Avenue," "Secret Affairs of Mildred Wild."

STAPLETON, MAUREEN. Born June 21, 1925 in Troy, NY. Attended HB Studio. Bdwy debut 1946 in "Playboy of the Western World," followed by "Antony and Cleopatra," "Detective Story," "Bird Cage," "Rose Tattoo" for which she received a Theatre World Award, "The Emperor's Clothes," "The Crucible," "Richard III," "The Seagull," "27 Wagons Full of Cotton," "Orpheus Descending," "The Cold Wind and the Warm," "Toys in the Attic," "Glass Menagerie," "Plaza Suite," "Norman, Is That You?", "Gingerbread Lady," "Country Girl," "Secret Affairs of Mildred Wild."

STARR, BILL. Born July 6 in San Francisco. Studied at HB Studio. Bdwy debut 1959 in "Take Me Along," followed by "Molly Brown," "All American," "Nowhere to Go but Up," "Something More," "Fade Out—Fade In," "High Spirits," "It's Superman," "Illya, Darling," "Drat! The Cat!," "A Funny Thing Happened on the Way to the Forum," "Via Galactica."

STATTEL, ROBERT. Born Nov. 20, 1937 in Floral Park, NY. Graduate Manhattan Col. Bdwy debut 1958 in "Heloise," followed by "When I Was a Child," "Man and Superman," "The Storm," "Don Carlos," "Taming of the Shrew," NYSF's "Titus Andronicus," "Henry IV," "Peer Gynt," and "Hamlet," LCR's "Danton's Death," "Country Wife," "Caucasian Chalk Circle," and "King Lear," "Iphigenia in Aulis," "Ergo," "The Persians," "Blue Boys," Bdwy in "A Patriot for Me."

STENBORG, HELEN. Born Jan. 24, 1925 in Minneapolis, Minn. Attended Hunter Col. OB in "A Doll's House," "A Month in the Country," "Say Nothing," "Rosmersholm," "Rimers of Eldrich," "Trial of the Catonsville 9," "Hot L Baltimore," Bdwy in "Sheep on the Runway."

STENDER, DOUG. Born Sept. 14, 1942 in Nanticoke, Pa. Graduate Princeton, RADA. Bdwy debut 1973 in "The Changing Room."

STEPHENS, GARN. Born in Tulsa, Okla. Graduate Calif. Western U. Pasadena Playhouse. Debut 1972 OB and Bdwy in "Grease."

STERLING, PHILIP. Born Oct. 9, 1922 in NYC. Graduate UPa. Bdwy bow 1955 in "Silk Stockings," followed by "Interlock," "An Evening with Richard Nixon and . . . ," OB in "Victims of Duty," "Opening of a Window," "Trojan Women," "Party for Divorce," "Party on Greenwich Ave.," "Peddler," "Summertree," "Older People."

STERNHAGEN, FRANCES. Born Jan. 13, 1932 in Washington, DC. Vassar graduate. OB in "Admirable Bashful," "Thieves' Carnival," "Country Wife," "Ulysses in Nighttown," "Saintliness of Margery Kemp," "The Room," "A Slight Ache," "Displaced Person," "Playboy of the Western World" (LC), Bdwy in "Great Day In the Morning," "Right Honourable Gentleman," with APA in "Cocktail Party" and "Cock-a-doodle Dandy," "The Sign in Sidney Brustein's Window.," "Enemies" (LC).

STEVENS, FRAN. Born Mar. 8 in Washington, DC. Attended Notre Dame, Cleveland Playhouse. Has appeared in "Pousse Cafe," "Most Happy Fella," "A Funny Thing Happened on the Way to the Forum," "How Now Dow Jones," "Her First Roman," "Cry for Us All," "On the Town," OB in "Frank Gagliano's City Scene."

STEWART, JOHN. Born May 21, 1934 in Brooklyn. Bdwy debut 1947 in "High Button Shoes," followed by "Love Life," "Happy Time," "King and I," "Grass Harp," "Bernardine" for which he received a Theatre World Award, "Sleeping Prince," "Waltz of the Toreadors," "Tattooed Countess" (OB), "Generation," "King and I" (JB).

STICKNEY, DOROTHY. Born June 21, 1900 in Dickinson, SD. Attended Northwestern U. Bdwy debut 1926 in "The Squall," followed by "Chicago," "March Hares," "Beaux Stratagem," "Front Page," "Milestones," "Philip Goes Forth," "Way of the World," "Another Language," "County Chairman," "On Borrowed Time," "Life with Father," "Life with Mother," "Small Hours," "To Be Continued," "Kind Sir," "The Honeys," "A Lovely Light," "Riot Act," "The Mundy Scheme," "Pippin."

STORCH, ARTHUR. Born June 29, 1925 in Brooklyn. Attended Bklyn Col., Glasgow U., Actors Studio. Bdwy debut 1953 in "End as a Man," followed by "Time Limit!," "Girls of Summer," "Look Homeward, Angel," "The Enemy Is Dead."

STRAIGHT, BEATRICE. Born Aug. 2, 1916 in Old Westbury, NY. Attended Dartington Hall. Bdwy debut 1934 in "Bitter Oleander," followed by "Twelfth Night," "Land of Fame," "Wanhope Building," "Eastward in Eden," "Macbeth," "The Heiress," "The Innocents," "Grand Tour," "The Crucible," "Everything in the Garden," OB in "Sing Me No Lullaby," "River Line," "Ghosts."

STRASSER, ROBIN. Born May 7, 1945 in NYC. Bdwy debut 1963 in "The Irregular Verb to Love," followed by "The Country Girl" (CC), "A Meeting by the River" (OB).

STRATEN, MARY M. Born Oct. 20, 1940 in Lewistown, Pa. Graduate CalStateU. Bdwy debut 1973 in "Cyrano."

STUART, LYNNE. Born Sept. 30 in Lakeland, Fla. Attended Tampa U., NY Col. of Music. Bdwy debut 1953 in "Kismet," followed by "New Girl in Town," "Bells Are Ringing," "High Spirits," "The Women."

STUTHMAN, FRED. Born June 27, 1919 in Long Beach, Cal. Attended UCal. Debut 1970 OB in "Hamlet," followed by "Uncle Vanya," "Charles Abbot & Son," "She Stoops to Conquer," "Master Builder," "Taming of the Shrew," "Misalliance," "Merchant of Venice," "Conditions of Agreement," "The Play's the Thing," "Ghosts."

SULLIVAN, JOSEPH. Born Nov. 29, 1918 in NYC. Attended Fordham, Am. Theatre Wing. Bdwy in "Sundown Beach," "Command Decision," "The Live Wire," "Country Girl," "Oh, Men! Oh, Women!," "The Rainmaker," "Best Man," "Fiddler on the Roof," "12 Angry Men" (OB).

SULLIVAN, LIAM. Born May 18, 1923 in Jacksonville, Ind. Attended Harvard. Bdwy bow 1951 in "The Constant Wife," followed by "Little Foxes," OB in "Anna K."

SUTORIUS, JAMES. Born Dec. 14, 1944 in Euclid, O. Graduate Ill. Wesleyan, AMDA. Bdwy debut 1970 in "The Cherry Orchard," followed by "The Changing Room," OB in "Servant of Two Masters."

SWANSON, BRITT. Born June 6, 1947 in Fargo, NDak. Attended HB Studio. Bdwy debut 1968 in CC's "King and I" and "My Fair Lady," followed by "Come Summer," "Shelter." Is member of Paul Taylor Dance Co.

SWANSON, GLORIA. Born Mar. 27, 1898 in Chicago. Bdwy debut 1945 in "A Goose for the Gander," followed by "Twentieth Century," "Nina," "Butterflies Are Free."

SWENSON, LINDA. Born July 29, 1945 in East Chicago, Ind. Graduate Oberlin Col., Columbia. Debut OB 1971 in "Blood," followed by "The Karl Marx Play."

SYMINGTON, DONALD. Born Aug. 30, 1925 in Baltimore, Md. Debut 1947 in "Galileo," followed by CC's "Caesar and Cleopatra," "Dream Girl," and "Lute Song," "A Girl Can Tell," OB in "Suddenly Last Summer," "Lady Windermere's Fan," "Rate of Exchange," "Shrinking Bride," "Murderous Angels," "An Evening with the Poet-Senator."

SYMONDS, ROBERT. Born Dec. 1, 1926 in Bristow, Okla. Attended Tex. U, UMo. With LC Rep in "Danton's Death," "Country Wife," "The Alchemist," "Galileo," "St. Joan," "Tiger at the Gates," "Cyrano," "Cry of Players," "Inner Journey," "The Miser," "Time of Your Life," "Camino Real," "Disintegration of James Cherry," "Silence," "Landscape," "Amphitryon," "Birthday Party," "Landscape," "Silence," "Scenes from American Life," "Play Strindberg," "Mary Stuart," "Narrow Road to the Deep North.," "Enemies," "The Plough and the Stars," "Merchant of Venice," and "A Streetcar Named Desire."

TANDY, JESSICA. Born June 7, 1909 in London. Attended Greet Acad. Bdwy debut 1930 in "The Matriarch," followed by "Last Enemy," "Time and the Conways," "White Steed," "Geneva," "Jupiter Laughs," "Anne of England," "Yesterday's Magic," "Streetcar Named Desire," "Hilda Crane," "Fourposter," "Honeys," "Day by the Sea," "Man in the Dog Suit," "Triple Play," "Five Finger Exercise," "Physicists," "Delicate Balance," "Home," "All Over," LCR's "Camino Real," "Not I" and "Happy Days."

TANNER, JILL. Born Oct. 18, 1943 in Bath, Eng. Attended RADA. Bdwy debut 1973 in "No Sex Please, We're British."

TANNER, TONY. Born July 27, 1932 in Hillingdon, Eng. Attended Webber Douglas School. Bdwy debut 1966 in "Half a Sixpence," followed by "No Sex Please, We're British," OB in "Little Boxes," "The Homecoming."

TARLETON, DIANE. Born in Baltimore, Md. Graduate UMd. Bdwy debut 1965 in "Anya," followed by "A Joyful Noise," "Elmer Gantry," OB in "A Time for the Gentle People," "Spoon River Anthology."

TARLOW, FLORENCE. Born Jan. 19, 1929 in Philadelphia. Graduate Hunter Co. OB in "Beautiful Day," "Istanbul," "Gorilla Queen," "American Hurrah," "Red Cross," "Promenade," Bdwy debut 1968 in "Man in the Glass Booth," followed by "Good Woman of Setzuan" (LC), "Inner City," "Medea."

TARPEY, TOM. Born June 3, 1943 in NYC. Attended Carnegie-Mellon U., LAMDA. Debut OB 1969 in "The Glorious Ruler," followed by "Crimes of Passion," "A Meeting by the River," Bdwy in "Othello," "Uncle Vanya."

TATE, DENNIS. Born Aug. 31, 1938 in Iowa City, Io. Attended IowaU. OB in "Black Monday," "The Blacks," "The Hostage," "Bohikee Creek," "Happy Bar," "Trials of Brother Jero," "Strong Breed," "Goa," "Electronic Nigger," "Black Quartet," "Life and Times of J. Walter Smintheus," "Jazznite," "Cherry Orchard," "Phantasmagoria Historia," Bdwy in "Les Blancs."

TAUBIN, AMY. Born Sept. 10, 1939 in NYC. Sarah Lawrence graduate. Bdwy debut 1968 in "The Prime of Miss Jean Brodie," OB in "Apollo of Bellac," "Double Talk," "Measure for Measure," "Rimers of Eldritch," "Dr. Selavy's Magic Theatre."

TAVARIS, ERIC. Born Apr. 8, 1939 in Fall River, Mass. Debut OB 1959 in "An Enemy of the People," followed by "The Prodigal," "In White America," "Butterfly Dream," "Macbeth," "Mummers and Men," "Androcles and the Lion," Bdwy in "The Lincoln Mask."

TAYLOR, CLARICE. Born Sept 20, in Buckingham County, Va. Attended New Theater School. Debut 1943 OB in "Striver's Row," followed by "Major Barbara," "Family Portrait," "Trouble in Mind," "The Egg and I," "A Medal for Willie," "Nat Turner," "Simple Speaks His Mind," "Gold through the Trees," "The Owl Answers," "Song of the Lusitanian Bogey," "Summer of the 17th Doll," "Kongi's Harvest," "Daddy Goodness," "God Is a (Guess What?)," "An Evening of One Acts," "5 on the Black Hand Side," "Man Better Man," "Day of Absence," "Brotherhood," "Akokawe," "Rosalee Pritchett," "Sty of the Blind Pig," "Duplex" (LC), "Wedding Band."

TAYLOR, GEORGE. Born Sept. 18, 1930 in London. Attended AADA. Debut 1972 in NYSF's "Hamlet," followed by "Enemies" (LC), Bdwy in "Emperor Henry IV."

TAYLOR, HOLLAND. Born Jan. 14, 1943 in Philadelphia, Pa. Graduate Bennington, Col. Bdwy debut 1965 in "The Devils," followed by "Butley," OB in "Poker Session," "The David Show," "Tonight in Living Color," "Colette."

TEAGUE, ANTHONY. Born Jan. 4, 1940 in Jacksboro, Tex. Bdwy debut 1963 in "110 in the Shade," followed by "No, No, Nanette."

THACKER, RUSS. Born June 23, 1946 in Washington, DC. Attended Montgomery Col. Debut 1967 in "Life with Father" (CC), followed OB by "Your Own Thing" for which he received a Theatre World Award, "Dear Oscar," Bdwy in "Grass Harp," "Heathen."

THEOHAROUS, TED. Born Jan. 23, 1930 in Sayre, Pa. Graduate CCNY, AADA. Debut OB 1954 with American Savoyards, followed by "How to Succeed in Business . . ." (ELT).

THOMAS, TONY. Born in Atlanta, Ga. Attended Temple U. Bdwy debut 1969 in "Henry V," OB in "Cities in Bezique," "The Pig Pen," "Orrin."

THOMAS, WILLIAM, JR. Born in Columbus, O. Graduate Ohio State U. Debut OB 1972 in "Touch," followed by "Natural," "Godspell."

THOMPSON, SADA. Born Sept. 27, 1929 in Des Moines, Iowa. Graduate Carnegie Tech. Debut OB 1953 in "Under Milk Wood," followed by "Clandestine Marriage," "Murder in the Cathedral," "White Devil," "Carefree Tree," "The Misanthrope," "USA," "River Line," "Ivanov," "The Last Minstrel," "An Evening for Merlin Finch," "The Effect of Gamma Rays On The Man-in-the-Moon Marigolds," Bdwy in "Festival," "Juno," "Johnny No-Trump," "The American-Dream," "Happy Days." "Twigs."

THORNE, RAYMOND. Born Nov. 27, 1934 in Lackawanna, NY. Graduate UConn. Debut OB 1966 in "Man with a Load of Mischief," followed by "Rose," "Dames at Sea," "Love Course," "Blue Boys."

THORNTON, ANGELA. Born in Leeds, Eng. Attended Webber-Douglas School. Bdwy debut 1956 in "Little Glass Clock," followed by "Nude with Violin," "Present Laughter," "Hostile Witness," OB in "The Mousetrap," "Big Broadcast."

THURSTON, TED. Born Jan. 9, 1920 in St. Paul, Minn. Attended Drake U., Wash, U. Debut 1951 in "Paint Your Wagon," followed by "Girl in Pink Tights," "Kismet," "Buttrio Square," "Seventh Heaven," "Most Happy Fella," "Li'l Abner," "13 Daughters," "Happiest Girl in Town," "Let It Ride," "Sophie," "Luther," "Cafe Crown," "I Had a Ball," "Wonderful Town" (CC), Bible Salesman" (OB), "Celebration," "Gantry," "Wild and Wonderful," Smith" (OB).

TIGAR, KEN. Born Sept. 24, 1942 in Chelsea, Mass. Harvard graduate. Debut OB 1973 in "Thunder Rock," followed by "Baba Goya."

TILLINGER, JOHN. Born June 28, 1938 in Tabriz, Iran. Attended URome. Bdwy debut 1966 in "How's the World Treating You?," followed by "Halfway up the Tree," "The Changing Room," OB in "Tea Party," "Pequod," "A Scent of Flowers," "Crimes of Passion."

TOMPKINS, TOBY. Born Sept. 8, 1942 in NYC. Yale graduate. Bdwy debut 1968 in "Man of La Mancha," OB in "Hail Scrawdyke," "The Cherry Orchard," "In White America."

TONER, TOM. Born May 25, 1928 in Homestead, Pa. Graduate UCLA. Bdwy debut 1973 in "Tricks."

TORRES, ANDY. Born Aug. 10, 1945 in Ponce, PR. Attended AMDA. Bdwy debut 1969 in "Indians," followed by "Purlie," "Don't Bother Me, I Can't Cope," OB in "Billy Noname."

TOVATT, ELLEN. Born in NYC. Attended Antioch Col., LAMDA. Debut OB 1962 in "Taming of the Shrew," followed by Bdwy 1972 in "The Great God Brown."

TRAPANI, LOU. Born Dec. 17, 1947 in Bklyn. Graduate Hofstra U. Debut 1970 OB in "Journey to Bahia," followed by "Hamlet," "She Stoops to Conquer," "Taming of the Shrew," "Misalliance," "Merchant of Venice," "And They Put Handcuffs on the Flowers."

TRAVOLTA, JOHN. Born Feb. 18, 1954 in Englewood, NJ. Debut 1972 OB in "Rain."

TRIBUSH, NANCY. Born Dec. 18, 1940 in NYC. Graduate Bklyn. Col. Bdwy debut 1961 in "Bye, Bye, Birdie," followed by "Happily Never After," "Oh, Calcutta," OB in "Riverwind," "Hang Down Your Head and Die."

TRONTO, RUDY. Born July 14, 1928 in Bklyn. Bdwy debut 1960 in "Irma La Douce," followed by "Carnival," "Man of La Mancha," OB in "Boys from Syracuse," "Secret Life of Walter Mitty," "Smile, Smile, Smile."

TRUMBO, NANCY. Born Sept. 23, 1945 in Volga, SDak. Graduate UColo. Debut OB 1973 in "The Secret Life of Walter Mitty" (ELT).

TSOUTSOUVAS, SAM. Born Aug. 20, 1948 in Santa Barbara, Cal. Attended UCal., Juilliard. Debut 1969 in NYSF's "Peer Gynt," followed by "Twelfth Night," "Timon of Athens," and "Cymbeline," OB in "School for Scandal," "The Hostage," "Women Beware Women," "Lower Depths."

TUNE, TOMMY. Born Feb. 28, 1939 in Wichita Falls, Tex. Graduate UTex. Bdwy debut 1965 in "Baker Street," followed by "Joyful Noise," "How Now Dow Jones," "Seesaw."

TURNER, JIM. Born Feb. 27, 1947 in NYC. Attended UAriz., HB Studio. Debut OB 1970 in "Blood," followed by "Don't Walk on the Clouds," Bdwy 1972 in "Dude."

ULLENDORF, JACQUIE. Born Mar. 4, 1945 in NYC. Attended AADA. Bdwy debut 1968 in "A Mother's Kisses," OB in "Babes in Arms," "How to Succeed in Business . . ." (ELT)

VALE, MICHAEL. Born June 28, 1922 in Bklyn. Attended New School. Bdwy bow 1961 in "The Egg," followed by "Cafe Crown," "The Last Analysis," "Impossible Years," OB in "Autograph Hound," "The Moths," "Now There's the Three of Us," "Tall and Rex," "Kaddish.," "42 Seconds from Broadway," "Sunset."

VALOR, HENRIETTA. Born Apr. 28 in New Cumberland, Pa. Graduate Northwestern U. Bdwy debut 1965 in "Half a Sixpence," followed by "Applause," "Jacques Brel Is Alive . . ."

VAN, BOBBY. Born Dec. 6, 1930 in The Bronx. Bdwy debut 1950 in "Alive and Kicking," followed by "On Your Toes," "No, No, Nanette."

VAN AKEN, GRETCHEN. Born Nov. 15, 1940 in Ridgeway, Pa. Graduate Emerson Col., Central Sch. of Speech, London. Bdwy debut 1964 in "Oliver!," followed by "Walking Happy," OB in "Digging for Apples," "Wanted.," "The Making of Americans."

VANDIS, TITOS. Born Nov. 7, 1917 in Athens, Greece. Attended Ntl. Theatre Drama School. Bdwy bow 1965 in "On a Clear Day You See Forever," followed by "Illya, Darling," "The Guide," "Look to the Lilies," "Man of La Mancha."

VAN GRIETHUYSEN, TED. Born Nov. 7, 1934 in Ponca City, Okla. Graduate UTex., RADA. Bdwy debut 1962 in "Romulus," followed by "Moon Besieged," "Inadmissible Evidence," OB in "Failures," "Lute Song" (CC), "O Marry Me," "Red Roses for Me," "Basement," "Hedda Gabler," "Othello."

VANLEER, JAY. Born June 24, 1931 in Cleveland, O. Graduate Western Reserve U. Bdwy debut 1972 in "Don't Play Us Cheap."

263

| Edmond Varrato | Marsha Warner | James Ray Weeks | Alyce E. Webb | Charles Weldo |

VARRATO, EDMOND. Born Nov. 25, 1919 in Blairsville, Pa. Attended State U., Theatre Wing. Bdwy debut 1948 in "Ballet Ballads," followed by "La Plume de Ma Tante," "Something More," "Pickwick," "Marat/deSade," "St. Joan," "Mike Downstairs," "Man of La Mancha."

VENUTA, BENAY. Born Jan. 27, 1911 in San Francisco, Cal. Attended Beaupre. Bdwy debut 1935 in "Anything Goes," followed by "Orchids Preferred," "Kiss the Boys Goodbye," "By Jupiter," "Nellie Bly," "Hazel Flagg," "Copper and Brass," "Dear Me, the Sky Is Falling," LC's "Carousel" and "Annie Get Your Gun," OB in "A Quarter for the Ladies Room."

VEREEN, BEN. Born Oct. 10, 1946 in Miami, Fla. Graduate HS Performing Arts. Debut 1965 OB in "Prodigal Son," followed by Bdwy in "Hair," "Jesus Christ Superstar" for which he received a Theatre World Award., "Pippin."

VESTOFF, VIRGINIA. Born Dec. 9, 1940 in NYC. OB in "The Boy Friend," "Crystal Heart," "Fall Out," "New Cole Porter Revue," "Man with a Load of Mischief," "Love and Let Love," Bdwy in "From A to Z," "Irma La Douce," "Baker Street," "1776.," "Via Galactica," "Nash at 9."

VILLA, DANNY. Born Sept. 13, 1934 in Berkeley, Cal. Bdwy debut 1969 in "Billy," followed by "Jesus Christ Superstar," "Cyrano."

WALKEN, CHRISTOPHER. Born Mar. 31, 1943 in Astoria, NY. Attended Hofstra U. Bdwy debut 1958 in "J.B.," followed by "Best Foot Forward" (OB), "High Spirits," "Baker Street," "The Lion in Winter," "Measure For Measure" (CP), "Rose Tattoo" (CC'66) for which he received a Theatre World Award, "Unknown Soldier and His Wife," "Iphigenia In Aulis" (OB), "Rosencrantz and Guildenstern Are Dead," "Lemon Sky" (OB), "Scenes from American Life," (LC), "Cymbeline" (NYSF), LC's "Enemies,". "The Plough and the Stars," and "Merchant of Venice."

WALKER, KATHRYN. Born in Jan. in Philadelphia. Graduate Wells Col., Harvard, LAMDA. Debut 1971 OB in "Slag," followed by "Alpha Beta."

WALKER, SYDNEY. Born May 4, 1921 in Philadelphia. Attended Conservatoire Nationale, Paris, Bdwy bow 1960 in "Becket," OB in "Volpone," "Julius Caesar," "King Lear," "The Collection," "A Scent of Flowers," "The Nuns," with APA in "You Can't Take It with You," "War and Peace," "Right You Are," "School for Scandal," "We Comrades Three," "The Wild Duck," "Pantagleize," "The Cherry Orchard," "The Misanthrope," "Cocktail Party," and "Cock-A-Doodle Dandy," "Blood Red Roses," with LCRep in "Playboy of the Western World," "Good Woman of Setzuan," "Enemy of the People," "Antigone," "Mary Stuart," "Narrow Road to the Deep North," "Twelfth Night," "The Crucible.," "Enemies," "The Plough and the Stars," "Merchant of Venice," and "Streetcar Named Desire."

WALLACE, ART. Born Sept. 21, 1935 in Oklahoma City. Attended Wash.U., Actors Studio. Bdwy debut 1963 in "No Place to Go but Up," followed by "A Joyful Noise," "Music Man" (CC), "Purlie," OB in "Tattooed Countess," "Flaholley" (ELT), "Hotel Passionato," "Now Is the Time for All Good Men," "Perfect Party."

WALLACE, LEE. Born July 15, 1930 in NYC. Attended NYU. Debut OB 1966 in "Journey of the Fifth Horse," followed by "Saturday Night," "Evening with Garcia Lorca," "Macbeth," "Booth Is Back in Town," "Awake and Sing," "Shepherd of Avenue B," "Basic Training of Pavlo Hummel," Bdwy 1972 in "Secret Affairs of Mildred Wild."

WALLACE, MARIE. Born May 19, 1939 in NYC. Attended NYU. OB in "Electra," "Harlequinade," "Bell, Book and Candle," Bdwy in "Gypsy," "Beauty Part," "Nobody Loves an Albatross," "Right Honourable Gentleman," "The Women."

WALTER, TRACEY. Born Nov. 25, 1950 in Jersey City, NJ. Debut OB 1972 in "American Gothics."

WALTZER, JACK. Born June 5, 1936 in NYC. Attended NYU. Bdwy debut 1956 in "The Matchmaker," followed OB in "Johnny Johnson," "To Damascus," "Silent Partner," "Waiting for Godot," "12 Angry Men," with LCRep in "After the Fall," "Marco Millions," "But for Whom Charlie," "Changeling," "Incident at Vichy," "Tartuffe," "Danton's Death," and "Country Wife."

WARD, DOUGLAS TURNER. Born May 5, 1930 in Burnside, La. Attended UMich. Bdwy bow 1959 in "A Raisin in the Sun," followed by "One Flew over the Cuckoo's Nest," OB in "The Iceman Cometh," "The Blacks," "Pullman Car Hiawatha," "Bloodknot," "Happy Ending," "Day of Absence," "Kongi's Harvest," "Ceremonies in Dark Old Men," "The Harangues," "The Reckoning," "Frederick Douglass through His Own Words," "River Niger."

WARD, JANET. Born Feb. 19 in NYC. Attended Actors Studio. Bdwy debut 1945 in "Dream Girl," followed by "Anne of the Thousand Days," "Detective Story," "King of Friday's Men," "Middle of the Night," "Miss Lonelyhearts," "J.B.," "Cheri," "The Egg," "Impossible Years," "Of Love Remembered," OB in "Chapparal," "The Typists" and "The Tiger," "Summertree," "Dream of a Blacklisted Actor," "Cruising Speed 600 MPH," "One Flew over the Cuckoo's Nest.," "Love Gotta Come by Saturday Night."

WARNER, MARSHA. Born July 3, 1949 in Cleveland, O. Graduate Ohio U. Debut OB 1972 in "How to Succeed in Business . . ." (ELT)

WARREN, JENNIFER. Born Aug. 12, 1941 in NYC. Graduate UWis. Debut 1967 OB in "Scuba Duba," Bdwy 1972 in "6 Rms Riv Vu" for which she received a Theatre World Award.

WARREN, JOSEPH. Born June 5, 1916 in Boston, Mass. Graduate Denver U. Bdwy debut 1951 in "Barefoot in Athens," followed by "One Bright Day," "Love of Four Colonels," "Hidden River," "The Advocate," "Philadelphia Here I Come," "Borstal Boy," "The Lincoln Mask," OB in "Brecht on Brecht," "Jonah."

WARRICK, RUTH. Born June 29 in St. Joseph, Mo. Attended UMo. Bdwy debut 1957 in "Miss Lonelyhearts," followed by "Take Me Along," "Irene," OB in "Single Man at a Party," "Any Resemblance to Persons Living or Dead," "Misalliance," "Conditions of Agreement."

WATERSTON, SAM. Born Nov. 15, 1940 in Cambridge, Mass. Graduate Yale, Bdwy bow 1963 in "Oh, Dad, Poor Dad . . . ," followed by "First One Asleep Whistle," "Halfway up the Tree," "Indians," "Hay Fever," "Much Ado about Nothing," OB in "As You Like It," "Thistle in My Bed," "The Knack," "Fitz," "Biscuit," "La Turista," "Posterity For Sale," "Ergo," "Muzeeka," "Red Cross," "Henry IV," "Spitting Image," "I Met A Man," "Brass Butterfly," "Trial of the Catonsville 9," "Cymbeline," "Hamlet," "A Meeting by the River."

WATSON, DOUGLASS. Born Feb. 24, 1921 in Jackson, Ga. Graduate UNC. Bdwy bow 1947 in "The Iceman Cometh," followed by "Anthony and Cleopatra" for which he received a Theatre World Award, "Leading Lady," "Richard III," "Happiest Years," "That Lady," "Wisteria Trees," "Romeo and Juliet," "Desire under the Elms," "Sunday Breakfast," "Cyrano de Bergerac," "Confidential Clerk," "Portrait of a Lady," Miser," "Young and Beautiful," "Little Glass Clock," "Country Wife," "Man for All Seasons," "Chinese Prime Minister," "Marat/deSade," "Prime of Miss Jean Brodie," "Pirates of Penzance," "The Hunter" (OB), "Much Ado about Nothing."

WATSON, SUSAN. Born Dec. 17, 1938 in Tulsa, Okla. Attended Juilliard. OB in "The Fantasticks," "Lend an Ear," "Follies of 1910," "Carnival" (LC), CC "Oklahoma!," and "Where's Charley?," Bdwy in "Bye Bye Birdie," "Carnival," "Ben Franklin In Paris." "A Joyful Noise," "Celebration," "Beggar on Horseback" (LC), "No, No, Nanette."

WATTERS, HAL. Born Feb. 20, 1943 in Oklahoma City. Graduate UOkla., Juilliard. Bdwy debut 1969 in "Celebration," OB in "Six," "From Berlin to Broadway."

WEBB, ALYCE E. Born June 1, 1934 in NYC. Graduate NYU. Bdwy debut 1946 in "Street Scene," followed by "Lost in the Stars," "Finian's Rainbow," "Porgy and Bess," "Show Boat," "Guys and Dolls," "Kiss Me, Kate," "Wonderful Town," "Hello, Dolly!," "Purlie," OB in "Simply Heavenly," "Ballad of Bimshire," "Trumpets of the Lord," "Streetcar Named Desire" (LC).

WEEKS, JAMES RAY. Born Mar. 21, 1942 in Seattle, Wash. Graduate UOre., AADA. Debut 1972 in LCR's "Enemies" "Merchant of Venice," and "Streetcar Named Desire."

WEIL, ROBERT E. Born Nov. 18, 1914 in NYC. Attended NYU. Bdwy bow in "New Faces of 1942," followed by "Burlesque," "Becket," "Once upon a Mattress," "Blood, Sweat and Stanley Poole," "Night Life," "Arturo Ui," "Love Your Crooked Neighbor" (OB), "Beggar on Horseback" (LC), "Lenny."

WEINER, ARN. Born July 19, 1931 in Brooklyn. Attended Pratt, LACC. Bdwy debut 1966 in "Those That Play the Clowns," OB in "Come Walk with Me," "Saving Grace," "Come Out, Carlo," "Evenings with Chekhov," "Sunset."

WELBES, GEORGE M. Born Sept. 14, 1934 in Sioux Falls, SD. Graduate USD. Debut 1968 OB in "Oh Say Can You See L.A.," followed by "The Other Man," "Oh! Calcutta!," "One Flew over the Cuckoo's Nest."

WELCH, CHARLES. Born Feb. 2, 1921 in New Britain, Conn. Attended Am. Th. Wing. Bdwy bow 1948 in "Cloud 7," followed by "Make a Million," "Donnybrook," "Golden Boy," "Breakfast at Tiffany's," "Married Alive," "Darling of the Day," "Dear World," "Follies.," "Status Quo Vadis."

WELDON, CHARLES. Born June 1, 1940 in Wetumka, Okla. Bdwy debut 1969 in "Big Time Buck White," followed OB by "Ride a Black Horse," "Long Time Coming and a Long Time Gone," "Jamimma.", "River Niger."

WELLS, TONY. Born Aug. 23, 1940 in Parsons, Kan. Graduate Oberlin., Boston U. Bdwy debut 1973 in "Shelter."

WESTON, JIM. Born Aug. 2, 1942 in Montclair, NJ. Attended Manchester Col., AADA. Bdwy bow 1969 in "Red, White and Maddox," followed by "Lovely Ladies, Kind Gentlemen," "Grease," OB in "She Loves Me," "Ballad of Johnny Pot," "A Gun Play."

Grenna Whitaker   Walter Willison   Beatrice Winde   Noel Young   Nancy Zala

WHEEL, PATRICIA. Born in NYC. Has appeared in "Cyrano," "The Tempest," "Arms and the Man," "Little Brown Jug," "Stars Weep," "Browning Version," "Cry of the Peacock," "Gertie," "Sacred Flame," "Soldiers," "Butterflies Are Free," "Voices.," "The Women."

WHITAKER, GRENNA. Born Mar. 22, 1948 in NYC. Graduate Queens Col. Debut OB 1972 in "Safari 300," Bdwy 1973 in "The River Niger."

WHITE, CHARLES. Born Aug. 29, 1920 in Perth Amboy, NJ. Graduate Rutgers U., Neighborhood Playhouse. Credits include "Career," "Cloud 7," "Gypsy," "Philadelphia, Here I Come," "Inherit the Wind," "Comes a Day," "Front Page."

WHITTLE, JAMES. Born Oct. 25, 1939 in Bisbee, Ariz. Attended Pasadena Playhouse. Debut OB 1964 in "Long Voyage Home," followed by APA's "War and Peace," "Wild Duck," "You Can't Take It with You," "Pantagleize," "The Misanthrope," and "Cocktail Party," "Merchant of Venice" (LC).

WHITTON, PEGGY. Born Nov. 30, 1950 in Pennsylvania. Debut OB 1973 in "Baba Goya."

WHYTE, DONN. Born Feb. 23, 1941 in Chicago. Attended Northwestern. Debut 1969 OB in "The Brownstone Urge," followed by "Foreplay," "One Flew over the Cuckoo's Nest."

WIDDOES, KATHLEEN. Born Mar. 21, 1939 in Wilmington, Del. Attended Paris' Theatre des Nations. Bdwy debut 1958 in "The Firstborn," followed by "World of Suzie Wong," "Much Ado About Nothing," OB in "Three Sisters," "The Maids," "You Can't Take It with You," "To Clothe the Naked," "World War 2-1/2," "Beggar's Opera."

WILCOX, RALPH. Born Jan. 30, 1951 in Milwaukee, Wisc. Attended UWisc. Debut 1971 OB in "Dirtiest Show in Town," Bdwy in "Ain't Supposed to Die a Natural Death."

WILDER, DAVID. Born Dec. 26, 1936 in The Bronx. Graduate CCNY. Studied at Juilliard. Bdwy debut 1968 in "Zorba," followed by "Man of La Mancha," "1776," "On the Town."

WILKERSON, ARNOLD. Born Apr. 6, 1943 in San Francisco. Attended RADA. Bdwy debut 1968 in "Jimmy Shine," OB in "Hair," "Don't Bother Me, I Can't Cope."

WILKINSON, KATE. Born Oct. 25 in San Francisco. Attended San Jose State Col. Bdwy debut 1967 in "Little Murders," followed by "Johnny No-Trump," "Watercolor," "Postcards," "Ring Round the Bathtub," "Last of Mrs. Lincoln," OB in "La Madre," "Earnest in Love," "Story of Mary Surratt," "Bring Me a Warm Body," "Child Buyer," "Rimers of Eldritch," "A Doll's House," "Hedda Gabler," "Real Inspector Hound."

WILLIAMS, DICK. Born Aug. 9, 1938 in Chicago. Debut 1968 OB in "Big Time Buck White," followed by "Jamimma," Bdwy in "Ain't Supposed to Die a Natural Death."

WILLIAMS, DORIAN. Born in Pontiac, Mich. Juilliard graduate. Debut 1972 OB in "Safari 300."

WILLIAMS, ELLWOODSON. Born June 17, 1937 in Jacksonville, NC. Graduate Tenn. AIU. Debut OB 1968 in "Cadillac Dreams," followed by "Land beyond the River," "Voice of the Gene," "Jerico-Jim Crow," "Duet in Black," "Adding Machine," "A Man's a Man," "Cry the Beloved Country," "Mercury Island," "Middle Class Black," "Ceremonies in Dark Old Men," "Murderous Angels," Bdwy 1971 in "Two Gentlemen of Verona."

WILLIAMS, TENNESSEE. Born Mar. 26, 1911 in Columbus, Miss. Graduate UIowa. Debut 1972 OB in his own play "Small Craft Warnings."

WILLIAMSON, NICOL. Born Sept. 14, 1938 in Hamilton, Scot. Bdwy debut 1965 in "Inadmissable Evidence," followed by "Plaza Suite," "Hamlet," "Uncle Vanya," "Nicol Williamson's Late Show" (OB).

WILLIARD, CAROL. Born Nov. 5, 1947 in Pgh, Pa. Graduate Carnegie-Mellon U. Debut OB 1973 in "The Orphan."

WILLIS, SALLY. Born Oct. 9, 1948 in Milford Haven, S. Wales. Graduate Sussex U., LAMDA. Debut OB 1973 in "El Coca-Cola Grande."

WILLISON, WALTER. Born June 24, 1947 in Monterey Park, Calif. Bdwy debut 1970 in "Norman, Is That You?," followed by "Two by Two" for which he received a Theatre World Award, "Wild and Wonderful," "Pippin."

WILSON, ELIZABETH. Born Apr. 4, 1925 in Grand Rapids, Mich. Attended Neighborhood Playhouse. Bdwy in "Picnic," "Desk Set," "Tunnel of Love," "Big Fish, Little Fish," "Sheep on the Runway," "Sticks and Bones," "Secret Affairs of Mildred Wild," OB in "Plaza 9," "Eh?," "Little Murders," "Good Woman of Setzuan" (LC), "Uncle Vanya."

WILSON, MARY LOUISE. Born Nov. 12, 1936 in New Haven, Conn. Graduate Northwestern. OB in "Our Town," "Upstairs at the Downstairs," "Threepenny Opera," "A Great Career," "Whispers on the Wind," "Beggar's Opera," Bdwy in "Hot Spot," "Flora, the Red Menace," "Criss-Crossing," "Promises, Promises," "The Women."

WINDE, BEATRICE. Born Jan. 5 in Chicago. Debut 1966 OB in "In White America," followed by "June Bug Graduates Tonight," "Strike Heaven on the Face," Bdwy bow 1971 in "Ain't Supposed to Die a Natural Death" for which she received a Theatre World Award.

WINKWORTH, MARK J. Born July 19, 1948 in Michigan. Graduate Hofstra U. Bdwy debut 1973 in "The Changing Room."

WINN, KITTY. Born 1944 in Washington, DC. Graduate Boston U. Bdwy debut 1969 in "Three Sisters," followed by "Hamlet" (NYSF).

WINSTON, HATTIE. Born Mar. 3, 1945 in Greenville, Miss. Attended Howard U. OB in "Prodigal Son," "Day of Absence," "Pins and Needles," "Weary Blues," "Man Better Man," "Billy Noname," "Sambo," Bdwy in "The Me Nobody Knows," "Two Gentlemen of Verona."

WINTER, EDWARD. Born June 3, 1937 in Roseburg, Ore. Attended UOre. With LCRep. in "Country Wife," "Condemned of Altona," and "Caucasian Chalk Circle," "Waiting for Godot," Bdwy in "Cabaret," "Birthday Party," "Promises, Promises," "Night Watch.," "Follies."

WISEMAN, JOSEPH. Born May 15, 1919 in Montreal, Can. Attended CCNY. Appeared in "Abe Lincoln in Illinois," "Journey to Jerusalem," "Candle in the Wind," "Three Sisters," "Storm Operation," "Joan of Lorraine," "Antony and Cleopatra," "Detective Story," "That Lady," "King Lear," "Golden Boy," "The Lark," LCRep's "Marco Millions," "Incident at Vichy," "In the Matter of J. Robert Oppenheimer," and "Enemies," OB in "Duchess of Malfi," "Last Analysis."

WITHAM, JOHN. Born Apr. 3, 1947 in Plainfield, NJ. Graduate AMDA. Debut 1972 OB in "Two if by Sea.", followed by "Comedy."

WOOD, STUART CRAIG. Born Oct. 3, 1945 in Washington, DC. Graduate Carnegie Tech, Wayne State U. Bdwy debut 1970 in "Lovely Ladies, Kind Gentlemen," OB in "Young Abe Lincoln," "Secret Life of Walter Mitty" (ELT).

WOODS, JAMES. Born Apr. 18, 1947 in Vernal, Utah. Graduate MIT. Bdwy debut 1970 in "Borstal Boy," followed by "Saved" (OB), "Conduct Unbecoming," "Trial of the Catonsville 9," "Moonchildren" for which he received a Theatre World Award., "Green Julia" (OB), "Finishing Touches."

WOODS, RICHARD. Born May 9, 1930 in Buffalo, NY. Graduate Ithaca Col. Bdwy in "Beg, Borrow or Steal," "Capt. Brassbound's Conversion," "Sail Away," "Coco," "Last of Mrs. Lincoln," OB in "The Crucible," "Summer and Smoke," "American Gothic," "Four-In-One," "My Heart's In The Highlands," "Eastward In Eden," "The Long Gallery," "The Year Boston Won The Pennant" and "In The Matter of J. Robert Oppenheimer" (LC), with APA in "You Can't Take It With You," "War and Peace," "School For Scandal," "Right You Are," "The Wild Duck," "Pantagleize," "Exit The King," "The Cherry Orchard," "Cock-A-Doodle Dandy," and "Hamlet."

WRIGHT, E. H. Born Aug. 14, 1950 in Jersey City, NJ. Attended Rutgers U. Bdwy debut 1972 in "Wild and Wonderful," OB in "Thoughts,"

WRIGHT, TERESA. Born Oct. 27, 1918 in NYC. Bdwy debut 1938 in "Our Town," followed by "Life with Father," "Dark at the Top of the Stairs," "Mary, Mary," "I Never Sang for My Father," OB in "Who's Happy Now," "A Passage to E. M. Forster."

YOHN, ERICA. Born in NYC. OB in "Agammemnon," "Circle of Chalk," "Ascent of F6," "Dream of Love," "Lysistrata," "Middle Man What Now," "Heel of Achilles," "Empire Builders," LCRep's "Yerma," "Caucasian Chalk Circle," and "Danton's Death," on Bdwy in "That Summer, That Fall," "Lenny."

YORK, MICHAEL. Born Mar. 27, 1942 in Fulmer, Eng. Attended UCollege Oxford. Bdwy debut 1973 in "Out Cry."

YOUNG, ASTON S. Born June 6, 1930 in NYC. Debut 1965 OB in "The Old Glory," followed by "Outside Man," "Arms and the Man," "Benito Cerino," "Trials of Brother Jero," "Strong Breed," "Man Better Man," "Jamimma."

YOUNG, JOE. Born June 5, 1905 in NYC. Bdwy debut 1944 in "Laughing Room Only," followed by "Once upon a Mattress," "Enter Laughing," "Great Airplane Snatch" (OB), "The Sunshine Boys."

YOUNG, NOEL. Born in Salt Lake City, U. Graduate UMon. Bdwy debut 1972 in "Fun City."

ZALA, NANCY. Born July 10, 1936 in NYC. Graduate St. Andrews U. Debut OB 1967 in "In Circles," followed by "I Am a Camera," "Woman at the Tomb," "O Marry Me," "Medea."

ZORICH, LOUIS. Born Feb. 12, 1924 in Chicago. Attended Roosevelt U. OB in "Six Characters in Search of an Author," "Crimes and Crimes," "Henry V," "Thracian Horses," "All Women Are One," "Good Soldier Schweik," "Shadow of Heroes," "To Clothe the Naked," "Sunset," Bdwy in "Becket," "Moby Dick," "Odd Couple," "Hadrian VII," "Moonchildren," "Fun City."

OBITUARIES

Tod Andrews (1953)

John Call (1971)

Leo G. Carroll (1959)

WILLIAM P. ADAMS, 85, stage, radio, and tv actor, died in NYC Sept. 29, 1972. He had appeared with E. H. Sothern, Julia Marlowe, John Barrymore, and in such plays as "If I Were King," "Hamlet," "Lysistrata," and "Paris Bound." He had served as president of AFTRA. Surviving are his widow, former actress Eleanor Wells, and a daughter.

MAX ADRIAN, 69, Irish-born stage and film actor, died Jan. 19, 1973 in his Surrey, Eng., home. He had a long and varied career in London, and appeared in NY with The Old Vic, and in "College Sinners," "Candide," "Mary Stuart," "The Lesson," "The Deadly Game," and "By George," a one-man performance impersonating Shaw. No reported survivors.

TOD ANDREWS, 51, stage, film, and tv actor, died Nov. 6, 1972 of a heart attack in his Beverly Hills home. Born Ted Anderson, he was known professionally for a while as Michael Ames. Had appeared on stage in "Summer and Smoke" for which he received a Theatre World Award, "Mr. Roberts," "Come On Up," "My Sister Eileen," "Storm Operation," "Mrs. Kimball Presents," "Public Relations," "That Old Devil," "A Girl Can Tell," "Sabrina Fair," and "Cactus Flower." His tv series include "Ironsides," "The Bold Ones," "The F.B.I.," and "The Gray Ghost." His widow and three children survive.

GUY ARBURY, 65, stage, film, and tv actor, was found dead of stab wounds in his NY apartment on Dec. 26, 1972. His Broadway debut was in 1935 in "Star-Spangled," subsequently in "The Good Neighbor," "Young Mr. Disraeli," "Hamlet," "Henry IV," "Kiss and Tell," "Tea and Sympathy," "Auntie Mame," "Goodbye Charlie," "First Love," and "Touchstone," among others. No reported survivors.

ROBERT ARMSTRONG, 82, stage and film actor, died Apr. 20, 1973 in Santa Monica after a short illness. Appeared on Bdwy in "Boys Will Be Boys," "Shavings," "Honey Girl," "Is Zat So?," "Sleep No More," before going to Hollywood where he appeared in over 100 films. His widow survives.

JOHN BANNER, 63, stage, film, and tv actor, died Jan. 28, 1973 in his native Vienna from an abdominal hemorrhage. He was a well known actor in pre-Hitler Germany, and came to NY in 1939. Appeared in "From Vienna," and "Pastoral," in many films, and for six years was the popular Sgt. Schultz on tv's "Hogan's Heroes" series. His widow survives.

HUGH BEAUMONT, 64, London's most successful producer, died Mar. 22, 1973 in his London home. He had also often been a co-producer on Bdwy with such productions as "A Man for All Seasons," "School for Scandal," and "Irma La Douce," among many others. No reported survivors.

SALLY BENSON, 71, writer, died July 19, 1972 in Woodland Hills, Calif., after a long illness. Her short stories about Judy Graves became the popular "Junior Miss" on Bdwy, radio, and tv. She adapted Tarkington's "Seventeen" for Bdwy, and based her play "The Young and the Beautiful" on F. Scott Fitzgerald stories. She also wrote many screenplays. A daughter survives.

DAN BLY, 37, stage manager, died Feb. 2, 1973 in Winston-Salem, N.C. Surviving are his wife, actress Patricia Conolly, and a daughter.

HELEN BONFILS, 82, producer, and patron of the theatre, died June 6, 1972 in Denver, Colo., after a long illness. Among the plays she helped bring to Bdwy were "Enter Laughing," "King Lear," "Comedy of Errors," "The Killing of Sister George," and "Sleuth." There are no immediate survivors.

LOUIS BOREL, 66, stage and film actor, died in his native Amsterdam sometime during Apr. 1973. Appeared in Holland, Germany, and England before his Bdwy debut in 1941 in "Candle in the Wind," followed by "Made in Heaven," "Idiot's Delight," and "My Name Is Aquilon." Returned to Amsterdam in 1949. No reported survivors.

JOHN BURRELL, 62, director, and former chairman of The Old Vic board of directors, died Sept. 28, 1972 of a heart attack in Urbana, Ill., where he was director of the Krannert Center for the Performing Arts. On Bdwy he directed "Peter Pan" with Jean Arthur, and "Mr. Pickwick." He co-directed The Shakespeare Festival Academy in Stratford, Conn., and was an executive director for CBS-TV. His widow and a daughter survive.

JOHN CALL, 64, actor, died Apr. 3, 1973 of a heart attack in his NYC home. After his Bdwy debut in 1934 in "Sailor Beware," appeared in "Father Malachy's Miracle," "Merchant of Yonkers," "As You Like It," "Be So Kindly," "But for the Grace of God," "The Flying Gerardos," "So Proudly We Hail," "Bet Your Life," "Bloomer Girl," "Pipe Dream," "A Touch of the Poet," "Oliver," "Pickwick," "A Time for Singing," "Comedy of Errors," "Hamlet," "Any Resemblance to Persons Living or Dead," "Henry V," "Measure for Measure," "Taming of the Shrew," "Much Ado about Nothing," "Midsummer Night's Dream," "Merchant of Venice," and "Romeo and Juliet." His widow and son survive.

CYNTHIA CARLIN, actress and tv producer, died Feb. 23, 1973 after a brief illness in NYC. She had appeared in several Broadway productions, over 250 radio shows, and produced several shows for television. Surviving are her mother, and brother.

ALAN CARNEY, 63, vaudeville, nightclub, stage, tv and film comedian, died May 2, 1973 of a heart attack after winning the daily double at Hollywood Park track. Made his Bdwy debut in 1954 in "Fanny." A brother and sister survive.

GINNA CARR, 35, musical comedy and burlesque actress, died of cancer July 13, 1972 in Hollywood. Surviving are her husband, comedian Joey Faye, and her mother.

LEO G. CARROLL, 80, English-born stage, film, and tv actor, died Oct. 16, 1972 after a long illness in Hollywood. Made his Bdwy debut in 1912 in "Rutherford and Son," followed by "The Constant Nymph," "The Perfect Alibi," "The Green Bay Tree," "Petticoat Fever," "Masque of Kings," "Two Bouquets," "Angel Street," "The Late George Apley," "Druid Circle," "You Never Can Tell," "Jenny Kissed Me," "Mary Rose," "Lo and Behold!," "O Borrowed Time," "Someone Waiting," and "The Pleasure of His Company." Appeared over 40 films, and on tv's "Topper" and "Man from U.N.C.L.E." series. Survived by his wido and a son.

MELVILLE COOPER, 76, English-born stage, film, and tv actor, died of cancer March 29, 1973 in Woodland Hills, Cal. Made Bdwy debut in 1935 in "Laburnum Grove," followed by "Jubilee," "The Merry Widow," "While the Sun Shines," "Firebrand of Florence," "Pygmalion," "Gypsy Lady," "The Haven," "An Inspector Calls," "The Liar," "Day after Tomorrow," "Make a Wish," "Much Ado about Nothing," "Escapade," "My Fair Lady," "Hostile Witness," and "Charley's Aunt (1970). A daughter survives.

CHARLES CORRELL, 82, actor, died Sept. 26, 1972 of a heart attack in Chicago. He was Andy on the "Amos 'n' Andy" radio show for more than 30 years. He is survived by his widow, former dancer Mercedes McLaughlin, and four children.

NOEL COWARD, 73, English-born stage, film, and tv actor, playwright, songwriter, composer, and director, died of a heart attack March 26, 1973 in his villa in Jamaica, BWI. A master of sophisticated comedy, he wrote 27 plays including "Private Lives," "Blithe Spirit," "Cavalcade," and "Bittersweet," and appeared in several of them on Bdwy: "The Vortex," "This Year of Grace," "Private Lives," "Design for Living," "Tonight at 8:30," "Nude with Violin," and "Present Laughter." In 1970 he was knighted by Queen Elizabeth. His most famous songs are "I'll See You Again," "A Room with a View," "Mad Dogs and Englishmen," and "I'll Follow My secret Heart." There were no immediate survivors.

WALLY COX, 48, Detroit-born stage and tv actor, night club entertainer, and writer, died of a heart attack Feb. 15, 1973 in his Los Angeles home. After performing in night clubs as a comedian, he made his Bdwy debut in 1950 in "Dance Me a Song." His greatest acclaim was as "Mr. Peepers" in the tv series, and on "Hollywood Squares." He is survived by his third wife, and a daughter by his first wife.

WILLIAM CRAGEN, 62, actor and director, died June 29, 1972 in Arnolds Park, Iowa where he had been an actor-director of the summer theatre for 13 years. He appeared on Bdwy in "White Steed," and "Country Wife," and in numerous radio and tv shows. Surviving is his widow.

WALTER CRAIG, 71, musical comedy singer-dancer-actor, and radio and tv program executive, died July 5, 1972 in Montclair, N.J. He appeared on Bdwy in "Jack and Jill," "Queen High," and "Greenwich Village Follies." His most successful network show was "The $64,000 Question." His widow and a daughter survive.

HOWARD S. CULLMAN, 80, philanthropist, Broadway "angel," commissioner of the Port of New York Authority, died June 29, 1972 after a long illness in his NY home. He won a reputation as a civic leader and crusader, and over the years invested in over 300 Broadway productions. Surviving are his widow and four children.

CLAIRE DEVINE, 82, former musical comedy actress, died Apr. 22, 1973 in her home in Dumont, NJ. After many years in vaudeville and musical comedy, she became a wardrobe mistress for several Bdwy productions, her last being "Fiddler on the Roof." She retired five years ago. A daughter survives.

BRANDON DE WILDE, 30, stage, film, and tv actor, died July 6, 1972 in Denver, Colo., as a result of injuries suffered in a traffic accident. At 7 he made his Bdwy debut in "A Member of the Wedding," subsequently appearing in "Mrs. McThing," "The Emperor's Clothes," and "A Race of Hairy Men." He appeared in several films, and starred in his own tv series "Jaimie." He is survived by his second wife, and a son by his first.

ROBERT EMMETT DOLAN, 64, stage, screen, tv composer, conductor, and producer, died of a heart attack Sept. 26, 1972 in Westwood, Calif. He gained prominence as the composer and conductor of some 27 Bdwy shows, including "Good News," "Strike Me Pink," "Hooray for What," "Leave It to Me," "Very Warm for May," "Louisiana Purchase," and later wrote "Texas, Li'l Darlin'," "Foxy," and "Coco." He scored more than 50 films. Two sons survive.

ETHEL EVERETT, 63, tv and radio actress, died April 2, 1973 in her NYC home. She began her career on radio in 1931, and later was prominent in "The Goldbergs" series. On tv she appeared in "Big Story," "Studio One," and "As the World Turns." Her mother and brother survive.

MARY FINNEY, 68, character actress, died of emphysema Feb. 26, 1973 in her NYC apartment. Her Bdwy debut was in 1950 in "Southern Exposure," followed by "The Cellar and the Well," "Make a Wish," "Gentlemen Prefer Blondes," "The Children's Hour," "The Magic and the Loss," "The Honeys," "Janus," "Happy Hunting," "Whisper to Me," "Too Much Johnson," and "First Impressions." For the last five years she had been a secretary. No reported survivors.

SARA FLOYD, 78, retired actress, died of a stroke Aug. 16, 1972 in Englewood, N.J. She had appeared in 34 Bdwy productions, including "Atlas and Eva," "Mourning Becomes Electra," "The Man Who Came to Dinner," "Show Boat," and "Inherit the Wind." A nephew and two nieces survive.

CARL FRANK, 63, retired stage, radio, and tv actor, died Sept. 23, 1972 in his home at Cruz Bay, St. John, V.I. Was a member of the Mercury Theatre, and appeared in such Bdwy productions as "Paths of Glory," "Boy Meets Girl," "A Sound of Hunting," and "The Shrike." He had been a radio announcer for several series, and appeared in tv series "Naked City," "I Remember Mama," and "Edge of Night." Surviving are his widow, son, and a daughter.

RUDOLF FRIML, 92, Prague-born composer, died Nov. 12, 1972 in Hollywood. He composed over 30 operettas, including "Rose Marie," "The Vagabond King," "The Firefly," and "The Three Musketeers." His fourth wife, and two sons and a daughter survive.

BERTA GERSTEN, 78, Polish-born actress, died Sept. 10, 1972 in NYC. Star of many Yiddish productions, she made her Bdwy debut in 1954 in "The Flowering Peach," followed by "A Majority of One." A son survives.

DR. BENJAMIN A. GILBERT, 67, died of cancer July 9, 1972 in his home in NY. For 42 years he had been house physician for Broadway theatres. Surviving are his widow, a son and a daughter.

THEO GOETZ, 78. Vienna-born stage, radio, and tv actor, died of a heart attack Dec. 29, 1972 in NY. Appeared on Bdwy in "Swan Song," "Family Portrait," and "The Golem." Had been a regular on radio and tv's "Guiding Light" series since 1947. His widow survives.

MINNA GOMBELL, 81, stage and film actress, died Apr. 14, 1973 in Santa Monica, Cal. ~~n~~ Bdwy, she appeared in "Indestructible Wife," "Indiscretion," and "Nancy's Private ~~ffair~~" before going to Hollywood in 1930. She made over 100 films. No reported survivors.

Melville Cooper (1940)

Noel Coward (1960)

Brandon De Wilde (1962)

Miriam Hopkins (1951)

Luba Lisa (1965)

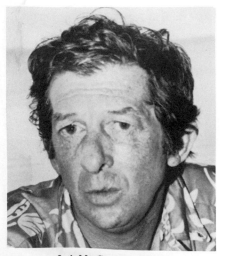

Jack MacGowran (1969)

WALTER N. GREAZA, 76, stage, radio, film and tv actor, died June 1, 1973 in a NYC hospital. Born in Minn., he made his 1927 Bdwy debut in "Love in the Tropics," followed by over 30 productions, including "We the People," "Judgment Day," "Wednesday's Child," "If This Be Treason," "To Quito and Back," "Ceiling Zero," "Now You've Done It," "Room Service," "A New Life," "Wallflower," "Temper the Wind," "The Visitor," "The Overtons," and "Roman Candle." On radio he was Inspector Ross of "Crime Doctor" for 9 years, and the editor in "Big Town." He was a regular on tv's "Edge of Night" series. He served as assistant executive secretary of Actors Equity for 8 years. His first wife, actress Mary Young, died in 1947, and his second, actress Helen Ambrose, died in 1966. No reported survivors.

ABEL GREEN, 72, editor of Variety, died May 10, 1973 of a heart attack in his NYC home. He was a top theatrical-trade reporter before joining Variety, and succeeded Sime Silverman its founder-editor in 1933. He remained its editor until his death. He wrote "Show Biz: From Vaude to Video" with Joe Laurie, Jr., the screenplay "Mr. Broadway" about the life of Mr. Silverman, and edited "The Spice of Variety." His widow, two brothers, and a sister survive.

CLIFF HALL, 78, stage, vaudeville, radio, and tv comedian, died of cancer Oct. 6, 1972 in Englewood, N.J. For over 30 years he was straight man for Jack Pearl (Baron Munchhausen), including 15 years in their radio series. Appeared on Bdwy in "Ziegfeld Follies," "No Time for Sergeants," "The Music Man," "Lord Pengo," "Here's Love," and "Sherry." A son survives.

RICHARD HALLIDAY, 67, critic, producer, and manager, died after surgery March 3, 1973 in Brasilia, Brazil. Denver-born, he became story editor for Paramount Pictures before becoming a Bdwy producer of "The Sound of Music," "Jennie," "Daughter of Silence," "Annie Get Your Gun," and "South Pacific" on tour. He also produced Mary Martin's tv specials. Surviving are his widow, actress-singer Mary Martin, and a daughter.

GLADYS HANSON, 89, retired stage and film actress, died Feb. 23, 1973 in her native Atlanta, Ga. At an early age, she became a member of the Henry Miller Co., subsequently appearing as Ophelia to E. H. Sothern's Hamlet, in "The Spoilers," "The Queen's Husband," "The Judge's Husband," "Richelieu," "If I Were King," "Builder of Bridges," "Evensong," "Mary Goes to Sea," "Raffles," "Our American Cousin," "The Governor's Lady," "Mecca," and her last play in 1939 "Brown Danube." A daughter survives. She was the widow of playwright-producer Charles Emerson Cook.

IRVING HARMON, 66, burlesque and musical comedy actor, died of cancer Mar. 19, 1973 in NYC. He had appeared on Bdwy in "Gypsy," "Do Re Mi," and "A Funny Thing Happened on the Way to the Forum." Surviving are a brother and sister.

HAROLD HASTINGS, 56, musical director of "A Little Night Music," died May 30, 1973 of a heart attack in his home in Larchmont, N.Y. After serving as musical director for many radio and television shows, he became musical director for such Bdwy productions as "Pajama Game," "Damn Yankees" for which he received a "Tony" Award, "New Girl in Town," "Top Banana," and "The Selling of the President." Surviving are his widow, and two daughters.

DOROTHY HINCKLEY, age unreported, retired actress, died Nov. 23, 1972 after a long illness in Maplewood, N.J. She had spent 36 years on the stage before retiring. Her husband, Robert H. Blair, survives.

MIRIAM HOPKINS, 69, stage and film actress, died of a heart attack Oct. 9, 1972 in a NY hotel. She made her Bdwy debut as a dancer in 1921 in "The Music Box Revue," subsequently appearing in "Garrick Gaieties," "Excess Baggage," "The Camel through the Needle's Eye," "Lysistrata," "Knife in the Wall," "Home Towners," "Jezebel," "The Perfect Marriage," "The Skin of Our Teeth," "Message for Margaret," and "Look Homeward, Angel," her last in 1958. She was in over 35 films. She is survived by her adopted son, and a sister. She was married and divorced four times.

URSULA JEANS, 66, British stage and screen actress, died Apr. 21, 1973 in a nursing home near London. After many years on the British stage, she made her Bdwy debut in 1933 in "Late One Evening." Her second husband, actor Roger Livesey, survives.

CECIL KELLAWAY, 79, stage and film character actor, died Feb. 28, 1973 in Hollywood. Born in South Africa, he later appeared on stage in Europe, Australia, and U.S. His last Bdwy role was in 1960 in "Greenwillow." Appeared in over 75 feature films. His widow and two sons survive.

HERBERT KENT, 96, English-born actor, died Mar. 13, 1973 in NY. Made his Bdwy debut in 1912 in "Pomander Walk," subsequently appearing in many plays. Surviving is his wife, former actress Ada Kent.

MARY LANGE, 60, stage and film actress, died Apr. 20, 1973 while vacationing in Coral Gables, Fla. After appearing in a series of "Ziegfeld Follies," she went to Hollywood and appeared in several films. She retired in 1938 when she married Frank A. Kolb of Standard Oil. Her husband and a son survive.

ERNITA LASCELLES, 87, English-born actress and author, died June 23, 1972 in Buckingham Valley, Pa. Was a leading lady on London stage before coming to U.S. in the 1920's for the Theatre Guild. Among the plays in which she appeared were "Back to Methusalah," "From Morn to Midnight," "Madras House," and "The Weavers." She wrote several plays, including "Fire," that were produced both in London and NY. She was the widow of actor Herbert Walter Ranson. Two daughters survive.

LUBA LISA, 31, actress-singer, was killed in an airplane crash near Colchester, Vt., on Dec. 15, 1972. She appeared in "Carnival," "I Had a Ball" for which she received a Theatre World Award, "I Can Get It for You Wholesale," "West Side Story," "Your Own Thing," and "They Don't Make 'Em Like That Anymore." Surviving are her parents, and a brother.

LILLIAN LITTLE, 66, character actress, died July 30, 1972 in NYC. She had appeared with the American Actors Co., and in "Death of a Salesman," "Auntie Mame," and "Queen after Death." She was director for the Lighthouse Players. A sister survives.

JACK MacGOWRAN, 54, one of Ireland's foremost actors, died Jan. 30, 1973 in a NYC hotel. He was appearing in the Lincoln Center Repertory Theater's production of "The Plough and the Stars." He had appeared previously in NY in "Juno," "Gandhi," and "MacGowran in the Works of Beckett." Surviving are his widow, and a daughter.

LESTER MACK, 66, stage, film, and tv actor, died Oct. 11, 1972 in a NY hospital. Among the plays in which he appeared are "Period of Adjustment," "The Moon Is Blue," "Mister Roberts," and "Solid Gold Cadillac." He played in several tv series, including "Love of Life," "Untouchables," "Wyatt Earp," and "Naked City." His widow survives.

LAURITZ MELCHIOR, 82, one of opera's greatest Wagnerian tenors, died Mar. 18, 1973 in a Santa Monica hospital following an emergency gall bladder operation. He was hailed throughout his career as a thrilling actor with a great voice. The Danish-born singer made his Metropolitan Opera debut in 1926 in "Tannhauser," and retired in 1950. He appeared in several films. Surviving are a son and daughter.

J. CARROL NAISH, 73, stage, film, radio, and tv actor, died Jan. 24, 1973 in a La Jolla, Cal., hospital. He appeared on Bdwy in "Shanghai Gesture," "The Broken Chain," "Scotland Yard," "A Memory of Two Mondays," and "A View from the Bridge." He was a master of dialects, and appeared in over 250 films. Perhaps his greatest popularity came as Luigi in the radio series "Life with Luigi." Surviving are his widow, former actress Gladys Heaney, and a daughter.

LARRY OLIVER, 93, stage, film, and tv actor, died Jan. 22, 1973 in Englewood, N.J. Among the many plays in which he performed are "The Wall Street Girl," "Torch Song," "The Farmer Takes a Wife," "The Next Half Hour," "Twinkle Twinkle," "Rosalie," and "Born Yesterday" in which he played Sen. Hedges 1,689 performances, and recreated the role for the film. No reported survivors.

REGINALD OWEN, 85, stage and film actor, died of a heart attack Nov. 5, 1972 in Boise, Idaho. His career spanned over 70 years, beginning in his native England. His Bdwy debut was in 1924 in "The Carolinian," followed by "Androcles and the Lion," "The Importance of Being Earnest," "The Play's the Thing," "Skin Deep," "The Marquise," "Three Musketeers," "Candle Light," "Out of a Blue Sky," "Petticoat Influence," "Child of Manhattan," "Affairs of State," and "A Funny Thing Happened on the Way to the Forum," his last role in 1972. He appeared in numerous films. His third wife survives.

LEW PARKER, 65, stage, film, radio, and tv comedian, died of cancer Oct. 27, 1972 in a NYC hospital. Began his career in vaudeville, and performed on Bdwy in "The Ramblers," "Girl Crazy," "Ballyhoo," "Red, Hot, and Blue," "Heads Up," "Rainbow," "Are You with It?," "The Front Page," "Ankles Aweigh," "The Armorous Flea," "Spring Is Here," "Hellzapoppin." Recently he was appearing as the father of "That Girl" tv series. Surviving are his widow, comedienne Betty Kean, and a daughter.

Reginald Owen (1960)

JAMES PATTERSON, 40, stage, film, and tv actor, died of cancer Aug. 19, 1972 in a NYC hospital. He had appeared off-Bdwy in "Brothers Karamazov," "Epitaph for George Dillon," "Zoo Story," "The Collection" for which he won an Obie, at Lincoln Center in "Silence" and "Amphitryon," on Bdwy in "Conversation at Midnight," "Inadmissible Evidence," "The Birthday Party" for which he received a Tony, and "Wrong Way Light Bulb." He is survived by his widow, actress Rochelle Oliver, and a son.

WAUNA PAUL, 61, former actress and producer, was killed in an auto crash Mar. 31, 1973 on the Island of Ibiza, Spain, where she had lived for 10 years. She had appeared on Bdwy in "Girls in Uniform," "Father Malachy's Miracle," "Uncle Harry," "Kindred," and "Embezzled Heaven." She produced several plays in London. Surviving is her mother, actress Josephine Brown.

KATINA PAXINOU, 72, Greek stage and film actress, died of cancer Feb. 22, 1973 in Athens. With her husband, actor-director Alexis Minotis, she helped found the Greek National Theatre, and they became its stars. Her Bdwy debut was in 1942 in "Hedda Gabler," and she subsequently appeared in "Sophie," "House of Bernarda Alba," "Electra," and "Oedipus Tyrannis." Among her many films was "For Whom the Bell Tolls" which won her an Oscar. Surviving are her husband, and a daughter.

LAURA PIERPONT, 91, actress, died Dec. 11, 1972 in New Canaan, Conn. She began her career at 6, subsequently appearing in such plays as "Madame Butterfly," "Wonder Bar," "Village Green," "Winged Victory," "The Women," "State of the Union," "Sleepy Hollow," "Leading Lady," "The Smile of the World," "Two Blind Mice," "Time out for Ginger," and "J.B.," her last in 1958. She was the widow of actor Taylor Granville. No reported survivors.

GEORGE PRUD'HOMME, 71, stage and film actor, died in Los Angeles June 11, 1972 of complications from a massive brain tumor. He had also used the name of George Pembroke, and appeared in such plays as "Paradise Lost," "We, the People," "Lady Windermere's Fan," and "The Time of Your Life." No reported survivors.

IRENE PURCELL, 70, retired stage and film actress, died July 9, 1972 in her Racine, Wisc., home. Among her Bdwy roles were "Cross Roads," "The Ladder," "Dancing Partner," "Accent on Youth," and "The First Apple." She retired in 1941 when she married Herbert Fisk Johnson, manufacturer of Johnson's Wax and other products. He survives.

James Patterson (1962)

ISABEL RANDOLPH, 83, stage, film, radio, and tv actress, died after a long illness Jan. 11, 1973 in Burbank, Cal. Appeared on Bdwy in "The Noose," and "Bird of Paradise," among others, and was a regular on the "Fibber McGee and Molly" radio series. She last appeared as Dick Van Dyke's mother in his tv series. Two daughters survive.

ANDY RAZAF, 77, composer and lyricist, died Feb. 3, 1973 in a North Hollywood hospital. In addition to over 1,000 songs, he wrote for such Bdwy shows as "Lew Leslie's Black Birds," "Keep Shufflin'," and "Connie's Hot Chocolates." Surviving is his widow.

OLIVE REEVES-SMITH, 77, English-born actress, died July 20, 1972 in NYC. Her Bdwy debut was in 1916 in "The Better 'Ole," followed by "Aloma of the South Seas," "The Constant Nymph," "Jubilee," "Love from a Stranger," "Whiteoaks," "The Wookey," "The Doughgirls," "Bloomer Girl," "The Male Animal," "Pigeons and People," "Richard of Bordeaux," "Three Live Ghosts," and her last, "My Fair Lady." She was the widow of actor Fuller Mellish, Jr. A sister survives.

CARL BENTON REID, 79, stage, film, and tv actor, died Mar. 15, 1973 at his home in Hollywood. Among his Bdwy credits are "The Cherry Orchard," "The Iceman Cometh," "Life with Father," "Strange Bedfellows," "Fiesta," "Foreign Affairs," "Her Man of Wax," "Papa Is All," and "The Little Foxes." He went to Hollywood in 1943 and played in many films. He retired in 1966. Surviving are his widow, former actress Hazel Harrison, and a daughter.

HARRY RICHMAN, 77, song-and-dance man on stage, film, and in night clubs, died Nov. ? 1972 in Hollywood. He starred in several editions of George White's "Scandals," "Vari? s," "Sons O' Guns," "Queen of Hearts," "Ziegfeld Follies," "Music Hall Varieties," "Inter? ?onal Review," "Say When," "New Priorities of 1943." He appeared in several movies, on ?o, and had his own night club "Club Richman." He was married and divorced three times.

Laura Pierpont (1952)

269

Edward G. Robinson (1963)

Margaret Webster (1960)

Ed Zimmermann (1969)

EDWARD G. ROBINSON, 79, Romanian-born stage and film character actor, died of cancer Jan. 26, 1973 in a Hollywood hospital. His acting career began as Emanuel Goldenberg in 1912 after preparing to become a lawyer. He changed his name in 1922. His Bdwy appearances were in "Under Fire," "Under Sentence," "The Pawn," "The Little Teacher," "First Is Last," "Night Lodging," "Poldekin," "Idle Inn," "The Deluge," "Banco," "Peer Gynt," "The Adding Machine," "Royal Fandango," "The Firebrand," "Androcles and the Lion," "Man of Destiny," "Goat Song," "The Chief Thing," "Henry Behave," "Juarez and Maximilian," "Ned McCobb's Daughter," "Brothers Karamazov," "Right You Are if You Think You Are," "The Racket," "Man with Red Hair," "Kibitizer," "Mr. Samuel," and "Middle of the Night," his last in 1956. He made 101 films, and became typed as a gangster. His second wife, and a son by his first wife survive.

TOM RUTHERFORD, age unreported, stage and film actor, died Jan. 6, 1973 in Vienna. Made his Bdwy debut in "New Faces of 1936," subsequently appearing in "He Who Gets Slapped," "Murder without Crime," and "Laura," among others. For the last ten years he had been in retirement in Salzburg. No reported survivors.

IRENE RYAN, 70, vaudeville, film, tv, and stage actress, died Apr. 26, 1973 of a stroke in Santa Monica, Cal. Began her career at 10 as Irene Noblette in vaudeville, and was active until her death. She is probably best known as "Granny" of the "Beverly Hillbillies" tv series. She made her Bdwy debut Oct. 23, 1972 in "Pippin." No close survivors.

ART SMITH, 73, stage, film and tv actor, died of a heart attack on Feb. 24, 1973 in a West Babylon, NY hospital. His Bdwy debut was in 1930 in "Broken Dishes," followed by "Golden Boy," "Anna Christie," "An Enemy of the People," "Rocket to the Moon," "Volpone," "West Side Story," "A Touch of the Poet," "Machinal," "Diff'rent," and "All the Way Home," among others. A Son survives.

SALA STAW, 66, Polish-born actress, died of cancer Nov. 3, 1972 in Torrance, Cal. She came to the U.S. in 1927 and appeared with Eva Le Gallienne's Civic Repertory Theatre, and the Federal Theatre Project. She also starred in her one-woman show "The Five Queens." She was founder and director of the Foundation for Classic Theatre and Academy. Surviving are her husband, Otto Albertson, and a son.

ROBERT STORY, 47, actor, was shot and killed Feb. 13, 1973 while working as a night clerk in a NYC hotel. He had appeared in "Beautiful People," "Nat Turner," "Shadow of a Gunman," "Waiting for Lefty," "Twelfth Night," and "Prologue to Glory," all off-Bdwy. His mother and a brother survive.

AKIM TAMIROFF, 72, Russian-born versatile stage and film character actor, died Sept. 17, 1972 in Palm Springs, Cal. Came to U.S. in 1923 with the Moscow Art Theatre, and stayed. He appeared mostly in films, but was on the stage in "Wonderbar," "Miracle at Verdun," "Candle Light," and "Rashomon." No reported survivors.

CHARLES TAZEWELL, 72, actor and author, died June 26, 1972 in his Chesterfield, N.H. home. Among the plays in which he appeared on Bdwy are "They Knew What They Wanted," "Lucky Sam Carver," and "Sugar Hill." He wrote many radio and tv scripts, including "Hollywood Hotel" and "Mayor of the Town." His greatest fame was probably from his Christmas story "The Littlest Angel." For many years he operated the Brattleboro (Vt.) Little Theatre. His widow survives.

FREDERIC TOZERE, 71, stage and film actor, died Aug. 5, 1972 in his NYC apartment. He made his Bdwy debut in 1924 in "Sweet Little Devil," and subsequently appeared in over 50 plays, including "Stepping Stones," "Journey's End," "Key Largo," "Watch on the Rhine," "Outrageous Fortune," "In Bed We Cry," "Signature," "A Rich Full Life," "Murder in the Cathedral," "It Can't Happen Here," "St. Joan," "King of Friday's Men," "Tower Beyond Tragedy," "First Lady," "Caligula," "Daughter of Silence," and "Little Boxes," his last in 1969 off-Bdwy. There are no immediate survivors.

HELEN TRAUBEL, 69, internationally famous Wagnerian soprano of the Metropolitan Opera, died of a heart attack July 28, 1972 in her Santa Monica, Cal., home. After leaving the Met in 1953, she appeared on Bdwy in "Pipe Dream," in night clubs, and several films. Surviving is her husband William Bass.

WADE WARREN, 76, retired actor, director, and broadcasting executive, died Jan. 14, 1973 in Englewood, NJ. He became an executive with NBC in 1930, and eventually became involved with tv productions. On Bdwy he was featured in "The Captain and the Kings," "Arturo Ui," and "Galileo." No survivors reported.

ARLENE WALKER, 54, former actress, and casting director of Young and Rubicam, died Apr. 15, 1973 in her NYC home. After appearing in over 1500 radio, and 500 tv shows, she made her Bdwy debut in 1966 in "The Wayward Stork" in 1966. She was the widow of William J. Percival.

MARGARET WEBSTER, 67, actress and director, died Nov. 14, 1972 in her London home. She was the last member of a 150-year-old theatrical family, and began her career in 1917. Her Bdwy appearances were in "The Seagull," "Family Portrait," "The Trojan Women," "Othello," "The Cherry Orchard," "Henry VIII," "John Gabriel Borkman," "Pound on Demand," "Alice in Wonderland," "The High Ground," and "The Brontes," a one-woman show. She directed many Bdwy and London productions, including operas, and Shakespeare plays. There are no immediate survivors.

ROBERT WEEDE, 69, Broadway and Metropolitan Opera baritone, died July 9, 1972 in Walnut Creek, Cal. He began his career as a singer at Radio City Music Hall in 1933, and debuted at the Met in 1937. His final performance at the Met was during the 1944–5 season. His greatest national recognition came with his Bdwy appearance in "The Most Happy Fella," followed by "Milk and Honey," and "Cry for Us All." Two sons survive, singers Richard, and Robert Jr.

ALFRED H. WHITE, 89, retired actor, died Aug. 22, 1972 in Ft. Lauderdale, Fla. He appeared in many Yiddish productions and vaudeville, before beginning his 5-year run in "Abie's Irish Rose" using his real name of Alfred Weisman. He also appeared in the 1937 revival. Two daughters survive.

ED ZIMMERMANN, 39, stage, film, and tv actor, died of a heart attack July 6, 1972 in York, Maine where he was appearing in "Who Killed Santa Claus?" His Bdwy credits include "Luther," "The Right Honourable Gentleman" "Venus Is," "A Day in the Death of Joe Egg," "A Patriot for Me," "Not Now Darling," and "The Philanthropist." Surviving are his widow and a daughter.

Index

272

284